# Milton in Italy

*Contexts*
*Images*
*Contradictions*

# medieval & renaissance texts & studies

VOLUME 90

# Milton
# in Italy

## Contexts
## Images
## Contradictions

Edited by

MARIO A. DI CESARE

Medieval & Renaissance texts & studies
Binghamton, New York
1991

**Library of Congress Cataloging-in-Publication Data**

Milton in Italy : contexts, images, contradictions / edited by Mario A. Di Cesare
        p. cm. — (Medieval & Renaissance texts & studies : v. 90)
    Papers from the 3rd International Milton Symposium, held in Vallombrosa and Florence, June 1988.
    Includes index.
    ISBN 0-86698-103-9
    1. Milton, John, 1608–1674–Knowledge–Italy–Congresses. 2. Milton, John, 1608–1674–Journeys–Italy–Congresses. 3. Poets, English–Early modern, 1500–1700–Biography–Congresses. 4. English poetry–Italian influences–Congresses. 5. Italy in literature–Congresses. I. Di Cesare, Mario A. II. International Milton Symposium (3rd : 1988 : Vallombrosa, Italy, and Florence, Italy) III. Series.
PR3592.I8M55 1991
821'.4–dc20

Special
Collections
PR
3592
I8
M55
1991x

91–23811
CIP

This book is made to last.
It is set in Goudy Old Style, smythe-sewn
and printed on acid-free paper
to library specifications.

Printed in the United States of America

The endpapers reproduce the map of Italy from John Speed's *Prospect of the Most Famous Parts of the World* (1627). It is likely that Milton had access to Speed's atlas when planning his Italian journey. Reproduced courtesy of the Library of Congress. Photograph by Phil Gerace.

In Memoriam

Leo Miller

*Miltonist*

*Gentleman*

*Independent Scholar*

# Contents

# Illustrations

# Acknowledgements

The tale is long and pleasant. My main thanks go to those who shared the trials of decision, month by month as we considered abstracts and read papers and prepared for the Symposium, and then afterwards as we assembled this volume: Roy Flannagan, Neil Harris, and Gordon Campbell. Being one of the Gang of Four with them was a remarkable and memorable experience.

Warm thanks to all the members of our informal editorial board, who generously read and commented on papers, many of them for both the symposium and this volume: Cedric Brown (Reading), Dennis Danielson (British Columbia), J. Martin Evans (Stanford), Neil Forsyth (Lausanne), John Hale (Otago, New Zealand), Judith Herz (Concordia, Montreal), Albert C. Labriola (Duquesne), Barbara Lewalski (Harvard), Diane McColley (Rutgers-Camden), Mary Ann Radzinowicz (Cornell), Stella Revard (Southern Illinois), John R. Roberts (Missouri), John T. Shawcross (Kentucky), Kathleen Swaim (Univ. of Massachusetts-Amherst), Mindele Treip (Cambridge), and Michael Wilding (Sydney). The late Leo Miller, who is recognized in the dedication, also served generously and well. All worked hard and selflessly.

Special thanks to Estella Schoenberg, who, on her own initiative, located the map which we use for the endpapers and who arranged for the photography.

Thanks also to the many MRTS staffers who participated in various stages of composition and production with their usual sense of urgency and responsibility: Lori Vandermark, Lee Hoskins, and Judith Sumner, and Linda Ciano, Jennifer Glennon, Karen Guest, Kristen Lippert, Liz Madden, and Michelle Tessler.

Finally, particular thanks to two dedicated and talented members of the MRTS editorial staff: Michael Pavese, who imposed a judicious measure of order on the book, and Michael Horan, who made the index.

# Introduction

THIS BOOK BRINGS TOGETHER THIRTY-TWO ESSAYS on Milton and the Italian world. The subject has both attracted and eluded analysis, mainly because there is so much to do, and yet it has seemed hard to make much of it — that is, to see it clearly and simply and unambiguously. Scholarship seems driven to force Milton's journey into neat categories; witness this comment in an expert chronicle of the climate of opinion:

> Nel 1638-'39 completò la sua educazione con un lungo viaggio sul continente, secondo l'uso rinascimentale. . . . Soggiornò . . . in Italia . . . ottenendo grande successo nei circoli intellettuali.[1]

The suggestion that Milton completed his education with a grand tour on the continent in the usual Renaissance mode may be attractively simple, but it is also reductionist, misleading, and even irrelevant. Certainly it is an unlikely description of that independent spirit. As for the "great success he obtained," is it best situated in *intellectual* circles? The comment no doubt reflects the writer's notion that writing and reading Latin hexameters and other verses are best defined as intellectual pursuits. One wonders about the fact that much of the early poetry — presumably the verses Milton recited and which were received with such esteem in the Italian academies — reflects broadly his readings in and experience of classical Greek and Roman poetry, Renaissance Latin poetry, the great Italian poets, and some minor contemporary poets. Out of those recitations and that esteem, he will maintain in the *Reason of Church-Government* not long after returning home, came the resolve to write in his own language, to achieve something in his native tongue

---

[1] *Dizionario Letterario Bompiani degli Autori di tutti i tempi e di tutte le letterature* (Milan: Bompiani, 1957), 2:746.

which "aftertimes ... should not willingly let ... die."[2] The links are hardly obvious. But then little in Milton's life or works is obvious.

The "Italian element in Milton's verse" has exercised more than one incisive critic and careful scholar. Even before going to Italy, Milton thought he might be temperamentally unsuited to Italy, because (to adapt the famous phrase in *Paradise Lost* 9.44-45) "an age too late, or cold / Climate" damped his "intended wing." In *Mansus*, he describes himself as "A young pilgrim sent from a Hyperborean region" ("Missus Hyperboreo iuvenis peregrinus ab axe").[3] The same hint of lingering envy of those blessed with warmth and sunshine lurks in other contexts – for instance, in his longstanding concern about proper pronunciation as expressed in the following principle from *Of Education*:

> their [Latin] speech is to be fashion'd to a distinct and cleer pronuntiation, as neer as may be to the *Italian*, especially in the vowels. For we Englishmen being farre northerly, doe not open our mouthes in the cold air, wide enough to grace a Southern tongue; but are observ'd by all other nations to speak exceeding close and inward: So that to smatter Latin with an english mouth, is as ill a hearing as law French. (CPW 2:382-83)

The Italian experience was multifarious and hardly limited to the journey itself. Milton brings Latin with him (along with several other languages), a kind of passport to the internationalism or supranationalism of at least one level of contemporary European culture. But he also brings his northern English consciousness, sharpened by an awareness of the alienness of this older world, this world that remained Catholic and tied to a past that seemed both oppressive and decadent. One aspect of this consciousness, expressed as follows in the *Areopagitica*, has been emphasized often:

> I could recount what I have seen and heard in other Countries ... when I have sat among their lerned men ... and bin counted happy to be born in such a place of *Philosophic* freedom, as they suppos'd England was.... (CPW 2:537)

---

[2] CPW 1:810. Further references to the *Complete Prose* will be incorporated, parenthetically, in the text.

[3] *Mansus*, 24. I cite Milton's poetry from Hughes's text; the translation of the bits from *Mansus* is mostly my own. The whole passage glances wistfully at the sunny warmth of Manso's southern world.

The other side of this coin is his own sense that his Muse is alien: "longinquam ... Musam" he describes her in *Mansus*, and "gelida vix enutrita sub Arcto" ("poorly nourished under the frozen Bear"), which "rashly dared to flit through the Italian cities" ("Imprudens Italas ausa est volitare per urbes" [29]).

*Longinqua* and *imprudens* — the two words convey forcefully and with a certain poignancy that sense of alienness and exclusion which we must confront and which therefore confounds any attempts to deal simply with Milton's involvement in the Italian world. One of the most important aspects of this subject is simply this: you *cannot* see it so simply and clearly. The contexts and images produced by Milton's involvement with Italy mesh with contradictions also, and not just the contradictions inevitable when a Protestant northerner wanders about in a southern Catholic land. Some of these contradictions occupy many of the contributors to this volume.

§

This book is entitled *Milton in Italy*, but the contributors do not limit themselves to the literal year of the Italian sojourn or attempt to deal with Milton's influence on Italian literature or culture. The stay in Italy, beginning in the summer of 1638 and lasting about a year, informs most of this book, but Italy was in certain senses important to Milton's cultural consciousness and intellectual effort during much of his life. In this context, *Italy* is meant broadly and accommodatingly, just as it was in the Third International Milton Symposium on which this volume is based.[4] Like the symposium, this book assumes that the Italian experience is a matter of mind and spirit even more than a literal journey, an *itinerarium mentis* as much as the risky journey of a stranger in a strange land. Italy for Milton encompasses both ancient Rome and the seat of papist iniquity, classical culture, Renaissance Humanism, and the oppressiveness spawned by the Counter-Reformation. It includes Vergil

---

[4] The Third International Milton Symposium was held in Vallombrosa and Florence in June 1988. For Roy Flannagan's full and lively account of the weeklong meeting and for summaries of most of the more than one hundred papers given there (including earlier versions of most of the papers printed here), see MQ 22 (1988): 69–108.

and Dante, Horace and Petrarch, Cicero and Ficino, Ariosto and Michelangelo, Tasso and Machiavelli, Galileo grown old, the art and music that flourished all around him during his journey, the poetasters who feted him, St. Peter's as Pandemonium, the scholars and the academies which welcomed him, and the Jesuits who posed a danger to him.[5] Milton had the classical tradition in his bones; his sense of that tradition need not have been Italian except that he went there and he understood the power and beauty of the language and its claim on the classical heritage and all that the heritage implied. We must not under-rate the political and religious problems, of course, but we must not overrate them either.

Though this is a big book with thirty-two essays and though at least as many more papers on Milton's Italian world were presented at Vallombrosa and Florence at that remarkable June symposium, these papers aim to open up rather than close off the multiple complexities of the subject. The papers range far and wide, some arguing with each other, all pursuing and then passing beyond stimulating questions. The organization of the volume is simple enough – after a brief section which treats the journey specifically and broad questions of culture and contradiction, the papers are grouped into natural categories: images of the shaded wood at Vallombrosa, the telescope and the vistas opened out upon a glorious sight, and the Italy of the Counter-Reformation with its cycles of censorship and repression; contexts of art and music; contexts of literature and language, historiography, and classical culture and the contemporary culture of the academies.

The volume begins with essays which reflect on complexities and contradictions, examining what the Italian experience might mean to this northern European Puritan Englishman aspiring to be an Italianate Humanist (Corns) and who learned to define himself and his liberty against an Italy that was both familiar and foreign: Milton in Italy was "an oxymoron in search of the higher resolution of paradox" (Woods). Dustin Griffin challenges the notion that the journey was a moment of consecration to literature, while Diana Benet examines the genre of the "escape from Rome" as Englishmen's self-definition in a critical time. The section

---

[5] He tells us in the *Defensio secunda* (CE 8:124) that he was warned against returning to Rome because of plots being laid against him by English Jesuits ("parari mihi ab Jesuitis Anglis insidias, si Romam reverterem").

ends with a paper that follows Milton through Milan and the Pennine Alps (Cinquemani).

Some of the papers quarrel with each other directly or indirectly — arguing whether or not Milton ever went to Vallombrosa while also surveying and analyzing what the Etruscan shades and Etruscan history offer, what the elusive and brilliant simile might mean, and what attractions Vallombrosa had for later visitors (Harris, Mulder, Huttar, Chaney). A different image illuminates the next papers as they probe the art and science of seeing, the modes of discourse astronomical and poetic (Herz, Friedman). This section closes with another kind of image — the *imprimaturs* (or permissions to print) which embody "the Inventors and the originall of Book-licencing" (CPW 2:505) — and the inverted image of that *imprimatur* in Milton's own outlaw pamphlet *Areopagitica* (Shullenberger).

Three papers on art balance three on music, but with different structures. There are detailed discussions of allegorical ceiling cycles and speculations about their role in England during the second quarter of the century and, by inference, about their impact on Milton's own aesthetic development (Treip), on the one hand, and, on the other, a close textual reading of the iconography of Genesis in the Creation mosaics of San Marco in Venice and in Milton's poem (McColley). Both approaches are queried implicitly by the argument that Milton viewed Italian art hesitantly, perhaps even hostilely, and that he emerged from the journey with "a strong attraction to the visual image combined with a deep ideological suspicion of it" (O'Connell). The papers on music are similarly balanced. Polly Mander explores the the music of *L'Allegro* and *Il Penseroso* in terms of humanist ideals and Horatian principles, while the two other papers in this section focus on specific kinds of music — Paul Stanwood on the Orpheus legend, especially via Monteverdi, and Margaret Byard utilizing an eye-witness account to describe in detail the music of Rome and then to speculate on the echoes and imitations that can be heard in Milton's "advent'rous song."

The largest group of papers inevitably concerns literature mainly. Three papers scrutinize classical contexts — moments of Horatian self-presentation in both English and Latin poems (Brown); the etymological implications of *dis* and the network of prefixes in *Paradise Lost* (Forsyth); and the implications of the Horatian *carpe diem* theme (Sano). Several papers vigorously explore Milton's connections with the great Italian epic poets: Boiardo's *Orlando Innamorato* is linked to *Paradise Regained*

(Ross); the great triad — *Orlando Furioso, Gerusalemme Liberata,* and *Paradise Lost* — is studied in terms of formal patterns of divine intervention (Eriksen). David Reid investigates the differences in the ways that Tasso and Milton treat the reflection of oneself in another in love and the pursuit of the self in despair or self-hate. Robert Entzminger deals with Tasso's *Aminta* as foil to Milton's *Comus,* showing how Milton accomplishes a political reorientation of the genre. Wyman Herendeen explores Milton's puritan historiography and its genealogy in Machiavelli, Guicciardini, and others. Michael Spiller examines the background and uses of that very social trope, the apostrophe, in Milton's sonnets, while Anna Nardo looks at the academic sonnet in Italy and what Milton learned, directly or indirectly, from it. Stella Revard investigates the "Italian Pindar," Gabriello Chiabrera, brought to Milton's attention by Carlo Dati; Estelle Haan shows Milton composing a "written encomium" in his poem *Mansus.* The final papers provide searching explorations of Milton's command of language, his lexicography, his extraordinary vocabulary, and the peculiar character of his dictionary (Miller); and of the multivalence of polyglot Milton's language-interest as he makes his choice of English a message as well as a medium (Hale).

But this bare outline is meant simply as an invitation to the rich and varied feast offered here; my thumbnail sketches can do no more.

§

Implicit in any study of Milton's Italian contexts is the problem of language, always cardinal to the experience of travel to a foreign place, whether actual or imaginary. Milton's linguistic abilities are legendary; he brought Latin as a passport to an international world; he read and wrote Italian easily. Yet we wonder: Where did Italian itself finally fit in? Was Italian a step away from Latin? Is the sense of the vernacular itself crucial to his understanding? Carlo Dati testified in several places that Milton loved Italian quite as much as Latin. In a letter of December 1648, Dati links Milton's love of Italian with his command of the language, saying that he writes in "Toscano, sapendo che la mia Lingua è a lei si cara, e familiare che nella sua bocca non apparisce straniera" (French, 2:221–22). Dati had earlier given more than one reason for this love and this fluency. In a letter of November 1, 1647, he praised Milton's "dote singulariss*. di rauuiuare le lingue morte, e le straniere far proprie" ("the extraordinary ability to bring dead languages to life and to make foreign languages your own") as well as his deep affection and esteem for Italy itself: "Conobbi ancora in quale stima fosse appò di Lei la mia Patria..." (French, 2:202).[6]

Like any sensitive traveller, Milton understood profoundly the sense of the alienness of other tongues, the full and proper force of *barbarus*[7] with its deterrent implications, the wall of estrangement necessarily there. That sense comes out, piercingly at times, even when the context is controversy. In *Apology against a Pamphlet*, he points to the "native *Latinisms* of *Cicero*" and to the "lofty nakednesse of your *Latinizing* Barbarian" (CPW 1:934-35). While the latter is a common threat to all, the former is a measure or standard, the frustration of every aspiring Latinist who is just beginning to realize that he or she can never make it a completely native tongue.[8]

On September 10, 1638, Milton wrote to the Florentine priest and philologist Benedetto Bonmattei a letter which discusses in interesting ways certain of his concerns about language. His aim is to urge Bonmattei to deal at length with both pronunciation and the history of letters in Italian. But he writes the letter in Latin, an act which embodies his sense of *imperitiam, & inopiam*, his lack of skill in Italian and his need for the *venerandam ... matrem* from Latium itself (French, 1:385). The wit does not completely hide his ambivalence about language, his vacillation between great but dead languages and lowly vernacular ones, his desire to see the vernacular language dignified, given proper status.

---

[6] Milton insisted on this *stima* (esteem), ascribing it to the richness of Italian culture and to its breadth and humaneness. In *Defensio secunda*, he emphasized the special attraction of Italy as the home of *humanitas* and of civilization: "Verum ego Italiam ... ut ... humanitatis ... & civilium doctrinarum omnium hospitium & noveram antea, et expertus sum" (CE 8:114). The controversial context of this assertion does not detract from its force or clarity. And the uncommon extravagance is a happy reminder of how warm responsiveness is bred by a sojourn in sunny Italy. — In a letter to Carlo Dati, April 1647, he recalls the generous response to his outspokenness: "veniam ... meae ... olim apud vos loquendi libertati, singulari cum humanitate, dare consuevistis" (French, 1:374); the final word, implying a habit of spirit, is the highest praise of all.

[7] It means, basically, a foreigner, one whose language is not the language of the natives. See particularly the use of the word in *Of Education*, CPW 2:373.

[8] In *Areopagitica*, assailing the "pure conceit of an *Imprimatur*," he expresses a well-defined counter-sense of his own language: "our English, the language of men ever famous, and formost in the atchievements of liberty, will not easily finde servile letters anow to spell such a dictatorie presumption English" (CPW 2:505).

In the letter, Milton argues that where Plato saw portents of civil disorder in variations and disorder of dress, the far more important and substantial danger to a civilization lay in the decay of language: "errorem loquendi usu, occasum ejus Urbis, remq; humilem & obscuram subsequi" (French, 1:383). The debasement of language he sees as part and parcel of the decline, an embodiment of the loss of freedom: "& ad servile quidvis jam olim paratos incolarum animos haud levi indicio declarant." Here too he describes the vernacular in terms almost as attractive as he would use to describe Greek and Latin, which he specially loves, noting how attached he is to Florence, the Arno, the Fiesolan hills: "quin sæpe Arnum vestrum, et Fæsulanos illos colles invisere amem," and, carried away, he avows his deep and excelling love for Bonmattei's country, a love not to be outdone by anyone: "vestræq: Nationis ita amantem, ut non alius, opinor, magis" (1:384).

It was just a few days later, on September 16, 1638, according to the manuscript *Atti dell'Accademia degli Svogliati*, that Milton read before the Accademia degli Svogliati, no doubt with Bonmattei present (he was a member of the Accademia), "una poesia Latina di versi esametri molto erudita" ("a very learned Latin poem in hexameter verse").[9] Whether these happy experiences among the academics in Florence led to his resolve to write in his own vernacular is not completely clear; the evidence in the manuscript *Atti* refers, on three different occasions, specifically and only to Latin poems, but there is no way of knowing if these are also the poems referred to in Milton's account in *The Reason of Church-Government*. They might be. Or there might have been other poems, in Italian or perhaps in Greek. In any case, Milton's own version of the matter bears repeating in some detail:

> But much latelier in the privat Academies of *Italy*, whither I was favor'd to resort, perceiving that some trifles which I had in memory, compos'd at under twenty or thereabout (for the manner is that every one must give some proof of his wit and reading

---

[9] French, 1:389. On March 17, 1639, he read "nobili versi latini" (French, 1:408); a week later, he read "diverse poesie latine" (French, 1:409). The terms are interesting and invite a good deal of speculation. At the first meeting recorded, Milton read a poem in hexameters or heroic verse; in the second reference, *nobili* also suggests heroic verse or hexameters, while the word *diverse* in the third reference may allow for something less exalted: perhaps elegiac verses such as those *Ad Leonaram Romae canentem* (Hughes, 130-31).

there) met with acceptance above what was lookt for, and other things which I had shifted in scarsity of books and conveniences to patch up amongst them, were receiv'd with written Encomiums, which the Italian is not forward to bestow on men of this side the *Alps,* I began thus farre to assent both to them and divers of my friends here at home, and not lesse to an inward prompting which now grew daily upon me, that by labour and intent study (which I take to be my portion in this life) joyn'd with the strong propensity of nature, I might perhaps leave something so written to aftertimes, as they should not willingly let it die. These thoughts at once possest me, and these other. That ... there ought no regard be sooner had, then to Gods glory by the honour and instruction of my country. For which cause, and not only for that I knew it would be hard to arrive at the second rank among the Latines, I apply'd myself to that resolution which *Ariosto* follow'd against the perswasions of *Bembo,* to fix all the industry and art I could unite to the adorning of my native tongue ... to be an interpreter & relater of the best and sagest things among mine own Citizens throughout this Iland in the mother dialect. That what the greatest and choycest wits of *Athens, Rome,* or modern *Italy,* and those Hebrews of old did for their country, I ... might doe for mine: not caring to be once nam'd abroad ... but content with these British Ilands as my world.... (CPW 1:809-12)

The passage is remarkable, not to say breathtaking, in its sweep, in the audacious move from that remote base, from remembered esteem and honor among another, distant people. Not the least of its striking sureties is Milton's own soaring confidence; like the pilgrim Dante in the limbo of the poets (*Inferno* 4), Milton is staking out a place of his own in the great company of Homer and Vergil and Tasso, of Sophocles and Euripides – the epic and dramatic poets – and claiming his title to be "doctrinal and exemplary to a Nation" (815). The extraordinary thing is the direct link he alleges with the Italian experience, with the acceptance granted to "some trifles which I had in memory," borne through that Muse and language felt to be alien and resistant.[10]

---

[10] The renewed reference to the Academies further on in the preface (819) defines the centrality of the Italian experience in ratifying his career and his hopes.

Whether or not Don Wolfe is right (CPW 1:742 f.), that the aim of the autobiographical preface is to announce his great poetical works (and Wolfe makes this theme the argument of his annotations), the controlling point is that Milton places himself squarely within the tradition of the great poets and affirms his place in the name of the vernacular.[11]

§

Let me close these remarks with one example of the Italian element in Milton's work which has gone little remarked: Ariosto's *Orlando Furioso*, a work which few Miltonists would at first blush think to be relevant.[12] I do not suggest influence, but I do wonder about the possibility of deep and fundamental similarities between these two poems, outwardly so different.

If there is such a possibility, it would appear to be an improbable possibility. Among critics and historians, especially those of the Anglo-Saxon persuasion, the *Orlando Furioso* has been and still is often thought to be frivolous and unserious: a delightful poem based mainly on Ovid, a game whose only concern is to exercise an omnipresent and corrosive irony. Recent criticism, however, not only rejects such readings but also argues an integral and multi-faceted seriousness, placing Ariosto's poem squarely within its own time — "the poem of Europe," says Barbara Reynolds.[13] The poem, she argues, is harshly critical of contemporary corruption in politics and society, committed to a remarkably advanced view of feminine status, and clear- and even cold-eyed in its

---

[11] The acute self-consciousness which Wolfe rightly perceives here is not so modern as Wolfe suggests (736); cf. Robert Durling, *The Figure of the Poet in Renaissance Epic* (Cambridge: Harvard Univ. Press, 1966) on Ovid, Petrarch, Chaucer, and especially Ariosto. I have argued elsewhere that Milton's decision to write *Paradise Lost* in English was like Dante's and Ariosto's; perceiving the agency of language to be intensely ideological, Milton aimed finally at forging a new style, a unique style, an instrument worthy of epic, a mode of poetic discourse which might raise the vernacular to the levels of the Greek and Roman hexameter; and that this attempt was both brazen and traumatically liberating. See "Interrupted Symmetries: *Terza Rima*, Heroic Verse, First Lines, and the Style of Epic," *Mediaevalia* 12 (1989 for 1986), especially 275-78.

[12] Except as object of attack: see most (wrongheaded) commentaries on *Paradise Lost* 1.16, Milton's accurate translation of Ariosto's line cited below.

[13] In the introduction to her translation, *Orlando Furioso (The Frenzy of Orlando): A Romantic Epic*, 2 vols. (Baltimore: Penguin Books, 1975-77).

definition and representation of life in this world and its exigencies.

But an *apologia* for this poem is not my intent here; considering the improbable possibility *is*. Notice the following about the *Orlando*. Ariosto announced boldly that he was going to sing "cosa non detta mai in prose nè in rima"—"Things unattempted yet in prose or rime," in Milton's accurate translation. Ariosto's title, *Orlando Furioso*, challenges us with an oxymoron — the sublime hero of the *chansons*, Roland, defender of the faith, right arm of Charlemagne, heroic martyr at Roncesvalles — somehow overcome by folly or madness (for the love of a pagan princess) or with the kind of *furor* which, Ficino reminds us, Plato ascribed to poets. Ariosto persisted, despite vigorous pressure, in composing his work in his native Italian rather than Latin. He created a poem which militantly asserted itself against the epic tradition while fully claiming its own place in the tradition. His contemporaries were troubled by his determined rejection of common generic norms and by the powerful and innovative accomplishment of his verse. He endowed his female characters with richness and complexity and diversity (they are often more interesting than the males) quite uncommon and unexpected in chivalric poetry or narrative generally. He insisted on autonomy as maker of his poem, establishing not one but three centers or narrative themes, balancing these coolly with each other, not allowing full dominance to any and bringing them together in a fragile harmony at the very end. All of these things annoyed as much as they pleased contemporaries and critics. Many were equally annoyed by his casual inversions of heroics, his insouciant disdain for the sublime conventions of the tradition, and his deliberate heterodoxy.

*Mutatis mutandis*, everything here applies, in its own way, to Milton and his *Paradise Lost*.

Note further that both poems begin with division, inherent in their very titles, each an oxymoron: *Orlando Furioso* and *Paradise Lost*. Both poems present discomfiting, even intractable, problems of structure and order — a nearly relentless centrifugal force and the demand for continual control, unabating exercise of will and tact. Read as narrative, both *Orlando Furioso* and *Paradise Lost* appear episodic, loose, disjointed; they are fervently centrifugal, leading us away again and again from their centers. The necessity for *felt* authorial control strikes one immediately in each poem. At the very outset, the violations of tradition by both poets define this necessity. But enough; a careful Miltonic reader of Ariosto will find much more.

Perhaps, then, the improbable possibility becomes an impossible probability – that the Puritan poet of the cold northern climate found and cherished and absorbed much from the cordial Italian and his dazzling poem.[14]

---

[14] In *Of Reformation*, Milton ranked Ariosto with Dante and Petrarch (CPW 1:559); in the passage quoted earlier from the *Reason of Church-Government*, he applauded Ariosto's decision to write in the vernacular (CPW 1:810-12). For the story of Ariosto's decision as told by Sir John Harington, see the excellent modern edition of Harington's translation, *Ludovico Ariosto's Orlando Furioso Translated into English Heroical Verse . . .*, ed. Robert McNulty (Oxford: Clarendon Press, 1972), 571. The *Commonplace Book* cites Harington's translation. If we follow conventional methods of *Quellenforschung* or "influence"-study, there are few "traces" of Ariosto's work in Milton. But I suggest that conventional methods do us little good; that "influence" is a term we should banish completely from literary study and reserve for the more squalid aspects of political life, as in "influence-peddling"; that bemusement with Tasso, especially on account of the rich question of the "sense variously drawn out," coupled with the ignorance of Ariosto's work prevalent in English studies, is the main reason for neglect of Ariosto by Miltonists. We leave Ariosto to Spenserians, where the "influences" are, it would appear, "obvious." But the kind of kinship I have in mind is stronger between Ariosto and Milton than between Ariosto and Spenser. It is not a question of facts and links; it is a question of poetry.

# Abbreviations

| | |
|---|---|
| AJPh | *American Journal of Philology* |
| Arthos | John Arthos, *Milton and the Italian Cities* (New York: Barnes and Noble, 1968) |
| Budick | Sanford Budick, *The Dividing Muse: Images of Sacred Disjunction in Milton's Poetry* (New Haven: Yale Univ. Press, 1985) |
| CE | *The Works of John Milton,* ed. Frank Allen Patterson et al., 18 vols. + 2 vols. index (New York: Columbia Univ. Press, 1931–1940) |
| Colie | Rosalie Colie, *The Resources of Kind: Genre-Theory in the Renaissance,* ed. Barbara K. Lewalski (Berkeley: Univ. of California Press, 1973) |
| CPW | *The Complete Prose Works of John Milton,* ed. Don M. Wolfe et al. (New Haven: Yale Univ. Press, 1953–1982) |
| Darbishire | *The Early Lives of Milton,* ed. Helen Darbishire (London: Constable, 1932) |
| Diekhoff | *Milton on Himself: Milton's Utterances upon Himself and His Works,* ed. John S. Diekhoff (New York: Oxford Univ. Press, 1939; New York: Humanities Press, 1965) |
| ELH | *English Literary History* |
| Fish | Stanley Fish, *Surprised by Sin: The Reader in "Paradise Lost"* (Berkeley: Univ. of California Press, 1967) |
| Fowler | *The Complete Poems of John Milton,* ed. John Carey and Alastair Fowler (London: Longman, 1968) |
| French | *The Life Records of John Milton,* ed. J. Milton French, 5 vols. (New Brunswick, NJ: Rutgers Univ. Press, 1949–1958; New York: Gordian, 1966) |
| Hanford | James Holly Hanford and James G. Taaffe, *A Milton Handbook,* 5th ed. (New York: Appleton-Century-Crofts, 1970) |
| Hughes | *John Milton: Complete Poetry and Major Prose,* ed. Merritt Y. Hughes (New York: Odyssey Press, 1957) |

LCL          Loeb Classical Library
Lewalski     Barbara Kiefer Lewalski, *Milton's Brief Epic: The Genre, Meaning, and Art of "Paradise Regained"* (Providence, RI: Brown Univ. Press, 1966)
Martindale   Charles Martindale, ed., *John Milton and the Transformation of Ancient Epic* (Totowa, NJ: Barnes & Noble Books, 1986)
Masson       David Masson, *The Life of John Milton: Narrated in Connexion with the Political, Ecclesiastical, and Literary History of His Time*, 7 vols. (London: MacMillan & Co., 1881-1894; New York: Peter Smith, 1946).
MacCaffrey   Isabel Gamble MacCaffrey, *"Paradise Lost" as "Myth"* (Cambridge: Harvard Univ. Press, 1959)
MLN          *Modern Language Notes*
MLR          *Modern Language Review*
MP           *Modern Philology*
MQ           *Milton Quarterly*
MS           *Milton Studies*
N&Q          *Notes & Queries*
Parker       William Riley Parker, *Milton: A Biography*, 2 vols. (Oxford: Clarendon Press, 1968)
Prince       F. T. Prince, *The Italian Element in Milton's Verse* (Oxford: Clarendon Press, 1954)
Ricks        Christopher Ricks, *Milton's Grand Style* (Oxford: Oxford Univ. Press, 1963)
Sells        Arthur Lytton Sells, *The Paradise of Travellers: The Italian Influence on Englishmen in the Seventeenth Century* (Bloomington: Indiana Univ. Press, 1964).
Shoaf        R. A. Shoaf, *Milton: Poet of Duality: A Study of Semiosis in the Poetry and the Prose* (New Haven: Yale Univ. Press, 1985)
Variorum     *A Variorum Commentary on the Poems of John Milton*, gen. ed. Merritt Y. Hughes (New York: Columbia Univ. Press, 1970- )
Wilson       A. N. Wilson, *The Life of John Milton* (New York: Oxford Univ. Press, 1983)

# Milton in Italy

*Contexts*
*Images*
*Contradictions*

THOMAS N. CORNS

# John Milton: Italianate Humanist, Northern European Protestant, Englishman

THIS ESSAY ENGAGES ISSUES OF RHETORIC, addressing the polemical implications of Milton's representation, not only of other peoples, but of the English, and considering the way in which the self-image he produces variously proclaims its cultural affiliations. Milton's invocation of images of Italy and of the values and associations of Italianate culture are particularly complex.

Hostile images of foreigners certainly antedate the mid-seventeenth century, but it is during that period that these images are rapidly extended, refined, and achieve a general press circulation. We need postulate no deep plotting in explanation. For political and economic reasons, England, and particularly revolutionary England, enters into conflicts with several of its neighbors, such as the Scots and the Dutch and with a number of other peoples, most obviously the Irish, who are less rivals than potentially or actually a subject and expropriated race. Simultaneously, a new awareness of the possible importance of public opinion, and of the role of the press in controlling it, initially lead to surges in more straightforward propaganda, and later, in the Cromwellian ascendancy of the 1650s, in the development of what we would now recognize as a subtler form of news management.

Generally, the deleterious representation of others in the pursuit of English interest takes a simple form, even in otherwise subtle writers. As Banton had observed, racial theory as it obtained in the early modern period has little of the insidious scientism of its nineteenth- and twentieth-century manifestations.[1] Thus, against the background of Anglo-Dutch rivalry, spilling over into open war, so subtle a poet as Marvell happily rehearses a litany of familiar anti-Dutch sentiment. They

---

[1] Michael Banton, *Racial Theory* (Cambridge: Cambridge Univ. Press, 1987), 2, 8–9.

live, fittingly enough, in a dunghill of a country, scarcely land at all: "This indigested vomit of the Sea / Fell to the *Dutch* by just Propriety." They habitually eat that wretched food, the pickled herring, and, unsurprisingly given their circumstances, foster alien, outlandish and perverse creeds and sects: "Hence *Amsterdam, Turk-Christian-Pagan-Jew*, / Staple of Sects and Mint of Schisme grew."[2] Again, Cromwellian propagandists extended and consolidated hostile images of the Scots into a model of stereotypical assumptions which obtain in England to this day. What do the English know of the Scots? That they are fiercely appetitive and speak a comic version of the language. As *Mercurius Politicus* attempts to make Cromwell's Scottish campaign a focus of national, rather than sectional, interest, Nedham offers the persistent reiteration of a stereotypical notion of the blue-bonneted "guid people" of Scotland poised to raid the property-owners of England.[3] Milton, too, had played these tunes in his official publication on behalf of the English republic, *Observations upon the Articles of Peace* (1649), which functioned as part of the ideological preparation for the Cromwellian campaign in Ireland, which was distinguished in turn by the extraordinary savagery (by British standards) of the massacres at Drogheda and Wexford. The propaganda initiative served as theoretical precursor to the expropriation of the Irish Catholic landowning classes. Milton's racial image of the Irish suggests their unqualified barbarism, primitivism even, combined with an inability to benefit from instruction. They are "sottish . . . indocible and averse from all Civility and amendment" (CPW 3:304), little better than animals and to be treated as animals. What Milton has to say about Italy sits interestingly alongside the simplicities of Marvell and Nedham and of his own portrayal of the Irish.

Certainly, hostile stereotypical notions of Italy were available in English popular culture of the early modern period. Consider, for example, the assumptions about Italian life which constitute the premises of *The White Devil* or *The Unfortunate Traveller*. As Nashe has a character observe:

Italy, the paradise of the earth and the epicure's heaven, how

---

[2] "The Character of Holland," lines 7-8, 34, 71-72, *The Poems and Letters of Andrew Marvell*, ed. H. M. Margoliouth, rev. Pierre Legouis and E. E. Duncan-Jones, 2 vols. (Oxford: Clarendon Press, 1971), 1:100-101.

[3] *Mercurius Politicus*, persistently in the issues for 1650 and elsewhere.

doth it form our young master? It makes him to kiss his hand
like an ape, cringe his neck like a starveling, and play at heypass,
repass, come aloft, when he salutes a man. From thence he
brings the art of atheism, the art of epicurising, the art of whor-
ing, the art of poisoning, the art of sodomitry.[4]

Milton sometimes uses such popular associations when it serves the
polemical moment. In *Areopagitica*, for example, he disputes the argument that censorship improves the moral climate with the sally, "If the
amendment of manners be aym'd at, look into Italy and Spain, whether
those places be one scruple the better, the honester, the wiser, the
chaster, since all the inquisitionall rigor that hath bin executed upon
books" (2:529–30). His comment only works if his reader subscribes to
the received view of honesty and chastity in Italy (and Spain). Again, in
an image scintillating with a barbed wit, he describes the appearance of
a title-page once it has been through the intricacies of the Florentine or
Roman licensing procedures and bears all the right imprimaturs:

Sometimes 5 *Imprimaturs* are seen together dialogue-wise in the
Piatza of one Title page, complementing and ducking each to
other with their shav'n reverences, whether the Author, who
stands by in perplexity at the foot of his Epistle, shall to the
Presse or to the spunge. (2:504)

Milton's depiction of the scene trades upon English assumptions not
only about the high incidence of a monkish clergy in Italy, but also
about the nature of Italian manners. The "complementing and
ducking" is rather like the cringing and heypassing of Nashe's description—phoney, affected, and essentially "unEnglish."

Elsewhere in *Areopagitica* Italians appear as victims of popery and as
exemplars of the sort of decline popish prelates and their Presbyterian
imitators would foster in England:

I have sat among their lerned men, for that honor I had, and
bin counted happy to be born in such a place of *Philosophic*
freedom, as they suppos'd England was, while themselvs did
nothing but bemoan the servil condition into which lerning

---

[4] *The Unfortunate Traveller and Other Works*, ed. J. B. Steane (1971; repr.
Harmondsworth: Penguin, 1978), 345.

amongst them was brought; that this was it which had dampt the
glory of Italian wits; that nothing had bin there writt'n now these
many years but flattery and fustian. There it was that I found and
visited the famous *Galileo* grown old, a prisner to the Inquisition, for thinking in Astronomy otherwise then the Franciscan
and Dominican licencers thought. (2:537–38)

Milton is, for modern academic readers, at his most attractive here.
Especially in the pamphlets of the early 1640s, however, references to
Italy generally function somewhat differently, though we find a pointer
in Milton's parenthesis about his own familiarity with Italian academies.
Seemingly he has achieved an ingress that constitutes a rare honor for
an Englishman: announcing his cultural credentials lends an authority
to his analysis of the intellectual life of continental Europe.

Several such announcements appear in his antiprelatical pamphlets,
and they serve well that sort of cultural rank-pulling that informs his
strategy against bishops in general and Joseph Hall in particular. While
Smectymnuus offered qualified, learned, and sober refutations of the
enemy, often couched in terms approaching deference, Milton acts on
the old assumptions of Martin Marprelate, that the bishops are lechers,
dullards, idlers, gluttons, and clowns.[5] The construction of the hostile
image works in part through the associated process in which he defines
himself as smarter, better informed, and, perhaps most important, more
cultured. Consider the polemical significance of the cultural values
inscribed in this passage, in which he is giving an account of Athanasius's views on the relative status of scripture and patristic writing:

> The very first page of Athanasius against the Gentiles, averres the
> Scriptures to be sufficient of themselves for the declaration of
> Truth; and that if his friend *Macarius* read other Religious
> writers, it was but φιλοκάλως *come un virtuoso*, (as the Italians
> say), as a lover of elegance.... (*Of Reformation*, CPW 1:564)

This quoting in Greek and glossing in Italian may seem a little
pretentious, and the idiom, "as the Italians say," carries an implication
that he has *heard* them say it, not merely read it in England. In terms
of the documentation of his argument, both Greek and Italian are

---

[5] See my "Obscenity, Slang and Indecorum in Milton's English Prose," *Prose
Studies* 3 (1980): 5–14.

redundant, but they function rhetorically. Milton, in refuting the arguments of prelatical antiquarians, is careful to do so in terms which suggest his own learning. While *Of Reformation* offers an argument for the simple clarity of the Gospels over the convolutions of patristic writing, it does so with every show of its author's culture and scholarship. Thus, Milton not only cites Dante and Petrarch and Ariosto (in my experience, a literary species of evidence without precedent in this debate), but he adds they are "three the famousest men for wit and learning, that *Italy* at this day glories of" (558): Milton not only knows these Italian writers, but he also knows what Italians contemporaneously think of them. Again, when he imparts to his readers a view of the Jesuits which all thinking English Protestants probably subscribed to already—that they corrupt youth and learning—he adds "and I have heard many wise, and learned men in *Italy* say as much" (586).

Milton's shrewdness as polemicist is often understated. Even in his first pamphlet he showed a smart capacity to anticipate the responses of the enemy. Sure enough, when the prelatical apologists get around to answering him, their game plan is to suggest that he is a half-educated parvenu, ill-prepared to tangle with his betters. The anonymous *Modest Confutation* of his *Animadversions* on Bishop Hall offers a biographical fantasy of Milton as a dissolute and ignorant B.A.[6] The Miltonic response is to reiterate his credentials as Italianate humanist. George Thomason did not date his copy of the *Modest Confutation*, nor was it registered. There is some evidence, however, to support the view that it appeared while Milton was composing *Reason of Church-Government* (CPW 1:863–64), which contains an episode of autobiography unique within the polemical writing of the English civil war (1:805–23). In a much-quoted passage Milton once more invokes the Italian experience:

> But much latelier in the privat Academies of *Italy*, whither I was favor'd to resort, perceiving that some trifles which I had in memory, compos'd at under twenty or thereabout (for the manner is that every one must give some proof of his wit and reading there) met with acceptance above what was lookt for, and other things which I had shifted in scarsity of books and conveniences to patch up amongst them, were receiv'd with written Encomi-

---

[6] Anon., *A Modest Confutation of a Slanderous and Scurrilous Libell, Entituled, Animadversions* (London, 1642), passim.

ums, which the Italian is not forward to bestow on men this side the *Alps.* . . . [etc.] (1:809–10)

The whole passage meets nicely the attempted character-assassination of his enemies, but once more the parenthesis, as he leans to his readers to advise us, in passing, how one behaves in an Italian academy, carries the full cultural charge.

There are similar though less developed passages elsewhere in the early prose—for example, in his invocation of Italian practise in naturalizing loanwords (*Animadversions*, 1:667), or his regret that Bishop Hall seems not to know the Italian satirists (*Apology*, 1:915). References to Italy and Italian culture become much less frequent in later vernacular prose, though he resumes them in Latin polemic addressed to a continental audience. Of course, there may be a simple psychological point: the recollection of the Italian journey may have faded, whereas earlier he may have thought about it frequently. I think, however, the relative decline in the importance of such allusions may reflect a shift in his role in the English political scene. In his early writing, Milton is engaged in what I have elsewhere termed a quest for respectability.[7] The appropriate intertext for those early works is dominated by that laboriously produced stereotype of the radical as low-class, uneducated, and unpropertied, and Milton works long and hard to distance himself from that notion. The self-image he produces of himself as Italianate humanist offers a stratagem of some importance, but it is one which, in a sense, he does not need in his republican prose, where a certain triumphalism displaces whatever cultural edginess may earlier have obtained.

But Milton adopts other roles, both in his early prose and later. When the exigencies of polemic require, Milton can play the patriot, asserting England's role in the forefront of the Reformation, calling on Europe to witness its political achievement, and praising the virtues, both literary and cultural, of the English tongue. As a student, Milton had adroitly assumed the role of apologist for the English language: "At a Vacation Exercise in the College," with its resounding invocation, "Hail native language," in the context of its original performance probably played opportunistically on an undergraduate audience's

---

[7] "Milton's Quest for Respectability," *MLR* 77 (1982): 769–79.

reservations about classical language acquisition. Later, when he wants
to build a vision of a native English reforming zeal (though perverted by
episcopacy), he persistently invokes almost as a role-model the figure of
Wyclif, "our Country m[a]n" who "open'd the eyes of *Europe*" to the
spirit of Reformation (*Doctrine*, 2:232; see also 1:704, 2:502, 553). In a
spurious argument in *Areopagitica*, he tries to demonstrate that licensing
is "unEnglish" because English, "the language of men ever famous [for]
liberty," contains no such tyrannous words as "imprimatur" (2:504–5).
Of course, English is and always was replete with words for bondage,
thraldom, serfdom, and so forth. The republican *nom de guerre* adopted
on the title page of his Latin defences, "Joannes Miltonus *Anglus*,"
accords well with the posture.

Sometimes a rather different European perspective emerges. Milton
offers himself as heir to and co-worker in the European reformation, a
direction most explicitly developed in his divorce tracts, and particularly
in *The Judgement of Martin Bucer*, but implicit in much of his more
technical and more heterodox theological writing. Again, the posture
serves the polemical purpose. When Milton's views on divorce attract
the savage attentions of Presbyterian and allied divines, he demonstrates
the cultural and doctrinal continuities between himself and those
European divines most respected by English Calvinists. With obvious
relish, he lists as a coda to his own most thorough account analogous
arguments from "a faire number of renowned men, worthy to be [the
Presbyterian divines'] leaders," and predominant among them are the
luminaries of the Northern European reformation, Luther, Calvin, and
their associates (*Tetrachordon*, 2:707). Not Italy, but the northern
Germanic states are offered as a spiritual home.

One person may indeed play many parts, nor, if he is as complex as
Milton and if he is responding cunningly to the requirements of political controversy, do the parts necessary follow serially. Milton's ways of
representing himself to his readers—or, perhaps more accurately, to his
perceived readers—sometimes lack an ultimate coherence but rarely lack
skill, as we may see in his prose allusions to Italy and its culture, and
his energetic self-presentation occasions the assumption of various roles,
among them, the Italianate humanist, the European Protestant, and
John Milton, Englishman.

University College of North Wales—Bangor

SUSANNE WOODS

# "That Freedom of Discussion Which I Loved": Italy and Milton's Cultural Self Definition

**M**ILTON IN ITALY WAS AN OXYMORON in search of the higher resolutions of paradox: a Protestant in the center of Catholicism, a poet among liturgists, a young man enthusiastic about humanist learning among older men for whom the optimisms of Petrarch, Ficino, and Bembo had declined into a wary sophistication. In this ferment of cultural contradiction, Milton learned to define his own freedom by reacting dialectically to Italy as both familiar and foreign environment. In the process he affirmed his literary vocation, learned to express a national identity, and helped redirect England's vision of liberty.

We know that Milton's Italian experience boosted his sense of poetic vocation. The "literary parties" in Florence, the attention of Manso in Naples, and even the religious debates in Rome helped confirm that he was "destined ... from a child to the pursuits of literature" (1:822).[1] What has received less attention is the Italian journey's role in helping Milton to understand himself as an Englishman, and in particular to define the identity of his culture as one which characteristically valued and pursued liberty. That identity, in turn, became central to Milton's sense of his combined poetic and political vocations. Much of this understanding developed from his discovery of where he felt at home, who or what he felt as alien to him personally, and what he came to define as characteristically English.

The famous description of his Italian adventure in the *Second Defense* suggests that Milton experienced two levels of "homecoming": first

---

[1] Citations are from CPW, except for citations from *The Second Defense of the English People*, which are used, for the greater familiarity of their translation, from Merritt Y. Hughes. Citations from CPW appear in the text by volume and page number; citations from *The Second Defense* in Hughes appear in the text by page number and column letter (a or b). *The Second Defense* may also be found in CPW 4:612–20.

the return to Florence from Rome, where he "was received with as much affection as if [he] had returned to [his] native country," and finally the return to his actual "native country, after an absence of about one year and three months." Milton describes his return home to England as coinciding with (and prompted by) "the time when Charles, having broken the peace, was renewing what is called the episcopal war with the Scots, in which the royalists being routed in the first encounter, and the English being universally and justly disaffected, the necessity of his affairs at last obliged him to convene a parliament" (830a). The first homecoming is from Rome to Florence, from the defenses he felt himself forced to make of "the reformed religion in the very metropolis of popery" to the "literary parties" that confirmed his natural vocation (829a, b). It contrasts for Milton an alien popish culture with a familiar literary one. The second homecoming, from Italy to England in May, 1639, also highlights a cultural contrast, in part between foreign Europe and native England, but also, interestingly, setting "the English" against "the royalists."

In Florence Milton has learned to define himself confidently as a literary man, and on his return to define being English as the pursuit of liberty. It was, he tells us, "the melancholy intelligence" of civil strife in England that truncated, though it did not immediately end, his travel abroad (he "thought it base to be travelling for amusement abroad while ... fellow citizens were fighting for liberty at home"). And he claims it was the opportunity to promote liberty that spurred him to his pamphleteering when he returned:

> I saw that a way was opening for the establishment of real liberty; ... that the principles of religion, which were the first objects of our care, would exert a salutary influence on the manners and constitution of the republic.

The *Concordance to Milton's English Prose*[2] gives many direct references to Italy in the pamphlets, and to Rome as both place, ancient and modern, and symbol. I want to focus on three of Milton's earlier English prose works, two written within three years of his Italian experience, to show how quickly he incorporated the complexities of

---

[2] *A Concordance to Milton's English Prose*, ed. Laurence Sterne and Harold Kollmeier, Medieval & Renaissance Texts & Studies, vol. 35 (Binghamton, NY, 1985).

this experience into his cultural self definition. The first is Milton's earliest anti-prelatical tract, *Of Reformation* (May 1641), which indicates how Milton began to define differently his images of Rome and Florence as he sought to affirm an English national identity based on (Protestant) liberty. *The Reason of Church Government* (early 1642) and, most familiarly, *Areopagitica* (November 1644), illustrate particularly telling connections Milton made between his Italian experience and his identity as a rhetorician of religious and civil liberty. In the process Milton helps to define anew the English idea of freedom, connecting it to language and the "freedom of discussion" he had enjoyed, interestingly, in Italy.

A central strategy in *Of Reformation* is to appeal to an English nationalism identified with Protestantism and the authority of Scripture and a free conscience, in opposition to a tyrannical papacy firmly and specifically tied to Rome. The split between Rome and Florence in Milton's own mind is evident from the authority he uses to prove his points about Rome, ancient and modern. Rome is the "womb and center of apostacy" (1:547) ever since the emperor Constantine, who "marr'd all in the Church." Milton's denigration of Rome's imperial Christianity gains Tuscan reinforcement as "the opinion of three of the famousest men for wit and learning, that *Italy* at this day glories of": Dante, Petrarch, and Ariosto. Milton's admiration for Italy sustains itself by dividing south from north, by allowing Rome to represent repression, tyranny and antichrist, and Florence to represent reason and knowledge, indeed to confirm Milton's opinion of Rome. His argument in the first part of *Of Reformation* is that England is at a crossroads: it can go back to the dangers and oppressions of Rome, as the "antiquarians" would direct, or forward to the fulfillment of its Reformation heritage, beyond Italy altogether.

The second part of *Of Reformation* continues Milton's appeal to English nationalism and his dualistic use of Italian example. Its underlying logic is to argue that just as the popes subjected all of Italy to Rome (1:577–79 and 594–95), so the English prelates would subject free Englishmen to Romish oppression and exile: "What numbers of faithfull, and freeborn Englishmen, and good Christians have been constrain'd to forsake their dearest home, their friends, and kindred, whom nothing but the wide Ocean, and the savage deserts of *America* could hide and shelter from the fury of the Bishops" (1:585). To these godly exiled free English Protestants, Milton asserts, the prelates even prefer

"Jesuits, who are indeed the onely corrupters of youth, and good learning; and I have heard many wise, and learned men in *Italy* say as much" (1:586).

Throughout both parts of *Of Reformation* Florentine humanism and Milton's Italian conversations remain important authorities for the rejection of Rome and for his warning against the Romish direction of English prelaty. What he claims as episcopal rapine he associates with denial of England's particular parliamentary liberty (1:590 and 592–93). The work concludes with a patriotic assertion of English liberty, civil as well as religious ("there is no Civill *Government* that hath beene known ... more divinely and harmoniously tun'd, more equally ballanc'd as it were by the hand and scale of Justice, then is the Common-wealth of *England*"), and with Milton's poetic vision of an England reaping "*Nationall Honours* and *Rewards*," instructed by the figure of the poet (1:599, 616).

Though Milton's pamphleteering may be "the use ... but of [his] left hand" (1:808), *Of Reformation* illustrates and *Reason of Church Government* affirms that it will carry important rhetorical lessons from his Italian experience: it will be in the vernacular, it will move toward eloquence, it will speak of liberty, and it will assert the identity of its author. In *Reason of Church Government* Milton presents himself as primarily a poet, and makes his famous "covenant with any knowing reader" that he will fulfill his poetic promise, and in the English vernacular, once he has matured and England has "enfranchised herself from this impertinent yoke of prelaty, under whose inquisitorious and tyrannical duncery no free and splendid wit can flourish" (1:820). Milton's vernacular ambitions, central to his nationalism, are another illustration of the debt his cultural identity owed to Italy. *Church Government* credits "the private academies of Italy" with bolstering Milton's belief that he was destined to be a poet who "might perhaps leave something so written to aftertimes, as they should not willingly let it die" (1:809, 810). The connections Milton makes in this pamphlet between poetic and divine inspiration are themselves eloquent English, which Milton attributes to Italian example: he has chosen, he says, to follow "that resolution which Ariosto applied against the persuasions of Bembo, to fix all the industry and art [he] could unite to the adorning of [his] native tongue" (1:811).

In *Church Government* Florence and Rome come home to England as symbols for poetry and debate, and as devices for self-affirmation, the one by approval and the other by contrast, the one by identity, the other by difference. In line with the dialectical model for Renaissance self-fashioning, which posits identity with and differentiation from an entrenched culture, Milton has managed to articulate his own identity in the clarifying environment of a foreign experience set in the very home of humanism, which in *The Second Defense* he calls "the seat of civilization and the hospitable domicile of every species of erudition" (827b) where, nonetheless, under Popery, the natives must exercise a "composed and wary magnanimity" (819b).

A crucial result of the Italian journey, suggested throughout his pamphlets but perhaps clearest in *Church Government*, is that the humanist-educated Milton remains an admirer of Italian erudition but is also driven to identify himself and his values fully and characteristically with England. He may cite Dante and Petrarch against Constantine and bask in praise from the Florentine academies, but even comfortable Tuscany raises professed Catholics who must nod toward Rome. The English rebellion against prelaty makes Milton profoundly a patriot, and, more importantly, patriot of a country whose culture he imagines coincides precisely with his own values. It does not much matter whether he "really" believed that the English cultural identity corresponded with his own—there is some evidence that he did not. The important point is that in his earliest pamphlets Milton assumes that identification as his rhetorical stance, and makes the assumption of free discourse his personal contribution to the evolution of English ideology.

This is abundantly clear in *Areopagitica*, a work whose central strategy is to identify with the wise patriotism of the parliament to whom the pamphlet is ostensibly addressed and to define civil liberty as inherent in the English character. Milton makes interesting direct use of his Italian experience in this most eloquent of his pamphlets. As he contrasted oppressive Rome with a homecoming to enlightened Florence, so he contrasts his present audience, Parliament, with the oppressive tyranny of a prelatical monarchy. He offers his pamphlet as evidence of, as well as injunction toward, free discourse: "When complaints are freely heard, deeply considered,and speedily reformed, then is the utmost bound of civil liberty attained that wise men look for." Then, in blatant disregard for the pamphlet's own lack of license, he continues: "To which, if I now manifest by the very sound of this which I shall utter, that we are already in good part arrived, and yet from such a steep disadvantage of tyranny and superstition grounded into our principles as was beyond the manhood of a Roman recovery" (2:487).

Milton's contrast between Italian oppression and English liberty newly defines liberty not as the freedom from disorder so beloved by the Tudor and Stuart monarchies, but as the freedom to assert individual conscience over hierarchical authority, a dissenter's argument. If we set *Areopagitica*'s assumptions and arguments into a broader historical context, it further suggests the importance of Milton's Italian experience to his redefinition of liberty. Freedom in renaissance England had been, most simply, the citizen's right to participate in affirming public order under the law.[3] The English were traditionally proud of their status as freemen (as opposed to villeins or serfs) and associated it with a government of laws and with the characteristic generosity and lack of self interest that the words "free" and "liberal" had come to connote. Since generous behavior usually comes from those who can afford it, however, freedom is always associated with free agency, with the ability of a person to act without concern for self and without a personal sense of imposed restraint or deprivation. This is about as close as English renaissance notions of liberty come to modern ones. The Elizabethans and Jacobeans would have been astounded, not to say appalled, at the almost casual way the British, Americans, and most Europeans are currently allowed to speak against their governments.

The tradition of dissent that erupted during the English civil wars was based primarily on belief in the integrity of individual conscience informed by Scripture, an essentially protestant position that Milton affirms in *Church Government*. The dissenting pamphlets of the civil war and commonwealth periods therefore laid the groundwork for changes in the English idea of freedom that became established in the eighteenth century and were enunciated, for example, in the American Bill of Rights. Milton is among the most liberal and eloquent of those dissenters, who include such libertarian extremists as John Lilburne the leveller, Gerard Winstanley the "true leveller" or "digger," and that most dangerous group of radicals, the Quakers.[4] Unlike most of these, who

---

[3] See, e.g., Joel Hurstfield, "The Paradox of Liberty in Shakespeare's England," in *Freedom, Corruption and Government in Elizabethan England* (London, 1973), 50–76.

[4] In addition to the discussions of these theorists in CPW, especially vol. 2, see

get their dissenting posture by setting themselves against contemporary English self-definition, Milton assumes an English tradition of freedom that incorporates his ideas, and sets them against what he claims to be the recent, alien, practices of the Stuart monarchy and episcopacy.

The strategy in *Areopagitica* is to identify these recent monarchic practices, including censorship, with foreign tyranny symbolized by a Rome-dominated Italy, and so continue the identification of true Englishness with what is actually a revised notion of liberty. "Men will . . . see what difference there is between the magnanimity of a triennial parliament and that jealous haughtiness of prelates and cabin counsellors that usurped of late, whenas they shall observe ye in the midst of your victories and successes more gently brooking written exceptions against a voted order than other courts . . . would have endured the least signified dislike at any sudden proclamation" (2:488–89).

The free exchange of ideas he urges by flattery here is central to Milton's portrait of the good and moral life, uncloistered, which combines humanist erudition with protestantism—strong features of Milton's personal identity confirmed in Florence and Rome. The principle of knowledgeable choice is central to his view of both personal and political liberty. Political scientist Charles Geisst has examined apparent contradictions in Milton's political thought and concluded that they can be understood as resolving in an ethical system that underlies both his theological and political thought and depends upon the ability of human reason to distinguish good from evil and choose the good. In a fallen world this is only possible with education. Geisst concludes that, according to the evidence of *Areopagitica* among other pamphlets, Milton believed that "by his proliferation and actions as a free agent, man found himself in need of a civil society. The agency by which man functions in this society and at the same time worships God is reason. When reason becomes perverted through extraneous forces, it must be rectified by human means, viz. by education."[5] Education brings knowledge, but without the grace of free exercise of individual conscience there is no true liberty. As Geisst comments, to Milton a "man without a conscience was a man in bondage . . . no better than a fool or a slave.

Perez Zagorin, A *History of Political Thought in the English Revolution* (London, 1954).

[5] Charles Geisst, *The Political Thought of John Milton* (London, 1984), 29.

This is the cornerstone of Milton's political theory."[6]

In *Areopagitica* Milton contrasts such civil libertarian "English" protestantism to a panorama of censorship from ancient Greece to the present, concluding with an Italian model of the imprimatur system. Although Florence was for Milton the good Italy as Rome, symbolically at least, was the bad, he uses both Florentine and Roman imprimaturs as examples of Italian censorship, leading to elegant ridicule: "Sometimes five imprimaturs are seen together, dialoguewise, in the piazza of one titlepage, complimenting and ducking each to other with their shaven reverences, whether the author, who stands by in perplexity at the foot of his epistle, shall to the press or to the sponge" (2:504). It is this model "that so bewitched of late our prelates and their chaplains with the goodly echo they made," Milton claims, that it provoked the use of similar censorship dialogues in England, "so apishly Romanizing that the word of command still was set down in Latin ... perhaps, as they thought, because no vulgar tongue was worthy to express the pure conceit of an imprimatur, but rather, as I hope, for that our English, the language of men ever famous and foremost in the achievements of liberty, will not easily find servile letters enough to spell such a dictatory presumption English" (2:505).

Coming as it does from the most eloquent Latinist of his generation, this is perhaps disingenuous, but the terms of Milton's assertion are clear. English is the language of free men. To be English is to value and assert liberty. To write in English is to write freely. *Areopagitica* is arguably the first fruits of the vernacular eloquence, described in *Church Government*, that Milton hopes one day to exercise as a poet. Several of the flights of poetic prose that occasionally elevate *Areopagitica*'s rhetoric to the high style are tied directly to Milton's cultural articulation of English freedom. It is "our sage and serious [English] poet Spenser," a "better teacher than Scotus or Aquinas," who invites us to "see and know, and yet abstain" from intemperance. And it is prophetic Milton who sees

in [his] mind a noble and puissant nation rousing herself like a strong man after sleep and shaking her invincible locks ... an

---

[6] Geisst, 36–37.

eagle muing her mighty youth and kindling her undazl'd eyes at the full midday beam; purging and unscaling her long-abused sight at the fountain it self of heav'nly radiance (2:556).

The vision of his own enlightened "puissant nation" comes by contrast with what Milton has "seen and heard in other countries," most notably Italy.

> I have sat among their learned men . . . and been counted happy to be born in such a place of philosophic freedom as they supposed England was, whilst themselves did nothing but bemoan the servile condition into which learning amongst them was brought; that this was it that had damped the glory of Italian wits; that nothing had been there written now these may years but flattery and fustian (2:537-38).

The locution here is revealing: "a place of philosophic freedom *as they supposed* England was." Only in such subtleties is Milton's consciousness of his own subversion clear. And even with those signs of subversion, Milton presents the Florentine lesson as above all a lesson in the interconnectedness of his English identity, freedom, and true eloquence.

Milton learned in Italy that "erudition" was not enough. The pursuit of truth was not possible without the religious and political freedoms that permitted it. A life as God's poet must wait for maturity through political action aimed at free inquiry. *Of Reformation* sets out the premises of Milton's national identity in contrast to Rome and with the support of Florence. In *Church Government* and *Areopagitica* Milton found ways to challenge what Louis Montrose calls the dominant ideology without seeming to challenge a traditional English cultural identity.[7] Milton continues to identify English prelaty with Rome, while the appreciation of freedom and eloquence he found in Florence he attributes to Parliament and his English audience generally. On a broader level, Milton sets Italy as a whole, with its history, oppressions, and aspirations, against a vigorous and increasingly enlightened England.

---

[7] Louis Adrian Montrose, "*A Midsummer Night's Dream* and the Shaping Fantasies of Elizabethan Culture: Gender, Power, Form," in *Rewriting the Renaissance*, ed. Margaret W. Ferguson, Maureen Quilligan, and Nancy J. Vickers (Chicago: Univ. of Chicago Press, 1986), 65-87.

But Milton was no fool. He knew perfectly well that the parliamentarians he was praising would cheerfully continue to ban books on, for example, divorce. *Areopagitica* was itself an assertively unlicensed book. His rhetorical strategy shows him conscious of ideological reality and determined to change it, on the surface by what Stanley Fish calls the rhetorical rather than dialectical mode,[8] but substructurally by challenging traditional English ideas of freedom, responsibility, and governance. Milton's Italy moves from experience to strategy, and it is no longer Milton defining his own Englishness in *Areopagitica*, but Milton challenging England to define itself.

The full effect of Milton's efforts would not be felt until the debates on freedom that were so strong a feature of eighteenth-century British and American cultural self-definition. Yet the true English eloquence he confirmed in himself in Italy and turned on his own apparently unheeding parliament continues to resound its conviction, as well as its ironies: "It is the liberty, Lords and Commons, which your own valorous and happy counsels have purchased us, liberty which is the nurse of all great wits. This is that which hath rarefied and enlightened our spirits like the influence in heaven; this is that which hath enfranchised, enlarged and lifted up our apprehensions degrees above themselves." And then the challenge to become what Milton claims his English parliamentary auditors already to be: "Ye cannot make us now less capable, less knowing, less eagerly pursuing of the truth, unless ye first make yourselves, that made us so, less the lovers, less the founders of our true liberty" (2:559).

In his early pamphlets Milton brings to England that freedom of discussion which he so loved in Italy. "For me I have determin'd to lay up as the best treasure, and solace of a good old age, if God voutsafe it me, the honest liberty of free speech from my youth" (1:804), he declares in *Church Government*. In *Areopagitica* he asserts a personal and national identity not much reflected in the public policy of his own time, but resonant still in English speaking cultures.

Franklin and Marshall College

---

[8] Stanley E. Fish, *Self-Consuming Artifacts: The Experience of Seventeenth-Century Literature* (Berkeley: Univ. of California Press, 1972), 1–77 and passim.

DUSTIN GRIFFIN

# Milton in Italy:
# The Making of a Man of Letters?

C RITICS TODAY ARE INCREASINGLY CONCERNED about a writer's
literary career, not just the inward career (the momentous decision to be a poet, aspirations and frustrations, the sense of
inward ripeness, the conscious achievement), but the outward: what to
publish, when to publish, in what format, through what printer or
bookseller, for what audience. To think about bookseller, audience, and
career is to focus on the writer as professional. And although the term
"professional" has not been thought appropriate, Miltonists have in
recent years looked at Milton's place in the "literary system."

Richard Helgerson, for example, has proposed that we think of
Milton not as a gentleman amateur writer nor as a professional, but as
a "laureate" poet, who sees poetry as his vocation, devotes his life to its
service, and aspires to a Virgilian progress.[1] But Milton's 1645 volume,
in Helgerson's view, is rather a deferral of epic ambition than a fore-
shadowing of the great epic work to come after 1660. His analysis of
Milton's self-presentational gestures yields the conclusion that Milton in
1645 is still an occasional poet, dependent on the older patronage
system, linked by collaboration, commendatory poems, and publisher to
a world of cavalier gentleman-poets. By contrast, Thomas Corns argues
that the 1645 volume is not so much a deferral of the future as a timely
re-assertion—against contemporary attacks that he was only an ignorant
sectary—of Milton's status as a liberal humanist scholar.[2]

My larger concern, reflected in my subtitle, is with Milton's status as
a writer not just in the ideal "literary system" but in the practical world

---

[1] *Self-Crowned Laureates: Spenser, Jonson, Milton, and the Literary System* (Berkeley:
Univ. of California Press, 1982).

[2] Thomas N. Corns, "Milton's Quest for Respectability," *MLN* 78 (1982): 769-79;
"Ideology in the *Poemata* (1645)," *MS* 19 (1984): 195-203.

of print culture. Despite the work of Helgerson and others, I don't think we yet fully understand Milton's role in his culture as a public writer. We don't even have adequate terms to define a learned writer who received a government salary, signed contracts with booksellers, owned rental property, and loaned money at interest. As Helgerson himself shows, Milton combines aspects of amateur, professional, and laureate. And his categories, derived from Elizabethan practice, make less and less sense as the seventeenth century unfolds. Corns's terms reflect not socioeconomic realities but the polemical tactics of Milton and his opponents. My specific concern, signalled by my title, is with Milton's Italian journey of 1638-1639. What difference did that journey make, in the context of Milton's first published volume in 1645, and of his long public career, from the first poems in the 1620s to the final works of the 1670s?

We are all familiar with William Riley Parker's answer. "Beyond doubt the Italian experience brought a turning point in Milton's development as an artist." The journey "confirmed and clarified his confidence, so that an 'inward prompting' could grow daily within him. After Italy, Milton knew what he had to do. In a sense, travel limited and confined his hitherto vague ambitions. He returned home content to be only the greatest of English poets."[3] Parker's thesis complements that of J. W. Saunders, who in a book on *The Profession of English Letters* (1964) argued that Milton was "converted" by his Italian trip, discovering that he was at once a citizen of the international world of letters and an intensely English writer, and finding in the Florentine academies a model for the "fit audience ... though few" that he would seek to address.

We can understand that biographers might wish to see the Italian journey as Milton's conversion, and his consecration. It seems to represent a pilgrimage to the Mediterranean sources of the Renaissance, to the home of Dante, Petrarch, Ariosto, and Tasso, and of the Latin writers before them. It represents a revelation of beauty and warmth to a young man from a distant and marginal northern land, a "cold / Climate" that may not have felt conducive to poetry.[4] It may serve—

---

[3] Parker, 1:179, 180.

[4] Cf. *Mansus*, 24-29, where Milton says he has been "gelida vix enutrita sub Arcto" (poorly nourished under the frozen Bear).

though a bit late—as Milton's coming of age (at the age of 28), the end
of the prolonged first phase of his life, and the announcement of the
beginning of the real literary career. It enables the biographer, worried
as much as Milton is about the late beginning, to declare that his hero
is now on his way toward the great literary achievements for which
Milton is remembered. Such a view of the Italian journey is in fact vali-
dated by Milton himself, who in autobiographical reflections, especially
in the 1650s, looked back on the days in Italy as a period of crucial
encouragement.

Furthermore, it is reasonable to suspect that it was the Italian
journey which placed firmly in Milton's mind some important literary
models after which he would pattern his own work. Milton himself
wrote not long after his return from Italy of Tasso's *Jerusalem Delivered*
as a "diffuse" model of the epic he imagined writing one day. And he
explicitly vowed to follow Ariosto as a writer who determined not to
write in Latin but to adorn his native tongue.[5] To some extent Milton
went on to imitate Italian writers. Scholars such as F. T. Prince have
pointed to the "Italian element" in Milton's verse. Andreini's *Adamo
Caduto* is properly included among the many sources and analogues of
*Paradise Lost.* In the end, it is true, the Italian writers do not seem
significant models for Milton's great poems. He would have been
familiar with their work in any case, without making a trip to their
homeland. Even so, to discuss them in Italy with fellow writers may
have made an indelible impression.

But for all its attractions, this view of Milton's Italian journey seems
to me open to question, on three grounds: (1) it is built on too little
testimony from Milton, and doesn't take adequate account of the
rhetorical context of the famous few words with which he remembered
Italy; (2) it tends to glamorize the literary world of Italy in the 1630s,
and glosses over the extraordinary differences between that world and
Milton's own literary milieu in mid-seventeenth-century England; (3) it
implies a temporal and causal link—for which there is inadequate
evidence—between Milton's alleged "conversion" and his later literary
career. Let me take up these three points in order.

1. We have misread Milton's own testimony. It is surprising to re-

---

[5] *The Reason of Church-Government,* in CPW 1:811–13. All references to Milton's
prose are to this edition.

discover how little Milton said about the importance of Italy. All inter-
preters go back to the same two passages, in *The Reason of Church-
Government* and especially in the *Second Defense*, where Milton remarks
on his encouraging reception in the Florentine academies, his visit to
Holstenius in Rome, and to Manso in Naples. We need to remember,
furthermore, that Milton was not simply recording biographical data; he
was constructing an artful *defense* of his moral and literary character.
Elsewhere, when the context and the decorum are pastoral, as in "Epitaphium Damonis," his Italian acquaintances appear as shepherds named
Menalcus and Lycidas. We know these to be useful literary fictions. The
autobiographical remarks in the prose are likewise not confessional
asides; they are no less carefully designed to achieve a specific rhetorical
purpose. His purpose is polemical and apologetic, that is, to argue a
controversial case, and to establish his own credentials as a controversialist. "I'd rather not write contentiously," he in effect claims in 1641;
"I'd rather devote myself to the kind of work that the Florentines
encouraged in me." Corns is right, I think, to suggest that the passage
in *The Reason of Church-Government* is designed to refute charges that
Milton was poor, ambitious, and ignorant. It declares instead that
Milton is a man with a gentleman's means, decorous modesty, and a
gentleman's education.[6]

The passage in the *Second Defense* is prompted by inflammatory
charges that he fled from Cambridge to Italy, to find a hiding place in
the "refuge or asylum for criminals." On the contrary, Milton claims, I
went to the "lodging-place of *humanitas* and of all the arts of civilization" (1.609). It is not only the extravagance of Milton's description that
should make us assess his words carefully for their evidentiary value.
Milton was quite ready, in another rhetorical context, to deprecate Italy
as a land of servility, flattery, and fustian, when his purpose (in *Areopagitica*) was to dissuade Parliament from abolishing native English
liberties.

Indeed, we need to use care whenever we find Milton reflecting
retrospectively on the shape of his career. At various times in his life he
looked upon the prose tracts of the 1640s, for example, as (a) an end in
themselves (*Second Defense*) and even a culminating achievement (*First
Defense*); (b) the training for some later great work; and (c) an unfortu-

---

[6] Corns, "Milton's Quest," 777.

nate interruption or deferral of his epic career (*The Reason of Church-Government*).

2. The Parker thesis tends to glamorize the Italy Milton saw, and to obscure the point that he could find little in contemporary Italian culture that he could use in England. The Italy that Milton saw was not the Italy of Dante, or Petrarch, or Ariosto, or Tasso. As Masson carefully noted long ago, the late 1630s represented a low point in Italian literature.[7] Since Tasso had died in 1595 Italy had produced no great writer. After Marino, Chiabrera, and Tassoni had died in the 1620s and 1630s, the writers who remained were minor figures and dilettantes. A later literary pilgrim like Boswell could meet giants like Voltaire and Rousseau in France and Switzerland; in Italy Milton could find (apart from Galileo, if he saw him) poets no more significant than Jacopo Gaddi, Carlo Dati, and Antonio Malatesti. As Johnson suggested later, the Italians gained more from the relationship than Milton did. The commendatory poems he exchanged connect him not with writers of any stature, but with Antonio Francini, Giovanni Salzilli, and a writer named Selvaggi, so minor that neither Masson nor Parker could discover his first name.[8] Their formal literary compliments—and Milton learned to ape the Italian style—are notoriously "extravagant."[9] The academies in Florence and Rome were mere shadows of their fifteenth-century antecedents, little more than clubs of gentlemen amateurs. Their members included some serious scholars, but when they met in the academies it was not to present their scholarship, but "mostly to listen to poems and to hear discourses on religion and morality and decorum."[10] A recent historian notes in their discourses commonplace contents and an "air of self-congratulation."[11] Though Milton's languages included French and Italian along with a number of classical tongues, theirs were limited to Italian and Latin. He apparently gave requisite proof of his wit and won praise not by reciting *Il Penseroso* or

---

[7] Masson, 1:712.

[8] Edward Chaney has recently proposed that "Selvaggio" was in fact an English Benedictine monk, David Codner, who in Italy sometimes called himself Matteo Selvaggi. See *The Grand Tour and the Great Rebellion* (Geneva: Slatkine, 1985), 244-48.

[9] Parker, 1:172, 177.

[10] Arthos, 12.

[11] Arthos, 20.

*Lycidas* or a speech from *Comus*, the great early works which we rightly remember and honor. Instead, it was probably one of Milton's early Latin prolusions or poems, formal academic exercises recalled now for an "academic" occasion. Milton himself called them "trifles." For political reasons (i.e., papal and Spanish influence in Counter-Reformation Italy) discussions were limited to safe topics.[12] Milton himself noted in *Areopagitica*—where his topic is free speech in England—that the members of the Florentine academies "did nothing but bemoan the servil condition into which learning amongst them was brought" (1.537–38).

This hardly sounds like the ideal community of writers, free citizens of the republic of letters, the fit audience though few, that some commentators imagine, or the model for Milton's later outspoken addresses to Parliament or the governments of Europe. Upon reflection, we might note that it is the social dimension of the academies that Milton emphasizes. As he says, they promoted "humane studies" but also encouraged "friendly intercourse."[13] Perhaps Milton was primarily delighted with the academies because he had spent much of his youth in solitary study. But upon his return home he could not expect to find or construct an English equivalent. The system of education he designed in 1644 was based not on the Florentines but on his own education at St. Paul's and on the writings of Vives and other Renaissance humanists.

What else did Italy offer Milton? A model of church and aristocratic patronage, in the persons of Cardinal Barberini and Giovanni Battista Manso. Although Milton could say (in *Mansus*) that he hoped some day to find such a friend as Tasso had found in Manso, he gave no indication either before or after his trip to Italy that he seriously sought out any kind of client-patron relationship in the older Renaissance fashion. Italy also offered an example of a culture dominated by the Roman church, in which Italian or English Jesuits might well plot against free-speaking Englishman. Even if such a culture promoted and protected literature, it could only confirm Milton's Protestant and anti-prelatical principles.

Furthermore, even if Ariosto and Tasso offered literary landmarks by

---

[12] Arthos, *passim*.

[13] *Second Defense*, in CPW 4.1.615–16. Milton proposed for his own country "the learned and *affable* meetings of frequent Academies" (1:819, my emphasis).

which Milton might steer his own course, in one important respect they enacted a social role that was wholly alien to the mature Milton. Both Ariosto and Tasso belonged to a sixteenth-century court-based culture in which writers were dependent upon patrons who provided employment, hospitality, and even literary direction. Ariosto received regular orders from one cardinal who employed him and was advised by another to write in Latin.[14] Tasso, in Milton's own words, left up to one of the Italian princes "the chois of whether he would command him to write of *Godfrey's* expedition against the infidels, ... or *Belisarius*, ... or *Charlemain*" (*The Reason of Church-Government*, 1.814). By contrast, only in his capacity as Latin Secretary did Milton take marching orders from Cromwell. In purely literary matters he was his own master. His promptings were "inward." Just a few lines before he notes that Tasso deferred to a prince of Italy, Milton declares that his own mind proposed her own subjects (*The Reason of Church-Government*). And in later years Thomas Ellwood's famous remark about *Paradise Regained* was received not as instruction but as a lucky and fruitful jest.

   3. There is inadequate evidence to support a causal link between the trip to Italy and the pattern of his career after 1660. Upon his return from Italy in the spring of 1639 Milton, despite his alleged conversion, took up a life similar to his life before Italy. It is difficult to find evidence of any "turning point." As Milton says, he rented a house for himself and his books, and "devoted myself to my interrupted studies" (4.1.621). The "academy" he opened was not a literary society but a school for young boys. It would be six years before he would publish his first collection of *Poems*, and twenty-eight years before he would publish *Paradise Lost*. What intervened of course was the 1640s, and their claims upon Milton's pen. We can only speculate what Milton would have done if he had been left to pursue his private studies. The famous literary program announced in *The Reason of Church-Government* (1642) has suggested to some that Milton would have turned to epic, or tragedy, or ode. But even that declaration must be read carefully. Milton covenants with the "knowing reader" to deliver,

---

[14] Milton especially notes with approval (and emulates) "that resolution which *Ariosto* followed against the perswasions of *Bembo*, to fix all the industry and art I could unite to the adorning of my native tongue" (*The Reason of Church-Government*, 1.811).

at an unspecified future date, some carefully unspecified work. Whether he has in fact laid particular literary plans is open to question.[15] In any case, the announced rhetorical purpose of the literary agenda is to assert (somewhat illogically, one might think) Milton's "right" to "meddle" in matters concerning prelacy (1.823).[16] And it seems reasonable to suspect that if uninterrupted he might simply have devoted himself to such projects as his *History of Britain* and his *Logic*, both begun in the 1640s, or the Latin dictionary.[17] Interestingly enough, this is precisely the sort of work done by the scholars of the Florentine academies.

As it is, Milton turned to polemical prose in the early 1640s, and when at last he returned to poetry in 1645 it was to bring out a volume of occasional verse consisting almost wholly of poems written prior to his Italian journey. So we cannot conclude that the alleged discovery and confirmation of his vocation in Italy led directly to any solid literary results. But we might suspect that, in an odd way, the Italian journey rather confirmed an older pattern than provided a new one. Can we perhaps see the 1645 *Poems* as Milton's *Italian* volume—the work of a gentleman amateur and private scholar? In this light, the Italian journey does not mark the crucial watershed in Milton's literary career. On the contrary, it reflects and reinforces older habits and patterns that Milton was later to outgrow. Even the allegedly new self-confidence that Parker points to seems already apparent in the Milton of *Lycidas* and *Comus*. He didn't need the Florentines to tell him he was a good poet. For the most part, Italy offered Milton very little that he could use or re-create in England, and little that significantly shaped his later career. If anything, his trip to Italy prolonged the pattern of private studies that Milton had established in the 1630s. It would take the violent dislocations of 1649 and of 1660, with their interruptions, gratifications, and ultimate disappointments—to dislodge Milton from a course that might have led him to an Italianate career as "a Gentleman of Great Note for

---

[15] Scholars disagree about the degree to which this covenant points toward the major poems.

[16] It is worth noting that in the same sentence appears Milton's claim—often challenged by critics—that he was "Church-outed by the prelates."

[17] When about 1649 Milton thought he had "an abundance of leisure," he turned not to poetry but to his unfinished *History* (Second Defense, 4.1.627).

Learning" (as Ellwood called him in 1662),[18] who wrote only learned treatises and occasional and complimentary poetry for circulation among his private friends.

Although at the end of his career he in fact published a number of books that resemble the sort of work produced in the Florentine academies—the *History of Britain*, the little treatises on grammar and logic—Milton after 1667 should be thought of, not as a Italianate gentleman scholar, but as a public author or man of letters.[19] I use the latter term here not in its Italian sense of elegant man of learning—though the minutes of one academy may refer to him as a *letterato inglese*[20]—but in its developing English sense of a public or career writer. He carefully saw his works into print in the format he thought best, revising when necessary for a second edition. He cultivated a kind of public persona, and published three of his last works with a portrait as frontispiece. He didn't worry about the shape of a laureate career and a satisfyingly epic climax, but (as Johnson admiringly reported) in his last years "did not disdain the meanest services to literature."[21] Though he signed contracts with booksellers, he did not apparently need the money, and may well have published simply because (as Johnson suggested) he took "delight in publication."[22] His labors, like those of Adam in Eden, were his pleasure. To understand Milton's mature and developed sense of his role as a writer, we need more answers, I suggest, than those provided by the Elizabethan literary system, the temporary demands of polemic and controversy, or the Florentine academies.

New York University

---

[18] French, 4:367.

[19] Was Milton perhaps attracted to print in part because the Italian academicians thought it honorable to publish? The contemporary *Apes Romanae* (Bees of Rome) lists a total of 450 published authors in Rome in 1631-1632.

[20] French, 5:385.

[21] "Life of Milton," in *Lives of the Poets*, ed. G. B. Hill, 3 vols. (Oxford: Clarendon Press, 1905), 1:147.

[22] "Life of Milton," 1:149.

DIANA TREVIÑO BENET

# The Escape from Rome: Milton's Second Defense and a Renaissance Genre

S UBSTANTIAL DISCREPANCIES EXIST between Milton's account
of his Italian trip in the *Defensio secunda* and some facts
known by his biographers: Milton claims he spoke out against
Roman Catholicism in Italy, and yet he was entertained by men within
the church hierarchy. He says he was threatened by a Jesuit plot in
Rome because he defended his religion, but he remained in the city for
two months. Milton's most intriguing inconsistency, however, concerns
his travels during the beginning of England's troubles. He declares that
he "thought it base" to be abroad "at my ease for the cultivation of my
mind" while his fellow-citizens fought for liberty at home (CPW
4.1.618–19);[1] nevertheless, he lingered in Italy for eight months after
he heard of the problems facing his compatriots.

Interest in Milton's discussion has centered especially on two issues,
his reference to a Jesuit plot in Rome and his reaction to the news of
war in England. Regarding the latter, Clavering and Shawcross suggested, over twenty years ago, that Milton altered only his intention to visit
Sicily and Greece, places where he expected to amuse himself, but did
not change his intention "to pursue further education primarily in
Italy."[2] Recently, A. N. Wilson has modified this interpretation only
slightly: Milton "claims that the news from England altered his purpose
in being abroad"[3]—what had begun as a pleasure trip became a serious

---

[1] All quotations of Milton are from CPW 4.1; of DuMoulin, from "Selections
from DuMoulin, *Regii sanguinis clamor*," in CPW 4.2. Subsequent quotations of both
authors are cited in the text using the standard abbreviation CPW and giving volume,
part, and page number.

[2] Rose Clavering and John T. Shawcross, "Milton's European Itinerary and his
Return Home," *Studies in English Literature* 5 (1965): 50.

[3] Wilson, 78.

period of preparation for the civic role the young man expected to play at home. As for the Jesuit plot, John Diekhoff expressed reservations in 1939:

> Finally, it is the biographers of Milton (those who admire him inordinately and those ... who do not) that have made much of Milton's claim to courage in Rome. Milton himself only tells us that he was warned of a Jesuit plot, that he ignored the warning, and that by the will of God nothing came of it. We are meant, of course, to deduce his courage and his honesty, but we are left to make as much or as little of the plot as we will.[4]

But a recent article concludes that Anthony Wood, the author of *Athenae Oxonienses*, was "probably in a good position to know" that Milton's claim in *Defensio secunda* "to have boldly criticized Roman Catholicism in Rome itself" was truthful.[5]

While these topics continue to provoke interest, their underlying inconsistencies cannot be resolved as matters of truth or falsehood. Besides, from the perspective of the *raison d'etre* and purpose of Milton's Italian story, its veracity is irrelevant: the author discusses his trip in the *Second Defense* because Peter DuMoulin had suggested (in *The Cry of the Royal Blood to Heaven Against the English Parricides*) that he fled to Italy in disgrace from Cambridge. In the context of DuMoulin's work, Milton's travel story sheds its status as questionable autobiography and comes into focus as part of a purposive polemical response. The chief pressures to which Milton responds in the *Second Defense* are unflattering characterizations of himself and of his Italian sojourn in *The Cry*. These depictions coincide with Milton's own sense of a particular vulnerability to criticism. His representation of his travel experience is meant to counter DuMoulin's personal attack and to assert his regard for Italy and for his friends there against the generally negative English view of that country. These motives help to shape the *Second Defense* and divide the Italian material in two parts, each part

---

[4] Diekhoff, xxxii. He cautioned that "no man who writes much of himself can always know or always tell the literal truth in what he relates, whatever he may omit. ... Milton is perhaps especially likely to mislead in passages in which he is replying to pamphlet attacks upon himself" (xxix).

[5] Allan Pritchard, "Milton in Rome: According to Wood," *MQ* 14 (1980): 95.

responding to a charge made in *The Cry*. In one section, Milton avails himself of a Renaissance genre that transforms the unprepossessing image of himself created by his antagonist. The "Escape from Rome" of popular literature is useful to Milton because it enables him, simultaneously, to echo the public disapprobation of Italy, to remain true to his own esteem and affection for that country, to express his scorn for Roman Catholicism, and to present himself as utterly heroic.

§

The *Defensio secunda* (1654) is a response to *Regii sanguinis clamor* or *The Cry of the Royal Blood* (1652) and is, in part, Milton's effort to counter Peter DuMoulin's personal attack. Milton realized that he was vulnerable to criticism because he had been in Italy and had stayed there after the troubles began in England. Indeed, DuMoulin had come uncomfortably close in *The Cry* to the sensitive area: "They say that the man was expelled from his college at Cambridge because of some disgrace, that he fled shame and his country and migrated to Italy. When the rebellion broke out, he was recalled from Italy into England with the hope of a new state of affairs" (CPW 4.2.1050). Milton feared that his remaining in Italy could be used against him, if discovered; consequently, he made the Italian trip the defiant centerpiece of a self-presentation tailored to refute DuMoulin's charges. He knew, as his antagonist had reminded him, that Italy had two facets in the public imagination:

> But why to Italy . . . ? Another Saturn, I presume, I fled to Latium that I might find a place to lurk. Yet I knew beforehand that Italy was not, as you think, a refuge or asylum for criminals, but rather the lodging-place of *humanitas* and of all the arts of civilization, and so I found it. (CPW 4.1.609)

One writing problem Milton confronted in the *Second Defense* was how to deal with the Italy he admired and the Italy indicated by his opponent and imagined by the English public. Englishmen of the sixteenth and seventeenth centuries were fascinated, whether they "harped more constantly on the attractions or the repulsiveness with which they credited the Italian world."[6] Sir Edwin Sandys, for instance, granted Italians some virtues, but maintained that "the whole Country is strangely overflowne and overborne with wickednesse, with filthinesse of speech, with beastlinesse of actions."[7] Notwithstanding this kind of opinion, Italy was admired also as a center of civilized values. Joseph Hall recognized the country's immense cultural allure and, at the same time, its supposed decadence when he argued that Italy could corrupt even mature travelers who went there for the sake of their education, travelers, that is, like John Milton: "For what discouragements shall they find from the love of studies in those parts which are most sought to for civility? Who knows not that they are grown to that height of debauchment as to hold learning a shame to nobility?"[8]

Milton decided to capitalize on Italy's reputation as a cultural mecca to counter DuMoulin's first and most obvious accusation, that of ignorance:

> One was found, after learning had been banished outside their land, who would dare to write Latin, a great hero, forsooth, whom they might pit against Salmasius—John Milton. (CPW 4.2.1050)

It is well known that Milton responded to the charge of ignorance by fashioning the "autobiographical sketch" in the *Second Defense* as "a deliberate attempt to show his high place in the world of learned and creative men."[9] But it has not been recognized that this attempt is almost entirely confined to his remarks on Florence:

> In that city, which I have always admired above all others because of the elegance, not just of its tongue, but also of its wit, I lingered for about two months. There I at once became the friend of many gentlemen eminent in rank and learning, whose

---

[6] John Walter Stoye, *English Travellers Abroad. 1604–1667* (London: Cape, 1952), 109.

[7] Edwin Sandys, *Europae speculum. Or, a View of Survey of the State of Religion in the Westerne parts of the world* (London: T. Cotes, 1638), 27.

[8] Joseph Hall, "*Quo Vadis?* A Just Censure of Travel, As it is Commonly Undertaken by the Gentlemen of our Nation," in *The Works of the Right Reverend Joseph Hall, D.D.*, ed. Philip Wynter (1893; repr. New York: AMS Press, 1969), 9:537–38.

[9] Don M. Wolfe, introduction to CPW, 4.1.259.

private academies I frequented—a Florentine institution which deserves great praise not only for promoting humane studies but also for encouraging friendly intercourse. (CPW 4.1.615-16)

Milton here identified the men who entertained him, welcoming him into their intellectual circles. Including their names, he complimented his friends and underlined his own credibility, but he suppressed some details in order to keep his account above reproach from any detractor: Milton did not mention that in Florence he "found himself happily a member of a Roman Catholic literary set." He did not identify his friend Coltellini as "the official censor at the Uffizi. Two other members of the group, Chimentelli and Bonmatthei, whom Milton mentions with especial warmth, were Catholic priests."[10] Obviously, Milton used the Italian reputation for learning to counter the charge made against him of ignorance; but he also used his experience in Florence to record his admiration for the whole country and to express his affection for those who befriended him in Italy.

§

Milton knew that Italy also figured in the popular mind as iniquitous. Every major Italian center was suspect to the English, and "Individual cities were associated with specific evils. Florence represented a certain type of political activity judged immoral. . . . Venice represented the evil of licentiousness. . . . Above all, Rome was England's danger."[11] The papal city was the focal point of the English attraction-repulsion, as Bishop Hall's metaphor reveals: "That Courtesan of Rome, according to the manner of that profession, sets out herself to sale in the most tempting fashion: here want no colours, no perfume, no wanton dresses."[12] Though obviously inviting, the calculatedly attractive lady was reputed also to be dangerous in 1599. "Roman pollicies" against

---

[10] Wilson, 82.

[11] The association of Florence with immoral political activity was due to "Duke Alessandro Medici who ruined the Republic, Catherine de Medici who ruined the kingdom of France and contrived St. Bartholomew's massacre, Machiavel who ruined Europe" (Stoye, *English Travellers*, 109).

[12] Hall, *Quo Vadis*, 533.

religious enemies were "things manifest and ordinary," and included "their *persecutions*, their *confiscations*, their *tortures*, their *burnings*, their secret *murthers*, their general *massacres*."[13]

As the center of Catholicism, Rome titillated the Protestant English imagination, in which a readymade villain led a cast of thousands in nefarious or superstitious activities: the pope is "a Devill"; "*Judas* was put in trust with a greate deale of the Devils businesse; yet not more than the Pope."[14] He presides over a profitable city of spurious shrines and relics where all things are for sale, where there are "cerain fixed shops and *Marts of miracles*, in one place a shop of miracles for *barrennesse*, in another, a shop for the *tooth-ache*."[15] The superstitious inhabitants of Rome "spend themselves, times, goods, lives, fortunes in ... ridiculous observations." The pope and his priests "have brought the common people into such a case by their cunning conveyances, strict disciplines, and servile education, that upon pain of damnation they dare not break the least ceremony, tradition, edict."[16]

Apart from the hatred many Protestants felt for everything about Catholicism, English suspicion of Rome had been fuelled in the sixteenth century by the Church's active desire to see Mary Stuart on the throne of an excommunicated Elizabeth, the Jesuits' undercover activities in England, and the close ties between Spain and Rome. One by-product of the charged religio-political situation between England and Italy had surfaced in popular literature: the "Escape from Rome" narrative was a Renaissance genre produced in England by the conjunction of many factors, including complex international and domestic political affairs; an aggressive Roman Catholicism; a religious fear bordering on hysteria; English xenophobia; and the various political, local, and personal pressures that compelled certain individuals at different times to assert, enhance, or defend their reputations. Moreover,

---

[13] Edwin Sandys, 103-4.

[14] Thomas Adams, "The White Devil," in *In God's Name: Examples of Preaching in England 1543-1662*, ed. John Chandos (New York: Bobbs-Merrill, 1971), 181; 180.

[15] *John Donne's Sermons on the Psalms & Gospels With a Selection of Prayers and Meditations*, ed. Evelyn M. Simpson (Berkeley: Univ. of California Press, 1967), 151.

[16] Robert Burton, *The Anatomy of Melancholy: What it is, with all the kinds, causes, symptoms, prognostickes & severall cures of it*, ed. Holbrook Jackson (1932; repr. New York: Random House, 1977), 3:367.

the narrative may also have been produced by some men who, instead of responding designedly to public or private situations, wished simply to record actual conditions or events they experienced in Rome: as we shall see, the boundaries between fact and fiction are blurred by a number of factors. The "Escape" (whose name I take from one of the paradigms cited below) is a part of the great mass of Renaissance travel literature written by a "multitude of robust extraverts, merchants, sailors, and travellers, who were going about their lawful or unlawful occasions all over the seven seas."[17] It may properly be seen as a type of popular literature because, beyond the common setting of the narratives, the various examples of the genre depend upon (or exploit) a particular cultural perspective to achieve their effect and, most significantly, because they share a distinctive plot. Milton uses the "Escape from Rome" to replace DuMoulin's characterization of him in *The Cry* with a more attractive image and to forestall criticism about his sojourn abroad. In this effort, the long-standing and negative English image of Italy, and especially of Rome, was a boon to the polemicist.

§

Perhaps because DuMoulin's charge of ignorance is so clearly stated, scholars have not noticed the second, and largely implicit, slur on Milton. He is likened to various small animals throughout *The Cry*. Beginning in the dedicatory letter to Charles II, the author deliberately diminishes him with a little self-reflexive flourish. Salmasius, Charles is told, is preparing an attack that will

> silence Milton for us, and will give him a castigation just as he deserves, "A monster, horrible, deformed, huge, and sightless." Though, to be sure, he is not huge; nothing is more weak, more bloodless, more shrivelled than little animals such as he, who the harder they fight, the less harmful they are. (CPW 4.2.1045)[18]

---

[17] Douglas Bush, *English Literature in the Earlier Seventeenth Century. 1600–1660* (Oxford: Clarendon, 1962), 190.

[18] Although some scholars now believe the dedicatory letter to be the work of Alexander More, its problematic authorship is not relevant to my present subject.

Subsequently, Milton is lessened by the "doubt, whether [he is] a man, or a worm" (1050); he is squashed by a sentence that links him successively with "a monster," a dragon, and "the serpent to be bruised under our feet" (1051). Milton is a "gallows-bird" (1051) or one of the "hounds" (1052). The diminishing images reach their climax in the scurrilous verses at the end of the pamphlet:

> Do you, you dung-heap, you blockhead, do you dare to gnaw away at men of Salmasius' caliber? Now let the mouse scourge the elephant, the frog revile the panther; let the foolish shrew-mouse twitch the mane of the lion, the ape scoff at the bear, the fly at the kite. . . . let scarabees defile the sacred bird of Jove and pollute Jove himself with their white droppings.
> (CPW 4.2.1078–79)

> Oh, if you were so greatly feared by all as you are cursed, then you would be more terrible than Hercules. . . . by your name mothers would frighten their nurslings; infants would tremble at you as a wolf-man who would eat little boys.

> It is well that as a public enemy, fierce with your threats, slyer than Sinon, more savage than Busiris, more fierce than a tigress seeking her whelps, you are yet less warlike than a scared rabbit.
> (1080)

Though the small animals' efforts to contest with the larger are laughable, their mettle might seem admirable. But DuMoulin stresses the difference between words and deeds to underline his opponent's utter unfearfulness. Even children cannot be frightened by a "scared rabbit," no matter how fiercely he threatens. Persisting and peaking, the small-animal imagery reveals its purpose at last as it leads to direct accusation. DuMoulin declares to Milton that the thought of the gallows "now shakes your wicked heart with fear, now strangles your wicked breath in your throat . . . and often breaks your sleep with fearful phantoms"

---

Whether it is the work of More or of DuMoulin, the letter is wonderfully consistent with the body of *The Cry* in its treatment of Milton. See Paul W. Blackford, preface to "Selections from DuMoulin," CPW, 4.2.1037.

(1080–81). Artfully, DuMoulin uses the gathering imagery to accuse Milton of cowardice.

Milton's hypersensitivity to DuMoulin's criticism springs from his realization of vulnerability. It is inaccurate to say that he "fends off an attack which as such his opponent has not made"[19] when he writes:

> Although I claim for myself no share in this [military] glory, yet it is easy to defend myself from the charge of timidity or coward-ice, should such a charge be leveled. For I did not avoid the toils and dangers of military service without rendering to my fellow citizens another kind of service that was much more useful and no less perilous. (CPW 4.1.552)

From this direct response to DuMoulin, with its admission that he did not fight, Milton advances to the equation of his polemical activities with warfare:[20]

> Wherever liberal sentiment, wherever freedom, or wherever magnanimity either prudently conceals or openly proclaims itself, some make haste to applaud, others conquered at last by the truth, acknowledge themselves my captives. (555)

> I think my war is over.... I must wage a posthumous war as well, and with a familiar enemy whose attacks I easily sustained when they were fierce and vigorous. (559–60)

Surely, the author who battles against fierce and vigorous attacks, triumphs, and takes captives cannot be accused of cowardice. I have argued that Milton's presentation of Florence was entirely positive, with the city figuring as "the lodging-place for *humanitas*" as well as the temporary domicile of the learned Milton. But the other Italy, the Italy

---

[19] Donald A. Roberts, preface and notes to *A Second Defence of the English People* in CPW 4.1.552n.

[20] Milton's use of heroic imagery in the *Second Defense* has been noticed before, by Joseph Wittreich, Jr., and by Annabel Patterson, for instance, but neither has seen it as arising, at least in part, from Milton's need to answer DuMoulin's attack. See Wittreich, " 'The Crown of Eloquence': The Figure of the Orator in Milton's Prose Works," in *Achievements of the Left Hand: Essays in the Prose of John Milton*, ed. Michael Lieb and John T. Shawcross (Amherst: Univ. of Massachusetts Press, 1974). See also Patterson, "The Civic Hero in Milton's Prose," *MS* 8 (1975): 71–101.

of the popular imagination, could be used to combat DuMoulin's "scared rabbit"; Rome was the natural background for a courageous Milton.

§

When English travelers from the late sixteenth century onward to Milton's day related their experiences in Rome, they only added particular details to the city that already existed in the popular imagination. With impressive frequency, they told a story whose plot was as simple as that of any morality play, and which was bound to appeal to their anti-Catholic countrymen. The Englishman's nationality and religion transform him into the Protestant-hero of his narrative. This hero arrives in the city of idolatry and superstition where attempts will be made to harm him spiritually or physically. He is in grave danger as long as he stays. But the English hero, protected perhaps by the invincible shield of the true faith, prevails. He escapes the threat of contamination or death to tell his triumphant story.

Anthony Munday was probably the first to publish an "Escape from Rome" narrative. A brief look at his book in its context suggests the political and personal exigencies that helped to create the popular genre at the same time that it indicates the welter of confused or questionable motives that were to plague (even while they informed) the type. Munday wrote *The English Romayne Life* after he had been a witness for the Crown against Edmund Campion and the other Jesuits executed in England in 1582. The book was his proof that he and Thomas Nowell had lived at the English College in Rome for some months in 1578. Munday's travels began simply out of a "desire to see straunge Countreies,"[21] but he and his friend were robbed. In order to persuade them to travel to Rome, "Roman soldiers" in Paris gave him and Nowell money and letters of introduction to the College. The attempts to convert the Englishmen continued persistently from their first evening in Rome, Munday asserts. When a priest took him aside for a

---

[21] Anthony Munday, *The English Romayne Lyfe* [1582], ed. G. B. Harrison (London: John Lane, 1925), 2.

long talk, his common sense told him that he was in danger and must appear, at least, to participate in the religious life of the College.

Munday maintains that others would have done the same "if they were at *Roome*, and behelde the mercilesse tiranny executed on the members of Christe, God not having endued them with the spirit of perseveraunce, to suffer and abide the like."[22] God's unwillingness that Munday should be a martyr made him, instead, an undercover agent within the enemy camp. His Rome consists primarily of the interior of the English College and the churches he visited, and he includes many details meant to show the total corruption of the Church. Particularly, in setting down the tale of which he is the only possible hero, Munday purports to describe the priests' concoction of falsehoods to cozen the ignorant.[23] Despite the fact that he was no martyr, Munday is still the creditable Protestant-hero of his narrative because, as he tells it, he remained untouched by the iniquity he describes; his faith was tried but he never abandoned it. He returned home to bear witness against the papists, but others did not escape Rome's physical and spiritual perils. Munday ends with the story of one Richard Atkins who came "to rebuke the great misorder" of the Englishmen at the College, was taken by the Inquisition and eventually burned to death. He reports the events in some detail to show the fate he avoided because God did not say "*I will that thou shalt suffer this.*" Atkins's death was glorious, but Thomas Nowell did not escape what Munday describes as the greater danger: he lost the true faith.[24]

According to Munday's own narrative, he is the sighted hero among the blind on their "dunghil of most irksome & noysom smell." But G. B. Harrison, his twentieth-century editor, reminds us that perhaps all the facts might tell another, different, story. Munday does not mention that he was trusted enough by the men at the College to carry messages and pictures from Rome to English Catholics. He does not mention that, two years after his return, he became a paid spy "and was taken on

---

[22] Ibid., 65.

[23] Munday says, for example, that the friars occasionally throw into the dark vaults of St. Pancratia dog, hog, or sheep bones to be found by pilgrims. They then identify the bones as belonging to "Saint *Fraunces*, Saint *Anthonie*, Saint *Blase*, or some other Saint that pleaseth them to name" (*Romayne Lyfe*, 58–59).

[24] 100; 65; 63.

the staff of Richard Topcliffe, the notorious anti-recusant agent, as informer and pamphleteer." He does not say that his veracity as a witness was questioned, notably by Luke Kirbie before his execution on the scaffold. Clearly, Munday's "word is very unreliable. On his own showing, he was a glib and facile liar who served himself well on all occasions."[25]

Obviously, the "Escape from Rome" was conceived by Munday as a mode of self-presentation and self-justification in the public forum. As such it could be useful to a liar who needed to assert his probity: since his escape supposedly precluded verifiable event or persecution, how could his authority be challenged? But we cannot safely conclude that the genre attracted only Renaissance liars because Edward Webbe, its next practitioner, would seem to have had no discernible reason to invent. Munday's travels took place in 1578 and his account was published in 1582. Webbe, a sailor whose extensive travels took him as far as Russia, was in Rome in 1588 and published *His Travailes* in 1590. It promptly went through three editions. Compared to Munday's very detailed and lengthy story, Webbe's escape narrative is brief, consisting only of one long paragraph. Webbe says he was "nineteene daies in trouble with the Pope, and the English Cardinall Doctor Allen"; after they let him go, he "was againe taken by ye English Colledge and put there into the holy house three daies, with a fooles coat on my backe, half blewe, halfe yellowe, and a cockescomb with three bels on my head, from whence I was holpen by meanes of an English-man whom I found there, and presented my petition and cause to the Pope: who againe set me at libertie."[26] Before he got to Rome, Webbe had been taken prisoner in Russia by the Tartars, and eventually ransomed. Perhaps we can assume that he enjoyed inventing adventures for himself but, with equal reason, we might assume that Webbe had enough exotic material without inventing the brief Roman interlude. *His Travailes* present the reader with the possibility that Protestant Englishmen, persecuted and endangered in reality, found it difficult to "Escape from Rome."

---

[25] 61; v; vi; viii.

[26] Edward Webbe, *His Travailes* [1590], ed. Edward Arber (London: n.p., 1869), 30–31.

Perhaps accounts like Webbe's made travelers like George Sandys expect trouble and, consequently, describe their departure from the city as perilous and difficult. Sandys ends a book (first published in 1615) that details his travels in the Turkish Empire, Greece, and Egypt with a rather thin "Escape from Rome." The heat, he remarks,

> enforced us to house our selves in an Inn some fifteen miles distant from *Rome*, unto which we rid in the cool of the evening. Having stayed here four days (as long as I durst) secured by the faith and care of Mr. *Nicolas Fitz-Herbert*, who accompanied me in the surveying of all the Antiquities and Glories of that City, I departed to *Siena*.[27]

Since Sandys does not mention any particular trouble it is impossible to understand why he thought he needed the protection of an exiled Roman Catholic or why he did not "dare" to stay longer than four days.[28] Nothing happened to Sandys, but his fearful expectation that something *could* happen fits his very brief narrative into the pattern of danger, courage, and escape.

For Fynes Moryson in his *Itinerary* (published in 1617), Rome was only one stop on his extensive travels. In 1594, he was there for about four days as a tourist, wishing merely to see as much as possible of the city in that brief time. And yet his narrative not only fits but seems to exult in the "Escape" pattern. Moryson figures as a spirited Englishman, an insouciant hero who enjoys nothing more than outwitting the Roman Catholics. When he arrived to see the sights, he made daily payment for his food and lodging, "so being ready upon all events of danger, and having no carriage to trouble us, we hoped if need were to escape."[29] Concern for his safety compelled him to seek the protection of the English Cardinal Allen. Allen, explains Moryson, had become

---

[27] George Sandys, *Sandys Travels, Containing an History of the . . . Turkish Empire* [1615], 7th ed. (London: John Williams, 1673), 240.

[28] Sells, 183.

[29] Fynes Moryson, *An Itinerary Containing His Ten Yeeres Travell through the Twelve Dominions of Germany, Bohmerland, Sweitzerland, Netherland, Denmarke, Poland, Italy, Turky, France, England, Scotland, & Ireland* [1617], 4 vols. (Glasgow: James MacLehose, 1907), 1:301.

more cordial to his countrymen since the English defeat of the Spanish Armada made "reducing England to papistry" an unlikely proposition. The Cardinal gave his protection on condition that Moryson would hold his tongue and "abstaine from offence. Onely for his duties sake, hee said, that hee must advise me, and for the love of his Countrey intreate me, that I would be willing to heare those instructions for religion here, which I could not heare in England."[30]

Keenly aware of the need for discretion, Moryson accomodated himself to the situation by agreeing to hear mass. As soon as he assented to Cardinal Allen's conditions, he says, he was surrounded by Englishmen and priests offering to serve as guides. He agreed. But "I well knew," he remarks, "that such guides would be very troublesome to me, for they (according to the manner) disputing of Religion, I must either seeme to consent by silence, or maintaine arguments ful of danger in that place."[31] Having told the would-be guides where to find him, and feeling that he was physically safe thanks to the Cardinal, he moved immediately to different lodgings. Thus neatly, with a self-satisfying ruse, Moryson claims he evaded attempts on his faith.

Considering that he was in Rome so briefly, Moryson describes a lot of successful trickery on his own part against the Romans.[32] After only four days in the city, as Easter approached, priests came to his inn to register every person "to know if any received not the Communion at that holy time." Moryson prepared to leave for Florence at once. Before going, however, he says he played one last elaborate trick to satisfy his curiosity. Having sent ahead his two Dutch companions to wait for him in the suburbs of Rome, he went to the Jesuits' College "attired like an Italian." There he asked to see Cardinal Bellarmine. Before "this man so famous for his learning," Moryson claims to have passed himself off

---

[30] 1:259; 260.

[31] Ibid., 1:260.

[32] Moryson feels the Italians are bound to "ridiculous observations" and, consequently, alert for the smallest deviation from ritual or tradition. When he and his friends rode on mules to visit the major churches, for example, they asked directions from a man whose surly reply was, "What doe you ride to heaven, and we poore wretches goe on foote without shooes to visit these holy Churches. By this we found our errour, and were glad that we had passed that day without further danger" (1:275). Once he avoids worshipping the Holy Stairs "which Christ ascended in Pilate's house at Jerusalem" by dodging into a nearby church, supposedly preferring to worship there. He walks in one door and out another (1:224).

as a Frenchman come to Rome "for performance of some religious vowes." He tried to flatter the "Champion of the Popes" by asking permission to return at "vacant houres to enjoy his grave conversation."[33] Bellarmine courteously granted the bogus Roman Catholic's request and, within the hour, pleased with himself, Moryson galloped toward Siena. This Protestant-hero did not merely escape unharmed from the dangerous city; as he went, he claims that he tweaked the toes of the seven-headed beast. Again, though Moryson reports that he felt threatened, nothing actually happened. Like Webbe and Sandys, he has no apparent reason to lie. However, Moryson's attitude and antics seem so playful that, if genuine, they suggest that he did not take the Roman peril seriously; but whether true, false, merely exaggerated, or partly invented, they show the potential self-enhancement available to the protagonist of the "Escape from Rome." An Englishman who dresses like an Italian and passes himself off as a Frenchman to a Cardinal "famous for his learning" is an extraordinary creature, real or imaginary, and not a bad image to present to the English world.

William Lithgow traveled in 1609 and published his account in 1632, just six years before Milton began his travels. Lithgrow was very anti-Roman Catholic and gave his experience the marginal heading *My Escape from Rome*. He says he was in the city for twenty-eight days and "hardly escaped the hunting of those blood-sucking Inquisitors." "And to speke trueth, if it had not beene for Robert Meggatt ... who hid me secretly for three dayes in the top of his Lords Pallace, when all the streets and ports of Rome were layd for me, who conveighing me away at the fourth mid-night, and leapt the walles of Rome with me, I had doubtlesse dyed."[34] Lithgow does not explain why, particularly, he was hunted but his rabid anti-papist stance might explain his assumption (founded or unfounded) that he was of interest to the Inquisition. In this case, given Lithgow's fanatic hatred of Catholicism and the absence of any specific details, we may conclude that paranoia alone could produce the pattern of danger, courage, and escape.

The next Escapee from Rome was Sir Edward Herbert, who travelled

---

[33] Moryson, *An Itinerary*, 1:303; 304.

[34] William Lithgow, *The Totall Discourse of the Rare Adventures & Painefull Peregrinations of Long Nineteene Years Travayles from Scotland to the Most Famous Kingdomes in Europe, Asia and Affrica* [1632] (Glasgow: James MacLehose, 1906), 18.

in late 1614–early 1615 and wrote his account in the 1640s. He never finished his *Autobiography*, which remained unpublished until 1764, but his story is of interest, nonetheless. First, Herbert tells about being congratulated at the English College as the sole visiting Englishman courageous enough to acknowledge his Protestantism.[35] Then he describes his second trip to Rome, telling how he

> saw the Pope in consistory, which being done, when the Pope being now ready to give his blessing, I departed thence suddenly; which gave such a suspicion of me, that some were sent to apprehend me, but I going a bye way escaped them, and went to my inn to take horse, where I had not been now half an hour, when the master or regent of the English College telling me that I was accused in the Inquisition, and that I could stay no longer with any safety, I took this warning very kindly; howbeit I did only for the present change my lodging, and a day or two afterwards took horse, and went out of Rome towards Siena, and from thence to Florence.[36]

Herbert's account leads the reader again to the issues of self-presentation and veracity. No one who reads Sir Edward "will be inclined to give much credence" to the account written by the self-centered and self-satisfied man.[37] But even if it is self-promoting fiction, Herbert's story is of value, indicating how popular the genre had become, how current and useful it was to a man wishing to create a courageous image. Moreover, it demonstrates yet again the scant material that could be fashioned into the "Escape from Rome" narrative.

Writing about travel narratives from Bacon's *New Atlantis* to Swift's *Gulliver's Travels* Jenny Mezciems points out the "interdependence between fact and fiction in travel narratives mostly of the Renaissance period" and reminds us of the difficulty faced by the author:

> One of his problems, at the very time of widened horizons and opportunities in the Renaissance, was that travel narrative traditionally belonged to fantasy. The new material, however factual,

---

[35] Edward Herbert, *The Autobiography of Edward, Lord Herbert of Cherbury*, ed. Sidney Lee (1886; repr. New York: Dutton, 1906), 82–83.

[36] 83–84.

[37] Diekhoff, xxxii.

was strange, and therefore romantically exciting; readers themselves would give the narrative the status of literature … and accomodate it within an existing literary tradition. But in this tradition travellers from Odysseus onwards were conventionally liars or poetic inventions, and their accounts real only as myth is real.[38]

In addition to the latitude created by readers' expectations, we have seen that other pressures might inspire the writer to embellish or invent: the genuine expectation of danger, religious paranoia or a fertile imagination, as well as the occasional necessity to maintain one's good character or perhaps the occasional compulsion to self-aggrandizement. Additionally, of course, there is the possibility that some writers of escape narratives simply recorded actual events.

§

By the time Milton went to Italy in 1638, several factors had helped to diminish tensions between England and the Papal States. The combined presence of Henrietta Maria on the throne and the absence of a parliament from 1629 had led to a relatively peaceful period of about ten years for English Catholics. Rome reciprocated with a fairly tolerant attitude toward visiting Englishmen; the Queen was, after all, the godchild of Pope Urban. From December 1634 to June 1641, there was a papal agent at her court in London and a Queen's Resident representing her in Rome from June 1636 until mid-May 1640.[39] In addition to this virtual exchange of ambassadors, relations between the Romans and the English were improved by being under the particular care of Cardinal Francesco Barberini. The pope's nephew and a Secretary of State, Barberini had been officially appointed Cardinal Protector of England and Scotland in 1626. The extent of Barberini's involvement with the English court and his awareness of the state of affairs in England was impressive. He was in close communication and continual negotiations with Henrietta Maria and members of her entourage

---

[38] Jenny Mezciems, " 'Tis not to divert the Reader'; Moral and Literary Determinants in Some Early Travel Narratives," *Prose Studies* 5 (1982): 2, 3.

[39] Gordon Albion, *Charles I and the Court of Rome. A Study of Seventeenth-Century Diplomacy* (Louvain, 1935), 149–50.

especially because of her wish that Urban create an English cardinal.[40]

It is likely that Milton found a hospitable Rome when he traveled there. In about December 1639, however, after he had returned to England, the public restraint about Roman Catholicism inspired by the Queen's position gave way: "When it became certain that a Parliament would be called, voices were raised against the Papists all over the Realm."[41] The Long Parliament itself was the chief forum used to signal the end of even a sham religious toleration. Cornelius Burges preached a sermon on November 17, 1640 to the House of Commons, marking their public fast. Some of his remarks seem to have been directed at the Queen's chapel, the center of Roman Catholic worship in London:

> Beloved, let me speake freely, for I speake for God, and for all
> your safeties. You cannot be ignorant of the grosse Idolatry daily
> increasing among us, and committed not (as adultery) in Corners
> onely, but in the open light; people going to, and coming from
> the Masse in great multitudes, and that as ordinarily, openly,
> confidently as others go to and from our Churches.[42]

Less than five months later, in a sermon to the Commons marking another public fast, Samuel Fairclough referred to the "Froggs and Jesuits of *Rome*" in the nation: "Oh therefore hast their ruine, and your owne triumph; though *Rome* was not built in one day, yet may it be, nay it shall be destroyed in a day."[43] In the early 1650s, when Milton wrote the *Second Defense*, anti-Roman Catholicism was still the standard. Given his opinion of the Roman faith, his need to assert his courage against DuMoulin's attack, and his awarness that his uncurtailed sojourn in Italy made him vulnerable to criticism, it is not surprising that he turned to the "Escape from Rome."

---

[40] 323.

[41] 337.

[42] Cornelius Burges, "A Responsibility to Punish. A Sermon preached . . . on November the 17th., 1640," in *In God's Name: Examples of Preaching in England 1543–1662*, 347.

[43] Samuel Fairclough, "A Call for Blood. The Troublers Troubled, or Achan Condemned and Executed. A Fast Sermon preached before the House of Commons on 4th April, 1641," in *In God's Name*, 373.

Milton's account of his brush with danger is brief but strategically placed:

> Although I desired also to cross to Sicily and Greece, the sad tidings of civil war from England summoned me back. For I thought it base that I should travel abroad at my ease for the cultivation of my mind, while my fellow-citizens at home were fighting for liberty. As I was on the point of returning to Rome, I was warned by merchants that they had learned through letters of plots laid against me by the English Jesuits, should I return to Rome, because of the freedom with which I had spoken about religion. For I had determined within myself that in those parts I would not indeed begin a conversation about religion, but if questioned about my faith would hide nothing, whatever the consequences. And so, I nonetheless returned to Rome. What I was, if any man inquired, I concealed from no one. For almost two more months, in the very stronghold of the Pope, if anyone attacked the orthodox religion, I openly, as before, defended it. Thus, by the will of God, I returned again in safety to Florence.
>
> (CPW 4.1.618-19)

Milton's statement about his fellow-citizens reveals his strategy. The military imagery declares him a hero. "Stronghold," "attacked," "defended," and "safety" in this context make him a Protestant soldier, a courageous parallel to the English people fighting for freedom at home. Far from being abroad "at his ease for the cultivation of his mind," Milton braved a great danger to go to Rome, where "For almost two more months" he defended the orthodox religion. His very absence from England, which might be construed to his discredit, Milton transforms into the successful foreign campaign of a warrior.

A reader has noticed an omission in Milton's account: "In sharp contrast to his exuberant references to literary friends and associations in Florence is Milton's limited mention of like experiences in Rome. He notes by name only Luc Holste or Holstenius."[44] There are other omissions: Milton does not tell his reader that, on his first trip to Rome, he was entertained at the English College. He does not reveal

---

[44] Donald A. Roberts, preface and notes, 618n.

that Lucas Holstenius was Cardinal Francesco Barberini's secretary and librarian, or that he met him at the Vatican library. There is no mention of the fact, either, that he was Barberini's guest. Milton does not say that, during his second trip to Rome, he

> attended a splendid concert at the Cardinal's residence. Milton described it, in a letter to Lucas Holstenius. . . . he was flattered when the Cardinal made his way through the crowds and . . . asked Milton to call on him privately the next day, and this was clearly a success.[45]

In fact, according to his account, during his second stay in Rome, Milton did only two things: he defended the faith, deliberately placing himself in great peril to do so, and he succeeded in surviving the danger by his providential escape. Milton answered DuMoulin's charge of cowardice with an astute version of the "Escape from Rome."

§

Inevitably, Escape narratives from Munday to Milton reflect the troubled history of England and Rome, a combative Protestantism, events surrounding the authors, and their personal situations. The Rome presented by these authors did not differ materially from the city in the mind of the pew-bound English. But they had been there and returned. Contemporary circumstances shaped the Escape narratives into a common structure whose spirit expressed the deep-seated English fear of an aggressive, corrupt Rome, a structure that appealed to the equally deep-seated conviction that Protestantism (being "true") deserved the victory over Catholicism. Naturally, the Protestant heroes, armed with the true faith, were impervious to Rome's threats and machinations. They never wavered before the error and danger constituting the city they saw. Their experiences defined Rome in terms familiar to their Protestant readers: it was the lair whose trappings could threaten but never ensnare the righteous.

Did Milton embed in the *Second Defense* a clue to his artful disposition of selected events when he wrote that he "should like to be *Ulysses*" (CPW 4.1.595)? The foregoing has shown the difficulty of distinguishing between fact and fiction in "Escape from Rome" narratives.

---

[45] Wilson, 89.

Without sufficient, verifiable information, it is impossible to answer tantalizing questions about biographical truth. But we can assert with confidence that in the *Defensio secunda* Milton created an image to oppose an image, deliberately fashioning a doughty Protestant hero to eradicate a scared rabbit.

To counter DuMoulin's insinuations, Milton needed to prove himself an educated and courageous man. Moreover, his antagonist had reminded him of the form Italy took in the contemporary imagination: he had to reckon with the English (and his own) hostility to the center of Roman Catholicism in spite of his personal affection for Italy and for his Italian friends. Milton responded to these pressures with a finely-articulated piece of polemical writing. Whatever the truth of his extended stay and of the Jesuit plot, the "Escape from Rome" enabled him to accomplish several objectives. He used the vulgar ideas of Italy and of Rome, especially, to create a heroic persona with which to counter the prosaic and unmilitary facts that he remained abroad after the fighting had begun in England, and that he did not fight in the war at all. The popular genre enabled him to express his conviction that the work he did (defending "the orthodox religion") was as courageous as, and more important than, physical warfare. There is more than one way to do battle, and the effort Milton claims to have begun in Rome he carried on in England, indisputably, after the war. By providing him a frame that gave his experience a heroic cast, the Escape narrative enabled Milton to express, in the *Defensio secunda*, a whole complex of feelings and attitudes about Italy, its culture, its people, and its religion. Florence became the name and location for everything Milton found delightful and admirable in Italy; Rome he sacrificed to longstanding English fears, to his disapproval of Roman Catholicism, and to his controversialist's need to present himself as a soldier the equal of those who fought at home. To consider Milton's Italian story as mere autobiographical sketch is to scant its subtle artistry and its brilliance as a polemical rejoinder.[46]

New York University

---

[46] A research grant from Georgia State University enabled me to complete this essay, and I am grateful to Dean Clyde W. Faulkner and Professor Virginia Spencer Carr for their assistance in obtaining it. For help with the essay itself, I wish to thank John Shawcross, who made useful suggestions on an earlier version.

A. M. CINQUEMANI

# Through Milan and the Pennine Alps

ALTHOUGH, IN THE SECOND DEFENSE, Milton mentions Milan only as a city he "proceeded through" on his way to Geneva it must have interested him more than those words imply.[1] Having studied the church fathers only a year or two before, he would certainly have associated Milan with St. Ambrose; even more so, the poet, whose *Paradise Lost* was so profoundly influenced by the *City of God*, and who called his theological treatise *De doctrina christiana*, would have thought of St. Augustine. Milan was also the city where the "famous renowner of Laura" had lived (1353–1361), himself inspired by the *Confessions*. And in his poem to Manso, written on his departure from Italy, Milton reflects on Chaucer's Viscontean visits: "Quin et in has quondam pervenit Tityrus oras" ("And Tityrus also long ago made his way to these shores").[2]

A curiosity significant to the "reconstruction" of Milton's visit is that it was (very nearly) Borromean, or "Manzonian," Milan through which Milton passed. If he took the route that had been established by the end of his century, he approached Milan from Verona by way of the towns of Castel Novo, Desenzano, San Marco, Brescia, Ponte di San Pietro, Palazzolo sull'Oglio, Canonica d' Adda, and "Colombardo" (Cologno Monzese?), avoiding *bravi* and gypsy predators all the way.[3] Like Renzo Tramaglino, who, in the *Promessi Sposi* of Manzoni, enters Milan on St. Martin's day, in November, 1628 (that is, not quite eleven years earlier), Milton must have walked or ridden between the hedges

---

[1] *The Second Defense of the People of England*, trans. Robert Fellowes, in Hughes.

[2] *Manso*, line 34, in Hughes.

[3] Nicolas de Fer, *Cartes nouvelles et particulières pour la guerre d'Italie* (Paris: Chez l'auteur, 1705). See the map *Routes des Postes d'Italie*.

on the Stradone di Loreto (present-day Corso Buenos Aires), skirting the Lazzaretto, where, seven or eight years before his arrival, as many as 15,000 plague victims were hospitalized at a given time, and entered the city through the Porta Orientale. There he might have observed the houses about which Minucci had complained ninety years earlier, houses of "the most ugly form, without architectural distinction."[4] He would have proceeded, like Renzo, down the Corso di Porta Orientale to the Corsia dei Servi (present-day Corso Venezia and Corso Vittorio Emanuele), which, just beyond the famous bakery El Prestin di Scansc, led (and still leads) to the Duomo. It is not even unlikely that Milton stayed at an inn near the center, like the Osteria della Luna Piena in Via Armorari, athwart the Ambrosiana.[5] He would have been wise to avoid the Quartiere di Porta Romana, nearby, where, in the Palazzo Trivulzio, the devil was said to live.[6]

Only seven years had passed since the great "Manzonian" plague was declared ended (2 February 1632), and only nine since the so-called *untori*, who had presumably caused the plague, had come to a terrible end. The plague, as well as famine and mercenaries, had brought the population of 130,000 (in 1631) down to 60,000 or 70,000. It was a time of war between Spain and France; Milan, at this time under Spanish administration, was therefore involved. This city of 800 *ettari* (almost 2,000 acres) was ruled, in 1639, by Gian-Giacomo Prince Trivulzio, a general of the cavalry, who had been created cardinal by Pope Urban VIII. Approximately 25,000 men were under his command, not only Spaniards, but Germans, Swiss, Neapolitans, and Lombards.[7] The population suffered; the mood was somewhat paranoid, as is suggested by Paolo Morigia several years before Milton's visit

---

[4] A. Minucci, *Descrizione d'un viaggio fatto nel 1549 da Venezia a Parigi* (Turin, 1862), 397. This and the other lines translated from Italian in this paper are mine.

[5] See Alessandro Manzoni, *I Promessi Sposi* (Milan: Hoepli, 1936), 11:174-75; Giuseppe Bindoni, *La topografia del romanzo I Promessi Sposi*, 2d ed. (Milan: Villardi, 1951), 14-20, 60-66; Alberto Lorenzi, *La Milano dei Promessi Sposi* (Milan: Serie Città di Milano, 1969), 19, 48; Giampaolo Dossena, *Guida ai misteri e segreti di Milano* (Milan: Sugar, 1967), 14; Carlo Torre, *Ritratto di Milano* (1674; reprint, Milan: Arnaldo Forni, 1973), 323-78. For the Prestin di Scansc and the Osteria della Luna Piena, see *I Promessi Sposi*, 12:183, and 14:209 ff.

[6] Bruno Caizzi and Aldo Ballo, *Milano dell'età spagnola* (Rome: LEA, 1960), 15.

[7] V. Forcella, *Milano nel secolo XVII* (Milan: Tarra, 1898), 19-20, 59-70.

when he hesitates, in his *Sommario*, to describe the Castello Sforzesco in detail because he "might begin to be suspicious to the princes."[8] Cantù characterizes the public mood of this period quite negatively: "no other sentiment, then, in men's hearts but cowardly fear; no other example but that of submission and baseness, made respectable with the name of prudence."[9] Thus Spanish, Counter-Reformation, militaristic Milan would probably not have encouraged a sense of security in the young English Protestant.

Yet Milan was an ancient imperial city with memories of the paleochristian era, and it clearly had not lost its appeal. In spite of the effects of war, plague, and the Spanish occupation, it retained most of the happy features earlier praised by Morigia: it was still "a glorious country, its air being extraordinarily clean, its land most fertile, its wines most light, the water healthy."[10] Count Onofrio Castelli had observed, in 1635, four years before Milton's arrival (yet after the plague), that Milan was extraordinary in being an ancient city that had remained great while the others had fallen: "it never fails to be a great city, always maintains itself as great; and if it comes to be devastated quickly revives to greatness."[11] Although, as the ambassador Redaelli complained, the city was in grievous debt, the taxes high, and the poverty of its inhabitants attributable to "so many disorderly military billets,"[12] Milan, long famous for its superior armor, still produced arms, wrought and spun gold, silks, damasks, and felt hats, all, however, under the protectionist control of Spain.[13] One result of this flow of goods was a colony of merchants, some of them English. A curious passage in a seventeenth-century book on fashion suggests that English influence, at least in polite society, was considerable in Milan in 1639, probably because of

---

[8] Paolo Morigia, *Sommario delle cose mirabili della città di Milano* (Milan: J. delli Antonii, 1609), 68.

[9] Forcella, 37.

[10] Morigia, 71.

[11] *Consviderationi del Conte Onofrio Castelli sopra dve delle singolari doti della città di Milano* (Milan: Ghisolfi, 1635), 3.

[12] Raffaele Bagnoli and Franco Fava, *Milano: Il tramonto delle Signorie* (Milan: Famiglia Meneghina, 1984), 118.

[13] Galeazzo Gualdo Priorato, *Relatione della città e stato di Milano* (Milan: L. Monza, 1666), 131.

the presence of merchants and their families. For the Milanese women had begun to adopt, and the men admire, the English fashion in skirts:

> The skirt or petticoat (to say it pleases is not enough), beneath the doublet latched with moiré silk, [was] so short that it left part of the legs exposed to lookers-on; with stockings of purple silk interlaced with gold that, worn loose, neglectfully, and flounced, seemed to fall above the feet; on which were little golden shoes, with a finger's-width of leather heel below, and above, two rose-buds the color of the stockings. They say I have held her of England, I mean the ladies of that country, in high esteem, who wear their skirt[s] in this way.[14]

Since Milton admits, in the *Second Defense*, to having consulted with (presumably) English merchants on his way back to Rome, there is no reason to think he did not have the same sort of contact with their counterparts in Milan.

Other wonders remarked by seventeenth-century travelers like Paolo Morigia remained: the Duomo, whose incomplete façade did not hide the remnants of the old cathedral, Santa Maria Maggiore, still visible within (did that sight take root in Milton's imagination: the "Fabric huge / [That] Rose like an Exhalation," the project for three hundred years of the Veneranda Fabbrica?); the Ospedale Maggiore, constructed by Ludovico Il Moro; the Lazzaretto; the Episcopal Palace; the Castello Sforzesco, "in beauty, size, and strength impregnable."[15] That Milton witnessed these monuments, relics for the most part of the Viscontean and Sforzan past, but reminders also of the prominence of Milan in the establishment of Christianity, cannot be doubted. Whether he was moved at the sight of monuments that might refer to motives in his own intellectual and spiritual development is not clear. An attachment to such "relics" might seem a sort of unprotestant superstition.

Still, the works that Milton was to write in the years following his Italian visit, in particular the antiprelatical and divorce pamphlets and

---

[14] Giovanni Sonta Pagnalmino, *Carozza da nolo overo del vestire e vsanze alla moda* (Venice: Giacomo Bortoli, 1655), 47. Sonta Pagnalmino refers to the year of Milton's visit, 1639. Concerning the fashion of "sweet neglect," cf. Herrick's "Delight in Disorder."

[15] Morigia, 68.

the two *Defenses*, are studded with references to Constantine, St. Ambrose, and St. Augustine, all of whom loom large in Milanese history. Even thirteen centuries after them, Milton's Milanese contemporaries were keenly aware that "in all the Holy Roman Church, spread out around the world, only four men were designated Doctors, of whom our city was made illustrious by two [Ambrose and Augustine]."[16] Of course, Milton's references to Constantine are hardly approving: it was through his influence that "the Church that before by insensible degrees welk't and impair'd, now with large steps went down hill decaying."[17] Perhaps, if he thought of Constantine in Milan, he associated him only with the visible signs of decay, and nothing else. But it is difficult to be in the Ambrosian city and not think of Ambrose. Moreover, one suspects that Ambrose had already exerted a permanent influence upon Milton, since several of his basic theological concepts were drawn from him.[18] It was, however, the "political" Ambrose who might have interested Milton during his visit to Milan. He later seemed impressed by Ambrose's contentions with Roman power, though he found the bishop's own power unseemly:

> Not an assembly, but one *Bishop* alone, Saint AMBROSE of *Millan*, held Theodosius the most Christian Emperor under excommunication above eight moneths together, drove him from the Church in the presence of his Nobles, which the good Emperor bore with heroick *humility*, and never ceas't by prayers, and teares, till he was absolv'd, for which coming to the Bishop with *Supplication* into the *Salutatory*, some out Porch of the Church, he was charg'd by him of tyrannicall madnes against GOD, for comming into holy ground.[19]

Did Milton's intellectual/historical interest translate itself into a sense of place? His unsureness about the salutatory (in the passage above) seems to imply that Milton did not associate the account in *Of*

---

[16] Ibid., 84.

[17] *Of Reformation*, in CE 3:25.

[18] See, for example, C. A. Patrides, *Milton and the Christian Tradition* (Oxford: Clarendon Press, 1966), 18, 95, 99, 174, and passim.

[19] *Of Reformation*, in CE 3:70–71.

*Reformation* with a church he had, it must be assumed, actually seen: Sant'Ambrogio. Can he have looked at the atrium of Sant'Ambrogio basilica and not thought of Theodosius prostrating himself before Ambrose, of Augustine hesitating to interrupt Ambrose's studies? Was he not reminded of the election of that remarkable layman? Could he have failed to think of the struggles between Catholic and Arian? It is difficult to believe that Milton made his way through Milan oblivious to the paleochristian churches built by Ambrose, harking back to the conversion of St. Augustine, built on the sites of martyrdom (Sant'-Ambrogio, San Lorenzo, San Nazaro, San Simpliciano; Santa Tecla and the baptistery of San Giovanni alle Fonti had already been razed in 1639).

Could Milton have passed through Milan and not thought of the *Confessions*, books 5-9? If he was interested in monuments at all, he would certainly have sought out the little church of Sant'Agostino; every Milanese thought (mistakenly) that "here this saint [Augustine] received the water of baptism from St. Ambrose, with Adeodatus his son and Alipius his companion."[20] (Neither Milton nor his contemporaries could have known, as present-day scholars agree, that Ambrose actually baptized Augustine in the baptistery of San Giovanni alle Fonti, whose ruins were discovered in 1942.) Opposite the basilica of Sant'Ambrogio was the site of Petrarch's house (presently at Via Lanzone, 53), a short distance, to have the story of Milton intersect with that of Manzoni, from the house in which Bernardino Visconti, the "Innominato," lived (Via Lanzone, 2), and from the monastery of Santa Valeria, where, during Milton's visit, the penitent (actual) Nun of Monza still suffered. Whether Milton was interested at all in the artistic, architectural, and intellectual contributions to Milan of, let us say, Leonardo and Bramante (the *Cenacolo*, Santa Maria delle Grazie, and so on) is an open question. Milton is curiously silent about art.

The Tuscan form of Italian that Milton no doubt had learned might not have prepared him for Milan, where Milanese dialect was widely spoken. It was not used in a merely familial, social sense but also for literary satire. For example, the pretensions and vacuity of the Milanese *accademie*, which promoted the use of Tuscan Italian, were held up to

---

[20] Torre, 172.

scorn in satirical compositions in dialect.[21] "Above all," said Carlo Maria Maggi a generation after Milton, "keep our language free from filth" ("Sora el tut tegnii ben la nostra legna / Netta di immondizi").[22] Thus, if Milton stayed in Milan for any length of time, he might have needed to refer to a work such as the *Varon Milanes* (1606) of Giovanni Capis, a sort of Italian-Milanese dictionary, or the *Prissian de Milan* (late sixteenth century) of Giovanni Ambrogio Biffi, to understand such terms as "nagot" ("niente," nothing) and "a oùr a oùr" ("a tempo," in time).

Milton would probably not have found the *accademie* of Milan as stimulating as those he had visited further south. Considering that the Accademia dei Lincei in Rome had published a work as important as Galileo's *Istoria e dismostrazioni intorno alle macchie solari* in 1613, and the Crusca of Florence the *Vocabolario* in 1612, there is little to be recommended in the seventeenth-century Milanese production. It is unlikely that Milton would have found a Milanese Benedetto Buon- mattei with whom to correspond concerning, let us say, the *questione della lingua*. Carlo Maria Maggi, who might have served that function, was, at the time, only nine years old. However, there was no lack of Milanese schools (the Palatine, the Brera) or *accademie* (the Animosi, the Arisofi, the Incerti, the Infuocati, the Inquieti), none of them of special literary significance, not even the latter, which was formed in 1594 by the Marchese di Caravaggio "to the end of treating important subjects."[23] Unfortunately, the most prestigious member of the In- quieti, and one of the greatest intellectuals of seventeenth-century Milan, the polymath Ludovico Settala, correspondent of Galileo and Justus Lipsius, had died six years before Milton's visit. And of course he was a century too late to meet Cardan, who seems, with his "subtleties," to have been a sort of joke to Milton.[24]

Although Federico Cardinal Borromeo had died in 1631, the cultural and philosophical influence of this scholar, *literatus*, and

---

[21] Bagnoli and Fava, 84.

[22] Ferdinando Giannessi, *Il declino spagnolo*, vol. 11 of *Storia di Milano* (Milan: Fondazione Treccani degli Alfieri, 1958), 416.

[23] Forcella, 90–99; Bagnoli and Fava, 84–85.

[24] "Subtleties beyond Cardan," *Animadversions*, in CE 3:114.

antiquarian was still felt in 1639 in the Ambrosian Library. Milton, who had had Holstein show him about the Vatican Library, might indeed have been interested in the Ambrosiana.[25] This public library, which had opened its doors in 1609, contained the 30,000 printed books and 15,000 manuscripts collected during his lifetime by Cardinal Borromeo. The collection included such works as the palimpsest of Plautus and of Cicero, Arabic and Syriac versions of the Bible, the *Ilias picta* (a fifth- or sixth-century Byzantine manuscript), the 1470 Venetian edition of Virgil (with Petrarch's marginal notes in his own hand), the 1471 edition of Boccaccio, the Gothic Bible of Ulfilas, and the correspondence between Pietro Bembo and Lucrezia Borgia. It would soon contain the *Codice Atlantico* of Leonardo.[26]

Cardinal Borromeo had also established, in the same building, an art museum (now the Pinacoteca of the Ambrosiana), an Accademia delle Belle Arti, a print shop capable of printing books in oriental characters, and three colleges: the Collegio Trilingue, the Collegio degli Alunni, and the Collegio dei Dottori, one of whose members was Giuseppe Ripamonti, who was writing his account of the recent plague, *De peste* (1640), at the time Milton was in Milan. Whether Milton might have met him, historian of the Council of Trent and defender of Catholic doctrine, is doubtful.[27]

The greatest paintings the Pinacoteca Ambrosiana would ever contain were already part of the collection in 1639. If Milton remained more than a day or two in Milan, he might have heard of and seen the private collection of the Canon Manfredo Settala, son of Ludovico. The *palazzo* in Via Pantano of this "Italian Archimedes," as he was called,

---

[25] See Manzoni's account of the Ambrosiana in the earlier seventeenth century in *I Promessi Sposi*, 22:318-22.

[26] Giorgio Chittolini, "La città storica," *Milano*, 9th ed. (Milan: Touring Club Italiano, 1985), 209-14. There is a fairly complete account of the holdings of the Ambrosiana in 1698/99 in Bernard de Montfauçon, *The Antiquities of Italy*, 2d ed. (London: J. Darby, 1725), 8-16.

[27] For a sampling of Ripamonti's work, see *Alcuni brani delle storie patrie*, trans. C. T. Dandolo (Milan: Arzione, 1856). Giuseppe Gargantini's *Cronologia di Milano* (Milan: Editrice Lombarda, 1874), 247, indicates that Ripamonti took up the task of writing the history of the plague on 23 December 1635. See also Bagnoli and Fava, 86-87, 127; Giannessi, 428. One of the *dottori* of the Collegio was, curiously enough, called Giovanni Antonio Salmazio, apparently no relation to Claude.

was frequented by foreign visitors throughout the year. It was certainly the most famous "salon" of seventeenth-century Milan. One wonders if Milton made the acquaintance of this best known of living Milanese intellectuals, eight years his senior, whom Giannessi describes "illustrating, explaining, and discussing with a fervor that clearly combined science and necromancy, ingenuous curiosity and proud encyclopedism."[28] The Settala collection, which was absorbed by the Ambrosiana in 1751, was destroyed during World War II.

If the "men of letters who had it from [Milton's] daughter" were correct in reporting to Voltaire that Milton had seen Andreini's *Adam, or Original Sin* during his visit to Milan, one would expect the performance to have occurred in such a place as the *palazzo* of Manfredo Settala. (Of course, Voltaire's claim is taken with a grain of salt because he first locates the performance in Florence and because the facts, not reported elsewhere, have never been corroborated.)[29] If Voltaire was correct, Milton's stay in Milan, assumed to have taken place in May, 1639, could not have been short.

Assuming Milton did have some time in Milan, one would expect him to be interested in purchasing books. Although Milanese book publishing, once illustrious, was, because of the repressive measures of the Counter-Reformation and the disorders of war, generally in a state of decline during the period of Milton's visit, he might still have found something of value in the book shops in Piazza Mercanti. There, between the Palazzo dei Giureconsulti and the Palazzo della Ragione, in the shadow of the statue of Philip II (which Manzoni describes as being on the point of saying, "I'm just coming after you, you rabble")[30] books of "singular elegance" published by Federico Agnelli and Giovan Battista Bidelli and printed by Ghisolfi were available.[31] However, the future writer of the *Areopagitica* would have found no book that did not reflect the "plots and packing of Trent." This is suggested in a letter sent in 1567 by Pietro Galesino to Carlo Cardinal Borromeo. He assures the Cardinal that booksellers in Milan will have to abide by the

---

[28] Giannessi, 435.

[29] See French, 1:378–80.

[30] Trans. Archibald Colquhon, *The Betrothed* (New York: Dutton, 1961), 12:174.

[31] Forcella, 142, 250; Giannessi, 437.

rules of the Counter-Reformation. They must have "a book or inventory of all the books stocked in the shop, subscribed by both a deputy of the archbishop and the father-inquisitor," and they must not "sell books not listed in the inventory, nor sell Bibles in translation or common books concerning the controversies between Catholics and heretics." Booksellers were not permitted to buy books that were still "to be purged," and were not allowed to "buy books for themselves or for others in Germany and in other places suspected of heresy."[32] Milton must have been happy to leave Milan and head for Protestant Geneva.

Masson imagines Milton, after his "rapid transit ... across the northern Lombard plains," "crossing the Alps by St. Bernard" and taking a "last look at Italy beneath."[33] Since he made his way along Lake Geneva, Milton might just as easily have taken the Simplon as the Great St. Bernard route into Switzerland; the former had been in use since the fourteenth century.[34] If so, Milton's route would have taken him through the Porta Comasina or the Porta Tenaglia in Milan to Saranno, Varese, Laveno, across the Lago Maggiore to Domodossola, and then, by the Simplon Pass, to Brig and the Rhone Valley. In Geneva he could, as Masson puts it, delight "in a breath of fresh Protestant theology after so long a time in the Catholic atmosphere of Italy."

State University of New York<br>The College at New Paltz

---

[32] Mario Bendiscioli, *L'età della riforma cattolica*, vol. 10 of *Storia di Milano* (Milan: Fondazione Treccani degli Alfieri, 1957), 467.

[33] Masson, 1:831.

[34] George B. Parks, *The English Traveler to Italy* (Rome: Edizioni di Storia e Letteratura, 1954), 517-19.

*Images*

JOHN R. MULDER

# Shades and Substance

> ... he stood and call'd
> His Legions, Angel Forms, who lay intrans't
> Thick as Autumnal Leaves that strow the Brooks
> In *Vallombrosa*, where th'*Etrurian* shades
> High overarch't imbow'r ...
>
> (PL 1.300–304)

THE EPIC SIMILE DEVELOPED FROM HOMER'S simple metaphor into the very signature of the grand epic manner and reached its apogee in *Paradise Lost*, where it achieved an almost magical "multiplicity and precision of logical, actual, and visual correspondence."[1] The lines that refer to leaves and shades in Vallombrosa occur in the description of Satan's moving to the edge of the fiery flood where he first beholds and next addresses his followers, who then begin to stir at his command.[2] The entire passage is richly ornamented with similes that move in pairs: Satan's shield is like the moon, his spear taller than a pine; the angel forms are like leaves in autumn and like sedge on the Red Sea; they are numberless as a plague of locusts and more numerous than the Goths invading from the North.

Although *Paradise Lost* now appears to us with the patina of a literary classic, the Miltonic style is self-consciously modern—most notice-

---

[1] These are the criteria for the success of the developed literary simile as given in the *Princeton Encyclopedia for Poetry and Poetics*, ed. Alex Preminger (Princeton: Princeton Univ. Press, 1974), 768.

[2] Although lines 300–304 of book 1 are my object, their context is the cluster of similes that refer to Satan's size and the number of his followers, in lines 283–355. Quotations from Milton's poems are taken from Hughes.

ably so in the ways in which the similes foreground the poet in the act of writing and thus the reader in the process of reading. One instance of this is the quick shifting of tenses as the poet moves from Satan's prehistory to his own day—in which the Tuscan artist explores the sky, leaves strow the brooks, trees embower, and Orion vexes the sea—and alludes in passing to historical events that came between Satan's past and our present. We go back and forth between a world before and beyond our time and space to the world we know now, and we range across the latter, from Norwegian hills to Lybian sands; numerous details carry a historical freight: Arno, Rhene, and Danube, Ammiral, General, and Sultan, Fiesole, Vallombrosa, and Etruria.

This shifting of times and tenses is one instance of a baroque play with perspectives; another is the poet's moving in and out of the characters of his making; the point of view changes from *seeing with* Satan to *looking at* him. The first epic simile in *Paradise Lost* conveys this strikingly.[3] During Satan's first speeches of defeat and defiance we identify with a human voice; then we are made to see him from the outside and learn that the voice is that of a monster of inhuman and dangerous dimensions. Our perception, it is implied, may be mistaken as the poet mixes the little and the large, the strange and the familiar. Satan's shield is first "massy, large and round," but the introduction of Galileo's telescope—the instrument for enlarging our vision—makes Satan's shield seem remote, small, and vague; the size of his spear is somewhere between a mast and a wand; his armies are like leaves, sedge, or insects, but also like barbarian hordes that cover continents.[4]

Add to these changes the sudden shifts in tone that evoke contrary moods. The terror of Satan as Briareos, or Typhon, or Leviathan leads into the pathetic tale of the unwary pilot who mistakes the sea beast for an island and about whose fate the poet leaves us agonizingly in the dark while "wished morn delays."[5] The quiet of the Tuscan artist at a cool nocturnal distance contrasts with Satan's "torrid Clime" that

---

[3] 1.203-8.

[4] 1.284-94, 302-12, 338-43, 351-55. The most detailed and illuminating consideration of Milton's references to Galileo, astronomers, and astronomy is by Neil Harris, "Galileo as Symbol: The 'Tuscan Artist' in *Paradise Lost*," *Annali dell' Istituto e Museo di Storia della Scienza di Firenze* 10 (1985), 3-29. Harris sees the "Tuscan artist" as "a Satanic Image" (16).

[5] 1.203-8.

"smote on him sore besides." The contrary music and the change of
moods are especially obvious in the paired similes of the fallen angels as
leaves and sedge. The scene that Satan beholds changes for the reader
into an overlay of scenes; we see, in quick succession, a burning lake,
an autumn valley, a sea after a storm, and a drowning cavalry. (The
logical link between event and similes is the stress on the number and
disorder of the fallen.) In the first simile the scene is still, pastoral,
autumnal, elegiac; the second, in a series of lengthening clauses, unfolds
a baroque scene of tumult in defeat and joy in victory and ends with an
emphatic summation that combines description and judgment: "so thick
bestrown / Abject and lost lay these."

The overlay of scenes constitutes an overlay of perspectives and thus
of judgments. Through all the scenes runs a dividing line: on the one
side are the fiery flood, the brook, and the sea, on the other is the safe
shore; on the one side loss, on the other continuity; on the one side are
the fallen angels, leaves, sedge, the cavalry of Busiris, and on the other
are Satan, trees, Moses and the Israelites. Satan beholds the evidence of
his ruin but fails to understand it; the Israelites behold their salvation
and praise God. Ironically, however, in the reader's perspective both
Satan and Moses stand in the same place; Satan too has been allowed
to part the flood and reach safety—the God who saves His elect in
history also allows the damned to do their worst throughout history.[6]

The analogy between Satan's "miraculous" escape and the salvation
of Israel through the parting of the waves has been suggested earlier, in
1.222-24:

> on each hand the flames
> Driv'n backward, slope thir pointing spires, and roll'd
> In billows, leave i' th' midst a horrid vale.

Only faith can resolve the reader's ambivalence by rightly ordering the
circles of perspective because the real center is only implied: Satan's
"salvation" is a mere parody of God's type; the salvation of Israel is the
type itself, but it has had to be completed, in the poet's and the reader's
time, by the salvation through the Greater Man, the antitype that God
had in mind before time was.[7]

---

[6] That Satan is a parody of Moses is again suggested in the similes of 1.338-55;
there Satan and Moses are alike instruments of God's punishment of the impious.

[7] In the poet's rendering of Satan on the shore, Satan is at the center of a series

But what do the shades of Vallombrosa have to do with salvific history? A few lines sketch a rural haunt as the eye moves from leaves below to trees above—with a hint of pillar, arch, and temple—and comes round again with the active "imbow'r." What link is there between this cool enclosure and hell's fiery vault? The logical connection is clear: the simile conveys number, abjection, and loss.[8] It conveys also what might have been—dumb endurance of numbing pain—had Satan not been there to call his followers to "order." The simile recalls its antecedents in Homer, Virgil, and Dante,[9] and resonates with the echoes of its origin in antiquity. In the tradition before Milton, the simile likens human mortality to the process of change and recurrence in nature and thus conveys a classic, secular, and stoic acceptance of transience. In the case of these fallen angels, however, the loss is moral and spiritual, and the poet soon evokes a more militant conception of life in the subsequent allusion to Exodus. Vallombrosa also calls up the biblical Valley of the Shadow of Death and suggests the insubstantial outline of these lost forms.[10] Given this play on *umbra*, shadow, and shade, may we translate "*Etrurian* shades" into "the shades of the departed Etruscans"? When all the other similes make a judgment or imply the judgment of Providence, may we pass judgment on the Etruscans too? If Busiris was an overreacher, patterned after that Satan who aspired too high, does "High overarch't" allude to the arch of Pride's ascent and fall? Etruria was, like Egypt, a vanished culture, its language unknown, speaking only through monuments designed for the perpetuation of memory—a culture

---

of allusive circles, the largest of them being God's providential design, here only hinted at; in that design, however, the Son is at the center while Satan careens on the widest circumference.

[8] Isabel Gamble McCaffrey comments: "The idea of barrenness . . . generates many of the images of the fallen angels and the landscape of Hell" (McCaffrey, 126).

[9] C. M. Bowra cites a longer list of antecedents in *From Virgil to Milton* (London: Chatto & Windus, 1945), 240-41. See also S. Baldi, *Folte come le Foglie o lo Scudo di Satana* in *Comparative Dimensions: English, German and Comparative Literature Essays in Honour of Aurelio Zanco*, ed. M. Curreli and A. Martino (Saste, 1978), 221-40.

[10] Ps. 23.4: "Yea, though I walk through the valley of the shadow of death, I will fear no evil: for thou art with me." The reference is ironic: Satan, though in the valley of death, fears no evil but embraces evil as his good; he and his followers are of God forsaken. Harris, "Galileo," 26 n. 66, underlines the importance of the Junius-Tremellius Bible.

of tombs. What place may the Etruscans have occupied in Milton's typology of history? Do these shades have a substance?[11]

§

The history of the Etruscans has been gradually recovered; how they have been perceived (or, their place in historical thought) has only recently been a topic in Etruscology.[12] In their case, it has been especially difficult to distinguish between fact, legend, and invention. They seem to have been an alien tribe that slowly becomes visible among the Italic tribes of the Villanovan periods.[13] Their language, though still undeciphered, is clearly not Indo-European. They may have come from Asia Minor; their culture, of pre-Hellenic origin, may derive from ancient earth-cults. They appear as "a strange fragment of primeval Asia in the midst of a European landscape."[14] In the seventh century BC they were the dominant people in the regions north of Rome, and they became one of the powers the early Romans had to overthrow to gain control of the Mediterranean basin. There have been three major versions or myths of their history: one version and two Renaissance

---

[11] Since Milton's time, ancient Egyptian texts have become intelligible, but Etruscan writing still keeps its secrets. It survives in some ten thousand epigraphic records; although the texts are legible—the Etruscan letters derive from a Greek alphabet of Western type—their meaning remains elusive ("Etruscan: Language," *Encyclopedia Brittannica*, 1984 ed.).

[12] Alain Huss, in *Les Etrusques et leur destin* (Paris: Picard, 1980), 309 ff., gives a brief survey of the Etruscans in historical thought. Giovanni Cipriani made a thorough study of the Etruscan image in Renaissance Florence: *Il mito etrusco nel rinascimento fiorentino* (Florence: Leo S. Olschki, 1980). As subsequent notes will attest, I have made ample use of Cipriani's work.

[13] "Perhaps" ought to accompany every assertion about the Etruscans; their Asiatic origin is by no means uncontested. Recently, Etruscologists have argued that the prehistoric origins of the Etruscans were Mediterranean. Michael Grant has called Etruscology "a bibliographical nightmare." The selected bibliographies in the following studies may give the lay reader a convenient means of access: Michael Grant, *The Etruscans* (London: Weidenfeld and Nicolson, 1980); Ellen MacNamara, *The Etruscans* (New York: Dorsett Press, 1973); Larissa Bonfante, ed., *Etruscan Life and Afterlife: A Handbook of Etruscan Studies* (Detroit: Wayne State Univ. Press, 1986); Emeline Hill Richardson, *The Etruscans* (Chicago: Univ. of Chicago Press, 1976).

[14] Sibylle von Cles-Reden, *The Buried People: A Study of the Etruscan World* (London: Rupert Hart-Davis, 1955), 13.

versions; of the latter pair, one is republican, the other monarchical in inspiration.[15]

In the Roman account of the national past, Etruscan kings ruled the city for a century (616-619 BC) till Rome revolted against the tyranny of Tarquinius Superbus.[16] When Porsenna, king of Etruria, attempted to subdue the city on behalf of the exiled Tarquin, he so admired the heroic resistance of its citizens that he concluded a treaty instead, in the belief that Rome and Etruria were destined to live in mutual amity and esteem. Beginning with the siege and sack of Veii (396 BC),[17] Rome gradually absorbed the Etruscan city-states, although certain cities— among them Virgil's native Mantua—remained Etruscan down to imperial times.[18] Roman writers often refer to the Etruscans' observance of religious rites, to their practice of divination, and to the importance they placed on the cult of the dead—their tombs, notably that of Porsenna, became legendary.[19]

The image of Rome so dominated the medieval imagination that the Etruscans were forgotten; in Dante's day the better class of Florentines, like Brunetto Latini, claimed Roman descent.[20] The early humanists, however, traced the origin of Florence to Latini's despised Fiesole. Salutati and Bruni remind their fellow citizens that the civic patrimony was Etruscan before it became Roman and that the Florentine love of

---

[15] Grant, *Etruscans*, lists the scattered references to the Etruscans in ancient Greek authors—twenty-seven references in all—and in ancient Latin authors—twenty-six references in all (296-300). The Roman account of the national past intended here is essentially that of Livy.

[16] The revolt was said to have been sparked by the rape of the matron Lucretia by Sextus, youngest son of Tarquinius Superbus—a narrative touch reminiscent of epic invention.

[17] Veii fell after a ten-year siege—another echo of the literary epic. The Etruscans were not granted Roman citizenship until 89 BC.

[18] T. R. Glover, *Virgil* (1904; repr. New York: Barnes & Noble, 1969), 13. Glover cites Virgil: "Mantua, rich in ancestry . . . and her strength is of Tuscan blood" (*Aeneid* 10.198, 203).

[19] Pliny the Elder (*Natural History*, bk. 36, chap. 19, 91-93) cites Varro's description of Porsenna's tomb, crowned with pyramids and bells. Pliny disapproves of Porsenna's vainglorious monument, calling it *vesana dementia*, an insane folly that exhausted the resources of the kingdom, and *impendio nulli profituro*, an expense of profit to no one, except to the architect (LCL, 10:72-73).

[20] *Inferno* 15.61-78.

freedom and hatred of tyranny have an Etruscan source.[21] Bruni's mythical Etruria was a loose federation of city-states, each governed by an elected magistrate and a council; exhaustion, rather than conquest, accounted for their decline, but the best of their culture had passed to the Romans. This transfer was to repeat itself in time, but in reverse—Bruni argues that the strength of Rome has now been exhausted and that Florence, having renewed its ancient splendor, is again the moral *patria* of all Italians.[22]

The quattrocento myth of republican Etruria changed radically in the next century. As archeological discoveries brought to light the tombs, statuary, and frescoes of the Etruscans (notably in the necropolis of Tarquinia), an increasingly learned and aristocratic Florence came to admire the Etruscans for their art and architecture, for the grandeur of their power rather than their spirit of freedom.[23] Under Lorenzo the Magnificent Florence again became the dominant power in Italy. Although republican forms of government survived, they were void of power, now vested in the figure at the head. The resurrected image of an ancient Etruscan monarchy accompanied the concentration of power in the principate. In the work of the notorious Annio da Viterbo, the magistrates of the twelve Etruscan city-states became eleven little kings with a twelfth king ruling over all; Annio's Etruscans were Italy's oldest inhabitants, brought there by Noah himself, and instructed by him in religious wisdom.[24] Egidio Antonini, also *da Viterbo*, continued Annio's line: his Etruscans came from Chaldea, and their religious mysteries and history parallel those of ancient Israel.[25] When, after the Savo-

---

[21] Cipriani, 3-12.

[22] Bruni transferred to the Etruscans all that the Middle Ages had admired in Rome: ancient lineage, virtue, prudence, learning, and wisdom.

[23] Werner Keller, *The Etruscans* (New York: Alfred A. Knopf, 1974), 411-12; Franco Borsi, ed., *Fortuna degli etruschi* (Milan: Electa editrice, 1985), 36-37; Cipriani, 29-32.

[24] Cipriani, 33-36. Annio da Viterbo, born Giovanni Nanni (1432[?]-1502), pretended to be the first editor of the original works of seventeen ancient authors, which he said he had discovered in Mantua; his commentaries were meant to demonstrate their authenticity. Though soon accused of forgery, he did find defenders; some scholars have inclined to the charitable view that he was a credulous man, acting in good faith; see the entry under NANNI in *Biographie Universelle*, ed. M. Michaud (Paris, 1854).

[25] Cipriani, 53-55.

narola "interlude," the Medici reestablish their power, they consistently promote the monarchical version of the Etruscan myth to legitimize their reach for power. Leonardo Salviati, on the occasion of the corona-tion of Cosimo I as Grand Duke, delivered a speech that mentioned how "the noble province [of Tuscany] takes joy in your recovery of your ancient crown"—*della tua antica corona recuperata.*[26] Ever after, the Medici styled themselves *Magni Duces Etruriae,* thus giving their preemi-nent power a past and, with it, the sanction of ancient tradition.

§

The young Milton once refers to Etruria as "infamous for sorceries,"[27] but elsewhere the context of his Etruscan references is always laudatory. Old Etruria was Virgil's birthplace; new Tuscany was the home of Dante, of Petrarch, and the Diodatis. Florence was to prove almost a second home to Milton. The friends he made there seem to have accepted the limits of their political freedom as inevitable.[28] The exam-ple of Milton's correspondent, the learned priest Buonmattei, is typical; at fifteen, before thinking of taking holy orders, he had entered the service of Grand Duke Ferdinand I. When the Duke died, Buonmattei composed and published the offical funeral oration as public orator of the Florentine Academy.[29] And yet, Milton later records that the Floren-tines he had met were conscious of their "servile condition ... which had dampt the glory of Italian wits."[30] When he came to compose *Paradise Lost,* Milton had learned much about the ways and means of power in the battle he had fought and lost against monarchical rule in

---

[26] Cipriani, 109.

[27] In *quintum novembris* mentions *veneficiis infamis Hetruria* (5); in *Mansus* (4) Milton refers to Etruscan Maecenas; in the Argument to *Epitaphium Damonis* he recalls that, on his father's side, Charles Diodati was descended from the Etruscan city of Lucca (*ex urbe Hetruriae Lucca paterno genere oriundus*).

[28] The friends are identified in Parker, 1:170-73.

[29] For Milton's letter to Buonmattei see *Milton's Private Correspondence (1627-1638)* in CPW 1:328-32.

Buonmattei is the subject of a long and thorough essay in *Dizionario biografica degli italiani* (Rome: Istituto della enciclopedia italiana, 1960); vol. 31, the last volume to appear to date, goes from *Cristaldi* to *Dalla Nave.* For names beyond this last the work of Michaud is still useful though dated; see n. 24.

[30] *Areopagitica,* in CPW 2:537-38.

his own country. As Latin Secretary, he had composed nearly a dozen letters to Ferdinand II, the reigning *Magnus Dux Etruriae*.[31] But Milton could hardly have been unaware that, for all their titular dignities and papal and royal connections, the Medici princes pursued power arrogantly, often cruelly, and sometimes murderously.[32]

All we know of Milton's experience after his Italian tour must lead to the conclusion that *"Etrurian* shades" imply the image of vainglory. And yet, the recall of the historical and biographical context will not account for the peculiar evocative power of his shady valley; as the commentary grows, meanings multiply. The poet's "High overarch't" is literally appropriate because the Etruscans were—mistakenly—credited with the invention of arch and vault.[33] Such overarching may justly refer to Etruscan pride, since monumental grandeur habitually provokes the scorn of the poet in *Paradise Lost*. The association of the great Etruscan tombs with monarchy allows us to infer that, in Milton's typology of history, Etruria is parallel to Egypt. There is, however, in Milton's allusion no hint of judgment or condemnation; his lines convey only the pathos of transience. To conclude: do we meet here another instance of Milton's extraordinary ability to express affection, admiration, and regret for some part of mortal experience or achievement that his "higher argument" compels him to disavow?

Drew University

---

[31] For the letters to the Grand Duke see *State Papers*, in CPW vol. 5, part 2: 557-58, 616-19, 625-26, 641-42, 652-55, 801-2, 812-13, 821-25, 867-69.

[32] Umberto Dorini, *I Medici e i loro tempi* (Florence: Nardini, 1982); five members of the family were murdered by other members.

[33] The first vault, built of baked clay, was probably Assyrian; see MacNamara, *Etruscans*, 66-74.

NEIL HARRIS

# The Vallombrosa Simile and the Image of the Poet in Paradise Lost

IN THE FIRST BOOK OF *Paradise Lost*, within the bounds of a single verse paragraph (283–330), Milton twice describes either Satan or his followers with extended similes that draw explicitly on the landscape of Florence or its surroundings. As the fallen archangel rises from the burning lake and steps out onto the fiery shore of Hell, his shield is like "the Moon, whose Orb / Through Optic Glass the *Tuscan* Artist views / At Ev'ning from the top of *Fesole*, / Or in *Valdarno*, to descry new Lands, / Rivers or Mountains in her spotty Globe" (1.287–91).[1] This arresting image is generally attributed to an encounter with the "famous *Galileo* grown old, a prisner to the Inquisition, for thinking in Astronomy otherwise than the Franciscan and Dominican licensers thought," visited by Milton on his Italian journey of 1638–1639, and mentioned in *Areopagitica*.[2] The subject of this essay is instead the second of these similes, which I likewise term "Florentine," though it refers to a place a little distance away. It occurs in Milton's description of how Satan:

> ... stood and calld
> His Legions, Angel Forms, who lay intrac't
> Thick as Autumnal Leaves that strow the Brooks
> In *Vallombrosa*, where th' *Etrurian* shades
> High overarcht imbowr; or scatterd sedge
> Afloat, when with fierce Winds *Orion* armd
> Hath vext the Red-Sea Coast, whose waves orethrew
> *Busiris* and his *Memphian* Chivalrie,

---

[1] I cite the poetry from Milton, *Complete Poems*, ed. B. A. Wright, introduction and notes by Gordon Campbell (London, 1980). References to the prose are to both CE and CPW.

[2] CE 4:330; CPW 2:538.

While with perfidious hatred they persu'd
The Sojourners of *Goshen*, who beheld
From the safe shore thir floating Carcasses
And broken Chariot Wheels: so thick bestrown
Abject and lost lay these, covering the Flood,
Under amazement of thir hideous change.
He calld so loud, that all the hollow Deep
Of Hell resounded. . . .                                    (1.300-315)

We are at once aware of Milton's huge debt to and rivalry with his peers. Though short similes on the same subject occur in Homer (*Iliad* 2.468 and 800, 6.146-49) and Bacchylidis, it is in imitation of Virgil that a comparison of soldiers, spirits or devils becomes *de rigeur* in classical and Renaissance epic. In his version Milton retains the bipartite structure of the simile in the *Aeneid*, where the dead, waiting to cross the Styx, are likened to leaves that fall at the first touch of autumnal frost, and to birds that gather in vast clusters to migrate to sunnier shores (6.309-12);[3] but his leaves are already fallen and the birds are

---

[3] The previous analogues of Virgil's simile are discussed in R. G. Austin's commentary on book 6 of the *Aeneid* (Oxford: Oxford Univ. Press, 1977), 130-31, and by Brooks Otis, *Virgil: A Study in Civilized Poetry* (Oxford: Oxford Univ. Press, 1963), 410-12. The most comprehensive study on the analogues of Milton's simile is by Sergio Baldi, "Folte come le foglie (e lo scudo di Satana)," in *Comparative Dimensions: English, German and Comparative Literature Essays in Honour of Aurelio Zanco*, ed. M. Curreli and A. Martino (Cuneo, 1978), 221-40, reprinted in Baldi, *Studi Miltoniani* (Florence: Università degli Studi, Istituto di lingue e letterature germaniche . . . [1985]), 65-81.

Without attempting a complete bibliography, the following works comment on the Vallombrosa simile: Anon., *Essay on Milton's Imitations of the Ancients* (London, 1741), 23; James Whaler, "The Miltonic Simile," *PMLA* (1931): 1034-74, 1046-47; "Hibernicus," *N&Q* 184 (1943): 85; C. M. Bowra, *From Virgil to Milton* (London: Macmillan, 1945), 240-41; Geoffrey H. Hartman, "Milton's Counterplot," *ELH* 25 (1958): 1-12, reprinted in his *Beyond Formalism* (New Haven and London: Yale Univ. Press, 1970), 113-23; John M. Steadman, "The Devil and the Pharoah's Cavalry," *MLN* 75 (1960): 197-201; J. B. Broadbent, *Some Graver Subject: An Essay on "Paradise Lost"* (London: Chatto & Windus, 1960), 85-86; Christopher Ricks, *Milton's Grand Style* (Oxford: Oxford Univ. Press, 1963), 123-24; Anne D. Ferry, *Milton's Epic Voice: The Narrator in "Paradise Lost"* (Cambridge, Mass.: Harvard Univ. Press, 1963), 74-78; Marjorie H. Nicolson, *John Milton: A Reader's Guide to His Poetry* ([London]: Thames and Hudson, 1964), 191-92; Isabel G. MacCaffrey, *"Paradise Lost" as "Myth"* (Cambridge, Mass.: Harvard Univ. Press, 1967), 124-26; A. S. P. Woodhouse, *The Heavenly Muse: A Preface to Milton* (Toronto: Univ. of Toronto Press, 1972), 213-15;

substituted by the sedge on the Red Sea. Further analogues in major texts are the damned *mal seme d'Adamo* in the *Inferno*,[4] the pagan hordes in Ariosto,[5] and Tasso's devils.[6] In terms of an application of the simile to the fallen angels, there are also biblical texts such as Isaiah 34.4: "And all the hoste of heauen shal be dissolued, and the heauens shal be folden like a boke: and all their hostes shal fall as the leafe falleth from the vine, and as it falleth from the figtre" (Geneva Bible);[7]

---

Christopher Grose, *Milton's Epic Progress: "Paradise Lost" and Its Miltonic Background* (London and New Haven: Yale Univ. Press, 1973), 163-65; Harold Bloom, *A Map of Misreading* (New York and Oxford: Oxford Univ. Press, 1975), 130-38; J. P. Holoka, " 'Thick as Autumnal Leaves': The Structure and Generic Potentials of an Epic Simile," *MQ* 10 (1976): 78-83; Linda Gregerson, "The Limbs of Truth: Milton's Use of Simile in *Paradise Lost*," *MS* 14 (1980): 135-52, 144-46; Claes Schaar, *The Full Voic'd Quire Below* (Lund, 1982), 58; Charles Martindale, *John Milton and the Transformation of Ancient Epic* (London and Sydney: Croom Helm, 1986), 5-6. See also the essays by Chaney, Huttar, and Mulder in this volume.

[4] *Inferno* 3.112-14, first cited by H. J. Todd in his edition of 1801.

[5] *Orlando furioso*, 16.75: "Che meglio conterei ciascuna foglia, / Quando l'autunno gli arbori ne spoglia" ("I should do better to count all the leaves of which the autumn strips the trees") first cited by Todd. In the same poem the wicked Gabrina is as fickle as a "foglia / Quando l'autunno è più priva d'umore, / Che'l freddo vento gli arbori ne spoglia, / E le soffia dinanzi al suo furore" (21.15), translated in Harington as "She more light than leaves in Autumne season, / That ev'ry blast doth blow about and change"; but this image derives rather from Ovid, *Heroides*, 5.109-10: "Tu levior foliis tunc cum sine pondere succi / Mobilibus ventis arida facta cadunt" ("You are flightier than the leaves when, without the weight of their sap and dried up by the volatile winds, they fall"); cf. also Boccaccio, *Filocolo*, chap. 3 "Tu, mobile giovane, ti se' piegato, come fanno le frondi al vento, quando l'autunno le ha d'umore private" ("You, fickle youth, you gave way, as the leaves do to the wind, when the autumn has deprived them of their life-spirit"). The image of the dying leaf recurs in a description of Bradamante's armour: "Era la sopraveste del colore / In che riman la foglia che s'imbianca / Quando del ramo è tolta, o che l'umore / Che facea vivo l'arbore le manca" (32.47) ("The covering was of that color that remains in a leaf that whitens when it is stripped from the tree, or when the spirit that made the tree alive fails it"); but Ariosto also transforms the Virgilian simile into a description of a season: "Tra il fin d'ottobre e il capo di novembre, / Ne la stagion che la frondosa vesta / Vede levarsi e discoprir le membre / Trepida pianta, fin che nuda resta, / E van gli augelli a strette schiere insembre, / Orlando entrò ne l'amorosa inchiesta ..." (9.7) ("Between the end of October and the beginning of November, in the season when the fearful plant sees its leafy dress fall away, until it remains naked, and the birds flock together in thick clusters, Orlando took up his loving search").

[6] *Gerusalemme liberata* 9.66 (first cited by Todd), repeated at *Conquistata* 10.68.

[7] In his commentary Jerome writes: "et tabescat omnis militia vel fortitudo coelorum ... in similtudinem foliorum, quae appropinquante frigore, arentia atque

but Milton certainly knew many other instances of the *frondium casus*, some of which have yet to be discovered by his critics.[8]

---

contracta de vinea et ficu defluunt" (in Migne, *Patrologia latina* 24.370) ("all the armies and might of the sky withers . . . compared to leaves, which, as the cold arrives, dried up and shrivelled, fall from the vine and the fig"). I cite the Geneva Bible from the facsimile of the 1560 edition with an introduction by Lloyd E. Berry (Madison: Univ. of Wisconsin Press, 1969).

[8] In his *Poetices* Scaliger dedicates a page to examples of the *frondium casus* (2d ed. [Heidelberg, 1581], 711), including, besides the usual Virgil, this otherwise unnoticed example from Claudian: "Conveniunt animae: quantas violentior Auster / Decutit arboribus frondes, aut nubibus imbres / Colligit, aut frangit fluctus, aut torquet arenas" (*De raptu Proserpinae* 2.308-10) ("The dead gather together: as many as the leaves that the rougher south wind shakes from the trees, or showers it brings from the clouds, or waves it breaks, or sands it blows about"). An important and likewise unmentioned analogue occurs in Apollonius Rhodius, who combines waves and leaves to describe the Colchian forces: "countless as the waves of the stormy sea when they rise crested by the wind, or as the leaves that fall to the ground from the wood with its myriad branches in the month when the leaves fall [φύλλα χαμᾶζε περικλαδέος πέσεν ὕλης | φυλλοχόῳ ἐνὶ μηνί]—who could reckon their tale?" (*Argonautica* 4.214-17, trans. R. C. Seaton, LCL).

Besides the example given below at note 10, Boiardo has various examples in the *Orlando Innamorato*: "Ma tante foglie non lascia una pioppa / Là nel novembre, quando soffia il vento, / Quanti ènno e cavallier" (2.11.52) ("But a poplar does not lose as many leaves, in November when the wind blows, as there were knights"); "Quel populaccio tremando se crola / Come una legier foglia al vento fresco" (2.16.8) ("That wretched people gave way in terror, like leaf in a strong breeze"); "Or la battaglia è ben stretta e ricolta, / Né abatte il vento sì spesso le fronde, / . . . / Come son spessi e colpi de le spade" (2.17.47) ("Now battle is well and truly joined, and the wind does not shake the leaves down so thickly . . . as are thick the blows of the swords"); "la gran folta / Com'una foglia ad ogni vento volta" (2.30.50) ("the great throng, turned like a leaf in every blast").

From other Italian epics, I cite Alamanni, *Avarchide*: "e qual l'aride fronde, / Poi chè il calor estivo già vien meno, / Nel tardo Autunno, d'Aquilone al fiato, / Caggion, nudo lassando il tronco amato: / Tal da colpi di lui cader si vede / Gente infinita" (ed. Florence, 1570, 5.13) ("And like dry leaves, once the summery heat has failed them, in late Autumn at the blast of the North wind, fall, leaving the beloved tree bare, so at his strokes were seen to fall infinite numbers"); Trissino, *L'Italia liberata dai Goti*, to describe the numbers of the Goths: "E come suole ombrosa, e folta selva / Di faggi, o d'olmi, o di robuste quercie; / Quando l'autunno vuol dar luogo al verno, / Coprir di frondi tutto quanto il suolo, / Tal chè non può vedersi erba, nè terra" (ed. Verona, 1729, canto 10, p. 106) ("As when a thick and shady wood, of beeches or of elms or of strong oaks, when autumn wants to give way to winter, habitually covers the whole ground with leaves, so that neither grass nor earth can be seen"; cf. also canto 18, p. 181, and 26, p. 283); Graziani, *Il Conquisto di Granata*: "Tante giamai da le silvestri piante / Non caggiono l'Autunno aride fronde" (ed. Modena, 1650, 2.58) ("As many dry leaves do not fall in Autumn from the plants of the wood"; cf. 25.48).

A superficial, and rapidly discarded, reading of Milton's simile takes this compound image to be primarily extrinsic from the main narrative, introduced so as to allow a moment of distancing and relief.[9] This initial impression of a delightful *excursus* is syntactically reinforced by the symmetry of *calld* (300) and *calld so loud* (314) (a harmony reiterated within the simile by *strow* and *bestrown*), marking the interruption and consequent resumption of the principal action. From a single point of likeness, the *thickness*[10] of the leaves or sedge on the water compared to the angels on the lake of fire, a brief pastoral interlude transports the reader away from the anguish of Satan's followers to the vision, if fleeting, of a pleasant sylvan landscape; but, despite the potency of the suggestion, it is an illusion of escape.

In critical writing on Milton it has often been assumed that, just as the encounter with Galileo may have inspired the previous simile of the "Tuscan Artist," so its companion piece draws on a visit allegedly made by the English poet to Vallombrosa in the autumn of 1638; and this

---

To the English epigones, besides Marlowe, *Tamburlaine* 2, 3.5.3, cited by Bowra, I add 1, 4.1.30-32—"could their numbers countervail the stars, / Or ever-drizzling drops of April showers, / Or withered leaves that Autumn shaketh down."

[9] The main studies on the Miltonic simile remain those by James Whaler, "The Miltonic Simile," *PMLA* 46 (1931): 1034-74; "The Grammatical Nexus of the Miltonic Simile," *Journal of English and Germanic Philology* 30 (1931): 327-34; "Compounding and Distribution of Similes in *Paradise Lost*," *MP* (1931): 313-27; "Animal Simile in *Paradise Lost*," *PMLA* 47 (1932): 534-53. In the first of these Whaler stresses the function of relief: "In the midst of a scene of strife, pain or crisis the poet may use for illustration an image that carries suggestions of tranquillity" (1036); cf. Hartman, "Milton's Counterplot." On the simile, see also L. D. Lerner, "The Miltonic Simile," *Essays in Criticism* 4 (1954): 297-308, and Gregerson, "The Limbs of Truth."

[10] In the previous canon I have so far found only one example where the link with the fallen in the context is the *thickness* and not the number of the leaves; cf. Boiardo, *Orlando Innamorato* 2.7.17: "Come al decembre il vento che s'invoglia, / Quando comencia prima la fredura: / L'arbor se sfronda e non vi riman foglia; / Cossi van spessi e morti alla pianura" ("As in December the wind blows up, when the cold first comes, the tree loses its leaves and not one remains, so thick do the dead fall to the ground"); but it is unlikely that Milton knew this example, since Berni's *Rifacimento* and the late sixteenth-century "raffazzonamento" of Boiardo in which Milton knew the text (cf. Harris, "John Milton's Reading of the *Orlando Innamorato*," *La Bibliofilia* 88 [1986]: 25-43) both alter the nature of the comparison: "Come il Dicembre il vento, che si annoia / La terra, e agli anima' to' la pastura, / Cascan le foglie, e par che'l mondo muoia, / Cosi cascano i morti alla pianura" (Berni 2.7.22) ("As when in December the wind that troubles the land and takes the pasture from the animals, the leaves fall, and it seems that the world is dying, thus the dead fall to the earth").

biographical prior assumption, though there is no formal evidence to substantiate it, has undoubtedly jaundiced the consequent interpretation. Bishop Newton declares the Miltonic version to be "far superior to the other [by Virgil] as it exhibits a real landskip";[11] while more recent scholars have argued both that in various aspects of his description of Hell the poet "was drawing on visual memory as well as upon imagination and conflating actual sense impressions with literary reminiscence,"[12] and that to "the suggestion in the first half of this compound simile Milton adds the memory of a leafy scene visited a quarter of a century before, allowing himself this one image of pure beauty in a series whose note is not beauty, but desolation rising to terror."[13] However, just as in the earlier simile the image of the astronomer hardly suits that of Galileo as Milton found him thirty years earlier, sick, blind, and imprisoned not in Fiesole, nor, strictly speaking, in the Val d'Arno, but at Arcetri,[14] so various small, but significant, historical discrepancies make it unlikely that the poet could have visited Vallombrosa in the autumn. Though he spent the whole summer of 1638 in Florence, probably arriving in early July, and though his presence is recorded at a meeting of the Svogliati academy in mid-September,[15] by the end of same month, or by early by October, when the leaves fall in the high Tuscan valley, Milton had already departed on his journey south to Rome and Naples. The discrepancy is a trifling one; but it does indicate that Milton's Vallombrosa is artificial in at least its imagining of the

---

[11] *Paradise Lost. A Poem, in Twelve Books. The Author John Milton . . . with Notes of Various Authors, by Thomas Newton,* 8th ed., 2 vols. (London, 1775), 1:34.

[12] Nicolson, *John Milton,* 194; cf. 192. "Milton's mind went back to his Italian journey for the first comparison . . . [quotation]. Anyone who has scuffed through autumn leaves knows how numberless they seem, but in Vallombrosa . . . , famous district of woods and forests near Florence, they were even more impressive than in England." On the challenge to Milton's veridicity in the description of Vallombrosa, first made by Mrs. Piozzi in her *Observations* (London, 1789), that "the trees are all evergreen in those woods" (2:50), which brought a reply from Wordsworth in 1834, see E. Chaney in this volume.

[13] Woodhouse, *The Heavenly Muse,* 214. In his commentary on the text Alastair Fowler remarks on the previous simile that the "apparently supererogatory geographical details may be Milton's indulgence of fond memories" (London, 1968), 479.

[14] Baldi, *Lo scudo,* 72; N. Harris, "Galileo as Symbol: The 'Tuscan Artist' in *Paradise Lost,"* *Annali dell'Istituto e Museo di Storia della Scienza di Firenze* 10 (1985): 3–29, 13–14.

[15] Cf. French, 1:371–89 and 5:385; Harris, "Galileo as Symbol," 5–6.

season, and that these Italian landscapes are not genuine memories of the scenes of his Continental tour. Nevertheless, the critical interpretation that relates these two similes to the biography of the poet possesses its own legitimacy, above all because the main source of our information about the Italian tour is Milton himself, who, besides the famous passage in *Areopagitica*, describes it at length in the *Defensio secunda* (1654), while the panegyrics of Florentine or Roman acquaintances are prefixed to the *Poems* (1645). Just as much as the classical or Renaissance epics, these writings constitute a *corpus* of text Milton knows his "fit audience" will use to read *Paradise Lost*; therefore, it would be as dangerous to deny that the poet wishes to evoke the issue of autobiographical experience, whether real or imaginary, as, on the other hand, to insist rigidly that the allusion to Italy is no more than fond and idle reminiscence.

If these two famous similes are images set by the poet to entrap and momentarily entangle the reader,[16] in the previous comparison of Leviathan mistaken by the "Pilot of som small night-foundered Skiff" (1.204) for a safe haven, Milton has warned us to beware of fair inviting appearances, or to risk the worst. His Vallombrosa is no charming idyll, but a mirror for Hell and all its potentialities. In the *Institutiones* Quintilian praises ἀνταπόδοσις, or strict correspondence between the comparison and the text,[17] and in this respect Milton emulates the Virgilian archetype in manipulating both simile and context to produce significant correspension. This point was obvious to his early critics, such as the anonymous author of the *Essay upon Milton's Imitations of the Ancients*, who wrote that "the falling of a Shower of Leaves from the Trees, in a Storm of Wind, very well represents the Dejection of the Angels from their former Celestial Mansions; and their *faded Splendor wan*, is finely expressed by the paleness and witheredness of the Leaves";[18] while elsewhere the characteristic metonymy of *shades* for *trees* reiterates the "darkness visible," the "high overarcht" of the

---

[16] Cf. Fisch.

[17] *Institutiones* 8.3, par. 74-77.

[18] *Essay*, 23; cf. ibid. "Milton's Comparison is by far the exactest; for it not only expresses a Multitude, . . . but also the Posture and Situation of the Angels. Their lying confusedly in Heaps, covered with the Lake, is finely represented by this Image of Leaves in the Brooks."

branches over the streams, the ceiling of Hell "vaulted with fire";[19] like the leaves, the angels are cut off from the source of life and consequently wither, while, particularly with the Virgilian *autumni frigore* in mind, Milton's Hell contains extremes of ice as well as of fire.

While seeming to imitate the Homeric simile *à queue longue*,[20] Milton's comparison comments in detail on its context. Though the autobiographical content is fictitious, the simile is a manifestation of an authorial presence within the epic. By this expression I do not mean a naively biographical relationship between simile and, in this case, the poet's continental travels; I mean his consistent exploitation of the simile throughout the poem as a device to reinforce our sense of a distinct controlling intellectual presence, or the figure of the intrusive narrator, whom we recognize as a persona of the historical Milton.[21] In the *Topica* Aristotle states that, since its primary function is to exemplify and to illustrate, the simile should draw on materials or situations familiar to the reader.[22] Again it is helpful to contrast Milton's viewpoint in the simile with that of his classical models. In the Homeric texts some divergence is perceptible between the epic world of the Trojan conflict, or the wanderings of Odysseus, and the common-

---

[19] Broadbent, *Some Graver Subject*, 86.

[20] On Milton's use of classical models for the simile: cf. D. P. Harding, *The Club of Hercules, Studies in the Classical Background of Paradise Lost* ([Urbana]: Univ. of Illinois Press, 1962); Martindale, *John Milton*. On the Homeric simile: cf. G. P. Shipp, *Studies in the Language of Homer*, 2d ed. (Cambridge: Cambridge Univ. Press), 208; Michael Coffey, "The Function of the Homeric Simile," *American Journal of Philology* 78 (1957): 113-32. In recent years the critical discussion on Virgil's dialogue with his Greek models and use of multiple corresponsion has been intense; cf. Otis, *Virgil*; David West, "Multiple-correspondence Similes in the *Aeneid*," *Journal of Roman Studies* 59 (1969): 40-49, and "Virgilian Multiple-correspondence Similes and their Antecedents," *Philologus* 114 (1970): 262-75; Roger A. Hornsby, *Patterns of Action in the "Aeneid": An Interpretation of Vergil's Epic Similes* (Iowa City: Univ. of Iowa Press, 1970); Gordon Williams, *Technique and Ideas in the "Aeneid"* (New Haven and London: Yale Univ. Press, 1983); R. O. A. M. Lyne, *Further Voices in Vergil's "Aeneid"* (Oxford: Oxford Univ. Press, 1987).

[21] On the image of the narrator: cf. R. Durling, *The Figure of the Poet in Renaissance Epic* (Cambridge, Mass.: Harvard Univ. Press, 1965); but Oliver Lyne's discussion of univocal and multivocal epic in *Further Voices* of the Virgilian text is applicable, with certain differentiations, to the Renaissance model.

[22] *Topica* 8.1.157a: "For clearness, examples and illustrations should be adduced, the examples being to the point and drawn from things which are familiar to us, of the kind which Homer uses" (trans. E. S. Forster, LCL).

place or everyday happenings depicted in many of the comparisons, though a fundamental homogeneity of aspect between poet and story is barely disturbed; in the *Aeneid*, however, where the chronological gap between the heroic age of the action and the Augustan setting is approximately a thousand years, the Virgilian narrating presence is more conspicuous, especially in similes that are distinctly "Roman" in their choice of material;[23] finally, in *Paradise Lost*, we are never allowed to forget the huge gulf of time between an action at the beginning of the created world and focal point of a narration set in late seventeenth-century, post-Restoration England. Milton's similes might well range through a large and varied number of biblical, mythological, or historical events; but, in order to illustrate the lost and, at least for the present, irretrievable archetype of the prelapsarian universe, the analogue necessarily refers to man's fallen condition, the one known to both the poet and his readers. In our two Florentine similes, present or present perfect tenses in the verbs underline the contemporaneity of the images (in the first *view* and *descry*, in the second *strew* and *imbowr*, followed by *hath vext* and three past tenses for the scene from Exodus). Through the particular cosmology invented by Milton to explain the eternal spring of the unfallen world, the autumn invoked in the description of the Tuscan valley is as postlapsarian as the poet's choice of tense.

§

If in their comparisons Homer and Virgil in the main draw on the landscapes of Greece and Italy, with only an occasional exception, the scenery remains generic rather than specific; Milton on the contrary not only takes his similes from the whole of the known world (a landscape of the mind though, never seen, but derived from his reading and study), but he also enhances his images by a choice of concrete locations. The topographical multiplicity and consequent exclusion of universal symbols (in *Paradise Lost* specific names are post-lapsarian or an accommodation) confirm the non-Edenic and post-Babelian nature of Milton's geography; but the same features extend and deepen the commentary on the text, since the names and places inevitably possess further meanings and associations. When Milton situates his simile of

---

[23] Williams, *Technique*, 166.

the falling leaves in the shady Italian valley, the naming of "Vallom-brosa," celebrated in Ariosto's *Orlando Furioso* as "una badia / ricca e bella, nè men religiosa, / e cortese a chiunque vi venia" (22.36),[24] he not only breaks with tradition, but also introduces a new dimension into the relationship between the simile and its context.

At a preliminary and semantic level, the ominous etymology of the place name was observed by Patrick Hume in 1695: "It [alian]. In the Shady Vale. *Valombrosa* is a famous Valley in *Tuscany*, so named of *Vallis* and *Vmbra* Shade, remarkable for the continual cool Shades, which the vast number of Trees that overspread it, afford";[25] but the surface word-play is extended by an unmistakable allusion to the biblical "Valley of the Shadow of Death" (Psalm 23.4 in the Geneva Bible and Authorized Version).[26] The parallel between the two texts is closer than the standard English translation of the Psalm reveals, since biblical scholarship now questions the Masoretic pointing of the Hebrew as *shadow of death*, and prefers a different one meaning *deep darkness*.[27] Though in the Septuagint this formulaic phrase, which is frequent in certain books of the Old Testament, is translated as σκιά θανάτου as is the case in the Greek New Testament when Isaiah 9.2 is quoted at Matthew 4.16 and Luke 1.79, Renaissance biblical philologists and

---

[24] The name *Vallombrosa* appears only in the final 1532 text, and in the versions of 1516 and 1521 this verse reads *Valspinosa*. Giovanni Villani, *Cronache . . . nelle quali si tratta dell'origine di Firenze* (Venice: Zanetti, 1537), 4:16, gives a brief account of the life of St. John Gualbert "il primo hedificatore della badia, et religione dell'ordine di valembrosa, onde molte grandi & riche badie sono discese in Toscana" ("the first founder of the Abbey, and of the Vallombrosan Order, to which many large and rich monasteries in Tuscany owe their origin"). A long life of the founder was published in Florence in the year after Milton's visit; cf. Diego de'Franchi, *Historia del Patriarcha S. Giovanni Gualberto Primo Abbate & Institutore del Monastico Ordine di Vallombrosa* (Florence: Landini, 1640). The "order of *vallis umbrosa* or the Monks of the Shadowy Valley" is mentioned by Alexander Ross; cf. Πανσεβεια, *or, a View of all Religions in the World: with the Severall Church-Governments, from the Creation, to these Times*, 3d ed. (London: Saywell, 1658), 283. From 1634 through to 1640 the original Monastery of Santa Maria in Vallombrosa was undergoing extensive reconstruction; cf. *Vallombrosa nel IX centenario della morte del fondatore Giovanni Gualberto 12 luglio 1073* (Florence: Giorgio & Gambi, 1973).

[25] Hume, *Annotations on Milton's Paradise Lost* (London: Tonson, 1695), 19.

[26] Cf. Steadman, *The Devil*; Schaar, *The Full Voic'd Quire*, 58.

[27] C. A. and E. G. Briggs, *A Critical and Exegetical Commentary on the Book of Psalms* (Edinburgh: Clark, 1907), 1:209-12; *Hebrew and English Lexicon of the Old Testament* (Oxford: Oxford Univ. Press, 1959), 853.

translators were aware of the ambiguity in the Hebrew. The Junius-Tremellius Bible, from which Milton cites Psalm 23.4 in *De doctrina*,[28] translates "Etiamsi ambularem per vallem lethalis umbrae, non timerem malum,"[29] instead of the *in medio* [or *valle* in modern texts] *umbrae mortis* endorsed by the Vulgate, and, in a note at Job 10.20-21, "abivero ... in terram tenebrosam et lethalis umbrae," elucidates with the marginal gloss: "umbrae lethalis, id est umbrosissimam." Likewise, in a note on Matthew 4.16, Erasmus observes that the Hebrew is a "unica dictio ... composita ex umbra & morte, ut intelligas altissimam caliginem, qualis est apud inferos."[30] On the other hand, if the echo of the biblical text confirms the sinister and menacing import of the *valle ombrosa*, it also moves it into a different context. The Psalm is a poetic expression of hope in darkness, of faith in God's succour, and, according to the Junius-Tremellius Bible, of renewal.[31]

A second analogue exists in the abrupt contrast between the Hell of the setting and the beautiful Tuscan valley of the simile, where nevertheless the etymology of the name, and sinister affinities between similitude and referent, all stress likeness rather than difference, and therefore recall another beautiful but evil valley in biblical texts, described by Milton in his catalogue of the infernal deities when he singles out Moloch, who made "his Grove / The pleasant Vally of *Hinnom*, *Tophet* thence / And black *Gehenna* calld, the Type of Hell" (1.403-5). Biblical exegesis frequently dwells on the paradox between the loveliness of the valley of Hinnom (or of the Sons of Hinnom), and the horrors of the rites there performed at the high altars of Tophet (cf. *Paradise Lost* 1.392-96); but Jerome found the beauty to be the very cause of corruption "quod subjaceat Siloe fontibus, et amoenitate sui, quia locus

---

[28] CE 17:248; CPW 6:378.

[29] On Milton's use of this Protestant Latin Bible, first published in 1575 (I cite from the 1623 Hannover edition); cf. John Carey in CPW 6:45, and Harris F. Fletcher, "The Use of the Bible in Milton's Prose," *University of Illinois Studies in Language and Literature* 14 (1929).

[30] Erasmus, *Annotationes* in the *Novum Testamentum* (Basel: In Officina Frobeniana, 1542), 26.

[31] On verse 23.3 "Animam meam quietam effecit, ducit me per orbitas iustitiae," the Junius-Tremellius Bible glosses: "Animam meam, id est, me languentem, mea infirmitate labefactum, & planè confectum instaurat: regenerationis symbolam" ("My soul, that is, my languishing self, afflicted by my weakness, and wholly broken down, he restores: a symbol of regeneration").

irriguus est, populum provocaverit ad luxuriam, quam idolorum cultus sequitur"[32] ("it lay beneath the fountains of Siloe, and by its beauty, because there was plenty of water, it would have turned the people towards pleasure, and the worship of idols followed thereupon"). Erasmus also formulates the one and the other as part of the same equation, describing Tophet as a "locus delitiarum ... qui prius alliciebat amoenitate, postea factus est abominandus"[33] "a place of beauty ... that first enticed by its loveliness, and afterwards became one to be abominated."

Seventeenth-century English writers furnish lengthy and colorful descriptions of the place, some of which undoubtedly recall Milton's Italian valley: George Sandys speaks of it as "heretofore most delightfull, planted with groves, and watered with fountaines,"[34] while Raleigh pictures the idol of Moloch as a "man-like brazen body, bearing the head of a Calfe, set up not far from Jerusalem, in a Valley shadowed with woods called *Gehinnon* or *Tophet*."[35] Even if he had never visited Vallombrosa, Milton knew the Italian valley to be the site of a famous monastery, so an analogy between Catholic idolatry and the horrible shrines of Tophet suits his polemical purpose all too well. The later fortunes of Tophet offer further analogies with the application of our simile to its context: after the destruction of the shrines and the felling

---

[32] "Commentariorum in Jeremiam Prophetam," 32.35, in Migne, *Patrologia latina* 24:897–98; cf. Migne 24:735, 26:66.

[33] Erasmus, *Annotationes*, 53.

[34] George Sandys, A *Relation of a Journey begun An: Dom: 1610*, 2d ed. (London: Barrett, 1621), 186.

[35] Sir Walter Raleigh, *The Historie of the World* (London: Burre, 1614), 494. Further descriptions of the Valley of Hinnom and Tophet in English writers can be found in Samuel Purchas, *His Pilgrimage or Relations of the World and the Religons observed in all Ages and Places discovered, from the Creation unto this Present*, 4th ed. (London: Stansby, 1626), 86, and in Thomas Fuller, A *Pisgah-Sight of Palestine and the Confines thereof, With the History of the Old and New Testament acted thereon* (London: J. F., 1650), 133. A more sober account appears in Franciscus Quaresimus, *Historica Theologica et Moralis Terrae Sanctae Elucidatio* (Antwerp: ex officina Plantiniana Balthasaris Moreti, 1639), 2:274: "vallis Gehennon est profunda, pulchra ac spatiosa, olim hortis, vineis atque arboribus consita, quae alluitur et fecondatur aquis fontis Siloë, & torrentibus Cedron. In valle ista erat insignis idololatriae lucus, Topeth appellatur" ("the valley of Gehenna is deep, beautiful and spatious, once planted with gardens, vineyards and trees, washed and watered by the brooks of Siloe, and by the streams of Cedron. In this valley was a grove famous for idolatry, called Tophet").

of the groves by "good Josiah" (1.418), the valley of Hinnom became the rubbish tip of Jerusalem, where fires were kept burning to destroy the refuse, and thus in the New Testament *gehenna* is a term for the fiery torments of Hell. The innumerable fallen angels that are the subject of the simile is a reminder that, just as the neighboring valley of Jehosaphat will be the place of God's judgment, so Tophet and Gehenna were set aside for his vengeance: "Therefore beholde, the daies come, saith the Lord, that it shal no more be called Tópheth, nor the vallei of Ben-Hinnóm, but the valley of slaughter; for thei shal burye in Tópheth til there be no place" (Jeremiah 7.32, Geneva Bible).

Third, in terms of a spiritual typology, the specific location of the simile at Vallombrosa carries on the symbolic identification, begun in the previous simile, of Florence with Sodom. In the structure of his simile Milton alludes to the prophecy in the book of Revelation of how the ministry of the two witnesses must end in violence, martyrdom and death.

> And when they have finished their testimonie, the beast that cometh out of the bottomles pit, shal make warre against them, and shal ouercome them, and kill them.
>
> And their corpses shal lie in the stretes of the great citie, which spiritually is called Sodom and Egypt, where our Lord also was crucified (Revelation 11.7-8, Geneva Bible).

The second half of the Vallombrosa simile, with the brilliant syntactical transition from the sedge on the Red Sea to the flotsam and jetsam of the Pharoah's proud cavalry, is undeniably Egypt. The landscape of Sodom before its destruction offers an obvious correspondence with the simile, since, on the authority of Genesis 13.10, "the Sodomites sometimes inhabited a pleasant and fertile valley, watered by the Jordan, which Moses compareth *to the garden of the Lord, and the land of Aegypt,* for pleasure and plenty."[36] The Protestant interpretation of Revelation also introduced an Italian connection into this text, since in their exegesis the "great city" was not Jerusalem but Catholic Rome, as

---

[36] Purchas, *His Pilgrimage*, 83; cf. Genesis 13.10: "So when Lot lifted vp his eies, he sawe that all the plaine of Iordén was watered euerie where: (for before the Lord destroyed Sodóm and Gemoráh, it *was* as the garden of the Lord, like the land of Egypt, as thou goest vnto Zóar)" (Geneva Bible).

Junius's highly successful commentary makes explicit: "Sodome signifieth most licentious impietie and iniustice; Egypt most cruell persecution of the people of God; and Ierusalem signifieth, the most confident
glorying of that Citie, as it were in true religon, being yet full of falshood and vngodlinesse. Nowe who is ignorant that these things doe
rather and more agree vnto Rome, than vnto anie other Citie."[37]

   Milton's interpretation of Sodom as a symbolic and spiritual entity,
and the double allusion to a foreign city such as Florence, show his
debt to Dante and the *Divina Commedia*. The tribute is manifest in
explicit imitation, since, where in the classical poets the citation of
specific placenames is the exception rather than the rule, Dante takes
some pains in various comparisons to provide a concrete location.[38]
Moreover, as an innovation with respect to the classical model discussed
above, similes of the *Commedia* suggest a discreet distinction of aspect
between referent and comparison, so as to highlight a chronological
difference within the authorial viewpoint. Throughout the course of the
poem the principal character of the *Commedia* is the author himself, the
first-person *io*, during the time it takes him to journey through the three
realms; but the imagery of the similes draws rather on an authorial

---

   [37] I cite from the translation of Junius's commentary on Revelation in the Latin
text, extracted and published as *A Briefe and Learned Commentarie vpon the Reuelation
of Saint Iohn the Apostle and Euangelist, applied vnto the Historie of the Catholike and
Christian Church . . . translated into English for the Benefit of those that vnderstand not
the Latine* (London: Richard Field for Robert Dexter, 1592), which replaced the original
commentary in editions of the Geneva Bible published after 1599; cf. Berry, Introduction to facs. Geneva Bible, 15. The 1560 Geneva annotations are equally polemical: the
beast "is, the Pope which hathe his power out of hel and cometh thence. He sheweth
how the Pope gaineth the victorie, not by Gods worde, but by cruel warre," and the
city means "the whole iurisdiction of the Pope, which is compared to Sodom for their
abominable sinne, and to Egypt because the true libertie to serue God is taken away
from the faithful: and Christ was condemned by Pilate, who represented the Romaine
power which shulde be enemie to the godlie."

   [38] Examples of detailed topography in the similes of the *Inferno* are 12.4 (landslide
on the Adige), 16.99 (waterfall at Acquaqueta), 15.4 (dykes in Flanders or on the
Brenta), 122 (palio at Verona), 18.28 (the Roman jubilee), 21.7 (the Venetian Arsenal),
29.46 (hospitals in Valdichiana, Maremma, and Sardinia), 31.136 (the Carisenda tower
in Bologna). Reference to Florence in an extended simile is, if anything, conspicuous
for its absence and occurs only at 19.17 (a font in San Giovanni broken by Dante to
save a drowning child). On the similes in the *Commedia*; cf. Luigi Venturi, *Le similitudini dantesche ordinate, illustrate e commentate*, 3d ed. (Florence, 1911); Oreste Alla-
vena, *Stile e poesia nelle similitudini della Divina Commedia* (Savona, 1970).

experience in which we find mentioned the places and scenes of Dante's later exile and wanderings. The English poet imitates this distinction of aspect in the temporal dichotomy of the two Florentine similes, which, despite their historical discrepancies (evident mainly to the scholar), serve to introduce momentarily the image of the younger "Milton" on his travels, an image at once questioned by the disturbing affinities with the context, and set aside in favor of the narratorial figure that dominates elsewhere in *Paradise Lost*, that of an older, deeply afflicted, but poetically mature "Milton."

Criticism of poets who interfere unnecessarily in their story, and thus make their presence obvious and unwelcome, begins in the *Poetics*, where Aristotle praises Homer's realism in keeping what the poet tells us is his own self to the minimum necessary to link dialogue and introduce episodes.[39] In the sixteenth century this criticism was discussed by Castelvetro, whose commentary on the *Poetics* distinguishes between the *rassomigliatore*, who obeys the Homeric norm and avoids interposing a narrating self between the reader and the story, and the *predicatore*, who, doing the opposite, usurps the roles of the characters and becomes a partisan in the action.

> Che diremo noi del poeta, in quella parte dell'epopea nella quale egli nè narra azzione nè introduce persona a favellare, ma giudica le cose narrate, o riprendendole, o lodandole, o tirandole a utilità comune e ad insegnamenti civili e del ben vivere? ... conciosa cosa che giudicandole e parlandone come che sia, si mostri persona passionata e laquale v'abbia interesse, e perciò si toglia a se stesso la fede e si renda sospetto a' lettori d'essere poco veritiere narratore.[40]

---

[39] Aristotle, *Poetics* 1460a5-11: "Homer . . . alone among epic poets is not unaware of the part to be played by the poet himself in the poem. The poet should say very little in his own character, as he is no imitator when doing that. Whereas the other poets are perpetually coming forward in person, and say but little, and that only here and there, as imitators, Homer after a brief preface brings in forthwith a man, a woman, or some other character—no one of them characterless, but each with distinctive characteristics" (trans. Bywater). A similar opinion is voiced by Plato in the *Republic* § 393.

[40] Lodovico Castelvetro, *Poetica d'Aristotele vulgarizzata e sposta*, ed. W. Romani (Bari: Laterza, 1978), 2:161-69; cf. also Paolo Beni, *In Aristotelis Poeticam Commentarii* (Padua, 1613), "Controversia LXXXV: Num iure affirmet Aristoteles Epico quam paucissima dicenda: & Num haec laus Homero debeatur."

What shall we say then about the poet, in that part of the work
where he does not describe some action or introduce someone to
speak, but passes judgement on what has been told so far, either
telling it again, or praising it, or showing its usefulness in terms
of acquiring moral improvement and a better way of life? ...
since judging and talking about it in this way, he shows himself
to be involved therein and with some personal interest, thus
destroying his own credibility and making the readers suspect
that he is no longer a truthful story-teller.

This criticism has a curiously familiar ring! When Dr. Johnson sets
forth strictures on the cardinal proems in books 1, 3, 7 and 9 of
*Paradise Lost* as beautiful superfluities that no one would want to
lose,[41] his objection is the same; likewise, when A. J. A. Waldock
accuses Milton of tugging at the reader's sleeve and warning him against
believing the literal sense of the text, albeit unconsciously, the critic is
repeating Aristotle. On the other hand, such criticism fails to recognize
how, though he certainly infringes on the classical norm, Milton is
structuring his poetical *apologia* according to the archetype of Dante's
*Commedia.*

In the *Convivio,* before launching into the commentary on his own
poems, Dante states that, like the servants at a feast, he must first
remove two *macule* from the bread he intends to offer his guests, or, in
other words, allay two doubts that might come into the mind of his
reader. Whereas the second, that the commentary might prove excessive-
ly prolix, does not interest us, the first is the classical objection that
"parlare alcuno di sé medesimo pare non licito"[42] ("it is not right for
one to speak of oneself"). Dante agrees that, in the main, such conduct
is reprehensible in a writer; but, he argues, there are circumstances in
which one has to make one's own life and deeds the focus of the
narrative, such as when "grandissima utilitade ne segue altrui per via di
dottrina" ("great profit follows for others by learning from it"), and he
instances Augustine's *Confessions,* or when one must speak in one's
own defense because no one else will stand up to do so:

---

[41] "Milton," in *The Lives of the English Poets,* ed. G. Birkbeck Hill (Oxford:
Oxford Univ. Press, 1905), 1:175.

[42] D. Alighieri, "Il Convivio," in *Opere minori,* ed. C. Vasoli and D. De Robertis
(Milan and Naples: Ricciardi, 1988), 1.2.2 and 14.

quando senza ragionare di sé, grande infamia o pericolo non si
può cessare; e allora si concede per la ragione, che de li due
sentieri prender lo men reo è quasi prendere un buono. E questa
necessitate mosse Boezio di sé medesimo a parlare, accio chè
sotto pretesto di consolazione escusasse la perpetuale infamia del
suo essilio, mostrando quello essere ingiusto, poichè altro scusatore non si levava.[43]

when without speaking of oneself, much disgrace and danger
cannot be stopped; and in such a case it is allowable, for the
reason that, between the two paths, to take the less bad one is
almost to take a good one. Such a necessity moved Boethius to
speak of himself, so that under the pretext of a consolation he
spoke out against the lasting disgrace of his exile, and showed
that it was unjust, since no one else stood up to defend him.

Read in the light of this remark, Milton's use of Dante justifies the
strong narratorial presence in *Paradise Lost* as a self-defense of the poet
himself, *poichè altro scusatore non si levava.*

Reference to the *Commedia* likewise associates Florence with Sodom
as a symbol of violence against the righteous man and poet. In an
earlier article I argued that the mention of *Fesole* in the previous simile
of the "Tuscan Artist" alludes to Dante's encounter in canto 15 of the
*Inferno* with Brunetto Latini, who approaches running over the burning
sands of the third *girone* and is recognized only with difficulty by his
former pupil.[44] The Renaissance commentators on the *Commedia*, in
whose editions Milton read his Dante, are unanimous that sodomy is
the vice that condemns Latini to this part of Hell.[45] Landino points
out the appropriateness of the rain of fire: "È ancora conueniente che
gli punisca col fuoco, perchè tal pena ueggiamo ch'apparecchiò Iddio a
Sodoma & Gomorra"[46] ("It is appropriate that they be punished by

---

[43] Ibid., 13.

[44] Harris' "Galileo as Symbol," 24–25.

[45] I cite the text of the *Commedia* from *Dante con l'espositione di M. Bernardino
Daniello de Lucca* (Venice: Pietro da Fino, 1568), mentioned by Milton in the "Commonplace book" (cf. CE 18:162; CPW 1:418); and the comments of Landino and Velutello from *Dante con l'espositioni di Christoforo Landino, et d'Alessandro Velutello*
(Venice: Sessa, 1564).

[46] Ibid. While there is no disagreement among Renaissance commentators, more

fire, since that is the punishment we know God carried out for Sodom and Gomorrah"). The encounter leads to a powerful condemnation of Florence, and of Dante's political enemies there, who will force the poet into exile, and whom Latini contemptuously designates the *bestie fieso- lane*.

> Ma quello 'ngrato popolo maligno,
> Che discese da Fiesole ab antico,
> Et tien'ancor del monte & del macigno,
>     Ti si farà per tu' ben far nimico;
> Et è ragion, che tra gli lazzi sorbi
> Si disconuien fruttare il dolce fico.     (15.61-66)

But that ungrateful spiteful people, that formerly came down from Fiesole, and still keeps something of the mountain and its hardness, for your good actions will become an enemy; and this is right, for among bitter briars the sweet fig will not give fruit.

The violence of Sodom—an epic subject Milton includes among the various summaries of plots for biblical and historical dramas in the Trinity College manuscript[47]—towards Lot and his family, who escape before the city's destruction by sulphur and fire from Heaven, is thus re-enacted in the conduct of Florence towards her greatest poet. The doom of the city in Genesis, where the "smoke of the country went up as the smoke of a furnace" (19.28, Geneva Bible), and the incandescent rain and sands of the *Inferno*, both furnish analogues for the "burning marl" and "fiery deluge" of Milton's Hell that as "one great Furnace flam'd," and that makes Beelzebub (like Brunetto Latini) unrecogniz- able.[48]

---

recently there has been a lengthy discussion of Brunetto Latini's sin; cf. Tiziano Zanato, "Su *Inferno* XV e dintorni," *Rivista di letteratura italiana* 6 (1988): 185-246.

[47] CE 18:233-34.

[48] Latini's defective sight (15.16-19) and the condemnation of the Florentines as *orbi* (15.67) both allude to the blindness that strikes the Sodomites (Genesis 19.16; cf. Zanato, 201-2), mentioned by Milton in *Eikonoklastes* (CE 5:67; CPW 3:342); whereas, vice versa, Dante's difficulty recognizing the *cotto aspetto* of his former teacher was attributed by the Renaissance commentators to the deformity wrought by this sin; cf. Velutello: "che difficilmente lo conoscesse, significa che questo vitio deforma tanto l'huomo, che più tosto per bestia, che per huomo si fa conoscere, perchè di quella tien i costumi, & di questo solamente l'aspetto" ("that he recognized him with difficulty

In the posthumous *Responsio ad Ioannem Miltonem*, Saumaise advances the nasty slander that on his travels Milton was debauched by his sodomite Italian friends.[49] Inversely, despite the undoubted pleasure he took in some of his Italian acquaintances and in their friendly reception of him, one part of the Englishman's mind, as was common in other Protestant tourists of the period, viewed himself as a righteous man travelling among the cities of the iniquitous (thus his outspokenness in matters of religion and clash with the Jesuits).

The implicit condemnation of Florence as a new Sodom in the *Commedia*, and the warning as to Dante's imminent expulsion, identify the poet as a type of the righteous man, estranged from his fellow citizens, who enjoys God's personal protection.[50] In canto 15 the commentaries of both Velutello and Daniello cite the earlier indictment of Florence by the glutton Ciacco, who accuses its inhabitants of deafness to justice: "Giusti son due, ma non ui sono'ntesi: / Superbia, inuidia & avaritia sono / Le tre fauille, ch'hanno i cuori accesi" (6.51-53) ("There are two just men, but they are not harkened to: pride, envy, and greed are the three flames that have lit their hearts").[51] While the

---

signifies that this vice so deforms man, that rather as a beast, than as a man is he known, because he has the manners of the first and only the appearance of the second"). — The "Egyptian" half of the simile also offers extensive corresponsion with the context, beginning with the pun on "inflamed sea" (300) and "Red-sea Coast" (306). Satan's escape from the burning lake mimics that of the Israelites (cf. Mulder in this volume), as does his stance on the "safe shore," gazing at the wreckage of an army for whose destruction he is responsible. The analogy with Moses becomes more explicit in the following simile, the locusts called up by the "potent Rod / Of *Amrams* Son in *Egypts* evil day" (338-39) compared to the "bad Angels" who respond to "th'uplifted Spear / Of thir great Sultan" (347-48), since in Exodus the same rod closes the sea over the pursuing Egyptians (cf. Exodus 14.16, 21, 26-27; *Paradise Lost* 12.210-12). A parody of the biblical text demonstrates Satan's capacity for dissimulation and prepares the way for similar reversals of type.

[49] French, 1:417.

[50] At Genesis 18.20-32 Abraham bargains with God as to the number of righteous men who will suffice to save Sodom; cf. CE 3:278; CPW 1:861. On the contrast between the *lazzi sorbi* and the *dolce fico*, Velutello writes: "tra quello inhumano, e duro popolo, non era conueniente, che la uirtù del Poeta si esercitasse, perchè sarebbe stato un dar le margarite a porci, non potendosi le uirtù ne gli animi bestiali, & efferati inserire" ("amongst that unkind and hard people, there was no chance for the virtue of the poet to work, since this would be throwing pearls before swine, given the resistance of these wild and brutish hearts to all virtue").

[51] Cf. also *Purgatorio* 16.121-26.

three just men of the Bible are named at Ezechiel 14.14, 20, the identity of Dante's two *giusti* became and remained a matter for debate amongst medieval and Renaissance commentators, as it is today;[52] but both Landino and Velutello suggest Dante himself (together with his fellow poet Cavalcanti), while Daniello in addition argues that the two men remain unknown to their fellows (not "they are not listened to"). Milton's personal interest in the doctrine, popular in Reformation theology, of the single just man can hardly escape a reader of *Paradise Lost*: in book 11 Michael shows to Adam, first Enoch:

> The only righteous in a World perverse,
> And therefore hated, therefore so beset
> With Foes for daring single to be just,
> And utter odious Truth.                    (11.701–4)

and then Noah, "the onely Son of light / In a dark Age, against example good, / Against allurement, custom, and a World / Offended; fearless of reproach and scorn, / Or violence" (11.808–12); while elsewhere in the text an outstanding example of constancy is provided by the single refusal of the angel Abdiel to bow to the corrupting falsehoods of Satan (5.803–6.43). This cast of mind means that Milton certainly recognized the significance and the symbolism of the poetic self in the *Commedia*.

Dante's choice of two, rather than three, *giusti* is inevitably also a reminder of the witnesses slain in Revelation, whose corpses are left unburied in the streets of the great city to the rejoicing of the ungodly; but after three and a half days "the spirit of life *coming* from God, shal enter into them, and they shal stand vp vpon their fete: and great feare shal come vpon them which sawe them" (11.11, Geneva Bible). During the Reformation the interpretation of this text was a matter of bitter polemic: traditional Roman Catholic exegesis, authoritatively summarized in Bellarmine's *Disputationes*,[53] argued that the witnesses were

---

[52] Cf. Z. G. Baranski, "*Inferno* VI.73: A Controversy Re-examined," *Italian Studies* 26 (1981): 1–26.

[53] Robert Bellarmine, *Disputationes . . . de Controversiis Christianae Fidei adversus huius Temporis Haereticos*, 2d ed. (Ingolstadt: Sartor, 1588), vol. 1, controversia 3, "De Romano Pontefice," bk. 3 "Disputatio de Antichristo." Gordon Campbell argues that in the lost "Index theologicus" Milton gathered material for a reply to this work; cf. "Milton's 'Index Theologicus' and Bellarmine's 'Disputationes De Controversiis

Enoch and Elia, whose recognizable return to earth would mark the coming of Antichrist and the beginning of the last days; but Protestants, who claimed that Antichrist was the pope of Rome, declared them to be the martyrs of the true Church whose sufferings and deaths had occurred in the various ages of history.[54] Pareus's commentary, cited by and well known to Milton,[55] holds the exposure and mockery of the bodies to be the persecution of their writings and the ridicule of their teachings:

---

Christianae Fidei Adversus Huius Temporis Haereticos'," MQ 11 (1977): 12-16. See also Bellarmine's Apologia . . . pro Responsione sua ad Librum Iacobi Magnae Brittaniae Regis, cuius Titulus est, Triplici Nodo Triplex Cuneus (Rome, 1610), ch. 10, 154, "De sede & duratione Antichristi," ch. 11, 160, "De Henoch, & Helia."

[54] In divinam Apocalypsin S.Apostoli et Evangelistae Johannis commentarius, 2d ed. (Heidelberg: 1622), cols, 475-76: "Prophetiam intelligamus hic non strictè praedictionem futurorum: sed latè praedictionem doctrinae propheticae & apostolicae. Hanc illi obscuratam & proculcatam ab Antichristo, renovatâ prophetiâ vindicabunt, cordatè praedicabunt atque restituent Ecclesiae, idque Christo hoc eis dante, hoc est, spiritu heroico & donis eos armante, ut regnum Antichristi toto orbe Christiano ceu φεώημα inexpugnabile firmatum & roboratum, cordatè oppugnent, & concutiant fortiter" ("We interpret the prophecy here as not limited strictly to future events, but as a general prediction of prophetic and apostolic doctrine. These men will avenge with renewed prophecy [the Church] obscured and trampled on by Antichrist, they will preach from their hearts and restore the Church, and, Christ having given this to them, that is having armed them with heroic spirit and gifts, so that against the realm of Antichrist or garrison, which is unconquerably strong and fortified, they fight with their hearts and smite it powerfully"). At 478: "Sicut autem oppressio Ecclesiae non facta est momento, nec initio fuit gravissima, sed paulatim incrementa fecit, donec sub pedibus Antichristi prorsus depressa iaceret sancta civitas: sic duorum testium praeconium adversus eum non semper fuit aequaliter evidens & efficax" ("Just as the subjugation of the Church did not happen in any one moment, nor was it serious at the beginning, but gradually increased until finally the sacred city lay wholly thrown down beneath the feet of Antichrist, so the outcry of the two witnesses against him was not always equally evident and effective"). Also the English divine John Bale, The Image of Both Churches, after the Most Wonderfull and Heavenly Revelation of Sainct Iohn the Euangelist, Containing a Very Fruitfull Exposition or Paraphrase upon the Same (London: Thomas Cast, s.d.), views the two as the "witnesses of gods ueritie in all ages" (fol. 16), who have "continued with the people of God since the death of Steeuen, for the most part secretly and unknown to the world" (fol. 11v).

[55] In the divorce tracts Milton makes frequent reference to writings by Pareus, while in the Reason of Church-Government, he states that "the Apolcalyps of Saint John is the majestick image of a high and stately Tragedy, shutting up and intermingling her Solemn Scenes and Acts with a sevenfold Chorus of halleluja's and harping symphonies: and this my opinion the grave autority of Pareus commenting that booke is sufficient to confirm" (CPW 1:815); cf. also the preface to Samson Agonistes.

Cadavera testium sunt non tantum eorum corpora, quibus
frequenter talia ad literam contigerunt . . . sed & eorum nomina,
quae anathemate ferit, & eorum libri, quos haberi, legi, vendi
prohibet, igne exurit, denique etiam familiae, quas quibus potest
modis infames reddit & opprimit.[56]

The corpses of the witnesses are not only their physical bodies,
as the literal meaning here and elsewhere has it, . . . but also their
names, which are outlawed in bulls, as well as their books, which
are forbidden to be owned, read or sold, or are burnt in fires,
and finally also their families, which are defamed by all possible
means and oppressed.

The echo of the apocalyptic text in the structure and in the application of the simile in Vallombrosa therefore identifies the narrating
Milton of *Paradise Lost*, like Dante before him, with the witnesses and,
in more general terms, with the image of the just man. If, in the first
half of the simile, the ambiguity of the "Shady vale" recalls the personal
situation of the poet "On evil days though fall'n, and evil tongues; / In
darkness, and with dangers compast round, / And solitude" (7.26–28);
the second half, with the wreckage of the Egyptian chivalry, shows that
God's vengeance has been, and again will be, actuated. In the *Readie
and Easie Way to Establish a Free Commonwealth* (1660) Milton condemns the imminent Restoration as "chusing . . . a captain back for
Egypt";[57] thus the allusion to Revelation is one of ominous foreboding
for his victors, since the resurrection of the witnesses was a symbol for
the renewal of their cause by others.[58]

---

[56] Pareus, *Commentarius*, col. 493. A standard popularizing gloss such as Richard
Baxter's *Paraphrase in the New Testament, with Notes Doctrinal and Practical*, 2d ed.
(London, 1695), concurs in a political interpretation: "Say some, They shall literally be
cast out inhumanely buried; say others, They shall be politically slain, deposed,
silenced, imprisoned, and cast by as dead and useless. And not only their persecuting
enemies, but the deluded rabble and people, shall see their oppression and insult over
them, and not suffer them to be restored, or honoured."

[57] CE 6:194; CPW 7:163 (cf. Numbers 14.2–3); cf. "Letter to a Friend": "when so
great a part of the Nation were desperately conspir'd to call back again thir Egyptian
bondage" (CE 6:101; CPW 7:325).

[58] Baxter, *Paraphrase*: "And this will seem, to carnal men, to be Gods disowning
them, and all that they did: But the same sort of Men shall be raised again, and revive
their work with more success, and again silence the deluded insulting enemies."

In other biblical texts the withering of a leaf is a metaphor for the sterility of sin: "all our righteousness *is* as filthy cloutes, and we all do fade like a leafe, and our iniquities like the winde haue taken vs away" (Isaiah 64.6, Geneva Bible);[59] and likewise barren trees or vines are consigned to the flames of God's anger;[60] but perhaps the antitypes, the leaves that do not fall or wither, are more significant. In Milton's rendering of the first Psalm "done into verse in 1653," the image of a tree growing by fresh waters occurs as a similitude for the righteous man who "hath not walkt astray / In counsel of the wicked."

> He shall be as a tree which planted grows
> By watry streams, and in his season knows
> To yield his fruit, and his leaf shall not fall,
> And what he takes in hand shall prosper all.
> Not so the wicked, but as chaff which fannd
> The wind drives, so the wicked shall not stand
> In judgement, or abide their trial then,
> Nor sinners in th'assembly of just men.[61]

A similar antitype occurs in the final chapter of Revelation, where the ambivalent and shady Vallombrosan brooks have an antithesis in the "pure riuer of water of life, cleare as crystal, proceding out of the throne of God, and of the Lambe," where on "ether side of the riuer, was the tre of life, which bare twelue maner of frutes, & gaue frute euerie moneth: & the leaues of the tre *serued* to heale the nations with" (22.1-2).[62] In his commentary on these verses Pareus observes that

---

[59] Cf. Ezechiel 17.7-9, 19.12; Isaiah 1.28-30; Jeremiah 8.13.

[60] Cf. Malachi 4.1; Matthew 3.10, 7.16-20; Luke 3.9. Note also the image of corrupt trees and fruit at Matthew 3.10; Luke 6.43, and the extended comparison at Jude 12.3: "These are spottes in your feasts of charitie when they feast with you, without all feare, feding themselues: cloudes *they are* without water, caryed about of windes, corrupt trees & without frute, twise dead, & plucked vp by the rootes. *They are* the raging waues of the sea, foming out their owne shame: *they are* wandring starres, to whome is reserued the blaknes of darkenes for euer" (Geneva Bible).

[61] Cf. "For he shal be like a tree planted by the riuers of waters, that wil bring forthe her frute in due season: whose leafe shal not fade: so whatsoeuer he shal do, shal prosper" (Geneva Bible); cf. Proverbs 11.28, Jeremiah 17.7-8.

[62] The image draws on Ezechiel 47.12 "And by this riuer vpon the brinke thereof, on this side, & on that side shal growe all fruteful trees, whose leafe shal not fade, nether shal the frute thereof faile: it shal bring forthe new frute according to his moneths, because their waters runne out of the Sanctuarie: and the frute thereof shal

"cum aliarum arborum folia arescant, cadant, pereant: haec arbor perpetuò foliis virebit"[63] ("when the leaves on other trees dry up, fall and perish: this tree will flourish with eternal leaves").

University of Florence

---

be meat, & the leaf thereof shal be for medecine" (Geneva Bible); cf. *Paradise Lost* 5.652 "By living Streams among the Trees of Life."

[63] Pareus, *Commentarius*, cols. 1223-24.

CHARLES A. HUTTAR

# Vallombrosa Revisited

**M**ILTON'S ITALIAN JOURNEY, kept in memory for a quarter-century, left its mark on *Paradise Lost* in a number of fine details. More than one reader has seen in his Eden hints of Italian gardens, paintings, and topography.[1] His description of Hell may owe something to geothermal features of the landscape near Naples or near Florence or both; his Pandemonium, to the Basilica of St. Peter in Rome; and a series of epic similes, concentrated in about twenty lines in book 1, contains several explicit references to Florence and its environs—"*Fesole*," the Val d'Arno, "the *Tuscan* Artist," and Vallombrosa (284-304).[2]

Let us examine one of these similes and try to observe the impact of Milton's Italian experience on the composition of his poem.

> He [Satan] stood and call'd
> His Legions, Angel Forms, who lay intrans't
> Thick as Autumnal Leaves that strow the Brooks
> In *Vallombrosa*, where th' *Etrurian* shades
> High overarch't imbow'r. . . .          (300-304)

The simile continues, shifting from Italy to Egypt and eventually from

---

[1] Hannah Disinger Demaray, "Milton's 'Perfect' Paradise and the Landscapes of Italy," *MQ* 8 (1974): 33. On the gardens, she cites Joseph Addison. See also Henry J. Todd, ed., *The Poetical Works of John Milton*, 7 vols. (London, 1809), 3:86.

[2] Marjorie Hope Nicolson, "Hell and the Phlegraean Fields," *University of Toronto Quarterly* 7 (1938): 500-513 (Naples); Irwin R. Blacker, "Did Milton Visit Hell?" *Seventeenth-Century News* 9 (1951): 54 (near Florence); Rebecca W. Smith, "The Source of Milton's Pandemonium," *MP* 29 (1931): 187-98. Other possible traces of the Italian journey in *Paradise Lost* are mentioned in Robert Ralston Cawley, *Milton and the Literature of Travel*, Princeton Studies in English, no. 32 (Princeton: Princeton Univ. Press, 1951), 127-28. My text for Milton's poetry is Hughes.

topographical to historical reference and from description to moral evaluation, before its conclusion:

> ... so thick bestrown
> Abject and lost lay these, covering the Flood,
> Under amazement of thir hideous change.
>
> (311–13)

There are four explicit points of resemblance between the angelic forms and the leaves: they lie on the water's surface, they are inert or lifeless ("intrans't"), they are crowded together in great numbers, and they have undergone a severe change in appearance. To these we may add a fifth similarity, an implicit one: both the angels and the leaves have got where they are by falling, consequent upon a separation from their life-giving source. And here we begin to see the economy of Milton's similes[3] at work, for the thought of a fall invites us (considering the subject of the whole poem) to a metaphorical as well as a literal interpretation, from which it is a quick step to perceive the angels as the enemies of God, defeated and doomed. Milton makes these latter points more nearly explicit when he introduces a new vehicle in this complex simile, likening the angels to the drowned hosts of Pharaoh (306–11); but the ideas are already implicit in the Vallombrosa segment of the simile to a greater degree than is generally appreciated, as the first part of this paper will show.

Yet such an interpretation is problematic, for the Vallombrosa lines have at the same time a melodic sound, unlike the harsher lines that follow, and have thereby a pastoral quality that would seem inconsonant with any implications of death or judgment. Indeed, readers have found here a hint of the earthly paradise, or "an ironical contrast" between "the beauty of the 'shady valley' " and the ugliness of Hell, or a "moment ... of relief or distancing," of "maximum contrast" but without

---

[3] Concerning this well-established idea see James Whaler, "The Miltonic Simile," *PMLA* 46 (1931): 1034–74; L. D. Lerner, "The Miltonic Simile," *Essays in Criticism* 4 (1954): 297–308; Ricks, 118–32; Christopher Grose, *Milton's Epic Process: Paradise Lost and Its Miltonic Background* (New Haven: Yale Univ. Press, 1973), 140–69; John Hollander, *The Figure of Echo: A Mode of Allusion in Milton and After* (Berkeley: Univ. of California Press, 1981), 114–20; Charles Martindale, *John Milton and the Transformation of Ancient Epic* (Totowa, NJ: Barnes and Noble, 1986), 119–32; and Neil Harris in the present volume.

irony; while for yet another critic, the movement of thought in the poem has been temporarily suspended while we enjoy an idyllic description far removed from the simile's ominous tenor[4]—suspended, perhaps, by the force of the poet's happy memories of his sojourn in Italy. The second part of my paper will address itself to this conflict between message and tone.

## I

To follow Milton at work in this passage we must first remind ourselves of the epic tradition he inherited. Who first saw in the leaves of fall, or the fall of leaves, an emblem of mortality were a question above anti-quarianism. Glaucus, encountering Diomede in battle before Troy, used the simile to express an ancient fatalism: to live and then die, being succeeded in turn by new generations, is the human lot (Homer, *Il.* 6.146-49).[5] Here the leaves are already fallen, matted on the forest floor, composting. Homer's successors, Virgil (*Aen.* 6.309-10) and Dante (*Inf.* 3.112-16), extended the theme of mortality by likening dead leaves to ghosts in the underworld, but they present the leaves in motion: passive (as they were in Homer) and not under their own control, but broken loose from the tree and being carried randomly to earth. Virgil also mentions the frost which causes the leaves to fall, and this metaphorically reinforces the theme of death. Tasso in his turn applies the leaves simile not to ghosts in Hell but to devils being driven back to Hell by Michael (*Ger. Lib.* 9.66.5-6)—glancing, in so doing, at an analogue from the scriptural tradition, Isaiah's much briefer compari-son of the discomfiture of God's enemies to the fall of leaves.[6] Some-

---

[4] For earthly paradise cf. Mary Shelley, *Rambles in Germany and Italy*, 2 vols. (London: Edward Moxon, 1844), 2:138, and Wordsworth as cited in Robin Jarvis, "Shades of Milton: Wordsworth at Vallombrosa," *Studies in Romanticism* 25 (1986): 493-94. "Ironical": Douglas Bush, "Paradise Lost," *A Milton Encyclopedia*, ed. William B. Hunter, Jr., et al., 9 vols. (Lewisburg: Bucknell Univ. Press, 1978-83), 6:77. "Distancing": Geoffrey H. Hartman, "Milton's Counterplot," in *Beyond Formalism: Literary Essays 1958-1970* (New Haven: Yale Univ. Press, 1970), 113, 118. Idyllic: A. S. P. Woodhouse, *The Heavenly Muse: A Preface to Milton*, ed. Hugh MacCallum (Toronto: Univ. of Toronto Press, 1972), 214.

[5] None of Homer's successors follows his lead in using this *topos* as a device for characterizing a speaker.

[6] "All their hostes shal fall as the leafe falleth from the vine, and as it falleth from

what outside this tradition stand Seneca, who in drama, not epic, offers autumn leaves as one of five rapid-fire comparisons for a multitude of spirits summoned up from the realms of the dead, and two narrative poets who are concerned with mere numbers, not mortality, in their comparisons of an innumerable host of warriors to autumn leaves.[7]

As we would expect, Milton, who has announced his intention to outdo his predecessors, is no mere perfunctory imitator of these models.[8] He weaves together carefully selected elements to make a fabric uniquely suited to his own purposes. His application of the leaves *topos* to devils may follow Tasso, but he adds the word "Legions" with its New Testament resonance,[9] a word which in its primary meaning also

---

the figtre" (Isa. 34.4). *The Geneva Bible* (1560), facsim. ed. by Lloyd B. Berry (Madison: Univ. of Wisconsin Press, 1969). Subsequent biblical quotations are from this text.

[7] "Non tot caducas educat frondes Eryx" (Seneca, *Oedipus* 600); the other four images (601–7) are the waves of the sea and the flowers, bees, and returning birds of spring. (Citations of ancient authors in the present paper, unless otherwise noted, are from the Loeb editions.) In discussing this passage in relation to Milton's simile and earlier exemplars of the *topos*, Sergio Baldi, "Folte come le Foglie (e lo Scudo di Satana)" (1978), collected in his *Studi Miltoniani* (Florence: Università, 1985), 65–81, notes that Seneca goes beyond Virgil by localizing the references to nature in his simile. Apollonius Rhodius also joins the image of countless waves to that of falling leaves (*Argonautica* 4.216–18); Ariosto confines his comparison to a brief, unextended simile (*Orl. Fur.* 16.75.7–8). Both poets may echo Homer, *Il.* 2.800 (where, however, the leaves are not explicitly autumnal) or 2.468 (where they are explicitly not autumnal).

I omit passages by Marlowe and Bacchylides, mentioned by C. M. Bowra in his survey of the *topos* (*From Vergil to Milton* [London: Macmillan, 1948], 240–41): Marlowe's because his numberless leaves are still alive on the tree, and Bacchylides' because (like an even more recently discovered fragment, possibly by Pindar) Milton could not have known it, though it is likely that Virgil did (see Mary R. Lefkowitz, "Cultural Conventions and the Persistence of Mistranslation," *Classical Journal* 68 [1972]: 36, and Lefkowitz, *The Victory Ode: An Introduction* [Park Ridge, NJ: Noyes Press, 1976], 99–100). The *topos* is discussed more fully by Claes Schaar, *The Full Voic'd Quire Below: Vertical Context Systems in* Paradise Lost, Lund Studies in English, 60 (Lund: Gleerup, 1982), 54–59. I also omit a passage which Richard J. DuRocher (*Milton and Ovid* [Ithaca: Cornell Univ. Press, 1985], 155–56) considers parallel to Milton's simile: *Met.* 3.729–31, where Ovid, in the story of the dismemberment of Pentheus, borrows Virgil's frost motif and emphasizes the violence of the leaves' separation from the tree; but neither detail is in Milton. An especially detailed comparison of the Homer and Virgil passages with Milton's may be found in James P. Holoka, " 'Thick as Autumnal Leaves'—the Structure and Generic Potentials of an Epic Simile," *MQ* 10 (1976): 78–83.

[8] See *Paradise Lost* 1.13–16 and Harold Bloom, *A Map of Misreading* (New York: Oxford Univ. Press, 1975), 135–38.

[9] Luke 8.30. Milton uses the Luke 8 story more explicitly in *Paradise Regained*

glances at Ariosto's army. In placing the scene in Hell Milton follows older models; in emphasizing the innumerable quantity of the leaves he follows Virgil, Seneca, Tasso, and Ariosto; and in asking us to visualize them no longer falling but massed together—"sodden devitalized rotting" is the way one critic describes their state[10]—he follows Homer. His borrowed leaves, at any rate, carry with them already the accumulated associations of death, defeat, and wickedness which will become more explicit in the biblical reference later in the simile.[11] To these, in the particular context of *Paradise Lost*, Milton adds associations of sin and its consequences, the wasting of autumn[12] and, more inclusively, the general fruitlessness which is the fruit of sin.[13]

To parallel his fallen angels, lying on the lake's surface, Milton masses his leaves on water, rather than the forest floor, as in Homer. This leads to another significant element in his simile, one for which he may have taken a hint from Seneca but which, so far as the epic tradition is concerned, is his original contribution. I refer to the geographical exactness:[14] it is not generic water that he gives us or a generic forest,

---

4.626-32, in the context of a long passage on the various falls of Satan. See also lines 562, 605-6, and 619-20; in the last of these passages, based on Luke 10.18, Milton again uses the word "autumnal" to invoke the seasonal metaphor.

[10] Irene Samuel, *Dante and Milton* (Ithaca: Cornell Univ. Press, 1966), 76.

[11] John M. Steadman, "The Devil and Pharaoh's Chivalry," *MLN* 75 (1960): 198 and 200-201, shows how these associations, though still only implied up to line 304, are reinforced by the exegetical tradition on Isa. 34.4 (cf. note 6 above).

[12] MacCaffrey, 126. Milton's "Autumnal Leaves" in book 1 thus anticipate the tilting of the earth and the consequent change of seasons in book 10, occurring as a result of the Fall of Man.

[13] Alastair Fowler, "Introduction" [to *Paradise Lost*], in Fowler, 436.

[14] Observed—as Baldi notes (68)—by Newton in his 1749 edition of *Paradise Lost*. Milton's geographical reference provides a link with the later development of the *topos*, since it was in the Arno valley near Florence that Shelley was inspired to write his "Ode to the West Wind" in 1819. To study that later development is beyond the scope of the present essay; a good beginning is made by Hollander, 95-98, 115, 121-22, 128-29; see also János Riesz, "Falling Leaves: Some Reflections on the Nature and Function of the Image in Lyric Poetry," *Yearbook of Comparative and General Literature* 33 (1984): 49-58. To the texts they cite may be added these lines by Dante Gabriel Rossetti: "How then should sound upon Life's darkening slope / The ground-whirl of the perished leaves of Hope, / The wind of Death's imperishable wing" (*The House of Life* 1.4.12-14; ed. Paull Franklin Baum [Cambridge, Mass.: Harvard Univ. Press, 1928], 70). In a later sonnet, again expressing a mood of despair at contemplation of the beloved's death, Rossetti uses a similar image: "my life unleaved" (1.25.11; ed. Baum, 101).

but "the Brooks / In *Vallombrosa*, where th' *Etrurian* shades / High overarch't imbow'r." Milton is not merely indulging a personal fondness for his Italian memories. On the contrary, with remarkable efficiency he contrives that every noun, verb, and adjective in that added pair of lines should contribute its bit to the overall tone of the simile. Of brooks and bowers we will speak later. "Overarch't" echoes the reference six lines before to the fiery "vault" that surrounds Satan as he walks.[15] "Shades" is much more than a habitual or formulaic metonymy for trees or foliage:[16] besides being a synonym for "ghosts," the word hints at an imagined identification of the Italian landscape with this region of darkness visible. There is even an echo of the "dark wood" which for Dante denoted both the lost condition of fallen humanity and the environs of Hell's mouth (*Inf.* 1.2). Reinforcing these connotations is the etymology of the otherwise innocent place name Vallombrosa, a name that might also evoke, for an ear trained on the Authorized Version—or, for that matter, the Prayer Book psalter or the Geneva version—"the valley of the shadow of death."[17]

That leaves another place name, "*Etrurian*," which strangely enough has received hardly any comment beyond the gloss that it is a Latinate way of designating Tuscany, the region in which Vallombrosa (as well as Florence) is located. But "*Etrurian* shades" does not merely "evoke some ghostly images of a civilization long dead," for in Florence when Milton visited it the sense of its distinctively Etruscan heritage was very much alive.[18] Furthermore, by the implications of his reference only

---

[15] J. B. Broadbent, *Some Graver Subject* (London: Chatto and Windus, 1960), 86.

[16] B. A. Wright, " 'Shade' for 'Tree' in Milton's Poetry," *N&Q* 203 (1958): 205–8.

[17] Psalm 23.4; Milton could be confident of his readers' familiarity with this phrase, which is identical in all three versions mentioned. Cf. Steadman, 201; Broadbent, 86; Edward Le Comte, *A Milton Dictionary* (New York: Philosophical Library, 1961), 344; Louis L. Martz, *The Paradise Within* (New Haven: Yale Univ. Press, 1964), 112; and the more detailed discussion by Neil Harris, "Galileo as Symbol: The 'Tuscan Artist' in *Paradise Lost*," *Annali dell'Istituto e Museo di Storia della Scienza di Firenze* 10.2 (1985): 26–27, who points out that the meaning of the Hebrew phrase in Psalm 23.4, reinforced by such contemporary scholarship as that of Beza and Tremellius, is even closer to "vall'ombrosa" than the familiar English translation.

[18] Martz, 112. On Etruscan survival see Giovanni Cipriani, *Il mito Etrusco nel rinascimento Fiorentino*, Biblioteca di Storia Toscana Moderna e Contemporanea, Studi e Documenti, 22 (Florence: Leo Olschki, 1980); *"Mito" Etrusco e ideologia Medicea*, Annali della Facoltà di lettere e filosofia, Univ. Siena, vol. 2 (Florence: Leo Olschki, 1981); Gabriele Morolli, *"Vetus Etruria": il mito Etruschi . . . da Vitruvio a Winckelmann*

fourteen lines earlier to one of the ancient Etruscan cities, Faesulae, which Neil Harris has shown carries ominous associations from Dante as well as from its geography and history,[19] Milton has alerted us to the possibility of sinister overtones in "*Etrurian.*" And considering the general tenor of the leaves simile, "*Etrurian*" is a specially apt term, for most of the distinctive features of ancient Etruscan culture, as set forth by authorities well known to Milton, had what would be for him associations of the demonic.[20] The Etruscans' general reputation was

---

(Florence: Alinea, 1985); and the essay by John R. Mulder in the present volume. Prior to the fifteenth century, Etruscan civilization had for some time largely been ignored; see, for example, Anthony Luttrell, "Caprania before 1337: Petrarch as Topographer," in *Cultural Aspects of the Italian Renaissance: Essays in Honour of Paul Oskar Kristeller*, ed. Cecil H. Clough (Manchester: Manchester Univ. Press, 1976), 11. The creation of the *Magnus Ducatus Hetruriae* in 1569 reflects a revival of interest in the Etruscan heritage, in a context of Florentine patriotism. Barely fifteen years earlier the first Etruscan artefacts had been unearthed, and Cosimo I, the first Grand Duke, took an interest in the excavations and in Etruscan antiquities (James Cleugh, *The Medici: A Tale of Fifteen Generations* [London: Robert Hale, 1976], 285). Etruscan studies continued—on a casual basis, however, until the early eighteenth century, when the rediscovery and publication of Dempster's *De Etruria regali* began a continuing tradition of academic Etruscology. Dempster's work was written between 1616 and 1625 (Massimo Pallottino, *The Etruscans*, trans. J. Cremona, rev. ed. by David Ridgway [Bloomington: Indiana Univ. Press, 1975], 24) and formally presented to the Grand Duke Cosimo II. (It is important to note, however, that according to Eric Cochrane, *Florence in the Forgotten Centuries 1527-1800* [Chicago: Univ. of Chicago Press, 1973], 140, 386-87, the Etruscan enthusiasm of this period was not shared by all Florentines.) In the year preceding Milton's visit, Curzio Inghirami published in *Ethruscarum antiquitatum fragmenta* ("Francofurti" [Florence], 1637) the artefacts he had discovered in 1634-35 on a farm near Volterra. Inghirami's work was controversial, and he returned to the fray with *Discorso sopra l'opposizioni fatte all'antichità Toscane* (Florence, 1645).

[19] Harris, 14-16.

[20] Giulio Buonamici, *Fonti di storia Etrusca tratte dagli autori classici* (Florence: Leo Olschki, 1939), in a classified compilation (in Italian) of references to Etruria and the Etruscans in ancient sources, devotes fifty-five pages to religion and divination (297-351—chap. 4). See also Thomas Dempster, *De Etruria regali*, 2 vols. (Florence, 1723-2[6]), lib. 3. Modern historians corroborate and supplement these points: see Georg Wissowa, ed., *Paulys Real-Encyclopädie der classischen Altertumswissenschaft*, neue Bearbeitung (Stuttgart: J. B. Metzler, 1894-1919), 6:725-30; R. A. L. Fell, *Etruria and Rome* (Cambridge: Cambridge Univ. Press, 1924); R. S. Conway, "Italy in the Etruscan Age. A. The Etruscans," *The Cambridge Ancient History*, ed. J. B. Bury et al., 12 vols. (Cambridge: Cambridge Univ. Press, 1923-39), 4:415-21; Cyril Bailey, "Roman Religion and the Advent of Philosophy," *The Cambridge Ancient History*, 8:448-51; Werner Keller, *The Etruscans*, trans. Alexander and Elizabeth Henderson (New York:

that of a "nation ... devoted beyond all others to religious rites"; folk etymology variously derived their name from words meaning sacrifice.[21] Their superior "knowledge of the ceremonies relating to divine worship" was widely acknowledged; to them Roman religion owed much of its lore concerning civic rituals and the religious aspects of civic architecture, its priestly organization (the college of pontiffs), its concepts of the afterlife, and especially, as Renaissance dictionaries routinely emphasized, its arts of divination.[22] The Romans had their own augurs, but for the most important prognostications they would bring in Etruscan experts, trained in the so-called "Etruscan Discipline" whose miraculous revelation is narrated by Ovid.[23] To one of their specialties, the interpretation of thunder and lightning,[24] Milton alludes in *In quintum Novembris* (23) when he links the Etruscan thunder-god Summanus with the wicked plots of Satan. For this and other examples of

---

Knopf, 1974); Mauro Cristofani, *The Etruscans: A New Investigation*, trans. Brian Phillips (New York: Galahad Books, 1979), 91-121; Larissa Bonfante, "Daily Life and Afterlife," *Etruscan Life and Afterlife*, ed. Larissa Bonfante (Detroit: Wayne State Univ. Press, 1986).

[21] Livy 5.1.6 ("gens ... ante omnes alias eo magis dedita religionibus"); Isidore, *Etymologiae* 9.2.86 and Dionysius of Halicarnassus, *Antiquitates Romanae* 1.30.3 (cited by Pallottino, 138); Iudocus Hondius, *Nova et accurata Italiae hodiernae descriptio* (Amsterdam, 1626), 79.

[22] Dionysius of Halicarnassus, 1.30.3 (τῆς ἐμπειρίας τῶν περὶ τὰ θεῖα τεβάσματα λειτουργιῶν). Rituals: M. Verrius Flaccus and Sextus Pompeius Festus, *De verborum significatione*, with notes by A. Augustinus, J. Scaliger, et al. (Heidelberg: P. Santandreanus, 1593), sig. O6ᵛ; Leone Baptista Alberti, *De re aedificatoria* (Paris, [1512?]), fol. 53ᵛ (lib. 4. cap. 3); W. F. Jackson Knight, *Vergil: Epic and Anthropology*, ed. John D. Christie (New York: Barnes and Noble, 1967), 222-23. Architecture: Alberti, fols. 83ʳ, 98ᵛ, 100ʳ (lib. 4. cap. 3, 7.3, 7.4); Giovanni Rosino, *Antiquitatum Romanorum corpus absolutissimum*, ed. nova by Thomas Dempster (Geneva: G. Cartier, 1620), 11; Bailey, 449-50; Fell, 52; Cristofani, 107-8. For Renaissance dictionaries, see e.g. Ambrosius Calepinus, *Dictionarium* (Venice: apud Aldi Filios, 1552), sig. 2m8ᵛ; Carolus Stephanus, *Dictionarium historicum, geographicum, poeticum ...* (Ursellis: C. Sutorius, 1601), 816. See also Rosino, 274, 287.

[23] Lucan, *Pharsalia* 1.584; Dio Cassius, *Historia Romana* (Loeb ed., 1:77 and 191); cf. W. Warde Fowler, *The Religious Experience of the Roman People* (London: Macmillan, 1911), 309, and Cristofani, 92. Ovid's account is found in *Met.* 15.553-59; see also Buonamici, 309-15.

[24] Pliny, *Naturalis historia* 2.138-44; Seneca, *Quaestiones naturales* 2.32, 41, and 45; Claudian, *In Eutropium* (Loeb ed., 1:139); Servius Grammaticus, *In Vergilii carmina commentarii*, ed. G. Thilo and H. Hagen, 3 vols. (Leipzig: Teubner, 1923), 1:492. See also Buonamici, 326-36.

the "black art" found in Roman tradition, the humanist Sebastian Franck in his *Weltbuch* blames the Etruscan "books of magic."[25] Long before, Cicero had ridiculed the practices in question (*De divinatione* 1.33, 2.23), and the early Church in its turn banned them. "Empty delusions," Arnobius called them, "and the nutriment of empty de-sires," sprung from the "mother of superstition, Etruria," and their practitioners became a byword for perfidious unreliability.[26] The Etrus-cans were also charged with offenses against morality. They had long had a reputation for shameless sexual indulgence.[27] Arnobius castigat-ed the "loathsomeness" of their initiation rites, and Tertullian blamed them for introducing into Rome "public shows in the name of reli-gion."[28] Etruria gave to Rome the Bacchanalia, gladiatorial combat, the mass slaughter of war prisoners as a public spectacle, and ritual human sacrifice.[29] Much of the Etruscan religion was rooted in a detailed and vivid doctrine of the afterlife, far more so than that of Greek or Italic religion, and not only Roman but medieval Christian conceptions of hell, especially the iconography of demons and of torment, owe much to the Etrurian shades.[30]

There is a further association that would make "*Etrurian*," for Milton, yet more sinister. The role of the Etruscans in founding the ancient Roman pontifical college might symbolically make the Roman Catholic Church their heirs; the possibility would hardly escape the poet who could punningly describe the bridge-building skill of Sin and Death as "wondrous art / Pontifical" (*PL* 10.312-13). In his youthful anti-

---

[25] Sebastian Franck, *Weltbuch* (1534), fol. 77ʳ ("der schwartzen kunst").

[26] Arnobius of Sicca, *The Case Against the Pagans*, trans. and ed. George E. McCracken, Ancient Christian Writers, no. 7-8, 2 vols. (Westminster, Md.: Newman, 1949), 1:173, 2:508 (*Adversus gentes* 2.62, 7.26). Rosino, 290.

[27] W. V. Harris, *Rome in Etruria and Umbria* (Oxford: Clarendon Press, 1971), 19 and 119-20, cites relevant ancient texts. But cf. Bonfante, 234-35.

[28] Arnobius, 2:427 (*Adversus gentes* 5.18); Tertullian, *De spectaculis* 5 ("spectacula . . . religionis nomine").

[29] Dempster, 1:340; W. Fowler, 346-47; Conway, 420-21.

[30] Fell, 18; R. S. Conway, "The Etruscan Influence on Roman Religion," *Bulletin of the John Rylands Library* 16 (1932): 384-90; W. F. Jackson Knight, *Roman Vergil*, rev. and enlarged ed. (New York: Barnes and Noble, 1971), 257; Keller, 408-9. Earlier recognition of this connection is demonstrated by the ninth-century Rémi d'Auxerre, *Comentum in Martianum Capellam*, ed. Cora E. Lutz, 2 vols. (Leiden: E. J. Brill, 1962-65), 1:178.

Catholic poem *In quintum Novembris* Milton made this very association when he noted that Satan, flying to Rome to awaken his servant the pope, would pass "Etruria, notorious for its sorceries."[31] If Etruria was the "generatrix et mater superstitionum," as Arnobius had put it, her lineal descendant might well appear to be what Milton himself once called "the worst of superstitions,... Popery."[32] By the early seventeenth century, the ideology identifying superstition with the Church of Rome, and perhaps especially with monasticism, had gone beyond polemic to become embedded in ordinary language, as a few moments' study of the relevant *Oxford English Dictionary* entries will show. Familiarized over a long period through such widely known works as Cranmer's *Catechism*, Calvin's *Institutes*, and the *Book of Homilies*,[33] this synonymy was well established in the popular mind. If extended to include a Church of England only partially reformed, it accounts for the majority of the appearances of *superstition* and its derivatives in Milton's works across more than thirty years, as recorded in more than three columns of Patterson's *Index*.[34] The Etrurian connection is made explicit in the following contemporary comment, in a pamphlet attack on the pluralism of the Restoration church:

> You are the greatest Juglers and Deceivers in the world; and you laugh among your selves, (as the *Thuscan* Soothsayers) and confer Notes, as that Pope with his Cardinal, saying, *How much gain doth this Fable of Christ bring us?*—and poor souls should avoid you as the shadow of death.[35]

---

[31] Line 51 ("veneficiis infamis Hetruria"); the translation is John Carey's in Fowler, 46.

[32] *Of True Religion* (1673), CE, ed. Frank Allen Patterson, 6:180.

[33] Cranmer (1548): *OED*, s.v. "superstitiousness." Calvin (ET 1561): *OED*, s.v. "superstitious"; see also Ford Lewis Battles's subject index to his translation of the *Institutes*, ed. John T. McNeill, Library of Christian Classics, vols. 20-21, 1 vol. in 2 (Philadelphia: Westminster, 1960), 2:1703-4. *Homilies* (1547): *OED*, s.v. "superstition," 1b; see also *Certaine Sermons or Homilies appointed to read in Churches, In the time of the late Queene Elizabeth* (London: John Bill, 1623), 36-37, where the reference is especially to monastic establishments: "the innumerable superstitions that hath bene in strange apparel, in silence, in Dormitory, in Cloyster, in Chapter..." (37).

[34] Frank Allen Patterson, *An Index to the Columbia Edition of the Works of John Milton*, 1 vol. in 2 (New York: Columbia Univ. Press, 1940), 2:1897-98.

[35] Thomas Ken (?), *Ichabod* (Cambridge: for J. Greaves, 1663), 63.

Another Etruscan legacy would be the Mons Vaticanus itself, where according to Pliny the Elder[36] the Etruscans once practiced their religion on the site now occupied by the great Basilica of St. Peter. A guidebook of 1625 gave the information that in ancient times the Vatican was outside Rome proper, in the Etruscan dominions.[37] Milton would know, too, the current etymology deriving *Vatican* "from *Vaticinium*, a fore-telling."[38] Nor would it have escaped him that, at the time of his visit, it was a Tuscan who reigned as pope. Perhaps, then, one reason Milton thought of Vallombrosa as being "overarch't" by "*Etrurian* shades" is that it was the site of a monastery, an especially dark representative of a benighted church, for which he shows in his writings the greatest contempt.[39]

## II

But that brings us to the crux of the matter. Milton has introduced a simile to enhance his description of the fallen angels lying in great profusion and disarray on the burning lake. He has borrowed a traditional figure of autumnal leaves, extended the simile with a pointed comparison between the demons and the vanquished Egyptian host, and added a short passage particularizing the locale of the fallen leaves. He has loaded this addition with place names and other words resonant of evil, death, and Hell, thus packing into his simile far more information about Satan's legions than the mainly descriptive comparisons of his sources. Milton has, however, allowed the same passage to have other overtones as well, hinting at a pleasant rural scene, a *locus amoenus*. It is done partly by a geographical allusion—Vallombrosa, even in

---

[36] *Naturalis historia* 16.237. A citation of this reference, contemporary with Milton, is by Rosino, 21.

[37] Johann Heinrich von Pflaumern, *Mercurius Italicus* (Augsburg: A. Apergeri, 1625), 201.

[38] Thomas Godwin, *Romanae historiae anthologia* (1614), rev. and enlarged ed. (London: T. J. for Peter Parker, 1668), 8. Cf. Aulus Gellius 16.17 (Loeb ed., 3:184-87); Hondius, 134.

[39] Cf. Michael Lieb, "Milton among the Monks," in *Milton and the Middle Ages*, ed. John Mulryan (Lewisburg: Bucknell Univ. Press, 1982), 103-14.

autumn, is a far cry from Hell's "many a dark and dreary Vale" (2.618);
partly by sheer melody, the liquid consonants and open back vowels;[40]
and partly by imagery. Bowers and brooks abound in Milton's poetry
and nearly always they give a blameless delight. Brooks are the favored
places of good spirits in A Mask, of the Pensive Man, of the unfallen
Adam in Paradise (where even the attribution of "mazy error" cannot
mar their intrinsic goodness [PL 4.237-40]), and of the heavenly Muse
in Sion. Milton's bowers also, though always shady, are usually paradis-
al and pastoral. Even when in PL 4.690 and 701 his language evokes
Spenser's and Homer's morally censurable bowers, it yet leaves no spot
or blame behind. The "blissful Bower" in which Milton places Adam
and Eve is not unnatural, like Spenser's (FQ 2.12), but

> a place
> Chos'n by the sovran Planter, when he fram'd
> All things to man's delightful use; the roof
> Of thickest covert was inwoven shade. . . .
>                               (4.690-93)

The language may hint at artifice ("inwoven" and, in 699-703,
"wrought," "mosaic," "inlay," "broider'd," "Emblem"), but that serves
only to underscore the inherent goodness of nature's artificer, contrasting with the spirit of furtive and unrestrained sexual license that imbues
Homer's treatment of Zeus in a parallel passage in the Iliad.[41] Uriel's
words in innocently directing Satan to the same place echo the language
of the Vallombrosa simile:

---

[40] Including the name "Vallombrosa" itself (cf. Holoka, 81), whose use primarily
for euphony in Ariosto's Orlando Furioso (22.36.3) Milton would recall. Kitty Cohen
notes the "contrast" between the "music of 'Vallombrosa' " and the "hardening" of
consonants later in the passage (The Throne and the Chariot: Studies in Milton's Hebra-
ism [The Hague: Mouton, 1975], 54).

[41] Douglas Bush, commenting on the particular line (Il. 14.348) to which Milton
alludes (PL 4.701 and 9.1039-41), notes that the reproof implicit in the Homeric
passage is present in Milton's account of Adam and Eve's lovemaking after the fall, but
not before (Paradise Lost in Our Time: Some Comments [Ithaca: Cornell Univ. Press,
1945], 105-6). Perhaps the closest divine parallel to the Edenic bowers would be the
angels' "blissful Bow'rs" in Heaven (11.77).

> That spot to which I point is *Paradise*,
> *Adam's* abode, those lofty shades his Bow'r.
>
> (3.733–34)

Indeed no "bower," even in fiction, was ever "shadier"—nor "more sacred" (4.705–6). Paradise was "a happy rural seat of various view" (4.247),

> Both where the morning Sun … smote
> The open field, and where the unpierc't shade
> Imbrown'd the noontide Bow'rs;       (4.244–46)

the alternatives are equally desirable. Of great attractiveness to Milton's Pensive Man are "*arched* walks of twilight groves, / And *shadows* brown," where "in close covert by some Brook" he might be "hid[den] from Day's garish eye" (*Il. Pen.* 133–34, 139, 141, emphasis mine). Surely the poet who could conceive of a fitting seat for "deity"

> Under the shady roof
> Of branching Elm Star-proof       (*Arc.* 88–89)

would be susceptible to having similar imaginations stirred among the overarching shades near Florence as they had been some half-dozen years before at Harefield. It must be acknowledged that the elm bower in *Arcades* seems to owe something verbally to the entrance to Hell in Virgil (*Aen.* 6.282–83) and the deceptive wood of Errour in Spenser (*FQ* 1.1.7). And Spenser lies behind the "ominous Wood" where Comus practices magic "in thick shelter of black shades imbow'r'd" (*A Mask* 61–62). The words "ominous" and "black" offer explicit direction, but apart from this sole instance, in Milton's early poetry (including the early books of *Paradise Lost*) the bower scene, like that of brooks, connotes blameless delight.[42]

There is, however, a cluster of three passages in book 9 where the language of book 1 is echoed in a way that seems to mock any notion

---

[42] See also 5.230, 375–76. Even the contrast at the end of book 8 between Adam's bower and Raphael's better-lighted residence, while it points to a difference between man and angel—if all goes well, a temporary difference—does not thereby imply a moral judgment. Passages in the Nativity Ode might be thought to provide another counterexample, but neither the "arched roof" of the "deceiving" Oracles (175)—perhaps a cave is intended—nor the Nymphs' "twilight shade of tangled thickets" (188) has much in common with the "high overarch't," open Tuscan walks.

of its innocence. In the first, having eaten the fatal fruit, Adam seizes Eve's hand and leads the way "to a shady bank, / Thick overhead with verdant roof imbowr'd" (9.1037-38). This episode ends with the pair awaking to "guilty shame" (1058). Adam now feels the need to hide, not from the garish sun but from the "dazzl[ing]" glory of "heav'nly shapes" which were wont to visit him (1082-83):

> O might I
> ... live ... in some glade
> Obscur'd,[43] where *highest* Woods *impenetrable*
> *To Star or Sun-light*, spread thir *umbrage* broad,
> And brown as Evening: Cover me ye Pines,
> Ye Cedars, with *innumerable* boughs
> Hide me, where I may never see them more
>                              (1084-90, emphasis mine)

—or, what Adam is perhaps thinking, may never more be seen: that at least is why he later flees "among / The thickest Trees" (10.100-101), not realizing, of course, since seasonal change is yet unknown to him, that eventually their unleaving would expose him again.[44] In the words "Cover me," Adam is linked with those who will desperately seek to evade the Last Judgment:

> Then shal they beginne to say to the mountaines, Fall on vs: and to the hilles, Couer vs.
> For if they do these things to a grene tre [as Christ speaks, he is being led to Calvary], what shalbe done to the drye?

In Luke 23.30-31, as in *Paradise Lost*, the fall of leaves is associated with spiritual death and impending judgment.[45]

---

[43] Echoing Dante's "selva oscura" (*Inf.* 1.2) but reversing Dante's wish to find the way out of it.

[44] This deceptive quality of the shade under which Adam and Eve hid was a point made in the exegetical tradition on the Genesis story: see D. W. Robertson, "The Doctrine of Charity in Mediaeval Literary Gardens: A Topical Approach through Symbolism and Allegory," *Speculum* 26 (1951): 26, quoting and commenting on a long passage by Hugh of St. Victor on the allegorical meaning of the transitory and hence deceptive leaves.

[45] John H. Lauck, II, "*Paradise Lost* IX.1084-90 and Luke 23:28-30," *American Notes and Queries* 21 (1983): 132-33, notes the first part of this allusion and relates it to another idea, that of verses 28-29, but does not comment on the "grene"/ "drye"

In the third passage, the desire to hide their shame leads the pair into an Indian figtree, a many-trunked plant which grows to make "a Pillar'd shade / *High overarch't*, and echoing Walks between" (9. 1106-7, emphasis mine). The shade is so deep that loopholes must be cut to admit light (1110). Possibly in happier circumstances an "*Indian Herdsman*" might unoffendingly find cool shelter here from a heat which since Adam's fall has become oppressive (1108-9), but the attempt of the guilty pair to cover their shame is wholly inadequate as a shelter from the inquiries of their Judge or even from their own inward storms.

As Hollander has pointed out,[46] the key words in these passages from book 9 that are carried over from the Vallombrosa simile in book 1 bring with them a freight of doom. Yet this observation is too simple, for we have noted intervening passages in book 4 whose brooks and bowers remain innocent, uncontaminated by the earlier use of those images. May we say that the images in question have, in book 1, become infected by their infernal environment and thus carry forward into later sections of the poem both innocent and sinister possibilities, and that which of these will be "caught" in a new setting depends on that new context? The postlapsarian situation of book 9 brings out connotations of evil which, in the same images in book 4, remained inapplicable. We cannot exclude them from our minds, of course, but their operation is only to remind us of the innocence which the scene still, at this point, retains, and of the fragility of that innocence: "the evil meaning is consciously and *ominously* excluded."[47] Then as we move to book 9, enough of the old innocence clings to the same images to remind us of what might have been, had Adam stood firm, and thus by irony to intensify the sense of loss these bowers now represent. Back in the Vallombrosa passage, the balance is different. The contamination

---

imagery in verse 31. On this verse the Geneva margin reads, "If the innocent be thus handled, what shal the wicked man be?" The contrasting tree images may be traced to Psalm 1.3-5, where the righteous person "shal be like a tre planted by the riuers of waters, . . . whose leafe shal not fade. . . . The wicked are not so, but . . . shal not stand in the Iudgem[e]nt."

[46] Hollander, 49.

[47] Ricks, 110 (my italics); see his whole discussion, 109-16. Cf. A. Bartlett Giamatti, *The Earthly Paradise and the Renaissance Epic* (Princeton: Princeton Univ. Press, 1966), 299-313.

has begun, to be sure, but the idyllic quality of "brooks" and "im-bow'r" is comparatively much stronger than it will be in book 9.

The tension created by the presence of this pastoral quality in a simile depicting devils is a reflection of what we may well guess to have been Milton's mixed feelings about his Italian journey. Vallombrosa with its monastery, and Catholic Italy at large, certainly represent in Milton's mind an institution which, on paper and in the abstract, he holds in contempt. Yet at the same time they represent happy memories of hospitality and the obligations of a guest toward people who have treated him well.[48] To Milton the militant Protestant, Italy was a place of religious darkness and personal danger,[49] but to Milton the promising young humanist it was a place of cultural brilliance and of a gratifying reception. And the men he met there were often hard to classify as belonging to one Italy or the other. A priest or a cardinal, perhaps, might in theory be of the devil's party, yet on experience prove to be a

---

[48] Cf. Milton's letters to Carlo Dati (CE, 12.50) and Lucas Holstenius (12.38–44); Defensio secunda (CE, 8.122–24); Reason of Church Government (CE, 3:235–36); and the materials collected by French, 1:371–78, 382–401, 408–9; 5:385–89; Parker, 1:171–78. Edward Chaney, The Grand Tour and the Great Rebellion (Geneva: Slatkine, 1985), 249–51, discusses the question of the evidentiary value of Milton's own statements about his Italian experiences. See also Arthos, 53–55, 68–69, 101–3; Sells, 77, 197; and Leo Miller, "Milton Dines at the Jesuit College: Reconstructing the Evening of October 30, 1638," MQ 13 (1979): 142–46.

[49] Cf. Defensio secunda (CE, 8.124) and discussion by Diekhoff, xxx–xxxii. See also Parker, 2:827; Arthos, 101; Miller, 144. Milton may well have been apprehensive about his personal safety, based not only on the hints of Sir Henry Wotton concerning the need for circumspection, when in Rome, to avoid "offence of others" and at the same time of one's "own conscience" (quoted by French, 1:362), but also on such more lurid warnings as that published by Lewis Owen in 1626 (A True Relation of the State of All the English Colledges ... in All Forraigne Parts, 24) warning English travelers "to forbeare going to Rome, or any other place, where any Inquisition for Religion is; or else to walke very circumspectly, for feare of falling into their hands.... For many men of meere curiositie to see Rome, haue lost their liues for it; or else haue been constrained to make their Religion their Hackney horse, to saue their liues." Ten years after Milton's journey John Raymond, in An Itinerary Contayning a Voyage, Made into Italy (London: Humphrey Moseley, 1648), counseled that heat, bandits, and "the horrible (in Report) Inquisition" were all "evitable dangers" and the last may be "prevented by discretion": "As there is connivance at the Luterani (for so they terme us) so tis rashnesse to proclaime ones opinion, weaknesse to disclose it" (sig. A11ᵛ–12ʳ). See also R. S. Pine-Coffin, Bibliography of British and American Travel in Italy to 1860 (Florence: Leo Olschki, 1974), 23–25.

kindred spirit. Even Etruria, for all its negative connotations, must be applauded for its role in fostering arts and letters both in ancient times and in the modern rebirth.

This was an important lesson that Milton brought home from his travels, though it may have taken a few years to assimilate. In the heat of controversial writing Milton might care little for such careful and diluting qualifications. But in his mature master work, where the utmost integrity is demanded, it would not do to pretend that things are less complicated than they are. Vallombrosa could not be allowed to have an exclusively negative connotation, tempting as it might be for the sake of the argument. That is why we find, at the heart of the simile, ideology tempered by experience. It is not the least important legacy of Milton's sojourn in Italy.

Hope College

EDWARD CHANEY

# The Visit to Vallombrosa: A Literary Tradition

> Vallombrosa! of thee I first heard in the page
> Of that holiest of Bards. . . .
> W. Wordsworth, "At Vallombrosa"[1]

MORE THAN A THOUSAND METERS ABOVE SEA-LEVEL, ON A pine-clad prominence at the north-western edge of an impressive chain of hills known as the Pratomagno, is perched a somewhat austere building known as the "Paradisino." From here, on a clear day, one can peer westward across the complex valleys and streams which wind down into the upper Arno, or Casentino, and make out Brunelleschi's cupola some twenty miles away in Florence. In exceptional weather, other features of the great city through which the Arno flows on its journey to the Mediterranean may also be discerned. "Col sereno," says the guidebook (though here a lively imagination is surely a prerequisite), it is even possible to perceive the sea itself.[2]

There is no doubting the real presence of the buildings immediately beneath one, for the Paradisino perches directly above the spreading bulk of the monastery to which it belongs, the once great convent of Vallombrosa which gave its name to one of Italy's most powerful religious orders. Between the date of its foundation in the early eleventh century and its decline and suppression in the nineteenth, this monastery became the home of innumerable distinguished clerics and played host to travelling clergy and laity alike. Among the latter, especially during the past two hundred years, have been many well-known foreigners whose visits to Vallombrosa and its Paradisino are well documented.

---

[1] *Memorials of a Tour in Italy, 1837* (London, 1842).

[2] *Guida d'Italia del Touring Club Italiano: Toscana*, 4th ed. (Milan, 1974), 367.

But although the Paradisino functioned for centuries as the monastery's retreat and guest-house—latterly indeed as a hotel—only one commemorative plaque is affixed to its facade. Erected in the summer of 1925, this late (pre-War) example of Anglo-Italian collaboration—the work of the sculptor, H. Anderson and poet, Ugo Ojetti—fulsomely celebrates the visit of a seventeenth-century English Protestant, albeit a significantly Italianized one:

Nel 1638
Qui dimoro
il sommo poeta inglese
Giovanni Milton
studioso dei nostri classici
devoto alla nostra civiltà
innamorato di questa foresta e di questo cielo
30 Agosto 1925[3]

Both the erection and wording of so prominent and confidently specific a plaque was, and is still, consistent with contemporary scholarship. In the then standard, six-volume life of Milton, the great Scots scholar, David Masson, powerfully endorsed the notion that Milton visited Vallombrosa. "Among all Milton's excursions round Florence," he wrote,

none seem to have been remembered by him more fondly; his

---

[3] "In 1638, the great English poet, Giovanni Milton, student of our classics, devotee of our civilization, in love with this forest and this sky, stayed here"; see The Times, 28 August 1925, 1 and 3 September 1925 (the latter carrying a photograph of the unveiling of the plaque which includes a sculpted relief portrait of Milton in profile); see also A. Sorani, Marzocco 30 (6 September 1925), n. 36, pp. 2-3. For this and other aspects of the monastery, see Carlo A. Kovacevich, L'Abbazia di Vallombrosa (Rome, 1951); A. Allodoli, in L'Abbazia di Vallombrosa nel pensiero contemporaneo, introduction P. Bargellini (Livorno, 1953), and Vallombrosa nel IX centenario della morte del fondatore Giovanni Gualberto 12 luglio 1073 (Florence, 1973), the latter especially detailed on the rebuilding of the abbey from 1637. A useful bibliography on Milton and Vallombrosa is to be found in Neil Harris's unpublished Ph.D. dissertation: "Milton's 'Sataneid': The Poet and the Devil in 'Paradise Lost' . . ." (Univ. of Leicester, 1985). I should like to thank both Drs. Harris and Gordon Campbell for their help and encouragement in preparing this article for the press. For a timely tip about the Beckford papers I thank the ever-helpful Jean-Pierre Mialon of the Bodleian Library. As ever, I would like also to thank Joe Trapp and Anglo-Florentine friends, Harold Acton, Mark and Heather Roberts, and the Thomson-Glovers.

mention of it has added much to the prior poetical celebrity of the spot; and in the Convent of Vallombrosa they still cherish, it is said, the legend of his visit, and profess even to show relics in authentication.[4]

As if referring the reader to a primary source, Masson then cites Wordsworth's notes to "At Vallombrosa," a subject to which I shall return. More recently, William R. Parker's still standard two-volume biography further supports the view that Milton returned to England enriched with "memories of ... 'autumnal leaves that strow the brooks / in Vallombrosa, where th'Etrurian shades / High overarched embower'." Indeed, Parker seeks to confirm this by asserting that "the excursion [to Vallombrosa] was popular with travellers."[5] Almost all subsequent accounts have taken the visit for granted.

## I

In this paper I shall argue that Milton never actually visited Vallombrosa but merely borrowed its picturesque name, probably from Ariosto's *Orlando Furioso*—which by September 1644 he had read at least twice—to promote an appropriate atmosphere in a particular scene of *Paradise Lost*.[6] I believe that Ariosto's references to the "rich and beautiful badia" of Vallombrosa—or Valspinosa as he had even more arbitrarily named this fictive French abbey in the first two editions of *Orlando*—however inviting ("cortese a chiunque venia"), they would

---

[4] Masson, rev. ed. (London, 1881), 1:789.

[5] Parker, 2:825.

[6] I have briefly examined this subject in *The Grand Tour and the Great Rebellion: Richard Lassels and the "Voyage of Italy" in the Seventeenth Century* (Geneva and Turin: Slatkine, 1985), 51. Though he presumably read the Italian original also, what is thought to have been Milton's copy of Harington's 1591 translation of *Orlando Furioso* survives with the marginal note on p. 405: "Questro libro due volte Io letto, Sept. 21. 1642"; see Parker, 1:251 and 2:884. It is amusing to note that in even owning a copy, Milton was being less pious than at least one supposedly less Puritanical contemporary. Nicolas Ferrar, of Little Gidding fame, ordered his to be burnt prior to his death, asserting that "the having an *Orlando* in the house is sufficient ground to have it burnt down over ye [ye?] heads, that truly feare God." Milton's predilection for "magniloquent" names (what T. S. Eliot referred to as his "solemn game") is discussed in B. Everett, "The End of the Big Names: Milton's Epic Catalogues," in *English Renaissance Studies Presented to Dame Helen Gardner*, ed. J. Carey (Oxford, 1980), 254-70.

never have sufficed to persuade Milton to depart from his otherwise entirely conventional Grand Tour itinerary and make the extremely arduous detour to the remote monastery which genuinely went under this name.[7] Parker could see "no reason to doubt that Milton actually visited Vallombrosa," because he thought that an excursion there was a relatively routine part of the seventeenth-century tourist's itinerary. But far from being "popular with travellers" and thus part of a general pattern into which Milton's particular pilgrimage might have fitted unobtrusively (albeit uncomfortably, given Parker's conventional view of Milton's inflexible Protestantism), no Englishman is known to have visited Vallombrosa during the whole of the sixteenth and seventeenth centuries.[8] Nor, with the fascinating exception of Don Enrico Hugford, who in 1743 went so far as to become Abbot of Vallombrosa, have I found evidence of any Englishman, or woman, visiting the monastery in the first three quarters of the eighteenth century.[9]

Merging with a rapidly evolving European travel literature of the late eighteenth century, the legend that Milton actually visited Vallombrosa spawned its own literary tradition, stimulating countless cultured, and

---

[7] Ariosto, *Orlando Furioso*, ed. N. Zingarelli, 5th ed. (Milan, 1954), 595. For the 1516 and 1521 readings, see the Debenedetti-Segre edition (1960). The long-standing popularity of Ariosto's poem in England is suggested by the choice of the name Orlando by the parents of the composer, Orlando Gibbons in 1583, or those of Traherne's patron, Sir Orlando Gibbons in the seventeenth century, and demonstrated by the number of editions of Harington's translation between 1591 and 1634. William Higgins's mid-eighteenth-century retranslation may have boosted interest at a time relevant to the discussion which follows, though by then *Paradise Lost* was itself a favorite with all but Johnsonians.

[8] For the conventional nature of Milton's tour, see J. W. Stoye, *English Travellers Abroad 1604–1667*, 2nd ed. (New Haven-London, 1989), 156; cf. Chaney, 251.

[9] For Hugford, see T. Sala and F. Tarani, *Dizionario storico biografico dell' Ordine di Vallombrosa* (Florence, 1929), 1:306 and John Fleming, "The Hugfords of Florence: Part I," *Connoisseur* 135 (1955): 106–10. At St. John's College, Oxford, there is an attractive portrait drawing of Hugford by his pupil Lamberto Gori done on vellum in 1757. It was brought back from Florence in 1759 by John Duncan, Fellow, and presented by him to the College. He also presented St. John's with the large scagliola image of John the Baptist above the fireplace in the hall by Gori. It was Hugford, working apparently in the Paradisino itself, who developed the important craft of scagliola-work as a fine art, his brother Ignazio acting very effectively as his agent. Gori and his pupil, Stoppioni, are mentioned by Joseph Forsyth in his interesting account of improvements in scagliola manufacture at Vallombrosa in *Remarks on . . . Italy in the years 1802 and 1803*, 2nd ed. (London, 1816), 83–84.

subsequently, less cultured tourists to follow in the allegedly holy bard's supposed footsteps. The earliest travelogues to include accounts of Vallombrosa seem to have been French. Curiosity might have been stimulated by Ariosto's implicit Francophilia, Orlando—post Pulci and Boiardo—being the Italianized name for the *Chanson*-singing Roland, and Vallombrosa, being a similarly Italianized monastery somewhere in Charlemagne's France. More significant, however, may have been the fact that Benedictinism in France enjoyed a strong revival in seventeenth-century France, especially after the foundation of the scholarly congregation of Maurists in 1618. This revival encouraged a renewed religious and antiquarian interest in ancient monasteries such as Vallombrosa, which was unparalleled in post-Reformation England.[10]

Only one French account of Vallombrosa I have found pre-dates Milton's Italian journey, but its place and date of publication (Paris 1634), and its distinguished provenance and popularity throughout Europe make it a major rival to Ariosto's *Orlando* as the possible source for Milton's famous reference.[11] Written by a servant of the zealously anti-Protestant, Henri de Bourbon, Prince de Condé, the *Voyage de Monsieur le Prince de Condé* describes a tour of Italy begun in Montpellier in the summer of 1622 and completed a year later. Condé and his entourage spent the night of Friday, 27 January 1623 at Vallombrosa. As if echoing Ariosto, the *Voyage* account describes the "tres-belle Abaye dans de tres-fascheuses montagnes pleines de neige," as "fort beau & riche." It was noticed that higher up there was a Hermitage, "d'une seule cellule, fort beau, mais la demeure en est afreuse." The monks belong to the Benedictine order, "reformez par Sainct Gualbert," and it was observed that the beautiful church contained some fine relics.[12]

In 1691, the renegade Franco-Italian priest, Gabriel d'Emiliane, to

---

[10] Urban VIII attempted to revive Benedictinism in Britain with the *Bull Plantata* in 1633; see D. Lunn, *The English Benedictines: 1540–1688* (London-New York, 1980), 112-14. The 1630s saw a slight revival in the fortunes of the religious orders in England, but the horrors of the 1640s wiped out such development. For all his reputation as an apostle of freedom, Milton never protested on behalf of the slaughtered Catholic saints of his own country, even though some of his friends may have been Catholics. In this respect, the despised Charles I showed both greater courage and toleration towards a religion of which he did not himself approve.

[11] *Voyage de Monsieur le Prince de Condé en Italie depuis son partement du Camp de Montepellier, iusques à son retour en sa maison de Mournon* ... (Paris, 1634).

[12] *Voyage de Monsieur ... de Condé*, 170-72.

help demonstrate that he was now a good Protestant-in-exile, worthy of the Whiggish patronage of Earl of Nottingham, published a travelogue with the sensational title of *The Frauds of Romish Monks and Priests, set forth in eight Letters.*[13] Just as Jean Mabillon and Michel Germain had done in April 1686, d'Emiliane approached Vallombrosa from Camaldoli. After the thick snow which surrounded Camaldoli, the initial descent into warmer and more fertile terrain was welcome. It also encouraged d'Emiliane to notice variations in the type of tree which grew at the different altitudes, providing us with useful seventeenth-century evidence for our encounter a century later with enlightenment concern about the scarcity of "fallen leaves" in a predominantly coniferous area.[14] As this best-selling account seems to have been the earliest in English and was probably the first full-length traveller's description of Vallombrosa published in any language, it is important as a source for the increasingly elaborate setting into which Milton qua *wandervoegel* was to be placed. After his brief simmering by Johnsonian sceptics, this nature-trekking Milton was stirred into a leafy setting, brought to the boil by disbelief-suspending Romantics, to end up so solidly fixed in a

---

[13] 125-30. The preface is signed by "G.d'E. E.A.P." which I believe stands for "Gabriel d'Emilien Ecclesiae Anglicanae Presbyter," as suggested by an anonymous hand in the Bodleian Library's copy of the second edition, also of 1691. Bodley's catalogue, however, ultimately following J.-M. Querard (*Les Supercheries Litteraires devoilées* [Paris, 1869], 1:1234), which in turn has been followed by Wing and most other bibliographies, asserts that Gabriel d'Emiliane is the pseudonym for Antoine Gavin. There is no evidence for this and indeed, given the chronologically and geographically distinct careers of each of these former Catholics, the deduction is entirely implausible. My own copy of the fifth edition (London, 1725) also has "Emilliane" pencilled in on the title page.

[14] Though Neil Harris has thoroughly documented the grim literary connotations of "shady valleys," the more straightforward pre-Romantic dislike of anywhere that was not flat, fertile, and sunny seems to have been overlooked in discussions of Milton's visit. The Vallombrosan pines were admired qua cash crop from the start, though the presence of other trees, including deciduous species, was noticed as early as 1510 in Taddeo Adimari's *Vita de S. Giovanni Qualberto glorioso & institutore del ordine di Valembrosa* (Venice), fol. 8; see Harris, 278. See also, for an interesting survey of pastoral poetry which modifies but does not persuade me to abandon my view of the essentially negative seventeenth-century response to the wilder aspects of nature, see James Turner, *The Politics of Landscape: Rural Scenery and Society in English Poetry 1630–1660* (Cambridge, Mass., 1979). I nonetheless thank Professor Turner for his views on this paper. For Michel Germain's account of his and Mabillon's 1686 visit to Vallombrosa, see *Correspondence inedite de Mabillon et de Montfaucon avec l'Italie*, ed. M. Valery, 3 vols. (Paris, 1846), 1:245-46.

gelatinous accumulation of detail contributed by unquestioning nineteenth-century scholars and literati, that it was not until the age of
deconstruction (by coincidence), on the three hundred and fiftieth
anniversary of his Italian journey, that the poet was finally lifted free of
the legend. In view of its potential value in understanding the evolution
of this legend, I quote from d'Emiliane's *Frauds* at length:

> knowing that the Abby of *Valombrosa*, which is chief of another
> Order of Monks, very famous in *Italy*, was not above a days
> Journy from thence, we all of us Travelled thither. We went
> down Hill for some miles, and afterward, coasted about the
> *Apennin*, by a very pleasant Way.... All these sides of the
> Mountains are exceeding rich, as abounding with all sorts of
> *Fruit-Trees*.... After half a days Journy, we were obliged to mount
> the *Apennin*, for four Miles together, through very stony and
> rugged ways, until we came to Vallombrosa, in Latin *Vallis
> Umbrosa*. This Place in indeed a Vally with respect to the Tops
> of the Mountains, that raise themselves a great height above it;
> but if we compare it with the level of the Country that lies
> beneath it, it is a very high Mountain, and very cold, for there
> are no Fruit-Trees to be seen here, except only some *Chesnut-
> Trees*, and a few *Apple-Trees*. The great Forests of *Pine* and *Fir-
> Trees* that encompass it, in former times rendred the place very
> Dark and Shady, which was the occasion of giving it the name of
> *Valombrosa*.

At this point, d'Emiliane gives the reader a potted account of San
Giovanni Gualberto's commendable refusal to avenge the death of his
brother, which led instead to his becoming a monk and founding the
Vallombrosan Order.[15] D'Emiliane then returns to "my Solitude of
Vallombrosa" and provides us with a particularly detailed description of
the Paradisino, then still known as the Hermitage, though since the visit
of the Prince de Condé, together with the monastery itself, considerably
enlarged:

> We arrived at this famous Abby, where are some of the most
> magnificent and sumptuous Buildings that can be. One of the

---

[15] Ibid., 128.

*Florentine* Gentlemen that was with me had a Brother there, who was the chief Person there, next to the Abbat, for whose sake we were very Civilly received. The Monks here lead a very commodious and pleasant life; when they are weary of living in this Desert, they make an Enterchange with the Monks of *Florence*, and thereby enjoy the pleasing variety of living one part of the year in the Country, and other in the City. They have cut down for a quarter of a League round their Monastery all the great Fir-Trees that Shadow'd it, to give themselves more air, and to make the place more Healthy. The next Morning we were led to the Hermitage of S. *John Gualbert*, which is about half of League distance, from the point of a little rock which lifts up it self in the midst of a Vally, being very craggy on every side. In getting up to it, we went round the Rock, as by a winding Stairs, for the space of one quarter of an hour, at the end of which, we found our selves at the Top of the Rock, where the Hermitage is; which consists of a very neat Chapel, curiously gilt and painted all over, and a very handsome Set of Lodgings, well Wainscoted and Painted all within, with a Garden of a moderate size, so that the whole is a meer Jewel. There is no monument left here of the ancient Cell of this Saint, all the building being new and modern: there is always a Father Hermit that dwells here, with a Converse Brother to serve him. Whenever the Hermit dies, the Abbots of that Congregation *Valombrosa*, at their general Chapter, make choice of a Monk of Exemplary Life, and a lover of Solitude, to reside there. The great Abby is to furnish him all necessaries of Life: He has a very fine Library full of choice Books when he has a mind to Study; and indeed the Hermit that was then in possession of the place, was a Man of competent Learning, and appeared to me a very honest Man. He made us a very fine Discourse about the Contempt of the World, and the Advantages of Retirement and Solitude: Tho' indeed there was no great need of it, for we were already, without all that, so Charmed with the Beauty of this Hermitage, that in case there had been more of the same cut, Nature, rather than Grace, would easily have persuaded us to become Hermits, in order to enjoy an easie and pleasant Life, without either care or trouble. The Monks of *Valombrosa* have extremely relaxed their strictness of their first Institution. They are Clothed in Black, and profess the Rule of S. *Bennet*, tho' indeed they observe but little of it. The next day we set out very betimes in the Morning towards Mount Alverne [La Verna].[16]

Despite the frequent republication of d'Emiliane's account during the first half of the eighteenth century, the earliest evidence of native English interest in Vallombrosa I have found is a letter written by Horace Walpole in May 1752 to one of his favorite correspondents, the British Envoy to the Court of Tuscany, Sir Horace Mann. It is highly significant that Walpole attributes the recent "passion" for Vallombrosa to Milton's having "mentioned it" in *Paradise Lost*, our first indication that those apparently topographical lines were to become an essential part of the poet's biography. He asks Mann for a copy of a print of the monastery which he has recently seen at the house of a friend though he writes: "I don't think it gives much idea of the beauty of the place."[17] If by the latter remark, Walpole were trying to persuade Mann, who in thirteen years' residence in Florence had never visited Vallombrosa, that during his thirteen months in the same city (between 1739–1740), he, Walpole, *had* done so, he was to be more candid as an old man.[18] Replying in 1791 to a letter from Mary Berry who had been "disappointed of going to Volombroso" on her Grand Tour, Walpole admits that he had never been there himself. Now that "Milton has made everybody wish to *have seen it*," he also regretted this, though half a century earlier it had probably never occurred to him to undertake the journey.[19]

Notwithstanding Walpole's mid-century reference to a Milton-induced passion for Vallombrosa, the earliest manifestation of such a passion dates from the 1780s. The fact that this occurs in what was to have been the literary debut of that self-consciously original travel-writer and novelist, the millionaire dilettante, William Beckford, suggests that

---

[16] Ibid., 128–30.

[17] *Yale Edition of Horace Walpole's Correspondence*, ed. W. S. Lewis et al. (London, 1960), 20:317: "but you know what a passion there is for it in England, as Milton has mentioned it." The print belonged to Thomas Barrett-Lennard, who had presumably acquired it during his 1749 residence in Florence; ibid., 75.

[18] Chaney, "From the Alps to Anglo-Tuscany," *Bollettino del C.I.R.V.I.* 3.5: 155.

[19] *Walpole Correspondence*, ed. cit., 21:357. For Mary Berry's travels, see *Extracts of the Journals and Correspondence of Miss Berry from the year 1783 to 1852*, ed. Lady Theresa Lewis, 3 vols. (London, 1865).

there cannot have been many British travellers who had preceded him to this remote spot. Based on his European tour of 1780-1781, after a complementary second tour in 1782, Beckford completed his extraordinarily precocious *Dreams, Waking Thoughts, and Incidents; in a Series of Letters* early in the following year.[20] One of these "Letters," ostensibly written in Florence on 23 October 1780 and addressed to an unnamed but idealized amalgam of Alexander Cozens, his charismatic art teacher,

---

[20] The Bodleian Library copy of *Dreams* (Arch. H. d. 14, now housed with the newly catalogued Beckford archive formerly in the possession of the Duke of Hamilton), contains a letter from Beckford to G. Clarke dated 1833 and an inscription by Clarke explaining that it was one of four surviving copies, "the whole of the impression with the Exception of these four copies were purposely burnt at Fonthill in 1801." The relevant section of the original manuscript diary is now Bodleian Library, MS Beckford d. 4. The absent Vallombrosan account should be between fols. 71v-72r, which includes letters dated 22 and 26 October, the 23rd not featuring. Since Beckford claims to have stayed the night at Vallombrosa, it is impossible that he could have written letters on the 22nd and 23rd from Florence so that in this respect both the *Dreams* and *Italy* editions are internally inconsistent. A genuine (MS) letter from Florence to Alexander Cozens is dated 15 October, the next, the 26th is from Siena. What Beckford wrote on the 26th from Siena tends to confirm that his printed Vallombrosa "letter" was written with Courtney, as well as Cozens, in mind: "Think where I was this time last year—happy and sequestered with my love Wm.—." The three other copies referred to by Clarke are named as belonging to Beckford himself, Earl Spencer and Samuel Rogers. In fact the Bodleian possesses two other large-paper copies formerly belonging to Beckford. Both the Beckford copies are heavily annotated with autograph alterations and abridgements done in anticipation of the published edition which finally appeared together with accounts of the later European journeys in two volumes in 1834.

That Beckford was contemplating reissuing his *Dreams* long before he actually did so is revealed in an anecdote recorded in the poet Thomas Moore's *Diary*; the entry also reveals the extent of contemporary prejudice against Beckford. In October 1818, Samuel Rogers forwarded the news that Beckford was delighted with *Lalla Rookh* and hinted that Moore might prepare Beckford's travels for the press, earn himself around a thousand pounds for his labours. Moore's reaction was that "if he were to give me a hundred times that sum, I would not have my name coupled with his"; *Rogers and his Contemporaries*, by P. W. Clayden, 2 vols. (London, 1889), 1:273-74. Given the cult of Beckford in the first half of this century, the republication of *Dreams* by Guy Ghapman as *The Travel Diaries of William Beckford*, 2 vols. (Cambridge, 1928); by Robert J. Gemmett (Cranbury, NJ, 1971), with relevant letters and useful introduction by which we can date Vallombrosan passage to the winter of 1781-82 from Beckford's correspondence with his editor, Samuel Henley; and most recently of an edited abridgement by Elizabeth Mavor (Harmondsworth: Penguin, 1986), it is surprising that the Vallombrosan passage has not been remarked upon hitherto in connection with Milton. It is no less odd that Beckford still features so little in the secondary literature on Romanticism.

and William Courtney, the boy with whom he had fallen in love the previous year, began as follows:

> Do you recollect our evening rambles last year, upon the hill of pines; and the dark valley [at Fonthill], where we used to muse in the twilight? I remember, we often fancied the scene like Valombrosa; and vowed, if ever an occasion offered, to visit its deep retirement. I had put off the execution of this pilgrimage from day to day till the warm weather was gone; and the Florentines declared I should be frozen if I attempted it. Every body stared, last night at the opera when I told them, I was going to bury myself in fallen leaves, and hear no music but their rustlings. Mr.— [the Rev. John Lettice, Beckford's necessarily complaisant tutor] was just as eager as myself to escape the chit-chat and nothingness of Florence: so we finally determined upon our expedition, and mounting our horses, set out this morning, happily without any company, but the spirit which led us along.[21]

Beckford describes the difficult journey in characteristically melodramatic style. At one stage of "rocky steeps shattered into fragments," the travellers were tempted to turn back; the temperature indeed dropped when they ascended into "the forests of pine," but their "fresh aromatic odour" revived Beckford's spirits.[22] His imagery (if not his proto-Romantic prose style) becomes more Miltonic as he approaches the sacred spot, so that on arrival, the reader is presented with a fully-fledged example of the literary tradition which enshrines Milton's Vallombrosan visit as historical fact at the very birth of that tradition. So "advanced" is Beckford's imaginative description, that it raises—as if deliberately—almost all the issues which are addressed in the course of this paper (including, given the absence of the passage from the relevant surviving manuscript, even a degree of doubt about his own expedition). Even his laboured emphasis on the prevalence of deciduous autumn leaves, the reward for his deliberate postponement of the excursion from Florence, seems intended to counter the later, leaf-related scepticism about Milton's visit:

---

[21] *Dreams*, 181.
[22] Ibid., 182.

The cold to be sure was piercing; but, setting that at defiance, we galloped on, and issued shortly into a vast amphitheatre of lawns and meadows, surrounded by thick woods beautifully green. Flocks of sheep were dispersed on the slopes, whose smoothness and verdure equal our English pastures. Steep cliffs, and mountains, cloathed with beech to their very summits, guard this retired valley. The herbage, moistened by streams which fall from the eminences, has never been known to fade; and whilst the chief part of Tuscany is parched by the heats of summer, these upland meadows retain the freshness of spring. I regretted not having visited them sooner, as autumn had already made great havock amongst the foliage. Showers of leaves blew full in our faces as we rode towards the convent, placed at an extremity of the vale, and sheltered by remote firs and chesnuts, towering one above another. Alighting before the entrance, two fathers came out, and received us into the peace of their retirement. We found a blazing fire, and tables spread very comfortable before it, round which five or six over-grown friars were lounging, who seemed, by the sleekness and rosy hue of their countenances, not totally to have despised this mortal existence.[23]

Escaping from the friars, "who made a shift to waddle after," Beckford soon found himself at liberty among decaying beeches, "listening to the roar of the waterfall which the wood concealed." There follows a passage which was retained with only minor alterations in the widely-read 1834 edition:

The dry leaves chased each other down the steeps on the edge of the torrents with hollow rustlings; whilst the solemn wave of the forests above, exactly answered the idea I had formed of Valombrosa,

> — where the' *Etrurian* shades
> High overarch't imbowr.

The scene was beginning to take effect, and the Genius of Milton

---

[23] Ibid., 182–83.

to move across his favourite valley, when the fathers arrived puffing and blowing, by an easier ascent than I knew of.[24]

At this point, anticipating Coleridge's reaction to the persons from Porlock, Beckford adds another sentence he was later to suppress: "Pardon me, if I cursed their intrusion, and wished them as still as Gualbertus." "You have missed the way," cried one of Beckford's puffing monks, adding significantly for our purposes:

the Hermitage, with the fine picture by Andrea del Sarto [now in the Accademia in Florence] *which all the English admire* [italics mine], is on the opposite side of the wood; there! don't you see it on the point of the cliff?[25]

When in November 1821, Samuel Rogers asserted that "nobody I know has been to Vallombrosa," he may have been stimulated to do so by his friend Wordsworth's soon-to-be-published *Memorials of a Tour, 1820*, which expressed an as yet unfulfilled longing "to slumber, reclined on the moss-covered floor" in the "shadiest wood" of Vallombrosa. (Ironically, this is not only reminiscent of Beckford's recollections of his conversations in Fonthill gardens, but uncannily like the style he had parodied in *Modern Novel Writing* of 1796: "Here stretched supinely on a bed of moss, the late Lord Mahogany would frequently pass the sultry hours of the day.")[26] In the process of promoting himself as pioneer, however, Rogers must either have forgotten Beckford's 1783 account, have regarded Beckford as so extraordinary as not to count or, conceivably, have suspected Beckford's account to be fictional.[27] In any

---

[24] Ibid., 185; cf., 1834 ed., p. 217 where the Milton quotation is corrected.

[25] Ibid., 185.

[26] *Modern Novel Writing or the Elegant Enthusiast and Interesting Emotions of Arabella Bloomville*, by the Right Hon. Lady Harriet Marlow, 2 vols. (London, 1796), 70-71. The description of the grounds of Mahogany Castle in chapter 6 is a fascinating essay on a landscape garden in which "the hand of [Payne] KNIGHT had assisted." In view of what follows regarding Parsons and Mrs. Piozzi, it is interesting that *Modern Novel Writing* was at first thought to be the work of fellow Della Cruscan, Robert Merry; see André Parreaux, "The Caliph and the Swinish Multitude," in *William Beckford of Fonthill 1760-1844*, ed. F. M. Mahmoud (1960; Port Washington, NY-London, 1972), 1-15.

[27] It is worth noting that in a letter to Byron describing his 1817 visit to Fonthill, Rogers wrote that "the woods recalled Vallombrosa . . ."; see L. Melville, *The Life and Letters of William Beckford* (London, 1910), 239.

event, it seems likely that directly or by report, Beckford's vivid Vallom-brosan set-piece became known soon after it was printed and encouraged incipient English interest in a place already rendered sacred by Miltonic citation. It is indeed probable that Beckford was in the minds of Miss Berry and Walpole when they articulated their regrets at not having visited "Volombroso."

We know of at least one eighteenth-century Vallombrosan visit undertaken as a direct result of Beckford's interest, that of the great landscape painter, John Robert Cozens, the unstable son of the exotic Alexander. Almost two years after the ostensible date of Beckford's description, and twelve months after separating from Beckford in Naples during the latter's second great Italian tour, Cozens travelled north to Florence and then rode out to Vallombrosa to spend the 24th of September sketching in the vicinity of the monastery.[28] To an unrealistic extent, Cozen's drawings all depict decidedly deciduous trees, which might suggest that Beckford was conscious of an otherwise unrecorded debate on Milton's fallen leaves a decade or so before Mrs. Piozzi referred to the problem in print. The following day Cozens was back in Florence, sketching the Villa Salviati (though not the one I believe Milton had in mind when he remembered "the Tuscan artist" and his "optic glass" in *Paradise Lost*). A month later, he rejoined Beckford, now on his third Grand Tour, in Geneva, where significantly he was sighted alighting from a coach by Miss Berry.[29]

---

[28] All seven of J. R. Cozens's sketch-books, formerly in Beckford's collection, were sold by the Duke of Hamilton at Sotheby's on 29 November 1973 (see sale catalogue), and are now in the Whitworth Art Gallery, Manchester; see Francis Hawcroft, "Grand Tour Sketchbooks of John Robert Cozens, 1782-1783," *Gazette des Beaux-Arts* 91 (1978): 99-106. I thank Dr. Kim Sloan of the Mellon Centre in London for drawing these to my attention.

[29] Kim Sloan provides a useful account of J. R. Cozens in these years but is mistaken in saying that Cozens was not released by Beckford until early December (*Alexander and John Robert Cozens: The Poetry of Landscape* [New Haven-London, 1986], 150). Her source, Thomas Jones's *Memoirs* (*Walpole Society* 32 [1946-48]: 114), is quite specific in recording that Beckford "left *Naples* for *Marsailles* leaving behind his Draughtsman Cousins Once more a free Agent and loosed from Shackles of fantastic folly and Caprice—" on 10 September 1782. The sketch of the Villa Salviati was done on 25 September 1783, the day after the Vallombrosan sketches; see *Walpole Society* 23, nos. 387-93. Beckford owned a copy of Giuseppe Zocchi's *Vedute delle ville e d'altri luoghi della Toscana* (Florence, 1744) which includes an etching of the larger Villa Salviati on the Via Bolognese (see Clive Wainwright's summary of the Sotheby's

While we can be reasonably sure that Cozen's 1783 expedition was inspired, and probably patronized, by Beckford, we can only hypothesize that knowledge of his *Dreams* may have encouraged William Parsons, Bertie Greathead, Mr. Biddulph and Mr. Piozzi to form a "party of pleasure" and travel from Florence to Vallombrosa two years later. Relevant to this hypothesis may have been Mrs. Thrale's visit to Fonthill on 27 June 1784, just two months prior to her departure for Italy with her Italian husband.[30] With the publication of Parsons' poem "Vallombrosa" in his *Poetical Tour* of 1787, and, two years later, of Mrs. Piozzi's own *Observations and Reflections*, with its report of this somewhat sceptical Vallombrosan expedition, the excursion-stimulating legend of Milton's visit really got underway.[31] By 1837, when the defiantly unsceptical, sixty-eight-year-old William Wordsworth came and composed "At Vallombrosa," which he prefaced with the relevant lines from *Paradise Lost* in exactly the way Parsons had done, the legend had become a fully established feature of Grand Tour mythology, featuring prominently even in the French travel literature.[32] Lamartine included mention of Milton with Dante, Boccaccio and Michaelangelo among the great poets, artists and political refugees whose cells he was shown.[33]

---

sale held in October 1975: *TLS* [19 December 1975]: 1524). It is this villa, which lies immediately beneath Fiesole and has a massive tower which Milton would have seen on his way in and out of the north of Florence, that I believe he had in mind when referring to the Tuscan artist and his optic glass.

[30] *Thraliana*, ed. K. C. Balderston, 2nd ed., 2 vols. (London, 1951), 1:598. In view of what Beckford and James Wyatt were to do with Fonthill a decade later, Mrs. Piozzi's comparison between the old (i.e., Palladian) Fonthill and eventually Wyattized Wilton is worth quoting in full: "We went to Wilton and also to Fonthill; they make an admirable & curious contrast between ancient Magnificence and Modern Glare: Gothic & Grecian again however, a Man of Taste would rather possess L^d Pembroke's Seat, or indeed a single Room in it—but one feels one should live happier at Beckford's." That Mrs. Piozzi was certainly aware of Beckford's literary talent is revealed by her praise of *Vathek*; at the same time, however, she more than once condemned the man as a "Professor of Paederasty" (*Thraliana*, 1:969, n. 2).

[31] Parsons, *Poetical Tour* (London, 1787), 84-101 (2nd ed., 2 vols., 1807, 1:125-48) and Hester Lynch Piozzi, *Observations and Reflections made in the course of a journey through France, Italy, and Germany* (1789), ed. H. Barrows (Ann Arbor, 1967), 164.

[32] Though his critical method apparently does not call for mention of Beckford, Parsons, nor the other precedents dealt with here, I cite, as the most recent study of this poem, Robin Jarvis, "Shades of Milton: Wordsworth at Vallombrosa," *Studies in Romanticism* 25 (1986): 483-504.

[33] See Charles Dedeyan, *Lamartine et la Toscane* (Geneva-Turin, 1981), 24. In a

By Wordsworth's day, the popular guidebooks and travelogues such as
Joseph Forsyth's of 1813 and Eustace's of two years later included
accounts of Vallombrosa and of Milton's supposed visit as a matter of
course. Most quoted *Paradise Lost*, while some, such as the anonymous
*Mementoes . . . of a Tour*, published in two volumes in 1824, incorporated into their descriptions their own full-length poems, the *Mementoes'*
surprisingly good forty-line meditation "Written at Vallombrosa, 1821"
in rhyming couplets being, I believe, a hitherto unnoticed precedent for
Wordsworth's contribution to what by 1837 was a fifty-year-old genre.[34] Indeed, if justice is to be done (given the priorities of our origina-
lity-obsessed century), this poetic tradition should be extended still
further back to Beckford's 1783 account (that he felt this himself might
lie behind his decision to publish the revised edition of *Dreams* in
1834). Beckford once commended Rousseau's "prose poems in praise
of nature." Whatever Milton would have thought of Rousseau, or, for

---

letter to Virieu, dated 1 March 1827, Lamartine described Vallombrosa as: "un
immense monastere, au sommet d'une montagne de l'Appenin, entoure de forets de
pins et de chataigniers. Voila ou j'irai souvent, comme y allait Milton, pour passer des
journee au printemps [sic; no thoughts of fallen leaves here]; mais je t'y voudrais!"
Lamartine was persuaded that "tous les grands poetes et tous les grands artistes de
l'Italie y sont-ils venus tous chercher un asile temporaire contre les miseres, contre le
desespoir ou contre les proscriptions dont la vie des hommes memorables est toujours
travaillee. On y montre la cellule de *Boccacce*, celle de *Dante*, celle de *Michel Ange*,
celles de differents proscrits des maisons rivales qui se disputerent la liberte ou la
tyrannie pendant les luttes des republiques du moyen age" (op. cit., 75). Three years
after his visit, Lamartine published his poem "L'Abbaye de Vallombreuse" (see *Harmonies Poetiques et Religieuses*, no. 11, in *Oeuvres Poetiques Completes*, ed. M.-F. Guyard
[Paris, 1963], 332–34, and N. Harris, op. cit., 194). While on the subject of famous
foreigners, one might mention that even Nietsche visited Vallombrosa, by this time
Milton's "visit" having become so well-known as to encourage even Germans (*L'Abbazia di Vallombrosa nel Pensiero Contemporaneo*, cit., 28–30).

[34] *Mementoes, historical and classical, of a Tour through part of France, Switzerland,
and Italy in the years 1821 and 1822* . . . , 2 vols. (London, 1824), 1:265–64; see
Appendix (below) for complete text of poem. In his more down-to-earth text, the author
merely explains that Vallombrosa is "a spot which Milton is said to have visited, and
from which he is supposed to have painted some of the scenic imagery in Paradise
Lost." The *Mementoes* was a widely distributed book which it is difficult to believe
Wordsworth did not know. It was reissued with fourteen quality engravings and a
cancel title page as *A classical and historical tour through France [etc]*, in 1826, and
again, as *A Tour through France, [etc]*, in 1827; see R. S. Pine-Coffin, *A Bibliography of
British and American Travel in Italy to 1860* (Florence, 1974), 186–87. I would greatly
welcome any suggestions as to who the author might have been. In all three issues, his
or her preface is subscribed: "London, Nov. 1823."

that matter, of Beckford, all three merged in the latter's Vallombrosan "Letter," which surely qualifies as a "prose poem" of great originality.[35]

In the wake of Beckford and Parsons, but still prior to the Napoleonic Wars, it seems to have been the ladies who responded most warmly to the literary legend. Once the British had rendered Italy safe for tourism again, it was the female travellers who seemed keenest to write about Vallombrosa. Admittedly, the radical Lady Morgan was responding to the reactionary Roman Catholic Reverend Eustace in her account and like Mary Berry (and perhaps Marianna Starke, who also corrected Eustace's exaggerated accounts of French destruction) failed to actually scale the hills to reach the monastery. As an admirer of Milton and the author of the pioneering biography of Milton's more genuinely freedom-fighting contemporary, Salvator Rosa, her account of Miltonic Vallombrosa (annotated by a fifteen-line political biography) is nevertheless of interest:

> Commanding this beautiful vale, rise the woods of Vallombrosa, with all that magnificence of scenery which left on the mind of Milton images which recurred to cheer his spirit, to freshen his fancy, and enrich his page, when blindness shut out nature from his view; and the persecution of despotism had left him lonely and unhonoured, in solitude, and in neglect.
>
> The scenery of Vallombrosa, caught even in the mistiness of distance, still has the character which, in Milton's days, distinguished its "Etrurian shades," and which, in far remoter times, lured the hermit's steps to its profound solitudes, and gave it its melodious name.[36]

Intrepid as ever (though now past sixty), Frances Trollope, with least famous son, Thomas, in tow, thought nothing of the journey to Val-

---

[35] The extent to which Beckford and his family were indeed anxious to maintain a low profile by the supression of the edition during and after the time of the Courtney scandal, is poignantly suggested by the aspiring author's original ambitions for *Dreams*: "You know," he wrote to his tutor, Lettice, in 1781 shortly before finalizing the Vallombrosan passage: "I have set my heart upon the success of this book" (*Dreams*, R. S. Gemmet ed., 19).

[36] Lady Sydney Morgan, *Italy*, 2 vols. (London, 1821), 2:145–46. Partly because she praises him in it, Byron praised Lady Morgan's book as "really *excellent*" in August 1821 (*Born for Opposition: Byron's Letters and Journals*, ed. L. A. Marchand [London, 1978], 8:186). For a brief life, see E. Suddaby and P. J. Yarrow, *Lady Morgan in France* (Newcastle-upon-Tyne, 1971).

lombrosa.[37] On an early May morning in 1841 she rode out of Florence, complaining first of her companions for rising so late and then of the "frightful" heat they all had to suffer as a consequence. She comments, somewhat ironically, on Ariosto's praise of Vallombrosan hospitality and notes that the ladies were not permitted to enter the monastery, apparently being entertained in the Foresteria (or Paradisino) above. Still more forcefully than Forsyth, she concludes from its "wonderful exactitude of description" that Milton's "sylvan scene" account of Eden in Paradise Lost "must have been written as a record of Vallombrosa." Quoting the relevant lines, she bestows on them the highest praise: that they surpass even Walter Scott's in "painting scenery with words."[38]

Published within a year of her visit, Mrs. Trollope's account may just have been known to Mary Shelley, who, though it was late October and "not the season for excursions," "could not resist the temptation of visiting Vallombrosa" in the autumn of 1842. Two years later she published a popular account of her visit which incorporates an observation on autumnal leaves to which I shall return.[39] Perhaps misled by references in Mary's Rambles to a "new and good road" and the "accommodation" laid on for women at the monastery's "forestiera," Elizabeth Barrett Browning, complete with Flush, Wilson and ever-indulgent Mr. Browning, was soon having herself hauled up to the monastery "along a 'via non rotabile' through the most romantic scenery ... in basket sledges drawn by four white oxen"; only to be drawn ignominiously back down again when the male-chauvinist monks refused to let her stay the three summer months she had intended.[40]

---

[37] Mrs. [Frances] Trollope, A Visit to Italy, 2 vols. (London, 1842), 219. I thank fellow travel literature enthusiast, Mildred K. Abraham of the University of Virginia Library, for informing me of Mrs. Trollope's expedition.

[38] Ibid., 222–23.

[39] Mary Shelley, Rambles in Germany and Italy, 2 vols. (London, 1844), 2:137.

[40] The Letters of Elizabeth Barrett Browning, ed. F. G. Kenyon, 3 vols. (London, 1897), 1:332–33; cf. several subsequent letters to others describing same excursion with different emphases and details, e.g., two oxen instead of four (341). Mary Shelley (loc. cit.) had written that: "No women are admitted within these sacred walls, but a forestiera is built adjoining for our accomodation," meaning in her case, coffee and the opportunity to dry her clothes. See the related problems encountered by George Eliot and her devoted escort at nearby Camaldoli in 1861 as told by Thomas Adolphus Trollope in What I Remember, 2 vols. (London, 1887), 2:275-78. For a guidebook

## II

Far from motivating Milton to seek out the real Vallombrosa, Ariosto's popularizing choice of this effective signifier of a non-specifically signified location, was surely in *itself* sufficient explanation for Milton's incidental use of the name in *Paradise Lost*. It would not have taken an especially learned or imaginative Grand Tourist, let alone one familiar with Greek, Latin and Italian, to conjure up classically leaf-strewn brooks when he read and heard of a place known as "shady valley."[41] No doubt proud Florentines would have informed Milton that the real Vallombrosa, the original monastery of their prestigious Vallombrosan order (and one their greatest living architect was rebuilding at considerable expense), was not in France but in their Grand Duchy, the recently revived ancient Etruria; hence its corrected location among "the Etrurian shades" in Milton's poem. (With de Franchi's monograph on San Giovanni wending its way through the Florentine censor collecting those "proud," "exorcising" *imprimaturs* Milton so abhorred, Vallombrosa would have been much talked of in the academic circles he frequented in late 1638 and early 1639.)[42] But like Ariosto, Milton was primarily

---

owned by the Brownings, see Maggs catalogue 849 (London, 1958), 20: *Nuova Guida ovvero descrizione storico-artistico critica della Città e contorni di Firenze*, compilata de Federigo Fantozzi (Florence, 1852).

[41] If more learned or imaginative explanations are required to account for Milton's Vallombrosan imagery, several are supplied in the late Sergio Baldi's important article, "Folte come le foglie (e lo scudo di Satana)," *Critical Dimensions . . . Essays in honour of Aurelio Zanco*, ed. M. Curreli and A. Martino (Cuneo, 1978), 221–41 (now reprinted in the very useful, if indexless, *Studi Miltoniani*, collected as a posthumous tribute to Prof. Baldi by his colleagues at the University of Florence [1985], 65–97). See also Neil Harris, especially 260–61, for Alexander Ross's 1658 reference to the "order of *vallis umbrosa* or the Monks of the Shadowy Valley."

[42] Gherardo Silvani is described as "Florence's greatest 17th-century architect" by Rudolf Wittkower in *Gothic vs. Classic* (New York, 1974), 80. Given his pre-publication knowledge of Buonmattei's *Della lingua Toscana* in September 1638, it is not impossible that Milton knew of de Franchi's book with its detailed illustrated account of Vallombrosa, prior to publication. In 1629, Averardo Nicolini, the Abbot responsible for employing Silvani for the rebuilding in progress at the time of Milton's visit, had published the folio: *Rituale Monasticon secundum consuetudinem monachorum, & monialium ord. S. Benedicti. Congreg. Vallisumbrose*. "Etruria" carried a variety of connotations for the cultured, the most ancient being somewhat sinister and thus suited to the satanic context Milton intended. More mundanely, however, as in Leandro Alberti's *Descrittione di tutta Italia* of 1550 (which, according to J. C. Boswell's survey of his

interested in the effect the name would have on his readers. Whether these were familiar with the relevant classical or Renaissance sources for the fallen leaves simile, they would have even less knowledge of the real Vallombrosa than himself. Milton nowhere claims to have visited Vallombrosa, or for that matter, Paradise, so that in contrast to the debate as to whether he visited Galileo—which he specifically claims to have done—here the burden of proof lies not with the sceptics, but with those who subscribe to what is merely an eighteenth-century tradition.

As with most other traditions, "documentation" to underpin the legend was soon forthcoming. If Milton could write fulsome and recently discovered thank-you letters to the Catholic convert librarian,

---

library, Milton probably owned), Etruria was simply the classically correct term for Tuscany which a poet was all the more bound to use since Cosimo I had lent it powerful, archaeologically supported political prestige in the mid-sixteenth century. It is surely worth noting in this connection that the world's foremost Etruscologist—the posthumous publication of whose book *De Etruria Regali* effectively pioneered the subject—was a British Catholic who had died in Italy little more than a decade before Milton's visit. Thomas Dempster (c. 1579-1625) was a Latin poet and the well-known editor and author of several distinguished books on subjects of great interest to Milton, a professor at Pisa and Bologna favored by Medici Grand Dukes and the Barberini Pope, Urban VIII, the colleague of Galileo, teacher of Giovanni Battista Doni and the focus of several Anglo-continental scandals, including one involving the Earl of Leicester's son, Sir Robert Dudley, the most distinguished Englishman resident in Tuscany at the time of Milton's visit. Milton would thus surely have known of Dempster and his works even if he may not have had access to his as yet unpublished treatise on the Etruscans which had been presented to Cosimo II but awaited its "discovery" at the hands of Thomas Coke, the early eighteenth-century Earl of Leicester, before being published. The most detailed post *D.N.B.* account of Dempster is to be found in A. M. Crinò, "Inediti su alcuni contatti Tosco-Britannici nel Seicento," *English Miscellany* 12 (1961): 158-70. Three recent studies deal with his pioneering place in Etruscology: G. Cipriani, *Il mito etrusco nel rinascimento fiorentino* (Florence, 1980); M. Cristofani, *Lo scoperto degli Etruschi* (Rome, 1983); and, in the year of the major Etruscan exhibitions in Florence, G. Morolli, *"Vetus Etruria": il mito degli Etruschi nella letteratura architettonica* . . . (Florence, 1985). Dempster's most important poem, *Musca Recidiva*, went through three editions during his lifetime which would in itself justify adding his name, along with that of James Gibbes, to those of Buchanan, Barclay and John Owen, whom Douglas Bush cites as "the only poets of British birth who achieved continental fame"; see *Variorum* 1:4-5 and my "English Catholic Poets in mid-seventeenth-century Rome," Appendix II, *The Grand Tour* . . . , 232-43. In the *Ragionamento funebre* published by the Accademia della Notte di Bologna in 1626, a year after his death, Dempster was praised by Ovidio Montalbani as the equal of Homer. As someone who would so assiduously recruit similar eulogies during his Italian tour twelve years later, perhaps Milton sought out Dempster's tomb in the great church of San Domenico on his way through Bologna.

Holstenius, for hospitality and for arranging a meeting with a cardinal, would he not have thanked his Vallombrosan hosts with a similarly Ciceronian epistle or two? Our fist recorded "sighting" of such letters dates from just prior to the 1866 dissolution of the monastery and was made by an incipiently redundant monk. The original manuscript version of "At Vallombrosa" reveals that Wordsworth had initially paused to wonder "if local traditions speak truth" on the subject of Milton's visit and indeed residence in a cell up at the *Paradisino*. Somewhat naively, he seems to have been won over by "the pride with which the Monk, without any previous question from me, pointed out [Milton's] residence," and thereupon decided to upgrade the legend to historical status in the published version of his poem, exclaiming almost impatiently:

The Monks still repeat the tradition with pride,
And its truth who shall doubt? for his Spirit is here
In the cloud-piercing rocks doth her grandeur abide,
In the pines pointing heavenward her beauty austere;
In the flower-besprent meadows his genius we trace. . . .[43]

---

[43] *The Poetical Works of William Wordsworth*, ed. E. de Selincourt and H. Darbishire, 5 vols., 2nd ed. (Oxford 19 ), 3:223. Wordsworth begins "At Vallombrosa" by quoting the lines with which he had begun, "Composed in the Simplon Pass," published in 1822 in *Memorials of a Tour on the Continent, 1820*: "Vallombrosa! I longed in thy shadiest wood / To slumber, reclined on the moss-covered floor." Though in their accounts of this tour, the standard biographies do not mention the fact (see M. Moorman, *William Wordsworth: A Biography*, 2 vols. [Oxford, 1965], 2:524-26; and S. Gill, *William Wordsworth: A Life* [Oxford, 1989], 394-95), Crabb Robinson declined to accompany the sixty-seven–year-old Wordsworth on his horseback pilgrimage to Vallombrosa, apparently leaving him at Pontassieve and excusing himself on the basis of having been there before (see *The Letters of William and Dorothy Wordsworth*, ed. E. de Selincourt, rev. ed. A. H. Hill [Oxford, 1982], 6:406). Robinson may even have helped provoke Wordsworth's indignant tone in "At Vallombrosa" by articulating his doubts about the Miltonic connection. He had joined "a party of pilgrimage" to Vallombrosa on 2 August 1830, and was to describe his experience in more down-to-earth, dare one say, intelligent terms than Wordsworth. Vallombrosa, he wrote, was:

of interest to English travellers, chiefly because one of our great poets has introduced its name into a simile. . . . It must be the delight which the sound gives to every ear susceptible of the beauty of verse, that excites a curiosity concerning the place, the name of which is so introduced. But as far as expectation is raised, that can only suffer disappointment from the visit, for with the present appearance of the valley, the description does not in the least agree. I could see but one little stream in it. It is by no means woody, and all

By the mid-1860s these monks must have been still more desperate to promote the international prestige of their convent in a last-ditch attempt to avert the forthcoming crisis. Thus we find one of them informing the gullible-sounding James Henry Dixon that:

> they had several letters that Milton addressed to the convent after his return to England. He said they were written in the purest Latin, but he could not show them, as he was not aware in what part of the library they had been placed.[44]

Though apparently no relation to Wordsworth's eponymous gardener, James Dixon would certainly have read the Laureate's poem and accompanying note, his enthusiasm for the topic being such that he soon sent in another contribution to Notes and Queries. In this he recalls being shown "a small organ on which Milton used to play":

> The keyboard was worn away. The venerable custodian said "We do not have a new one, out of respect to Milton". He then said, "It is the only old part: all the interior is new". The chapel which contains the organ is on the summit of the hill or mount called il Paradisino di Miltone.[45]

---

the trees now growing there (I presume that twenty years have produced no change) are pine or fir-trees, and of all trees the least adapted to arched bowers are the fir and larch. (Diary, Reminiscences, and Correspondence of Henry Crabb Robinson, ed. T. Sadler, 2 vols. [London, 1872], 2:98–99)

Wordsworth might almost be responding to his friend (and the deserved dedicatee of the Memorials) when he writes: "The fault-finders are themselves mistaken; the natural woods of the region of Vallombrosa are deciduous, and spread to a great extent; those near the convent are indeed mostly pines; but they are avenues of trees planted within a few steps of each other . . . plots of which are periodically cut down . . . My guide, a boy of about fourteen years old, pointed this out to me" (Poetical Works, 3:498). Privately, however, Wordsworth confessed to having been "somewhat disappointed at Vallombrosa." He was also to excise the description of Milton as "Holiest of Men" from the "Prospectus" to The Recluse.

[44] N&Q 11 (1873): 62: "I have passed three winters at Florence . . . when I was at Vallombrosa one of the Fathers stated that they had several letters . . . Since I was at Vallombrosa the convent has been disolved, and the buildings are now used for a Botanical and Agricultural College." The latter information enables us to date Dixon's Vallombrosan visit to before 1866.

[45] N&Q 8 (1876): 306. It is amusing to remember that Beckford claims to have "made a full stop at the organ" in Vallombrosa: "perhaps the most harmonious I ever played upon"; Dreams, 182. This is no doubt the "old" one mentioned on fol. 8v of

Meanwhile, however, a certain C. J. H. claimed to have outdone Dixon by seeing the letters themselves which were now in Florence. Prompted by an appeal for their discovery which had been published in *Notes and Queries* soon after Dixon's original article, C. J. H. writes: "A few years ago, when residing in Florence, I was shown two letters to the convent of Vallombrosa, both in an excellent state of preservation." "What became of these," C. J. H. continues nonchalantly, "I know not; probably they have been given away...."[46]

I vividly remember a lecture at the Warburg Institute given by Dr. Neil Harris, who wittily put the case for Milton's having visited Vallombrosa. In order to counter the sceptical argument first forwarded by Mrs. Piozzi's friends that the brooks of Vallombrosa could never have been leaf-strewn because "the trees are all ever-green in those woods," Dr. Harris concluded his lecture by flinging handfuls of recently gathered Vallombrosan beech-leaves at the stunned academic audience to demonstrate that devil-like deciduous "autumnal leaves" do in fact fall in Vallombrosa.[47] Today, Vallombrosa is indeed rich in beeches and other deciduous trees, but the extent to which this was always the case is not entirely clear. As we have seen, Gabriel d'Emiliane, writing in 1691, described the monastery as encompassed by "great Forests of Pine and Fir-Trees," a few chestnuts and apple trees excepted. As early as 1637, topographical engravings depict the monastery as surrounded almost exclusively by conifers, though the presence of oaks, chestnuts and, as we shall see, one beech in particular, was an integral part of the story of S. Giovanni Gualberto's eleventh-century foundation of the

---

an early nineteenth-century MS collection of Vallombrosan inscriptions in my possession: "L'organo antico era del celebre autore Onofrio che li trova dalla Congregazione [?] in Bibbiena[.] l'attuale e del Fronci Benedetto, fatto nel 1819...."

[46] *N&Q* 8 (1877): 117. Defenders of Milton qua Vallombrosan visitor, mainly against Todd's *Milton* (1801) 2:40, who quotes Mrs. Piozzi, and Brewer's *Dictionary of Phrase and Fable*, continue to appear in *Notes and Queries*, e.g., Jonathan Bouchier, *N&Q* 11 (1879): 463, and his supporters, pp. 488–89. The last of these was "H. W. New Univ. Club," who writes "I visited Vallombrosa in the spring of 1867, in company with a son of the poet Wordsworth, and can testify to the truth of Beckford's description of the convent as 'sheltered by firs and chestnuts towering one above another'." See also Aldo Sorani in *Saturday Review of Literature* 2 (1925): 318, which confirms that no trace of the letters survives but lends credence to their existence more than a century earlier.

[47] For more detail, see Neil Harris's Ph.D. dissertation, cited above, note 3.

monastery as told by Don Diego de Franchi at the time of Milton's visit to Florence.[48] A recent documentary history of *Vallombrosa e le sue Selve* shows that forestry was the monastery's major industry from the earliest times, the composition of the surrounding woods changing in response to economic demand from generation to generation. Between 1750-1753, during the prosperous Abbacy of Enrico Hugford, the monks not only distributed 229,761 loaves of bread to the local poor but, I had been pleased to read, also planted 40,300 beeches "on the neighboring mountains."[49] Unfortunately, the new history contradicts my less respectable source, recording that these beeches were in fact "abeti" or pines.[50] Be this as it may, when John Chetwode Eustace visited the abbey in 1802, he was still characterizing the woods as consisting "of firs thick and lofty" and, quoting Pope (as if to demonstrate that Vallombrosan imagery could be created independently of a Vallombrosan visit), "darksome pines that o'er yon rocks reclin'd."[51] In the second edition of his *Classical Tour*, Eustace appended to his account of Vallombrosa an exaggeratedly anti-French report taken from the *British Review*, which, in language itself borrowed from the first edition of Eustace's *Tour*, announced that the Napoleonic invasion had in the meantime been responsible for the total destruction of "the majestic abbey, the enchanting Paradisino" and the "sylvan scene" generally:

---

[48] *Historia del Patriarca S. Giovanni Gualberto primo abbate et institutore del monastico ordine di Vallombrosa* (Florence, 1640). This book took almost three years to wend its way through the bureaucratic procedures required to obtain the necessary imprimaturs. For the etchings, at least one of which seems to have been by Stefano della Bella, see A. Gabbrielli and E. Settesoldi, *Vallombrosa e le sue selve: nove secoli di storia* (Stia: Ministero dell'Agricoltura e delle Foreste, 1985). For a later but much better depiction of Vallombrosa, see that by Cicci dated 1750, from a set of 1833 acquatint views by Bury, illustrated in Nello Puccioni, *La Vallombrosa e la Val di Sieve inferiore*, Italia artistica no. 81 (Bergamo: n.d.), 27-28.

[49] Augustus Hare, *Florence* (London, 1884), 217.

[50] Gabbrielli and Settesoldi, 118.

[51] J. C. Eustace, *A Tour through Italy*, 2 vols. (London, 1813), 2:227-31. The Pope quotation is from *Eloisa and Abelard*. The author writes that *Paradise Lost* "is considered as the model of modern parks." For Eustace in Italy, see J. H. Whitfield, "Mr Eustace and Lady Morgan," *Italian Studies Presented to E. R. Vincent* (Cambridge, 1962), 166-89. While Marianna Starke took care to disabuse her readers of Eustace's exaggerated account of French destruction, Lady Morgan was so incensed as to launch a satirical onslaught on both him and *The British Review* (*Italy*, 2:146 n).

The forests and dells resound no more with the sound of the *church-going bell*, the wide spreading cedar, the darksome pine, the mournful cypress, no longer wave their aged brows to the embalmed air.[52]

Subsequent to this supposed destruction, however, Marianna Starke, the anonymous author of the *Mementoes*, Wordsworth, Frances Trollope, Mary Shelley and Elizabeth Barrett Browning, all seem to have found both monastery and surrounding woods in reasonable condition, with the latter still characterized by conifers (though in 1837 Wordsworth, provoked perhaps by Crabb Robinson's scepticism, drew attention to the presence of beeches in a letter to his daughter).[53] Mrs. Browning indeed, no doubt jaundiced by her reception at the hands of those unfriendly monks, consoled herself for her expulsion from Paradise by remembering how ghastly the food had been, complaining to Mrs. Jameson that, "they make their bread, I rather imagine, with sawdust of their fir trees."[54] Back in Florence, however, writing "Casa Guidi Windows" (and, no doubt, rereading her Wordsworth), her imagination reasserted itself more positively in favour of Miltonian Vallombrosa, not merely by belatedly emphasizing the prevalence of beeches there, but by bringing autumn forward a few months:

> The Vallombrosan brooks were strewn so thick,
> That June-day, knee-deep, with dead beechen leaves,
> As Milton saw them ere his heart grew sick,
> And his eyes blind. . . .

"We must think," she writes, addressing the mountains and the forests, that

> Your beauty and your glory helped to fill
> The cup of Milton's soul so to the brink
> He never more was thirsty . . .

---

[52] Eustace, *A Classical Tour through Italy, An. MDCCCII*, 2nd ed. 2 vols. (London, 1814), 2:215. *British Review*, no. 10, p. 383; cf. Beckford's *Italy; with Sketches of Spain and Portugal*, 2 vols. (London, 1834—but based on journeys of 1780 and 1782).

[53] Wordsworth, *Letters*, ed. cit., 6:406.

[54] Ibid., 333.

He sang of Adam's Paradise and smiled
Remembering Vallombrosa.[55]

According to the third edition of Augustus Hare's *Florence*, by 1890
large numbers of Eustace's aged trees had indeed been destroyed:

> But nowhere has the mad destruction of old trees in Italy been
> carried to such an excess as at Vallombrosa. An Englishman
> vainly offered to pay the fullest timber price for some of the
> finest trees which adorned the ascent from Pelago if they might
> be left standing in their places; his offer was refused, and every
> tree of any age or beauty was destroyed. The noble wood on the
> ridge of the hill, which sheltered all the young plantations, has
> been ruthlessly annihilated in the same way.[56]

I have not discovered who Hare's anonymous Englishman might be—
though the millionaire Anglo-Florentine exile, John Temple Leader, is
a possible candidate. He or Hare may have been inspired by Wordsworth's "The Pine of Monte Mario." This single pine tree (presumably
of the "Umbrella" type) was "saved from the sordid axe by Beaumont's
care," an act which stimulated in the poet "a gush of tenderness."[57]

An American who merits a mention in this context is George P.
Marsh, the former United States Minister at Constantinople and Turin
who spent the last twenty-one years of his life in Florence and then in
Rome—when the capital was transferred there—as minister to the new
kingdom of Italy.[58] He was a pioneering ecologist and author of a
fascinating book entitled *Man and Nature*, first published in 1864,
which included detailed documentation of the failures and achievements

---

[55] E. B. B., *Poems.*

[56] Hare, *Florence*, 3rd ed. (London, 1890), 2332. Hare, like Eustace and the earlier
key Italian travel writers, e.g., Richard Lassels in the seventeenth century and Henry
Swinburne in the eighteenth, was a Roman Catholic. For milder mention of Vallombrosan trees "felled by order of the Government" in 1891, see Virginia W. Johnson,
*The Lily of the Arno* (London, 1891), 110–11.

[57] Wordsworth's note to this poem, which precedes "At Vallombrosa" in *Memorials of a Tour in Italy, 1837*, explains that "a price had been paid for it by the late Sir
G. Beaumont, upon condition that the proprietor should not act upon his known
intention of cutting it down"; see F. Owen and D. B. Brown, *Collector of Genius: The
Life of Sir George Beaumont* (New Haven-London, 1988).

[58] *Dictionary of American Biography*, 21:297–98.

of the Italian authorities in the field of conservation in general, and warnings of the dire effects of deforestation in particular.[59] It was partly thanks to his influence that the National School of Forestry (the "Istituto Superiore Forestale Nazionale") was established in the monastery at Vallombrosa in 1867 (transferred to Florence in 1913), and it was here in the hotel which was established by the Croce di Savoia in the ancient Foresteria that he died on 23 July 1882.

To complete this saga with a definitive argument against Milton having seen even a thinly-strewn layer of autumnal leaves on a Vallombrosan brook, I should like to conclude with a second distinguished American Italophile who died at Vallombrosa, the sculptor and man of letters immortalized by Henry James, William Wetmore Story.[60] In an informative if somewhat *belle lettriste* essay entitled simply "Vallombrosa," first published in the April 1881 issue of *Blackwood's Magazine*, Story describes how, "in the latter part of last October" he was invited by an unnamed lady (probably his daughter Edith, wife of the Marchese Peruzzi dei Medici) to spend a few days with her and her family in "an old deserted house, built centuries ago by the Medici as a stronghold and hunting-box" about three miles from the famous monastery.[61] Story's account of this once castellated *villino* whose flanking towers had been "cruelly" levelled by the present government, as well as that of the

---

[59] This book was described by Lewis Mumford in *The Brown Decades* (New York, 1931), 78, as "the fountainhead of the conservationist movement." It was republished in a revised edition as *The Earth as Modified by Human Action* in 1874.

[60] H. James, *William Wetmore Story and his Friends*, 2 vols. (London, 1903); see also *Dictionary of American Biography*. Story died in his daughter's house at Vallombrosa in 1895 and like Marsh was buried in the Protestant Cemetery in Rome.

[61] Loc. cit., 483. As noted by James, Story's essay was "reissued as a volume of scarce more than a hundred pages in 1881" (2:330-33). The British Institute of Florence possesses a rare copy for notice of which I thank its librarian, Mark Roberts. James also notes that three miles for the distance between the monastery and the house at Lago is something of an exaggeration. Vallombrosa provided what James calls the "undertone" for Story's "short idyllic novel *Fiammetta*," published in 1886. It was written at the Lago di Vallombrosa during the summer of 1885 and, "in memory of those happy days in the 'Etrurian shades'," dedicated to Story's wife and daughter, to whom it had been read "on three beautiful mornings as we sat under the shadows of its whispering pines." For Medicean interest in (and presence at) Vallombrosa dating back to Landino's *Camaldulese Disputations*, see G. Volpi, "Lorenzo de'Medici e Vallombrosa," *Archivo Storico Italiano* 92 (1934): 2, 121-32, and C. Elam and E. Gombrich, "Lorenzo de'Medici and a Frustrated Villa Project," in *Florence and Italy: Renaissance Studies in Honour of Nicolai Rubinstein*, ed. P. Denley and C. Elam (London 1988), 481-92.

monastery itself, are well worth reading, but what is of primary interest here is that although this was late October, the autumnal leaves, even those of the most decidedly deciduous chestnuts, had not detached themselves from their trees. Story would no doubt have preferred them to have been strewing the brooks for, having quoted the inevitable lines, he refers frequently to the season as if willing nature to respond to art. But though it was mid-autumn, both birds and trees persisted in behaving as if it were summer. On one side of the monastery, "the sloping hills are dark with miles of serried firs; on the corner, they are golden-brown with glowing chestnuts."[62] Elsewhere in the same essay the leaves may have changed color but have clearly not yet lost their grip:

> Magnificent chestnuts throng the autumnal slopes, their yellow leaves glowing in the autumn sun. Sombre groves of firs, mar-shalled along the hillsides for miles, stand solemn and dark. Beech-trees rear at intervals their smooth trunks, or gather together in close and murmurous conclave.[63]

Meanwhile Vallombrosa's most distinguished tree, il Faggio Santo, supposedly flourishing after almost nine centuries, was famous for being even more reluctant than its non-miraculous colleagues to part with its leaves. From early in the eleventh century it would "put forth its leaves long before the others," thus sheltering S. Giovanni and his hut, and "was the last, when winter came, to shed its leaves on the ground."[64]

All this, of course, has been by way of emphasizing the impossibility of Milton's having seen—as distinct from imagined—Vallombrosa's leaves in their fallen state, even if, for some reason, he had ventured so far as Vallombrosa itself. That 1880 was not climatically unique is indicated by Mary Shelley's discovery of the same conditions in late October thirty-eight years later. She had hesitated to embark on the excursion from Florence, considering that autumn was "too far advanced" but when she arrived at Vallombrosa "the branches on noble forest trees ... spread over our path ... were [still] in the sear and yellow leaf," a state of affairs which prompted the observation that "the place [as distinct from its botanical behavior?] was the more consonant with Milton's

---

[62] Story, "Vallombrosa," 487.
[63] Ibid., 484.
[64] Ibid., 490.

verse."[65] No more than other nineteenth-century travellers, however, was she inclined to doubt so attractive a tradition as Milton's visit, quoting the inevitable lines with the best of them. Even after Masson's Methuselan *Life* had, in the form of an unprecedentedly precise chronology, unwittingly supplied the means to undermine the myth, the romantic *Story* was to implicitly postpone Milton's autumn to an impossibly late date—and describe conditions he hadn't seen himself—rather than forego the chance to dream (in print) of his hero's hillside wanderings:

> Here, among others, came Milton, in the flower of his youth, to gaze on this magnificent panorama, to store his mind with images and pictures—that long remained vivid when the outer windows of his sight were closed—to study in the library, to pace the terraces, to ponder the grand poem of his later years, and to leave behind him a memory dear to all who love English poetry. The landscape is still the same as when he saw it, and the leaves strew the hillsides as thickly as when he wandered among these shady groves. His shadow walks with every English traveller through the long corridors, where once the monks who are now but dust listened to his silvery tones, and wondered perhaps at this fair youth, with long and golden hair, who came from a far-away country, and spoke softly if brokenly in their tongue. The charm of this place long lingered in his mind . . . the impression made on his mind never left him.[66]

Milton was in Tuscany twice in his life, first during the summer of 1638, for a period of approximately two months ending sometime around mid-September, and second, during early spring of the following year. By the end of October 1638, a time of the year when—as Mary Shelley and Story both so eloquently testify—the deciduous leaves of Vallombrosa change color but do not yet fall, Milton and his servant had long since left Tuscany and were in Rome, being wined and dined by the English Jesuits.[67]

---

[65] M. Shelley, 135-37.

[66] Story, op. cit., 408.

[67] For identification of those with whom he dined (and of the 1645 *Poems'* "Selvaggi") see my *The Grand Tour and the Great Rebellion*, 282-83.

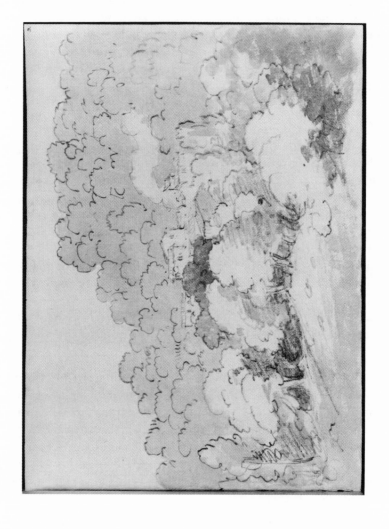

Fig. 1. J. R. Cozens, *View of Vallombrosa* (sketchbook vol. 6).
Courtesy of The Whetworth Art Gallery, University of Manchester.

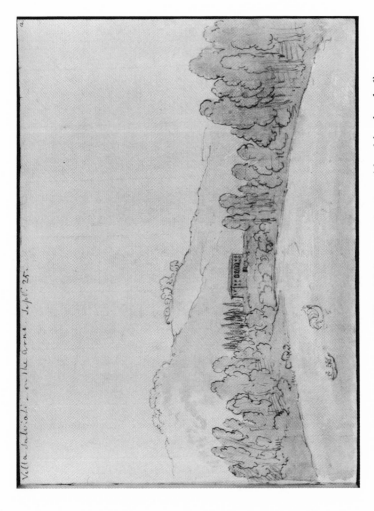

Fig. 2. J. R. Cozens, *Villa of Salviati on the Arno* (sketchbook vol. 6). Courtesy of The Whetworth Art Gallery, University of Manchester.

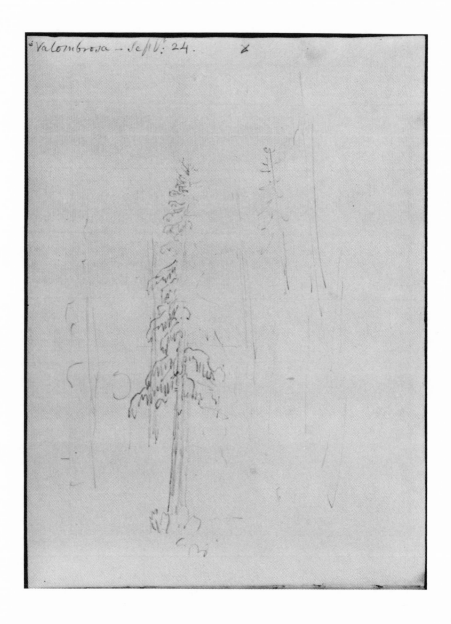

Fig. 3. J. R. Cozens, *Firtrees at Vallombrosa* (sketchbook vol. 6).
Courtesy of The Whetworth Art Gallery, University of Manchester.

## Appendix

"Written at Vallombrosa, 1821" from anon., *Mementoes, historical and classical, of a Tour through part of France, Switzerland, and Italy in the years 1821 and 1822 . . .*, 2 vols. (London, 1824), 1:264–65.

In these lone shades, where solitude e'er reigns;
Far from the world, and all its sick'ning pains,
Here let me muse, and hush'd be every strife,
Remote from man, and vain, delusive life:
Mid scenes which, erst, the classic muse did sing
And Milton soaring with sublimer wing.
Here may the heart, when sadd'ning thoughts inspire,
Flee from mock mirth, and into self retire;
Friendship betray'd may here some solace find
To heal the wound still rankling in the mind.
Here too may some fond youth of generous mould,
Whose heart responded to the tale he told,
Whose idol mistress to adore was pleasure,
His heart's chief life, and soul's best treasure,
Find a fit place to mourn his hapless lot
And sigh o'er love profaned and vows forgot.
Some one unfit to feel, just fit to feign,
A mimic love, to give another pain.
Whose fashion-phrase, or mode, or dress more spruce,
Or dashing vice, may offer some excuse
To show the bitter slight, or cold disdain,
Or words of scorn to love that pleads in vain;
To sink the soul, oppress it more and more,
And bleed the fainting heart at every pore.
Or here, perchance, may flee some maiden true,
Firm of resolve to bid the world adieu;
Of him she fondly loved, by fate bereft,
No hope, no joy, or peace, to her is left;
To memory's woes she gives the live-long day,
Weeps oe'r the past, and sighs her soul away.
Or here may pine some yet more hapless maid
Honour abused, and virgin faith betray'd:

Retirement best suits with wounded pride,
And woe that springs from shame who would not hide?
Like some fair vase of alabaster hue,
Of purest form, and exquisite to view,
If once defaced, deform'd, by hands profane,
Or lustre lost by some foul, tainted, flame,
The beauteous object, late the general pride,
To pity, scorn, neglect, is thrown aside.

Lincoln College, Oxford

JUDITH SCHERER HERZ

# "For whom this glorious sight?": Dante, Milton, and the Galileo Question

B
UT WHEREFORE ALL NIGHT LONG SHINE THESE, FOR WHOM /
This glorious sight, when sleep hath shut all eyes?"[1] That is
the question that grounds all others in the poem—it is Eve's
question, and Adam's, and the narrator's, and ours. To answer it only
to reinstate it as a question is the poem's dominating strategy. "Thinking in astronomy"—Galileo's crime in the eyes of the inquisition as
Milton described it in Areopagitica—generates questions in Paradise Lost
that remain unanswered and indeed unanswerable save by reiteration.
For Dante, by contrast, there could be nothing transgressive about
"thinking in astronomy"; the stars and the love that moves them are
one. But Galileo's presence in Milton's poem not only marks this
obvious difference between the two poets, it marks as well those points
at which their visions converge, as Milton both resists and rewrites his
predecessor in the epic of astronomy.

Galileo was also interested in Dante, although for reasons quite
different from Milton's. When he gave his 1588 lectures to the Florentine Academy on "La Figura, Sito e Grandezza dell'Inferno di Dante"
(lectures that were later to provide the first mention of Galileo in print
in a 1604 reference),[2] he was joining a technical debate that had begun
a century earlier in the work of Antonio Manetti. Manetti's conclusions,

---

[1] *Paradise Lost* 4.657-58. All subsequent references are to Fowler and are indicated
in the text of the essay.

[2] Filippo Valori, "Termini di mezzo relievo e d'intera dottrina tra gl'archi di casa
Valori," cited in Galileo, *Le Opere di Galileo Galilei*, Edizione Nazionale, ed. G.
Barbèra (Florence, 1934), 9:1. See also Stillman Drake, *Galileo at Work* (Chicago:
Univ. of Chicago Press, 1978), 475. Valori notes the "patriotic" aspect of the lectures:
"di salvare con buone ragioni il nostro Fiorentino e ribattere i motivi del nobil
Lucchese" (9:1).

along with those of Landino and Benivieni, were subsequently challenged in 1544 by the non-Florentine Alessandro Vellutello. Using
Archimedes and the mathematics of conic sections, Galileo concurred in
the measurements of Manetti, to the honor of Florentine Science. The
enterprise was at once scientific and literary, but the difference between
the two was more one of degree than of kind; Galileo suggests as much
at the start of his lecture when he contrasts the accomplishments due to
scientific observation and the even more wonderful results of the
"investigation and description of the site and shape of the Inferno,
which, buried within the bowels of the earth, and hidden from all
senses, is known to no one by experience."[3]

Galileo taking the measure of Dante's poem and, incidentally,
measuring the giants and Lucifer as well, provides both a wonderfully
evocative emblem for the figure of Galileo in Milton's poem and a way
of talking about Milton's relation to Dante.[4] It is from this perspective
of the dual presence of Dante and Galileo in *Paradise Lost* that I want
to join the long-standing debate over Milton's concern with the new
astronomy.[5] Was he interested in these issues only insofar as he could

---

[3] ". . . l'investigazione e descrizione del sito e figura dell'Inferno, il quale, sepolto
nelle viscere della terra, nascoso a tutti i sensi, è da nessuno per niuna esperienza
conosciuto." Galileo, pere, 9:31. The literary writings of Galileo, including commentaries on Ariosto ("Postille all'Ariosto") and Tasso ("Considerazioni al Tasso"), are
collected in *Opere*, vol. 9, along with the two lectures on *Inferno*.

[4] See Paget Toynbee, *Dante in English Literature* (London, 1909), 121-28, for a list
of allusions and parallels. For Milton's knowledge of Dante, see James Holly Hanford,
"The Chronology of Milton's Private Studies," *PMLA* 36 (1921): 251-314 and Ruth
Mohl, ed., *Commonplace Book* in CPW 1:365-67. Irene Samuel, *Dante and Milton*
(Ithaca: Cornell Univ. Press, 1966), provides the fullest account of the Dante/Milton
relationship. See her discussion of Milton's reading of Dante, and of the parallels
between the proems to books 1, 3, 7 and 9 and Dante's view of the role of the poet.
Kathleen Swaim, "Some Dante and Milton Analogues," *Renascence* 7 (1984): 43-51,
discusses Milton's Protestant reorientation of "this inherited literary material" (43). A.
J. Smith, *The Metaphysics of Love: Studies in Renaissance Love Poetry from Dante to
Milton* (Cambridge: Cambridge Univ. Press, 1985), emphasizes the contrast between
the two, especially their views of love: "The poet of the *Commedia* moves through love
to a clear intelligible vision of the love that sustains the universe; the ultimate proof of
love is that it draws the poet up to itself, impelling him by the lure of beauty to transcend his humanity. . . . Milton simply moves the opposite way, to the unsparing embodiment of love in the fallen world. The ultimate proof of the divine love he posits is
that it incarnates itself to prove the worth of our human nature" (326).

[5] See Marjorie Nicolson, "Milton and the Telescope," *ELH* 2 (1935): 1-32; Paul

moralize the problem and conclude with *his* starry messenger, the affable archangel, that he should "dream not of other worlds"? Or did that dream enter more deeply into his text, even at times colliding with the frequently repeated injunction to be "lowly wise"? Does the optic glass baffle or enable the poem's visionary enterprise?

That Milton knew these lectures is quite unlikely, but he may well have known of them, especially when one considers how Dante conscious most of Milton's Florentine aquaintances were, particularly those, like Carlo Dati, who provided his contact with Galileo. Here I am assuming the accuracy of Milton's statement in *Areopagitica*. That Galileo failed to mention this precocious but quite unknown English visitor is unremarkable. That Milton would fabricate the incident in the course of a defense of truth and intellectual freedom makes very little literary or moral sense. Moreover, the prose statement carries an historical weight very different from the mention of Vallombrosa in *Paradise Lost*. There the shadows, sounds and Dantean resonances of the Etruscan landscape give the word more the status of a found poem than of a biographical datum.

It is, however, a very nice coincidence that the first reference to Galileo in Milton's poem has him performing this very task—the mea-

---

Johnson, *Astronomical Thought in Renaissance England* (Baltimore: The Johns Hopkins Press, 1937); Kester Svendsen, *Milton and Science* (Cambridge, Mass.: Harvard Univ. Press, 1956); Thomas Kuhn, *The Copernican Revolution* (Cambridge, Mass.: Harvard Univ. Press, 1966). Johnson follows Nicolson in emphasizing Milton's interest in "descriptive astronomy" (285), and also argues for Milton's use of Galileo's *Dialogue*, as does Barbara K. Lewalski ("The Genres of *Paradise Lost*: Literary Genres as a Means of Accommodation," *MS* 17 [1983]: 88-92; *Paradise Lost and the Rhetoric of Literary Forms* [Princeton: Princeton Univ. Press, 1985], 46-50). Grant McColley, on the other hand, argues that the influence of Wilkins and Ross is more important ("Milton's Dialogue on Astronomy: The Immediate Principal Sources," *PMLA* 52 [1937]: 728-62). Svendsen characterizes Milton's interest in science as "broad . . . conventional" and stresses the medieval element in his scientific thinking. However, elaborating on a point of Nicolson, he argues that "Milton's breaking of the circle is a deliberate ambiguity, not only consistent with the theme but contributory toward the narrative design implied in the many other dualities, alternatives and options in characterization, setting and plot" (237). Lawrence Babb reiterates Svendsen's emphasis but then goes on to argue that whatever were Milton's original intentions in introducing the new astronomy, he ended up repudiating the whole line of inquiry (*The Moral Cosmos of Paradise Lost* [East Lansing: Michigan State Univ. Press, 1970], 91). For Webber, Harris, Flannagan, see note 15; also for Harris, see note 16.

suring of Satan—although with the advantage of a technology that Galileo was not to know of until twenty years after the lectures in Florence. In the exfoliating Tuscan-artist simile, the telescope is both subject and means as it opens an intertextual space that connects Milton's text to Dante's. The simile marks the poem's first great leap outside the confines of its narrative boundaries. It opens geographical and astronomical space and connects literary, historical, and providential time.[6] And it handles, with a typically Dantean brusqueness, the seductions of its own nostalgia. As Dante to Francesca, or to Cavalcanti, or to Brunetto, so Milton to the embowering shades, as later to the massed chivalry marching to the "Dorian mood of flutes and soft recorders," or to the fall of Mulciber, where that spacious, elegiacally evoked moment is harshly interrupted—"thus they relate / Erring." But that reprehended narrative voice remains within Milton's poem, much as it does within Dante's. Thematically, too, the simile repeats the Dantean topos of exile as it moves from the shore of the fiery lake through the fallen leaves in Dante's Virgilian Vallombrosa to the safe shore from which the sojourners of Goshen look back at the destroyed Memphian chivalry.[7] It is in this last transumption that the most resonant link between Dante and Milton is established. For Dante and for Milton exile is the condition of both poet and poem, although in Milton's text it is less Psalm 114 and its typologically read promise of recovery that resounds than Exodus 14 and its narrative of destruction.

Like his precursor, Milton constructs a narrative space beyond the

---

[6] See Malabika Sarkar, " 'The Visible Diurnal Sphere': Astronomical Images of Space and Time in *Paradise Lost*," MQ 18 (1984): 1-5, for a discussion of the relationship between images of space and time: "Both groups of images present the prelapsarian world of *Paradise Lost* as at once measurable and immeasurable" (5). Mildred Gutkin, " 'Knowledge Within Bounds': Spatial Imagery in *Paradise Lost*," *English Studies in Canada* 7 (1981): 282-311, discusses the paradoxical nature of the poem's spatial metaphors in an argument that emphasizes the "urgent, unspoken summons to proceed beyond limits" (291), a point that is crucial to my argument here.

[7] Harold Bloom provides the essential discussion of Milton's transumption of his precursors in this passage in A *Map of Misreading* (New York: Oxford Univ. Press, 1975), 130-38. Although Louis Martz's reference is not to Dante, his concern is with the theme of exile. His comment on narrative perspective in Eden implicitly evokes the presence of Galileo: "Alongside Satan or behind him, or looking over his shoulder we have the broader vision of the poet, who includes Satan within his view." *Poet of Exile: A Study of Milton's Poetry* (New Haven: Yale Univ. Press, 1980), 108.

reach of memory, even of language. Milton's awareness that his language has only the status of analogy derives in large part from Dante, whose epic vision involves a similar accommodation, but one which has an easier relationship with the language that imperfectly constitutes it. Thus, when Dante asks Beatrice to explain the spots on the moon, her reply is at once a cautionary tale on the limitations of the senses—"even following after the senses thou seest that reason's wings are short"[8]— and an outline of an experiment with mirrors and candles, followed by a discussion of the nature of alloys (the scientific discourse offered by way of countering the pilgrim's scientific mistake in supposing that the spots are caused by variations in rare and dense matter).

This almost prosaic discussion of the spots on the moon is not felt to be different in kind from the language that represents the mysteriousness of heaven. The extraordinarily new enterprise that the last canticle undertakes—"the waters I take were never sailed before" (2.7)—does not involve a distinction between literary and scientific discourse, for the metaphoric and literal are one. What the pilgrim realizes is that he sees and yet does not see at the same time: "It was clear to me then that everywhere in heaven is Paradise" (3.87–88). He encounters from the start an accommodated universe, for, as Beatrice explains, "it is necessary to speak thus to your faculty, since only from sense perception does it grasp that which it then makes fit for the intellect" (4.40–43). The poem thus becomes an analogy constructed upon an analogy in which scientific speculation has the same status as any other form of intellectual endeavor; the language of science rests effortlessly at its heart.

Indeed, for Dante, as for Galileo three centuries later, the heavens can be represented abstractly as the work of a divine geometer whose circles may be mathematically scrutinized even if their full measure cannot be taken. Although the last simile of the *Paradiso* turns the pilgrim into a failed geometer ("Like the geometer who sets all his mind to the squaring of the circle and for all his thinking does not discover the principle he needs, such was I . . . ": 33.133–36), it is, nonetheless, by means of a transcendent geometry that the poet finds an accommoda-

---

[8] *The Divine Comedy of Dante Alighieri*, ed. and trans. John D. Sinclair, 3 vols. (New York: Oxford Univ. Press, 1939–48), *Par.* 2.56–57. All subsequent references are indicated in the text of the essay.

tion for his vision so that his desire and will finally "spin like a wheel with even motion," within those immeasurable circles "revolved by the love that moves the sun and other stars." Furthermore, by building his source of authority into the poem and hence aligning his questions and answers, Dante frees his pilgrim from the problem of knowledge. The limitations of Dante's vision are simply a given, even as the poem as the vehicle of this vision keeps pushing beyond those bounds so that one finally sees that which no tongue can tell—at the last, the mute tongue of the infant "la lingua alla mammella" (33.108). From Milton's post-Copernican point of view, however, the language of science is no longer transparent; it has itself become the subject of scrutiny and implicated in the problematic of scientific speculation.

Liminally situating his inquiry between bounds and beyond—"knowledge within bounds; beyond abstain / to ask" (7.120-21)—Milton sets human memory and desire in relation to scientific speculation. For part of the dilemma implicit in the bounds/beyond injunction involves Adam's learning where to locate the break between self and all that is not self; it involves his learning how to read the conjunction in Raphael's explanation that he will describe creation in order to "glorify the maker, and infer / Thee also happier" (7.116-17). Thus scientific speculation is established as an aspect of Adam's humanness from the start. Unlike Dante's pilgrim, however, Adam must pose his questions even if there are no fully adequate answers available to him, for Milton's poem can only gesture towards the authority that Dante's takes for granted. The questions that Adam and Eve pose about the universe they are given to inhabit are only provisionally answered; more often they disrupt and divert the narrative. They create a discursive situation where the relation between the literal and metaphoric is blurred, where the over-going of boundaries is both a syntactic function and a thematic necessity.

Eve's question at the close of her second speech in the poem is thus a telling model of what is at once a narrative and an epistemological problem.[9] There, after her "mirror song," she poses the poem's most intractable question: "But wherefore all night long shine these, for

---

[9] See Earl Miner, "The Reign of Narrative in *Paradise Lost*," MS 17 (1983): 3-25, on the subordination of the lyric to the narrative in *Paradise Lost*.

whom / This glorious sight, when sleep hath shut all eyes?" (4.657–58).
In the eighteen preceding lines she had offered to Adam a bounded and
timeless universe: "With thee conversing I forget all time. . . ." Within
it Eve is to Adam is to Eve as first line is to last in a syntax of reflection, a playing out in language of the gaze in the pool that was her first
act, her first memory. Unlike that first scene there is here no space for
intrusion. Adam no longer disturbs the image in the pool but is himself
the fixed point that carries Eve's reflection back to her. Here there is
only a present and action is stasis. But suddenly, in one of those major
disruptions of voice frequently enough employed by the narrator, but
not usually by his creations, Eve sounds her own "but," breaking that
enclosure both syntactically and thematically. Lyric celebration yields to
scientific inquiry; all times of day may not please alike, nor may Adam
be her sole concern. For Eve, too, has a conjunction to negotiate, a self
and not-self to delimit (the scene at the pool enacts that necessity,
although ambiguously, as the happily resolved Narcissus allusion
suggests, despite the implication of desire deferred, of the private, erotic
and interior closed off).[10] Thus, her question provides a tonal contrast
that to a degree marks its impertinence. It has no containing discourse
and thus can instantly be subsumed by Adam. Nonetheless the contrast
between its prosaic formulation and the preceding lyric passage suggests

----

[10] This scene has been the subject of much interesting exploration recently,
especially from a feminist perspective. Christine Froula, "When Eve Reads Milton:
Undoing the Canonical Economy," *Critical Inquiry* 10 (1983): 321–47, argues that it
represents the silencing of a potentially autonomous Eve, with the result that "Milton's
poem constructs its gods and its speech on the bedrock of woman's silence." Mary
Nyquist, however, argues that Froula does not submit "the category of personal
experience to ideological analysis," in a reading that emphasizes the historical and
cultural significance of Eve's speech, "The Genesis of Gendered Subjectivity in the
Divorce Tracts and in *Paradise Lost*," in *Re-Membering Milton: Essays on the Texts and
Traditions*, ed. Mary Nyquist and Margaret W. Ferguson (New York and London:
Methuen, 1987), 99–127. She claims that Eve's speech "plays a role historically and
culturally in the construction of the kind of female subjectivity required by a new
economy's . . . sentimentalization of the private sphere" (120), that her "narrative
creates a space that is strongly if only implicitly gendered, a space that is dilatory, erotic,
and . . . private" (119). See also Patricia Parker, *Inescapable Romance: Studies in the
Poetics of a Mode* (Princeton: Princeton Univ. Press, 1979), 114–23, for a discussion of
"the 'staying' of Eve upon her shadow" as a threshold moment, as part of a pattern of
deferral and dilation.

the disruption implicit in the linking of the erotic and the speculative (the pool itself is such an image—reflecting Eve, reflecting the heavens), a linkage repeated throughout the poem and nowhere more emphatically than in Adam's attempts to rephrase that question for himself.

Once raised, the question remains a disturbing presence in the text. Adam answers rapidly, but neither seems completely satisfied with his response. For Eve a more appealing, although finally more unsettling, answer is provided in her dream that very night: it is she upon whom all creation waits, as Satan in Adam's voice returns, reflects, her words back to her—"heaven wakes with all his eyes, / Whom to behold but thee" (5.44-45). But that answer leads to the illusory ascent to heaven, the sudden fall, the awakening, and the tear. Moreover Adam, in his turn, asks the very same question of Raphael: why do the "numbered stars seem to roll / Spaces incomprehensible merely to officiate light / Round this opacous earth?" (8.19-23). At the end of Raphael's discourse, Adam declares himself "cleared of doubt," but the question has not been answered so much as rephrased, moral inquiry having been substituted for scientific. Although human memory, Adam's witness to his own creation, is then offered in place of the "fume" of speculation, it brings with it its own difficulties in Adam's persistent confusion over the boundaries between reason and passion, between bounds and beyond. The question remains, albeit bracketed, at the very end of the poem when Michael's last words to Adam place scientific knowledge— the names of all the stars, "all secrets of the deep, all nature's works" (12.578)—to the side of, although not necessarily in place of, "the sum of wisdom" which, as Adam concludes, is to "acknowledge my redeemer ever blest" (573). (What invigorates the piety of this conclusion is the political humanism at its center—"by small / Accomplishing great things, by things deemed weak / Subverting worldly strong" [566-68]).

This question that will not go away, that links the first conversation of Adam and Eve to their last moment in the garden, that ushers in, each time that it is recalled, a new stage in the unfolding of the narrative, can quite literally be called the Galileo question. It arises during the first day in The Dialogue Concerning the Two Chief World Systems as a result of Simplicio's assertion that "the sun, the moon, and the other stars, ... have no other use than that of service to the earth."[11] The

---

[11] Galileo, Dialogue Concerning the Two Chief World Systems: Ptolemaic and Coper-

replies of both Sagredo and Salviati, the one concerning the limits of the imagination, the other, the nature of the spots on the moon, have an obvious echo in Milton's poem, as do the words of Salviati (the position closest to Galileo's in *The Dialogue*) that whatever exists in the universe beyond the range of the telescope or the imagination is "continually singing encomium sin His praise" while engaged in the "perpetual occupation of all creatures in praising God."[12]

One can accumulate numerous echoes and allusions to Galileo's writing in Milton's poem—the dialogue form itself,[13] the linking of Orion with the discussion of the spots on the moon, the association of the telescope with a ship's mast in the discussion of the second day, references to comets, discussions of sunspots, the milky way, the moons of Jupiter, and the phases of the horned Venus.[14] The Galileo voice is heard also in many of the poem's speakers. Galileo's attack on the Peripatetics "forced into their strange fancies by attempting to measure the whole universe by means of their tiny scale," his scorn for those who "make use of that farrago of spheres and orbs composed by the astronomers," his insistence that "all human reasoning must be placed second to direct experience"[15] echo both in Raphael's warnings and in Adam's ongoing observations and calculations. There is little doubt that Milton knew Galileo's work, but how he read it and what weight he gave it in *Paradise Lost* still remains an open question. It has been several times suggested, by Joan Webber, for example, and most recently by Neil Harris and Roy Flannagan,[16] that by associating the new astronomy with Satan, Milton was in some measure repudiating the

---

nican, ed. and trans. Stillman Drake (Berkeley: Univ. of California Press, 1967), 59.

[12] *Dialogue*, 62.

[13] See note 4.

[14] The references to Galileo suggest that *The Starry Messenger*, "Letters on Sunspots," *The Dialogue Concerning the Two Chief World Systems*, and *The Assayer* were known to Milton. See the following passages for: comets 2.708, 4.256, 12.633; moons of Jupiter 8.149; Venus 7.366; new stars 7.383; milky way 7.577.

[15] Galileo, "Letters on Sunspots," in *Discoveries and Opinions of Galileo*, ed. and trans. Stillman Drake (New York: Doubleday Anchor Books, 1957), 142, 97, 118.

[16] Joan Webber, *Milton and His Epic Tradition* (Seattle: Univ. of Washington Press, 1979); Roy Flannagan, "Arts, Artists, Galileo and Concordances," *MQ* 23 (1986): 103–5; Neil Harris, "Galileo as Symbol: The 'Tuscan Artist' in *Paradise Lost*," *Annali del'Istituto e Museo di Storia della Scienza di Firenze* 10 (1985): 3–29

Galileo enterprise. But assimilating, even imitating, seems to me nearer the mark, for the polemic on the uses of knowledge that Milton built into his poem works ultimately to confirm his own artistic practice which depends upon the tension between certainty and doubt. Thus the dangers of Galileo's undertaking signalled in the cautionary phrases— "yet never saw," "less assured"—are the poet's dangers too, a jeopardy he acknowledges when, "escaped the Stygian pool," he seeks for ways to express holy light unblamed.

If the astronomer's dangers are the poet's, so, too, are his ambitions[17]—to make the universe manifest, to show creation celebrating the deity both lyrically and speculatively. The poet, however, unlike the astronomer, need not choose among competing world systems, and not simply because of his instinct for plenitude in contrast to the scientist's requirement of parsimony, as Robert Hinman described the choice in a discussion of Cowley's use of the new science.[18] For the problematizing of knowledge is not an unfortunate result but the essential condition of the poem's undertaking. Clearly Galileo's discoveries provided a source of expanded imaginative possibilities in their opening of the poem's space, but, even more crucially, they offered a means for the human actors in the poem to define their identity as a function of their search for ways to understand their universe. Such inquiry may be constrained by the recollection of Herbert's fleet astronomer, but it is also empowered by the abundance of imagination invested in "thinking in astronomy." Thus to the question, does the telescope baffle or enable the poem's visionary enterprise, the answer must be that it enables it precisely because it baffles it.

The phrase "thinking in astronomy" brings us back to Milton's recollection of his meeting with Galileo, a scene which is no doubt risky

---

[17] Harris also makes this point: "In the contrast between Dante entering the *selva oscura* at the height of his political fortunes and writing the *Divine Comedy* in poverty and exile, between Galileo the astronomer and Galileo the prisoner, Milton, who knew and compared at least two different editions of Boccaccio's *Vita di Dante*, found a pattern for the figure of the poet in *Paradise Lost*" (27). However, he argues that it was the "casus Galilei," not Galileo's science, that was important for Milton. Indeed, he suggests that the "Tuscan artist" is a Satanic image (16), that it does not refer to Galileo in particular but to Florentine astronomers in general.

[18] Robert Hinman, *Abraham Cowley's World of Order* (Cambridge, Mass.: Harvard Univ. Press, 1960), 37.

to invoke but one which is still, I suggest, a felt presence in the text. For it is not only Adam and Eve who have to negotiate the slippery fit between memory and speculation; Milton has to as well, particularly the memory of Galileo, musical son of a musical father, blind and under house arrest, yet still seeking to express his view of God's light "un-blamed," as Milton remembers it some twenty five years later, himself now old and "in darkness, and with dangers compast round." But the political and biographical resonances of the memory do not provide the only link between the two. It is more nearly the similarity of their intellectual projects that locates the Galileo presence in the poem.

As Bloom has argued, although "Milton and Galileo are late, they see more and more significantly" than their precursors.[19] In my read-ing, the crucial precursor is Dante, Galileo serving as a marker of difference. If Dante's pilgrim was given Aristotle, as redacted by Bea-trice, in order to make sense of his world, Adam is given the telescope and allowed to use it even at his peril. We are given the telescope too. That it is, in the first instance, trained simultaneously on Satan and the moon need not diminish it any more than its association with Raphael's vision need validate it. Certainly its use is qualified in book 5, but both poet and reader require it to register the magnitude of Raphael's flight (itself an index of God's intentions towards his newly created). That angels can see further than scientists or poets is, after all, no news.

Concordia University

---

[19] Bloom, 133.

DONALD FRIEDMAN

# Galileo and the Art of Seeing

W
E KNOW VERY LITTLE ABOUT MILTON'S encounter with
Galileo; but, understandably, his readers have inferred a
great deal. Their meeting could have taken place during
one of Milton's sojourns in Florence, in the late summer of 1638 or the
spring of 1639; but even that possibility was the object of a famous
challenge by S. B. Liljegren many years ago, on the twofold ground that
Milton made no mention of the meeting until some years later, omitting
mention of it in a number of writings seemingly more pertinent than
*Areopagitica*, and because Milton was not trustworthy (an argument he
based largely on the conviction that the poet had falsified the evidence
in accusing King Charles of plagiarism in *Eikon Basilike*).[1] The latter
charge has been adequately refuted; but the absence of any mention of
the Arcetri visit by Milton, Galileo, or their friends in any surviving
document remains puzzling, especially since, in a letter to Lukas Holste
written from Florence, Milton at least refers to other Italians whose
acquaintance distinguished his visit to Rome.[2]

---

[1] S. B. Liljegren, *Studies in Milton* (Lund, 1918), 3–36. Liljegren also charged that
it would have been exceedingly difficult for Milton to obtain access to Galileo at these
times; but Marjorie Nicolson, among others, has offered arguments and evidence to
counter Liljegren's assertions. There is a convenient summary of the debate in the
footnote to the lines in *Areopagitica* which mention the visit, to be found on page 538
of volume 2 of CPW. All citations of Milton's prose will be to this edition.

[2] CPW 1:332–36. In "Galileo as Symbol: The 'Tuscan Artist' in *Paradise Lost*,"
*Annali dell'Istituto e Museo di Storia della Scienza di Firenze* 10, 2 (1985): 3–29, Neil
Harris argues that while Milton probably did visit Galileo at Arcetri (he cites a mention
by Carlo Dati of "*un Cavaliere Oltromontano ricco non meno de' Beni di Fortuna, che di
Virtù,*" who behaved as if his utmost desire was to meet the astronomer), the phrase
in *Paradise Lost* (1.288), "Tuscan Artist" should not be understood necessarily as a
periphrasis for Galileo, because some of its associations are Satanic, as, for example,
Fiesole's being to the north of Florence. Harris recognizes the pervasive ambivalence of
Milton's view of Galileo's work, however.

We may never know whether the meeting ever did take place; and even if it did, we may never know more than we do now about what the two discussed, what their impressions were of each other, whether Milton was allowed to look through Galileo's telescope—even the inadequate and outdated instrument we have learned he then had at hand[3]—about all these things, we know almost nothing. But about the encounter between the two much can be said, if only because of the fact that Milton chose either to make the effort to secure access to the aged philosopher or to imagine a meeting between them. And if the latter, he imagined the experience so vividly that Galileo could serve eventually both as a nexus of an argument in a prose treatise written some five years after the Italian journey, and as a rich and various exemplum in an epic poem written perhaps twenty years afterward. We must also consider that Galileo is the only historical personage from Milton's era who is mentioned by name in *Paradise Lost*, a well-known fact whose interpretation may bear on the meaning of that encounter to the poet.

Galileo first appears in the epic pronominally, so to speak, as "the Tuscan artist"; and it is less well known—or at least less frequently noted—that the word "artist" occurs only here in the poem. In fact, it is the only occurrence of the word in the entire canon of Milton's English poems. It is also a word that he used altogether only three times in all his prose writings, and never after the composition of *Tetrachordon*.[4] The arts were, however, always much on his mind, and the characterizations of the liberal, mechanical, and mental arts in his works vary tellingly according to period, genre, and rhetorical situation and purpose. But about the artist himself, the figure and embodiment of those skills, intuitive graces, and understandings that Milton included in his supple definition of art, he seems to have felt, if not mere ambivalence, then a hesitant uncertainty that expressed deeper feelings of conflict and obscured identification. What does it mean, then, that two decades after

---

[3] In a letter to Fulgenzio Micanzio written from Arcetri on November 11, 1637, Galileo refers to his having by him only "il mio antico e scopritore delle novità celesti" (Galileo, *Opere*, Edizione Nazionale, ed. A. Favaro et al. [Florence, 1890], 17:220); cited in Harris, 14.

[4] My authorities are: *A Concordance to Milton's English Poetry*, ed. William Ingram and Kathleen Swaim (Oxford: Clarendon Press, 1972); and *A Concordance to the English Prose of John Milton*, ed. Laurence Sterne and Harold H. Kollmeier, Medieval & Renaissance Texts & Studies, vol. 35 (Binghamton, NY, 1985).

their physical encounter in Florence, and several years after the English poet entered into that same blindness which had overtaken the Italian scientist shortly before that meeting, Galileo emerged again from Milton's memory as "the Tuscan artist"?

For the otherwise-uncorroborated report of the Florentine visit in *Areopagitica* is adduced as part of the case against licensing prior to publication, and specifically in defense both of the ability of "the common people" to resist erroneous or scandalous argument, and of the powers of the learned ministry to thus educate and nurture their hearers. Lest his putative parliamentary auditors think the complaint of the learned against external interference with the newly-established freedom of publication shallow and self-serving, Milton recalls the pleasure he derived from the envious remarks of his Italian colleagues, who thought of England as a place of "*Philosophic freedom.*" He notes with slightly ironic and perhaps forced optimism that he sublimated his knowledge of the "Prelaticall yoak" under which England was then "groaning" in "a pledge of future happiness," since "other Nations" were so certain of the soundness of English liberty.[5] The climactic demonstration of the destructive power of censorship to damp the glory of the mind of a nation is Galileo, imprisoned by the Inquisition "for thinking in Astronomy otherwise than the Franciscan and Dominican licensers thought." Whether Galileo told Milton more of the tangled details of his trial, abjuration, and condemnation, and whether he knew the precise nature of the dispute or of the strange history of the Bellarmine documents,[6] it is clear that for his own polemic purposes Milton presents Galileo as the victim of an exercise of institutional power as absurd as it is immoral, an attempt bound to fail in the end, but capable of interrupting the work of individual and national reformation damagingly.

There is an irony that underlies the passion of his defense of the

---

[5] *Areopagitica*, in CPW 1:537–38.

[6] Recently Pietro Redondi, in *Galileo Heretico*, translated as *Galileo Heretic* by Raymond Rosenthal (Princeton: Princeton Univ. Press, 1987), has argued that Galileo's condemnation was based ultimately on his speculations about atomist doctrines and consequently on their implications for the dogmatics of the eucharist. Redondi adduces Vatican documents from the 1616 examination of Galileo to support his claim. He is not able, however, to explain fully the nature of Bellarmine's instructions to Galileo at that time concerning the allegedly heretical status of his Copernican arguments.

liberty of speculation, nonetheless. It is nearly a critical commonplace that until his trip to Italy, and in some senses throughout his poetic career, Milton was relatively untouched and perhaps unengaged by the genuinely revolutionary implications of developments in cosmology, astronomy, physics, and mechanics which we associate with the work of Kepler, Galileo, Gilbert, and, from a slightly different perspective, Copernicus. As commentators since Addison have pointed out, the cosmology of Milton's early poems and scholastic prose is fairly serenely Ptolemaic, not to say Aristotelian; his metaphors, images and analogic arguments show little impress of Copernican theory, inhabiting the geocentric universe of nested spheres quite comfortably.[7] It is equally a commonplace that the familiar "dialogue on astronomy" between Adam and Raphael in book 8 of *Paradise Lost*, while it exhibits an informed grasp not only of Copernican/Keplerian concepts but also of specific and crucial observations of Galileo, does not move to resolve the dispute between the two *Massimi Sistemi* which the astronomer had epitomized in the dialogue written in 1631.[8] Rather, it presents them only as possible explanations of what may be observed of the heavens from the perspective of earthborn men, and ends with the exhortation to "be lowly wise," since "heaven is ... too high / To know what passes there," and above all, because "to know / That which before us lies in daily life, / Is the prime wisdom."[9]

To be sure, Raphael's well-intended (indeed, God-sent) counsel to censor freedom of thought (which in this context is to be understood as the tendency of "the mind or fancy ... to rove / Unchecked"),[10] is not to be confused with Milton's own putative stand in the controversy between the traditional and the new cosmologies.[11] But it is something

---

[7] Addison's remarks can be found in *Spectator*, no. 297, for February 9, 1712. Similar judgments are rendered by Marjorie Nicolson in *Science and Imagination* (Ithaca: Cornell Univ. Press, 1956), 82–83; F. R. Johnson, *Astronomical Thought in Renaissance England* (Baltimore: Johns Hopkins Univ. Press, 1937); A. H. Gilbert, "Milton and Galileo," *SP* 19 (1922): 154; Kester Svendsen, *Milton and Science* (Cambridge, Mass.: Harvard Univ. Press, 1956), 237.

[8] *Dialogo di Galileo Galilei Linceo ... sopra i due Massimi Sistemi del Mondo Tolemaico, e Copernicano*, translated by Stillman Drake as *Dialogue Concerning the Two Chief World Systems—Ptolemaic and Copernican* (Berkeley and Los Angeles: Univ. of California Press, 1953); hereinafter cited as *Dialogue*.

[9] *PL* 8.172–73, 193–95. All citations of Milton's poetry will be to Fowler.

[10] *PL* 8.188–89. This characterization is, of course, Adam's.

[11] Barbara Lewalski, in *"Paradise Lost" and the Rhetoric of Literary Forms* (Prince-

of a puzzle that in choosing to introduce the matter of the dispute into the epic (and in considerable astronomical detail), he chose to articulate it as an opposition between conventional Ptolemaic description and a generalized Copernican hypothesis, reinforced by some of the more recent observational discoveries. The puzzle derives from the fact that an informed reader like Milton must inevitably have known that the argument had for some time been between the heliocentric theory of Copernicus and the bipartite geo- and heliocentric account of Tycho Brahe, whose mathematical demonstrations satisfied the requirements and saved the appearances as completely as did those of Copernicus and Kepler.[12]

Nor is it likely that Milton could have been unaware of the state of the debate; as F. R. Johnson showed convincingly fifty years ago, citing Digges and Harriot prominently among a host of other amateurs and scholars, the issues between the two competing systems were well known and vigorously addressed in England from the mid-sixteenth century on.[13] Their persistence is evident in Hobbes's visit to Galileo in 1635, Henry More's Copernican rhapsodics in "Psychathanasia," and in the founding stages of the Royal Society. The young Milton, in short, while basking in the admiration of the Italian Neoplatonic academies, and in the consciousness of the superiority of English liberties—in whose defense he was about to give up his plans for travel to Sicily and Greece and return to take up the work of his left hand in the pamphlet wars of the 1640s—saw Galileo primarily as a fallen hero in the wars of free scientific speculation. But the fundamental issues

---

ton: Princeton Univ. Press, 1985), 46–50, argues that Raphael's purpose is not to "demonstrate and defend a theory, but rather to help Adam discover . . . the terms that should govern scientific inquiry into the cosmos."

[12] B. Rajan, in *"Paradise Lost" and the Seventeenth-Century Reader* (London: Chatto and Windus, 1947), 152–53, notes Milton's apparent ignorance of the Tychonic theory with some severity; but Fowler, in his footnote to *PL* 8.117–22, finds evidence in Raphael's speech, 85–114, that Milton recognizes Tycho's contributions. A rather obvious explanation of Milton's choices would seem to lie in his knowledge of and homage to Galileo's *Dialogue*; Grant McColley, in "The Astronomy of *Paradise Lost*," *SP* 34 (1937): 209–47, comments on Milton's grasp of contemporary astronomical discussion, while Alan Gilbert, in "Milton and Galileo" (see above, n. 7), adduces numerous comparisons between the dialogue between Raphael and Adam and the exposition in Galileo's *Dialogue*.

[13] *Astronomical Thought in Renaissance England*, chapters 6, 8, 9.

over which those wars were being fought had not at this point engaged his moral imagination. He had probably not yet grasped, for example, the full significance of Galileo's opposition to the assumptions of an Aristotelian cosmology that insisted on ontological distinctions between the sub- and superlunary worlds. But they were assumptions that he would himself discard in imagining a universe made of "one first matter all."[14] For in Milton's mature arguments for the fundamental goodness of matter, his adherence to the doctrine of creation from out of divine substance rather than to the orthodox tenet of creation *ex nihilo*, and in what Christopher Hill has characterized as his participation in the belief in mortalism,[15] one can discern the basis for a sympathetic understanding of the reasons for Galileo's struggle against the physics of Aristotelian cosmology. That cosmology, circumscribed by its own fundamental assumption of a finite universe, could not account for change or motion except as a characteristic state of an object, and had to define that state in relation to an inherent teleology. It was therefore qualitative in its analyses, and tied to the data provided by immediate sense experience. Plato had seen that the cosmos could be understood in other terms, primarily those of mathematical, or at least conceptual, abstractions; but the consequence was a field of inquiry that was necessarily static, and one in which the objects of sense and the forms that gave them their real definitions were detached from each other in ways that could not be bridged by empirical investigation.

Galileo's daring venture was to imagine a dynamics in which physical realities could be submitted to mathematical analysis, thus allowing him to study the behavior of objects in the world as examples of quantities in relation to each other and to general laws of motion and stasis. As historians of science have often observed,[16] Galileo took his inspiration from Archimedes in his reliance on hypothesis: that is, the proce-

---

[14] *PL* 5.472.

[15] See *Milton and the English Revolution* (New York: Penguin Books, 1979), 317-23; subsequently (324-33) Hill discusses the historical antecedents and the contemporary analogues of Milton's ideas on the nature of material creation.

[16] Cf. Ernst Cassirer, "Galileo's Platonism," in *Studies and Essays in the History of Science and Learning, Offered in Homage to George Sarton* (New York: Henry Schuman, 1946), 277-97; Rene Dugas, *Mechanics in the Seventeenth Century*, trans. F. Jaquot (Neuchatel, Switzerland: Editions du Griffon, 1958), 18 ff.; Alexandre Koyré, "Galileo and Plato," *JHI* 4 (1943): 400-428; Pietro Redondi, *Galileo Heretic*, 65.

dure by which a natural philosopher could reason from states unknown in nature to known conditions of physical behavior, through Galileo's chosen technique of "putting questions" to the objects. His unique contribution was to intuit the potential consequences of introducing the concept of the relativity of motion into the contemplation of the heavens. Although his imagination was stirred by the possibility of understanding celestial motion through the application of mathematical law, the inescapable effect of such an application was to assert the ontological integrity of a universe hitherto divided by *a priori* qualitative distinctions.[17] Henceforth every advance in the understanding of the behavior of terrestrial objects carried with it implications for the understanding of the behavior of celestial bodies; thus the conceptual distance between the heavens and the earth was progressively diminished. A further consequence was that the qualitative valences of change and stability were also affected, and so, therefore, was the observer's sense of the true relationship between the planet from which he viewed the stars and sun and those objects of his surveillance. Insofar as Galileo made it more nearly possible to believe that the earth and the stars were governed by a single set of principles of motion, his discoveries and arguments spoke for an ontology consistent with Milton's view of the "one first matter" from which "all" was made.[18]

But it is doubtful that by 1638 Milton's thinking about such matters had been articulated fully enough to grasp the implications of Galilean mechanics. It is conceivable, too, that Milton's image of Galileo as a martyr in the wars of truth had to develop and gain vividness over the years between his trip to Italy and the publication of *Areopagitica*,

---

[17] Cf. A. Koyré, "L'apport scientifique de la Renaissance," in *Etudes d'Histoire de la Pensée Scientifique* (Paris: Presses Universitaires de France, 1966), 47: "Galilée est peut-être le premier esprit qui ait cru que les formes mathématiques étaient réalisées effectivement dans le monde" ("Galileo was, perhaps, the first thinker to believe that mathematical forms are actually realized in the world").

[18] Stillman Drake, in *Galileo at Work* (Chicago: Univ. of Chicago Press, 1978), 164, explains Galileo's rejection of the Tychonic cosmological system (which could explain the phases of Venus, as the Ptolemaic system could not) on the grounds that to suppose that the sun possessed power to move other planets while the earth did not was to "regard heavenly bodies as made of some different substance and regulated by different laws than those on earth." Galileo, against philosophers within the Aristotelian tradition, "contended that the only sound way to reason about the heavenly bodies was by analogy with terrestrial experience."

because the aura surrounding the ill and aged man he visited at Arcetri was dimmed to some extent by the irreducible facts of his abjuration and surrender to the dictates of the Inquisition. However harsh and uncomprehending Milton felt the church to be in its insistence on controlling natural philosophical inquiry by institutional dogma, he was also presented with the facts that the object of its intellectual tyranny was "imprisoned" in his own house, free to conduct experiments, to correspond, and to publish his scientific findings; although, to be sure, he was subject always to the constraints imposed by the Holy Office on any utterances in support of Copernican theory. Moreover, the young poet who had dramatized only four years earlier his passionate belief that even though the "corporal rind" be "immanacled" the "freedom of the mind" cannot be touched,[19] was confronted in Galileo (as figure or person) with the paradox of the age's most daring and unfettered intellect having betrayed that daring and assumed the mind's fetters, if only in public and for a moment. It is not altogether surprising, then, that it took some years for Milton to transmute Galileo into a tutelary genius of the Reformation of thought and belief to which his early pamphlets are dedicated.

The poet of *Paradise Lost* saw the meanings surrounding Galileo's life and work somewhat differently, although he never lost the sense of the complexity of their evaluation. Every allusion in the poem to Galileo and to his major discoveries, although clearly intended still to contribute to a sense of intellectual courage, its motives and implications, is also shadowed by implied doubts, or at least uncertainties, about the substance of scientific hypotheses, the validity of empirical observation, and particularly about the spiritual and psychic sources of invention. Milton's similes are notoriously multivalent, serving often to illuminate multiple perspectives on an ostensible subject. For example, when Raphael pauses at the gate of heaven before undertaking his didactic errand to Eden in book 5, his view of the earth is utterly unobstructed, so clear that he can see the cedars crowning the hill of Paradise. By comparison, the epic voice tells us, "the glass / Of Galileo, less assured, observes / Imagined lands and regions in the moon."[20] Apart from noticing how nicely Milton has balanced the apposition of the word

---

[19] A *Masque presented at Ludlow Castle (Comus)*, Fowler, 663–65 (*Poems*, 209).
[20] *PL* 5.261–63.

"assured" between Galileo and his telescope, we should remember that "confident," "certain," "sure of oneself," were lesser meanings at the time than "secure," "safe," "proved to be valid," and even "pledged" or "covenanted."[21] It is not only that Galileo, dealing in hypotheses and empirical observation, is less sure of his data and their meaning than is the angelic intellect, but also that his work is less intrinsically bound to the laws of nature than is Raphael's, even though its theories may coincide with truth.

Galileo had argued, in his persona as Salviati in the *Dialogue*, that although the human intellect is radically inadequate with regard to its understanding of "the multitude of intelligibles" (what he refers to as *extensive* understanding), in certain respects it can be thought to grasp a proposition with the certainty normally attributed to "Divine intellect." These propositions are understood, he says, "*intensively*," and among such propositions are mathematical hypotheses and proofs; for in comprehending them the human mind "succeeds in understanding necessity."[22] This is one of the arguments that was condemned by the papal commission charged with examining the *Dialogue*; nor is it difficult to see why. However guarded and selective Galileo is in making his point, that point is essentially an assertion that the created intellect can at times grasp reality with the fullness and depth of the intellection of God. That he finds this equivalence, albeit not solely, in the abstract propositions of mathematics is also, however, a sign of the measure of inherent instability that colors Galileo's evaluation of sense experience and *its* role in experimentation. It is that instability—what some students of Galileo have called "the ambiguity that was characteristic of [his] work as productive scientist"[23]—that Milton reflects in this passage. Thus the Tuscan artist sees "Imagined lands" in the moon, perhaps because he imagines them, or because the telescope presents images of them, or because his readers and believers imagine them, or because, finally, others have imagined them and Galileo has succeeded in observing them truly. Milton resolves this tangle no more definitively than Raphael decides between the two great systems of cosmology. What is at

---

[21] *OED*, s.v. A, l, 3, 5.

[22] *Dialogue*, 103.

[23] Cf. *New Perspectives on Galileo*, ed. Robert Butts and Joseph Pitt (Dordrecht and Boston: D. Reidel, 1978), vii.

stake for the poet, nevertheless, is the criterion of true judgment in adjudicating between the claims of perception and the claims of the imagination, which in the epic are tied always to the powers of inspiration, the gift of heaven or of the muse.

It seems to be clear, in any case, that the mists of doubt that surround the figure of the astronomer in this passage have gathered since we met him first in book 1, where, in one of the similes whose treacheries have been so skillfully exposed by Stanley Fish,[24] Satan's shield is compared to the moon, "whose orb / Through optic glass the Tuscan artist views / At evening from the top of Fesole, / Or in Valdarno, to descry new lands, / Rivers or mountains in her spotty globe."[25] Here the suggestion of possible bad faith, or at least of the mistaking of the willed for the rational, the imagined for the real, is concentrated in the single word, "to." Either Galileo has viewed the moon to the effect of having discovered new lands resembling those of his own planet, or he has devised experiments in optics so as to find something hitherto unknown. The latter possibility describes with remarkable accuracy the empirical procedure characteristic of Galileo's research; for, like the philosophical astronomers who were his immediate predecessors and contemporaries, he did not proceed inductively. His great discoveries in mechanics, for instance, flowed from the combined energies of his certainty that the phenomena of nature appeared in forms that might be understood, and his cumulative belief that it was essential to ask questions of those phenomena in a "language" that would elicit answers in those forms. (In many instances that language was mathematical.) Thus, typically, Galileo did not follow the Baconian model which has become the paradigm of modern experimental investigation, in which observations are accumulated until the data are sufficient to provide grounds for inferences that may reasonably explain recurrent behaviors. Rather, Galileo constructed by reason an explanation of phenomenal events that conformed to his ideas of physical laws, and then designed an experiment to test his explanation.[26]

---

[24] Most notably in *Surprised By Sin*; see 22–37 and passim.

[25] *PL* 1.287–91.

[26] See Cassirer, "Galileo's Platonism," 292. Cassirer attempts to explain the nature of Galileo's adoption of Platonic mathematical thought by describing it as a "physical Platonism": i.e., one in which a "logic of motion" could be constructed through the use of mathematics which Plato had seen, rather, as a way of abstracting reality from

This method gave him access to aspects of physical reality which would otherwise have been "invisible," since the conditions that test and reveal the laws that govern them do not occur in nature. That is, to understand the law of free fall it was necessary to imagine a body moving along a plane tangential to a sphere; but no measurements taken in an actual experiment could have yielded the necessary results because perfect planes and perfect spheres do not exist, except in the mathematical imagination. Galileo did free himself from governing Aristotelian concepts of motion to the extent of realizing the possibility of indefinite motion uninterrupted by an external force. But he failed to grasp the laws of inertia because he could not imagine infinite motion in a straight line, bound as he was still by the concept of perfect circularity as the basic form of the cosmos, and therefore as the necessary course of such motion.

So when Milton sets "the Tuscan artist" on "the top of Fesole / Or in Valdarno, to descry new lands," he presents an action in which the ideas of control and intent are involved in which ways that are deeply problematic. For "descry," both traditionally and contemporaneously with Milton, carried more strongly than "to see from a distance" the connotations of revealing or betraying (the word was still in touch with one of its roots in "crying out"), particularly something that it is unwise to discover.[27] The simile rehearses and intensifies our sense of the potential dangers of viewing by clashing the venerable name of the moon with its new description as the "spotty globe." Furthermore, it glances toward another danger, that of failing to distinguish between

---

the physical world of sense perception. He goes on to point out that Galileo referred more characteristically to the *Meno* than to the more widely-relied on *Timaeus* because in the former dialogue Socrates resorts to *hypotheses* in the construction of rational argument. Cassirer argues, further, that Galileo, while adopting Plato's method of "problematic analysis," grants it higher ontological status because of his discovery that physical principles may be true descriptions of natural laws even though they cannot be observed in actual occurrences in nature. Hans Blumenberg, while arguing that the views of Cassirer (and others) on Galileo's Platonism require severe modification, nevertheless assumes something like Cassirer's account of Galilean method when he says that "Behind [Galileo's] discoveries we see not the sober industry of the devoted experimenter who keeps on increasing his body of data until it surrenders its hidden formula to him, but rather the speculative anticipation that places its trust in nature's use of absolutely simple means to achieve its effects." Cf. *The Genesis of the Copernican World*, trans. Robert M. Wallace (Cambridge, Mass.: MIT Press, 1987), 407.

[27] *OED*, s.v. I, 2, c.

imposing an interpretive schema on the object of investigation and inventing the experiment—the "question"—that will force it to reveal its inner truths.

Milton's complicated view of the viewer is also revealed in the periphrasis, "the Tuscan artist." Almost all of the meanings of "artist" we have inherited appeared during the late Renaissance, from the 1590s to the middle of the seventeenth century; and in the generation of those meanings we can perceive the eddying cultural attitudes that are reflected, in part, in the figuration of Galileo in *Paradise Lost*. The first appearance of the artist as a master of all the liberal arts—a philosopher—is almost exactly contemporaneous with its first use in describing the skilled performer—the practical man as distinguished from the theorist. By a similar token, the alchemist is first called an artist by early Jacobeans, and the mechanic craftsman first by the subjects of Charles I. By the year of the king's execution the word has come to mean the cunning and untrustworthy master of artifice. But no one identifies a scientist as an artist until 1667—that is, until Milton does so in the first edition of *Paradise Lost*, in the passage in book 1 under discussion.[28] I suggest that in that locution he distills the attitudes—the admiration and apprehension, the assertion of empiric clarity and perceptual fragility—that the late English Renaissance focused on the new science.

Whatever the nature of the change in Milton's view of Galileo between his sympathetic memoir in *Areopagitica* and the less perspicuous images in the late epics, it cannot be accounted for wholly by considerations of genre, rhetorical situation, or didactic context. Northrop Frye remarked some years ago that Galileo seems to "symbolize for Milton the gaze outward on human nature, the speculative reason that searches for new places, rather than the moral reason that tries to create a new state of mind."[29] I think that is only part of the truth reflected in the several images of the philosopher we have been examining; for the speculative reason that Milton praises implicitly in the prose treatise is indeed parallel to the moral reason, and above all in its desire to create a new state of mind. Although at the time of the visit to

---

[28] *OED*, s.v. I, 1; II, 4, a; I, 3, b; II, 5; IV, 9; I, 2. Galileo himself, in a letter written to Antonio de Ville in 1635, used the phrase, *artisti scientifici*; the editors of the National Edition of the *Opere* gloss this usage as referring to "*professori delle scienze.*" Cf. Arthos, 45 n. 12.

[29] *The Return of Eden* (Toronto: Univ. of Toronto Press, 1965), 58.

Arcetri Milton may not yet have fully appreciated the bases of the conflict between the great systems, it is unlikely that he remained uninstructed in the significance of the relation between mathematics and the cosmology, the physics, and the celestial mechanics of Copernicus, Kepler, and Galileo. It is equally unlikely that he would have failed to perceive during his interview with the blind astronomer—let alone upon reading his recent dialogue or discussing both with his Italian hosts— what Alexandre Koyré has characterized as Galileo's intellectual foundations in Platonic philosophy.[30] Nor is it easy to believe that Milton would have been unable to grasp the bearing of assertions such as that in *Il Saggiatore* (1623), speaking of the book of the universe: this grand book "cannot be understood unless one first learns to comprehend the language and read the letters in which it is composed. It is written in the language of mathematics, and its characters are triangles, circles, and other geometric figures without which it is humanly impossible to understand a single word of it; without these, one wanders about in a dark labyrinth."[31] There are implications here that Galileo did not fully draw, implications for the relation between terrestrial and celestial mechanics, and thence ultimately for the desacralization of the heavens. But the significance of these lines for Milton's thinking lies in Galileo's assertion that both the visible and invisible universes are governed by pre-existent laws, to express which the intellect devises symbolic languages; and, further, that the visible world is at the same time a guide to the understanding of the cosmos and a sign of the existence of an order of things beyond the power of sight, but not beyond the power of imaginative projection and analysis.[32]

The dark labyrinth of which Galileo wrote was one that Milton knew well. He invoked it in the first work of his left hand upon his

---

[30] Besides "Galileo and Plato," see "Galileo and the Scientific Revolution of the Seventeenth Century," *Philosophical Review* (1943): 333-48; and *Galileo Studies* (Atlantic Highlands, NJ: Humanities Press, 1978), 108, 159.

[31] Quoted in the translation by Stillman Drake, in his *Discoveries and Opinions of Galileo* (Garden City, NY: Anchor Books, 1957), 238.

[32] Blumenberg is excellent on the ambivalent impact of the telescope, which at the same time extended the capabilities of the senses and revealed the existence of a reality that escaped those capabilities. He characterizes this as a challenge to "the postulate of visibility," the traditional view according to which the intelligible must be present to the senses, which are reason's only access to reality. See *The Genesis of the Copernican World*, 642-43, and part 6, passim.

return from Italy, *Of Reformation*, when he compared the brightness and plainness of truth with the "darkness and crookedness" of the human intellect, filmed with ignorance and "blear with gazing on ... false glisterings." To repair the ruins of the Fall would be to fulfill the purpose for which, as he says, "The *Wisdome* of God created *understand-ing*, fit and proportionable to Truth the object, and of it, as the eye to the thing visible."[33] For Galileo, as for Kepler, and ultimately for Newton, that proportionableness was found in universal mathematical laws, deduced truths that transcended the particular variables of observation and guaranteed both their necessary adherence to an intelligible truth and the links between earthly and heavenly mechanics. Such views did indeed hold the potential for causing a revolution in thought; but Galileo believed he had found a way to show that the discoveries of the mind and the discoveries of the eye were more deeply consonant than imagined even in the theory of the spheres. Thus, the discoveries of the moons of Jupiter and the phases of Venus did not prove the heliocentric hypothesis; they existed because mathematical laws, which could not be at variance with revealed truth, showed that they must exist: the telescope simply made it impossible for those who could not read the language of celestial mechanics to claim that what was not seen was not there. The governing theory of the structure of the visible universe, about to be displaced, resisted unassimilable ideas of change and motion because its basic premiss of a finite, spherical cosmos tended to equate perfection with its root meaning of "completed," and therefore, with the immutable. Indeed, despite Galileo's revolutionary willingness to entertain new concepts of motion (and its corollary, change) in the heavens, his universe remained finite, possibly because he could not imagine infinite motion in any mode other than the circular, and thus could not arrive at the concept of infinite rectilinear motion, the key to the law of inertia and the new universe of Newtonian physics. Nevertheless, Galileo was able to break the links between the cosmology of circular perfection and the laws of motion; in the *Dialogue*, Salviati challenges the Aristotelian identification of circularity and immutability as indelible attributes of celestial perfection,[34] arguing with conscious

---

[33] CPW 1:566.
[34] Cf. *Dialogue*, 18, 58, 367–68; and Koyré, *Galilean Studies*, 222–23 n. 122. Koyré, 222, asks, on Galileo's behalf, "why should not the life and changability [*sic*] of

perversity that recent signs of change in the heavens would, on Aristotle's showing, prove that the heavens are not perfect.

Something of the same profundity of the impulse to redefine, to
reform, received doctrines of spiritual and formal excellence resonates in
Raphael's explanation to Adam (PL 5.524), that God has made him
"perfect, not immutable." It is clear that by the time he composed
Paradise Lost Milton had also shaped a theory of creation and what one
might call a teleological ontology. Change—defined as growth, or ascent,
or return to the Creator—is central to Raphael's account of the design of
the created universe, and to its purpose or providential end as God has
set it out before the understanding of angels and human beings. If, at
the end of time, God will again be "all in all," resuming the integrity of
his substance out of which has exfoliated all creation and all time, then
history—as Milton wants his characters and his readers to know—is
intended to be a record of mankind's steady climb back up the ladder
of perfection from which it fell at the moment of mistaken choice in the
garden of Eden. To the prelapsarian Adam, Raphael explains that it is
from the "one almighty" that "All things proceed, and up to him
return, / If not depraved from good, created all / Such to perfection."
The connection between change and perfection is made here explicitly,
as is its dependence on maintaining the rectilinear course of change
toward the goal of its origins.[35]

The poet and the philosopher shared a belief in the fundamental
intelligibility of a created, providential universe; they also were suspended in an intrinsicate web of feelings about the senses and their percep-
tions. Both beliefs are registered in Milton's allusions to Galileo in
Paradise Lost. What lends those passages a further dark glamor may be
the poet's consciousness of the profoundly spiritual resonances of the
mind of the revolutionary, empiric, heretic. And this is not to speak at
all of the multiple ironies of their common blindness, the light that
Milton prayed for and came to see by, and which, in the writing of
Paradise Lost, enabled him to see the meaning of the work which twenty
years before he had thought was only a blazing instance of liberty of

---

the sublunary world be ... a greater perfection than the frozen immobility of the
heavens?" In The Assayer (Discoveries and Opinions, 263), Galileo declares archly that
he cannot accept Aristotle's designation of heavenly forms as "noblest" because he has
never read "the pedigrees and patents of nobility of shapes."

[35] "Depraved" takes its force from pravus, i.e., crookedness.

thought darkened by ignorance and doctrinal prejudice. In the midst of his own darkness, he could recognize belatedly the companionable visionary mind which had seen through the telescope to a truth infinitely remote and infinitely bright.

University of California—Berkeley

WILLIAM SHULLENBERGER

# "Imprimatur": The Fate of Davanzati

ILTON'S PRIMARY ANXIETY IN *Areopagitica* is about the possibility of mind control. The pamphlet directs attention to the ways in which control of printing, the means of production of thought in post-Gutenberg pre-electronic culture, can force the conscience and imagination in such culture. We misread *Areopagitica* if we neglect its status as an unlicensed, *samizdat* text.[1] It projects us into intellectual and political settings where the publication of what we call "literature" entails risk to more than reputation. As I revise this essay in February of 1989, the Ayatollah Khomeini's recent order for the execution of Salman Rushdie, author of *The Satanic Verses*, is a bewildering reminder of such risk. *Areopagitica*'s proper companion texts might include Rushdie's novel, along with the work of Solzhenitsyn and the suppressed Russian writers, Orwell among English writers, and Czeslaw Milosz's *The Captive Mind*, which document "the forc't and outward union of cold, and neutrall, and inwardly divided minds" (A 551)[2] forewarned by Milton. The stupefaction of independent judgment

---

[1] Milton published *Areopagitica* in direct violation of the Licensing Order of 1643. Although Milton risked less with his tract than do the authors of the underground texts of the Soviet bloc in our time, that he published it illegally and addressed it to Parliament in the wake of vigorous public attention to and denunciation of *The Doctrine and Discipline of Divorce* suggests that Milton was risking government censure or punishment in a battle of the books of an entirely different order than the ones we tend to wage in the academy. Abbe Blum's essay on Milton's stance as author and licenser is the most recent exposition of the political and legal implications of his publishing *Areopagitica* without official license. Blum judiciously reviews previous treatments of the state of English publishing law in the interregnum and of Milton's tactics in response to it. Abbe Blum, "The Author's Authority: *Areopagitica* and the Labour of Licensing," in *Re-Membering Milton: Essays on the Texts and Traditions*, ed. Mary Nyquist and Margaret W. Ferguson (New York and London: Methuen, 1988), 74-96.

[2] All quotations from *Areopagitica*, cited parenthetically with A, are taken from

and originality, self-censorship, the institutionalized hypocrisy which Milosz calls "Ketman,"[3] social despair: modern totalitarian governments would achieve a bureaucracy efficient enough to operate a system of thought-abortion as thorough as that anticipated by Milton. In interregnum England too much was happening too fast for Milton's anxieties to be realized. Christopher Hill, in fact, describes the collapse of censorship in 1641 and the consequent explosion of political texts in the interregnum as the most important event in seventeenth-century English literature.[4] The dragon's teeth had been sown, and sprung up armed men (A 492), even by the time Milton was writing his pamphlet. His visionary optimism indicates Milton's recognition that the dissemination of texts could no more be reversed than the orbits of Copernicus. Nevertheless, the memory of intellectual servitude imposed by Stuart royal prerogatives through the Court of Star Chamber, only recently challenged and shattered, must have fed Milton's apprehension about what the new presbyters might attempt, should they become fully established in the machinery of power. Milton foresaw that the future of thought control would lie in the anonymity of a self-reinforcing bureaucracy, perhaps a bureaucratic spectre of the very Parliament to whose higher, Areopagitical, sense of mission he makes his appeal.

Milton projects his concern about the possibility of bureaucratic control of thought onto the map of recent Italian intellectual history, which he satirizes as a monstrous nightmare of ecclesiastical tyranny. The Counter-Reformation Catholic Church appears in Milton's writing as a workshop for systems of intellectual control. Milton alludes to three nearly contemporary Italians in formulating his argument against linguistic and imaginative repression: Sarpi, Galileo, and Davanzati. Sarpi, "padre Paolo," is honored for his *History of the Council of Trent*, as "the great unmasker of the *Trentine* Councel" (A 501), a champion of truth, a Venetian Abdiel whose narrative of Counter-Reformation abuse of power provides the format for Milton's own polemical history

---

CPW, vol. 2, ed. Ernest Sirluck. All quotations from *Of Reformation*, henceforth cited parenthetically with OR, are taken from CPW, vol. 1, ed. Don M. Wolfe and William Alfred.

[3] Czeslaw Milosz, *The Captive Mind*, trans. Jane Zielonko (New York: Vintage Books, 1981), 54-81.

[4] Christopher Hill, "Radical Prose in Seventeenth-Century England: From Marprelate to the Levellers," *EIC* 32 (1982): 95-118.

of censorship.[5] Galileo serves in the pamphlet as a chilling example of the Inquisition's power over truthful and original thought, a Samson in shackles, "grown old, a prisner to the Inquisition, for thinking in Astronomy otherwise then the Franciscan and Dominican licencers thought" (A 538).[6] But what of Bernardo Davanzati Bostichi? Davanzati's name appears in the middle of Milton's historical argument about the origin and development of licensing (A 504). In this pamphlet where words have such potency of life as to generate armed men, and men may yield up such potency of life as to become their own epitaphs, Davanzati—not his book, *Scisma d'Inghilterra*—is cited as an example of an officially sanctioned text. The very anonymity of reference is part of Milton's point about the way in which licensing drains the lifeblood of intellect from the work of writing, but the reference is worth closer scrutiny. *Areopagitica* parades its remarkable erudition with gusto and control; of its multitudinous references, none seems superfluous. Of all the possible texts marked with the papal *imprimatur*, why does Milton cite Davanzati in particular? How does Davanzati figure in the ideology and the imagery of *Areopagitica*?

A Florentine classicist and gentleman of letters, Davanzati (1529–1606) was a member of the Accademia degli Alterati; his pseudonym, "il Silente." Concerned with the development of contemporary spoken Italian as an instrument of literary expression, Davanzati translated Tacitus's *Annales* and other works into the vernacular. Davanzati studied Dante as a precursor for his own projects in the vernacular, but Tacitus became his model for a concise, vivid, direct style at odds with the prevailing florid mannerism of the academic prose of his period. Davanzati's history of the English Reformation through the death of Mary Tudor, first printed in 1602 and reissued in Florence in 1638, would very likely have caught Milton's attention during his stay in Florence.[7]

---

[5] Ernest Sirluck, "Milton's Critical Use of Historical Sources," *MP* 50 (1953): 226–31.

[6] Galileo's intellectual bondage may even be parodied in Milton's description of "5 Imprimaturs . . . seen together dialogue-wise in the Piatza of one Title page, complementing and ducking each to other with their shav'n reverences" (A 504). Leo Miller has suggested that this personification alludes to the unusually crowded verso of the title page of Galileo's important *Dialogo* on the Ptolemaic and Copernican world systems. Leo Miller, "The Italian Imprimaturs in Milton's Areopagitica," *Publications of the Bibliographical Society of America* 65 (1971): 345–55.

[7] Ettore Allodoli, *Giovanni Milton e l'Italia* (Prato: Tip. C. & G. Spighi, 1907), 82.

Fletcher has determined that Milton's citation of the 1638 licensing permissives corresponds to the frontispiece of the 1638 edition. He has also argued that Milton's reference to Francis Bryan as Henry VIII's "vicar of Hell" (A 518) derives from Davanzati's text.[8]

Davanzati's narrative is historical biography dominated by the story of Henry's attempt to pressure Pope Clement VII into an annulment of his marriage to Catherine of Aragon. The narrative recounts the blossoming of schism out of the lust of the king, the deceitful erotic and religious seductions of Anne Boleyn, the ruthless yet ultimately self-destructive quest for power by Wolsey, Cromwell, and Cranmer. Davanzati counterpoints the note of tragic degradation with his descriptions of the saintliness of Catherine, and the exemplary martyrdoms of Thomas More, John Fisher, "primai lumi d'Inghilterra" ("the first lights of England")[9] and other monastics and clerics who refused allegiance to the king when he broke unity with the true Church, established himself as the supreme head of the English Church, dissolved the monasteries and plundered their riches, and betrayed his people. Davanzati concentrates on the illegitimate and blasphemous relationship and marriage to Anne Boleyn, the erotic intrigue, the long delay through legal and theological examination of and debate over Henry's marriage to Catherine, the pious and steadfast scrupulosity of Pope Clement VII, who refused to bow to Henry's pressure, persuasion, and threats. After the fatal marriage to Anne, the rest of Henry's reign and the entirety of Edward's reign amounts to an anticlimactic playing out of those forces which Henry's original lust and greed, fed by the ambitions of his ministers, set in motion. Mary's reign is represented as a brief return to sanity and sanctity which God did not see fit to sustain:

> Per questi, o altri nostri peccati, o perche a Dio non paressero le enormezze d'Arrigo ben purgate con si lieve vapulazione, ecco che la Reina in capo a cinque anni e quattro mesi del suo regno mori: infelice, per non aver grazia, come d'Arrigo figliuola, di figliuoli: e lasciato alla sua emula il Reame, perche nella

---

[8] Harris Fletcher, "Milton and Henry VIII's 'Vicar of Hell'," *JEGP* 47 (1948): 387–89.

[9] Bernardo Davanzati Bostichi, *Scisma d'Inghilterra con Altre Operette* (Milan: Dalla Società Tipografica de Classici Italiani, 1807), 67. All references to Davanzati, henceforth cited parenthetically with D, will be to this edition.

Religione lo travagliasse, il Cardinal Polo Legato morì dopo lei dodici ore.                                                        (D 127)

For these, either other sins of ours, or because it did not seem to God that the enormities of Henry were well expiated with such light penance, behold that the queen at the end of the fifth year and fourth month of her reign died: unfortunate, not to have had the grace of children, being the daughter of Henry: and she left the kingdom to her rival [Elizabeth], because she had tormented her in religion, the Legate Cardinal Pole died twelve hours after her.

This is where Davanzati ends his narrative. The spare style and jerky cutting are not quite consonant with the theological implications of the tale he tells, of great, potentially tragic, individuals driven and destroyed by mean desires, and acting them out on the unsteady stage of European politics. There seem to be two narrative impulses at work in the *Scisma d'Inghilterra*. The one, for which Davanzati's Tacitean mode of understatement seems well suited, is a Raymond Chandler-like fable of bottomless human corruption. The other, which is not fully realized, is a sort of deuteronomic sacred history of human sin and divine punishment and restitution.

Much of the unevenness and sketchiness of Davanzati's narrative can be explained by its derivation. Davanzati's text is a condensed translation of the Latin *De origini ac progressu schismatis Anglicani*, written by the English Jesuit Nicholas Sanders (1530-1581). Educated at Winchester College and New College in Oxford, Sanders joined the exile community of English Roman Catholics in Louvain in early 1559, with the accession of Elizabeth to the English throne. Already respected enough as a man of letters to have been offered the post of Latin Secretary to Mary Tudor in 1557, Sanders in exile turned his considerable intellectual energies to support the cause of English Catholicism and to work for the dethronement of Elizabeth. In various writings and reports on the state of the Church in England, he proved to be so energetic and effective a polemicist for the Roman Church that he was on several occasions considered for a Cardinalate. In 1579, Sanders was commissioned by Pope Gregory XIII to lead an expeditionary force into Ireland, to stir up Catholic insurrection against the English government. After nearly two years of largely unsuccessful hit and run action, Sanders died as a fugitive in the Irish hills, his loss in skirmishing mourned as a terrible waste of intellect by his friends in exile: "Our Sanders is more to us than the whole of Ireland" (DNB, 749).

Sanders left his manuscript on the Reformation in England unfinished, with little more than notes on the state of the English Church under Elizabeth. The text was edited and enlarged by Edward Rishton, a priest in Douai who was also an exile from Elizabethan England; Rishton's major contribution was an extensive treatment of the sufferings of Catholic martyrs under Elizabeth. De origine ac progressu schismatis Anglicani, incorporating Rishton's additions, was published first in Cologne in 1585, then in Rome in 1586.[10] It was diffused extraordinarily rapidly throughout Europe. A French translation appeared in 1587.[11] In 1588, the Jesuit Pedro de Ribadeneira, a friend of Sanders as well as the friend and first biographer of Loyola, translated the history into Spanish, adding material he had gathered from Spanish sources and from his own experiences in England.[12] The first Italian version of Sanders's history was written by the Dominican Girolano Pollini and published in Florence in 1591 and in Rome in 1595.[13] De origine became, in effect, the definitive Counter-Reformation account of the emergence of the Church of England. It provides the basis not only for Davanzati's text, but for a number of other translations and adaptations appearing in various European languages throughout the seventeenth century.[14] When, in 1679, Gilbert Burnet undertook his massive apologetic history of the Reformation in England, he saw it as his principal task to rebut Sanders's more scandalous charges and thus to

---

[10] Thomas McNevin Veech, Dr. Nicholas Sanders and the English Reformation, 1530–1589 (Louvain: Bureaux du Recueil, Bibliotheque de l'Universitè, 1935), 234. All references to Nicholas Sanders's text, cited henceforth parenthetically with S, will be to De origine ac progressu schismatis Anglicani. Libri tres. Quibus historia continetur maxime ecclesiastica, annorum circiter sexaginta, lectu dignissima, nimirum, ab anno 21. regni Henrici Octavi, quo primum cogitare coepit de repudianda legitima uxore serenissima Catharina, usque ad hunc vigesimum octavum Elizabethae, quae ultima est eiusdem Henrici soboles. Aucti per Edouardum Rishtonum & impresi primum in Germania, nunc iterum locupletius & castigatius editi (Rome, 1586).

[11] G. Constant, La Reforme en Angleterre I. Le Schisme Anglican. Henri VIII (1509–1547) (Paris: Perrin & Co., Libraires-Editeurs, 1930), 327.

[12] Veech, 237.

[13] Constant, 326.

[14] Fletcher, 389. Thomas H. Clancy, S.J., Papist Pamphleteers: The Allen-Persons Party and the Political Thought of the Counter-Reformation in England, 1572–1615 (Chicago: Loyola Univ. Press, 1964), 16.

destroy Sanders's influence on European understanding of the English Church:

From whence it is come that in this age that author [Sanders] is in such credit, that now he is quoted with much assurance: most of all the writers, in the church of Rome, rely on his testimony as a good authority. The collectors of the general history of that age follow his thread closely, some of them transcribe his very words. One Pollini, a Dominican, published a history of the changes that were made in England, in Italian, at Rome, anno 1594, which he should more ingenuously have called a translation or paraphrase of Sanders's History: and of late more candidly, but no less maliciously, one of the best pens of France has been employed to translate him into their language, which has created such prejudices in the minds of many there, that our Reformation, which generally was more modestly spoken of, even by those who wrote against it, is now looked on by such as read Sanders, and believe him, as one of the foulest things that ever was.[15]

Davanzati's history is one of those about which Burnet complains that it "should more ingenuously have been called a translation or paraphrase," a condensed Italian transcription of Sanders; in fact, a close reading reveals nearly exact verbal parallels throughout.[16] If we exam-

---

[15] Gilbert Burnet, *History of the Reformation of the Church of England*, ed. Nicholas Pocock, 7 vols. (Oxford: Clarendon Press, 1865), 1:4. Sanders's account has even now not been quietly laid to rest, or left to be the subject of curiosity and disputation within the academy. A conservative Roman Catholic press in the United States in 1988 reprinted David Lewis's nineteenth-century translation with Lewis's introduction and notes. The publication is not a scholarly edition but a paperback reprint describing Sanders's book, in its jacket notes, as "as truly great sourcebook of information on the Protestant 'Reformation' in England, an essential book used by writers about the history of the 'Reformation.' . . . In all, *The Rise and Growth of the Anglican Schism* provides an intimate look into the lives and times of the unsavory characters who produced the disastrous Protestant 'Reformation' in England. It is a unique book that cannot be ignored by anyone interested in the complete and true story of that sad, sad event." References to the English translation of Sanders's book, henceforth cited parenthetically with L, will be to *The Rise and Growth of the Anglican Schism*, trans. and introduction, David Lewis (London: Burns and Oates, 1877; repr. Rockford, Ill.: TAN Books & Publishers, 1988).

[16] Veech (237) follows Constant's assertion (326) that Davanzati's account is in fact

ine as an example the one passage in Davanzati to which Milton alludes in *Areopagitica*, we can see how closely it is modeled on Sanders's original text. Following Sanders, Davanzati has just presented the highly charged recognition scene, in which it is revealed that Anne Boleyn is in fact Henry VIII's daughter. Thomas Boleyn, having discovered that his wife has given birth to a daughter while he has been on ambassadorial duty for two years in France, wishes to repudiate and divorce her. Boleyn remains unmoved by the entreaties of his wife, and even by the more forceful persuasions of the king's representatives, until his wife confesses on her knees "che il Re per sua infinita sollecitudine, e non altri, l'aveva ingenerata" ("that the King, and no other, through his constant solicitude, had produced her [Anne]"; D 24). The king, in his visits to the mother, began to notice her older daughter, Mary, and to draw her into the decadent circle of his court,

e domandando una volta Francesco Briano nato de'Boleni (di tutti li scelleratissimi cortigiani, onde era la corte piena, il piu fine) chi si giacesse con la madre, e poi con la figlia, che peccato farebbe? ripose: il medesimo, che a mangiarsi prima la gallina, e poi la pollastra. Disfacendosi il Re per le risa, disse: Ben se' tu mio Vicario dell'Inferno (gia era costui per lo suo miscredere detto Vicario dell'Inferno del Re), onde cosi poscia ognuno il chiamo. Il Re essendosi tenuta la madre, e l'una figlia detta Maria Bolena, anche a quest'altra, detta Anna, volto l'appetito.
(D 24-25)

Inter hos insignis quidam nepos extitit Franciscus Brianus, eques

---

derived from Ribadeneira. In light of the tight verbal parallelism that exists between Sanders's and Davanzati's narratives, I think that this assertion needs to be examined. For further consideration of the intertextual problem, see Pedro De Ribadeneyra, *Hystoria Ecclesiastica del Scisma Del Reino De Inglaterra, En la qual se tratan las cosas mas notables que han sucedido en aquel Reno tocantes a nuestra Santa Religion, desde que comenco, hasta la muerte de la Reyna de Escocia* (Madrid: Manuel de Lyra, 1589). On the basis of intitial observations, I did not find the argument for Davanzati's derivation of his text from Ribadeneira's compelling. But the task of editorial reconstruction, involving a close study of the lines of transmission of Sanders's narrative in the different European languages, would be a different, and much larger, project than this one. Because the foundation text of *Scisma d'Inghilterra* is Sanders's narrative, whether or not it is mediated to Davanzati by Ribadeneira, I will concentrate on the significance of parallels and differences in the texts of Davanzati and Sanders.

auratus, ex gente & stirpe Bolenorum. Ab illo Rex quodam tempore quaefuit, quale peccatu videretur, matrem primum deinde filiam cognoscere? Cui Brianus, omnino (inquit) tale, o Rex, quali gallinam primum, deinde pullum eius gallinaceum comedere. Quod verbu cum Rex magno risu accepisset, ad Brianum dixisse fertur: Ne, tu merito meus es inferni Vicarius. Brianus enim iam prius ob impietatem notissimam, vocabatur Inferni Vicarius, post hoc autem, & Regius inferni Vicarius. Rex igitur cum, & matrem prius, & postea filiam Mariam Bolenam pro cocubina tenuisset, demum ad alteram quoque filiam Annam Bolenam, animum adijcere coepit.                                  (S 24)

Among these was one distinguished profligate, Sir Francis Bryan, of the blood and race of the Boleyn. This man was once asked by the king to tell him what sort of a sin it was to ruin the mother and then the child. Bryan replied that it was a sin like that of eating a hen first and its chicken afterwards. The king burst forth into loud laughter, and said to Bryan, "Well, you certainly are my vicar of hell." The man had been long ago called the vicar of hell on account of his notorious impiety, henceforth he was called also the king's vicar of hell. The king, who had sinned before with the mother and the elder daughter, turned his thoughts now to the other daughter, Anne.     (L 24)

David Lewis's English translation of Sanders adequately represents Davanzati as well. Davanzati typically condenses the narrative through subordination and parenthesis, so as to emphasize the essentials of Sanders's narrative. This anecdote, to which Milton refers, is more than a bit of casual innuendo. It depicts a king whose sexual appetite is insatiable and indiscriminate. It draws the Boleyn women into the erotic and blasphemous cynicism of the Henrician court, and identifies a Boleyn, Francis Bryan, as a pre-eminent figure in its corruption. It establishes Sanders's major theme: the Henrician Reformation originated in obscenity, in the perversion of the blood relationships established by family and of the spiritual relationships established by true religion. Writing in exile under the threat of Elizabeth's continuing persecution of the faithful, Sanders has a personal stake in embarrassing and discrediting Anne Boleyn's daughter, Elizabeth, as well as her religious establishment. Thus the virulent scandal-mongering against Anne and her family, including the assertion that she was Henry's daughter, is a particularly bold and effective feature of Sanders's polemical history. Davanzati follows Sanders's schema but eliminates certain of its details and the larger polemic context of the history to which Sanders constantly refers. Consequently Davanzati's abbreviated account (D 24-28), seems strangely second-hand and patched together, lacking in thematic coherence but oddly sensationalistic, like a tabloid article about what really goes on behind the scenes in the royal family.

Aiming toward a concise, nearly journalistic account of the English Reformation, Davanzati mutes the polemic intensity of Sanders. He tends to subdue Sanders's stridently articulated theme of the providential action of a God who rewards martyrs and allows the ambitious to suffer their own self-destruction. In his "riduzione," Davanzati has foreshortened the historical treatment of all the events which follow Henry's marriage to Anne and the original schism, and edited the accounts of Catholic English martyrs in order to give a somewhat more impersonal stress to the unfolding of events, placing them more squarely in the context of European power conflicts than in the tropological pattern of human sin and divine response which organizes Sanders's narrative. A typical, yet perhaps the most important, instance of Davanzati's editorial excision of Sanders occurs when the conflict between Henry and Clement VII goes beyond the point of compromise or concession. After relating Henry's secret marriage to Anne (S 92-94), Sanders interjects a vehement denunciation of the unjust divorce of Catherine, the unnatural incestuous marriage to Anne, and the obscene religious heresies bred by these errors, then returns to the historical narrative by quoting Clement VII's sentence of excommunication (S 102-03), which becomes, in effect, the confirmation and seal of Sanders's theological judgment. This passage is the rhetorical climax of Sanders's legal, theological, and historical argument:

Quare cum Henricus contra naturae quodammodo legem, post matrem Annae Bolenae cognitam, ausus sit filiam in uxorem assumere: quam impudenter obtendit, se non ausum esse Catharinam retinere, ne in Deum peccaret? quam impudenter etiam praetexuit, se credidisse, quod Pontifex authoritatem non habuerit Catharinae nuptias permittendi? . . . Nec tantopere mirandum est, si aut homo peccet, aut cum in profundum venerit, contemnat. Illud est mirandum, illud stupendum, si hominum infinita millia, non suam, sed alienam libidinem & hyprocrisin, non tantum aequo animo ferant, sed etiam suspiciant, laudent, colant, & ita colant, ut supra hoc fundamentum, fidem, spem, salutatemque suam exaedificent.

Omnes enim Anglicani protestantes, Lutherani, Zuingliani, Calvinistae, Puritani, & Libertini, ceteraeque omnes haereticae pestes, quibus Patria nostra misere periit, has turpissimas ac incestuosas Henrici & Annae Bolenae nuptias adorant, velut fontem Evangelii sui, matrem Ecclesiae suae, originem suae fidei.... Verum quidem est, per has nuptias aditum vobis patefactum esse ad omnem haeresim, omnemque nequitiam. Sed o immensam Dei bonitatem; qui, quod haereses vestras non alio partu quam per tam nefandas nuptias in lucem exire permisit, eo ipso declaravit, illas turpissimarum tenebrarum filias esse, ne aliter quam per opera tenebrosa procreari potuisse.                    (S 96-98)

Henry, therefore, who, against the law of nature in a certain sense, dared to marry the daughter of the mother he had defiled, was simply shameless when he pretended that he durst not keep his wife Catherine because he feared to sin against God; shameless also when he feigned to believe that it was not in the power of the Pope to sanction his marriage with Catherine.... Nor is it to be much wondered at that a man should fall into sin, or that he should be contemptuous when he comes into the depths of it; but this is marvellous and astonishing, that multitudes of men should endure patiently, not their own lewdness, but that of another—not only endure it patiently, but respect it, praise and honour it, and honour it so far as to build upon it their belief, their hope and salvation.

Now, all English Protestants—Lutherans, Zuinglians, Calvinists, Puritans, and Libertines—honour the incestuous marriage of Henry and Anne Boleyn as the wellspring of their gospel, the mother of their Church, and the source of their belief.... Certainly it is true that this marriage has opened a door to every heresy and to every sin. Oh, the infinite goodness of God! He would not suffer these heresies of yours to come forth in any other way than through this incestuous marriage, thereby showing them to be the fruits of darkness, and that they could not be had but by deeds of darkness.                    (L 99-101)

Sanders's personal stake in the story is evident here; for him, the monstrous progeny of Henry's marriage is both the many-headed monster of the heretical English Church and the hypocritical and lethal Queen Elizabeth whom Sanders spent his life in exile seeking to discredit and depose. It is no wonder that Elizabeth sought the suppression abroad of at least one version of Sanders's history,[17] or that the English responded to Sanders by a politic and contemptuous silence.[18]

There is no translation or paraphrase of this crucial diatribe in Davanzati's narrative, for Davanzati consistently eliminates passionate and meditative commentary of this sort. Distanced personally and politically from the events which shaped the life of Sanders as well as his nation, and concerned with achieving a style "stringato, sobrio, conciso" (EI, 410), Davanzati thus reduces the typological inflections that make Sanders's story a highly personalized version of sacred history. Finally, Davanzati does not recount the bloody aftermath of the schism under Elizabeth as Rishton chronicles it; he rounds off the tale as he has begun it, abruptly, with the death of Mary, as if to acknowledge that the Anglican schism is implicitly complete when Catholicism's last hope of renewal in England is defeated. Although Davanzati, with a few elisions, follows Sanders's account of the deaths of Mary and Pole verbatim, he ends his book without translating the eerily biblical final notes of Sanders's account: "quin & Cardinale Polo, post duodecim fere horas eodem ipso die, ex hac vita migrante, mox hora Satane & potestas tenebrarum Angliam occupavit" (S 358); ("Cardinal Pole also, on the same day, and about twelve hours after the queen, departed this life. Then came the hour of Satan, and the power of darkness took possession of the whole of England"; L 233). Although elements of typology, hagiography, and martyrology survive in Davanzati's Scisma, his exercise of Tacitean compression combines with a Machiavellian realism to transform the magniloquent sacred history, the invective, and the righteous indignation of Sanders's text into a tale that is more like a secular political melodrama.

How then do Davanzati, and Sanders more subliminally, figure in the argument of Areopagitica? Initially the historical content of Davanzati's text is less prominent in Milton's presentation than the status and nature of that text as a licensed publication. In his citation of the

---

[17] Constant, 327.
[18] Burnet, 4.

*imprimatur*, Milton makes of Davanzati a two-fold symbol: the lifeless product of an authoritarian system of textual production, and the embodiment of an understanding of history that opposes his own. The implicit antipode of Milton's outlaw pamphlet, Davanzati's text exemplifies the officially sanctioned history of received ideas. Whereas Milton's pamphlet is engaged in making history, he refers to a book at least two removes from the events it refers to: not only is it a belated attempt to codify and thus to stonify history, it is the secondary derivative of a text written by an "apishly Romanizing" (A 504) Englishman in the imperialist language of Latin. History survives in Davanzati's book as the dead letter, and the Latin *imprimatur* is its death warrant and epitaph. In terms of the ideological dialectic of the pamphlet, Davanzati's text exhibits the mode of censorship traced by Thomas Kranidas as "Imperial Roman, medieval, popish, Spanish, associated with corrupt, irrational, and fearful tyrannies," as emphatically as Milton's aligns itself with the "Greek, Republican Roman, and English [mode], associated with strong free commonwealths."[19] Milton sharpens the dialectic by his performative stance. His pamphlet asserts that it be read as if it were heard, with the proclamatory presence and vigor of speech challenging men of thought to action, scorning the limp deference to authority of a written text whose author accepts that his very identity depends on his censors.[20]

The symmetrical contrast between *Areopagitica* and *Scisma d'Inghilterra* can be further clarified by comparison of their use of sources.

---

[19] Thomas Kranidas, "Polarity and Structure in Milton's *Areopagitica*," *ELR* 14 (1984): 182.

[20] Margreta de Grazia, in "The *Areopagitica*'s 'Gross Conforming Stupidity'," an essay presented to the MLA, December 1984, presents the ways in which *Areopagitica* presents itself as spoken word. Milton's rhetorical strategy here seems to invite a deconstructive reading which would associate "written" texts like Davanzati's with absence and death, and texts disguised as "speech" like Milton's with logocentric authority and presence. But *Areopagitica* complicates such a reading. By its typographical emphasis on its own title page and on the citations of imprimaturs, it insists on its own printed existence. It also does so in drawing the famous extended analogy between the life of men and the life of reason incarnate in books: "For books are not absolutely dead things, but do contain a potencie of life in them to be as active as the soul was whose progeny they are" (A 492). Thus Milton confers on books, printed texts, the vitality and authority which Derridean critics would lead us to believe books can claim only when they veil their own textuality and masquerade as speech. My thanks to William Reading of Syracuse University, who questioned me about this issue.

Milton's historical argument about the origin and development of licensing and censorship is based on the work of the Italian Pietro Sarpi even as Davanzati's history is derived from the Latin text of the Englishman Sanders. Whereas Davanzati draws on Sanders freely and exclusively—one might say, in keeping with Milton's tone, "apishly"—yet without the courtesy of citation, Milton acknowledges his debt to "Padre Paolo" (A 501). Furthermore, as Sirluck has demonstrated, Milton checks Sarpi's account for accuracy and corrects his precursor in light of other source material, including the *Ecclesiastical History* of Socrates Scholasticus and the complete text of Martin V's papal bull of 1418 on excommunication of readers of prohibited books.[21]

The most striking revision of his precursor lies not in factual corrections but in Milton's appropriation of a text whose ultimate purposes are at odds with his. Sarpi does not in principle object to licensing, but to its ecclesiastical abuse: "Sarpi altogether approves of licensing; his point is that the licensing power ought to belong to the church only in matters of religion, and that in secular affairs it properly belongs to the state, from which the church has usurped it."[22] Milton's radical transformation of Sarpi's premises is characteristic of the iconoclastic pressure upon his sources which was the lifelong habit of his imagination. It is also in keeping with the thematic progressivism of *Areopagitica* itself, which champions opinion in good men as knowledge in the making (A 554), and understands history, and Reformation itself, as a collaborative project open to the future. Milton discovers in Sarpi's Erastian criticism a partially disclosed truth about the spiritually devastating consequences of licensing; his work involves making that truth explicit and uncompromised.

Although Milton makes no reference to Sanders's founding text on the English schism, it initially seems puzzling to imagine that a polemicist so learned as Milton would not be acquainted with a book so widely circulated and notorious. However, Sanders's book seems to have been more available in the vernacular translations than in its original Latin. Its vitriolic denunciations of the Tudors, of the schismatic English Church, and of the heresy and turpitude of its members, earned Sanders the nickname among the English of "Dr. Slanders" (L xxii), and

---

[21] Sirluck, 228.
[22] Ernest Sirluck, introduction to *Areopagitica* in CPW 2:503.

ensured that the book would be contemptuously ignored and actively suppressed in England. The text was first translated into English by David Lewis in 1877. Gilbert Burnet himself, taking up the scholarly cudgel against Sanders, answered his charges by reference not to the original *De origine ac progressu schismatis Anglicani*, but to Pollini's Italian translation and to Maucroix's more recent French translation;[23] this indicates how difficult it might have been to obtain or to read Sanders himself.

In a pamphlet which displays its vigorous erudition in multiple citations, Milton's suppression of reference to Sanders may also be strategic. Milton would have found ironic support for his assertion of the vigor of the free English intellect in the fact that the Counter-Reformation looked to an Englishman to lead its historical assault on the reformed English church. Yet Sanders's text is Latin, in the intellectual framework of *Areopagitica* "apishly Romanizing," "the language of repression and falsehood," as Kranidas has put it.[24] Insofar as it is a Roman Catholic critique of the English reformation under the Tudors, it exercises the one type of ideological expression which Milton would specifically exempt from his proposed policy of toleration: "Popery and open superstition, which, as it extirpats all religions and civill supremacies, so it self should be extirpat" (A 565). Yet Milton would have found in Sanders more than in Davanzati an ideological adversary worthy of aggressive refutation. Sanders's polemic intensity, his satiric resort to *ad hominem* argument, and his orotund Latin periods have their counterparts in Milton's political prose. Milton shares with Sanders a belief that history is providentially informed, yet he would have despised Sanders's version of that history. Writing to generate authentic reform and life-giving schism in England, Milton implicitly struggles with the false established version of the English schism for which Sanders is primarily responsible: "Let her [Truth] and Falshood grapple; who ever knew Truth put to the wors, in a free and open encounter. Her confuting is the best and surest suppressing" (A 561).

Yet the suppressing of Sanders is not complete because there is in his argument a germ of truth which Milton cannot honestly confute. Paradoxically, Milton the radical reformer implicitly shares with the

---

[23] Burnet, 4; Veech, 234.
[24] Kranidas, 177.

papists Sanders and Davanzati the judgment that the Tudor reformation went wrong. Yet *Areopagitica*, with its patriotic concern to win moderate Erastian support in the English Parliament,[25] offers only veiled reference to the failure of the Tudor religious settlement. If we take Milton's reference as a cue to peruse Davanzati's history, we can reconstruct Milton's critique. Milton cites Wycliffe, not Henry VIII or Cromwell or Cranmer, as the original torchbearer of reformation (A 553). His one reference to Henry VIII, demonstrating how corruption disseminates itself in high places, however tight the government's policy on control of printing, is drawn from Davanzati and Sanders (A 518). As we have seen above, this reference, to Francis Bryan as Henry's "Vicar of Hell," leads into the thicket of the very sort of scandal which Milton would not hesitate to exploit at the expense of his enemies. The anecdote about Bryan discovers a nest of incest, rapacity, and blasphemy that engenders corrupted policy and religion. Following Sanders, Davanzati thus creates an image-complex similar to those which appear in Milton's own denunciations of prelatical and royal dissolution. Perhaps Milton's allusion to this particular anecdote and its context in Davanzati's story indirectly signals Milton's recognition of and disgust with the moral disorder and the royal greed that engendered the established English Church, and ensured its breakdown.

*Of Reformation* had been more explicit and more politically focussed in its diagnosis of where reform went wrong in England. True reformation of discipline, or church order, was betrayed by the prelatical desire for power: "Henry VIII's quarrel was with Supremacie; the Bishops, who though they had renounc'd the Pope, they still hugg'd the Pope-dome, and shar'd the Authority among themselves" (OR 528). Henry freed the English Church from its bondage to Rome, but the primary structural problem of an ecclesiastical hierarchy enmeshed in the machinery of worldly power and the wealth it protected survived as a pallid imitation of the Roman system. Henry's appropriation of the Church's wealth and property failed to be an act of genuine reformation because it simply reversed the relation of church to state condemned by such free-thinking Italians as Sarpi: the Tudor reform freed the temporal authority from ecclesiastical tyranny by institutionalizing a political church under a temporal tyranny. The temptation of power under such

---

[25] Sirluck, CPW 2:176-77; Hill, 159-60.

a regime insured that English prelates would resist genuine reform and produce as fruits of the spirit only such a "queazy temper of luke-warm-nesse, that gives a vomit to God himself" (OR 537). In this respect, then, Milton shares with his ideological antagonists the judgment that the Tudor reformation was a betrayal of true religion: in Milton's opinion, of true reformation, and in the Catholic assessment, of the one true church.

Milton secures his ideological positioning of Davanzati's *Scisma* by placing it in the network of primary images which embody the argument of *Areopagitica*. Truth assumes human form in *Areopagitica* through organic images which bespeak athletic vitality, virility, motion, flow, and fertility. Harry Smallenberg has demonstrated how both argument and syntax witness to the nonconformity, the uncontainability of truth in action, of truth as action.[26] Falsehood exposes itself in images of stasis, gluttony, mechanism, and perversion. Whereas the spirit of truth works progressively toward dynamic unity, falsehood is, in Milton's image-making, the arch-schismatic, fearful of change, active in processes of mutilation, abortion, and dismemberment.

The reference to Davanzati appears at the center of the fiercest satiric invective in Milton's pamphlet. It is introduced by the account of how "the Councell of Trent, and the Spanish Inquisition engendring togeth-er brought forth, or perfeted those Catalogues, and expurging Indexes that rake through the entrails of many an old good Author with a vio-lation wors then any could be offer'd to his tomb" (A 502–503). Milton exposes the elements of monstrous generativity, anal compulsion, pagan omen-hunting, and necrophilia in this tridentine act of bibliographic transgression. Imagery of mechanistic reproduction emerges with Mil-ton's own reproduction of the official stamps which crowd the flyleaf of Davanzati's text, as well as that of George Conn, a Scottish papist whose licensed history of the Scottish Church provides a neat comple-ment to Milton's allusion to Davanzati.[27] Milton's subsequent personi-fication of the "five *Imprimaturs* seen together dialogue-wise in the Piatza of one title page, complementing and ducking each to other with their shav'n reverences" (A 504), reinforces the sense of mindless mecha-

---

[26] Harry Smallenberg, "Contiguities and Moving Limbs: Style as Argument in *Areo-pagitica*," *MS* 9 (1976): 169–84.

[27] Miller, 349–54.

nism, with the system of thought control reduced to parody by the implicit comparison of the self-important licensers to the bobbing and gyrating parts of an automaton.[28] But the most chilling and powerful image is the climax of Milton's satiric sequence:

> Till then Books were ever as freely admitted into the World as any other birth; the issue of the brain was no more stifl'd then the issue of the womb; no envious *Juno* sat cross-leg'd over the nativity of any mans intellectuall off spring; but if it prov'd a Monster, who denies, but that it was justly burnt, or sunk into the Sea? But that a Book in worse condition then a peccant soul, should be to stand before a Jury ere it be borne to the World, and undergo yet in darknesse the judgment of *Radamanth* and his Collegues, ere it can passe the ferry backward into light, was never heard before, till that mysterious iniquity provokt and troubl'd at the first entrance of Reformation, sought out new limbo's and new hells wherein they might include our Books also within the number of their damned.                    (A 505–506)

The chthonic terror of the classical underworld, the malevolent opposition of supernal powers, the eschatological immediacy of the Book of Revelation's disclosure of "the mysterious iniquity" of the whore of Babylon (Revelation 17:5), the systemic terrorism of Dante's *inferno*, are all invoked in order to provoke horror at a system of repression of thought which is not simply abortive of intellectual life but a blasphemous inversion of the movement toward life and toward light which is the promise of the spirit of truth.

Milton's primary example of the officially licensed text, Davanzati's book figures in this image system as the abortive offspring of the orthodox system of control. Because its own life of thought has been stamped out by the mechanisms of bureaucratic judgment, it exists already only as a footnote, consigned to imaginative limbo by the very seal of its approval. The *imprimatur* stamped on Davanzati's text reduces the potency of living speech, with its power to make history, to the stony

---

[28] Thomas Corns sees this passage in a more sinister light as "an Italianate drama of Machiavellian iniquity and the evil exercise of corruptly acquired power" (*The Development of Milton's Prose Style* [Oxford: Oxford Univ. Press, 1982], 92). My sense is that the parodic automatism of the passage renders that iniquity somewhat absurd.

tablets of law, whose power is to fix history in the patterns of a dead past. Davanzati's *Scisma* thus serves Milton's purpose as the model text of the negative poetics of the Counter-Reformation, a testament to the "pure conceit" (A 505) of a faceless system of control, evidence of its totalitarian power to make or erase history, to abort texts before they have been written, to "sponge" identity by a stamp and a signature.

Although imagery of perversion and bodily defilement occurs frequently in the cycles of gluttony and excretion that vivify Milton's invective against "obscene, canary-sucking prelates," "the new-vomited Paganisme of sensuall Idolatry," "the bottle of vitious and harden'd excrements" that is the essence of episcopacy (OR 549, 580, 524),[29] in *Areopagitica* his particular anxiety about the thought control implicit in efficient licensing materializes in the vehemence of his images of abortion and mutilation. If he conceives of his own text as carrying a "potencie of life" (A 492), virile and athletic in keeping with the truth he champions, he also acknowledges the fate of truth among inimical men, who "hewd her lovely form into a thousand peeces, and scatter'd them to the four winds" (A 549). Whereas the images of cross-legged Juno and Rhadamanthine judgment embody the practice of licensing as intellectual abortion, a stifling of the mind's life in the womb of conception, the images of dismemberment and mutilation carry the implicit threat of castration.[30] In this symbolic schema, Davanzati's book serves as the antithesis of Milton's virile text; the inverted image of *Areopagi-*

---

[29] In his study of rhetoric in *Of Reformation*, Michael Lieb explores parallels to Milton's calculated obscenities in other Puritan polemics and finds justification for them in the precedents of classical and biblical rhetoric. "Milton's *Of Reformation* and the Dynamics of Controversy," in *Achievements of the Left Hand: Essays on the Prose of John Milton*, ed. Michael Lieb and John Shawcross (Amherst: Univ. of Massachusetts Press, 1974), 72-75.

[30] My intention is not to rake through the entrails of Milton's psycho-sexual anxieties, but to make sense of how images freighted with associations with the life process, and with threats to it, function in a pamphlet whose concern is the vitality of the intellect. Even without leaning heavily on Freud, we can see that fertility and "potencie of life" are associated with the image of the body which is Milton's primary symbol in *Areopagitica* of vital truth, and the threats to truth are represented in degradations of that body image which contain an element of sexual menace. The association of the manifest images of dismemberment with the latent content of castration may seem strained in light of the feminine gender of the "truth" referred to here. Yet the gender of truth is shifting throughout the pamphlet, as in the reversal achieved by this passage's extended analogy to the myth of Osiris.

tica's preoccupation with intellectual freedom, it materializes Milton's anxiety about the loss of such freedom. Derivative and lifeless, severed by its official approval from the field of intellectual ferment into which Milton's pamphlet sallies forth and disseminates itself, sowing seeds of thought like dragon teeth, Davanzati's is in effect a castrated text. In contrast to the authoritative "signature event" of his own title page, which declares its independence not only of any licensing procedure but even of its own printer,[31] Milton typographically highlights the sanctioned flyleaves of Davanzati and Conn, exposing them as relics of thought control in which the papally appointed licensers display and mystify their authority. That one of Conn's papal licensers is named "Belcastro" (A 504) may not be a deliberate irony, but it subtly plays so well into Areopagitica's imagery of potency and impotence, mutilation of truth and intellectual emasculation, that it partly justifies Milton's inclusion of Conn's text as an anonymous companion-piece to Davanzati's book.

In embedding Davanzati's sterile text in his own, then, Milton presents the two possible fates of the work of thought in an age of mechanical reproduction. St. Paul's instruction to the church at Corinth that "the letter killeth, but the spirit giveth life" (2 Corinthians 3:6) could be the implicit epigraph of Areopagitica. As Milton contrasts the dead letter of authorized history to the living spirit of his pamphlet, he contrasts a past which is closed, determined, interpretable, to a future which is breaking in, open, yet to be explained. In Davanzati's derivative history of the Anglican schism, Milton wants his readers to see textual and historical fixation; in the deathly stasis of the sanctioned name, without intellectual substance or context, Milton suggests that officially approved history creates an authoritative version of the past at the expense of the living word. Milton's text, ambitious to be understood as spoken, living, transforming words of spirit, counters the dead letter of orthodox history with the proclamation that "God is decreeing to begin some new and great period in his Church, ev'n to the reforming of Reformation it self" (A 553). The Reformation, that is, is only just under way, not yet conformable to the retrospective closure which can reduce it to written history. Aligning himself with the prophetic British reformers Wycliffe (A 553) and Knox (A 534), Milton in Areopa-

---

[31] Blum, 81–82.

*gitica* argues that true reformation must involve an unmaking of history as it has been written in such texts as Davanzati's in order to clear the way for the truth which authorized history has dismembered.[32]

The work of unmaking history as written in order to open history to the action of truth involves Milton in what we might call the politics and poetics of schism. He plucks out the titular key term of Davanzati's and Sanders's texts, reverses its implications, and proceeds to ring paradoxical changes on it. As Milton wrote in *Of Reformation*, England's schism is not with the Church of Rome, but with the reformed churches of the Continent: "we are no better than a schisme, and a sore scandal to them" (OR 526). By the same logic of paradox which asserts that "a man may be a heretick in the truth" (A 543), Milton demonstrates that the ready if not easy way to ecclesiastical unity in a truth at war with orthodox conformity is through schism: "there must be many schisms and many dissections made in the quarry and in the timber, ere the house of God can be built" (A 555). "Christian faith," he reminds us, "was once a schism" (A 529). What the orthodox regard as schism is thus a fundamental act of faith, holding the mind open to the possibility of truth, to present and future revelation.[33] Insofar as the full truth will only be restored and revealed in unity and splendor by the very act of God at the Second Coming (A 549), Milton's trust in the dynamics of schism is a theology of hope, a faith in the iconoclastic

---

[32] In describing the rhetorical action of *Areopagitica*, Stanley Fish discloses how the pamphlet unmakes "truth as received" by the reader in order to be "the occasion for the trial and exercise that are necessary to the constituting of human virtue"; "Driving from the Letter: Truth and Indeterminacy in Milton's *Areopagitica*," in *Re-Membering Milton*, 242. Fish understands the field of this action as the private self of the reader: "Licensing and the premature closure of a weak reformation are alike forms of a single temptation, the temptation to substitute for the innumerable and inconclusive acts that go to make up the process by which the self is refined and purified some external form of purification that can be mechanically applied" (244). In thus rendering private the action of the pamphlet, he neglects its attempt to incorporate its reformed reader into the body politic of a revolutionary Christian England and its attempt to reform the public understanding of the writing of history itself, which are primary motives for Milton's writing.

[33] See Sanford Budick's analysis of "schism" as the political corollary to Milton's theologically grounded strategy of analytic division, in his excellent *Dividing Muse*. In his discussion of *The Reason of Church Government*, Budick writes, "quiet schism, Milton argues, is mysteriously healthful to the church body. To try to outlaw it altogether, to fail to tolerate it in some moderate form, is paradoxically to cause a fatal breach in church government" (39).

God who will continue restlessly to work through human history, making and unmaking, until he has remade the stubborn human heart and community in his own image.

The tragic story of the interregnum years in England, the disintegration of the radical coalition of schismatics and the sectarian formation of new orthodoxies, the ideological and spiritual loneliness Milton felt in the years following the Restoration, would demonstrate to him how perilous the politics of schism could be. And yet truth has its own necessity. The strenuous argument of Areopagitica is motivated by the very possibility that a "Nation of Prophets" (A 554) would prove to lack the self-discipline and the tolerance necessary to bear witness to that truth. Alert to the risks of freedom, Milton was not one either to retreat from history into a cloistered virtue, or to answer its dangers with the "rigid externall formality" (A 564) of a licenser's stamp, and all that it implies. And so the fate of Davanzati, ironically enough, is to be preserved as a monitory footnote to the "lively and vigorously productive" Areopagitica—a better fate, perhaps, than the intellectual oblivion to which Milton testifies that Davanzati's papal authorizers had consigned him, and in which an indifferent aftertimes would willingly have let him die.[34]

Sarah Lawrence College

[34] My thanks to Judith Kicinsky and William Haines, Research Librarians at Sarah Lawrence College, to the Rev. David Green and the Rev. Frederick Shriver, respectively Director of St. Mark's Library and Professor of Church History at the General Theological Seminary, and to the staff of the Shakespeare Institute, University of Birmingham, England, for assisting my research on this project.

Contexts
Artistic
Musical

DIANE MCCOLLEY

# Edenic Iconography:
# Paradise Lost and the Mosaics of San Marco

O F THE PUBLIC, MONUMENTAL CREATION CYCLES that Milton probably saw on his Italian journey, one that is particularly close to *Paradise Lost* iconographically is the Creation Dome of the Basilica of San Marco in Venice. During the spring of 1639, Edward Phillips tells us, Milton "spent a month's time in viewing of that stately city."[1] Seventeenth-century Venice—a city "stately" in both senses of the word—had the noble loveliness we can still see and a long-standing reputation for vice. Boccaccio described it nearly three centuries earlier as "vinegia dogni bructura ricevitrice," which a popular seventeenth-century translation renders "the receptacle of all foule sinne and abhomination."[2] Thomas Coryate calls it "the fairest Lady, yea the richest Paragon and Queene of Christendome," a glorious Virgin "because it was never conquered," but counsels his countrymen to "beware the Circean cups, and the Syrens melody" of the "seducing and tempting Gondoleers of the Rialto."[3]

The city carried on, then as now, a tourist industry that permitted

---

Research for this essay was aided by a grant from the Research Council of Rutgers, The State University of New Jersey.

[1] Phillips, *The Life of Milton*, in Hughes, 1029. Quotations from *Paradise Lost* are also from Hughes.

[2] Giovanni Boccaccio, *Decameron*, ed. Charles Singleton from autograph MS. Hamilton 90 (Baltimore: Johns Hopkins Univ. Press, 1974), 284, lines 31–32; *The Modell of Wit, Mirth, Eloquence, and Conversation*, trans. anon. (London, 1625), 130. The 1620 edition of the latter is available in reprint, with introduction by Edward Hutton (New York, 1940). Vittore Branca in his edition of the *Decameron* (Florence, 1951) notes that the "blason" of Venetian "corruption" so common in the sixteenth century must have been alive in the fourteenth ("È il 'blasone' della 'corruzione' veneziana che diverrà comunissimo nel '500 ma che già doveva essere vivo nel '300") but attributes it in Boccaccio's case partly to political rivalries (1:480 n. 3).

[3] Thomas Coryate, *Coryats Crudities* (London, 1611), 160, 158, 168.

access to many public buildings, and descriptions of the Basilica of San
Marco and its Treasury[4] catalogue precious ornaments with an admiration of sheer wealth reminiscent of Milton's Mammon,

> the least erected Spirit that fell
> From Heav'n, for ev'n in Heav'n his looks and thoughts
> Were always downward bent, admiring more
> The riches of Heav'n's pavement, trodd'n Gold,
> Then aught divine or holy else enjoy'd
> In vision beatific.                                    (1.679-84)

San Marco apparently had a similar effect on Coryate, who gives few
details of the mosaics but speaks of the "pavement ... made of sundry
little pieces of Thasian, Ophiticall, and Laconicall marble," and, in
1644, on John Evelyn, who says almost nothing of the marvellously
crafted Scriptural subjects of the great domes and storied walls, but
remarks that "the floor is all inlaid with agates, lazulis, chalcedons,
jaspers, porphyries, and other rich marbles, admirable also for the work;
the walls sumptuously encrusted, and presenting to the imagination the
shapes of men, birds, houses, flowers, and a thousand varieties." He
notes much else, as well, of the preciousness of marbles, gold, and other
riches for which Milton's bard says men have "Rifl'd the bowels of thir
mother Earth / For Treasures better hid" (1.686-87), and noncommit-
tally reports the rare favor of being admitted to the Treasury to see

> the cap, or coronet, of the Dukes of Venice, one of which had a
> ruby set on it, esteemed worth 200,000 crowns; two unicorns'
> horns; numerous dishes and vases of agate, set thick with pre-
> cious stones and vast pearls; divers heads of Saints enchased in
> gold; a small ampulla, or glass, with our Savior's blood; a great
> morsel of the real cross; one of the nails; a thorn; a fragment of
> the column to which our Lord was bound, when scourged; the
> standard or ensign, of Constantine; a piece of St. Luke's arm; a
> rib of St. Stephen; a finger of Mary Magdalen; numerous other
> things, which I could not remember. But a priest, first vesting
> himself in his sacerdotals, with the stole about his neck, showed

---

[4] See for example Girolamo Bardi Fiorentino, *Delle Cose Notabili Della Citta di
Venetia, Libri II* (Venice, 1587); and Francesco Sansovino, *Venetia Citta Nobilissima et
singolare, Descritta in XIIII. Libri* (Venice, 1581).

us the gospel of St. Mark (their tutular patron) written by his own hand, and whose body they show buried in the church, brought hither from Alexandria many years ago.[5]

The decorations of the Palazzo Ducale (of which the Basilica was the chapel) represent qualities of Venetian politics both compatible with and antithetical to Milton's Reformed and parliamentarian views. On the one hand, they celebrate a republican spirit and a resistence to the hegemony of papal Rome that Milton applauded. On the other, their glorification of Venice and her Doges as deified conquerors and the use of religious imagery to ennoble political ambition are incompatible with the thought of the poet who would a decade later support the assassination of overweening monarchs. Milton's references to Venice in his political prose twice approve its "immovable" Senate but warn against instituting the "fond conceit of somthing like a duke of Venice."[6] He expresses highest praise for Pietro Sarpi, thrice calling him great: "the great and learned *Padre Paolo*" who was the "great Venetian Antagonist of the *Pope*" and "the great unmasker of the *Trentine* Councel."[7]

Much as her politics gave both satisfaction and warning, Venice also offered an example of the "gay Religions full of Pomp and Gold" (1.372) that English Protestants deplored, made nearly irresistible by the incomparably beautiful anthems and psalm-settings of Claudio Monteverdi. For many reasons, the morally earnest John Milton no doubt had occasion to employ the advice of Henry Wotton, who had been King James's ambassador to Venice, that "I pensieri stretti, & il viso sciolto" —confined thoughts and an open countenance—would keep his person and his conscience safe,[8] and to cultivate that capacity for seeing and

---

[5] Coryat, 213; *The Diary of John Evelyn*, ed. William Bray, 2 vols. (Washington and London, 1901), 1:197–98.

[6] *Proposalls of certaine expedients for the preventing of a civill war now feard, & the settling of a firme government* (1659), ed. Robert W. Ayers, in CPW 336, and *The Readie & Easie Way to Establish a Free Commonwealth* (1660), in 7:436 and 446. Milton recommends that members of Parliament sit for life, using the Venetian Senate as an example.

[7] *Of Reformation*, ed. Don M. Wolfe, in CPW 1:595 and 581; *Areopagitica*, ed. Ernest Sirluck (1959), 2:501. Father Paolo is the religious name of Pietro Sarpi (1552–1623), who battled against the secular power of the Vatican as incompatible with the spiritual purposes of the church.

[8] Wotton, in a letter to Milton of 13 April, 1638, in *The Student's Milton*, ed. Frank Allen Patterson (New York: Appleton-Century-Crofts, 1930), 45.

knowing and yet abstaining that Venice, with her infinite airy charm, is especially suited to exercise.

Within this context, the Creation mosaics of the Basilica offer a breath of unambiguously fresh air. Unlike Renaissance humanist painters of Adam and Eve, who usually make the Fall their primary act, the devisers of the San Marco program read Genesis, in part, as Milton did: not confining the story to crime and punishment, but celebrating creation and regeneration as well. They include several features that appear rarely in the visual arts, but prominently in Milton's poem. These features affirm the original goodness of God's works, including Eve, and the repentance and regeneration of both Eve and Adam.

The ways the San Marco mosaics expand the creation story may be observed by comparison with the thirteenth-century mosaics of the Baptistry in Florence, which, with the exception of the first scene, have a more conventional iconographic program. The series begins with the Christ-Logos, in the heavens, blessing a creation, to which the dove of the Holy Spirit descends, that includes earth, water, sun, moon, six single representative animals (ox, goat, hart, ram, lion, and horse), four large symmetrical smiling fish, and Adam and Eve. Then, as in Genesis, the narrative starts over and represents the Creation of Adam, the Creation of Eve, the Fall, the Judgment, the Expulsion, Labor, the Sacrifices of Cain and Abel, and the Murder of Cain. No birds or animals (except the Serpent) appear with Adam and Eve, and the Creator sits apart and does not touch them. In this typical progression of events, the creation of woman leads directly to the Fall, and the postlapsarian scenes show its terrible effects. *Paradise Lost* and the San Marco mosaics, in contrast, dwell lovingly on details of creation and renewal.[9]

Interpretations of Genesis in the visual arts display variegated images of our first parents. From among these, we can sort out at least two general interpretations: one, that creation, and especially human senses and sexuality, and more especially woman, were primordially flawed, but in a way made fortunate by redemption, provided one firmly rejected the

---

[9] I do not, of course, mean to claim that Milton was "influenced" by particular works of visual art. His primary external sources were the Bible, nature, and literary predecessors. The San Marco mosaics share with Milton's epic a regenerative interpretation of Genesis that we can see more clearly by comparing iconographic analogues.

enticements of the flesh (or by sensuality, provided one firmly rejected the straight path of redemption); and two, that creation and humanity, including woman, were primordially excellent, wounded by the Fall, but redeemed wholly, as naturally incarnate beings in a material world whose beauty and limitations could help, rather than hinder, the growth of the spirit. Sixteenth- and seventeenth-century Italian art, though "humanist" in its glorious rendering of the human body and the depths and nuances of erotic feeling, leans to the former interpretation, or expresses disconcertingly mixed feelings: in Raphael's beautiful ceiling painting for the Stanza della Segnatura in the Vatican apartments,[10] for example, Eve is delicious but dangerous, and the Serpent is a mirror image of her. In Tintoretto's two Venetian versions of the Fall (fig. 1), the tension between Adam's hunched and shadowy disobedience and Eve's light-bathed, assured sensuality is devastating.[11] Because of their virtuosity and dramatic power, such aesthetically attractive but morally murky Renaissance humanist versions probably provide the commonest impression of visual interpretations of Genesis today. They imply an opposition between spirit and flesh that has roots in patristic commentary, which sometimes allegorizes Adam as Reason and Eve as Passion, but they depart from the iconographic tradition of most medieval manuscripts and Reformation Bibles. Theologically and iconographically speaking, they anomalously perpetuate a misogynous and divisive view of the creation story. Typically, they focus on the Fall, and confine their interest to the human figures, leaving out both the Creator and the rest of the creation; if other species are included they are usually emblems of the human passions thought responsible for the Fall, rather than fellow inhabitants of a diverse and entertaining world.

Illustrations in English Reformation Bibles, by contrast, usually neglect erotic beauty but show an earthy and zestful pleasure in the abundance of creation and place responsibility for the Fall either squarely on Adam or on Adam and Eve together as equal partners in both disobedience and regeneration. One may compare, for example, the

---

[10] Raphael, *The Fall*, reproduced in Roland Mushat Frye, *Milton's Imagery and the Visual Arts* (Princeton: Princeton Univ. Press, 1978), fig. 198.

[11] Tintoretto's two versions are in the Scuola Grande di San Rocco (fig. 1) and (now) in the Galleria dell'Accademia (Frye, fig. 173).

Fig. 1. Jacopo Tintoretto, *The Fall of Man.* Scuola Grande di San Rocco, Venice. Alinari/Art Resource, NY.

*Fig. 2.* John Speed, *Geneologies.* © The British Library.

illustration to the widely circulated Speed geneologies (fig. 2),[12] in
which Adam and Eve participate equally in the Fall and presumably in
redemption (though the Pauline text attributes each of these to "one
man"). They are surrounded by winsome beasts, some emblematic of
the Fall but others simply present: lions, squirrel, fox, cat, a handsome
ox, a herd of sheep, birds on the wing, a dog, a cow, and a pair of
camels. A frontispiece used in both the Geneva and Authorized Bibles
shows both a mutual Fall and, by means of banners, equal participation
in restoration;[13] animals include numerous birds and fish, the
hart—symbolic of the soul's desire for God (Ps. 42)—monkey, tortoise,
crocodile, and pairs of bears, lions, tigers, horses, elephants, camels,
goats, pigs, rhinoceroses, unicorns, foxes, sheep, cattle, dogs, and others.
The same attributes—visual equality and mutuality in the Fall and the
presence of other creatures—may be found as well in frontispieces or
headpieces to Genesis in many English Bibles and in series of engravings published for insertion by the binder. These, like the San Marco
mosaics, keep continuity with the iconographic traditions of medieval
manuscripts, which often present a mutual Fall and give loving attention
to the diversity of creatures, and their engravers sometimes add motifs
that suggest the possibilities of regeneration.[14] The Italian humanists,
on the other hand, by following more nearly the patristic, allegorizing
tradition, were more misogynous, more focussed on sin and less interested in the beauty and diversity of the rest of creation. Such distinctions help us see what implications Milton chose, cast aside, or combined in his living mosaic of words made flesh and song.

Like *Paradise Lost* and like medieval creation series in many forms,
the San Marco mosaics typologically encompass the whole Bible. The
Old Testament stories in the west atrium favor Noah, Abraham, and

---

[12] In 1610 John Speed obtained the right for ten years to insert his genealogies
into every edition of the Authorized Version, a practice which continued until at least
1640: note to A. W. Pollard and G. R. Redgrave, *A Short-Title Catalogue of Books
Printed in England, Scotland, & Ireland and of English Books Printed Abroad, 1475–1640*
(London, 1926; second edition, revised and enlarged, begun by W. A. Jackson and F.
S. Ferguson, completed by Katharine F. Pantzer, London: The Bibliographic Society,
1986), no. 23039.

[13] Frontispiece to Genesis, reproduced in Frye, fig. 109, from the Geneva Bible of
1583.

[14] For a fuller commentary on the implications of English Bible illustrations see
McColley, "The Iconography of Eden," in *MS* 24 (1988): 107–21.

Joseph, who strongly prefigure redemption, and prepare for the interior, with its empathetic depictions of the life of Christ and its great domes of the Ascension and the gift of the Spirit at Pentecost. Because of its location and vivid color contrasts, the Creation dome in the west atrium is clearly visible; situated just inside the south door of the west façade, it is low and flooded with afternoon sunlight. If one enters the central door and looks right, what one sees centered under the arch from that angle is the marriage of Adam and Eve. This visual first impression corresponds to the regenerative emphasis of the whole program and of Milton's poem. Although the figures do not have the fleshy verisimilitude of Renaissance paintings, the dome is richly beautiful. The figures, if anatomically naive, are appealingly linked to the rest of humanity by virtue of their unpretentious simplicity; and the scenes are full of praise for the diversity of being and for a Creator compassionately and intimately engaged in making, blessing, and renewing life.

The iconographic program of the Creation dome (fig. 3) has been traced to the Cotton Genesis, a fifth-century Greek manuscript now mostly in cinders in the British Library.[15] Although the mosaics were repaired in the nineteenth century in ways some critics deem ruinous, we are assured by Otto Demus, the primary expert on them, that the iconography remains intact.[16] The program is composed of twenty-six images arranged in three concentric circles, always beginning on the east. Around the whole composition runs an inscription describing ardent cherubim praising with serene voices in the flaming radiance of Christ, and four angels with flame-like wings fill the pendatives beneath the dome. The images begin with the dove of the Holy Spirit brooding

---

[15] MS. Cotton Otho B VI. See Kurt Weitzmann, "The Genesis Mosaics of San Marco and the Cotton Genesis Miniatures," in Otto Demus, *The Mosaics of San Marco in Venice, II: The Thirteenth Century* (Chicago: Univ. of Chicago Press, 1984), chap. 4. The relation between the miniatures and the mosaics was first observed by J. J. Tikkanen. Weitzmann and Herbert Kessler have since made a close study of the manuscript and of the relations between other manuscripts and monumental forms and concluded that the Cotton manuscript is indeed the chief source, with a few iconographic changes increasing Christological elements. An important addition, from the point of view of this essay, is the Judgment, with Adam and Eve kneeling, a motif taken from Middle Byzantine Last Judgments (107). The Last Judgment at Torcello, near Venice, is an example.

[16] Demus, 76. This work, in four volumes of two parts each, offers a full photographic record of the mosaics of the Basilica, most of the photographs newly taken by Ekkehard Ritter, and extensive historical and iconographic scholarship.

Fig. 3. *Creation Dome*, Basilica of San Marco, Venice. Alinari/Art Resource, NY.

Fig. 4. The Creation of Eve. Detail, Creation Dome, San Marco.
Alinari/Art Resource, NY.

Fig. 5. Detail, *Creation Dome,* San Marco. Alinari/Art Resource, NY.

upon the waters, followed by the separation of light from darkness, represented as two spheres from *each* of which pour six rays of light. We may remember how in *Paradise Lost* God "light from darkness by the Hemisphere / Divided"—so Milton divides his lines—and how morn goes forth "array'd in Gold / Empyreal" while "from before her vanisht Night, / Shot through with orient Beams" (7.250-51 and 6.12-15). Raphael commends *both* day and "ambrosial Night with Clouds exhal'd / From that high mount of God, whence light and shade / Spring both" (5.642-44), affirming the goodness of the whole creation's savory variety.

The San Marco Creator is represented as Christ-Logos, with cruciform aureole and cross-tipped staff. This version was to be the preferred one during the Middle Ages and the Reformation when an anthropomorphic God was portrayed at all, because artists who respected the commandment against visual represention of the invisible God found warrant in the doctrine that the Son was the agent "by whom all things were made"[17] to represent the Creator in his incarnate form. He is accompanied by the angels or personifications of the six Days. At the blessing of the first five, the Days receive white robes, while at their feet a river runs, complete with a leviathan, and beside them birds appear to be preparing to obey the command to increase and multiply.[18] In the next panel the animals appear in pairs, unlike Renaissance versions that use single animals emblematically to suggest reasons for the Fall. The pairing suggests that, like Milton, the mosaicist values reproductivity.

Next, conflating Genesis 1 and 2, come the shaping of Adam "out of the dust of the ground" and the sanctification of the seventh Day, who kneels to be blessed by the Lord who is now resting on his throne. He then animates Adam, giving him a winged soul, and leads him by the hand into Paradise, where two trees and the personifications of the four rivers await him.

In the outer and lowest circle, similarities to *Paradise Lost* become especially striking. Adam names the animals as Milton describes them, "Approaching two and two" (8.350); "they rejoice / Each with thir kind," as Milton's Adam says while pleading for a fit mate, "Lion with

---

[17] From the Nicene Creed; I quote from The Book of Common Prayer of 1559, in the Folger edition, ed. John E. Booty (Washington, 1976), 250.

[18] The suggestion is Weitzmann's, 111.

Lioness, / So fitly them in pairs thou hast combin'd" (8.392-94). In the mosaic, Adam's hand appears to rest on the lioness's head.

In keeping with their affirmation of creativity and procreativity, the most obvious difference between this and other Genesis cycles, and the greatest similarity to Milton, is the mosaics' non-mysogynist treatment of Eve. Apart from the inescapable fact that in the biblical narrative she fell first for the Serpent's fable and tempted Adam, they give her dignity equal to Adam's. Western versions of the Creation of Eve usually show God, midwife-like, delivering her whole from Adam's side or raising her up from behind him. The San Marco creation of Eve (fig. 4) follows Genesis 2 literally: the Creator extracts a rib from Adam—you can see the skin, still attached, pulled like taffy—and molds, or sculpts, Eve with the loving care of an artist: the Vulgate rendering of the "edification" or building of Eve is clearly figured. This rare motif of God as Artifex attentively forming Woman appears in one Renaissance painting that I know of, by Paolo Veronese, who worked in Venice and so knew the San Marco interpretation.[19]

It is this rarer but more scriptural image, not the predominant one, that Milton chooses: the Creator appears, Adam says, in a glorious *shape*,

> Who stooping op'n'd my left side, and took
> From thence a Rib, with cordial spirits warm,
> And Life-blood streaming fresh; wide was the wound,
> But suddenly with flesh fill'd up and heal'd:
> The Rib he form'd and fashion'd *with his hands*;
> *Under his forming hands* a Creature grew,
> Manlike, but different sex.
> (8.465-71; italics added.)

The emphatic repetition suggests that Milton consciously chose and stressed the forming of Eve as a separate work of art attentively made.

Having thus made Eve, the San Marco Creator presents her to Adam, his hand on her shoulder. Here Milton differs, since Eve comes "Led by her Heav'nly Maker, though unseen, / And guided by his voice" (8.485-86), an event the mosaicist could not very well represent; nevertheless, both declare her "divinely brought" (8.500) and Adam's

---

[19] Veronese's *Creation of Eve* is in the Art Institute of Chicago.

gesture expresses his response in Genesis as Milton's words do: "I now see / Bone of my Bone, Flesh of my Flesh, my Self / Before me; Woman is her Name, of Man / Extracted" (8.494-97).

Of the numerous ways of representing the Fall, those usually chosen for Reformation Bibles either give Adam and Eve equal responsibility for the choice, or else give Adam primary responsibility, while in the one favored by Italian Renaissance artists Eve is portrayed as erotic seductress and Adam as uxoriously overwhelmed: Tintoretto's deeply disturbing versions show a sexually enticing Eve with a tense but collapsing Adam (fig. 1). The San Marco Fall keeps to a literal interpretation that refrains from casting undue blame on woman or sexuality. Eve is tempted separately, while Adam nearby gazes absent-mindedly away. She then plucks the fruit and gives it to Adam. There is no representation of Eve eating the fruit; as in Reformation Bibles, Adam's eating is the Fall. The separate temptation, shared by Milton and the mosaicist, is much increased both spatially and psychologically in *Paradise Lost*. Milton represents a separation founded on vulnerable libertarian principles. Eve eats first, with Adam well removed, a plot that gives both Adam and Eve greater individual moral responsibility (however misused) than conflated versions. By presenting to Adam an Eve who has already eaten the fruit, Milton incorporates the tragic dilemma felt in the humanist paintings, but he elevates this dilemma, in both the separation colloquy and the temptation of Adam, to incorporate a complex mutuality and to suggest that Adam and Eve and all men and women since are capable of doing better.

After the covering with fig leaves, hiding, and denial of guilt, the San Marco series continues with two motifs rare in western Genesis cycles but crucial to *Paradise Lost*. At the Judgment, Adam and Eve kneel repentantly; after it in *Paradise Lost* both "forthwith to the place / Repairing where he judg'd them prostrate fell / Before him reverent, and *both* confess'd / Humbly thir faults, and pardon begg'd" (10.1098-1101, emphasis added). Milton's "both," and the equal posture and expression of Adam and Eve in San Marco, are significant; many works, including Antonio Rizzo's sculptures in the Doges' Palace,[20] show fallen Adam in an agony of remorse, but fallen Eve wearing a more ambiguous expression, with perhaps a degree of sly reservation. Milton,

---

[20] Antonio Rizzo, *Adam and Eve*, reproduced in Frye, figs. 187-88.

as if to refute a conventional assumption, strongly affirms the view that Eve is equally, soberly sorry: "nor *Eve* / Felt less remorse: ... both confess'd / Humbly thir faults, and pardon begg'd" (11.1097-1101).

To complete the regenerative emphasis of the scene and its equal treatment of Adam and Eve, the Christ-Logos clothes each of them (fig. 4): but we actually see him clothing Eve, as compassionately and attentively as we have seen him creating her. Robing is a scriptural symbol of regeneration: "he hath clothed me with the garments of salvation, he hath covered me with the robe of righteousness" (Isa. 62:10). (Fra Angelico, in his *Annunciation with the Expulsion*, shows Adam and Eve clothed not in animal skins but in the white garments of the Book of Revelation.) In *Paradise Lost* the Judge

> then pitying how they stood
> Before him naked to the air, that now
> Must suffer change, disdain'd not to begin
> Thenceforth the form of servant to assume,
> As when he wash'd his servants' feet, so now
> As Father of his Family he clad
> Thir nakedness. ...
> Nor hee thir outward only with the Skins
> Of Beasts, but inward nakedness, much more
> Opprobrious, with his Robe of righteousness,
> Arraying cover'd from his Father's sight.
> (10.211-23)

The Argument to book 10 also underscores the Son's compassion and Eve's inclusion in regeneration: he "in pity clothes them both."

In *Paradise Lost*, however, there occurs between the Judgment and clothing of Adam and Eve and the climactic moment when, at the end of book 10, they fall on their knees, a long dramatic scene during which Adam and Eve work through the effects of fallenness and recognize the message of hope.

The San Marco Expulsion differs markedly from the familiar motif of the angel with flaming sword chasing a terrified pair; instead the Christ-Logos, with his hand on Adam's shoulder, guides them through the gate of Paradise. Milton, of course, makes Michael their guide, who takes them by the hands; it is the gentleness of the guide and the equal dignity of Adam and Eve that Milton and the mosaic share. In the panel depicting labor, as Kurt Weitzmann points out, Eve seated with her spindle resembles images of the Virgin Enthroned.[21]

Finally, the postlapsarian sequence, continuing in the tympanum of the southwest entry to the nave, includes the unusual motif of the begetting of Cain and the birth of Abel surmounted by the injunction to "increase and multiply." Although one is inevitably aware of the misconception and the violent effects of sin Cain will enact, the commendation completes the blessing on human love and procreation that began with the presentation of Eve to Adam one sees upon entering the great west door. Milton, however, removes the ambiguity by celebrating the marriage bed *before* the Fall, one of many motifs he startlingly sanctifies in this way.

Comparison with the visual arts can help us see the justice and charity of Milton's choice of the tradition that rejoices in original blessedness and in repentance, over the insurgent tradition that makes the Fall central and implies that woman, sexuality, and a sense of the beauty of creation are primordially and continually dangerous. Although both the mosaics and the poem also depict sin and loss, the resounding emphasis in both is on creation and redemption; and this affirmation assumes the goodness and the capacity for regeneration of Eve as well as Adam. The mosaics have a down-to-earth cleanness about them that corresponds to Milton's moral sense better than lusher but morally ambivalent versions do; yet the beauty of those humanist paintings gleams, purified, in the innocent sensuousness of Milton's unfallen Adam and Eve. Milton, of course, treats the creation and the story of Adam and Eve in a far more amplified way than a visual artist can: he has the expansiveness and the music of a language receptive to all languages and a dramatic epic form open to infinite reverberations. The Creation as Raphael recounts it in book 7 combines the medieval artist's delight in detail with an Ovidian exuberance and with the power and awesome processes of the Book of Job. Milton incorporates into his Paradise the visual delight, the erotic intensity, and the nuances of human emotion that the Renaissance painters used to adorn our great progenitors. But he does so while Adam and Eve are still in the state of innocence, with "Sanctitude severe and pure ... in true filial freedom plac't" (4.293–94) enjoying "Love unlibidinous" (5.449), trusting and

---

[21] Weitzmann, 116.

free of suspicion, jealousy, possessiveness, inchastity, or duplicity. His achievement is to combine, in scenes *before* the Fall, but applicable to regeneration, all the affirmation of the flesh, the psychological complexity, and the drama of Renaissance painting with all the love of innocence, the pleasure in the diversity of living things, and the sense of deep involvement of the Creator with the creation found in the strand of medieval tradition represented by the mosaics, and so achieve full integration of the human and the divine.

When Milton describes the roof and floor of the nuptial bower of Adam and Eve, he both acknowledges the art form of the mosaicist and reverses the relation of art to nature in it; artists wrought flowers in stone, but the flowers of Paradise themselves "wrought / Mosaic" (4.699–700). *Paradise Lost* is wrought of the living word with its capacity for severe sanctitude and limitless freedom, probing drama and infinite music. But the mosaicist in his exuberance shares with Milton an ability to call forth a pleasure in living things that is durably fresh, to evoke love of innocence, and to stir up hope for the renewal of blessedness.

Rutgers University—Camden

MICHAEL O'CONNELL

# Milton and the Art of Italy:
# A Revisionist View

THE GREATEST DIFFICULTY WE HAVE IN INTERPRETING Milton's Italian sojourn comes, paradoxically, of the fact that the institution of tourism, travel for the sake of seeing things one has known hitherto only in books, is an unbroken tradition from Milton's day until our own. We too hope to add to our "acquired learning the observation of foreign customs, manners, and institutions," as Edward Phillips said his uncle wished to do when he decided to cap his years of study with a trip to Italy.[1] Like Milton, we want to see the ruins of ancient civilizations and the monuments of our own. Like him, we hope to get some practice in speaking the foreign languages we have learned at home. An informed modern tourist carries, as Sir Francis Bacon advised, "some Card or Book describing the Country, where he travelleth; which will be a good Key to his Enquiry."[2] We often follow, or intend to follow, Bacon's advice to keep a diary of our travels. Like Milton, we use introductions to foreign friends of friends in the hope that we will be taken places and shown things most tourists never see, and we too would consider it a coup if we met a foreign dignitary of the fame and stature of Galileo. In short, we participate in a tradition of tourism that connects us with the early seventeenth century. And because of this we assume we know what Milton wanted to see in Italy and why he wanted to see it.

We presume, therefore, that viewing the artistic heritage of Renaissance and baroque Italy, as well as the remains of antiquity, was prime

---

[1] "The Life of Milton," in Hughes, 1027.

[2] "Of Travaile," *The Essayes or Counsels, Civill and Moral*, ed. Michael Kiernan (Cambridge, Mass.: Harvard Univ. Press, 1985), 57; "Of Travaile" was added in the 1625 edition of the *Essayes*.

among the reasons Milton visited Florence, Rome, Naples, and Venice. In his encyclopedic Milton's *Imagery and the Visual Arts*, Roland Mushat Frye makes this assumption explicit from the beginning: an interest in and knowledge of the visual arts was a part of the mental culture of every cultivated Englishman, and John Milton was assuredly such an Englishman.[3] Frye may betray a moment's hesitation when he attributes to Milton's Florentine friends the need to stimulate an interest in art in their English guest; such friends "would certainly have encouraged him to take an interest in art, for such an interest was considered essential to the complete gentleman of the time."

The seventeenth century being what it was, it is unthinkable that men such as Gaddi, Dati, and Frescobaldi (to mention only the Florentines of whom we know most) would not have seen to it that Milton was introduced to the fine arts. The same is true of his friend Giovanni Battista Manso, the Marquis of Villa in Naples, and Lucas Holstenius, the curator of the Vatican collec-

---

[3] *Milton's Imagery and the Visual Arts: Iconographic Tradition in the Epic Poems* (Princeton: Princeton Univ. Press., 1978), 23–31. Similar assumptions stand behind the article "Milton and the Arts of Design" in *A Milton Encyclopedia*, ed. William B. Hunter, Jr. (Lewisburg, PA: Bucknell Univ. Press, 1978), s.v. "Arts": "Milton's prose and poetry reveal a considerable knowledge and appreciation of the arts of design: painting, sculpture, architecture, and gardens." The article suggests that Milton's "sensitivity to continental art and his observation of how it permeated the European scene may have had much to do with his deciding on the universal subject of man and woman rather than King Arthur as the subject for his epics," and that having seen so many visual representations of biblical narrative, "no doubt he longed to do the same in literature." While the article makes some interesting suggestions, it fails to acknowledge the influence of iconoclasm on English habits of mind. The two books on Milton and the Italian baroque do not depend in their arguments on an assumption of direct influence of visual art on Milton: Roy Daniells, *Milton, Mannerism, and Baroque* (Toronto: Univ. of Toronto Press, 1963), and Murray Roston, *Milton and the Baroque* (London: Macmillan, 1980). Daniells argues that "the great controlling ideas of form which imbued the collective mind of the period" (87) gave shape to the architecture of the Roman baroque and to Milton's major poems; he also argues that thematic concerns "with unity, power, majesty, splendour, with the demonstration of divine invincibilty and triumphant faith" tie Milton's poetry with the work of Bernini, Borromini, and Cortona (146). Roston derives the baroque vision from the revolution in the way the cosmos was understood and sees Milton sharing a new sense of God, space, and the spiritual world with the great baroque artists. He briefly notes that Milton's Roman sojourn coincided with a period of intense activity by these artists (48–49), but his argument does not depend on Milton's specific engagement with the Roman baroque.

tion, in Rome. With friends such as these, Milton could have gained entrance virtually everywhere, and must be presumed to have seen a great deal.[4]

Frye is surely right about the ability of such friends to open the palazzi, and hence the art collections, to an English visitor. But a further question lurks in the first phrase: in regard to visual art, what indeed was the seventeenth century for a Protestant Englishman? The education of a modern tourist constitutes painting and sculpture as significant both as aesthetic experience and as a means of knowing past cultures. But can we be sure the same was true of the English tourist in Italy in the 1630s? No doubt Milton's acquaintances in Florence, Rome, Naples, and Venice did encourage him to take an interest in art, for painting and sculpture were central elements in contemporary Italian culture. And no doubt they escorted him to various collections of paintings and (if he was willing) to churches, where much of the sacred art of the past two centuries was to be found. Milton must have looked at paintings, frescoes, and sculpture in these cities and been told what he ought to think of them. But how did he react to what he was shown?

The most perplexing element of Milton's sojourn in Italy in the years 1638–1639 remains his utter silence about the art we presume he must have seen. It is a silence he maintains in his later accounts of his travels, the most significant of which is the biographical section of the *Defensio secunda*.[5] Granted the purpose of this account is not to record his mental life during his travels but to defend, some twelve years after the fact, the probity of his life generally and the intellectual and social respectability of his acquaintance during the journey. But nowhere in his subsequent writings does he refer to a painting or a piece of sculpture or to an artist whose work he acknowledges having seen. Given his

---

[4] Frye, 24–25. On the circle of Milton's Italian friends, see in particular Arthos, which remains the best treatment of the intellectual milieu and climate Milton encountered in Florence, Rome, Naples, and Venice. Arthos makes no claims for Milton's encounters with the visual arts, noting that developments in music and musical entertainment might rather have contributed to his ideas of a dramatic poem (58); he similarly passes over consideration of Venetian painting "because in other circumstances Milton does not offer us enough indications of his interests there" (118).

[5] The biographical sections of the *Defensio secunda* (1654) are included in Hughes, 827–29. For the documentary record of Milton's Italian journey, see French, 1:360–421.

silence on art, we are left entirely in the realm of speculation. Frye grounds his work on the assumption that Milton was familiar with the general tradition of European sacred art and that he brought that familiarity to completion during his travels in Italy.[6] His book gives us a Milton reassuringly like us in his Italian sojourn, cognizant of the general tradition of sacred art and familiar with the paintings and sculpture we know. And in its comprehensive listing of visual analogues to Milton's poetry, it can thereby seem to settle the question of his knowledge of art and the visual character of his imagery.

I want to attempt some speculation based on two senses of difference. First, I want to assume that in spite of the cultural continuum between seventeenth-century tourism and our own, there are significant differences between what the well-educated traveler of the 1630s might have sought in travel and what we seek. And second, I want to insist on a synchronic difference between England and Italy in the way the visual imagination was valued and deployed in the century leading up to Milton's sojourn in Italy. A painting in the Pitti Palace in Florence can illustrate something of this latter difference. In the Sala dell'Iliade, amid mostly Italian paintings extending from the early sixteenth to the mid-seventeenth century—including works by Raphael, Andrea del Sarto, Veronese, Titian, Carlo Maratti, and Artemisia Gentileschi—is a portrait of Queen Elizabeth attributed simply to the "scuola inglese" of the cinquecento. Fynes Moryson, an English traveler, saw what must have been the same painting in 1594 when he visited the Palazzo Vecchio; significantly, it is the only painting he specifically notes. He was surprised to see it, but says "the Duke of Florence much esteemed her picture, for the admiration of her vertues."[7] In its present setting, amid the rich complexity of high Renaissance, mannerist, and baroque Italian

---

6 "Travelers in Milton's time, blessed with more leisure and encouraged by the social and cultural ideals of the well-educated gentleman, saw many more works of art than most modern tourists, even intelligent ones. . . . When Milton's earliest biographer says that in Italy he saw 'the rarities of the place' and when his nephew John Phillips [sic] writes that 'he met with many charming objects,' I think the evidence permits us to assume with some confidence that among those 'rarities' and 'charming objects' he included the masterpieces of art with which the cultivated Englishman was expected to be familiar" (Frye, 30–31).

7 *The Itinerary of Fynes Moryson* (Glasgow: James MacLehose, 1907), 1:322. The painting is catalogued in Roy C. Strong, *Portraits of Queen Elizabeth I* (Oxford: Clarendon Press, 1963), 76 (as Painting 74), and is reproduced on page 77.

painting, it appears primitive in the extreme, as though from a different era or an entirely different culture. The portrait is in the flat, unmolded, and shadowless mode typical of Elizabethan representation, in its stylization more icon than portrait.[8] It does not attempt to portray the subjectivity of the sitter. It is, in fact, unlikely that Elizabeth ever sat for the portrait; the painting shows one of the recognizable "masks" of the queen that became a standard means of representing her. The anonymity of the artist of the portrait also serves to emphasize that the social position of painters in England was significantly different from what it was in Italy, where artists enjoyed a certain social prestige and the most famous were subject even to a cult of personality. While contemporaneous with other paintings in the room, the portrait of Elizabeth *is* in a real sense an artifact from another culture. While late sixteenth- and early seventeenth-century England remained in other respects culturally contiguous with Italy, in the visual arts it was virtually a separate world.

The reasons for this must be sought in the religious cultures of the two countries. England became iconoclast in the 1540s, and though the policy was briefly reversed under Mary, it was reaffirmed by Elizabeth and remained powerfully in effect even despite Laudian attempts to reverse it in the 1630s. With very few exceptions the churches had been stripped of their paintings, reliefs, and statues in the middle of the sixteenth century.[9] All that remained readily accessible of the rich legacy

---

[8] Strong notes that the primary concern of portraits of Elizabeth was not with portraying her likeness but with conveying "an image 'full of glory,' an icon calculated to evoke in the eyes of the beholder those principles for which the Queen and her government stood" (*Portraits*, 34). "If the impenetrable mask of the Queen's majesty is to be linked with anything," Strong suggests, "it looks back across the centuries to the holy countenance of majesty of the Byzantine and the medieval emperors and shares with them a common debt to sacred imperialism" (41). See also Strong's *The English Icon: Elizabethan and Jacobean Portraiture* (London: Routledge and Kegan Paul, 1969) on the general tradition of iconic portraiture.

[9] Margaret Aston, *England's Iconoclasts*, vol. 1, *Laws against Images* (Oxford: Clarendon Press, 1988), especially chapter 6; John Phillips, *The Reformation of Images: Destruction of Art in England, 1535–1660* (Berkeley: Univ. of California Press, 1973); on the Laudian attempt to reverse this policy and the Puritan reaction it evoked, see chapters 8 and 9. See also Strong's brief sketch of this destruction in *The English Icon* (1–3). Frye's assertion that "the great visual heritage [of medieval English art] was still to be encountered in stained glass, wood carving, and stone sculpture in most parish churches, colleges, cathedrals, and even public buildings" (23) considerably underestimates the destruction that had taken place; most of this great visual heritage had been destroyed. Much of what remained would fall victim to Puritan iconoclasm in the 1640s.

of medieval art was the stained glass that had in most cases been spared because of the expense of obtaining clear glass to replace it. The vast majority of Englishmen, even well-educated ones, had very little experience of painting and sculpture—and virtually no experience of religious art. In fact, the failure of Laud's attempt to reverse iconoclast policy testifies to the success of that policy over the previous ninety years. Portraiture and emblem books are two exceptions, but exceptions that in a sense prove the rule. Portraiture, secularized and separated from the earlier tradition of portraying donors with patron saints or worshipping the religious mystery, continued to serve a dynastic and memorializing function (and we should recall that Milton's father had his son painted at the age of ten). Emblem books, as Huston Diehl has recently argued, were not incompatible with Protestant ideology; their significance lies in their status as products of the printing press and Renaissance humanism.[10] The stylized emblem remains under the dominance of the word, and in fact serves as a memento or remembrancer of a verbal formula. But only the royal family and a very few of the upper nobility assembled collections of paintings.[11] Because visual art exclusive of portraiture had been subject to religious disapprobation since the 1540s, it is arguable that what connoisseurship existed was charged with ideological

---

[10] "Graven Images: Protestant Emblem Books in England," *Renaissance Quarterly* 39 (1986): 49–66.

[11] On collecting in the Elizabethan and Jacobean periods, see Strong, *English Icon* (43–50), which is supplemented by Susan Foister, "Paintings and Other Works of Art in Sixteenth-Century English Inventories," *The Burlington Magazine* 103 (1981): 273–82. On the purchase of paintings in Italy by and for English aristocrats in the seventeenth century, see John Walter Stoye, *English Travellers Abroad, 1604–1667* (London: Jonathan Cape, 1952), 211–18. Prince Henry, James I's son, appears to have been the first member of the royal family to engage in connoisseurship, an activity in which his brother Charles followed him both as prince and king. For the extent of the royal collection, see Oliver Millar, ed., *Abraham van der Doort's Catalogue of the Collections of Charles I*, Walpole Society, vol. 37 (Glasgow: The Univ. Press, 1958–60). Thomas Howard, earl of Arundel, also assembled an impressive art collection. A notable exception to what I have said of only royalty and the upper nobility assembling collections of paintings would be John Donne, who appears to have had twenty-five or thirty paintings in the Deanery of St. Paul's, including in his private chambers such religious paintings as the Virgin, Mary Magdalen, the Virgin and St. Joseph, and the Entombment of Christ. See Ernest B. Gilman, *Iconoclasm and Poetry in the English Reformation: Down Went Dagon* (Chicago: Univ. of Chicago Press, 1986), 119–22. The fact that Donne confined the religious paintings to the private chambers of the Deanery would seem to confirm their potentially objectionable character.

and political significance by the 1630s. Charles's patronage of Rubens and Van Dyk had the creation of major political images as its end. The existence of religious paintings in the royal collection, moreover, may well have given impetus to Laud's unsuccessful attempt to reimpose visual images upon English worship. For the rest of society, iconoclast attitudes remained the norm, emphatically so among the Puritan left, and such interest in visual art as there was would align one with Laudian and royalist—or papist—sympathies.

Because its turn to iconoclasm had occurred before Renaissance styles had penetrated its culture, England remained, except for royal patronage, isolated from mannerist and baroque developments in painting and sculpture. If an Englishman was to become at all familiar with the traditions of representation that Frye applies to *Paradise Lost* and *Paradise Regain'd*, it could only be by travel on the continent. But how prepared were English travelers to absorb this vast tradition? The greatest barrier was not the problem of access—for much of it was public in the churches, and even private collections appear to have been surprisingly available to curious foreigners—but the habits of mind the traveler brought with him. The art of Catholic Europe was not culturally neutral, something to be seen and appreciated aesthetically. It was, rather, part of the sacramental complex of Catholic worship and belief, a structure that included relics, liturgical ceremony, sacraments, and the dogmas of the Counter-Reformation. One habit of mind is evident in the word that Moryson typically uses to refer to religious pictures; they are "images" and sometimes "graven images," even when he appears to refer to paintings.[12] Compared to other travelers, Moryson is fairly tolerant of the "images" he lists in the churches of Venice, but his very use of the word has behind it a memory of the biblical injunction against idolatry in the second commandment: "Thou shalt make thee no graven image, nether anie similitude of things that are in heauen

---

[12] See, for example, *The Itinerary*, 1:167-69, 177. Moryson takes note of two Latin inscriptions which point out that the viewer does not worship the image but the God whom the image merely portrays. One reads, "Nam Deus est quod Imago docet, sed non Deus ipse / Hanc videas, sed mente colas quod cernis in ipsa: That which the Image shewes, is God, itselfe is none, / See this, but God heere seene, in mind adore alone." To Moryson, however, this only shows "how they worshipped Images in a more modest though superstitious age."

aboue, nether that are in the earth beneth, nor that are in the waters
vnder the earth" (Exodus 20.4; Geneva translation).[13]

The scholarly William Bedell, who came to Venice in 1608 as
chaplain of the English embassy headed by Sir Henry Wotton, was
appalled by the ubiquity of religious art he saw around him:

> If ever there were any Citty, to which the Epithets would agree,
> which St. Luke gives to Athens, (which he calls κατείδωλον
> [given to idols]) this is it. Such a multitude of idolatrous statues,
> pictures, reliques in every corner, not of their churches onely, but
> houses, chambers, shopps, yea the very streets, and in the coun-
> try the high wayes and hedges swarme with them. The sea it self
> is not free; they are in the shipps, boats, and water-marks. And
> as for their slavery and subiection to them, it is such, as that of
> paganisme came not to the half of it.[14]

At the same time Bedell notes the contrast between the "beggary" of
English churches and "the glittering churches and monasteries of Italy,"
and worries that the impressive appearance of the latter may be "noe
small cause of the perversion of soe many of our young Gentlemen that
come into these parts." Indeed, this concern that the impressive visual
character of Italian religion may seduce young Englishmen runs just
below the surface of accounts of travel there. Another traveler a few
years after Bedell was similarly struck by the dangerous beauty of
contemporary Roman churches, "Wherein is inserted all possible
inuentions, to catch mens affections, and to rauish their vnderstanding:
as first, the gloriousnesse of their Altars, infinite numbers of images,
priestly ornaments, and the diuers actions they use in that service;
besides the most excellent and exquisite Musike of the world, that
surprizes our eares. So that whatsoeuer can be imagined, to expresse
either Solemnitie, or Deuotion, is by them vsed."[15] Works of religious

---

[13] *The Geneva Bible*, facsimile of the 1560 edition (Madison: Univ. of Wisconsin
Press, 1969). The Authorized Version retains the reading of "graven image": "Thou
shalt not make unto thee any graven image, or any likeness of any thing that is in
heaven above, or that is in the earth beneath, or that is in the water under the earth."

[14] Letter of Bedell to Adam Newton, in *Two Biographies of William Bedell*, ed. E.
S. Schuckburgh (Cambridge: Cambridge Univ. Press, 1902), 229.

[15] "A Discourse of Rome," in *Horae Subsecivae: Observations and Discourses*
(London, 1620), 389-90. The work is attributed to Gray Brydges, fifth Lord Chandos,

art, "images," form a part of this complex of seductive beauty that seems designed to entrap the mind and turn it to idolatry.

From a modern perspective, one is struck by how little English travelers in the early decades of the seventeenth century have to say about particular artists or specific works of art. They can refer to the Scuola di San Rocco or the Church of the Madonna del Orto in Venice without mentioning Tintoretto.[16] They can visit the seven pilgrimage churches of Rome without taking note of any works of art. Art, clearly, was not something they sought out. Michelangelo, who by this time was an unavoidable culture hero in Italy, is almost the only artist who is mentioned by name. What travelers do remark on are relics and occasionally the general effect of the architecture. Relics, in fact, have a curious fascination for English Protestants; they list them almost obsessively, frequently recording their abhorrence of the superstition involved in the honoring of them and, less frequently, their skepticism over their validity.

Protestant wariness of idolatry obviously stands behind this lack of involvement with visual art. Except for portraits, mythological scenes, and the occasional landscape, the art in Italy was religious—by far the largest part of the whole. One may infer from writers like Vasari that Italians were able to treat religious art with a combination of aesthetic regard and devotion. But among the English any tradition of integrating aesthetic and devotional interests had been broken by Reformation iconoclasm, and in its place the wariness of attitudes like Bedell's prevailed. As well as being generally unsympathetic, if not hostile, to religious art, they were also untrained in habits of perception, not only of its iconology but also of the complexities of mannerist and baroque styles. The differences between these styles and that of the High Renaissance are never noted by English travelers; one gathers that they were

---

but William Cavendish, second earl of Devonshire, and Thomas Hobbes are also candidates for its authorship. On Hobbes's claim to authorship, see Edward Chaney, *The Grand Tour and the Great Rebellion*, Biblioteca del viaggio in Italia (Geneva: Slatkine, 1985), 302–3.

[16] As Fynes Moryson does, *The Itinerary*, 1:179, 185. He mentions the subject of two of Tintoretto's paintings in Madonna del Orto, but not the painter; San Rocco, he says, passes the rest of the *scuole grandi* "in ceremonies and pomp," but ignores its paintings. The only artist Moryson mentions in Venice is "the famous painter Titiano" (182).

not perceived. It is possible, of course, that a traveler inclined toward sympathy with religious art—one thinks of Richard Crashaw—might well have trained his eye by intense exposure to what he could see in Italy. But one need only note the reaction of inexperienced modern museum-goers to realize how unlikely it is that Protestant English travelers, even intelligent and otherwise well-educated ones, would have made much of the art they were taken to see.

There is, however, one English traveler in the mid-seventeenth century who is a partial exception to what I have described above. John Evelyn, some twelve years younger than Milton and touring Italy six years later, differs in several significant ways from the English travelers who recorded their travels before him. Evelyn appears to have been the first English traveler consistently to mention the contemporary Italian art he saw in his travels. He obviously used guidebooks—and later refers to them to touch up the record he made in his diary.[17] He appears to know what there is to see in a city and sets out to see it, even rather systematically. Though undeniably of a less scholarly and literary cast of mind than Milton, Evelyn is indefatigably curious. He knows who the masters of Renaissance and baroque art are (though he too does not distinguish the styles). His reactions to their works are not profound; frequently his modern editor can trace them directly to the guidebooks Evelyn used—or is using to refresh his memory and fill out the diary. But he did employ the nineteen-year-old Carlo Maratti, whom he calls "my Paynter," to copy paintings and antique sculpture he fancied (including the reliefs of the sack of Jerusalem in the Arch of Titus).[18] He is equally responsive to architecture, taking note, for example, of buildings by Palladio. Though not precise in his judgments about styles—"gothick" is his word for any older, non-classical style, encompassing both what we would term gothic and romanesque—he invariably comments on the architecture of the buildings he has seen and frequently on the materials of which they are made.

What is most significant about Evelyn for comparative purposes is that he does not express any of the earlier Protestant revulsion at the elements of Catholic worship and devotion. While there can be no

---

[17] See E. S. de Beer's discussion in the introduction to his edition, *The Diary of John Evelyn* (Oxford: Clarendon Press, 1955), 1:85-101.

[18] Ibid., 2:223, 247.

doubt about his orthodox Anglicanism, he does not typically comment negatively about relics and ceremonies. He reports on what relics are to be found, or the ones he has seen, in various churches, but without insistence about papist superstition. At most he allows himself a "they say" or "it is reported" and occasionally offers a mildly skeptical dissent over a particularly dubious claim. But for the most part he accepts them as elements of the system of Italian religious expression. He is also eager to view Catholic rites and has no qualms about attending mass or witnessing processions. In his comment on Christmas Eve in Rome he combines a traditional Protestant suspicion of friars with a new (and for him characteristically eager) curiosity:

> On Christmas-Eve at night I went not to bed, by reason that I was desirous to see the many extraordinary Ceremonyes perform'd then in their Churches, as mid-night Masses, & Sermons; so as I did nothing all this night but go from Church to Church in admiration at the multitude of sceanes, & pageantry which the Friars had with all industry and craft set out to catch the devout women & superstitious sort of people with, who never part from them without droping some mony in a vessell set on purpose: But especialy observable was the pupetry in the Church of the Minerva, representing the nativity &c; thenc I went & heard a Sermon at the Apollinare by which time it was morning.
>
> On Christmas day his holynesse sa<y>ing Masse, the Artillery at st. Angelo went off: and all this day was exposd the Cradle of our Lord: [at Santa Maria Maggiore]. (2:290–91)

To catch the full significance of Evelyn's way of keeping Christmas, we should recall that this same year, 1644, was the first in which Parliament had banned celebration of the feast in England as a remnant of popish superstition. Holy Week similarly found Evelyn "running from Church to Church" to view various processions and at St. Peter's to see the most sacred relics there, the veil of Veronica and the spear of Longinus. In May Evelyn was at the Vatican again to see the pope receive the ambassador of Lucca, "After which I was presented to kisse his Toe, that is his embrodr'd Slipper, two Cardinals holding up his Vest & Surplice, so as sufficiently bless'd with his thumb & two fingers for that day I returnd home to dinner" (2:391). The mild irony in the concluding clause appears enough, for Evelyn, to deflect whatever disapproval he might be subject to for having kissed the pope's toe.

Evelyn's acceptance of sacred art with little apparent residue of iconoclastic sentiment is of a piece with his tourist's interest in Catholic ceremonial and relics. Not that the art inspired devotion in him any more than the ceremonial. He comments on it as he comments on architecture or antique sculpture; an aesthetic spirit appears to govern his acceptance of both ceremonial and art. But he did collect some paintings on religious subjects, among them a copy made by Carlo Maratti of Correggio's *Madonna and Child with Saints Catharine and Sabastian,* expressly borrowed for the purpose from Cardinal Barberini.[19]

I bracket Milton between these two sorts of English travelers in Italy not only because they stand on either side of his own travels in time but also because they represent two possibilities of English response to the art he too must have seen. In time Milton is closer to Evelyn; Frye uses Evelyn as illustrative of how a contemporary reacted to the art of Italy. But Evelyn is an exception who may allow us to get a more precise fix on Milton's position. In a number of important respects Milton and Evelyn are opposites. Evelyn, a Royalist, went to the continent in 1643 to avoid the Civil War then in progress; Milton returned from Italy in 1639, earlier than he had wished, because he thought it shameful, as he put it in the *Defensio secunda,* to be traveling while his countrymen were fighting for liberty at home. Milton's interests were primarily literary; an unusual feature of his sojourn is his attendance at Italian literary societies.[20] Though Evelyn responded to an invitation to the Accademia degli Umoristi, he did not otherwise seek out literary men in Rome or Florence. Milton very likely left Rome when he did to avoid Holy Week and Easter in the city; at the same time, it is hard to imagine him paralleling Evelyn's interests in processions and relics, let alone kissing the pope's toe. This does not mean that Milton necessarily avoided visual art, but since most of that art was tied to Catholic worship and devotion, it seems likely that their enthusiasms diverged here as well.

---

[19] See W. G. Hiscock, *John Evelyn and His Family Circle* (London: Routledge and Kegan Paul, 1955), 14. Evelyn also bought Maratti's *Church and Reason Submitting to Faith* and *Cross on a Book.*

[20] See Stoye, *English Travellers,* 223-24.

In his account of his travels in the *Defensio secunda*, moreover, Milton aligns himself with an earlier sense of what travel to central Italy was like for the English. Papal territory under Clement VIII (1592–1605) and Paul V (1605–1621) was inhospitable to Protestants, and it was necessary to take certain measures to guard one's religious opinions from the Inquisition. At Loreto Fynes Moryson spent the day fasting to disguise the fact that he was not seeking the indulgences connected with the shrine; similarly, at the gate of Rome he was apprehensive at meeting a company of English priests lest some who had been fellow scholars at Cambridge recognize him and know his religion.[21] The situation must have eased somewhat under Paul V, for in 1620 the anonymous writer of the *Discourse of Rome* says that "no *Englishman* is put into the *Inquisition*, vnlesse hee giue some publique offence."[22] Nevertheless, he concludes with several pages of advice on how loyal Protestants could avert danger in Rome, including avoiding churches during services; one might admit one's religion, but should eschew any vehemence or proselytizing. This is the Italy that Sir Henry Wotton experienced in the first and second decades of the century and of which he advised Milton: "i pensieri stretti, e il viso sciolto."[23] But under Urban VIII (Maffeo Barberini, 1623–1644), and his successor, Innocent X (1644–1655), Rome and the papal dominions became more open, even hospitable to the English. Whether by official or unofficial diplomatic policy, Cardinal Francesco Barberini, the eldest nephew of Urban, assumed the title Protector of the English Nation, the way in which Evelyn refers to him. In this role Barberini was known for the courtesy he showed English visitors. Milton felt flattered by the courtesies Barberini accorded him

---

[21] *The Itinerary*, 1:219, 223. Moryson (1:392) tells an amusing story of how he met a merchant at Voghera, in the duchy of Milan, who professed to be German. When Moryson spoke to him in German, the merchant protested "for want of the language" he was from the French-speaking border of Germany. Moryson then tried out French and discovered the merchant knew as little of that language. Concluding he wished to dissemble his nationality, Moryson resumed speaking Italian with him until the merchant's mistake of "repentiva" for "pentiva" discovered him to Moryson to be English. It was then all Moryson could do to persuade the man not to flee the inn thinking Moryson was a spy. On the changing conditions for English travelers in Italy after 1630, see Stoye, 175–95.

[22] *Horae Subsecivae*, 411.

[23] Wotton was passing on the advice given him by "an old *Roman* Courtier," Alberto Scipioni, whom he knew in Siena; French, 1:362.

and wrote to thank Lucas Holstensius for what he believed had been his agency in the attention he received. Milton was also welcomed at the English College and dined there in company with other Protestant Englishmen.[24] Nevertheless, in his account in the *Defensio* of the Italian sojourn, he gives the impression that he was in some danger while in Rome, that certain merchants warned him English Jesuits were hatching plots against his return to Rome from Naples. It seems likely that for polemical purposes Milton was considerably exaggerating whatever hostility he might have encountered.[25] Certainly the warnings did not deter him from returning to Rome and spending another two months there. Whatever the actual situation, Milton seems in this to be characterizing Rome as it had been for loyal Protestants two decades earlier; notwithstanding the courtesies he received, he was not going to delude himself into complacency about what Rome was, and what that meant, for a traveler of his religious convictions. If anything, the experience of Italy sharpened those convictions.

English attitudes towards art—and towards Italy—were clearly in a state of flux in the middle three decades of the seventeenth century.[26] Milton, in spite of his growing Puritan sympathies, need not be unequivocally linked with rigid iconoclast sentiment. But we do need to question the assumptions too easily made about what must have been Milton's appreciation of the visual culture he encountered in Italy. Because twentieth-century travelers have no difficulty sustaining an aesthetic interest in both poetic texts and visual art, it is easily assumed that such was the case for English travelers in the seventeenth century. But a difference must be acknowledged between the way the twentieth century understands generic distinctions, for visual objects as well as for verbal texts, and the way the seventeenth century understood them. To address only the question of visual art, a modern viewer may recognize differing original purposes for various kinds of painting, but these differences are not operative in contemporary aesthetic acceptance; a

---

[24] French, 1:391–92.

[25] As Stoye suggests, *English Travellers*, 181. See also Diana Benet's argument in this volume that the "Escape from Rome" had become a narrative *topos* of English Protestant travel literature.

[26] In mid-century, poets such as Herrick, Marvell, and Vaughan will begin to show an interest in painting. Marvell's "The Gallery" shows a particular awareness of continental traditions of painting.

landscape, a portrait, a Madonna and Child, a mythological scene, and a portrayal of sacred history may all be hung on the same museum wall. But historically each served a distinct cultural function in its original context. Even if a religious work has remained in its devotional setting, modern tourists approach it with differing assumptions and interests, as quattrolingual signs are frequently forced to remind them.

It is unlikely that the taxonomies of seventeenth-century viewers, whether Catholic or Protestant, were the same as ours. As noted above, portraiture served a memorializing and genealogical function and was not at all subject to iconoclastic strictures in England. The classically educated English apparently had no difficulty interesting themselves in antique sculpture in their travels. It may well be that contemporary representations of mythological subjects, whether painted or sculpted, were accepted as modern analogues of these antiquities. A significant factor in the acceptance of a mythological subject would be that no question of religious belief would enter in. But how would an explicitly ideological work be categorized; what reactions would it elicit? If Milton saw Pietro da Cortona's recently completed *Triumph of Divine Providence* in the Gran Salone of the Palazzo Barberini, could he have separated an appreciation of its magnificence from his apprehension that the triumph of Divine Providence is dependent on the Barberini pope and his efforts against Protestant heresy? Or given habits of mind fostered by a century of Reformation iconoclasm, would he have tended to associate its visual medium with its papist message? Landscape, on the other hand, clearly represented a type of painting that the English had little difficulty accepting, and it seems likely that this genre of painting has the most significance for Milton's verse.[27] But devotional images and representations of biblical subjects are another matter altogether. Here we need to face the likelihood that Milton's reactions to the art of Italy are substantially different from our own. Indeed, it is possible that Milton's profoundest reaction to the devotional and biblical art of Italy was negative, that it confirmed in him a reaction against the iconophile idea that sacred texts could be properly understood in terms of the visual.

From such a suggestion it may be thought that I wish to deny the entire relevance of Frye's visual contextualization of Milton's poetry and,

---

[27] See James Turner, *The Politics of Landscape: Rural Scenery and Society in English Poetry 1630–1660* (Cambridge, Mass.: Harvard Univ. Press, 1979), 21–35.

substituting cultural for literal blindness, endorse T. S. Eliot's notorious strictures on the visual quality of Milton's imagery. But while skeptical of Frye's idea of Milton's connoisseurship of the iconology of religious art, I want to propose that the experience of visual art in Italy did indeed leave a mark, but a deeply ambiguous one, on Milton's poetry. In his study of the role of the image in Western thinking W. J. T. Mitchell has recently called attention to the tension between spiritual and material images in Milton's treatment of Adam and Eve as the *imago dei* in *Paradise Lost* 4. He suggests that in lines 288–93 ("Two of far nobler shape erect and tall . . .") Milton "deliberately confuses the visual, pictorial sense of the image with an invisible, spiritual and verbal understanding of it."[28] The passage at first appears to indicate that Adam and Eve are images of God in their erect stature and nudity— almost as if, I would add, Milton is momentarily evoking the classical sculpture he had seen in Rome. The couple, "Godlike erect, with native Honor clad / In naked Majesty seem'd Lords of all." But then their resemblance to God becomes abstract and spiritual: "for in thir looks Divine / The image of thir glorious Maker shone, / Truth, Wisdom, Sanctitude severe and pure, / Severe, but in true filial freedom plac't." The image of God shines in them finally not in their resemblance to the sculpted gods of antiquity, but in the list of abstract spiritual attributes they share with the one true God. Is the resemblance to that God physical or in the sharing of spiritual qualities? Milton wants to have it both ways, Mitchell suggests: "Milton's poetry is the scene of a struggle between iconoclastic distrust of the outward image and iconophilic fascination with its power, a struggle which manifests itself in his practice of proliferating visual images in order to prevent readers from focusing on any particular picture or scene" (36). Milton similarly perplexes the issue of material and spiritual resemblance in Raphael's question whether his account of the war in heaven is a mere likening of spiritual to corporeal forms or whether in fact a more physical shadowing makes the two worlds "Each to other like, more than on Earth is thought." Whenever vision is thematized in *Paradise Lost*, it is as a troubling, troubled power. This is most evident in the final two books of the poem, in which Michael first presents visual images to Adam, the moral tenor of which the latter frequently misunderstands and misinter-

---

[28] *Iconology: Image, Text, Ideology* (Chicago: Univ. of Chicago Press, 1986), 35.

prets. Because "objects divine / Must needs impair and weary human sense" the angel changes from vision to verbal narration to complete the prophecy of divine providence.[29] In this Adam draws nearer to the Protestant reader who knows the same events as verbal narration. At the same time, the word proves the more reliable means of revelation because it interprets as it manifests.

But the poem that most fully represents Milton's intellectual life is also the one that in an oblique and sometimes paradoxical way bears most upon the broadening of that life that took place during the Italian sojourn. In *Paradise Regain'd* Milton finally winnows his mental experience and through Christ's renunciations expresses what has become essential and what extraneous to his moral and spiritual understanding. Travel and the experience of the visual are not expressly at issue in the poem. But they become instrumental in the temptations set before Christ and become an implicit part of what he, and Milton, renounce as inessential. Before the three temptations from the mountaintop, Satan begins by emphasizing Christ's lack of the experience of travel:

> The world thou hast not seen, much less her glory,
> Empires, and Monarchs, and thir radiant Courts,
> Best school of best experience, quickest insight
> In all things that to greatest actions lead.      (3.236-39)

Untraveled and inexperienced, he suggests, even the wisest man will remain timorous, irresolute, unadventuresome. Satan here no doubt enlarges on what had been in Milton's own mind when he proposed to himself the idea of traveling some thirty years earlier, a sense that travel will provide the experience that will draw one out of the solipsism of solitary study and direct him toward the greater world and its demands. (Thus understood, Satan's sense of the benefit of travel for the reclusive, contemplative temperament is emphatically confirmed by the two decades of Milton's life that followed his Italian year.) The three visions that Satan provides become a kind of travel, and Satan the cicerone for the sights he intends Christ should "see before thine eyes."[30]

---

[29] See in particular Gilman's discussion in his acute chapter on Milton in *Iconoclasm and Poetry*, 158-70.

[30] Though reading the visions differently, James Nohrnberg also links them to Milton's continental travel, " 'Paradise Regained' by One Greater Man: Milton's Wisdom Epic as a 'Fable of Identity,' " in *Centre and Labyrinth: Essays in Honour of*

But even before this, in the elaboration of the temptation of turning stone into bread in book 2, Satan presents an impressively visual temptation. The scene begins as a landscape; the site of Christ's rest at noon is described as a "shade / High rooft, and walks beneath, and alleys brown / That open'd in the midst a woody Scene; / Nature's own work it seem'd (Nature taught Art) / And to a Superstitious eye the haunt / Of Wood Gods and Wood Nymphs" (2.293-97). While Milton leaves it uncertain whether Nature or Art composes the scene, there can be no doubt that art takes over as Satan introduces a still life into the landscape:

> A Table richly spread, in regal mode,
> With dishes pil'd, and meats of noblest sort
> And savor, Beasts of chace, or Fowl of game,
> In pastry built, or from the spit, or boil'd,
> Grisamber steam'd; all Fish from Sea or Shore,
> Freshet, or purling Brook, of shell or fin,
> And exquisitest name.... (2.340-46)

The work of art then comes to apparent life and turns into a masque that includes music and dance—and even the sense of smell.[31] In effect, Satan's is the "superstitious eye" that would paint in the satyrs and nymphs that so frequently populate the landscapes of the Italian mannerist and baroque. He not only composes the still life, but then surrounds it with nymphs and naiades and the tall stripling youths "of fairer hue / Than *Ganymede* or *Hylas*." That the temptation is primarily aesthetic we cannot doubt from the fact that Christ has already rejected the temptation merely to satisfy hunger. Now he is being tempted to accept as reality what is only an image, like the birds who peck at the painted grapes in the famous story of Zeuxis.

In the three visions from the "specular Mount" that Satan presents to Christ's eyes, the mode of visual representation is expressive of the extrinsicality of moral understanding that characterizes Satan's sense of kingship. If Christ is to be a king, then he must concern himself with

---

*Northrop Frye*, ed. Eleanor Cook, Chaviva Hosak, Joy Macpherson, Patricia Parker, Julian Patrick (Toronto: Univ. of Toronto Press, 1983), 103.

[31] Frye notes the connection of the passage with still-life painting and plausibly ties it to the iconographic tradition of *vanitas*, *Milton's Imagery and the Visual Arts*, 338-39.

the military power represented by the Parthians, the impressively concrete empire that Rome is, or the institutionalized wisdom embodied in Athens. The power that each represents is something that can be portrayed and seen; the limitation of Satanic understanding is also the limitation of method. Paradoxically—or indeed the ultimate point of it all—the limitation of Satan's method also makes for the most impressive poetry of the poem; both in sound and in evocation of visual images, Satan's construction of the visions of Parthia, Rome, and Athens contrasts vividly with the minimalist poetry embodied in Christ's responses. In this deployment of poetic resources can be comprehended, I want to suggest, something of Milton's response to visual art during the Italian sojourn, at least what that response became in his reflection on it at the distance of the some thirty years that separate the journey from the poem. Satan's Rome is imperial Rome, the Rome that Milton could mentally imagine from such buildings he had seen as the Pantheon, the ruins of the Colosseum and the baths of Caracalla, and the arches of Constantine, Titus, and Septimius Severus.[32] But the magnificence of "great and glorious Rome,"

> With Towers and Temples proudly elevate
> On seven small Hills, with Palaces adorn'd,
> Porches and Theaters, Baths, Aqueducts,
> Statues and Trophies, and Triumphal Arcs,
> Gardens and Groves presented to his eyes,
>
> (4.34–38)

is as much the remembered splendor of the baroque Rome of Urban VIII, the city that Sixtus V, Paul V, and Urban had made the most impressive in Europe. The "strange Parallax or Optic skill" of Satan's "Airy Microscope" displays the inside as well as the outside of buildings. We might also understand this strange parallax as temporal as well as spatial. As Milton's cicerone no doubt had, Satan directs the eye toward "the skill of noblest Architects," the detail of "Carved work, the hand of fam'd Artificers / In Cedar, Marble, Ivory or Gold." The scene itself is like a monumental fresco conceived with striking visual ele-

---

[32] In reflecting upon Milton's experience of the ruins of Rome it is necessary to recall that much of what a modern traveler sees is the result of excavations carried out from the late nineteenth century until the present.

ments, such as the "Dusk faces with white silken Turbans wreath'd."
Christ can recognize the sumptuousness of the vision and still remain
"unmov'd." In doing so he makes what I take to be the essential
Miltonic distinction: the "grandeur and majestic show" do not, Christ
says, "allure mine eye, / Much less my mind." The eye is an inferior
power, capable of allurement, but even then subordinate to the discipline of the mind. In his reply Milton's Christ can summon up a
poetry of visual expressiveness; he remains steadfast,

> though thou should'st add to tell
> Thir sumptuous gluttonies, and gorgeous feasts
> On Citron tables or Atlantic stone,
> (For I have also heard, perhaps have read)
> Their wines of Setia, Cales, and Falerne,
> Chios and Crete, and how they quaff in Gold,
> Crystal and Murrhine cups emboss'd with Gems
> And studs of Pearl, to me should'st tell who thirst
> And hunger still.                                    (4.113-21)

The rhetorical flatness and elliptical grammar of the final phrase,
sustained by scriptural allusion, makes evident that what has gone
before—in Satan's own style!—is simply parody. Milton's Christ can see,
comprehend, and decisively reject what he has been shown. In response
to the vision of Athens, Christ also rejects, in visual terms, even the
verbal ornament of epithets applied to the Greek gods "thick laid / As
varnish on a Harlot's cheek."

In thus arguing for a relation between Milton's Italian tourism and
Christ's response to the tourism Satan thrusts upon him, I would agree
with Frye that Milton must indeed have seen a good deal of painting
and sculpture during his sojourn. But that seeing very likely occurred in
a different spirit than Frye implies. Milton's subsequent silence about
the painters and sculptors who occupied central positions in the culture
of Italy seems, finally, telling. They became for him not figures in their
own right, like Galileo or Ariosto and Tasso, but rather the anonymous
"noblest Architects" and "fam'd Artificers" of Satan's guided tour of
Rome. Though not a literal iconoclast, Milton became in 1649 the
figurative iconoclast who would strive through words to smash the icon

created to turn the executed king into a sainted martyr.[33] In the late 1630s his deepest sympathies lay with those who opposed Laud's attempts to turn the English church back toward the use of images.

If anything, those sympathies must have been confirmed during the stay in Italy; one constant of his recollections of the Italian year is his insistence on the steadfastness of his Protestant commitment in the face of Catholic challenge. A significant element of that challenge was a culture centered on the visual image, not only in painting and sculpture but in the whole baroque program of city building. In 1638–1639 Rome was at the height of this activity designed to assert in marble, plaster, paint, and stone the claims of the Catholic reform. St. Peter's had been dedicated eleven years before; Bernini was completing his monumental *St. Longinus* to commemorate one of its principal relics. Borromini was beginning San Carlo alle Quattro Fontane and the Oratory of St. Philip Neri. Pietro da Cortona had just completed his fresco of the *Glorification of the Reign of Urban VIII* in the Palazzo Barberini and was beginning SS. Martina e Luca. In Venice Santa Maria della Salute had been begun some six years before; the work of Tintoretto, completed a half century earlier, was everywhere to be seen. What would Milton have made of this widespread glorification of the image? It left its mark on his poetry, I suggest, in the deep attraction for the visual, an attraction made all the more poignant after the onset of blindness some fifteen years after the Italian tour. But at the same time it manifests itself in a deep suspicion of understanding gained through the image. Book 3 of *Paradise Lost* vindicates blindness in the essential impotence of human or angelic sight to approach the godhead. The pastoral landscapes of books 4 and 5 are positive expressions, but represent the fragility of innocence. Milton no doubt retained the humanist faith in the *visibilia* of creation as a revelation of God. But constructed images, whether the Pandemonium that recalls St. Peter's and other such monumental Roman churches as San Andrea della Valle and the Gesù or Satan's visionary tour of human culture in *Paradise Regain'd*, are foci of a strong disapprobation of an externalized representation, especially representation that purports to express the sacred. The legacy of what Milton saw during the Italian year is not

---

[33] See Richard Helgerson, "Milton Reads the King's Book: Print, Performance, and Making of a Bourgeois Idol," *Criticism* 39 (1987): 1–25.

finally a connoisseurship of sacred art and its iconographic traditions but rather the deep-seated tension between the visual image and the poetic word that lies at the heart of his major poetry.

University of California—Santa Barbara

MINDELE ANNE TREIP

# "Celestial Patronage":
# Allegorical Ceiling Cycles of the 1630s and the
# Iconography of Milton's Muse

## I

J H. HANFORD YEARS AGO RETRACED Milton's footsteps in Italy[1]
in a frustrated search to find factual evidence or written record
of paintings Milton might have seen (since Milton cites none in
his prose tracts or familiar letters, just as he mentions no specific
buildings, sights, or performances of plays or operas seen or music
heard there). Like Hanford, many others have nevertheless continued to
sense a powerful internal impact of Italian visual art on the descriptive
art of *Paradise Lost*. Hanford had cited the possible influence of "the
work of the great painters which must have confronted him everywhere," mentioning the Sistine Chapel and the Doge's palace in Venice.[2] Other areas also recently being taken into account are the great
Creation cycles in biblical illustrative art and medieval illustrations with
a typological content.[3] Renaissance paintings of a more abstruse intellectual kind—paintings with Christian-humanist programs of religious
and secular learning and typological patternings—offer another area of

I am indebted to Miss Jennifer Fletcher, of the Courtauld Institute, University of
London, for helpful discussions of the Rubens, Cortona and Gentileschi paintings, and
for arranging access to photographic collections at the Courtauld Institute.
[1] See Hanford, "Milton in Italy," *Annuale Mediaevale* 5 (1964): 49–63. Hanford
(5th ed.), appendix F, "Milton in Italy," 329–42, remains an indispensable source of
information and suggestions about Milton's Italian acquaintances and their interests.
[2] *John Milton, Englishman* (London: Victor Gollancz Ltd., 1950), 117–18.
[3] The "Raphael Bible" in the Vatican *loggie* would be an obvious example. D.
McColley, in a paper in this volume, discusses the Creation cycles in the dome of the
Basilica of San Marco in relation to Milton's Eden and Adam and Eve. Also see A. C.
Labriola, "The Medieval View of Christian History in *Paradise Lost*," in *Milton and the
Middle Ages*, ed. J. Mulryan (Lewisburg: Bucknell Univ. Press, 1982), 115–32.

possible influence. Raphael's Stanza della Segnatura in the Vatican, one of the allegorical showpieces of the High Renaissance, offers a complex illustration of one such compounded philosophical and religious message, bearing, as I have argued in detail elsewhere, close schematic, thematic, and iconographical relationships to Paradise Lost and to Milton's Muse, Urania.[4] Other efforts have also been made in recent years to go beyond the "backgrounds" approach to Milton's visual artistry, as afforded by Roland Frye's monumental study,[5] and to posit the influences of specific paintings on Paradise Lost. It is not to be supposed, either, that Milton looked at nothing more contemporaneous than the earlier works of art noted above. Paradise Lost also shows the impress of later "baroque" visual art—and not simply in the stylistic illusionism noted by Frye, or seen much earlier by Margaret Bottrall.[6] (Baroque descriptions are by no means always negatively contexted: there are "dive-bombing" archangels in Paradise Lost, for example Raphael [5.266 ff.], as well as the first great Satanic swoop [3.562 ff.], or the Caravaggesque battle effects in Hell.) Phillip Fehl has brilliantly analyzed the ways in which the intellectual "statements" made by the architecture of St. Peter's in Rome are reflected both accurately, and also in distortion, in architectural descriptions within Paradise Lost.[7] In a different medium, Margaret Byard has risked tracing a direct line of descent from Andrea Sacchi's "Divina Sapienza" painted figure to Milton's Urania [8] (the common progenitor, one may add, being Raphael's "Urania" panel in the Segnatura stanza).

---

[4] "Descend from Heavn'n Urania": Milton's "Paradise Lost" and Raphael's Cycle in the Stanza della Segnatura, ELS Monograph Series, 35 (Victoria, BC: Univ. of Victoria, 1985). The material on Raphael's Urania and associated emblems and emblem dynamics in the present essay develops material in this monograph. The present sections on the paintings of A. Sacchi and P. da Cortona formed the basis of more extended discussions of their iconography in a paper I gave at the CEMERS conference on "The Renaissance" (Binghamton, NY, 1987): "Milton and Allegorical Ceiling-cycles in Rome: 1638-1639."

[5] Milton's Imagery and the Visual Arts: Iconographic Tradition in the Epic Poems (Princeton: Princeton Univ. Press, 1978).

[6] Frye, plate, p. 172. Bottrall, "The Baroque Element in Milton," English Miscellany: A Symposium of History, Literature and the Arts, ed. M. Praz (Rome: The British Council, 1950), 1:31-42.

[7] See pp. 291-93 of "Poetry and the Entry of the Fine Arts into England: Ut Pictura Poesis," in The Age of Milton: Backgrounds to Seventeenth-Century Literature, ed. C. A. Patrides and R. B. Waddington (Manchester Univ. Press, 1980), 273-306.

[8] "Divine Wisdom-Urania," MQ 12 (1978): 134-37.

In the present paper, I shall have three interconnected aims. I wish to consider the background: the question of Milton's and other Puritan known artistic connections with visual arts, artists and art critics in Italy or England; to illustrate, from Raphael's influential Vatican cycle, the use of emblems and the processes of emblem dynamics in allegorical paintings—a language which we have now largely lost; and then to direct these enquiries to the important question of patronage, and to trace the process of the diverting of visual iconography in painting, including sacred iconography, to political uses during the 1630s, and the possible impact of this development on *Paradise Lost*. The thread I shall follow continues to be the figure of Urania (or her descendants) in four other Italian or Italianate cycles of this decade. It cannot be proved that Milton saw all of these paintings, although there is strong circumstantial evidence, as I show below, to connect him with some or all of them. Whatever the case may be, the themes and emblematic techniques of these cycles bear a meaningful relationship to certain of Milton's themes and emblematic descriptive techniques in *Paradise Lost*. Before proceeding, some further thought must first be given to the recurring question of why Milton did not think it necessary ever to mention paintings, if indeed his own art was affected in the ways suggested above.

One kind of answer to Hanford's frustrated questioning was interestingly afforded by Paul Kristeller in a recent lecture, in which he stressed the wide but predictable range of *topoi* employed in humanist writings, including letter-writing.[9] Usually destined for publication, such writings became a necessary mode of public self-presentation. Kristeller began by saying that the term "humanist" denoted a concern with the five arts, but excluded "Art." The trivium and quadrivium, the images of the ancient classics in whose garb the writer constantly dresses himself, literary theory and every aspect of the "sublime Art" of poetry, institutes of law, questions of science and education, advice for reading to students, libraries and books, news of public matters and public men, even the writer's own health—all these were admissible and expected subjects in writings which even when "personal" were constructed with an eye to creating a certain kind of image of the author for his contemporaries and for posterity. No one was more conscious than Milton of such a

---

[9] Plenary lecture, "Renaissance Humanism and its Significance," given at the CEMERS conference on "The Renaissance" (Binghamton, NY, October, 1987).

public image and such a destined role; his letters, inevitably published, inevitably followed suit. In the "Familiar Letters" or others,[10] almost all rhetorical in cast (not the sort of letters one might write home), or in the accounts of his European travels in his prose tracts, Milton's range of topics and his emphases are as above: his regular frequenting of the "private academies" of Florence, the "learned and superior men" met there, the "accomplished society" and "politeness" of Holstenius, the "warmth of friendship" shown him in Naples by Manso, the "honourable manner" to him of "so great a man" as Cardinal Francesco Barberini and the rare "opportunity of leisurely conversation" with him.[11] (In the letter to Holstenius Milton palpably is recording every detail of the three visits for the benefit of the future reader.) In these writings Milton indeed never mentions the performing arts, or the visual or applied arts—perhaps for the very reason that sightseeing for private pleasure, or private or "public entertainments" given by paid entertainers, were not considered to be fit material for serious humanist discussion or permanent record. "Art" was not in the "canon," as Kristeller has observed.

But the private side remains; and here we must draw different inferences. As Lee Jacobus and others have demonstrated, not only traditional music but the new styles (as in Monteverdi's operas) exerted a profound influence on "Lycidas" and probably on others of Milton's poems;[12] yet the only specific reference to Italian music in connection with Milton comes from Edward Phillips.[13] Milton attended a famous first performance of a contemporary opera at the Palazzo Barberini,[14] and other operas such as Doni's classical experiments[15] must have interested him keenly and may have had an impact on *Samson Agonis-*

---

[10] CE 12, ed. D. Clark, trans. D. Masson. Emphases (except with proper names) in all quotations from Milton are mine.

[11] Quotations (in English translation) from: *Pro populo anglicano defensio secunda* (*The Second Defence of the People of England*), ed. E. J. Strittmatter, trans. G. Burnett, in CE 8:123-25, and letter 9 to Lucas Holstenius (March 30, 1639), in CE 12:39-45.

[12] "Milton and Italian Monody" (Paper given at the Third International Milton Symposium, Florence, June, 1988).

[13] Darbishire, 59.

[14] *Chi soffre, speri*; music by Mazzocchi; sets by Bernini—no less!

[15] Combining monody (sung in *recitativo*) with the Greek choric model, so as to emphasize the words. See Hanford, 334-35 and nn. 10 and 11. Doni set Seneca's *Troades* to music for performance at the Barberini theatre.

*tes*; yet, while ancient tragedy is discussed in *The Reason of Church-Government*,[16] no contemporary model for tragedy is proposed, and in the brief reference Milton makes to the Barberini performance his emphasis is rather on its *magnificentiâ vere Romanâ* ("truly Roman magnificence")[17] than on its content (which evidently included the new *recitativo* styles). Similarly the case, one may judge, with visual art. There are no direct comments by Milton on paintings, any more than there are on contemporary music, drama or architecture; but that does not mean that none of these were seen or heard or appreciated by him.

However, a different and perhaps more central answer to Hanford's question lies in the essentially literary character and the abstract intellectual nature of much Renaissance painting. The *content* of the kinds of paintings under discussion here does very much fall within the humanist sphere of interests, and in one particular sense no special painterly orientation was necessary to assimilate their visual material into a literary context. Poetry and painting, in terms of their capacity to narrate a story (*istoria*) or convey an abstract idea (*concetto*) traditionally were interchangeable. Poetry is like painting in that it can describe visual scenes; and painting (it was constantly stressed) is like poetry, in that it can offer an intellectual argument: an "Idea" expressed through "symbolic images,"[18] the condensed symbolism of emblems, or through elaborate networks of these. Indeed, the "programs" for such paintings were most commonly drawn up by Renaissance humanist scholars or *literati*.[19] To "read" an allegorical painting was therefore a case of working back to recover the embedded allusions, usually literary and mythological in origin, and reinterpreting them in their new visual setting. It requires no special evidence to think that the learned Milton too could respond to the allusions in a "speaking picture" with ease and recognition, and interpret its new *invenzione* in just the way he could read and interpret a densely allusive Renaissance literary text which, in the Renaissance tradition of *imitatio*, constructed its own

---

[16] *The Reason of Church-Government urg'd against Prelaty*, in CE 3.1.237-38.

[17] Letter 9 to Holstenius, in CE 12:40-41.

[18] See E. H. Gombrich, *Symbolic Images: Studies in the Art of the Renaissance* (Oxford: Phaidon, 1972; 2d ed., 1978).

[19] For brief discussions of humanist painting programs and the early thesis of *ut pictura poesis* as applied to painting, see Treip, *Milton and Raphael*, appendix 1 and 72 n. 23.

argument against a background of mythological evocation from Virgil, Homer or Ovid. The grand allegorical painted cycle afforded a magnificent opportunity to make a new statement, to construct a topical argument, out of the mosaic of old allusions so frequently condensed into the symbolic personifications of emblem figures.

The kinds of emblematic representations which form the background to the present discussion had from antiquity to the Renaissance freely been interchanging places between literary and plastic or pictorial forms, the one copied back into the other, always recognizable, but most often modified, recombined or recontexted, in ways which qualified interpretation.[20] Even the individual emblem figure, the handy package of interchange between the literary and visual arts, contrary to popular supposition, never was a "fixed counter." As Cesare Ripa's simplified dictionary collections show,[21] the meaning of a particular emblem personification could be modified by altering some of its visual details; emblems could also acquire compound meanings by conflation with other emblems, as well as through recontexting, or being drawn into new "speaking" combinations with other emblems, either in emblem pictures themselves or expansions of those in painted "narratives." On each fresh occasion the viewer was to be his own interpreter, bringing to bear on the images his own portion of knowledge and interpretive recognition (as, with reference to paintings, over three centuries art critics such as Alberti, Adriani, Bellori, had never ceased to stress.)[22] The large allegorical canvas could further exploit already coded details and allegorical figures by bringing them into new "narrative" combinations and scenes, or create further innuendoes of tacit "argument" through manipulations such as foregrounding, marginalizing, changing the scale or focus, or joining up allegorical with human figures. The writer who has absorbed such emblematic antecedents and techniques makes special demands

---

[20] See n. 37 below.

[21] C. Ripa, Latin *Iconologia* (1593), illustr. (1603); in many Italian translations from 1613; redrawn and in French translations, 1630, 1636, 1644, 1677; in English translation and redrawn, 1709; plus others. Illustrations reproduced here are taken from the original vernacular editions of 1630 (Padua) and 1677 (Paris). Facsimiles may be consulted in the Garland series, "The Renaissance and the Gods" (New York and London, 1976), gen. ed. S. Orgel: *Iconologia: overo Descrittione d'Imagini* ... (1611); and *Iconologie, ou, Explication Nouvelle de Plusieurs Images* ... (1644), trans. J. Baudouin. These editions are used for quotations.

[22] Cf. Treip, *Milton and Raphael*, appendix 1 and 73 n. 36.

upon present day readers; their eyes need reeducation in the language and vocabulary of pictorial rhetoric. It is necessary to stress these matters, since it has not always been sufficiently obvious to what degree Milton's period and his own art were steeped in the language of emblems and in emblem aesthetics, and through how many avenues, apart from dictionary codifications, emblems may have reached him: via statues, inscriptions, medals, coins, devices; emblem books, emblem poems; as well as paintings, engravings, and, of course, allegorical masque "shows" (briefly considered below).[23]

## II

In the remaining parts of this essay I shall try to describe and illustrate—from five allegorical ceiling cycles forming a kind of chain of painterly derivations and modulations from Raphael earlier, on into the third decade of the seventeenth century (the decade of Milton's Italian visit), each with a central Urania or kindred figure or figures as presiding or strong presences—the relationships which I think these emblematic figures, set within the allegorical *invenzione* of their larger compositions, may bear to Milton's conception of his Urania and her role in *Paradise Lost*. The sequence takes on a special interest in that all five cycles were in buildings visited by Milton in Rome or known to him in London before his final blindness in 1652. These are, in Rome, the striking "Urania / Astrology" panel on the vault of the Stanza della Segnatura (c. 1507-1513)—Milton visited the Vatican at least once;[24] Andrea Sacchi's "Divina Sapienza" ("Divine Wisdom") ceiling (1633-1634) in the Palazzo Barberini; and Pietro da Cortona's "Divina Providenza" ("Divine Providence") ceiling (1633-1635; completed 1638), also in the Barberini palace; Milton probably visited this palace twice.[25] The remaining two Italian or Italianate cycles—almost contem-

---

[23] For a discussion of the emblem background and emblematic processes enacted in *Paradise Lost*, see Treip, " 'Reason is also Choice': The Emblematics of Free Will in *Paradise Lost*," forthcoming in *SEL* 31 (1991).

[24] For a discussion and bibliography on the circumstances of Milton's visit, the history and art-historical interpretations of the Stanza della Segnatura, and its iconographical program, see Treip, *Milton and Raphael*, chaps. 1-5.

[25] Milton's first visit was for the opera performance in February 1639; see Parker,

porary with Sacchi's and Cortona's—are in London. These are the Rubens Banqueting House ceiling at Whitehall (1628-1629; hung 1635); and Orazio Gentileschi's ceiling, "Peace with the Liberal Arts" (1638), in the Queen's House at Greenwich (removed in the mid-eighteenth century to Marlborough House, London). The English ceilings Milton may have known about early, through their close connections with contemporary masques and via his own association with Henry Lawes. But Milton may well have known these paintings more directly after 1649 in the changed circumstances of the Commonwealth, since both cycles were in buildings which seem to have been open to the public after the execution of the king.[26] Moreover, Milton after 1649 lived and worked in Whitehall for three years, before relinquishing his state posts in 1652; while the Queen's House was presently to be used for Commonwealth ceremonials, and Milton also had a certain connection, through state business, with the new owner, Bulstrode Whitelocke.[27] Of all this, more presently. It will be seen that, despite their close painterly connections and emblematic continuities, the messages conveyed by the iconographical programs of these five cycles change radically over the period in question, the process accelerating under the political pressures of the 1630s.


# III


The vault of Raphael's Stanza della Segnatura,[28] with its four heavenly personifications, linked in an endless circle, of Divine Poesy, Theology, Justice, and Philosophy (fig. 1), each heavenly emanation presiding over her human exemplars in an expanded scene dramatized on the corre-

---

2:828 n. 42. The second visit was a personal call on Cardinal Barberini on the following day: see letter 9 to Holstenius, CE 12:40-41.

[26] This opinion was expressed to me by Robert Fallon and is borne out by the excerpt cited from J. Evelyn's diary (see above and n. 75 below).

[27] See letter 41, Milton to Whitelocke (Feb., 1651), CE 12:326-27.

[28] The continuing fame of Raphael is to be remembered; his works became the aesthetic norm of the revived classicism of the seventeenth century; he was idolized by Vasari, whose Lives (Vite, 1550) continued its popularity late into the seventeenth century, and by the scholarly and influential Bellori (Vite, 1672, 1931; Imagini . . . da Rafaelle. . . , 1695, 1968; Vite inedite, 1942). These works, published late, were disseminated in lecture or other form before 1667.

sponding wall below (see fig. 2), offers the most spiritual Christian and humanist distillation of the classical Liberal Arts cycle that it is possible to imagine. The fifth female personification on the vault, a cosmic Urania, earlier identified as "Astrology" (fig. 3), of a much more commanding presence than the gentle astronomical Urania standing, back to us, on the Parnassus wall below (fig. 4), is seen on a panel set immediately between and just below Divine Poesy and Divine Philosophy. The triangular conjunction at once suggests Urania's mediating role between cosmic Muse, the Divine *numine afflatur* (Poesy's inscription), and Wisdom or Philosophy—a symbiosis which is paralleled in Milton's Muse, Urania. Writing *Paradise Lost* in his later years, Milton though blind could still hold before the inward eye such sacred images as these of Raphael.

The secret interplay of emblems in Raphael's fifth personification affords a signal illustration of the processes of emblem conflation and interaction. Urania bends down in rapturous contemplation over the starry transparent globe of the created universe, one hand leaning upon it. The globe (an orrery) relates her to the traditional astronomical Urania (a very early Tarocchi emblem shows a standing Urania, face averted, looking into a globe held in hand and holding compasses);[29] it relates her also to Astrology, who is shown as a divine figure in Ripa: crowned, sceptered, the sun of divine omniscience on her breast, hand on a large starry globe with zodiac (emblem, fig. 5). The astronomical Uranian crown of stars and starry dress (emblem, fig. 6) are secretly incorporated in the stars sprinkled over the Raphael figure's veil and dress; but her larger globe, the zodiac faintly sketched across it, relates her not only to Astronomy but also to Astrology (fig. 5). The Raphael Urania seems half to float in space, the position recollecting adjacent Poesy, with spread wings, on the vault (in fig. 2). As in that, or Ripa's winged Astrology with globe (alternative emblem, fig. 7), the wings say that these figures are celestial:

> On la peint avec . . . ses aisles, à cause que cette Science a cela de propre, d'eslever l'esprit aux connoissances les plus loüables & les plus hautes.[30]

---

[29] See K. Oberhuber et al., *Early Italian Engravings from the National Gallery of Art* (Washington DC: The National Gallery of Art, 1973), plate 24, p. 102.

[30] Baudouin (1644), 24; my translation.

She is depicted . . . winged, because this Science has the special property of lifting the mind to the most praiseworthy and highest understanding.

Yet these celestial figures retain their kinship with that humbler, earthbound Poesia who, seated on the ground, sings both of the heavens and earth (her divided globe, showing stars and land).[31] In contrast to the Urania or Astrology figures who, standing on earth, hold globe in outstretched hand (that is, they look up into the heavenly spheres; the faces are averted),[32] the position of the Raphael Urania in half figure *above* the globe of the Universe implies her authority over it, as do the similar superior positionings of the Tarocchi Theologia,[33] or Ripa's first Astrology figure (fig. 5). Finally, the unmistakable aura of Urania's loving care over what seems to be the newly created universe beheld in its fresh wonder[34] is reinforced by mysterious connotations of Divine Wisdom or Providence afforded by the *closed* books held away to her right and left by *putti*; for Divine Wisdom in emblems always is shown with a *closed* book (emblem, fig. 8),[35] while Human Understanding always holds an open book (emblem, fig. 9).

The above emblems and Raphael's surpassing expansions of them reflect long earlier processes of pictorial and literary conflation from at least the fourteenth century,[36] during which the iconography of the astronomical Urania gathered into itself the further attributes of Poesy and Divine Poesy, of Astrology—understood as the divine science of reading the stars and men's destinies—hence also, by Christianization, Urania-Astrology gathers to her the attributes of Divine Wisdom as manifest at the creation, and of Providence. All these are also the roles of Milton's mysteriously modulating Muse, constantly subsuming fresh meanings, in her various presences in the first three Invocations of

---

[31] Poesia, in the Tarocchi series: Oberhuber, plate 40, p. 120.

[32] On the standing and seated Uranias, see my appendix to the present essay.

[33] Oberhuber, plate 43, p. 123.

[34] G. P. Bellori's comment, *Descrizzione Delle Imagini Dipinte da Rafaelle d'Urbino* (Rome: 1695; facsimile, Farnborough, Hants.: Gregg International Publishers Ltd., 1968), 7.

[35] This emblem is not in the 1611 Italian Ripa, but is shown in the 1630 Italian edition. Cf. the figure with closed book (probably Urania) by Raimondi, after Raphael: see my appendix.

[36] See Treip, *Milton and Raphael*, chap. 6 and appendix 3.

*Paradise Lost* and in the cosmic sections of book 3. In these she is addressed as the Spirit of God presiding at the Creation (1.6–7, 19–22); as the Muse of Divine poetry and poetic inspiration (3.19), soaring high "Above th' *Aonian* Mount" (1.15: like Raphael's Divine Poesy); as "Sister" to "Eternal wisdom" (7.9–10); and as the cosmic Muse "rapt above the Pole" of the starry Universe (7.23).[37] However, in the Invocation to book 9, Milton refers to his Muse in rather different terms. Using the vocabulary of the court and of artistic patronage, he addressed her as his "Celestial *Patroness*":

> If answerable stile I can obtaine
> Of my Celestial Patroness, who deignes
> Her nightly visitation unimplor'd
> And dictates to me slumbring. . . .
>
> (9.20–23)[38]

Let us defer assessment of this singular change of styling until after consideration of the remaining cycles.

The themes and gracious but formal classicism of Raphael's "Urania" panel and surrounding paintings are revived in Andrea Sacchi's "Divina Sapienza" ceiling (fig. 10) in the Palazzo Barberini, painted in the "late classical" or "refined baroque" style (a simplified illusionism). Anne Harris[39] vigorously defends this simple, meditative, almost austere composition, the movement and design of which direct the viewer's eye to the adjacent Chapel, dedicated to the Holy Spirit.[40] The figures of Love and Fear riding apocalyptically across the top of the painting reinforce, perhaps, its tacitly invoked scriptural texts concerning Divine Wisdom's beauty and everlastingness (Wisdom of Solomon 7 and 8)[41]

---

[37] Various efforts, past and present, to restrict Milton's Muse to literary, Protestant-biblical, or theological associations miss the complex resonances in Milton's personal recontexting of his classical and Christian Muse onto "Sion's Hill." John Steadman, in chap. 3 of *Milton's Biblical and Classical Imagery* (Pittsburgh: Duquesne Univ. Press, 1984), emphasizes visual iconography in the traditions on which Milton drew.

[38] Quotations from *Paradise Lost* follow the text of H. Darbishire, ed., *The Poetical Works of John Milton* (London: Oxford Univ. Press, 1958).

[39] *Andrea Sacchi* (Oxford: Phaidon, 1977); see introduction and catalogue, item 17, 58–59.

[40] An actual view confirms Harris's impression (9): "What Sacchi has done is to imagine the room opened up with the vision appearing ahead of the spectator above the small private chapel."

[41] Harris (13 and n. 71; 11; 12–13; 41 and n. 77) discusses the Solomonesque

and the theme of soliciting by prayer entry through Wisdoms's gates (Proverbs 8)—the same texts as those cited by Milton in *The Reason of Church-Government*.[42] The enthroned yet somehow floating Divine Wisdom at center displays the regalia of Divine Astrology ( compare fig. 5): on her breast is a sun-jewel; her eyes look up but her face is averted, giving her an association with the emblem of Urania as well as that of Astrology. Her position high above a large globe recalls not only Astrology but, directly, the Urania of Raphael; the groupings of her attendants[43] also recalls Raphael's Parnassus. The posts of Wisdom's throne discreetly incorporate the Barberini crest (three bees). The evident compliment to the Barberini family in the attendant female Virtues, also in the use of the Barberini crest, is nonetheless subordinated to the central religious theme and figure of sacred Wisdom; what the painting primarily seems to say, is that that family which is to reign virtuously, beneficently, and lastingly must also first pray for Wisdom in ruling.[44] Milton could not but have been in sympathy with such a statement. If he saw both the Raphael and Sacchi paintings, the latter would have strongly reinforced the theme and visual impact of the former, so that what we may have embedded in *Paradise Lost* is a partly remembered visual sequence: the enraptured Raphael Urania, presiding providentially above the Universe; Sacchi's derivative, transported Divina Sapienza, also placed above a globe; and the Miltonic providential Muse, rapt above the pole—paintings, emblems, biblical texts, poem, in mutual dialogue of restatement and reinterpretation.

Cortona's slightly newer painting (fig. 11) in the Gran Salone nearby[45] presents a staggering contrast to Sacchi's. Cortona offered a

---

thesis of the room, confirmed in a contemporary document; the adviser was possibly Pallavicino.

[42] Preface to bk. 2, CE 3.1.240-41: "that the call of wisdom and vertu may be heard every where, as *Salomon* saith, *She crieth without, she uttereth her voice in the streets, . . . and in the openings of the Gates . . .* nor [is she] to be obtain'd . . . but by devout prayer to that eternall Spirit who can enrich with all utterance and knowledge."

[43] Reading to right from the figure of Divine Wisdom: Holiness, Purity, Perspicacity, Beauty. Reading to left: Beneficence, Divinity, Suavity (i.e., Harmony), Strength, Justice, Eternity, Nobility. The iconography is discussed by Harris, 10-11. Although Harris (10) cites parallels in Sacchi to Raphael's "Parnassus" and "Disputà," strangely, she does not make a connection with the Urania panel. M. Byard connects Milton with Sacchi, but neither with Raphael.

[44] Harris, 13.

[45] Discussed by G. Briganti, *Pietro Da Cortona: o della pittura barocca*, 2d ed.

deliberate antithesis, the challenge of baroque *colore* to Sacchi's *disegno*: a challenge reinforced by Cortona's emulation of Sacchi's title ("Divina Providenza" for "Divina Sapienza").[46] But Cortona's emphasis is not on Divine Providence. Virgilian allegories with large mythological figures of gods crowd the outer side panels, celebrating the suppression of heresies and the political and military victories under Pope Urban VIII. These mythological allegories and their boldly naturalistic treatment—gods and men consorting on equal terms—are strongly reminiscent of Rubens's almost contemporary paintings in Whitehall;[47] similarly recollective is the treatment of the figures in Cortona's center panel. The opulent, crowded surrounds here seem to funnel all the restless energies of their flying, writhing, illusionistic figures into the large, nearly empty space at the very center.[48] Above this open space loom three almost grossly inflated Barberini bees. In a dramatic sweep from bottom to left and upward, we see Divina Providenza, who, relegated to the bottom of the painting, gestures upwards toward Eternity at left. She, with an arching movement, holds out her crown of large stars above the empty space;[49] while overhead the three bees and a flying figure bearing the Cross Militant indicate clearly on whose absent head the immortal crown is to be placed.

Cortona's painting, it has been said, marks a form of secular breakthrough in allegorical painted cycles of the period.[50] Its far from discreet suggestions of the eternizing and apotheosis of Urban VIII clearly shocked the older painter Domenichino (himself an advocate of the

---

(Florence: Sansoni, 1982), 81–92. For details of the program (after a contemporary poem by F. Bracciolino [1566-1645] in praise of Urban VIII), see Briganti, 196–203.

[46] For a summary of their contrasting aesthetics, the relationship between the two ceilings, and the rivalries of their painters, see Harris, 8–10 and 43 n. 17; 10–11; and Briganti, 88–92.

[47] Similarly reminiscent are Cortona's mythological sequences on the ceilings of the Camera della Stufa and the Stanze dei Pianeti in the Pitti Palace in Florence.

[48] See R. Leone, "Il Soffitto di Pietro Da Cortona," in pamphlet, *Galleria Nazionale d'Arte Anticha* (Rome, 1980).

[49] The dynamics are strongly recollective of Rubens's "Apotheosis of James I" (fig. 13): there is a general sense among art historians that Cortona may indeed have been influenced by Rubens's work, possibly known to him via Rubens's paintings for Marie de Medici in Paris. There is little iconography to identify either of Cortona's allegorical figures: Divina Providenza has a small wand and a "glory" behind her head; Eternity's ostentatious crown of stars is more usually the attribute of Urania or Astrology.

[50] Comment by Jennifer Fletcher.

classical style), who hinted his disapproval in a guarded letter to Ange-
loni in September, 1640:

> Hò havuto caro della nuova pittura del Cortona scoperta.... A
> me sarebbe curioso solo il sapere l'ordine tenuto sopra tutta
> l'inventione dell'historie applicate: parmi havere inteso il capric-
> cio sia del Bracciolino sopra le lodi del Papa. Secondo quel poco
> che m'è stato significato, dubito che manchi, e che converrebbe
> più tosto a Principe secolare: non sò che mi dica: & io che non
> m'intendo, di qui principierei à giudicare.[51]

> I'm glad to have seen Cortona's new picture.... As for me, I
> would just be curious to know the plan in the overall "inven-
> tion" in the pictorial histories: I seem to have heard that the
> whimsical conceit may be Bracciolino's, in praise of the Pope.
> According to what little I have been given to understand, I'm
> afraid that it [the invention] may be deficient, and that it would
> better suit a secular Prince: I don't know what I'm saying: not
> being an expert.

One may be permitted to think that Milton would not greatly have
cared for Bracciolino's conceit, either.

## IV

Francesco Barberini's artistic coup in commissioning and acquiring a
major masterpiece in each of the two main opposed styles of painting of
the decade 1630-1640 needs to be set in its wider theoretical and
cultural context, since the Italian artistic scene was, briefly, also that of
the Stuart scene under Charles I.[52] The two rival ceilings, Cortona's
in the most opulent of "high Baroque" and Sacchi's in the tradition of
Raphael or the newly classicizing style which would become increasingly
prominent, taken together epitomized the most important aesthetic

---

[51] As quoted by Bellori in *Le Vite de' Pittori, Scultori e Architetti Moderni* (Rome, 1672); repr. in facs. (Rome: R. Istituto D'Archeologia E Storia Dell' Arte, 1931), 358. The translation is my own, kindly amended by Anna Bristow.

[52] On the Stuarts as art collectors, see F. Haskell, *Patrons and Painters: A Study in the Relations Between Italian Art and Society in the Age of the Baroque* (London: Chatto & Windus, 1963), 177-79; M. Whinney and O. Millar, *English Art, 1625-1714* (Oxford: Clarendon Press, 1957), 287-96.

*Fig. 1.* Raphael, Vault, Stanza della Segnatura. Fresco. Rome: Vatican.
Reproduced with permission of the Vatican Museum.

*Fig. 2.* Raphael, *Divine Poesy*. Detail on Vault. Seen above *Parnassus*. Frescoes.
Stanza della Segnatura. Rome: Vatican.
Reproduced with permission of the Vatican Museum.

*Fig. 3.* Raphael, *Urania.* Detail on Vault. Fresco. Stanza della Segnatura. Rome: Vatican. Reproduced with permission of the Vatican Museum.

*Fig. 4.* Raphael, *Parnassus*, showing lesser Urania and Erato. Fresco. Stanza della Segnatura. Rome: Vatican. Reproduced with permission of the Vatican Museum.

Fig. 6. C. Ripa, *Urania*. Engraving. From *Iconologie*, 1677.
Reproduced with permission of the Syndics of
Cambridge University Library.

Fig. 5. C. Ripa, *Astrology*. Engraving. From *Iconologie*, 1677.
Reproduced with permission of the Syndics of
Cambridge University Library.

Fig. 7. C. Ripa, *Winged Astrology*. Engraving. From *Iconologie*, 1677.
Reproduced with permission from the Syndics of Cambridge University Library.

Fig. 8. C. Ripa, *Divine Wisdom*. Woodcut. From *Iconologia*, 1630. Reproduced with permission from the Syndics of Cambridge University Library.

Fig. 9. C. Ripa, *Wisdom*. Woodcut. From *Iconologia*, 1630. Reproduced with permission from the Syndics of Cambridge University Library.

*Fig.* 10. A. Sacchi, *La Divina Sapienza* (Allegory of Divine Wisdom). Fresco. Rome: Galleria Nazionale d'Arte Anticha (Palazzo Barberini).

*Fig. 11.* P. da Cortona, *La Divina Providenza* (Allegory of Divine Providence). Fresco. Rome: Galleria Nazionale d'Arte Anticha (Palazzo Barberini).

Fig. 12. Rubens, *The Union of the Crowns*. Oil on canvas. London: Whitehall (Banqueting House). Crown Copyright: reproduced with the permission of the Controller of Her Majesty's Stationery Office.

*Fig. 13.* Rubens, *The Apotheosis of James I.* Oil on canvas. London:
Whitehall (Banqueting House). Crown copyright: reproduced with the
permission of the Controller of Her Majesty's Stationery Office.

*Fig. 14.* Rubens, *The Peaceful Reign of James I.* Oil on canvas. London:
Whitehall (Banqueting House). Crown copyright: reproduced with the
permission of the Controller of Her Majesty's Stationery Office.

Fig. 15. Gentileschi, *Peace with the Liberal Arts*. Oil on canvas.
London: Marlborough House; formerly in the Queen's House. Greenwich.
Crown copyright: reproduced with the permission
of the Controller of Her Majesty's Stationery Office.

Fig. 16. Gentileschi, *Urania*. Detail, side panel, *Peace with the Liberal Arts*.
London: Marlborough House. Crown copyright: reproduced with the
permission of the Controller of Her Majesty's Stationery Office.

Fig. 17. Marcantonio Raimondi, *Two Women with the Signs of Libra and Scorpio* (after Raphael). Engraving. Reproduced with permission of the Ackland Art Museum, The University of North Carolina, Chapel Hill.

*Fig. 18.* Wm. Marshall, Milton portrait, with four Muses incl. Urania.
Engraving. Photo from vol. 1 of *John Milton's Complete Poetical Works* (1943).
Reproduced with permission of University of Illinois Press, Urbana.

conflict of the day concerning painting. As Anne Harris has pointed out, the two styles could never be wholly separable (they were in fact at the time connected by a common illusionism, exaggerated in the baroque).[53] Nonetheless, the debate between them was sharp and publicly much aired. The classicizing party had the advantage of having the most distinguished academic art historians on their side, from Vasari to Bellori. The theoretical debate was not without profound implications for the other arts. Sacchi violently opposed Cortona and the *naturalisti*; the classicizing sculptor Duquesnoy in the same period opposed Bernini; Pallavicino, perhaps associated with the program for Sacchi's ceiling, wrote a thesis on the pure and simple style in prose. It is hardly to be supposed that critical issues of such wide importance as the foregoing were of no interest or relevance to the poet who was even then debating with himself "what the laws are of a true *Epic* poem": "whether the rules of *Aristotle* herein are strictly to be kept, or nature to be follow'd"—using not only Homer or Virgil as his guides, but also "the choycest wits" of "modern *Italy*."[54]

That Milton early had a clear conception of the wide implications of the classical style for all the arts is indicated by his, for the period, advanced statement in his letter to Charles Diodati in 1637; he there professes a "vehement love of the beautiful," saying that he searches constantly for a supreme image of ideal beauty: "ego hanc τοῦ χαλοῦ ἰδέαν veluti pulcherrimam quandam imaginem, per omnes rerum formas & facies: ... dies noctesque indagare soleo, & quasi certis quibusdam vestigiis ducentem sector"[55] (it is my habit day and night to seek for *this idea of the beautiful,* as for a *certain image of supreme beauty, through all the forms and faces of things* ... and to follow it as it leads me on by some sure traces which I seem to recognize). The classicizing Bellori in his influential lecture "L'Idea" was to express exactly the same platonizing thesis in art and for painting—the collecting of fragmentary traces of beauty from individual objects into one supreme

---

[53] See Harris, 43 n. 17. Summarizing loosely her distinction: baroque lavishness, energy, naturalism, secularism, and stress on surfaces, versus classical discipline, formal design, harmony, seriousness, and emphasis on deeper underlying content.

[54] *Of Education,* CE 4:286; *The Reason of Church-Government,* CE 3.1.236-37. Milton cites Castelvetro (a strict classicist); Mazzoni (defender of romance-allegorical epic); and Tasso (who adopts a median position).

[55] Letter 7 (Sept., 1637), CE 12:26-27.

image of beauty standing in the mind; and his theories would become standard dogma for Reynolds and other neoclassical painters.[56]

Further, in the tight circles of patrons, scholars, artists, and literary men of Florence or Rome which Milton found so congenial, cultural interests and activities closely overlapped. Vasari had been artist, architect, and also art critic and historian; Bernini was a painter as well as a sculptor and architect; literary men, both scholars and poets, were called on to advise on programs for paintings. To come nearer to Milton, the gifted Giovanni Battista Doni, whom Milton mentions in his letter to Holstenius and who had given a reading at the Svogliati Academy on the occasion when Milton also did, was not only classicist, orientalist, historian, but (like Milton) a musician, and a theorist on the development of musical drama. Milton's Italian friend, Carlo Dati, was among a number in that period to write a "Lives of the Painters." It is something of a current fallacy to imagine that cultivated Puritans were by their religious beliefs excluded from such diverse circles and broad cultural interests as the foregoing; they were not.

The equally close-knit cultural world of London exhibited similar widths of interests and versatilities, in Puritan and parliamentarian as well as Royalist circles; and there was a close overlap between London and Italy in cultural matters at this time. Francesco Barberini and his scholarly and artistic circle may be compared not only with the circles of Charles I or Buckingham, but very directly with the earl of Arundel and his circle. Each notable collector had his eminent scholar-librarian: Cardinal Barberini had Holstenius, Arundel had Junius Junior (who had been a Dutch pastor). Milton knew both scholars. The radical parliamentarian John Selden was a noted antiquarian; he published the "inscriptions" out of Arundel's famous collection,[57] which included ancient statues, fragments, and inscribed marbles, gems, and coins. The versatile Doni (to whose chair Milton's friend Carlo Dati succeeded) also had a parallel work to Selden's, a corpus of inscriptions.[58] If Italy

---

[56] See G. P. Bellori, "L'Idea del Pittore, dello Scultore e dell' Architetto," lecture of 1644 prefaced to Le Vite de' Pittori, Scultori e Architetti Moderni (1672), ed. E. Borea (Turin: G. Einaudi, 1976), 14, 17, 20.

[57] The work was entitled, Marmora Arundeliana (1629).

[58] See Hanford, 334.

had Vasari, Bellori, and other art historians, England had its Junius.[59]

We should remember the close associations of English and Italians, Catholics and Protestants, Puritans and Royalists, in matters of common cultural, artistic, scholarly, critical, and literary interests. We should not suppose that friends did not know of each other's diverse interests, or that scholars of different religious persuasions did not read each other's books. Rubens's London letters of 1629, expressing keen interest in Selden's recent scholarly publications but regretting that Selden's political involvements might be interfering with his scholarly output, convey a quite different picture, as well as a vivid impression of the richness of the English artistic scene:

> Certo in quest' isola iò non trovo la barbarie che si presuppone-rebbe dal suo clima tanto remoto dalle eleganze italiche, ansi confesso che per conto di pitture excellenti delle mani de maestri della prima classe, non ho giamai veduto una si gran massa insieme, come nella casa real et del gia ducca di Buckingham et appresso il conde d'Arundel una infinita di statue antiche et inscrittioni graeche et latine le quali V.S. havera vedute essendo publicate per Joannem Seldenum è commentate per eumdem assai dottamente secondo il valore di quel virtuoso e politissimo ingegno. Il cui trattato de Diis Syris, V.S. avera veduto stampato di nuovo ... ma io vorrei che si limitasse negli termini de la vita contemplativa sensa intricarsi nelle rumori politichi per gli quali sta preso con alcuni altri accusati di contumachia contra il Re nel ultimo Parlamento.[60]

Certainly in this island I find none of the crudeness which one might expect from a place so remote from Italian elegance. And

---

[59] F. Junius, the younger, *De pictura veterum* (1637); translated into English by Junius, 1638.

[60] Letter to Pieresc of Aug. 9, 1629, no. DCXVI in *Codex Diplomaticus Rubenianus* [*Correspondance de Rubens*], 6 vols., published in the original Italian, translated into French and annotated by M. Rooses and Ch. Ruelens (Anvers: J.-E. Buschmann, 1907), 5:152; the letter is no. 196 in the edition and English translation of R. Magurn, *The Letters of Peter Paul Rubens* (Cambridge: Harvard Univ. Press, 1955), 321–22. Selden's work on the Arundel marbles is again alluded to in Rubens's letter of Aug. 8, 1629, no. DCXV in the *Codex Rubenianus*, 5:148; no. 195 in Magurn, 320–21. The work of J. Selden referred to is *De Diis Syris syntagmata* (1617; 1627); Ben Jonson owned a copy.

I must admit that when it comes to fine pictures by the hands of first class masters, I have never seen such a large number in one place as in the royal palace and in the gallery of the late duke of Buckingham. The earl of Arundel possesses a countless number of ancient statues and Greek and Latin inscriptions which you have probably seen, since they are published by John Selden with commentaries by the same author, as learned as one might expect from such a distinguished and cultivated talent. You will doubtless have seen that his treatise, *De Diis Syris*, has just been reprinted.... But I wish that he had confined himself within the bounds of the contemplative life, without becoming involved in the political disorders which have brought him into prison along with several others accused of opposing the King in the last session of Parliament.

## V

Of all art forms in the 1630s, it is the Stuart masques—those grandiose allegorical ceilings descended to the stage—which constitute the most immediate point of contact between Milton and Italian iconographical painting. It is significant that the descriptive texts of several such masques (and thus their emblematic programs) appear to have been directly known to Milton, since *Comus* contains a number of echoes of Stuart masques of 1632–1634.[61] Such masques did not merely draw from emblematic dictionaries or devices; they seem often to have trans-posed whole scenes from allegorical paintings into their own emblematic costumes, sets, and "shows"—modulated into very different kinds of arguments. Conspicuous instances of such borrowings, some suggesting Raphael, occur in William Davenant's *Coelum Britannicum* (1634) and Thomas Carew's *The Temple of Love* (1635).[62]

---

[61] See Treip, "*Comus* and the Stuart Masque Connection," *ANQ* 2 (1989): 83–89.

[62] To the emblematic scenes and figures of Raphael's "Urania" poised above a globe, or "Divine Poesy" above "Parnassus," cf. these from the masques: "Eternity on a globe; his garment ... of a light blue, wrought all over with stars of gold" (*Coelum Brittanicum*, lines 1072–73); "Divine Poesy" with "garment ... sky-colour set all with

The masques appropriately bring us to the remaining cycles under discussion: Rubens's baroque sequence in the King's Banqueting House, and its companion piece in the Queen's House at Greenwich, Orazio Gentileschi's more refined classical cycle, "Peace with the Liberal Arts." These might almost have been planned by Charles I in a spirit of friendly rivalry to Francesco Barberini's two complementary and contemporaneous cycles in the Barberini palace. More intensely than those, however, both the programs created for Charles are imbued with latent or overt statements of political ideology, their iconography in this respect having intimate connections with the series of court masques from 1631-1639. Some idea of the public and traditional moral-emblematic content of the Rubens cycle is given by Roy Strong, who emphasizes its Protestant and British allusions and the connection of the Rubens program with the program of rule laid out by James I in *Basilikon Doron* (1599) for the benefit of his son.[63] But only the descriptive texts of the Stuart masques themselves, with their lavish allegorical emblematology, shared by the painted cycles, can give a full idea of the Stuart program of self-glorification and self-justification which it had also been laid upon Rubens and Gentileschi to commemorate in paint. The masques reveal with what almost contemptuous casualness the semi-sacred iconography of more earnest artists such as Raphael or Sacchi could be diverted to themes of personal glorification. The starry spheres, Eternities with their globes, divine Wisdoms, divine Poesies, all reappear in these later paintings, vying in eager adulation to praise and eternize the royal Stuarts. Or else, accompanying the emblems are personified Virtues in the shapes of gods and goddesses, who support or enforce the Stuart reign, while overthrown figures of Vices suggest the suppression of its enemies.

---

stars of gold, veil hanging down behind"—this figure "descends" from *above* a little Parnassus or "spacious grove of shady trees . . . afar off on a mount . . . a pleasant bower environed with young trees," from which "came forth a company of ancient Greek poets" (*The Temple of Love*, lines 70-82). See the stage directions in the texts of these masques, as printed in S. Orgel and R. Strong, eds., *Inigo Jones: The Theatre of the Stuart Court*, 2 vols. (Berkeley: Univ. of California Press, 1973), 2:579 and 600.

[63] See *Britannia Triumphans: Inigo Jones, Rubens and Whitehall Palace* (London: Thames and Hudson, 1981), 52-54. For other literature on Rubens's use of *Basilikon Doron*, see Strong, *Britannia Triumphans*, 42-54 and 68 nn. 48-65.

## VI

It would have been difficult in the 1630s for anyone with the slightest familiarity with the artistic scene of the court—certainly for Milton, since the earl of Bridgewater, commissioner of *Comus*, and Milton's friend, Henry Lawes, both had such close connections with the court—not to have heard of the famous and costly Rubens cycle, in progress for six years; its author was also an important diplomat to the English court, and its installation followed a few months after the production of *Comus*, which had its own political connections with the court. (Gentileschi, as long-standing resident painter to the court, had also achieved notoriety as possibly the most expensive and indulged continental artist in Charles's employ.)[64]

Rubens's cycle was commissioned in 1628; oil sketches submitted in 1629 and later indicate that its principal designs were closely followed, if not indeed directed, by the king. What may at once strike us about the Rubens paintings is that the numerous allegorical deities or divine Virtues involved have all been relegated to the peripheries, their central places in the Italian cycles now supplanted by the human figures of James or Charles. Thus the older subjects of divinely inspired Arts or Divine Wisdom or Providence have been translated into the secular argument of Divine Rule—a theme reinforced by all the tricks of illusionistic amplification. Mythologized subordinate allegories suggest (besides the ancient Briton and Protestant allusions posited by Strong) the suppression of sedition or armed insurrection by royal wisdom, temperate rule, and strength. The three central panels take a bolder line, asserting in strongly religious terms the divine character of the Stuart reign.[65] From 1635 the Banqueting House was no longer used for masques but kept quite empty, save for the audience-throne at the farther end. The hall thus gives the effect of an empty nave or basilica. The order in which the pictures appear as one passes under them, walking through the empty hall toward the throne, reinforces this

---

[64] Gentileschi's English career is sketched by R. Bissell, *Orazio Gentileschi and the Poetic Tradition in Caravaggesque Painting* (University Park, PA, and London: Pennsylvania State Univ. Press, 1981), 50–51.

[65] In the next section I follow, with some amplifications, the analyses of Julius Held in *The Oil Sketches of Peter Paul Rubens: A Critical Catalogue*, 2 vols. (Princeton: published for the National Gallery of Art by Princeton Univ. Press, 1980), 1:187–218.

impression. First, nearest the door (seen in reversed perspective), is "The Union of the Crowns" (fig. 12). Here the united diadems of England and Scotland are held from either side above the head of a robust infant (Charles, the inheritor of the New Reign; as well as the new united reign itself). The total scene evokes an "Adoration," as well as, in the disputing but reconciled mothers, a "Judgement of Solomon"; the enthroned James gravely presides, having made peace.

Centrally placed is the "Apothesosis of James I" (fig. 13), showing the aged king being lifted up from his throne toward Heaven by the allegorical figure of Justice, assisted by Religion and Faith. Two further allegorical figures placed higher hold the eternal crown above the monarch's head, while at the same moment *putti* remove the monarch's earthly crown: a scene to be echoed in poignantly different circumstances in 1649 in the exchange between Charles and Dr. Juxon on the scaffold.[66] And at the far end above the throne is "The Peaceful Reign of James I" (fig. 14). Here Peace and Plenty fearfully embrace each other to our left (the king's right); he extends his right arm towards them, averting his body from armed Insurrection with a firebrand at our lower right (his left); the latter is being suppressed by armed Minerva. In this complex and suggestive allegory, and in accordance with the "thought patterns of baroque art" and allegory,[67] various allusions to Solomon *pacificus*, to Jupiter hurling thunderbolts, and to Christ at the Last Judgement, all fuse. Although Rubens like Cortona paints naturalistically, his use of the sacred iconography is much more explicit, as well as secularly directed; this, coupled with his flagrant literalizing of the theme of human apotheosis (only adumbrated by Cortona), puts the exaltation of the Stuart reign on a quite different plane. Noble though the Rubens paintings are,[68] this form of art has crossed some ideological watershed.

---

[66] *Dr. Juxon:* . . . You haste to a crown of glory.
*The King:* I go from a corruptible to an incorruptible Crown, where no disturbance can be.
*Dr. Juxon:* You are exchanged from a temporal to an eternal Crown, a good exchange.

As quoted by J. Charlton, in *The Banqueting House, Whitehall* (London: HMSO, 1964; DoE, 1983), 9: taken from John Rushworth's *Historical Collections* (1659).

[67] Held, 1:194.

[68] Fehl, 301–2, defends Rubens's treatment as not sycophantic.

This conclusion is strengthened by the overt echoes in the Rubens cycle of the two religious ceiling cycles by Veronese in churches at Venice, particularly the typological Esther sequence in San Sebastiano. This shows, near the door, a "Presentation of Esther to Ahasuerus," then a central "Coronation of Esther," and above the altar "The Triumph of Mordecai" (true religion joins with Empire). Viewed in the strongly religious light of the Veroneses, as the visitor walks through Charles's hall empty like a nave, in parallel sequence the infant Charles becomes an infant Christ, inaugurating the new reign; the eternal crowning of his father and translation to Heaven, a Coronation or Ascension of the Virgin; while in the "Peaceful Reign" (the allusion the more recognizable from his own self-styling)[69] James presides like a "Prince of Peace"—or even a Christ at Judgement—above the throne-altar.[70] Viewed as a secular typology, the entire sequence constitutes a startling blasphemy—more blatant, perhaps, than anything Milton saw in Rome. The nature of the Puritan and parliamentarian response to this twisting of sacred iconography toward political propaganda and the implied exaltation of the Stuarts may be guessed at from Cromwell's cruel gesture in bringing the king to execution through the Banqueting House, so that he was forced to walk onto the scaffold passing under the ceiling asserting the Stuarts' eternal reign. Milton, immersed as he was in politics and living and working in Whitehall from 1649–1652, could scarcely have been unaware of the Rubens cycle and its propagandist implications. A little later in the Commonwealth, Cromwell himself was to give audience in the Banqueting House under the same paintings beneath which Charles had sat; for they were never taken down. Perhaps impossible to sell, they were also too valuable to lose.

To revert briefly to the masques: James Shirley's The Triumph of Peace (1634) occupies a rather particular place in the present argument. On the one hand, its themes (the allegorical "Visions" of the king's "Peace, Law and Justice") are intimately related to many of the motifs on the Rubens ceiling. On the other hand, this masque, one of those most closely echoed in Comus, also has strong connections with the

---

[69] James I's motto was "Beati Pacifici": he employed variations on this styling on many public occasions.

[70] Reproductions of the Veroneses may be seen in vol. 2 of T. Pignatti, Veronese, 2 vols. (Venice: Alfieri, 1976). The Rubens analogies to Veronese are suggested by Held, 1:188 and n. 2.

Commonwealth context. This most spectacular of all the masques was the lawyers' masque, with friends of Milton performing in it; many parliamentarians were associated, and by no means only in a spirit of suppressed criticism. While echoes of criticism of the king's policies may exist, especially in the anti-masques, there was also great interest in the masque for its own sake. *The Triumph of Peace* processed for hours in full costume from St. Paul's to Whitehall before its second performance in February, 1634; and John Selden (admired by Milton for his writings on Natural Law and divorce, and by Rubens for his book on inscriptions) rode on the floats, along with numerous other lawyers, the two Lawes brothers, and Bulstrode Whitelocke, noted Puritan constitutionalist and later Commissioner of the Great Seal in the Commonwealth Parliament. Whitelocke was an important member of the Council of State and one of Milton's direct superiors at Whitehall. Whitelocke with Selden were two of the four principal organizers of the masque, of which Whitelocke remained extremely proud. In recently discovered papers, he records in great detail his ingenious arrangements for its huge orchestras;[71] and later he published a minutely detailed and enthusiastic description of its "shows," as seen in the procession and masque.[72]

## VII

By another of the political-cultural ironies of the period, Bulstrode Whitelocke was after 1649 given the possession or use of the Queen's House at Greenwich; and it may therefore well have been he who was responsible for its excellent state of preservation, amidst the general neglect of the palace.[73] That this building after the execution of the

---

[71] See M. Lefkowitz, "The Longleat Papers of Bulstrode Whitelocke; New Light on Shirley's *Triumph of Peace*," *Journal of the American Musicological Society* 18 (1965): 42–60; *Trois Masques à la Cour de Charles I<sup>er</sup> d'Angleterre*, series "Le Choeur des Muses" (Paris: Éditions du Centre National de la Recherche Scientifique, 1970), 27–109.

[72] *Memorials of the English Affairs* (1625–60; London: Nathaniel Ponder, 1682). Whitelocke's account is reprinted in Lefkowitz, *Trois Masques*, 62–65; also in Orgel and Strong, 1:539–45.

[73] G. H. Chettle, *The Queen's House, Greenwich*, 14th Monograph of The London Survey Committee (London: National Maritime Museum, Greenwich, and London Survey Committee, 1937), gives the history of Henrietta-Maria's house during the interreg-

king was (like the Banqueting House) apparently open to the public is indicated by John Evelyn's diary for April 29, 1652:

> We went this afternoon to see the Queen's House at Greenwich, now given by the rebells to Bulstrode Whitlocke, one of their unhappy counsellors, and keeper of pretended liberties.[74]

That Milton must have known of the building and its contents at least by 1650 is certain; for, quite apart from his own connection with Whitelocke, the Queen's House during the interregnum was used for Commonwealth state occasions such as funerals.[75] Further, the "nine pieces" by Orazio Gentileschi which adorned its Great Hall were among the paintings of Charles I inventoried for sale by Cromwell's commissioners. But Orazio's "Nine Peeces in y$^e$ Ceeling," valued at £600, along with three other structural paintings either failed to sell or were removed from sale.[76] Thus "Peace and the Liberal Arts" remained undisturbed in situ for over a century.

Gentileschi's "Peace with the Liberal Arts" (or "Peace and the Arts"),[77] like the Rubens cycle, had an Inigo Jones ceiling and house for its setting. Again like the Rubens cycle, its theme connects it closely with Stuart politics and anxieties, as reflected in the masques of the same decade. In Albion's Triumph (1632) by Aurelian Townshend, a "triumphant" Peace sits in a cloud, "proclaiming her large benefits, and the world's ingratitude"; she subsequently commands, "Neptune to sea!" and "Bellona arm!" William Davenant's Britannia Triumphans

---

num, the documentation concerning the sale inventories for Gentileschi's and other paintings, and notes the Whitelocke connection—without, however, ascribing the preservation of this building or of Gentileschi's or other structural paintings in it to Whitelocke's influence.

[74] The Diary of John Evelyn, ed. A. Dobson, 3 vols. (London: Macmillan and Co., 1906), 2:55.

[75] Chettle, 38.

[76] Chettle, 36–37. A detailed description of the paintings and account of their subsequent removal (by 1744) to Marlborough House is given by R. Walker, Marlborough House: a Catalogue of Paintings and Engravings, Current Papers: Property Services Agency, Library Service (London: DoE, 1976), 1–10.

[77] See Bissell, 60–61; 90–97 (with plates), and J. Hess, "Die Gemälde des Orazio Gentileschi für das 'Haus der Königin' in Greenwich," English Miscellany, ed. M. Praz (Rome: The British Council, 1952). The paintings are in some places worn or doubtfully restored; and Hess and Bissell do not always agree in their readings of the iconography.

(1638) alludes to naval power—to be achieved through the recently extended Ship-money taxes—and relates "Naval Victory" to "Right Government" and "a real knowledge of all good arts and sciences."[78] Similarly, in the center panel of Gentileschi's painting a somewhat shadowy Peace hovers above a more forceful, crowned Britannia-like figure, seen waving her palm of Victory (fig. 15). Encircling these two central figures, and in the outer corners, are rather pedantic figures in small scale personifying various Liberal Arts, visual or applied Arts, and an assortment of Virtues. Their iconography seems confused, but we may take them to represent the benefits of Peace attendant on Victory. Certain details, such as the positioning of the enthroned Peace and the classical formality of the total circular design, may recall Raphael or Veronese. And we are forcefully reminded of Raphael, yet distanced from him, by the conspicuous and beautiful Urania (fig. 16), one of seven Muses painted in larger scale on the side panels. She is emblematically correct, with starry crown, gazing into an orrery held in her outstretched hand; she is shown seated on the ground. But this Urania, like her companion Muses and Arts, is functional—without a trace of the numinous. She *is* Astronomy, no more; the seated position probably is deliberately reductive. Her subordinate posture and positioning relative to the two central figures (she is placed as if seen below them) puts her in a situation of dependency, as does her marginal place in the side panel. In contrast to the allegorical figures in any of the other four cycles, she neither presides nor guides nor even assists, but humbly waits upon the royal crowned figure, center, and its overshadowing Peace; like her sister attendants, she directs her earnest gaze at the central figures, seeming to wait, depend upon, to "solicit" the royal patronage and protection. The erotic suggestiveness of her draperies, furthermore, like the languid postures of others of the attendant allegorical figures, bespeaks a certain trivializing; it evokes the sometimes daring dress of Henrietta-Maria's *tableaux* of ladies in the Queen's masques, or that "sweet disorder in the dress" which "kindles in clothes a wantonness" favored by Cavalier poets like Herrick and court portraitists like Sir Peter Lely.

---

[78] Orgel and Strong, vol. 2: *Albion's Triumph*, stage direction, lines 385–86, and lines 429–31, p. 457; *Britannia Triumphans*, stage directions, lines 22–23, 42, 47–48, p. 662.

Gentileschi's cycle marks the ignoble *terminus ad quem* of an earlier more high-minded era in painting, one whose original pious humanism would have been congenial to Milton. From High Renaissance earnestness in the expression of religious, moral, and educative values in painting, as seen in the "Urania" or "Divina Sapienza" of Raphael and Sacchi, the secular breakthough of Cortona's "Divina Providenza" illustrates the diverting of traditional emblematic values to a more ingratiating form of compliment; while his important English counterparts, Rubens and Gentileschi, show the overt adaptation of sacred or semi-sacred iconography to political propaganda and the personal glorification of a particular earthly regime. In keeping, allegorical Virtues or divine potencies who had earlier presided are in the latter three cycles pushed to the side, their central or celestial places usurped by the figures of earthly monarchs. Despite Milton's often reaffirmed enthusiasm for the arts of Italy, cradle of civilization, and despite the memories of Raphael or Sacchi which are perhaps subsumed in *Paradise Lost*, the Italianate artistic scene of the Stuarts, with which Milton had had such specific early association, must by a later date have presented itself to him in a much harsher light. The earlier paintings had praised the arts and their divine inspiration and wisdom in general, as nurtured by great men; the later paintings harnessed the arts and the gods in order to glorify the men themselves, and to assert their power and prerogatives.

If then in *Comus* Milton initiated a restrained Reformist dialogue with one important avenue of court compliment, the masque, it might be thought that in *Paradise Lost* he resumed a much more forceful iconographic critique. In *Comus* Milton necessarily had to be cautious, because—whatever else it may have been intended to communicate—*Comus* had a commissioner and patron to be suited and a designated task of celebration and compliment to perform. In *Paradise Lost* Milton was freed from any such obligations. In his epic he shows, by using similar personifications, that he still reveres the divine images of High Renaissance Christian-humanist art. But at the same time, Milton distances his divine Urania, hence his poem, from all those subservient Providences, Eternities, Peaces, or Uranias who in the 1630s in painted apotheoses or masque spectaculars had been made use of to flatter pope and king. By reversing the expected context of patronage in the lines from *Paradise Lost*, book 9, quoted earlier, Milton restores his Urania to her rightful roles and place in the Heavens, from which she had been rather ignominiously forced to descend. This "celestial Patroness"[79] indeed "dictates" the artist's theme—the patron's prerogative—but she "deigns" her free "visitation" "*unimplor'd.*" We may not be wrong in thinking that while "Patroness," "deigns," and "visitation" are all words implying a royal condescension, "unimplor'd" reverses the perspective, transforming the commercial transactions of political patronage into the free visitations of celestial grace. The lines revive for us the ambivalent situation of the radicalized poet who in 1654 could say with perfect truth (if not without a certain bitterness) that no one had ever seen *him* soliciting advancement or, with "supplicatory" looks, lobbying at the assemblies or doors of the powerful and great.[80]

Lucy Cavendish College
University of Cambridge

---

[79] The terms, "Patroness" or "Patron," are employed three times more by Milton: twice in the sense of "tutelary saint," "protector" or "intercessor" (*OED*), in "The Passion," line 29, and *PL* 3.219 (similarly to the usage at 9.21); and once negatively (of Satan) in *PL* 4.958.

[80] *Defensio secunda* (CE 8:136–37) with the G. Burnett translation (final line amended by myself): "me nemo ambientem, nemo per amicos quicquam petentem, curiae foribus affixum petitorio vultu, aut minorum conventuum vestibulis haerentem nemo me unquam vidit" ("no man ever saw me canvassing for preferment, no man ever saw me in quest of any thing through the medium of friends, fixed, with supplicatory look, to the doors of the parliament, or glued to the anterooms of lesser levées").

## Appendix:
## The Standing and the Seated Uranias

Milton's Urania with the poet soars "Above the flight of *Pegasean* wing" (7:4–5), like Raphael's winged Divine Poesy (in fig. 2) or Ripa's winged Astrology (fig. 7); but she also "descend[s] from Heav'n" to return the poet to a position "Standing on Earth" (7:1, 23). The standing Urania (as in the Tarocchi series, Oberhuber, plate 24, p. 102), globe held in hand but face averted, early became entangled with a Urania seated on the ground, also with globe (like the Poesia in the Tarocchi series, Oberhuber, plate 40, p. 120), and sometimes shown with face averted. (Raphael's Urania on the Parnassus [fig. 4, fifth to right] stands thus with back to us, lifted face turned away.) The conflations/divergences must indicate some now lost differentiations of meaning. L. Dussler (*Raphael: A Critical Catalogue of his Pictures, Wall-Paintings and Tapestries* [London and New York: Phaidon, 1971]), 74, noted the earlier mistaking of Erato (muse of lyric poetry, seated on the ground to the right of Apollo, her face turned to the side [fig. 4]) for Urania. We have noted that the Urania of Gentileschi, globe in hand, also is shown seated on the ground: either the earlier "mistake" is being perpetuated, or the positioning is deliberate; it perhaps indicates the astronomical Urania's more humble role than the celestial Urania's.

We may contrast with the seated Urania, not only the standing Tarocchi Urania, but the Urania shown standing, with averted face and *closed book* (see above in my text, and Divina Sapienza [fig. 8], for the significance of this), in the notable engraving, almost certainly representing Clio and Urania, by Raimondi after Raphael (fig. 17). (See *The Engravings of Marcantonio Raimondi*, ed. I. Shoemaker and E. Brown [Lawrence, KS, and Chapel Hill, NC: The Spencer Museum of Art, Univ. of Kansas, and The Ackland Art Museum, Univ. of North Carolina, 1981], 137–39, with plate 40; these two images are noted by E. Wind, *Pagan Mysteries in the Renaissance* [London: Penguin with Faber and Faber, 1967], 149–50 and fig. 38.) Here "Urania" is seen associated with a zodiac (as is Raphael's Urania); the zodiac (as in Ripa's Astrology) shows Libra and Scorpio. A similar astrological configuration, adapted but similarly placed, in a segment of a hemispheric band arching at the right of the scene, is to be seen in the Medina illustration to book 4 of the 1688 edition of *Paradise Lost* (*Paradise Lost. A Poem In Twelve Books*, 4th ed., illustrated [London: J. Tonson, 1688]). This is the book describing Raphael's flight to earth, for example, one of cosmological sections of the poem; Libra and Scorpio are also emphasized by Milton in book 3, in a cosmological section. (John Shawcross has kindly called my attention to this close parallel.) That Medina seems actually to have used Raimondi's scheme in illustrating *Paradise Lost* serves to suggest that the visual iconography of the emblematic Urania was specifically associated by others with Milton. The emblematic Urania had also appeared much earlier (see the lower left corner of the surround) in the Wm. Marshall engraving of Milton's portrait prefacing *Poems ... 1645* (fig. 18). This is reproduced in Fletcher's facsimile edition, *John Milton's Complete Poetical Works in Photographic Facsimile*, 4 vols. (Urbana: Univ. of Illinois Press, 1943), 1:153. Marshall's figure seems to conflate incoherently both traditions: Urania is portrayed with starry crown, large globe, averted face—yet seated. His Erato, upper right (also seated), herself seems to be confused with Urania: instead of a musical instrument she holds and looks into a globe. Again, the contemporary use of these emblems in such direct connection with Milton's poetry is significant.

M. N. K. MANDER

# The Music of L'Allegro and Il Penseroso

I N L'ALLEGRO AND IL PENSEROSO, Milton confronts fundamental issues concerning the value of poetry, while apparently debating various more superficial matters. A close examination of the "surface" debate enriches our understanding of the poem's profounder concerns, and I plan to consider specifically the contrast in the kinds of music represented in the poems. The musical discussion has been shown to be "indispensably related to form, content and meaning ... clarifying all three,"[1] and can be better understood if seen in the context of contemporary musical thought. That context is complex, but I shall attempt an outline.

I am not the first to see contemporary musical issues reflected in the poems. Sandra Corse finds "in the latter portion of each of these poems a clear exposition of the most exciting issue in music of the early seventeenth century, the debate which pitted monody against polyphony."[2] However, her account of the conflict between the "traditional" polyphony and the "new" monody oversimplifies both the musical situation and, in consequence, the discussion in the poems.

It was Monteverdi, in answer to the conservative Artusi, who introduced the terms "first" and "second practice" to describe the contrasting types of music which were under discussion.[3] In the "first practice" (of which Monteverdi cites Josquin and Ockeghem as examples and Willaert as a supreme example), the music is "not the servant, but the

---

[1] Nan Cooke Carpenter, "The Place of Music in L'Allegro and Il Penseroso," UTQ 22 (1953): 366. I have used Gordon Campbell's edition of Milton's poems throughout and Mrs. Campbell's translation of the Latin verse (from that edition).

[2] Sandra Corse, "Old Music and New in L'Allegro and Il Penseroso," MQ 14 (1980): 108.

[3] His brother, Giulio Cesare, explains this in an appendix to Claudio's Scherzi musicali (Venice, 1607).

mistress of the words."[4] In the light of humanist priorities, the "second practice" was to be preferred: that in which "the words are mistress of the music" (ibid). In the "second practice," Monteverdi includes both the newer kind of polyphony (that which gives the words priority) and the reciting style. Indeed, in the document which could be said to have started the debate,[5] Artusi condemns one of Monteverdi's polyphonic madrigals in the modern style. We need only to look at these madrigals, at the compositions of Cipriano de Rore, whom Monteverdi calls "the foremost reformer," at those of Luca Marenzio and Giaches de Wert, whom he cites as worthy followers, to see that monody was not the only means by which Plato's dictum concerning the priority of the text was honored in composition.

It would be nice to paint one background of musical theory and practice for L'Allegro and one for Il Penseroso, to let one poem speak for the "new" monody and the other for the "old" polyphony and thus to fit Milton neatly into place in the musical context of his time. The complexity I have indicated in musical developments renders this impossible. Yet the poems do reflect contemporary musical thought with all its contradictory elements, while drawing, appropriately, on centuries of musical philosophy.

One of the foremost advocates of the new monodic style was Guilio Caccini. If we look first at the passage from L'Allegro which has been closely compared with the actual wording of Caccini's Preface to the Nuove musiche, we are immediately confronted with a paradox. Milton speaks of:

> ... notes with many a winding bout
> Of linked sweetness long drawn out
> With wanton heed, and giddy cunning,
> The melting voice through mazes running.

It has been suggested[6] that this is a paraphrase of Caccini's account, in his description of monody, of "long winding points, simple or

---

[4] Monteverdi, Lettere, dediche e prefazioni, ed. de Pauli (Rome, 1973), 400-401.

[5] Giovanni Maria Artusi, L'Artusi overo delle imperfettioni della moderna musica (1600).

[6] By Sandra Corse who notes the similarity but not the paradox ("Old Music and New").

double—that is redoubled or intertwined one with the other." Milton clearly has a very accurate idea of the style favored by the monodists, but I am dubious about the suggestion of a verbal echo, particularly as the hypothesis is based on a translation. Milton did not need to know Caccini's words, he just had to use his ears. It is neither here nor there whether he read the theoretical works of the proponents of monody. To be fired with enthusiasm he had only to listen to those English compos-ers who were working along the same lines, such as Nicholas Lanier and his friend Henry Lawes.

When we look at the climax of Caccini's account of the effects of monody, and compare this with the effects of the music of *L'Allegro*, we find the paradox I mentioned earlier. Caccini's culminating paragraph is worthy of patristic or Neoplatonic writers on music at their most ecstatic:

> La quale bellissima essendo, e dilettando naturalmente, allora si fa ammirabile e si guadagna interamente l'altrui amore, quando color che la posseggone e con lo insegnare e col dilettare altrui esercitandola spesso, la scuoprono e appalesano per un esempio, e una sembianza vera di quelle inarrestabili armonie celesti, dalle quali derivano tanti beni sopra la terra, svegliandone gli intelletti uditori alla contemplazione dei diletti infiniti in Cielo somminis-trati.[7]

> Which art, being excellent and naturally delightful, doth then become admirable and entirely wins the love of others when such as possess it, both by teaching and delighting others, do often exercise it and make it appear to be a pattern and true resem-blance of those never ceasing celestial harmonies whence proceed so many good effects and benefits upon earth, raising and excit-ing the minds of the hearers to the contemplation of those infinite delights which Heaven affordeth.

It is important to remember that "music" in this context is melody and word perfectly combined in song. Thus Caccini is speaking of that art of *musica* which (traditionally) the Greeks had mastered, but which had been lost, and which was capable of working miracles through its near

---

[7] Angelo Solerti, *Le origini del melodrama* (Turin, 1903), 69.

divine potential. I quote, incidentally, from John Playford's translation[8] of 1674.

The *locus classicus* of this concept of teaching and delighting, so dear to Renaissance humanists, is of course, Horace's *Art of Poetry*, which for Caccini is highly appropriate, for what he calls "song" like that which Horace calls *ars poetica*, is music and word in one. John Milton would have been familiar both with the original and with the theme in Renaissance writers on poetics such as Sir Philip Sidney:

> [Poets] do merely make to imitate, and imitate both to delight and teach; and delight to move men to take that goodness in hand without which delight they would fly as from a stranger, and teach, to make them know that goodness whereunto they are moved.[9]

We can understand why Milton would have embraced a musical trend which held these values. If we look now at the pair of poems, however, we may be surprised. The passage which most clearly reflects Caccini's description of the effects of monody is that at the end of *Il Penseroso*, describing the effect of polyphonic Church music:

> There let the pealing organ blow
> To the full-voic'd choir below
> In service high and anthems clear
> As may with sweetness through mine ear
> Dissolve me into exstasies
> And bring all Heaven before mine eyes.

Surely this is the very polyphony in which, according to Caccini, the ideal unity of ancient music is most conspicuously lacking? Verse anthems included solo passages, of course, but these would not be sung by "full-voic'd choir," which expression is more suggestive of "full anthems" which were choral (polyphonic) throughout. Unison choral singing was unknown at the time (apart from congregational singing, and Milton specifies a choir). The plot thickens when we turn back to *L'Allegro*, for if the opening describes the art of monody, none of the

---

[8] *An Introduction to the Skill of Music* (London, 1674), 55. Playford does not acknowledge his source.

[9] *Apology*, 103.

appropriate ennobling effects are achieved. It is almost as though Milton wished in L'Allegro to denounce the art of monody and in Il Penseroso to claim for polyphonic music precisely those qualities which Caccini would claim for monody. Yet Milton later shows himself, in the sonnet to Henry Lawes, to be well versed in, and sympathetic towards, those of the aims of the Camerata represented by Caccini.[10]

One possible explanation is biographical. The pair of poems was written before Milton's Italian journey. Perhaps by the time of the sonnet, a change had been effected in Milton's attitude by his increased experience and understanding of the new trends originating in Italy. It is clear that he took a keen interest in musical matters while in Italy in 1638, and it has been suggested that certain changes in musical references in his "At a Solemn Music" were inspired by this visit.[11] I offer this explanation as devil's advocate. Long before he went to Italy, Milton was intimately acquainted with Italian innovations, for he was surrounded in England by music inspired by them. He was born and bred among musicians. His father composed, and his father's house hummed with musical activity. He was friendly from an early age with Lawes, can hardly have failed to know Lanier, and must have been acutely aware of all the radical activity among song writers of the period. Milton knew what the monodists were aiming at when he wrote L'Allegro, and if we look more closely at the poem and its companion, at contemporary musical developments and at traditions of musical philosophy, we see that Milton was indicating neither ignorance of, nor antagonism towards, current musical developments. On the contrary, he reflects in his poems the complexities and paradoxes inherent in those developments, and the ideals on which they are founded.

Caccini in the Preface and Milton in Il Penseroso both speak of a state in which perfection is perceived by the listener. Both see the end of their art as being (in Sidney's words): "to lead and draw us to as high a perfection as our degenerate souls, made worse by their clayey lodgings, can be made capable of."[12] I could equally well quote anoth-

---

[10] MacDonald Emslie, "Milton on Lawes: The Trinity MS Revisions," in Music in Renaissance Drama, ed John H. Long (Lexington, 1968).

[11] Harinder S. Marjara, "Milton's 'Chromatic jarres' and 'Tuscan Aire,' " MQ 19 (1985): 11–13.

[12] An Apology for Poetry, ed. Geoffrey Shepherd (Manchester: Manchester Univ. Press, 1973), 104.

er passage from Caccini, who speaks of "il fine del musico, cioè di dilet-
tare e muovere l'affeto dell'animo ..." ("the musicians's end, that is to
delight and move the affections of the mind").

How does music or poetry (let us say *musica*) "practised" by musician or poet (let us say *vates*) have this effect? For the answer, I turn to
that supreme Neoplatonist, Marsilio Ficino, though the idea was so
fundamental to Renaissance thought that this is but one of countless
passages which I could have chosen:

> Est autem apud platonicos interpretes divina musica duplex
> alteram profecto in eterna dei mente consistere arbitrantur al-
> teram vero in coelorum ordine ac motibus qua mirabilem quen-
> dam coelestes globi orbesque concentum efficiunt. Utriusque vero
> animum nostrum antequam corporibus clauderetur participem
> extitisse: verum iis in tenebris auribus velut simulis quibusdam
> ac cunctiis [sic] utitur hisque imagines ut saepe iam diximus
> musicae illius incomparabilis accipit. Quibus in eius qua antea
> fruebatur harmoniae intimam quandam ac tacitam recordationem
> reducitur totusque desiderio feruet: cupitque ut vera musica
> rursus fruatur: ad sedes proprios revolare: cumque id se quamdiu
> tenebroso corporis habitaculo circumsepta est adipisci nullo
> modo posse intelligat: eam cuius his possessione frui nequit
> nititur saltem pro viribus imitare.[13]

According to the followers of Plato, divine music is two-fold. One
kind, they say, exists entirely in the eternal mind of God. The
second is in the motions and order of the heavens, by which the
heavenly spheres and their orbits make a marvellous harmony. In
both of these our soul took part before it was imprisoned in our
bodies. But it uses the ears as messenger, as though they were
chinks in this darkness. By the ears as I have already said ... the
soul receives the echoes of that incomparable music, by which it
is led back to the deep and silent memory of the harmony which
it previously enjoyed. The whole soul then kindles with desire to
fly back to its rightful home, so that it may enjoy that true music
again. It realises that as long as it is enclosed in the dark abode

---

[13] *Epistole Marcilii Ficini Florentini* (Venice, 1495), liber 1, 4r–4v.

of the body it can in no way reach that music. It therefore strives wholeheartedly to imitate it, because it cannot here enjoy its possession.[14]

The moment when Il Penseroso perceives "all heaven" is a moment of divine inspiration. The one inspired, epitomized by Pythagoras, is one of the chosen few, singled out because of their virtue for the task of promoting virtue in others. In the fifth elegy, Milton describes this poetic frenzy from personal experience:

> Quid tam grande sonat distento spiritus ore?
> Quid parit haec rabies, quid sacer iste furor?
> Ver mihi, quod dedit ingenium, cantabitur illo;
> Profuerint isto reddita dona modo.

What grand song will my spirit pour forth from open lips? What will this fury, this divine madness, bring forth? Spring, which gave the inspiration to me, will be the subject of my song. In this way, the gifts will be returned to repay spring.

And he describes the duty of the poet thus inspired:

[Poetic] abilities, wheresoever they may be found, are the inspired gift of God, rarely bestowed, but yet to some in every Nation: and are of power beside that office of a pulpit to inbreed and cherish in a great people the seed of *vertu* and publick civility, to allay the perturbations of the mind, and set the affections in right tune.[15]

The final metaphor here is appropriate: the perception of heavenly harmony is possible for the poet because of his harmony of spirit, and renders him capable of inspiring such harmony in others. Thus the poet takes on a prophetic role, and Il Penseroso fittingly asks that he may continue to study:

> Till old experience do attain
> To something like prophetic strain.

---

[14] Ficino, *On Divine Frenzy* in *Letters*, trans. Fellowship of the School of Economic Science (London, 1975), 1:45–46.

[15] *The Reason of Church-Government* in CPW 1:816.

"Strain," for its musical associations, is particularly appropriate.

Throughout the two poems there are frequent references to natural and rustic music. We have raven, lark, cock, singing milkmaid, and rebeck in *L'Allegro*. The word "mirth" which appears frequently had the now obsolete meaning of "musical performance, melody." The poem ends with a plea to Hymen to provide perfect music (which Milton calls elsewhere mixed "voice and verse"). Something is amiss, however. Although the power of the music is conveyed in traditional terms (it pierces the soul and is compared with the music of Orpheus), certain expressions arouse doubt concerning the music's quality. Take, for example, "wanton," "giddy," and "melting," which imply the sensual, slackening—even lascivious—sound which one would expect of "soft Lydian airs." Thus, although L'Allegro requests the perfect combination, he requires of this "mix'd power" the wrong effects. Finally, he shows his true colors:

> These delights if thou canst give
> Mirth, with thee I mean to live.

Remembering the connotations of "mirth," we realize that for the frivolous Allegro, music is little more than entertainment. I can best indicate the gravity of L'Allegro's error by quoting a letter of the influential music theorist Girolamo Mei to Vincenzo Galilei. In a censorious passage he says:

> Veggo per il fin del ultima vostra che voi avete oppinione che la musica debba havere per suo objetto il dilettare l'orecchio con l'armonia.

> Finally I see that you are of the opinion that the purpose of music must be to delight the ear with pleasing sound.[16]

This is not the worst possible abuse of music. According to tradition, music can exert a powerful evil influence. I quote Richard Hooker:

> In harmony, the very image and character of virtue and vice is perceived, the mind delighted with their resemblances, and brought by having them often iterated into a love of the things

---

[16] Girolamo Mei, *Letters on Ancient and Modern Music*, ed. Claude V. Palisca (Rome, 1960), 115.

themselves. For which cause, there is nothing more contagious and pestilent than some kinds of harmony; than some nothing more strong and potent unto good.[17]

L'Allegro's music, with its seductive, voluptuous quality, verges dangerously on the "pestilent" variety.

We have seen L'Allegro dismiss Il Penseroso as living among "horrid shapes . . . unholy." Il Penseroso correspondingly denounces L'Allegro, and it is interesting that he sees the latter's ideas as "numberless." This is a strong condemnation. Number is the foundation of order. According to Boethius

Omnia quaecumque a primaera rerum natura constructa sunt, numerorum videntur ratione formatur. Hoc enim fuit principale in animo conditoris exemplar.[18]

From the beginning all things whatever which have been created may be seen by the nature of things to be formed by reason of numbers. Number was the principal exemplar in the mind of the Creator.

Milton calls poetry "numerous writing," for it is by number or order in poetry and music that man imitates divine order.

The pensive nun, Melancholy, when she arrives, is described in words which have positive connotations. Her "even step" suggests rhythmic harmony, and it is not surprising that she is granted the ultimate reward of the virtuous:

> And hears the Muses in a ring
> Aye about Jove's alter sing.

This music of the heavens is variously represented by Milton (as by others) as music of the spheres, the stars, and the angels, but ascribing it here to the Muses, he emphasizes its association with divine inspiration. In the course of the poem, we are reminded of universal harmony by the words "consent" (applied to the elements) and "consort" (of the seas) and, as in L'Allegro, by the natural harmony of birdsong and the

---

[17] Richard Hooker, Laws of Ecclesiastical Polity (London, 1907), book 5, 38.1, p. 146.

[18] Boethius, De institutione arithmetica, ed. G. Friedlein (Leipzig, 1867), 1.2.12.

sound of the bee (which "doth sing"). Il Penseroso is alert to these natural harmonies, and when he asks for inspiration, it is in terms which suggest that it will be available to him because of his harmonious or virtuous disposition; he is in tune with, and thus susceptible to, divine influence:

> And as I wake, sweet music breathe
> Above, about or underneath,
> Sent by some spirit to mortals good.

We cannot, by now, doubt Il Penseroso's qualities, and the next line serves to emphasize these, reminding us of Melancholy's "even step": "But let my due feet never fail." The "even step" and "due feet" of Il Penseroso effect another contrast with L'Allegro, in which the characters "trip" and "dance." The terms in Il Penseroso suggest ordered rhythm, perhaps even perfect scansion—another instance of accord with divine order.

The passage which immediately follows has that magnificent description of polyphonic church music which I discussed earlier. It is the climax of the pair of poems; all that has gone before has prepared us for this request for divine inspiration. We cannot doubt that Il Penseroso's request of Melancholy is nobler than that which L'Allegro makes of Mirth. The two different kinds of poetic activity can most clearly be contrasted in the light of the continuation of the passage quoted earlier from the letter of Ficino, which is based on Plato's Phaedrus:

> Est autem haec apud homines imitatio duplex. Alii nanque votum numeris variorumque sonis instrumentorum coelestem musicam imitantur: quos certe leves ac pene vulgares musicos appellamus: nonnulli vero graviori quodam firmiorique iudicio divinam ac coelestem harmoniam imitantes intime rationis sensum notionesque in versum, pedes ad numeros digerunt hi vero sunt qui divino afflati spiritu gravissima quaedam ac praeclarissima carmina ore, ut aiunt rotundo prorsus effundunt. Hanc Plato graviorem musicam poesimque nominat: efficacissimam harmoniae coelestis imitatricem nam levior illa de qua pauloante mentionem fecimus vocum duntaxat suavitate permulcet. Poesis autem quod divinae quoque harmoniae proprium e motuum numeris gravissimos quosdam et ut poeta diceret delphicos sensus ardentius exprimit: . . .

Now with men this imitation is twofold. Some imitate the celestial music by harmony of voice and the sounds of various instruments, and these we call superficial and vulgar musicians. But some, who imitate the divine heavenly harmony with deeper and sounder judgment, render a sense of its inner reason and knowledge into verse, feet and numbers. It is those who, inspired by the divine spirit, give forth with full voice the most solemn and glorious song. Plato calls this solemn music and poetry the most effective imitation of the celestial harmony. For the more superficial kind which I have just mentioned does no more than soothe with the sweetness of the voice. It expresses with fire the most profound and, as a poet would say, prophetic meanings, in the numbers of voice and movement.

All this discussion of musical reference in the poems may have implied that they constitute a debate on musical matters. I hasten to correct any such implication. The different kinds of music merely contribute to the overall contrast between the poems. Neither is there, in my view, any element of "old" versus "new" in the types of music described, for, as I have shown, the humanist principle whereby the text should be paramount resulted in reform in both solo and polyphonic music. Similarly, although one passage might suggest monody and another polyphony, it would be simplistic to hold that L'Allegro stood for the one and Il Penseroso for the other, or that one poem described the "first practice" and one the "second practice." Far more important than the contrasting kinds of music in the poems is the contrast of attitudes to that art. The debate touches on Milton's profoundest convictions concerning the purpose of his art and the source of its power, and we have seen how these convictions were those of humanist poets and musicians alike. Monodists and polyphonists (and most musicians were both) held common ideals. While Milton's poems make no overt contribution to the complex musical debate, our appreciation of the pair is enriched if they are seen in the context of the intellectual climate of the day.

London

P. G. STANWOOD

# Milton's Lycidas *and*
# Earlier Seventeenth-Century Opera

F
EW CLASSICAL LEGENDS HAVE HAD such continuous importance and persistent appeal as the myth of Orpheus. Like his
many predecessors, Milton, too, was moved by the legend of
the supposed son of Apollo and Calliope, who inherits and thus
embodies the power of song and verse. Ovid's extended description of
the legend in books 10 and 11 of the *Metamorphoses* is perhaps the
hinge that makes his whole love epic function; a generation earlier,
Vergil had told the story in the latter part of his fourth *Georgic*, the
climax of that work and the culmination of even earlier traditions and
folk-tales.[1]

When Eurydice, the wife of Thracian Orpheus, dies from the bite of
a snake next to a river-bank as she tries to escape the pursuing Aris-
taeus, Orpheus laments her fate, singing to the accompaniment of his
lyre. Then he goes to the underworld, gaining entrance by lulling its
guards to sleep with his enchanting song, even casting a spell on
Charon the boatman and on all the shades. He convinces Proserpine
herself that he should have Eurydice again. With Pluto's consent,
Orpheus is permitted to lead Eurydice out of hell, but only on condition
that he should not look back; otherwise, he will lose Eurydice forever.
But unable to keep his promise, Orpheus steals a look, and Eurydice is
gone. Orpheus mourns his loss bitterly, and he weeps for seven months
beneath a cliff by the river Strymon; his lamentation fascinates even the
tigers and the oak trees. Since nothing can soften his sorrow, the
women of the Cicones, inhabitants of Thrace and devotees of Bacchus,

---

[1] See the collection edited by John Warden, *Orpheus: The Metamorphoses of a
Myth* (Toronto: Univ. of Toronto Press, 1982), especially the essays by Emmet Rob-
bins, "Famous Orpheus," 3–23, and W. S. Anderson, "The Orpheus of Virgil and
Ovid: *flebile nescio quid*," 25–50.

hideously punish him by tearing his body to pieces, throwing the flesh over the land, and allowing the severed head to float on the river Hebrus. As the water carries his head away, it calls out "Eurydice" and continues to sing. This legend has variations and numerous additions, especially in connection with Orpheus's parentage and his usually unhappy end. But the essential idea in all of these stories is that Orpheus brings harmony to all things and creatures by his inspired mingling of voice and words.[2]

Milton's earliest reference to the Orpheus legend is evidently in his elegy to Diodati (in 1629), the allusion to the one who skillfully causes the "Thracian lyre" to sound.[3] *Il Penseroso* (105-8) and *L'Allegro* (144-150) invoke the Orphean legend of "the hidden soul of harmony." In *Ad Patrem*, Milton exalts the poet who makes music with words, like Orpheus who sang not simply with his cithara but with his song, and so restrained rivers, gave ears to the oaks, stirred the ghosts of the dead to tears, and won high fame (52-55). Here is the familiar Renaissance idea that Orpheus the poet-singer subdued lower nature by causing the whole earth to listen to him in astonished wonder; Milton develops the notion substantially in the second and third invocations of *Paradise Lost*. In book 3, Milton compares his earlier description of Hell and then of Heaven with Orpheus's journey; and in book 7, he prays that "the barbarous dissonance / Of *Bacchus* and his Revellers" who destroyed Orpheus (32-33) may not also destroy him or disturb his effort to make known his "advent'rous Song" (1.13).

But it is in *Lycidas* (1638) that Milton makes the most extended use of the Orpheus legend, displaying the poet-prophet-teacher's "perfect songs" which caused "even the very trees, the bushes, and the whole woods" to pull up their roots and rush to hear him.[4] The central importance of Orpheus to *Lycidas* is fundamental to the purpose of the

---

[2] Because he journeyed to the underworld and emerged alive, he is also identified with the Prince of Peace, the Messianic king mentioned in Isaiah 9.6. See Eleanor Irwin, "The Songs of Orpheus and the New Song of Christ," in *Orpheus*, ed. Warden, especially 58-59; and Patricia Vicari, "*Sparagmos*: Orpheus among the Christians," 63-83. For further background, see also John Block Friedman, *Orpheus in the Middle Ages* (Cambridge, Mass.: Harvard Univ. Press, 1970), especially chap. 3, "Orpheus-Christus in the Art of Late Antiquity."

[3] Except where indicated, quotations from Milton are taken from Hughes.

[4] See Prolusion 7, about 1632 (Hughes, 629).

whole poem: Milton, of course, identifies himself with Lycidas, or Edward King, in whom is realized the figure of Orpheus, controlling and organizing nature, displaying the power of recovery and creativity. In using the legend of Orpheus in *Lycidas*, Milton also uses one of the most familiar themes of the first operas, and in his "monody," he provides a literary form that parallels the *via naturale alla immitatione* of contemporary musical style.[5]

Finding the Orpheus legend so congenial, Milton must not only have read the literature but also heard or known about the music in which Orpheus figures prominently: the Italian opera of the earlier seventeenth century, with its roots even earlier in Angelo Poliziano's *Orfeo*, a work composed for the city of Mantua in about 1480, lost but still talked about when Jacopo Peri wrote his *Euridice* in 1600, and Monteverdi, influenced by both these predecessors, in his *Orfeo*, first performed in 1607. Milton's knowledge of music surely included these earliest operas, appropriately dedicated to the legendary first singer and divine patron of dramatic music. Thus, he must also have appreciated the rage for homophonic or monodic music, the so-called *stile rappresentativo* (theatrical style), which Giulio Caccini (c. 1545–1618) described in his *Le nuove musiche* of 1602 and illustrated in his own version of Orpheus later in the same year. Not only did this legend perfectly suit the earliest music drama, but the "new music" offered an especially satisfactory way of interpreting the story. In this fashionable mode, a recitative style that sought a balance between song and speech, Milton must have discovered the usual role of Orpheus memorably redefined, and in a way also that must have seemed to him and others of his time reminiscent of ancient Greek theatre.

---

[5] The "natural way of imitation" attempted a style midway between song and speech, emphasizing the solo voice. See Nigel Fortune, "Italian Secular Monody from 1600 to 1635: An Introductory Survey," *Musical Quarterly* 39 (1953): 171–95, and also the more detailed study by Gary Tomlinson, "Madrigal, Monody, and Monteverdi's 'via naturale alla immitatione,'" *Journal of the American Musicological Society* 34 (1981): 60–108. See also Tomlinson's *Monteverdi and the End of the Renaissance* (Berkeley: Univ. of California Press, 1987), especially chap. 5, "Guarini, Rinuccini, and the Ideal of Musical Speech"; and Walther Dürr, "Sprachliche und musikalische Determinanten in der Monodie: Beobachtungen an Monteverdis 'Orfeo,'" in *Claudio Monteverdi: Festschrift Reinhold Hammerstein*, ed. Ludwig Finscher ([Heidelberg:] Laaber-Verlag, 1986), 151–62. Of course, Milton's Italian journey of 1638–39 followed his writing of *Lycidas*; but what he was to hear and learn of "the new music" made his understanding of it more compelling.

Milton wrote in his *Defensio secunda* (1654)[6] that after he had arrived at Venice in 1639, probably in April, he took care to have the books which he had collected during his Italian sojourn loaded on the England-bound ship. His biographer Edward Phillips writes in more detail, stating that Milton

> Shipp'd up a Parcel of curious and rare Books which he had pick'd up in his Travels; (particularly a Chest or two of choice Musick-books of the best Masters flourishing about that time in *Italy*, namely, *Luca Marenzo, Monte Verde, Horatio Vecchi, Cifa*, the Prince of *Venosa* and several others).[7]

These all were familiar composers, important to the development of the new music: Luca Marenzio (1553-1599) and Antonio Cifra (1584-1629) were already well known in England, Henry Lawes (1596-1662) having made use of the song titles and one or two performing directions from the latter's *Scherzi et arie* (Venice, 1614).[8] Orazio (Tiberio) Vecchi (1550-1605) composed the popular madrigal comedy *L'Amfiparnaso* (1597), and Don Carlo Gesualdo, prince of Venosa (c. 1561-1613), was

---

[6] See Hughes, 830 (in the 1654 edition, p. 86).

[7] See *Life*, 1694, xvi, in Darbishire, 59. Cf. Anthony à Wood's sketch: "After he had taken the degrees in Arts, he left the University of his own accord.... Whereupon retiring to his Fathers house in the Country, he spent some time in turning over Latin and Greek Authors, and now and then made excursions into the great City to buy books, to the end that he might be instructed in Mathematicks and Musick, in which last he became excellent, and by the help of his Mathematicks could compose a Song or Lesson" (Darbishire, 36).

[8] See under "Cifra" and "Lawes, Henry" in *The New Grove Dictionary of Music and Musicians*, ed. Stanley Sadie, 20 vols. (London: Macmillan, 1980), hereafter cited as *New Grove*. Henry Lawes dedicated his first book of *Ayres and Dialogues* (1653) to the daughters of the earl of Bridgewater, "most of them being Composed when I was employed by Your ever Honour'd Parents to attend Your Ladishipp's Education in Musick," that is, about twenty years earlier, or near the time of *Comus*, which Lawes wrote for Bridgewater's inauguration as Lord President of Wales. For Henry Lawes's connection with contemporary Italian music, see Willa McClung Evans, *Henry Lawes: Musician and Friend of Poets* (New York: Modern Language Association, 1941), 16-32. From 1612 (and perhaps earlier), Lawes was learning "of the fashionable world of court musicians, a world in which Coperario's influence swayed musical thinking, in which Campion was well established, and in which Ferrabosco was enjoying the height of his success" (21). Giovanni Coperario (that is, the Englishman John Cooper), it should be recalled, had returned from his visit to Italy sometime between 1604 and 1608, bringing with him the new methods of composition.

celebrated not only for his modernist harmonies but also for the murder of his first wife and her lover.[9] Claudio Monteverdi, who died at the age of seventy-six in 1643, is today the best remembered of this group, and the only one who was still living when Milton visited Italy, residing in Venice when Milton was there in 1639.

Milton had obvious and ample opportunity for becoming well acquainted with the latest fashions in Italian music. Lawes had already shown at least a general sympathy for it in his music for *Comus* in 1634 though his specific indebtedness may be disputed; but there is no doubt that Lawes knew Italian music, especially that of Marenzio and Monteverdi, for he had copied their music into his partbooks, evidently as a young man.[10] But what was this new music which could so easily be made to suit the requirements of the earliest operas? And how did Milton adapt it to his own poetic needs?

The *camerata* centered around Giovanni de' Bardi, which was active in Florence from 1573 to 1587, discussed the musical theories that helped lead to the development of opera. In an effort to recover Greek music and drama, which they presumed was entirely sung, Bardi and his colleagues studied every source they could find. They were primarily assisted by Girolamo Mei, the most learned theorist among them, and by Vincenzo Galilei, the father of the astronomer, and also by Caccini himself, who turned particularly to Mei for advice. Caccini set out their ideas in his influential *Nuove musichi*, already mentioned, and he also, incidentally, dedicated his *Euridice* to Bardi. It should be remembered that in 1581–1582 Vincenzo Galilei had written his *Dialogo della musica antica e della moderna* in which he espoused the principles common to the members of the *camerata*, which they saw as necessary steps for the appropriate development of music in their own time: (1) the sentiments of the text ought to be expressed by the widest possible vocal range; (2) only one melody at a time should be heard; (3) rhythm and

---

[9] Gesualdo surprised his wife and her lover Fabrizio Carafra, Duke of Andria, "in flagrante delicto di fragrante peccato." See Lorenzo Bianconi, "Gesualdo," in *New Grove*.

[10] See Evans, 19–21, and the article in *New Grove*. See also Harris F. Fletcher, *The Intellectual Development of John Milton*, 2 vols. (Urbana: Univ. of Illinois Press, 1956–61), especially 1, chap. 21, "Music in the Grammar School Period" and 2, chap. 19, "Music." Cf. Walter L. Woodfill, *Musicians in English Society from Elizabeth to Charles I* (Princeton: Princeton Univ. Press, 1953).

melody must follow the speaking voice of someone possessed by "a certain ease, a casual affection," or *sprezzatura*, a well-used term in music as well as in discussions of courtly conduct of the period.[11]

The elaborately polyphonic music of the sixteenth-century madrigal, customarily composed for five equal parts, gave way to madrigals written for a single voice and continuo, or else consort; the madrigal as a *concertato ensemble*, or a composition for several voices, was virtually dead by the early 1630s. Thus the term "madrigal" survived as a description of a solo song, usually accompanied by a figured bass. Although "monody" was not at first applied to this kind of music, it soon became the inclusive term for all music that featured a single voice. The word appears in 1635[12] in the important *Compendio del trattato de' generi e de' modi della musica* by Giovanni Battista Doni (1594–1647), whom Milton met on March 24, 1639, in Rome, where, incidentally, he had

---

[11] Castiglione is the first to write of *sprezzatura* in his *Il Cortegiano* (1528), well known in the English translation by Thomas Hoby (1561). But Caccini is the first to apply the term to music, in his preface to *Euridice* (1600), where he insists "that by means of it I approach that much closer to the essence of speech." He writes in his *Le nuove musiche* of "negligently" (that is, naturally) introducing dissonances in order to approach "speaking" tones. See Nigel Fortune, "Sprezzatura," in *New Grove*. On Caccini's personal rivalry as well as his musical differences with Peri, see Nino Pirrotta and Elena Povoledo, *Music and Theatre from Poliziano to Monteverdi*, trans. Karen Eales (Cambridge: Cambridge Univ. Press, 1982), 238–57. (First published as *Li due Orfei* [1969]). – Vincenzo Galilei's *Dialogo* was published in facsimile, ed. Fabio Fano (Rome, 1934).

[12] Francesco Patrizi (1529–1597) was first to use the term "monodia" in Italian, in his *Della poetica* (Ferrara, 1586), ed. D. Aguzzi Barbagli (Florence, 1969–70), 1:382, discovering the word in Plato's *Laws* 764D. "Dico monodia, non per lo canto di un solo de' coreuti, che con questo nome dicemmo che fu detto, né per la monodia lamentavele di Saffo, ma per quella monodia la quale Platone distinse contro alla corodia, la quale dicemmo essere canto di tutto il coro, in quelle parole che di suo adducemmo in questa sentenza." ("By monody I mean, not the song of only one member of the chorus, which was called by that name, nor the sorrowful monody of Sappho, but that monody which Plato distinguishes from choral song [*corodia*], which we define as being sung by the entire chorus, in those words of his which we quote in this context.") In his *Compendio* (Rome, 1635), Doni writes: "Dove mi son proposto solamente di alcuni miei pensieri intorno le musiche a una voce sola (che anticamente si dicevano monodie, o semplici ch'elle fussero o accompagnate con l'instrumento) e qualle che di più voci si compongono" (2:96) ("Therefore, I have only put forward some of my thoughts about musical pieces for one voice [which in antiquity were called monodies, either because they were 'simple' or accompanied by the instrument] and those musical pieces that are carried through by several voices").

recently—it seems very likely—heard the famous Leonora Baroni sing at Cardinal Barberini's concert. What Milton heard and the kind of music he sent back to England was evidently "monodic." At the same time, he could hardly have missed hearing what I should call "Orphean" opera, with its popular recitative style.

Of the many operas on Orpheus composed during Milton's time, the best and perhaps most celebrated is Monteverdi's "Favola in Musica," *L'Orfeo* (1607). It combines a pastoral setting in a richly interwoven and symmetrically designed libretto, with a happy ending, written by Alessandro Striggio (the younger, c. 1573-1630). Above all, Monteverdi provides one of the greatest monodies in contemporary musical litera-ture, the extraordinary aria of Orpheus, which lasts nearly nine minutes in the revised edition of 1615. With "Possente spirto," Orpheus begins his song, written in *terza rima*, to Charon, at the poetic and spiritual climax of the opera. Here, indeed, is one of the first of those "strongly characterized set pieces (prayer, incantation, lament) that reappear time and again in early opera."[13] Monteverdi drew upon his great experi-ence as a madrigalist and harmonist in what became a musical touch-stone of his age. He assured for himself an even greater reputation with his next opera of 1608 to a libretto by Ottavio Rinuccini (also the author of Peri's *Euridice*): most of the music of *L'Arianna* has not survived, but the portion which Monteverdi himself described as "la più essential parte dell' opera," the lovely monodic lament, has come down to us.[14] The "Lamento d'Arianna" moved its first audience to tears and established itself in the consciousness of every music-loving Italian. For years to come, composers remembered and imitated Monteverdi's lament; and "Lasciatemi morire" and "Possente spirto" became the great and model set-pieces of the new monodic style.[15]

One musicologist calls Monteverdi's impressive achievement, espe-

---

[13] See Iain Fenlon, "The Mantuan Stage Works," in *The New Monteverdi Compan-ion*, ed. Denis Arnold and Nigel Fortune (London: Faber and Faber, 1985), 275.

[14] See letter of March 21, 1620, quoted in Hans Ferdinand Redlich, *Claudio Monteverdi: Life and Works*, trans. Kathleen Dale (Westport, Conn.: Greenwood Press, 1952; repr. 1970), 101, and also *The Letters of Claudio Monteverdi*, trans. Denis Stevens (London: Faber and Faber, 1980), 197-98. Quotations from Striggio's libretto are taken from the 1615 text edited by Nigel Rogers for the London Baroque perfor-mance (on EMI Angel 4D2X-3964, London, 1984).

[15] Cf. Henry Lawes's *Ariadne* (1653, but composed perhaps in the late 1640s), and the comments at the end of the present article. See Evans, 161-66.

cially in *Orfeo*, "a highly stylized and hieratically formalized incantation, through which a superhuman singer soothes and subjects the forces of darkness. . . ."[16] This judgment might, I think, describe also Milton's achievement in *Lycidas*. "In this Monody," Milton writes at the beginning of *Lycidas*, "the Author bewails a learned Friend." Undoubtedly, Milton understood by "monody" the Greek literary form represented in the speeches of Andromache, Hecuba, or Helen in the *Iliad* (book 24), and elsewhere in classical literature, especially tragedy, and he was familiar with the tradition of the lamenting poet-singer. Obviously, he would have known the famous lament in Vergil's Second Eclogue and the earlier Theocritean poems. But he must have had in mind also the current musical sense of the term; certainly, he wrote a lament essentially for one voice (with a second commenting on the whole poem in the final verse paragraph, or *commiato* to the *canzone* stanzas that precede it), making use of the central imagery of the Orpheus legend. Many commentators have ignored or insufficiently appreciated the term "monody" at the beginning of the poem, or only briefly and inadequately described it; but I am sure it is a crucial key to understanding the poem. Some writers have discussed the "musical" qualities of *Lycidas*, and others have described its indebtedness to the madrigal.[17] But *Lycidas* is a monodic madrigal in the "modern" seventeenth-century sense; it has nothing in common with the old-fashioned five-part songs, or the polyphonal harmonies of earlier composers. Written just before Milton went on his Italian journey, *Lycidas* is a remarkable testament not only to Italian poetic form in its *canzone* structure and rhyme scheme, but also to Italian opera.

Monteverdi, of course, did not write the libretto of *Orfeo*: that was the younger Striggio's work, which, in the early years of opera, implied something more than collaboration. Because the new monodic music had as its principal intention the wringing of a deeper meaning from the texts, the poet often became more important than the musician in

---

[16] See Pirrotta and Povoledo, *Music and Theatre from Poliziano to Monteverdi*, 277.

[17] See, for example, "The Minor English Poems," in *Variorum* 2:637. See also Gretchen Finney, "A Musical Background for 'Lycidas,' " *Huntington Library Quarterly* 15 (1951–52): 325–50; Joseph A. Wittreich, Jr., "Milton's 'Destin'd Urn': The Art of *Lycidas*," *PMLA* 84 (1969): 60–70; Mortimer H. Frank, "Milton's Knowledge of Music: Some Speculations," in *Milton and the Art of Sacred Song*, ed. J. Max Patrick and R. H. Sundell (Madison: Univ. of Wisconsin Press, 1979), 83–98.

operatic collaborations. In this unequal partnership, "the words came to be regarded as the design and the music the colour."[18] While some libretti were naive and awkwardly written, others, and certainly Striggio's among them, possessed commendable clarity and literary power. Orpheus's long monody in act 3 begins with the appearance of "Speranza," or Hope.[19] She quotes Dante's famous line from the *Inferno* (3.9), part of the inscription on the lintel of the gate of Hell: "Lasciate ogni speranza, voi ch'entrate" ("Abandon all hope, ye that enter"). Vergil, of course, is the ultimate source, as he writes of the Sibyl who warns away Aeneas's companions just as he is about to enter the underworld: "Procul O, procul este, profani / conclamat vates" ("O away, stand away, the Sybil cried, you uninitiated ones" [*Aeneid* 6.258-59]). The boldness of the journey is justified by the heaviness of the loss or the overwhelming desire to learn the wisdom of the dead and find some prospect for the future. While Milton, as the "uncouth swain," does not similarly enter the underworld to visit Lycidas, he compares his dead friend with Orpheus, eventually also seeing himself in them, and managing to turn his poem into a metaphorical journey not only to the place of the dead but, at the last, of the living.

Like Orpheus rising from the place of death to life once more, "So *Lycidas*, sunk low, but mounted high . . . hears the unexpressive nuptial Song" (172, 176). In Striggio/Monteverdi's version, this new life is achieved through the intervention of Apollo, who ascends with Orpheus to Heaven, "Dove ha virtù verace / Degno premio di sè, diletto e pace" ("Where true virtue has its just rewards, joy and peace"). For Milton the apotheosis comes "Through the dear might of him that walk'd the waves." Striggio has given Orpheus a happy end, unusual for this legend, but it incidentally anticipates Milton's Christian resolution of his poem, and it also reinforces the strongly moral direction both of his Orpheus and of Milton's *Lycidas*. At the conclusion of act 4 of Monteverdi's opera, as Eurydice vanishes after her brief moments with Orpheus, the chorus explains what went wrong:

---

[18] Simon Towneley Worsthorne, *Venetian Opera in the Seventeenth Century* (Oxford: Clarendon Press, 1954; repr. 1968), 117.

[19] In Rinuccini's text for Peri's setting of *Euridice* (1600), Venus escorts Orpheus on his journey to the underworld. On the relationship of Rinuccini and Peri with Striggio and Monteverdi, see Tomlinson, "From L'Euridice to Orfeo," in *Monteverdi and the End of the Renaissance*, 131-41.

Orfeo vinse l'Inferno e vinto poi
Fu da gli affetti suoi.
Degno d'eterna gloria
Fia sol colui ch'avrà di sè vittoria.

Orpheus conquered Hell, but then was conquered by his passions. Worthy of eternal fame shall be only he who has victory
over himself.

The sentiment is a sound Renaissance interpretation of the Orpheus
legend; but it is also a good description of Milton's abiding belief,
implicit in the honest virtue that exalts Lycidas, the "spare Temperance"
that preserves the Lady in Comus, and above all the Love that "hath his
seat / In Reason," an idea fundamental to Paradise Lost, and further
elaborated in Raphael's parting advice to Adam to "take heed lest
Passion sway / Thy Judgment to do aught, which else free Will /
Would not admit" (8.635-37).[20] Milton could be moved by the Orphean monody, especially when the words of the song helped to expel
"the grim Wolf with privy paw" (129).

Milton's most important use of the Orpheus legend occurs in
Lycidas, his own monody, a lament that recalls the style of Monteverdi,
Peri, Caccini, and others. The poem is testimony to Milton's apprecia-

---

[20] Compare the final scene of the opera with Milton's "Tomorrow to fresh Woods,
and Pastures new." Milton's quiet and harmonious resolution of his poem refers, of
course, to the swain who must survive in the world without Lycidas. Yet Lycidas, like
Orpheus, continues to live, the one through Christian immortality, the other through
an Apollonian eternity. As Apollo ascends with Orpheus, the chorus sings reassuringly
of him: "Così va chi non s'arretra, / Al chiamar di Nume eterno, / Così grazia in ciel
impetra / Chi quaggiù provo l'Inferno / E chi semina fra doglie / D'ogni grazia il
frutto coglie" ("Thus goes he who does not hesitate at the call of an everlasting god;
thus he obtains grace in Heaven, who here below tasted the infernal. And he who sows
in sorrow shall reap the fruits of all grace"). Striggio's original ending of Orfeo in his
libretto of 1607 provides a Bacchanalian chorus which anticipates the death and
dismemberment of Orpheus, a conclusion in close accord with Vergil and Ovid. F. W.
Sternfeld argues that Monteverdi himself changed Striggio's sad ending for the happy
one of his opera, sometime before 1609, the date of the first published score. See his
"The Orpheus Myth and the Libretto of 'Orfeo,'" in Claudio Monteverdi: Orfeo, ed.
John Whenham, "Cambridge Opera Handbooks" (Cambridge: Cambridge Univ. Press,
1986), 20-33. Whenham gives Striggio's original version, 35-41.

tion of the new music; but his sonnet to Henry Lawes (of 1646) provides one more instance of his knowledge and approval of this kind of music; for Lawes's "well measur'd Song / First taught our English Music how to span / Words with just note and accent"; he, too, knew how to "honour" verse by fitting the music to the sense of the words, as his *Ariadne*, Milton indirectly says, happily proved. Although certainly less skillful than its model, Lawes's "O Theseus, hark! but yet in vain" is an obvious descendent of "Lasciatemi morire." Milton saw in Lawes's composition a noble achievement, and in lauding it, he implicitly compliments also the musical tradition from which it grew, remembering, one may suppose, his own indebtedness to the monodies of the earliest Italian opera.

University of British Columbia

MARGARET BYARD

# "Adventrous Song":[1]
# Milton and the Music of Rome

O N CHRISTMAS EVE [OF 1644]" wrote John Evelyn, "I went
not to bed.... I walked from church to church the whole
night in admiration of the multitude of scenes and pagean-
try.... I thence went and heard a sermon at the Apollinaire, by which
time it was morning.... On Christmas day his Holinesse sang masse,
the artillerie at St. Angelo went off.... We were invited by the English
Jesuites to dinner, and afterwards saw an Italian comedy acted before
the Cardinals." The festivities continued and ended "with the rare
musiq at the Chiesa Nuova" that he had described earlier in more
detail. "The sermon being finished," the singers "begun their motettos,
which in a lofty cupola richly painted, were sung by eunuchs and other
rare voices, accompanied by theorbos, harpsichor[d]s, and viols, so that
we were even ravish'd."[2] The Christmas celebration and the music that
Evelyn, the diarist, experienced five years after Milton's visit might be
very much what Milton himself would have heard on his first visit to
Rome in 1638. After all, a large part of the Roman ruins that so pas-
sionately interested the later visitor was still buried under dust, and
Milton would have had plenty of time in his two visits in 1638 and
1639 for Christian Rome, its events, and its music, as well as for antiquities.[3]

---

[1] "Sing Heav'nly Muse... / I thence / Invoke thy aid to my adventrous Song,"
*Paradise Lost* (1.6, 12-13). For the poetry I have used CE throughout.

[2] John Evelyn, *The Diary of John Evelyn*, ed. E. S. de Beer (Oxford: Clarendon
Press, 1955), December 24-25 (2:290-91) and November 8 (2:232).

[3] The suggestion was made by Leo Miller, distinguished Milton scholar, in a
conversation in Vallombrosa, June 14, 1988. Milton's first visit to Rome was late in
1638. He was probably there for the Eve of All Saints (October 31) and the Eve of All
Souls (November 1), when there was outstanding music in church services. His second
visit "belongs to the early winter of 1639"; he was there by February 27. See James H.
Hanford, *John Milton, Englishman* (New York: Crown, 1949), 82-83, 92.

An extraordinary variety of music flourished in Rome during the pontificate of Urban VIII (Maffeo Barberini), from 1623 to 1644. There was music for church services (oratorios and settings for the Mass and hours), for operas (secular and religious music dramas), for private house music in the palaces of the church and lay aristocracy, for informal festivities in the streets of Rome. It was music on a handsome scale, showy and dramatic, quite commensurate in artistry and achievement with the painting of Cortona or the architecture of Bernini; it was an integral part of the art of baroque Rome.[4]

These musical riches, one may suggest, add significantly to the music and epic magnificence of Milton's poetry, especially *Paradise Lost*, an epic in a form "unattempted yet in Prose or Rhime" and unique in its fusion of "Voice [song] and Vers."[5] From the preliminary "Verse" introduction, Milton emphasizes the music of his poem; he associates it with Homer and Virgil, whose epics were traditionally intoned or sung and depended on music for their effect as well as on verse or meaning. The music Milton heard in Rome would have, therefore, a special significance for him and would be the origin of many of the epic's musical echoes and imitations. One conjectures further that the highly dramatic and emotional appeal of Roman baroque music would make it uniquely apposite for the new mode of music-poetry, the "adventrous Song" that Milton created for his religious and moral epic.

It should first be emphasized that the poet who had written "On the Morning of Christs Nativity" and *Lycidas*, two of the most beautiful and musical poems in the English language, would come to Rome with the

---

[4] Histories of music in the seventeenth century identify Rome as one of the great musical centers of the Roman Catholic world. To appreciate the extent and character of Roman music, one has to follow the development of the various genres in the seventeenth century. Some examples germane to this development its purposes are given in this essay; brief additional references may be found in Manfred F. Bukofzer, *Music in the Baroque Era* (New York: W. W. Norton, 1947), 20–70, especially 64–69. Paul Henry Lang gives a brilliant account of the early baroque period in *Music in Western Civilization* (New York: W. W. Norton, 1947), 314–92. See also Claude V. Palisca, *Baroque Music*, Prentice-Hall History of Music Series, 3 (Englewood Cliffs, NJ: Prentice-Hall, 1968), 8–88, 103–19, and Donald J. Grout with Claude Palisca, *A History of Western Music* (New York: W. W. Norton, 1980), 303–4, 311-12, 322–25. See also Nino Pirotta and Raoul Menoncelli, "Rome: Renaissance and Baroque," in *The New Grove Dictionary of Music and Musicians*, ed. Stanley Sadie (London: Macmillan, 1980), 16:155–62.

[5] "Sphear-born harmonious Sisters, Voice, and Vers" ("At a solemn Musick" [2]).

sensitivity, knowledge, and ability of a musician. The familiar details about Milton's musicianship that one is apt to forget are given in the *Early Lives*:

> Musick he Lov'd Extreamely, and Understood Well; 'tis said he Compos'd.... [H]e diverted Himself with Performing, which they say he did Well on the Organ and the Bas-Viol.... [H]is Voice was Musically Agreeable.[6] [He was] highly delighted with all sorts of Music....[7] [He] had a delicate Tuneable Voice & had good skill.[8] Hee had an excellent Ear, and could bear a part both in Vocal and Instrumental Music.[9]

Now and then, Milton himself reports, he made excursions to London "to become acquainted with some new discovery in mathematics or music, in which I then took the keenest pleasure."[10] It was in music, Anthony à Wood adds, that Milton "became excellent, and by the help of his Mathematicks could compose a Song or a Lesson."[11] From his earliest days, beginning at home with his father, a well-known composer, Milton lived in a world of Elizabethan and Jacobean music.[12]

In Rome Milton might have heard a new form of singing that was the current excitement and fashion. For this expressive song, as this new mode was called, performers were required to sing in a single line or melody (in monody) texts written in direct, understandable language and to express their meaning clearly and understandably. Its purpose was to sing expressively and dramatically and thereby to affect the emotions of the hearer. We can imagine what the term "expressive song" means if we realize that the new manner of singing was later to be called "bel canto," more familiar in the emotional, florid song of

---

[6] Jonathan Richardson, "The Life of Milton" (1734), in *The Early Lives of Milton*, ed. Helen Darbishire (London: Constable, 1932), 202, 204.

[7] John Toland, "The Life of John Milton" (1698), in Darbishire, 194.

[8] John Aubrey, "Minutes of the Life of Mr. John Milton" (1681), in Darbishire, 6.

[9] Edward Phillips, "The Life of Mr. John Milton" (1694), in Darbishire, 32.

[10] *Defensio secunda* in CPW 4.1.614.

[11] Anthony à Wood, "Life of Milton" from *Fasti Oxoniensis* (1691–92), in Darbishire, 36.

[12] Ernest Brennecke, Jr., *John Milton the Elder and His Music* (New York: Columbia Univ. Press, 1938), 94–135; Sigmund Spaeth, *Milton's Knowledge of Music* (1913; repr. Ann Arbor: Univ. of Michigan Press, 1963), 28–56.

nineteenth-century opera. The new music that emphasized expressive song came into prominence in *drammi per musica*, both sacred and secular, that were presented in Florence and in Rome almost simultaneously in 1600.[13] It meant a striking change from the old music in which the interweaving of many voices and instruments completely obscured the meaning of the words.[14] Expressive dramatic singing would be known to Milton from the Italianate song of the English court masques,[15] but it was in Rome that Milton would hear the more spectacular and highly professional performances characteristic of the sophisticated music of the Barberini papacy.

Of special interest for Milton out of this varied symphony of music would be the oratorios, or musical prayer meetings. So named from the prayer halls or oratories of the churches in which they were held—the Church of St. Marcellus or the even more popular Chiesa Nuova of St. Philip Neri (Santa Maria in Vallicella)[16] (fig. 1)—these musical prayer

---

[13] A famous performance of Jacopo Peri's *L' Euridice*, a music drama, in Florence in 1600, first popularized expressive dramatic singing. Through Emilio de' Cavalieri's *Rappresentatione di Anima et di Corpo* (Representation of the Body and Soul), Rome could claim to have produced a similar work in the same year. See Robert Donington, *The Rise of Opera* (London: Faber, 1981), 130-42, 207-10; Bukofzer, 1-19, 118-20; Palisca, 30-36.

[14] Polyphonic writing in the old style, it must be emphasized, continued especially in church services. After the 1600s, music in "concerto" style was gradually introduced. In this form solo, choral singing, and instrumental music were variously combined. See Bukofzer, 64-68; Palisca, 8-54. The battle that ensued in Italy over the "old" and "new" music is presented by a friend, Giulio Caccini, in the preface to *Le nuove musiche* (1602) and by a militant enemy, G. M. Artusi: see *L'Artusi, ovvero, Delle imperfezioni della moderna musica* (1600), in *The Baroque Era*, Source Readings in Music History, 3 (New York: W. W. Norton, 1965), 33-34.

[15] Many of the composers and singers for the court masques were Italian or Italian-educated. Antonio Ferrabosco, of an Italian immigrant family and much admired by André Maugars, composed the songs for the early court masques. See Alfonso Ferrabosco the Younger, for songs for the masques of Ben Jonson in *Ferrabosco's Ayres* (London: Stainer, 1926), nos. 3, 11, 18-23. Nicholas Lanier composed the music for Ben Jonson's masque *Lovers Made Men* (1617). Ben Jonson himself wrote, "And the whole maske was sung after the Italian manner." See *Ben Jonson*, ed. C. H. Herford, Percy and Evelyn Simpson (Oxford: Clarendon Press, 1970), 7:454. Henry Lawes, who composed for court masques other than *Comus*, had a decidedly Italianate musical education. See Willa McClung Evans, *Henry Lawes* (New York: Modern Language Association, 1941), 21-32.

[16] In 1575 St. Philip Neri had a new church and oratory built on the foundation of the ancient church of S. Maria in Vallicella for the musical prayer meetings or

meetings had been instituted in the 1570s to attract the faithful during the Fridays of Lent, and they were known for the bravura singing in the new expressive mode.[17] Open to the public and, therefore, to Milton during his second visit, they were enormously and increasingly popular. Hundreds filled the spacious oratories; the overflow had frequently to stand outside.[18]

In the characteristic form of oratorio fully developed by the early seventeenth century, prayers and sermons were interspersed with a musical recitation and intoning of a narrative selected from the Bible. A narrator or *testes* explained the meaning of the episode; different singers created the roles involved, and for their impersonations music was composed by prominent musicians of the day. Few texts for the music for the early oratorios survive, but for later services, published after the 1640s, we have arias of great beauty. The poignant and lovely lament of Jephthah for his daughter in the oratorio *Jephthe* by Giacomo Carissimi (1605-1674) is considered "one of the most moving pages of the whole century" and is still performed today.[19]

By an extraordinary coincidence, André Maugars, French viola da gambist, visited Rome from 1638 to 1639, which were the years of Milton's visits. He was as interested in oratorio and all forms of music as Milton would have been, although it is difficult to imagine a character more diametrically opposite his own. Tallemant des Réaux, the French memorialist, calls Maugars "un fou scélérat" and "un joueur de viole le plus excellent mais le plus fou qui ait jamais été" ("A crazy scoundrel" and "the most excellent but craziest violist there has ever been").[20] As a musician, however, Maugars was much admired by Marin Mersenne in *L'Harmonie universelle* and by Jean Jacques Rousseau in *Dissertation sur l'Origine de la Viole*. Maugars's letter to a friend

---

oratorios that he instituted. The new church with its oratory has been called the Chiesa Nuova ever since. See "Philip Neri," *Encyclopaedia Britannica*, 11th ed., 19:389.

[17] Howard Smither, *A History of the Oratorio I: The Oratorio in the Baroque Era; Italy, Vienna, Paris* (Chapel Hill: Univ. of North Carolina Press, 1977); Palisca, 103-17; Frederick Hammond, *Girolamo Frescobaldi* (Cambridge, Mass.: Harvard Univ. Press, 1983), 88-92; Bukofzer, 123-28.

[18] Gretchen L. Finney, *Musical Backgrounds for English Literature: 1580-1650* (New Brunswick, NJ: Rutgers Univ. Press, 1961), 232-33.

[19] Palisca, 115-17; and Giacomo Carissimi, *Jephte*, Meridian-Harmonia Mundi, KE77-132, 1987.

[20] *Historiettes de* [Gédéon] *Tallemant des Réaux* (Paris, 1840), 3:108, 112.

giving an account of his visit to Italy in 1638 and 1639 and analyzing the music he heard in Rome (*Response faite à un curieux* ...) is valued and used widely by musicians and musical historians today;[21] it gives us brilliant insights and shows intelligent appreciation and careful reporting, perhaps because of his other career as translator and writer. His translations of Bacon's *Advancement of Learning* and *Considerations touching a War with Spain* enabled him to style himself translator in English to Louis XIII.[22]

It is in Maugars's letter that we find a lively account of an oratorio performed during Lent in March, 1638, a year before Milton's second visit. Milton would very likely have heard similar performances when he returned to Rome during Lent in 1639. (Maugars refers to the performance as *récitatif* because a great many of the narrative passages would be in an intoned musical speech or recitative.) Maugars entered the barn-like hall of the Order of the Holy Crucifix, attached to St. Marcellus, where there was

> une congrégation ... composée des plus grands seigneurs de Rome, qui par conséquent ont le pouvoir d'assembler tout ce que l'Italie produit de plus rare; et en effet, les plus excellens Musiciens se picquent de s'y trouver. ... Aux deux costez de l'Église, il y a encore deux autres petites Tribunes, où estoient les plus excellens de la Musique Instrumentale. Les voix commençoient par un Psalme ... et puis tous les instrumens faisoient une très bonne symphonie. Les voix après chantoient une Histoire du Viel Testament, en forme d'une comédie spirituelle, comme celle de Suzanne, de Judith et d'Holoferne, de David et de Goliat. Chaque chantre représentoit un personnage de l'Histoire et

---

[21] André Maugars, *Response faite à un curieux sur le sentiment de la Musique d'Italie, escrite à Rome le premier octobre 1639*, Avec notes et éclaircissements par Er[nest] Thoinan (Paris, 1865). Thoinan gives details from the title page of the original edition of 1639 or 1640, which is no longer available: André Maugars, Célèbre Joueur de Viole, Musicien du Cardinal Richelieu, Conseiller, secrétaire, interprète du Roi en langue anglaise, Traducteur de F. Bacon, Prieur de Saint-Pierre Eynac. *Response* has been edited and translated into English by Walter H. Bishop as "Maugars' *Response faite à un curieux sur le sentiment de la Musique d'Italie*," *Journal of the Viola da Gamba Society of America* 8 (1971): 5–17. According to its title, Maugars's *Response* is about the music of Italy; in actuality, it is almost entirely about the music of Rome. For the "twelve or fifteen months" Maugars spent in Italy, see Maugars, 26.

[22] For details of Maugars's career, see preface to Maugars by Thoinan, 1–22.

exprimoit parfaitement bien l'énergie des paroles. (Maugars, 29; see n. 20 above)

> a congregation ... made up of the greatest nobles of Rome, who, consequently, are able to bring together the best that Italy produces. And indeed, the most excellent musicians take pride in being there.... On the sides on the church, there are two other small galleries, where the best instrumentalists were placed. The singers would begin with a psalm ..., and then the players of instruments would furnish a very good symphony. Then there would be sung a story from the Old Testament, in the form of a religious drama, such as that of Susanna, Judith and Holofernes or David and Goliath. Each soloist represented a character in the story and gave perfect expression to the force of the words. (Bishop, 9)

In *Paradise Lost*, Milton was to write of the Angels in Heaven who took their golden harps "and with Praeamble sweet / Of charming symphonie" introduce

> Thir sacred Song, and waken raptures high;
> No voice exempt, no voice but well could joine
> Melodious part, such concord is in Heav'n.
>
> (3.367–71)

In this and in many other instances Milton uses Maugars's musical terminology.

Susannah and Judith and any other feminine roles were sung by castrati in their strong, high, penetrating voices.[23] Maugars cannot praise the singers enough, nor the instruments that accompanied them: harpsichords, lutes, violins, archlutes, organs (figs. 2 and 3). The music was followed last of all by the playing of the organist of St. Peter's, "ce grand *Friscobaldi*" [sic], who "fit paroistre mille sortes d'inventions sur son Clavessin, l'Orgue tenant tousiours ferme" (Maugars, 30) ("the great Frescobaldi, [who displayed] a thousand kinds of inventions on his

---

[23] "Il y a un grand nombre de *Castrati* pour le Dessus et pour la Haute-Contre..." (Maugars, 35) ("There are many castrati for soprano and counter-tenor singing ..." [Bishop, 12]). Alessandro Moreschi, castrato, sings in *Italian Vocal Music*, Asco Records, A-114, 1961.

harpsichord while the organ struck to the main tune" [Bishop, 9–10]).
The texts for Frescobaldi's harpsichord compositions, for example, are
developed with almost fantastic elaborations on the theme he has
chosen. There is a pattern of crescendos and decrescendos in cascades
of notes in a rising and falling design.[24] It is almost as if he were
reporting on Frescobaldi's playing when Milton writes

> his volant touch
> Instinct through all proportions low and high
> Fled and persu'd transverse the resonant fugue.
>                                  (11.561–63)

Such a performance for Milton in 1639 would be extraordinarily
important and suggestive. We know from the Cambridge Manuscript
that among other plans he intended to write a drama on a biblical
subject.[25] The oratorio would demonstrate to him how effective and
affecting a retelling of a biblical tale could be.

Maugars also attended the celebration for the feast of St. Dominic in
the Church of S. Maria sopra Minerva, famous even today for its music
(fig. 4). He gives us a vivid account of a musical setting of the mass in
"concert" form. By this he means that the new monodic and old
polyphonic styles were combined, that there was solo and choir singing,
with and without instruments, in elaborate and varying combinations.[26] In the church, Maugars recounts,

> il y a deux grands Orgues élevez des deux costez du maistre
> Autel, où l'on avoit mis deux choeurs de musique. Le long de la
> nef il y avoit huit autres choeurs, quatre d'un costé et quatre de
> l'autre, élevez sur des eschaffaux de huit à neuf pieds de haut.…
> A chaque choeur il y avoit un Orgue portatif.… Le maistre
> Compositeur battoit la principale mesure dans le premier choeur,
> accompagné des plus belles voix. A chacun des autres il y avoit
> un homme qui ne faisoit autre chose que jetter les yeux sur cette

---

[24] Hammond, 141–61. See also Girolamo Frescobaldi, *Harpsichord Music*, Harmo-
nia Mundi, 1143, n.d.; *Organ Music, Toccatas*, bk. 2, Orion, cassette 969, n.d.

[25] Hanford, 150–54.

[26] This was a relatively new form developed by Lodovico Grossi da Viadana which
borrowed from secular music drama and its popular expressive music. See Viadana's
*Cento concerti ecclesiastici* (1602), in *The Baroque Era*, 59–63, and Palisca, 63–71.

mesure primitive, afin d'y conformer la sienne.... Le contrepoint de la Musique estoit ... remply de beaux chants.... Tantost un dessus du premier choeur faisoit un récit, puis celui du 3me, du 4me et du 10me respondoit. Quelquefois ils chantoient deux, trois, quatre et cinq voix ensemble de différens choeurs, et d'autrefois les parties de tous les choeurs récitoient chacun à leur tour à l'envy les uns des autres. Tantost deux choeurs se battoient l'un contre l'autre, puis deux autres respondoient. Une autre fois ils chantoient trois, quatre et cinq choeurs ensemble, puis une, deux, trois, quatre et cinq voix seules; et au *Gloria Patri*, tous les dix choeurs reprenoient ensemble. (Maugars, 27–28)

there are two great organs built on either side of the main altar, where two choirs had been placed. Along the nave there were eight more choirs, four on each side, placed on scaffolding eight or nine feet high.... With each choir there was a portable organ .... The master composer gave the main beat in the first choir, accompanied by the most beautiful voices. In each of the others there was a man who did nothing but watch this original beat so as to conform his own to it.... The counterpoint of the music was ... full of beautiful melodic lines.... At times a soprano of the first choir would have a solo, then one in the third, the fourth and tenth would answer. At other times two, three, four and five voices of different choirs would sing together, or the combined sections of all the choirs, each in its turn, would have a solo in rivalry with the other sections. Now two choirs would contend with each other, then two others would answer. Or three to five choirs would sing together, then one to five voices alone. At the Gloria Patri, all ten choirs resumed singing together. (Bishop, 7)

It was a magnificent and elaborate presentation. One imagines all ten choirs, ten organs, and other instruments of the "symphony" rising to the *Gloria Patri* in a crescendo of sound that echoed and resounded throughout the church.

Services at St. Peter's were even grander. Another contemporary of Maugars's, Pietro della Valle, describes a vespers celebration for the feast of Peter and Paul in which he gives us a perfect example of the gigantism in Roman church music that has come to be referred to as the "colossal baroque."[27] There were "Cornetti 3, for the Cuppula and a great big piece of music. . . . I know not whether for twelve or sixteen choirs, with an echo choir at the top of the cupola, which I understand in the spaciousness of that vast temple made marvellous effects."[28]

Would Milton have attended such conventionally religious services as opposed to the public, non-liturgical oratorios? He would at least have heard about festive popular celebrations for saints' days. On his visit in 1644, John Evelyn, a high church Anglican but still a member of the "reformed" Church of England, seems to have gone everywhere and attended services freely.[29]

Perhaps we can better hear what della Valle heard at St. Peter's, or Maugars at the celebration for St. Dominic and at the Oratory of the Holy Crucifix, if we think of music of the eighteenth century, which is closer to twentieth-century taste. We are reminded especially of the great oratorios that are descendants of the Roman form—a choral singing of "Let there be light," a dramatic climax, fortissimo, from Haydn's Creation (Milton's Paradise Lost at two removes),[30] or a modern massive sing-along for Handel's Messiah. Recent scholars maintain that the early oratorios of Rome were "cramming, squeezing" full and that audiences for operas were in the thousands.[31] Productions would have been to scale.

We have also to realize that singers had developed the power and ability to project, as had instrumentalists using string and wind instruments of a bewildering number and kind. The demand created for church and lay performances for every day of the church year brought hundreds of musicians of virtuoso caliber to Rome from all over the

---

[27] The composers, Làng comments, "saw in the Mass and motet an excellent medium for colossal polychoral murals" (370). Bukofzer also defines such church services as the "colossal baroque" (64, 69).

[28] Pietro della Valle, Della musica dell' età nostra, as quoted by Flavio Testi in La musica italiana nel seicento (Milan: Bramante, 1972), 2:246–47, and n. 27. Della Valle's account is translated by Hammond, 83.

[29] In The Diary, Evelyn gives a detailed account of his visit in Rome from November 4, 1644 to January 26 or 27, 1645, 2:212–315.

[30] Haydn used passages from Paradise Lost that were translated into German and then translated back from this German text into English. See H. C. Robbins Landon and David Wyn Jones, Haydn, His Life and Music (Bloomington: Indiana Univ. Press, 1988), 316–26.

[31] Finney, 232–33.

continent.[32] The effect of majesty and opulence in Roman performances would come from their number and professional excellence, echoing
in the handsome spaces of palaces and churches that still overwhelm us
today.

One can imagine Milton crowded in with hundreds of others or
standing at the door of the Oratory of the Holy Crucifix. It is tantalizing
to realize that he was in Rome in the same year as Maugars and might
have heard the same kinds of performances.[33] As a musician, Milton
would have been overwhelmed, as other visitors were. Furthermore, we
can only believe that he remembered his experiences when he later
advocated "set and solemn Paneguries, in Theaters, porches, or what
other place, or way may win most upon the people to receiv at once
both recreation, & instruction," and again when he referred to the
Apocalypse of St. John as "the majestick image of a high and stately
Tragedy, shutting up and intermingling her solemn Scenes and Acts
with a sevenfold *Chorus* of halleluja's and harping symphonies."[34]
Maugars was profoundly moved: "Il faut que je vous avoue," he wrote,
"que je n'eus jamais un tel ravissement" (Maugars, 28). ("I must
confess to you that I have never experienced such rapture" [Bishop,
81]). Another contemporary observer says that the voice of Loreto
Vittori, castrato and composer, heard outside the Oratory of the Vallicella, "stirred his audience to indescribable exaltation, so that they could
scarcely breathe, and many had to loosen their garments."[35]

In contrast to the singing in the deeply religious oratorios, but just
as popular, were street celebrations that Milton would have been unable
to avoid.[36] "The whole population of Rome attended," says Lady
Sidney Morgan of a festival in the Carnival of 1639. A masked singer,
"Signor Formica," an *improvvisatore*, sang popular Neapolitan ballads to

---

[32] Maugars, 26; Arthos, 55-56; Bukofzer, 61, 62; Palisca, 113-24.

[33] For Milton's visits to Rome, see above n. 3. According to the *Response*, Maugars
was in Rome for "twelve or fifteen" months. He was there in 1638 and perhaps in
1639. The date of publication of his letter was either 1639 or 1640. See Maugars, 26.

[34] John Milton, *The Reason of Church Government*, in CPW 1.820, 815.

[35] Janus Nicius Erythraeus, *Pinacotheca* (Cologne, 1642), bk. 2, chap. 63, quoted
in Finney, 233.

[36] Arthos, 81-86 n. 2, and Hanford, *Englishman*, 92, on Milton's presence in
Rome for the Carnival of 1639.

the accompaniment of the lute, "of which he was a perfect master." In between ballads he presented his vials and salves to the audience, who delighted in his skills and "in the contrast between his beautiful musical and poetical compositions and those Neapolitan gesticulations in which he indulged." When Signor Formica finally unmasked, he was discovered to be Salvator Rosa, painter, poet, and musician, one of the most celebrated personalities in Rome.[37]

On a much grander scale, but equally lighthearted, was "the entertainment of truly Roman magnificence" that Milton attended at the theater of the Barberini Palace on February 27, 1639. It enabled him to see and hear all that Rome had to offer of the most spectacular and brilliant. This was, of course, Chi Soffre, Speri, a comic opera performed in the immense theatre of the newly completed Barberini Palace, the largest in Rome.[38] The amazement of the poet can be imagined as he would inevitably contrast the splendor of the Barberini theater with any similar structure in London. The Whitehall Banqueting House would be insignificant by comparison. He would find himself amid a festive audience of 3,000 or more, including princes of the church, the highest aristocracy along with their entourages, artists, musicians, and hangers-on.[39] Before him would be a stage vast enough to accommodate full-sized carriages and to represent any region from heaven to hell. For Chi Soffre, Speri, costumes, jeweled fantasies in brilliantly colored silks and satins, scenery, and magical scene changes were designed by Gian Lorenzo Bernini, the pope's artist and architect, unquestionably the greatest genius of the age.

The plot of Chi Soffre, Speri (by Guilio Rospigliosi, the future

---

[37] This famous personality and the occasion of the Carnival of 1639 have been frequently described. See W. M. Rossetti, "Salvator Rosa," Encyclopaedia Britannica, 11th ed., 23:720-21; Lady Cynthia Morgan, Life and Times of Salvator Rosa (London, 1824), 1:249-52, quoted in Arthos, 61-62.

[38] Hanford, 94. Arthos doubts that Chi Soffre, Speri was the entertainment that Milton attended (81-86 n. 2). By Milton's own account, however, he did attend a large Barberini entertainment that might have been Chi Soffre, Speri, where he would have heard operatic, expressive song. See French, 1:391-92. For Roman opera of the period, see Donington, 17-215.

[39] The first Barberini theater, which has since disappeared, may have opened onto the gardens. Actors and audience could expand from the theater into the open, hence the estimates of audiences as large as 3,500. See Arthos, 85; Hanford, 94; Finney, 229.

*Fig. 1.* The Church (Chiesa Nuova) and oratory of Santa Maria in Vallicella, from Giovanni Battista Falda's *Il Nuovo Teatro delle Fabriche, et Edificii in prospettiva di Roma moderna . . .* , Rome, 1665. Designed by Borromini, the oratory was the most popular in Rome, where churchgoers flocked to hear Loreto Vittori and other famous singers on Fridays during Lent. Courtesy of The Metropolitan Museum of Art, Harris Brisbane Dick Fund, 1931. 31.67.4, leaf 19.

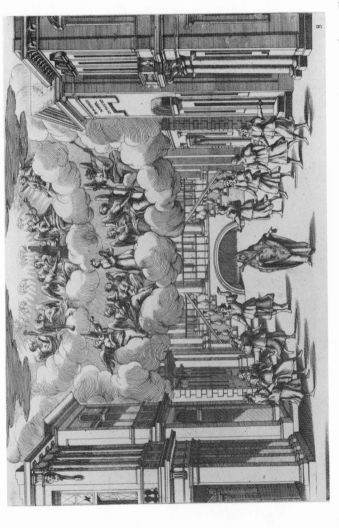

*Fig. 2.* The chorus and players in the "charming symphonie" receiving the saint in heaven in the music drama *Il Sant' Alessio*, performed at the Barberini Palace in 1632 and 1634, might well be assembled from the church groups André Maugars heard during his visit in 1638 or 1639. Included in the angelic performance are a lute, a shawm, an organ, violas, a cornetto, a timbrel, and a violoncello. Courtesy of The Metropolitan Museum of Art, Harris Brisbane Dick Fund, 1930. 30.58.5 (58).

*Fig. 3.* Music and ballet scene for the performance at the Casa Falconieri in Rome on the 25th of February, 1634, from V. Mascardi's *Festa Fatta in Roma . . .*, MDCXXXIV. The energetic chorus in the botton left corner is accompanied by a chitarrone, a violoncello and a harpsichord, popular and widely used instruments for chamber and church music. Courtesy of The Metropolitan Museum of Art, Harris Brisbane Dick Fund, 1930. 30.58.5 (93).

ALTRA VEDVTA DELLA PIAZZA DI S·MARIA DELLA MINERVA.

1 Chiesa di S·Maria dellae Minerva.    2 Obelisco inalzato da N·S·PP·ALESSANDRO VII.    3 Tempio della Rotonda.

Gio. Battif Falda dif e fec.    Per Gio·Iacomo Rossi in Roma alla pace et Piu del S·Pont.

Fig. 4. The church of Santa Maria sopra Minerva, built on the ruins of a Roman temple, from Giovanni Battista Falda's *Il Nuovo Teatro delle Fabriche, et Edificii in prospettiva di Roma moderna . . .*, Rome, 1665. It was here that André Maugars heard a service in "concert" form for chorus and groups of instruments, "the most celebrated and excellent performance I heard in Rome" (Maugars, 27). Courtesy of The Metropolitan Museum of Art, Harris Brisbane Dick Fund, 1931. 31.67.4, leaf 40.

Clement IX) consisted of an inconsequential succession of scenes—a pastoral scene among them, succeeded by a stage storm of thunder and lightning and concluding with a street fair complete with carts and carriages, charlatans and hawkers, and the motley of everyday Rome.

The music of the "variety" entertainment would be of intense interest for Milton, singer himself, lute player, composer of songs. The best-known composers of the day provided the songs and intoned musical speech (*recitativo secco*) for the five hours of the performance. To be heard at all through the space and noise of the enormous theater, performers had to sing at top voice, fortissimo, and for any female roles castrati alone with their highly developed lungs and large stentorian voices could produce sufficient volume. The storm scene would give an opportunity for the sharply contrasting drama and discord demanded in all genres of music.[40]

The astonishing reality of a Barberini-Bernini spectacle, another lively manifestation of the colossal baroque, would inevitably make a memorable impression on the poet. Can one not imagine that reminiscences would reappear in his poetry? One thinks inevitably of Satan's voice penetrating the vastness of hell and sounding above the hosts of fallen angels with the power of his single voice.

It was in the music of Leonora Baroni, star of solo singing in Rome in the 1630s, that Milton would hear expressive song more immediately in an artistically developed form. A highly professional musician, Leonora could be heard in Rome only in private concert, since women were excluded from all religious presentations; they were only allowed to attend Barberini entertainments when accompanying their husbands. Religious performances and lay entertainments were, of course, sung by men and boys.[41] Women singers, however, in *concerti delle dame*, had long been known in Italy. Characteristically composed of three singers who accompanied themselves on the harp, viola, and lute or theorbo, these trios were highly trained and excelled in the quality of their playing and singing. One such group was considered the "musical jewel" of the court of Ferrara, where Alfonso d'Este maintained a

---

[40] Hanford, *Englishman*, 93-95; Finney, 228-30; Arthos, 78-81; Byard, "Divine Wisdom—Urania," *MQ* 4 (1978): 134-37.

[41] Finney (230), citing Alessandro Ademollo, *I teatri di Roma nel secolo decimo-settimo* (Rome, 1888), 25 ff.

*concerto delle dame principalissime* for his own "private delectation." Enzo Bentivoglio, as ambassador from Ferrara to Rome, and Guido Bentivoglio, the cardinal of the Bentivoglio family, continued Alfonso's enthusiasm and sponsored *concerti delle dame* as part of their musical establishments.[42] Continuing in this tradition, Leonora was extraordinarily popular and admired by the cognoscenti of Rome, who besieged her or her patrons for invitations to her concerts. From the impressions they have left us of her personality and performance, she was one of the first of the *divas*.[43]

One has to imagine what this new musical experience would mean to Milton. Leonora's performance would give him, probably for the first time, an opportunity to hear a talented woman singing with professional skill and technique. In England music by women amateurs was everywhere; it was a primary part of a woman's education—for solo singing or taking a part in the universally popular madrigal groups.[44] But even in the masques, until their very late development, the singing was by male professionals. Best known of these was John Allyn (or Allin), who sang in the early masques, and later Henry Lawes, friend of Milton and composer of the songs for *Comus*.[45] Leonora's beautiful solo singing could not but enhance enormously the musicality we experience in the lyric passages Milton wrote for Eve.

Judging from the three Latin epigrams he wrote and intended for a

---

[42] Hammond, 6–7, 12–17; see also A. Newcomb, "Courtesans, Muses, or Musicians? Professional Women Musicians in Sixteenth-Century Italy," in *Women Making Music: The Western Art Tradition, 1150–1950*, ed. J. Bowers and J. Tick (Urbana: Univ. of Illinois Press, 1985), 90–115; Palisca, 16–19. The theorbo was a lute much lengthened to accommodate a second set of bass strings that increased its sonority. See Curt Sachs, *The History of Musical Instruments* (NY: W. W. Norton, 1940), 370–72.

[43] Maugars, 36–38; Arthos, 60–61.

[44] Dorothy E. Mason, *Music in Elizabethan England* (Charlottesville: Univ. Press of Virginia for The Folger Shakespeare Library, 1973), 1-35. In the 1560s, Thomas Whythorne, poet and composer, was music teacher for aristocratic and middle-class families. As music was considered essential for their education, he taught the women and children both practical and theoretical music. For the seventeenth century, we have Pepys's evidence that he is always resolving to practice and make his "wife do the like." Thomas Whythorne, *The Autobiography of Thomas Whythorne*, ed. James M. Osborn (Oxford: Clarendon Press, 1961); *The Diary of Samuel Pepys* (Berkeley: Univ. of California Press, 1971), 9:94 (February 27, 1668).

[45] John Allyn (or Allin) sang in the *Masque of Queens*, as Ben Jonson notes (*Ben Jonson*, 7:315). For Henry Lawes's performance in *Comus*, see Evans, 101-6.

volume of poetry dedicated to her, Milton may have heard Leonora more than once (perhaps at her own home or in the private apartments of one of the Barberini).[46] Would he have been invited by Cardinal Frederico Barberini? What makes the association of Milton and Leonora incongruous—incongruous for a puritan but not for a musician—is the gossip about Leonora's private life. Was she mistress of Cardinal Rospigliosi, later Clement IX, a favorite of the Barberinis, librettist for almost all their entertainments? Mazarin was known to be one of her admirers. Was she his mistress?[47]

We know, also from Maugars's extraordinarily vivid account of this *merveille du monde*, that her song was skillful, sophisticated, and deeply affecting. She sang to her own accompaniment on the theorbo or was accompanied by her mother on the lute or her sister on the harp. About her music he writes that

> elle l'entend parfaitement bien, voire mesme qu'elle y compose: ce qui fait qu'elle possède absolument ce quelle chante, et qu'elle prononce et exprime parfaitement bien le sens des paroles.... Elle chante ... avec une douce gravité. Sa voix est d'une haute estendüe, juste, sonore, harmonieuse.... (Maugars, 37)

> she understands [music] perfectly well, and even composes. All of this means that she has absolute control over what she sings, and that she pronounces and expresses the sense of the words perfectly.... She sings with ... gentle seriousness. Her voice is of high range, accurate, sonorous, harmonious.... (Bishop, 13)

Maugars not only attended Leonora's performances but was profoundly honored to be allowed to play with her himself. (Somewhat vaingloriously he records that he played in a Mass before twenty-three cardinals and, later, for two hours in a private concert for the pope. He only liked, he adds, to take out his viola da gamba for the purple.)[48]

What did she sing? Neither Milton nor Maugars mentions actual composers. She probably sang her own compositions or those of composers popular at the time, of Monteverdi, perhaps, whose works

---

[46] Maugars, 36–38.

[47] Maugars, 36 n. 1.

[48] For further details of Maugars's estimate of the artistry of this "marvel of the world" and for his own participation and performances, see Maugars, 36–38.

were among the "choice music" Milton sent home to England.[49] Both Milton and Maugars emphasize instead the effect of Leonora's singing. In his three epigrams Milton writes of his belief in the power of music. He found that God or some third mind or spirit was moving mysteriously in Leonora's throat; through her, mortals could gradually become accustomed to immortal tones. The power of her voice, in its age-old curative aspect, could have restored Tasso to sanity.[50] Maugars, too, was moved by the magic of her song as he heard her accompanied by her mother and sister. The ensemble

> me surprit si fort les sens et me porta dans un tel ravissement, que j'oubliay ma condition mortelle, et creuz estre desia parmy les anges, jouyssant des contentemens des bienheureux. . . . (Maugars, 37–38)

> had such an overwhelming effect on me and transported me into such ecstasy that I forgot my mortal condition and thought that I was already among the angels, enjoying the pleasures of the blessed. (Bishop, 13)

It is significant that Maugars and Milton, in his earlier poem "At a solemn Musick," emphasize the effect of music.[51] Both poet and musician must have been influenced by particular composers and by specific works they had heard, but their main interest seems to have been music's expressiveness, its ability to inspire, to excite, to move the emotions and passions. Even in his sonnet for Henry Lawes, Milton emphasizes Lawes's skill in setting words to music without distorting them and thereby adding to his music's effectiveness by humoring "best our tongue."[52] In their emphasis on expressiveness, Milton and Maugars, poet and musician alike, share the aim of all post-Tridentine art, most sumptuously and opulently presented in Rome in the paintings of

---

[49] Hanford, *Handbook*, 336.

[50] For a beautiful study and interpretation of the poems to Leonora, see Diane K. McColley, "Tongues of Men and Angels: *Ad Leonoram Romae canentem*," MS 19 (1984): 127–48. For Milton's three Latin epigrams to Leonora and their translation by Charles Knapp, see CE 1.228–31.

[51] Milton writes of music's power to pierce "Dead things with inbreath'd sense" and to present "That undisturbed Song of pure concent [harmony]" ("At a solemn Musick" [4–6]).

[52] "To Mr. H. Lawes on his Aires" (8).

Caravaggio and Cortona, in the architecture of Borromini and Bernini. This expressiveness was also the goal of the music I have attempted to describe.[53]

The music of Milton's experience in Rome is present, I would like to suggest, in *Paradise Lost* in the multifarious echoes and imitations of the music and musical sounds he had heard. In his brilliant and exact musical imagery Milton seems to point to actual musical performances almost as evocatively and specifically as Maugars and della Valle. We can hear the same "charming" symphonies that Maugars records in Milton's "Praeamble sweet / Of charming symphonie" (3.367-68) and in the Angels' "songs / And choral symphonies" (5.161-62). The antiphonal choruses of Maugars's "concert" (27) can be imagined in Milton's "Celestial voices ... / Sole, or responsive each to others note ..." (4.682-83).[54] One could assert that Milton's descriptions, of which these are only a few of multiple instances, are as much substantive evidence as the contemporary records.

Milton may well have imagined the poem's lyric and dramatic utterances as expressive song. We are reminded of the song of oratorio that moved Maugars so intensely in the poet's invocations. They are as much "voice" as they are "vers" in their rhythms, sonority and compelling tonality. Just as the invocation to book 3 is a praise of light, the invocation to book 1 is an evocation of the power of music:

> Of Mans First Disobedience, and the Fruit
> Of that Forbidden Tree, whose mortal tast
> Brought Death into the World, and all our woe,
> With loss of Eden, till one greater Man
> Restore us, and regain the blissful Seat,
> Sing Heav'nly Muse....          (1.1-6)

The drama of Satan's great "aria" to the sun, with its striking crescendo and decrescendo, is intensified if we imagine it as intoned musical speech:

---

[53] Roy Daniells, *Milton, Mannerism and Baroque* (Toronto: Univ. of Toronto Press, 1964), 170-93; John R. Martin, *Baroque* (New York: Harper and Row, 1977), 73-118. Like Maugars and Milton, Giulio Caccini, theorist and musician, declares in the preface to *Le nuove musiche* that the "musician's end ... is to delight and move the affections of the mind" (22).

[54] Spaeth, 113-21.

> O thou that with surpassing Glory crownd,
> Look'st from thy sole Dominion like the God
> Of this new World; at whose sight all the Starrs
> Hide thir diminisht heads; to thee I call,
> But with no friendly voice, and add thy name
> O Sun, to tell thee how I hate thy beams....
>
> (4.32–37)

This passage and others, notably his

> Sight hateful, sight tormenting! thus these two
> Imparadis't in one anothers arms
> The happier *Eden*, shall enjoy thir fill
> Of bliss on bliss, while I to Hell am thrust ...
>
> (4.505)

or Adam's

> O fairest of Creation, last and best
> Of all Gods works, ...
> How art thou lost, how on a sudden lost ...
>
> (9.896–97, 900)

would be strikingly appropriate for Loreto Vittori's powerful voice.

The pathos that Maugars described for us in Leonora's song and its high sweet gravity can be imagined in Eve's

> Forsake me not thus, *Adam*, witness Heav'n
> What love sincere, and reverence in my heart
> I beare thee ...                    (10.914–16)

or in her "O unexpected stroke, worse then of Death! / Must I thus leave thee Paradise?" (11.268–69).

Perhaps models for these passages can be found in music of the late sixteenth century (or earlier), but even without them we are compelled to respond to the beauty of their sound, their rhythms and sonorities. Through their music Milton adds profoundly to our experience in reading his poem and heightens our response to its meaning.[55]

---

[55] Anthony Quayle gives us a moving impression of the intoned musical speech that we can hear throughout the epic in his recital of the epic's first books: John

Even in the structure of the poem Milton seems to imitate the organization and architecture of baroque music. Contrasts of discord and harmony, characteristic of the texture of Roman music, and, indeed, of all baroque music, afford a framework for the epic, from the discordant cacophony of Hell at its beginning to the harmoniousness we experience at its conclusion.[56] This harmoniousness is strengthened by a strong musical association. Eve's "Such favour I unworthie am voutsaft" (12.622) and Adam's "Greatly instructed I shall hence depart" (12.557) are rephrased from the *Magnificat* and the *Nunc dimittis* that were always sung at vespers in the Roman Catholic and Anglican churches.

Crescendos and decrescendos that succeed each other throughout the poem are handsomely and magnificently presented, most notably in the crescendos to the alleluia for the victory in heaven and for the Creation. (One is reminded of the crescendo to the *Gloria* of the "concert" for St. Dominic that Maugars described.)[57]

> Up he rode
> Followd with acclamation and the sound
> Symphonious of ten thousand Harpes that tun'd
> Angelic harmonies: the Earth, the Aire
> Resounded, . . .
> The Heav'ns and all the Constellations rung,
> . . . the Harp
> Had work and rested not, the solemn Pipe,
> And Dulcimer, all Organs of sweet stop,
> All sounds on Fret by String or Golden Wire
> Temper'd soft Tunings, intermixt with Voice
> Choral or Unison. . . .
> Creation and the Six dayes acts they sung. . . .
>                     (7.557-62, 594-99, 601)

We can hear again the choruses and choirs of Rome in this resounding symphony in which even the constellations take part.

---

Milton, *Paradise Lost*, Books 1-4, read by Anthony Quayle, Caedmon, SWC-4004, n.d. Finney has pioneered in finding musical origins and associations for *Comus*, *Lycidas*, and *Samson Agonistes*. See *Musical Backgrounds*, 175-237.

[56] See Thomas B. Stroup, *Religious Rite and Ceremony in Milton's Poetry* (Lexington: Univ. of Kentucky Press, 1968), 3-47.

[57] Maugars, 28.

From his reminiscences of expressive music, the new and revolutionary musical mode of the seventeenth century, Milton creates the "adventrous Song" he intended. It is new and unattempted in that it goes far beyond the intoned musical speech of the narrator of classical epic in its imagery and allusions to contemporary musical forms and styles. It is altogether a new music-poetry that is to "raise" us through the indefinable transcendental power of music in which Milton still believed and "illumin" for us his great theme and purpose to "assert Eternal Providence" and "justifie the wayes of God to men."

The whole fascinating nexus of ideas involved in Milton's "adventrous Song" that this essay attempts to explore suggests that it had an additional and profound meaning for the development and evolution of Milton's art and that it helps to answer an unanswered question. During the many years that he meditated about a subject for composition one of Milton's choices was a drama on a biblical subject. His long choosing meant four different versions for this one topos, but all of those that have survived were for drama. Why did Milton change from drama to epic in the tradition of Homer and Virgil for his poem when he returned to poetry in the 1650s?

If Milton heard the many genres of music that were being presented in Rome, as we can only believe he did from the evidence in his epic, he would inevitably be most impressed by the oratorios and by their power and the intense emotional effect they had on the hundreds that crowded in to hear them. He would realize that oratorio would afford him a model for his poem. The narrator of the form could offer him a voice in which he could speak directly to his reader; the expressive music of its singers could be imitated in his music-poetry to enhance the emotional effect he sought. For these reasons and for the religious purpose that had evolved in Milton's mind and spirit, the oratorios of Rome led him from a biblical drama to a biblical epic. Drama, of course, could afford him the opportunity for music-poetry, but in oratorio he found a living and dramatic example of a powerful, expressive and beautiful form for his "adventrous Song."

New York City

*Contexts*
*Literary*
*Linguistic*

CEDRIC C. BROWN

# Horatian Signatures:
# Milton and Civilized Community

THAT MILTON CULTIVATED ARTS OF SELF-PRESENTATION, in society and literature, we all know. Evidence is abundant, from the "Vacation Exercise" through to the great epic in which authorial presence is so remarkable. I want to discuss an aspect of his self-presentation, visible throughout his career, though changing somewhat at different times; a kind of social self-imaging which has not attracted equal attention for all phases of his life but which may be called to mind by the Italian experience. I am referring to his recourse to the model of Horace in recording communications within what might be regarded as his ideal constituency, his "fit audience ... though few," the congenial and necessary society of liberally educated men.

I begin with an entry in an autograph book, an *Album Amicorum*. We have three surviving autograph entries in Milton's hand;[1] two use the same New Testament text. From 2 Corinthians 12.9 he took a motto expressing the paradox of grace: ἐν ἀσθενείᾳ τελειοῦμαι ("my strength is made perfect in weakness"). A scrupulously pious mark. The entry which furnishes my starting point is that recorded on June 10, 1639, in the book of Count Camillo Cerdogni (Cardouin), a Protestant Neapolitan exile living in Geneva, whom Milton encountered on his return journey. The first part of the entry is made by the last two lines of the Ludlow masque:

> if Vertue feeble were
> Heaven it selfe would stoop to her.

Another statement of grace; also, being a quotation of his own verse, a reminder that he is a poet. The context of the return from Italy suggests also another meaning: God has helped him through Babylonian lands.

---

[1] CE 18:271.

(Since elsewhere he refers not unproudly to his stout integrity when discussing matters of religion in Catholic Italy, it may be possible, paradoxically, to see a degree of self-satisfaction in this assurance of the need of divine aid.) The second part of the entry, over the signature *Joannes Miltonius, Anglus* is an adaptation of a well-known line from Horace, *Epistle* 1.11.27:

> Coelum non animum muto dum trans mare curro
> I change my sky but not my spirit when I travel across the sea[2]

The sentiment was familiar, a bit of a tag, used in the context of travel.[3] Sixteenth- and seventeenth-century editions of Horace record similar sayings in Latin sources, almost certainly imitating phrases from Greek.[4] Still, we seem to have here, in context, a reassurance of Protestant integrity—he is still John Milton, Protestant Englishman, and *his* part has been overtly celebrated in the book, as well as that of Providence.

Context might also have furnished other social meanings for the line. If for example Cerdogni acted as host, or showed kindness, he identified himself with the saving grace of Providence and thus found graceful thanks. Moreover, if Cerdogni was the cultivated man the entry took him for, he might have observed how different the situation of the English poet was from that of the Roman in his playful letter to Bullatius the traveller.

In his epistle Horace plays the gravely wise stay-at-home offering counsel to his friend gadding about abroad. Travelling can become an

---

[2] All translations are my own, unless otherwise indicated. Textual variants within the Latin texts of Horace are not significant for the brief examples used below. Despite John T. Shawcross, "Of Chronology and the Dates of Milton's Translation from Horace and the *New Forcers of Conscience*," *SEL* 3 (1963): 77–84, the question of which editions Milton used, of the dozens available in his own times, has not been satisfactorily answered, and in any case he probably used different ones at different times.

[3] See for example the parallel instance noted in Edward Chaney, *The Grand Tour and the Great Rebellion: Richard Lassels and the "Voyage of Italy" in the Seventeenth Century* (Geneva and Turin: Slatkine, 1985), 248.

[4] Sixteenth- and seventeenth-century annotators often saw a resemblance to Greek sayings, recorded for example in Aeschines and the Petrus Victorinus scholia on Cicero's familiar epistles, which teased the relationship between τρόπος (way of life, habit) and τόπος (place). See for example *Q. Horatius Flaccus ... Opera Dionysii Lambini ... interprete* (Paris, 1587), 266; *Q. Horatii Flacci, Poemata, quae extant, omnia ... studio et opera Gregorii Bersmani* (Leipzig, 1602), 371.

itch, something mindless and undiscriminating. Substantial pleasures can be found at home, about Rome. The mind needs above all reason (*ratio*) and prudence (*prudentia*); it may then praise foreign lands at a distance. Anyway, travelling over the sea makes no essential difference to men's souls: if they are reasonable and prudent, they were so before they started. Then, as often, Horace confirms an ironic undertone with a revelation in the ending. He is either at, or might as well be at, Ulubrae, a dull little town in the flat marshes, and, he boasts, the satisfactions Bullatius seeks in all his travels can easily be found there, to the man with a level mind, *animus aequus*.[5] If high philosophic advice has tipped over into amusing exaggeration, it may be because of sour grapes: this is after all a friend he is lecturing, and his friend is having all the fun. Not that the philosophy is devoid of seriousness; rather, it is registered in context as not immune from partiality in the speaker. The civilized philosopher must expect to listen to himself.

Recasting the Horatian line in the first person, Milton put himself into the part of the traveller, but in such a way as to claim all the wisdom at the disposal of Horace as speaker. His mind was principled in true religion before he went into Italy, and so has remained throughout his travels. The experience of Italy was thus in some sense a matter of indifference to him, with regard to his moral being. Whether this proud reassurance is an act of courteous consideration towards Cerdogni's Protestantism in exile; whether Milton intended to take from the Latin source an affable exaggeration, as if to suggest that Italy had left no essential impression on him; or whether, unlike Horace, he makes a heroic claim, unmodified by any self-deprecating irony, for himself as man of principle, these things are impossible to determine though teasing to think about. But all in all, taken as composite entry in its original context, the Geneva autograph entry projects both an ardently principled Protestant self-image and a social, urbane self-image. On this kind of occasion the fervent English reformer was content to take Horace into his signature.

---

[5] Is Horace playing with literal and metaphorical meanings of *aequus*? The Ulubrian marshes are level; the philosophic mind equitable, content.

§

I would like to put this nice moment of self-presentation into larger context, by looking at Horatian aspects of Milton's communications with certain kinds of audience in works before and after Italy. I will begin with later works, because they have been examined more often in this light.

Milton's sonnets of the 1640s and 1650s are, in many cases, self-consciously Horatian performances or have significant Horatian characteristics. This ground was zealously explored by Finley in a well-known article of 1937.[6] Milton allowed the modern European form of the sonnet some of the functions of Horatian ode; it is an interesting accommodation of genres. Of course this must not be put too simply. There had been all kinds of ways of imitating Horace, and the sonnet had already been put to various use. We know that Milton interested himself in the variety of Italian practice with the sonnet in the sixteenth and seventeenth centuries, and his visit to the Italian academies may well have renewed his awareness. But Horace's variety of practice with the ode often stands as distant model behind the variety of practice with the sonnet. When for example, Milton's sonnet can emerge as political statement, meditating present moments, as in "Captain or Colonel" or the Piedmont poem, we note that Horace made this possible for the ode, as in his laments for civil war and the various considerations of the destiny of Rome. Or the sonnet is turned to celebratory use, addressed to leading men, to Fairfax, Cromwell, and Vane—celebratory, yet moral and hortatory. These poems have been aptly compared especially with the later odes of Horace, particularly those of the fourth book, where he addresses many influential men about Augustan Rome.[7]

Mixed with these authoritative utterances about the destiny of the state we have sonnets depicting the cultivated social milieu of the poet. The artistic community is represented in the sonnet to Henry Lawes, for example. Though the final identity for the poet in that poem is that of Dante encountering Casella, one should note the Horatian celebration

---

[6] J. H. Finley, "Milton and Horace," *Harvard Studies in Classical Philology* 48 (1937): 29-73. I should perhaps add here that the present paper is not intended as an exhaustive account of Horatian imitation in Milton, but rather uses select examples to characterize certain modes of writing, suggesting particular writer-reader relationships.

[7] Editors compare *Ode* 1.1.32: *secernunt populo*.

of Lawes in the middle: "Thy worth and skill exempts thee from the throng."[8] But the examples which most people remember are the convivial poems addressed to young Lawrence and to Cyriack Skinner, two of them invitations to entertainment—modest entertainment, it is true, between times of study—and the third, to Skinner, on the experience of living with blindness, like the others but in a more confessional way a self-conscious monument to friendship. These are poems rich in cultural self-imaging.

Apart from considerations of subject and function, Finley discussed features of technique and manner. He noted resemblances in mode of address, as in the ending of "Captain or Colonel" or in the formulas which begin sonnets, as in the initial address to Lady Margaret Ley, or, more obviously, in the addresses to Fairfax, Cromwell, or Vane. Many such features were commonplace, but in some cases there is something which amounts to a Horatian signature, as in the opening:

Lawrence of virtuous father virtuous son

which cleverly adapts the formula of the opening of *Ode* 1.16:

O matre pulchra filia pulchrior
O lovely mother's more lovely daughter

And indeed the two invitation sonnets are imbued with Horatian mannerisms, capturing the spirit of civilized leisure, an idea to be shared between two men:

What neat repast shall feast us, light and choice,
Of Attic taste, with wine, whence we may rise
To hear the lute well touched, or artful voice
Warble immortal notes and Tuscan air?
    He who of those delights can judge, and spare
To interpose them oft, is not unwise.

He who can judge—as often in Horatian reminiscence an elite is created, both morally and artistically discerning, the educated core which Milton saw at the center of his liberal, reformed state.

Although it is not a sonnet but rather an elaborate Latin ode built upon ancient models, to suit its scholarly recipient, we should take into

---

[8] Quotations are from Fowler.

account here as belonging to the same generally Horatian kind of address the ode to Rous, the Oxford librarian. This is a poem which provides a notable example of confident humanist communication, in which touches of Horace play their distinctive part. Specifically, scholars have pointed to the formula about neatness of style (*munditia*, line 3), the calling on an unnamed god in the context of lament for the ravages of civil war (25-36), and the picturing of a true home for his poetry away from the barbarous noise of the crowd (*lingua procax vulgi*) near the end.[9] The urbane character of the whole should, however, be considered.

The poem accompanies a replacement copy of the 1645 *Poems* requested by Rous for the Bodleian, because the last one had for some reason not arrived with the other books, which were prose tracts. Milton makes his poem a celebration of rare, civilized discourse in times of barbaric strife. Whatever the state of Oxford and the country in 1647, Rous still cares about poetry. The ode is based upon the idea of shared experience and shared values. Its free, experimental play with strophic form is in itself a symptom of the recreation of relaxed scholarly activity. It also has a shape which expresses the passing from one quiet, untroubled world to the desire for another. In the first strophe the circumstances of composition of his earlier poems are remembered in idealistic pastoral terms; the poet was free, at play, *insons populi*, untainted (or unharmed?) by the crowd. The middle of the poem imagines a barbarous fate for the lost book of poetry, in lamentable times. But for the new copy to go into Rous' library is for it to enter into the very home of the Muses. In the final Epode he tells his book to look forward to a happy rest, all strife and envy having passed. Rous, like Hermes, is guide to those immortal regions. There the book will wait, a shade in a library, until true hearing may be found in better, more civilized times. This Rous, the true addressee of the poem, will understand. The generally Horatian character of the poem lies in its trust in goodwill and shared value in the recipient; it enacts the hope of continuing civilization in times of war.

These sonnets and the ode to Rous add up to something constant, and, as has often been pointed out, they bear a special burden of Miltonic self-presentation in the 1640s and 1650s, because they repre-

---

[9] See for example the notes collected in *Variorum* 1:327-31.

sent the only consistent body of poetry he achieved in those busy years. The image they project, an image to which the Horatian identity contributed no small part, is one of cultural authority. The experience of Italy, which confirmed his determination to be poet to the nation, the joining in pamphlet debates for liberty in the reformed state, his work for the Commonwealth government, his prominence in debate with great scholars on the European scene, many things added to the authority of Milton's voice. The fact that his invitational sonnets are to *young* men is symptomatic of his stance in the 1650s. Like the mature Horace of the fourth book of odes, Milton addresses the formable young from an established sense of personal example and experience.[10]

In the earlier phase of Milton's career, before Italy, there is no such comprehensive Horatian self-imaging, but there is, I think, a particular context for moments of Horatian friendship. That context is provided by Charles Diodati, or, perhaps, by the kind of companionship for which Diodati stands in his mind. As importantly, there are also moments even in early works in which Horace is deliberately invoked as a measure of knowing audience.

The image of Diodati is finally fixed in retrospect in the *Epitaphium Damonis*, a poem in which the memory of his dead friend and a sense of Italy are entwined. The discourse of this poem is thoroughly Virgilian; the pastoral genre itself speaks of friendship and community. The poem addresses itself to an intimate or cultured community, including, it would seem, to Italian friends.

The singer's appreciation of Damon is fully recalled in the poem in a progressive revelation coming closer and closer to the realization of pain through loss. From line 19 onwards there is a catalogue of virtues: fidelity to Protestant religion; "just" life; cultivation of learning; and finally, friend to a poet. Then the singer's personal loss is pictured: who will be his constant companion in work and play? These Horatian phrases follow:

---

[10] Of course these poems are not alone in projecting him as culturally authoritative, and cultural authority may, as in the Rous ode, be powerless in the business of the times. A parallel instance is provided for example by *The Reason of Church Government*, where he senses that his long digression of ethical proof, involving the revelation of high, idealistic plans for poetry, might only be understood by "the elegant and learned reader."

Quis me lenire docebit
Mordaces curas, quis longam fallere noctem
Dulcibus alloquiis. . . .

"Who will teach me to soften / eating cares? Who will beguile the long
night / with pleasant chatter?" Milton was fond of that Horatian formula about eating cares: it occurs, significantly, in L'Allegro, to which I
shall return.[11] The pleasant chatter, *dulcibus alloquiis*, is the other
tell-tale Horatian phrase.[12] At this place, reminiscence of Horace informs the picturing of carefree relaxation with an intimate friend, a
soul-mate, even within a poem controlled by the imitation of pastoral
elegy.

The hints of Horace in connection with a mood of social play are
not confined to the picturing of Damon. In the following section, as the
singer imagines friends coming to try to distract him from his grief and
to diagnose the causes of his melancholy—notice the careful reassurance
of the existence of a society of goodwilled friends about him—he gives
playful characterizations of them. Aegle, Baucis's daughter, is described
in an obvious reminiscence of Horace as "*Docta modus, citharaeque
sciens, sed perdita fastus*" ("Instructed in music, expert with the lute, but
ruined by scorn").[13] The poet presents himself as civilizing, and seeking his knowing audience, and in this context that which is antithetical
to the solitary and melancholic is apt to be associated with Horace.
From that point of view, seeing that Milton valued the light play of
some of the more inconsequential odes, it is perhaps not so much of a
surprise to find him in early career doing his experiment in metrical
translation with Ode 1.5, the frothy bit about Pyrrha.

L'Allegro, where social mirth is also contrasted with melancholy,
bears much more affinity with Horatian play than has often been
recognized. The mood is easy to fix:

And ever against eating cares,
Lap me in soft Lydian airs,

---

[11] *L'Allegro* 135; see Horace *Odes* 2.11.18 and 1.18.3-4. This is something of a set
phrase, and earlier annotators register many similar locutions in Greek: see for example
*Q. Horatii Flacci Poëmata . . . à Guilielmo Xylandro Augustano* (Heidelberg, 1575), 134;
Bersman, 61; Lambini, 58 and 122. See also *Variorum* 1:303.

[12] *Epode* 13.18; but this is also a set phrase, used by other writers: *Variorum* 1:303.

[13] *Ode* 3.9.10.

> Married to immortal verse
> Such as the meeting soul may pierce . . .
>
> (135-38)

and so on, claiming in the end such winning force for music that Orpheus himself could learn a thing or two about how better to have regained his Eurydice. The extravagance of happy fantasy is of course meant to be felt; both *L'Allegro* and *Il Penseroso* spin out fantasies, while hinting at sober realities. (Marvell's gently ironic poems about pastoral idyll and retirement took much from the art of Milton's twin poems.) In this respect the likeness to Horace goes beyond the banishing of eating cares, for it actually depends upon a sense of secure and intimate, knowing trust between poet and audience.

Critics have often accounted for this pair of answering poems from the example of academic debate. It may be. But it was Horace who was master at putting poems of opposing philosophies, mischievously, side by side. It was Horace also who was master of the comic art of allowing the pretenses of a speaker to be ironically punctured at the end, as in the well-known and here not irrelevant case of the second epode, *Beatus Ille*, where the whole picturing of country life so teasingly reminiscent of Horace's own Sabine farm is suddenly revealed as the pipedream of a city money-lender. *L'Allegro* and *Il Penseroso* have a similar, half self-deprecating, playful relationship with their audience, and that is why one can still quote Dr. Johnson as having got it so usefully wrong. "No mention is . . . made," he observed, with some ill-humor and a rather literal mind, "of a philosophical friend or pleasant companion."[14] The poems belong to, must have been addressed to, such a companion—that knowing companionship is implicit in the reading the poems demand. Is this in fact not coterie verse? Did Milton use Italian titles, one wonders, to confess affectations to a knowing friend, like Diodati? Both speakers, L'Allegro and Il Penseroso, correspond to familiar *personae* in Milton's verse of the late 1620s, in some of the more social of the Italian sonnets and Latin elegies.[15]

---

[14] *Lives of the English Poets*, ed. G. B. Hill (Oxford, 1905), 1:165-67.

[15] I am thinking of the poses adopted in some of the elegies, like the jovial ironic scholar of *Elegy 1*, the virile city-dweller of *Elegies 5* and 7, or the interesting mixture of *Elegy 6*, where in correspondence with Diodati Milton offers to match the outgoing, social *persona* of his friend whilst also playing up to his own habitual self-image, a

Let me press this point about a particular kind of self-imaging to an audience of friends in relation to other Horatian moments in the early verse and in connection with his longest poem written in Italy, *Manso*. There are for example two wonderful uses of Horatian ode in the Ludlow masque. They function as signals to an audience "not unwise." One instance has been noted before, and I have described it at length elsewhere.[16] In the section added to the Lady's last speech to the enchanter, "Shall I go on ..." (778-98), in which she threatens him with the sage and serious doctrine of virginity and says that she could raise herself to such enrapt utterance

That dumb things would be moved to sympathise
And the brute earth would lend her nerves, and shake ...

the nature of Comus's response confirms that Milton modelled the whole insert on the ode in which the celebrated phrase *bruta tellus*[17] occurs: 1.34. For Comus acknowledges himself shaken by the power of her words "as when the wrath of Jove speaks thunder." In Horace's somewhat playful ode, he is scared stiff by the sudden sound of thunder coming out of a clear sky and wonders thereupon whether it is not a sign to him personally to improve his religious attendances. The knowing reader of Milton's text will see that the allusion strengthens the conclusion that the power at stake is that of Truth, religious truth, itself. But Milton has, typically, I think, used Horace as a means of recognition, a shared experience between himself and the cultivated reader. Also, as in the Cerdogni autograph, the civilized wit of Horace stands side by side with an affirmation of his religious faith.

And Milton uses Horace similarly in another delightful allusion in the Elder Brother's notorious speech about the power of chastity (417-

---

caricature deliberately opposed to that of Diodati, of the serious, unsocial, and self-denying scholar. Some similar intimate play can also be found, for example, in the Italian *Sonnet* 2, in which Milton jocularly modifies his self-denying image, and of course this opposition of jocular and studious roles goes right back to the university prolusions, as for example to the Vacation Exercise, where the sober, fastidious student played for the nonce the jocular *comestor*.

[16] *John Milton's Aristocratic Entertainments* (Cambridge: Cambridge Univ. Press, 1985), 140-41.

[17] The phrase was much discussed by earlier editors not just because it was memorable but also because of uncertainty as to whether *brutus* means heavy or immobile. See for example the full discussion in Landini, 87-88.

74), which critics have sometimes taken without due sense of irony. "She that has that," says the boy, "is clad in complete steel, / And like a quivered nymph with arrows keen / May trace huge forests and unharboured heaths, / Infamous hills . . ." and so on. There are several signals to extravagance of thought here, in manner and context. Soberly speaking, chastity *is* no defense against physical attack. But the learned and elegant reader ought to register a version of Horace, *Ode* 1.22.1-8, *Integer vitae*:

> He that is unstained in life and pure from guilt needs not, Fuscus, the Moor's javelin or bow laden with poisoned arrows, whether he is going to make his way through the surf of the Syrtes or the unharboured Caucasus. . . .

The translator whose words these are, Wickham,[18] cross-refers his "unharboured Caucasus" (*inhospitalem Caucasum*) to Milton's "unharboured heaths, / Infamous hills." Posthumously Milton found an elegant reader, a translator of Horace.

How was it that Horace could say such an extravagant thing? Because when he was out walking in the woods, taking no notice of things about him, busy in fact with a love poem to a girl, Lalage, he suddenly came across a wolf in his tracks. And the wolf ran away. So of course if chastely erotic verse has such a marvellous effect, he will go on writing it. The irony in Milton's text is pointed up by allusion to comic irony in Horace; Horace is a signal of sophisticated, playful communication with a knowing audience.

A similar technique can be shown at the close of *Manso*. Milton confessed himself elegantly, familiarly, to Manso, as he could to no English lord and patron. In particular, he trusted him to read the self-deprecatory irony of the aggrandising ending of the poem. Even as he candidly reveals his great poetic ambition to the elderly aristocrat, Milton gracefully acknowledges that with him all is still to do. The final glorious vision of John Milton triumphant is fraught with ifs and whens—when, having written his British epic, he achieves old age, then perhaps some friend might do as Manso did for Marino, give him due

---

[18] *Horace for English Readers*, trans. E. C. Wickham (Oxford, 1903), 46. The phrase "infamous hills" has been seen as a further Horatian echo, of *infames scopulos* in *Ode* 2.3.20 (see *Variorum* 2:911).

rites, even have an effigy made; then perhaps John Milton will lie in peace of spirit; then perhaps even—"If one can be sure of such things and if rewards do really lie in store for the righteous in heaven"—the spirit of John Milton will go to some corner of that distant world and look down upon the doings of men, "tota mente serenum / Ridens" ("with my whole mind serenely smiling"), "Et simul aethereo plaudam mihi laetus Olympo" ("and with pleasure I shall applaud myself on etherial Olympus"). In this graceful mixture of candid revelation and humourous self-puncturing a note of Horatian irony has crept into the singing of the Virgilian heavens. The self-congratulation, somewhat preposterously, echoes the words of the Athenian speaker of Horace's first satire, the man who can never have riches enough—"At mihi plaudo" ("I am satisfied with myself"). Properly, I take it, young John Milton should more modestly be content with present benefits. As a social poem *Manso* bears a kind of Horatian signature.

Self-deprecation by ironic exposure is a frequent trick of Horace's and it can be found elsewhere in early Milton. For example, though the case is not one of specific verbal reminiscence of Horace, I suspect that the way to rescue *Haec ego mente*, the so-called recantation attached to Elegy 7, from what Bateson saw as the repellent effects of withdrawal from society, in a judgement as splendidly opposite to the truth as Dr. Johnson's statement about *L'Allegro* and *Il Penseroso*,[19] is to read carefully the tone of the extravagant last line. To claim with Diomedes the power to be able to frighten Venus probably registers with good humor an overstatement of his invulnerability to love. This is social poetry, that made as for friends.

If, despite such things as a recent volume of *Milton Studies* (19) devoted to the Latin poetry and advertising "The Urbane Milton," it is still quite common to underestimate his urbanity, it may be because it takes more than a little time to dislodge a long history of prejudicial comment about Milton the unsocial puritan. And, of course, critics have paid too exclusive attention to Milton's own declarations about the ambitious shape of his career as poet: he talks so much of turning to heroic kinds, to great works for the nation, that his creative engagement with other, more social kinds, is often somewhat underestimated. I am, of course, in the end using Horace both as a concrete reference and also as a kind of symbol for that urbane Milton.

---

[19] F. W. Bateson, *English Poetry* (London, 1950), 161.

I do not wish to overstate the case. There are other symbols of the playful and social Milton: we have already noted the uses of Virgilian pastoral, for example, to celebrate community, and in his early elegies for example he is often jocular in Ovidian vein. Horace is merely one identity for Milton, in certain, sometimes brief, contexts; it is not the enveloping Horatian identity of, say, a Ben Jonson or, even more, of an Alexander Pope. But Horace is touched more often, and with more consistent purpose, than is usually recognized, and it may be possible to say, in fact, that the symbol of Horace bears many of the same values as that of the whole Italian experience as represented in print, the documents of which he so carefully produced in the volume of 1645, in poems and commendatory matter, to suggest a monument to cultured communication. As Horace became signal of civilized communication in process, so Italy was used in later writings as proof of civilized communication he had known.

§

I want to turn now towards another repeated concern marked by reference to Horace, one which extends to *Paradise Lost*, thus to more public works and later years. The issue here is less an assumed kinship between poet and audience than a prescription about the right kind of audience. The concern about good audience is articulated in two poems already touched on, "Captain or Coronel" and *Ad Joannem Rousium*, but most famously it is registered in the gesture of anxiety expressed in *Paradise Lost* 7.31 about "fit audience ... though few."

In many of the examples we have already looked at of the uses of Horace as sign of shared cultural activity, there is a kind of celebratory trust in the goodwill and knowledge of a Manso, friends, or educated spirits watching or reading his masque. In these cases there may be reminiscence of Horace's general practice in social discourse in verse. In the somewhat different formulations about "fit audience," relatable to many statements in Milton about a readership elegant and "not unwise," reference is more to the authority of Horace's statements about audience, and the satires are used, especially perhaps 1.10, a poem defensively or prescriptively concerned with establishing true standards for poetic communication.

It may thus be symptomatic that, when he looks for ancient authorities for the good educative uses of satirical laughter, in the defensive *An*

*Apology*, Milton turns first to passages in two of Horace's satires (1.1.
24-6; 1.10.14-5) to explain, even though as he admits he could well
have used passages of Cicero and Seneca.[20] (He also commends Horace there for "wit and morality.") The famous phrase defining ideal
audience in *Paradise Lost* is modified from the tenth satire (line 74).
*Contentus paucis lectoribus* ("content with few readers") are Horace's
words; *doctis lectoribus* ("with learned readers") explains one early seventeenth-century editor,[21] though other interpretations of *paucis* are possible: the Frenchman Dacier, predictably perhaps, thinks of good taste,[22]
while a modern reader might simply assume that honesty and integrity
are the chief qualities in Horace's mind. One could take from Horace
and the annotators of Horace, as Jonson did so thoroughly, a concern
for how poetry was instructive and a recognition that communication
with the many was impossible.[23]

There is in fact a paradox to be registered, in connection with the
use of Horace to define audience: in social poems there could be
expressions of delight in the understanding of like-minded friends, like
Diodati, or of known cultured addressees. With poems of social kind,
security about audience leads to a kind of celebration. Conversely,
Horatian formulations about audience in works written in times of
adversity could also be associated with feelings of isolation and insecuri-
ty, even of fear and despair: when countrymen are deaf, there may be an
appeal from the poet to hearing in a civilized community. That fear may
be more or less accommodated by circumstance. The fear of harm from
the barbarous crowd in *Ad Joannem Rousium*, though expressing real
lament about times of civil war, is jocularly shrugged off, compensated
for, as it were, by the sense of value which Rous puts upon his verse. In
"Captain or Colonel" there is little hope that a royalist soldier will be

---

[20] CPW 1:903-4.

[21] Notes of John Bond in *Horatii . . . Poemata*, 2d ed. (Hannover, 1610), 238.

[22] " . . . gens choisis, gens de bon goust." André Dacier, *Remarques critiques sur les
oeuvres d'Horace* (Paris, 1687), 6:652-53.

[23] The questions of how Horace was read in the seventeenth century and how far
earlier editors and annotators shaped a reading of him are complex and fascinating
ones deserving of further analysis. See the recent preliminary review of these subjects
in Frank Stack, *Pope and Horace: Studies in Imitation* (Cambridge: Cambridge Univ.
Press, 1985), 1-17. I am also grateful to David Norbrook for allowing me to use his
unpublished paper, "Is Marvell's 'Horatian Ode' a Horatian Ode?" parts of which
discuss the contemporary reputation of Horace.

civilized or magnanimous enough to respond to poetry, though poetry there is given, ironically or not, immense judgemental authority. In *Paradise Lost*, where the poet figures himself as in prophetic isolation, trust in the proper hearing of the majority of his fellow countrymen has receded at least as far. Milton's admission there that he speaks only to the fit few seems less satisfied, *contentus*, than is the resignation of Horace as satirist in the tenth satire. Horace's poems ends in a celebratory naming of those he *wants* to hear; Milton, though of course he speaks rhetorically to those who will hear, presents himself as more secure in his possession of nightly visitations from his heavenly muse.

Pious and humanistically educated men provided his fittest constituency. Of his career as a whole, one notes how much he is on record as valuing an intellectual and spiritual companionship with audience, as if wishing for it always. He showed himself nervous when moving outside that audience. Of *Paradise Lost* we can even say that he provided within the poem a model of playful, intellectual discourse in the episode of Raphael's visit to Adam, which gives context to his "fit though few," so as to suggest not only the delight and profit of such discourse (whatever the special circumstances there) but also, subsequently, that the loss of such precious intellectual companionship is specially to be lamented—"No more of talk where God or angel guest / With man, as with his friend, familiar used / To sit indulgent ..." (9.1–3). Against the familiarity of the unfallen Adam with Raphael, we now have the solitary poet praying for protection against the madness of those with no ear for song: "But drive far off the barbarous dissonance ..." (7.32). The state of the world is measured by the possibility of harmonious communication.

In the end, then, if we trace Horatian formulations about audience right through to this famous place in *Paradise Lost*, we can see that the Roman poet provided a reference point for Milton in the crucial concern of how the civilizing poet could present himself to the community, and how, in return, the community might or might not relate to the civilizing poet. Horace defined an achievement in humanist communication, yet also, because he wrote about communication and stood so pre-eminently for that cultural achievement, he could be a kind of measure of the times. In the 1640s and 1650s, his most consistently Horatian phase, Milton's sonnets to great men, Fairfax, Cromwell, and Vane, are monuments to the possible power of poetry to exhort and persuade civilized men, while his sonnets to private friends are testimony to the continuation of a cultured community. In the Restoration period these Horatian transactions with the great and the socially cultured by name no longer seem possible. In *Paradise Lost*, a work of public spiritual instruction, the sense of vocation in the poet's role has sharpened the meaning of "fit ... though few": poets, like prophets, can minister only to those who will, or can, hear.

University of Reading

NEIL FORSYTH

# Of Man's First Dis

T HAT REMARKABLE FORWARD SHIFT OF STRESSES in the opening pentameter of *Paradise Lost* places special emphasis on
the first syllable of the long word *disobedience*:

Of **man's first dis**obedience and the **fruit** ...

The sound of the line initiates a series of *calembours* which makes the
announced subject of the poem not simply the moral offence of *disobedience*, important as Milton wants that to be, but a more fundamental
issue, one that reaches into the roots of language: it is about *DIS* and
what it signifies.

Milton was fond of using or making up negative words beginning
with *dis-*. For several such words, Milton appears as the first citation in
the *OED*, which suggests that some, at least, he invented. Examples are:
*disfigurement* (Comus 74), *disally* (Samson 1022), *displode* (*Paradise Lost*
6.605), and even *discontinuous* (PL 6.329).[1] In fact, he pushes the word-
play so far that an apparently neutral term like *discourse* is drawn into
the pattern of meanings, and so too is the power of making distinctions,
through which Milton figures God's creative word.[2] So he makes it that
much harder to tell God from Satan, and his serious play infects even
his own discourse. I shall first explore the network of prefixes in the
poem, with comments on the various words and the pressures exerted
by their etymologies, then establish the connection with Satan, and
finally see what difference it all makes.

---

[1] J. C. Gray, "Milton and the *OED* as Electronic Database," MQ 23 (1989):
66–73, to which the editor of MQ, Roy Flannagan, kindly alerted me.

[2] See Budick, who also shows also how Satan tries to confuse, and makes an
interesting link with Ramism.

# I

Christopher Ricks, in some of his most memorable paragraphs,[3] pointed to the accumulation of front-rhymes on *dis-* in the opening lines of book 9, the book of the Fall itself.

> No more of talk where God or angel guest
> With man, as with his friend, familiar used
> To sit indulgent, and with him partake
> Rural repast, permitting him the while
> Venial *discourse* unblamed: I now must change
> These notes to tragic; foul *distrust*, and breach
> *Disloyal* on the part of man, revolt,
> And *disobedience* on the part of heaven
> Now alienated, *distance* and *distaste*.[4]

The first word in this echoing series is the apparently harmless *discourse*, embedded in a phrase which asserts its innocence—*venial discourse unblamed*, and pointing back as the foil of a priamel[5] to the friendly chat just ended with Raphael. The line then completes itself after the colon, one of the strongest caesurae in the poem, by looking forward: "I now must change / Those notes to tragic." Nevertheless, the subsequent piling up of "sinful" *dis*-words threatens to reach back across the chasm of the caesura and contaminate that innocent *discourse*, anxiously flanked and protected though it is by *venial* and *unblamed*. Indeed the whole sequence (and indeed the whole of book 9) is introduced with the negative: *No more*, specifically *No more of talk*.

Ricks made nothing of the anxiety about *discourse* here, and that is an interesting measure of what has become available to critical perception in the past twenty-five years. Instead he noted the special effect of the "brilliantly unspoken pun" on *distaste*, aligned on the one hand with *distance* and meaning something like "revulsion," on the other

---

[3] Ricks, 69-72.

[4] *Paradise Lost*. 9.1-9, in Fowler. Subsequent references are to this edition and are incorporated in the text. "Lavinia *disespoused*" soon follows in line 17, another Miltonic neologism that marks an important theme of the poem and suggests one more potential parallel with Eve.

[5] For these terms, see Elroy L. Bundy, *Studia Pindacria*, University of California Publications in Classical Philology, vol. 18 (Berkeley, 1962; repr. 1986), nos. 1-2.

hand with the poem's constant reiteration of the Fall as the "tasting" of the apple: "On the part of man, *taste*; on the part of Heaven, *distaste*." Here too I think we might now extend the reach of this pun if we shift our sights from *taste* to *dis-*: the subject here, after all, is the archetype of human alienations, the original separation. The functions of the puns on *par-* have recently been explored in detail by R. A. Shoaf[6] (especially: *part*, *apart*, *separate*, and *pair*, *impair*, *repair*), and they reinforce and extend the poem's word-play on *dis-* which, in this passage, gets its basic meaning stated—*breach*.

The etymology of the prefix *dis-* lies in the Indo-European words for "two." It is related to Greek *dis*, "twice," and its basic meaning (according to the *OED*) is "two-ways, in twain," and hence "apart," as in *dialogue* or *diabolic*.[7] In English the vowel of the *dis-* prefix is normally short, but in French, through which some words passed in the Middle Ages (e.g., *descant*), it is lengthened (French *désaccord*, but English *discord*), and in Italian the vowel is always long. Sometimes, the *s* is assimilated, as in *different*, or it disappears, as in *divide*. In Latin, and so in English, compound words in *dis-* are frequently the opposite of words in *con-*, as in *discordia concors*. The prefix often has a privative, negative or reversive force, as in *displease*, *dissuade*, or *disaster*, in which sense, and given the vagaries of English spelling, it picks up the flavor of the unrelated Greek prefix *dys-*, meaning "unlucky" or "ill-," as in *dys-daemon*, "unhappy," or in English *dysentery*, *dyspeptic*, or (a modern coinage on the ancient medical model) *dyslexia*. Milton exploits this possibility for *disastrous twilight*, i.e., "ill-starred," in the lines which Charles II's censor apparently found subversive (2.593–96). In this negative or privative sense *dis-* remains a living prefix, having a readily understood meaning and generating new compounds such as *disestablish* ( a sixteenth-century formation), *disrobe*, or *disable*.

---

[6] Shoaf, especially 197, n. 54. The arguments of this book and of Budick's certainly complicate my own, but my main point is a much simpler one, perhaps a necessary preliminary to their more challenging style of argument. It is, incidentally, rather extraordinary that these two books, which both acknowledge the influence of Geoffrey Hartman, had the same editor at the same press, and were published in the same year, are yet entirely silent about each other.

[7] See Richmond Lattimore, "Why the Devil is the Devil," *Proceedings of the American Philosophical Society* 106 (1962): 427–29, and Neil Forsyth, *The Old Enemy: Satan and the Combat Myth* (Princeton: Princeton Univ. Press, 1987), 4–5, for the etymology of *diabolos* and *devil*.

In this sense also, via the *des-* form common to the Romance languages, there occurs some overlapping with another prefix *de-*, so that
Latin *dearmare* becomes in Old French *des-armer*, but *disarm* in English.[8] Thus to our family of words belongs Adam's horrified and profound word-play after the Fall (9.900–901):

> How art thou lost, how on a sudden lost,
> Defaced, deflowered, and now to Death devote?

Each of these words has its pun, reaching back for and playing on the
literal meanings. To understand the theological implications of *defaced*,
Stein cited a definition of sin in *De doctrina* 1.12 which includes the
phrase "a diminution of the majesty of the human countenance,"[9] and
Ricks neatly linked the human loss of face with the loss of God's
face.[10] And if we hear Adam saying *defaced* to Eve, it connects with
the moment (9.849) when he met her at the tree, and with her new-
found hypocrisy (i.e., "actor's language," Gk. *hypokrites*, actor):

> in her face excuse
> Came prologue, and apology to prompt,
> Which with bland words at will she thus addressed.[11]

Eve's speech is rounded off (886–87) with the standard epic formula:

> Thus Eve with countenance blithe her story told;
> But in her cheek *distemper* flushing glowed.

*Distemper* means here both a physical and mental disorder; as Fowler
notes, it is "a disturbance of the temperament of the bodily humours,"
but it is also the "intoxication" from which she is temporarily suffering.
Indeed the word picks up much of the range of related *tempus* words in

---

[8] See *de-* in the OED. *Defeat*, on the other hand, comes from Latin *dis-* + *facere*, to
undo, via Old French *des-* and the later French adaptation to *defait*. Contrast *defect*,
which comes direct from Latin, and from *de-* + *facere*.

[9] Arnold Stein, *Answerable Style: Essays on "Paradise Lost"* (Minneapolis: Univ. of
Minnesota Press, 1953), 8: compare *discountenanced* in 8.553, discussed below.

[10] Ricks, 140; see also 9.1080–82, "How shall I behold the face / Henceforth of
God or angel, erst with joy / And rapture so oft beheld?" Budick, 73, suggests *defaced*
could also refer to Milton's blindness. *Deface* comes from *dis-* + *facies*, via OF *desfacier*,
but *deflower* comes from *de-* + *flos*, as in LL *deflorare*; but. cf. OF *desflorir*.

[11] Surely "apology" functions as "prompter" here, not as Fowler has it "the actor
prompted."

the European languages (from *tempest* to *temper* to *temporary* to *time*).

On *deflowered* Fowler comments oddly: "Primarily metaphorical, though in a literal sense it would apply to the suggested seduction of Eve by Satan." The "metaphorical" sense is surely the one that implies the sexual seduction of Eve: the "literal" is that Satan had initially taken Eve to the tree from among her flowers. Of course, the sexual implications, as in the line "The flowery plat, the sweet recess of Eve" (9.440), are never far away.[12] *Devote* too, has a range of meanings: in its Latin sense it means "dedicated to a god by a vow," and here the god is both Death and the tree, to which Eve has just done "low reverence" (cf. *devout*),[13] so the word takes on the idea of "cursed." But since the sixteenth century, *devotion* has also had the secular meaning of enthusiastic attachment, which suggests betrothal, and so betrayal of Adam.

To sum up, then, *de-* and *dis-* are insistently the results of the Fall. As will by now be evident, the range of these words defines one of the informing plots of *Paradise Lost*, its Satanic movement from unity to separation and discord. The word *disobedience*, we may conclude, can carry such moral freight, however colorless it may seem, because Milton makes all these other words stand behind it.

## II

It is, in fact, Satan himself who makes explicit play with a pun on *dis-*. The word *discharge* forms part of a smirking string of puns on the newly-invented artillery (including *overture*: 1. open, 2. opening of negotiations or music, 3. hole or bore of the cannon; *touch*: already used three times before; and *loud*). What makes these puns so tiresome is the schoolboy knowingness which one hears in the speaking voice; one imagines the other devils tittering as the clever Satan delivers his taunting double-entendres (6.558-67):

---

[12] For Eve as Venus in her springtime garden, see my "Homer in Milton: The Attendance Motif and the Graces," *Comparative Literature* 33 (1981): 137-55. Herman Rapoport also explores the parallel with Botticelli's Primavera, *Milton and the Postmodern* (Lincoln: Univ. of Nebraska Press, 1983), 93-100.

[13] Compare 3.207-209, "To expiate his treason hath nought left, / But to *destruction* sacred and *devote*, / He with his whole posterity must *die*."

> Vanguard, to right and left the front unfold!
> That all may see who hate us, how we seek
> Peace and composure, and with *open* breast
> Stand ready to receive them, if they like
> Our *overture*, and turn not back perverse;
> But that I doubt, however witness heaven,
> Heaven witness thou anon, while we *discharge*
> Freely our part; ye who appointed stand
> Do as you have in *charge*, and briefly *touch*
> What we propound, and *loud* that all may hear.

To this level has the Satanic literalism been reduced, a crude and labored joke that depends on one meaning being missed by half of the audience. As Ricks well argues, it is the avoidance of this kind of extravagance that makes the passage at the beginning of book 9 so effective.[14]

Actually, Satan's joke turns back on himself, as part of the intricate ironies of his soliloquy on Mt. Niphates. He acknowledges there all that he was not prepared, or not able, to admit before: he was unable, for example, to distinguish two senses of the word *owe*, and therefore unable to *discharge* his "debt immense of endless gratitude" (4.52-57):

> Forgetful what from him I still received,
> And understood not that a grateful mind
> By owing owes not, but still pays, at once
> Indebted and *discharged*.

Satan remembers enough to tell the language of the money economy from that other system, the heavenly and unified one, in which debt and payment are the same. But since the soliloquy represents what it is like to be denied *grace*,[15] he cannot any longer enjoy a *grateful* mind.

---

[14] Ricks, 72. Edward Le Comte, *A Dictionary of Puns in Milton's English Poetry* (London: Macmillan, 1981), 45, adds "defecate" as a third meaning of *discharge*. This may be right; we definitely need "defecate" as a meaning of *disburdened* in 6.878 after the angels have been expelled at the end of the war in heaven: "Disburdened heaven rejoiced, and soon repaired / Her mural breach." Le Comte lists twenty-five words beginning in *dis-* which Milton exploits for puns.

[15] For play with the word *grace* in the poem, see Neil Forsyth, "Homer in Milton." Compare *Ad Patrem* 111-14, which includes both Greek *charis* and Latin *gratus* forms:

> At tibi, chare pater, postquam non aequa merenti

A more interesting example from the family of *dis-* words comes later in book 9, as one of Satan's "dark suggestions" (9.90) hidden "from sharpest sight" in the "wit and native subtlety" of the serpent. As part of the temptation of Eve, Satan links food (and sex), thought and knowledge through the repetition of the word *discernment*. First (9.571–74), in describing his supposed former state, he says:

> I was at first as other beasts that graze
> The trodden herb, of abject thoughts and low
> As was my food, nor aught but food *discerned*
> Or sex, and apprehended nothing high.

Then (9.679–83) the word defines the power of the tree, in one of the poem's adaptations of the Faustian tradition of forbidden knowledge:

> O sacred, wise, and wisdom-giving plant,
> Mother of science, now I feel thy power
> Within me clear, not only to *discern*
> Things in their causes, but to trace the ways
> Of highest agents, deemed however wise.

The address to the tree and its personification as a mother already encourage Eve to move closer to it, at least in thought, and then Satan hints at the need to know "things in their causes" and to question the wisdom of "the ways of highest agents" (i.e., God, who has forbidden the tree) in the light of the wisdom the tree itself can give. It is not usually noticed that these words also pose an implicit challenge to the voice of the narrator, who had claimed to be able to justify "the ways of god to men"—and the play-rhyme on *ways/wise* is typical of the Miltonic Satan's wit.

What most impresses Eve, apart from the fact that the serpent is not dead, is that he can speak reasonable words. As she muses a while, reflecting on what Satan has said, she again links eating and wisdom ("intellectual food" 9.768), and she also places Satan's word *discern* at the climax of an ascending series in which she rejects the idea of death, and in which the alliterations on *d* suggest another range of meanings:

---

Posse referre datur, nec dona rependere factis,
Sit memorasse satis, repetitaque numera grato
Percensere animo, fidaeque reponere menti.

> In the day we eat
> Of this fair fruit, our doom is, we shall die.
> How dies the serpent? He hath eaten and lives,
> And knows, and speaks, and reasons, and *discerns*,
> Irrational till then. For us alone
> Was death invented? Or to us denied
> This intellectual food, for beasts reserved?

Even as the alliteration makes a group out of *day-doom-die-dies*,[16] Eve's logic in the process of separating these words from each other, and so denying God's word. The alliterative pattern completes itself with *discerns-death-denied*, suggesting what Eve is really doing, or denying, beneath the surface of her thought.

In this word *discerns*, then, we find both the intellectual ability to distinguish one thing from another, and also (through the idea of judgment or discrimination) criticism, even literary criticism.[17] God said, "in the day ye eat thereof, you shall surely die," and Satan has got Eve to question that text, to divide its meanings, to interpret or read it, to be her own judge or critic. Satan, as it were, has just shown himself as the first literary critic, and Eve has quickly learned to be one too. The Greek words *krinein* (to judge) and *krisis* (judgment) are related to Latin *cernere*, as is the Latin *crimen* (judgment) and the English word for what Eve is about to commit—*crime*.

## III

Thus far I have confined my argument (more or less) to the fascination of etymological exploration, a staple of modern critical commentary on Milton. But now I want to go further than what a modern philologist

---

[16] The sequence even suggests a bilingual pun which reinforces the divine warning, since *dies* means "day" in Latin. In modern Cockney dialect, *day* and *die*, like *ways* and *wise*, have the same pronunciation.

[17] See Hebrews 4.12: "For the word of God is quick and powerful, and sharper than any two-edged sword, piercing even to the dividing asunder of soul and spirit, and of the joints and marrow, and is a discerner of the thoughts and intents of the heart." On the word *discerner*, William Gouge adds the conventional gloss: "we in English according to the notation of the Greek call such a one a *Critick*," *A Learned and Very Useful Commentary on the Whole Epistle to the Hebrews* (London, 1655), 450, quoted in Budick, 62.

would think of as etymology, in order to explore a different kind of word-play: likenesses of sound or other kinds of accidental similarities between words. Eighteenth-century writers and commentators, inventing a new and rigorous kind of classicism that the classical writers themselves might not have recognized, tended to disapprove of word-play, especially of this kind, as low or feminine. Witness Samuel Johnson's famous strictures on Shakespeare: "a quibble was to him the fatal Cleopatra for which he lost the world, and was content to lose it."[18] Johnson disapproved equally of Milton's "play on words, in which he delights too often."[19] Milton was, we know, extremely fond of etymological word-play, but he did not confine his delight to that restricted kind of pun. The poetic and intellectual tradition, from Plato's *Cratylus*, through the Roman rhetorician Varro, to medieval and Renaissance commentators on classical and biblical texts, tended to find equally significant what our philological and neoclassical training might refer to as "mere" phonetic similarities; indeed the two kinds of pun were not rigorously distinguished until the development of nineteenth-century historical linguistics.[20] Once we broaden the scope of the inquiry to

---

[18] Samuel Johnson, "Preface to the Plays of William Shakespeare," in W. K. Wimsatt, ed., *Johnson on Shakespeare* (Harmondsworth: Penguin, 1969), 68. Locke's condemnation of catachresis is an important stage in this development. Note especially: "Eloquence, like the fair sex, has too prevailing beauties in it to suffer itself ever to be spoken against. And it is in vain to find fault with those arts of deceiving wherein men find pleasure to be deceived," *Essay Concerning Human Understanding*, ed. John W. Yolton, 2 vols. (London and New York: Oxford Univ. Press, 1961), vol. 2, bk. 3, chap. 10, p. 106. See Paul de Man, "The Epistemology of Metaphor," *Critical Inquiry* 5 (1978): 13-30. For recent discussion of Shakespeare puns, see the essays in *Shakespeare and the Question of Theory*, ed. Patricia Parker and Geoffrey Hartmann (New York and London: Methuen, 1985), especially Margaret W. Ferguson, "*Hamlet*: Letters and Spirits," 292-309.

[19] Johnson, *Works*, 10.138, cited in Le Comte, *Puns*, viii.

[20] For the classical tradition, see most recently Frederick Ahl, *Metaformations: Soundplay and Wordplay in Ovid and Other Classical Poets* (Ithaca: Cornell Univ. Press, 1985); still very useful is W. B. Stanford, *Ambiguity in Greek Literature* (Oxford; Oxford Univ. Press, 1939), who begins from the observation that Aristotle felt ambiguity to be an unfortunate but inescapable aspect of language, but that poets often gloried in it. For the biblical and Renaissance approaches, see J. M. Sasson, "Word-play in the Old Testament," in *The Interpreter's Dictionary of the Bible*, supp. vol., gen ed. K. Crim (Nashville: Abingdon, 1976), 968-70, and Arnold Williams, *The Common Expositor* (Chapel Hill: Univ. of North Carolina Press, 1948), 230-32: "Starting with the assumption that all languages trace back to an original unity in Hebrew, the commentators were able with ease to derive Greek and Latin words from Hebrew. In common

include this kind of word-play, we can allow ourselves to hear that behind this collection of *dis*-words on which the poem lays such stress lurks another word—*Dis*.

Dis makes his appearance in *Paradise Lost* through the extended analogy between Eve and Proserpine. As the fatal temptation begins, Eve is tending her flowers (9.432–33),

> Her self, though fairest unsupported flower,
> From her best prop so far, and storm so nigh.

There is no mention of Proserpine here, but the lines recall the earlier allusion of book 4.270, the first in that prolonged negative catalogue of Paradises:

> Not that fair field
> Of Enna, where Proserpine gathering flowers
> Her self a fairer flower by gloomy Dis
> Was gathered, which cost Ceres all that pain
> To seek her through the world.

The two flower phrases linking Eve and Proserpine are among the many structural correspondences between books 4 and 9, and Milton reinforces the connection by another allusion to Ceres and Proserpine a few lines before; we need to remember "Her self a fairer flower" (4.270) in "Her self, though fairest unsupported flower" (9.432).[21] As she leaves his side for the last time still innocent, Eve is compared to various Roman females whom males found irresistible, among them Diana, "Pomona when she fled / Vertumnus," and "Ceres in her prime, / Yet virgin of Proserpina from Jove" (9.393–96).

The implications of this Greco-Roman myth as analogue for the Fall have been thoroughly explored by the commentators. Satan does not in fact "ravish" Eve, but their meetings are full of sexual suggestions, and

---

with Renaissance scholars generally the commentators were on the whole ignorant of sound shifts and phonetic laws, and they frequently confused the sounds of a language with the symbols used in writing it." A good example is that "the word *Heden*, or Eden, is ... both a proper name and the common noun meaning 'delight.' Pererius and Mercerus are sure that the Greek *hedone*, 'pleasure,' is derived from the Hebrew *Heden*."

[21] For extensive but often stimulating Derridean discussion of this pun, see Rapoport, "Milton's Lady of the Flowers," *Postmodern*, 59–100.

one of them is this insistent overlapping with the rape of Persephone by Hades/Pluto/Dis. The chain of well-known allusions leads back through Dante and Claudian to Ovid and Virgil, eventually to the *Homeric Hymn to Demeter*.[22] Milton's choice of *Dis* as the name for the Satan figure in the allusion follows the dominant tendency of the tradition. Thus Perdita's famous lines evoke the flowers that Proserpina let fall from "Dis's waggon," and in the *Tempest* masque Ceres says she has foresworn the "scandaled company" of Venus and Cupid

> since they did plot
> The means that dusky Dis my daughter got.[23]

It is only since the Romantics that it has become the fashion to give the older Greek form to mythological names.

*Dis* (long vowel) is probably a contracted form of *dives* ("rich"). The name is thus a Latin translation of Greek *Ploutos*, which indicates a common confusion between this god of wealth and *Plouton* (Pluto), another name for Hades, the traditional Greek king of the underworld. The confusion is encouraged by the standard overlapping of fertility concepts with the world of the dead.

> Let none admire
> That riches grow in hell; that soil may best
> Deserve the precious bane.

The evil (bane) of the present age of iron began with the mining of precious metals in *Stygiis ... umbris*, according to the Ovidian *locus classicus* for the commonplace,[24] so we might be tempted to hear in

---

[22] George deForest Lord, "Pretexts and Subtexts in 'That Fair Field of Enna,'" MS 20 (1984): 127-46, makes the extraordinary claim that Milton must have known (or "reconstituted") the *Homeric Hymn to Demeter*, which survives, as Lord admits, in only one manuscript, and that not catalogued in Moscow until 1777. He calls the relevant passage a "dissimile," a term I wish I had thought of.

[23] *Winter's Tale* 4.4.118; *The Tempest* 4.1.89. My thanks to my colleague, Margaret Tudeau Clayton, who points out the parallel with Caliban, "this thing of darkness" (5.1.275), "as disproportioned in his manners / As in his shape" (290-91), and also the "distempered" condition of Prospero when his recollection of the conspiracy disrupts the masque (4.1.145); see her "'How came that widow in?' The Vergilian Presence in *The Tempest*," part of her unpublished dissertation "Jonson, Shakespeare and the Figure of Vergil" (Cambridge University, 1986).

[24] *Metamorphoses* 1.125-42; cf. Spenser, *FQ* 2.7.17.

this Miltonic version an allusion to the meaning (and the name) *Dis*. Yet Milton appears to suppress that possibility here: his name for the god of riches is based on the Hebrew—*Mammon*. Thus the Roman name *Dis*, freed as it were from its etymology, may instead associate itself with the range of *dis-* words, and with death.

In Latin literature, *Dis* is the principle name for the king of the shades, and two other hellish puns in *Paradise Lost* depend on Milton's consciousness of this fact. Satan becomes aware of his new domain, and the *dis-* words accumulate here within the *d* sounds (1.56-67):

> round he throws his baleful eyes
> . That witnessed huge affliction and *dismay*
> Mixed with obdurate pride and steadfast hate:
> At once as far as angels' ken he views
> The *dismal* situation waste and wild,
> A dungeon horrible, on all sides round
> As one great furnace flamed, yet from those flames
> No light, but rather *darkness visible*
> Served only to *discover* sights of woe,
> Regions of sorrow, doleful shades, where peace
> And rest can never dwell, hope never comes
> That comes to all; but torture without end. . . .

The allusion to the entrance to Dante's Hell, where *Dis* is the name both of the inner city and the principal inhabitant, makes the covert presence of *Dis* in Milton's language even more apt. But the puns here are complex: *dismay* derives from *dis-* (*OED* definition 4) + *mag-* (*magan*, OHG, to be powerful), but there is no etymological link with *dismal*, in spite of their proximity in Milton's text. *Dismal* comes from OF *dis* + *mal*, and this from Latin *dies mali*, unlucky or evil days.[25] In this company, *discover* carries a subsidiary suggestion of the recognition of Satan's new nature as ruler of Hell.

The pun on *dismal* recurs when Adam is shown the murder of one son by another (11.466-70):

> Death thou hast seen
> In his first shape on man; but many shapes

---

[25] Le Comte lists both these puns, *Puns*, 46, but does not seem to notice Dis one.

Of death, and many are the ways that lead
To his grim cave, all *dismal*; yet to sense
More terrible at the entrance than within.

Michael's language recalls the Roman and Italian underworld quite closely, and one is surely required to hear, in Milton's alignment of death, the grim cave, and *dismal*, the name of the Roman god of the dead. The words, in fact, translate a formulaic phrase which the chorus sings at the end of several Greek tragedies: *pollai morphai ton daimonion* ("many are the shapes of the gods / divine power"). Through a multilingual pun Milton makes this "many shapes of death."

## IV

Virgil's *Aeneid* is the best place to begin exploring the Roman context. *Dis* is the name he normally gives to the king of the underworld, and the name therefore appears in those famous lines from the descent to the underworld in book 6 which provide the framework for the subsequent poetic tradition and which are dense with quotations or allusions in Milton. The Sybil explains to Aeneas how easy it is to get into the underworld, and how hard to get out:

> facilis descensus Averno:
> noctes atque dies patet atri ianua Ditis;
> sed revocare gradum superasque evadere ad auras,
> his opus, hic labor est.[26]

Easy the descent through Avernus: the gates of black Dis lie open night and day. But to retrace one's steps and escape to the upper air, that is the task, that is the struggle.

As in Milton, the *d*-s sounds make associations, this time among *Ditis*, *descensus*, and *dies*, and the passage immediately includes Persephone also. To make the journey downwards possible, says the Sybil, we need the golden bough, sacred to Proserpina, queen of the underworld, since she has ordained that it be brought to her as her special offering.

---

[26] *Aeneid* 6.126-29. I have used the edition of R. D. Williams (London: Macmillan, 1972). Translations are my own throughout this essay.

In Virgil, then, Dis and Proserpina are linked as joint rulers of the shades, deities to be propitiated and addressed. Once the proper sacrifices have been made, including a sterile cow "to thee, Proserpina" (6.251), the poem makes a brief new invocation (264-67), not now to the Muses but to the mysterious and primordial deities of the underworld:

> Di, quibus imperium est animarum, umbraeque silentes
> et Chaos et Phlegethon, loca nocte tacentia late,
> sit mihi fas audita loqui, sit numine vestro
> pandere res alta terra et caligine mersas.

You gods who rule over spirits, silent shades, Chaos, Phlegethon, wide realms of night and silence, let it be right for me to speak what I have heard; let it be permitted by your divine power to reveal what is buried deep in earth and darkness.

Then *Dis* himself is immediately mentioned, and his name picks up and completes the invocation to the *Di, quibus imperium est animarum*.

Aeneas and the Sybil now find themselves walking in the underworld, in the famous lines (6.268-74) that Dante evokes for the *selva oscura* at the beginning of the *Divina Commedia*:

> Ibant obscuri sola sub nocte per umbram
> perque domos Ditis vacuas et inania regna:
> quale per incertam lunam sub luce maligna
> est iter in silvis, ubi caelum condidit umbra
> Juppiter, et rebus nox abstulit atra colorem.
> vestibulum ante ipsum primis in faucibus Orci
> Luctus et ultrices posuere cubilia Curae.

They were walking in the darkness, shadowy figures in the lonely night, through the empty homes and vacant realms of Dis, like people going through the woods by the treacherous light of a dim moon, when Jupiter has hidden the heavens in shadows and black night has taken the color out of things. At the entrance itself, in the very jaws of Hell, Grief and avenging Guilt have placed their beds.

The jaws of Hell (here called *Orcus*, a Latin deity identified with Dis, and often used to mean the underworld)[27] introduce a catalogue of mythological and allegorical monsters[28] which ends appropriately enough with *Discordia demens* (6.280). A few lines later (6.309–14), Virgil and the Sybil encounter the large number of ghosts for which the simile of fallen autumnal leaves and migrating birds provides such a resonant analogy, echoing most notably in Milton's Vallombrosan allusion.

## V

The presence of Virgil's language in Ovid, Milton's main source for the story of the rape of Proserpine, further complicates his reference to Dis. Ovid tells the story in two places, *Fasti* 4.417–618 and *Metamorphoses* 5.341–661.[29] In the *Metamorphoses* the story is sung by the Muse of poetry herself, Calliope, and there is then a playful allusion to this song later when her son Orpheus stands in the presence of Proserpina and her husband, "lord of the shades," and appeals for their sympathy: "vos quoque iunxit Amor" (*Met.* 10.15–29).

Since Calliope sings in response to a challenge, her song becomes an explicit apology for poetry.[30] One of the daughters of Pieros sings about the battles of gods and giants, specifically the myth of the monster Typhoeus, another type of Satan, and how he put the gods to shame and rout. Calliope's reply wittily opens with the earthquakes caused by

---

[27] Williams compares *Aen.* 4.242. See *Ad Patrem* 118: "Nec spisso rapient oblivia nigra sub Orco."

[28] Milton echoes the passage at, e.g., *PL* 2.622–28.

[29] See the recent study by Stephen Hind, *The Metamorphosis of Persephone: Ovid and the Self-Conscious Muse* (Cambridge: Cambridge Univ. Press, 1987). Hind assesses the importance of the Homeric Hymn and other sources, and makes an intelligent contribution to the discussion of Richard Heinze's theory that Ovid's two versions are contrasted as elegaic versus epic. See also Richard J. Du Rocher, *Milton and Ovid* (Ithaca: Cornell Univ. Press, 1985).

[30] Calliope's performance in the song-contest provided Milton with much to enrich his poem. It forms part of the context for his own self-referential remarks on the nature of his poem, such as the proem to book 9, in particular the contrast between the long and tedious havoc of battles feigned and what his own celestial patroness dictates to him slumbering. For the tradition behind this repudiation of epic, beginning with Callimachus, and important in Ovid, see Hind, 128–31, esp. notes 21–32, 39, 40, and p. 165 n. 34. Milton's "Descend from heaven, Urania" finds an interesting analogue in Ovid's "ad mea perpetuum deducite tempora carmen" in 1.3–4.

the struggles of Typhoeus imprisoned under Etna. Worried that his roof may spring a leak and let in the light, Dis comes out from his "tenebrosa sede" (Met. 5.359) to have a look around Sicily. All is well, it seems; but before he can return to his kingdom Venus spots him and decides to take advantage of his vulnerability to extend her power to the realm of hell. In words that allude to and parody Virgil (as Ovid often does, and as is doubly appropriate here in this Heliconian response to the epic Pierid challenge), Venus says to her son Cupid: "arma manusque meae, mea, potentia" (Met. 5.365), and tells him to attack. He fires an arrow and it lands in the heart of Dis.

The passage (Met. 5.379–91) is important for Milton: among other things it is a fine instance of Ovidian (and so Miltonic) sound- and word-play. The tempo mounts until the three dental consonants at the end of the line (-dine Ditem) mark the moment of the arrow's penetration:

> "... iunge *deam* patruo!" *dixit* Venus, ille pharetram
> solvit et arbitrio matris de mille sagittis
> unam seposuit, sed qua nec acutior ulla
> nec minus incerta est nec quae magis au*d*iat arcum,
> oppositque genu curvavit flexile cornum
> inque cor hamata percussit harun*dine Ditem.*
>
> Haud procul Hennaeis lacus est a moenibus altae
> nomine Pergus, aquae: non illo plura Caystros
> carmina cygnorum labentibus au*dit in undis.*

"Join the goddess with her uncle," said Venus, and Cupid opened his quiver. At his mother's behest he picked from his thousand arrows the sharpest and surest and most responsive to the bow. Bracing his knee he bent the bow, and the barbed shaft struck deep into Pluto's heart.

Not far from the walls of Henna lies a deep pool of water called Pergus. Its music rivals the songs of the swans that Cayster hears on its gliding waters.

Again the songs of the swans, in this case the Homeric swans of Cayster, alert us to the self-referential aspect of the verse. The sound play (*audit in undis*) extends itself even into the apparently peaceful description of the *locus amoenus* with its eternal spring; as the passage continues, the use of the "blows of Phoebus" ("*Phoebus ... ictus*") for the sun's rays[31] recalls the deadlier archery of Cupid and maintains the narrative tension.

> silva coronat aquas cingens latus omne, suis que
> frondibus ut velo Phoebeo submovet ictus.
> frigora dant rami, varios humus umida flores:
> perpetuum ver est. quo dum Proserpina luco
> ludit et aut violas aut candida lilia carpit,
> dumque puellari studio calathosque sinumque
> implet et aequales certat superare legendo,
> paene simul visa est *dliectaque raptaque Diti:*
> usque adeo est propertus amor.[32]

A ring of trees girds the pool all around, and their leaves keep off the harsh rays of the sun. The branches provide cool shade, and the ground is moist with all kinds of flowers: the season is always spring. In this grove Proserpina was playing, gathering violets or white lilies. Eagerly, she filled her baskets and the folds of her robe, trying to pick more than her companions. Almost in one moment she was seen, she pleased, and Dis took her up—so swift is the rush of love.

Once again the tempo is carefully managed, preparing for the suddenness of the rape by the contrast with the peaceful setting. The shock of *raptaque Diti* is further increased by the chiastic sound pair that it makes with the *dilectaque* which immediately precedes.

The whole passage provides the model for Milton's equivalent, but much longer, description of the garden, via the list of negative parallels that begins, we recall (*PL* 4.268),

---

[31] See Charles Segal, *Landscape in Ovid's Metamorphoses* (Wiesbaden: Hermes Einzelschriften 23, 1969), 54, on the sun's arrows here; also Hind, *Metamorphosis*, 30–33.

[32] Besides the various sexual implications of flowers and laps, discussed in J. N. Adams, *The Latin Sexual Vocabulary* (London: 1982), 90, 207, and picked up in Milton's *deflowered* (*PL* 9.901), the pun on Latin *paene* and *pene*, the ablative of *penis*, is obviously relevant here; it is quite common in priapic poetry, and is discussed, along with much other Ovidian word-play, in Frederick Ahl, *Metaformations*, 20–21, citing a footnote in Gibbon to show general awareness of the pun.

> Not that fair field
> Of Enna, where Proserpine gathering flowers
> Her self a fairer flower by gloomy Dis
> Was gathered,

before we are brought back with a jolt to the point of view from which
we see the garden (285–86):

> From this Assyrian garden where the fiend
> Saw *undelighted all delight.*

Milton's play with *undelighted* we can now see both as suggested by
Ovid's *dilectaque* and as rounding off his sequence of negative comparisons by a typical ring or "aria da capo," linking back by the echo to
*gloomy Dis* in line 270.

Ceres eventually learns what has happened to her daughter, and goes
to Jove to insist she be brought back. Jove's reply concludes by granting
her request, on condition Proserpina has not eaten in the underworld
while she was there. What is interesting in Jove's speech is that, though
he is not named at this point, Dis comes into the narrative through a
Jovial pun.

> sed tanta cupido
> si tibi *discidii* est, repetet Proserpina caelum. . . .

Literally what he says is "if you really have such longing to separate
them, let Proserpina come to the upper world again. . . ." But the words
*cupido . . . discidii* playfully invoke both the name of the god who started
all the trouble, Cupid, and the name of Dis. They thus imply Demeter's
"desire for a Dis fall" (*Dis* + *cado*) as well as for a "cutting in two" (*dis-*
+ *scindo*) or marital separation—a disjoining.

The plucking of the fruit shows that Proserpina is, as it were, incur-
able, and the pomegranate, with its incorporated pun on *poma*, apple,
had already suggested to the mythographers the link with Eve.[33] Milton ignores that relatively trivial word-play, and focuses instead on the

---

[33] Sandys, *Ovid's Metamorphosis. Englished by G. S.. Mythologiz'd and Represented in
Figures: An Essay to the Translation of Virgil's Aeneis* (Oxford, 1632), 256, quoted by
Fowler ad loc 4.268–74, and by Lord, "Pretexts," 135. The serpent in the name
Proserpina, with its proposed etymology of "creeping forward," was also noted by
Sandys.

more important links between Dis and the discord which followed his attempt. But he nonetheless makes play with the word *fruit* and quickly makes the link with death explicit in those opening lines we may now hear again:

> Of man's first *disobedience* and the *fruit*
> Of that forbidden tree, whose *mortal taste*
> Brought *death* into the world, and all our woe.

# VI

Dante makes a similar though much briefer allusion to the Proserpina story. When he reaches the Earthly Paradise in the *Purgatorio*, he sees the young and lovely Matelda, herself an incarnation of the garden and its innocence, picking flowers in a beautiful springtime landscape. She reminds him, he says (28.49-51), of where and what was Proserpina in the time when her mother lost her, and she lost the spring:

> Tu mi fai rimembrar dove e qual era
> Proserpina nel tempo che perdette
> la madre lei, ed ella primavera.

You make me remember where and what was Proserpina at the time her mother lost her, and she the spring.

Proserpina was not normally associated with the loss of spring as such, and Dante has evidently noticed that Ovid, in his version of the story, says briefly that in the fair field of Henna, "perpetuum ver est."[34] Milton picks up and extends the comparison, but the ingredients are already here in Dante.

More important than his version of the Proserpina story, though, is the name *Dis* itself. In the *Inferno*, Dis (or rather *Dite*) is used first as the name for the lowest reach of Hell, which Virgil and Dante approach and enter in cantos 8 and 9:

---

[34] *Metamorphoses* 5.391 (see above). For discussion of Dante, see C. H. Grandgent and Charles S. Singleton, eds., *Dante Alighieri. La Divina Commedia* (Cambridge, Mass.: Harvard Univ. Press, 1972), 565; see also C. H. Martindale, *John Milton and the Transformation of Ancient Epic* (Beckenham, Kent: Croom Helm, 1986), 173.

> Lo buon maestro *disse*: "Omai, figliuolo,
> s'appressa la *città* c'ha nome *Dite*,
> coi gravi *cittadin*, col grande stuolo."

The good master said: "Now, my son, comes the city called Dis,
with its grave citizens and great garrison." (8.67–69)

The walls of Dis, the Hell of willful sin, are defended by the rebel
angels and contain immediately within the arch-heretics and their
followers, those who defied their maker and renounced his truth; so it
is appropriate that Dante's *cittadin* picks up and brings together the two
words *città* and *Dite*. The inhabitants are, in their pride, personifications
of its fierce and defensive independence.

This is, *a fortiori*, true of the eponymous ruler of the city, the vast
and frozen figure of Satan himself, whom Dante also calls *Dite*. We
hear about him early on, in the plan of Hell, at the central point of the
universe (11.64–65). And Dante finally sees him, or more correctly
*realizes* that he is seeing him, in the last great canto of the *Inferno*:
"There is Dis," says Virgil, "and there the place where you must put on
the armour of fortitude" (34.20–21):

> "Ecco *Dite*," *dicendo* "ed ecco il loco
> ove convenien che di fortezza t'armi."

There he is, a traitor in each set of jaws, his three faces echoing Virgil's
"deos, Erebumque Chaosque / tergeminamque Hecaten, tria virginis
ora Dianae" (*Aeneid* 4.509–10: "gods, Erebus and Chaos and threefold
Hecate, the three faces of maiden Diana"), but in this context an
infernal parody of the Trinity. He is still, upside down in the ice of
Cocytus, except for the ominous and rhythmic flapping of his wings.
Down this repulsive body, Virgil and Dante must climb, to the center
of the universe, into his very arse, in order to emerge back into the
bright world of light. This immobile figure is the opposite of Milton's
active and busy Satan, but for that very reason he functions as a kind of
shadow, a still point from which to measure the energy of his rival.[35]

Among the reasons for Dante's choice of *Dite* as the most numinous
name for his Satan (whom he also calls Lucifer and Beelzebub, but at

---

[35] See Irene Samuel, *Dante and Milton: The "Commedia" and "Paradise Lost"*
(Ithaca: Cornell Univ. Press, 1966).

less significant moments), we should probably cite two. Allegorical implications can extend themselves out more readily from a center which already unites the chief Roman name for the king of the underworld and the Christian figure of the devil; indeed the whole picture of the Inferno borrows more from Roman tradition than Christian, at least in its physical or tactile aspects. The second reason is more interesting, but it requires that we hear the *Divina Commedia* in its own language, not in English translation. For there is a potential play on the words *Dite* and *Dio*, Dis and God—a much more far-reaching pun than is suggested by the equivalent Latin words, where Dis *is* one of the gods, not the opponent of the one God himself.

One example must serve. In canto 11, where we first learn the name of the eponymous king of the *doloroso regno*, that name is flanked by six occurrences of the word *Dio*, three before and three after. There are practical reasons why God's name should be mentioned so often in this canto, but they are as nothing beside the fact that this is the place at which Dante tells us Satan's seat is at the exact center of the universe. He reinforces this symbolic centrality by arranging the six occurrences of the word *Dio* around the central *Dite*, making a symbolic seven in all.

## VII

God and the Devil are frequently aligned with each other in *Paradise Lost*, and the more one pursues the parallels the more one wonders what the difference (so to speak) can be. Milton and his tradition usually maintain the distinction in both narrative and theological ways, so that the likenesses between them are to be accounted for by Satan's mimicry—his effort to equal God.[36] This principle extends to the act of creation itself; but since Milton imagined creation as differentiation, circumscribing with golden compasses, and dividing day from night, or "The waters underneath from those above / Dividing" (7.268-69), one may ask who is imitating whom. No doubt this concept of creation is connected to the effort of Ramist logic, and Puritan politics, to recuper-

---

[36] See John Steadman, *Milton's Epic Characters* (Chapel Hill: Univ. of North Carolina Press, 1968), 160-73. He shows, for example, that Milton used the Latin of the Tremellius-Junius Bible (*me aequabo excelso*) rather than the more widespread *ero similis altissimo* to translate "I will be like the Most High" in Isaiah 14.14.

ate for God's party the power of just division and discernment. An
important image, we have seen, is the two-edged sword which pierces
"even to the *dividing* asunder of soul and spirit, a *discerner* of the
thoughts and intents of the heart," which figures the word of God in
Hebrews 12.4.[37] Milton plays with this paradox in his witty analogy
for divorce, "which like a divine touch in one moment heals all, and
like the word of God, in one instant hushes outrageous tempests into a
sudden stilnesse and peacefull calm."[38] He even makes divorce and
creation equivalent: "by all consequence to *dis-joyn* them, as God and
nature signifies and lectures to us ... by the first and last of all his
visible works: when by his *divorcing* command the world first rose out
of Chaos, nor can be renewed again out of confusion but by the separating of unmeet consorts."[39] In the parallel passage in *Paradise Lost*,
Christ's first speech as creative word substitutes for "outrageous tempests" the *discord* of the troubled waves and the deep (7.216-17):

> Silence, ye troubled waves, and thou deep, peace,
> Said then the omnific Word, your discord end.

We have to reckon, then, with a more or less explicit contrast in
Milton's thought between creative division and discord, but a contrast
in which the key terms may overlap or threaten each other. Milton even
enjoys the game this allows him to play.

The Satanic infection, then, is not equivalent to the presence of *dis-*
words in the language, just as *twoness* is not inherently fallen or sinful.
But twoness is dangerous. It is indeed the very source of the problem
for Adam—his desire not to be one alone. The poem is a meditation on
the problem of duality, how two can come to be from one (in its

---

[37] See above; also Budick, 57-67, and Shoaf, 24-25.

[38] *Divorce*, 2.17, CPW 2.333; see Lana Cable, "Coupling Logic and Milton's Doctrine of Divorce," MS 15 (1981): 143-59.

[39] *Divorce* 1.10, YE 2.273. The *OED* under *disjoin* 3 also cites "That marriage
therefore God himself disjoins," *Divorce* 8.42. Contrast the subtle speech with which
Eve offers the fruit to Adam (9.883-85). It ends with some clever nonsense about
"deity" and "fate," including an understated threat of divorce which is, in the context,
unbearably ironic:

> Lest thou not tasting, *different degree*
> *Disjoin* us, and I then too late renounce
> *Deity* for thee, when fate will not permit.

metaphysical form, a recurrent theme in Donne), and what the consequences are, moral, metaphorical, and linguistic.

The danger extends also to *discourse*. The first use of the word in the
poem, as for many of the themes, is in Hell—specifically by those devils
who prefer philosophy to heroic (and "partial") song. The complicated
syntax of these lines (555-65), as much as their dialectical or polarized
content, suggests what the problem is:

> In discourse more sweet
> (For eloquence the soul, song charms the sense)
> Others apart sat on a hill retired,
> In thoughts more elevate, and reasoned high
> Of providence, foreknowledge, will and fate,
> Fixed fate, free will, foreknowledge absolute,
> And found no end, in wandering mazes lost.
> Of good and evil much they argued then,
> Of happiness and final misery,
> Passion and apathy, and glory and shame,
> Vain wisdom all, and false philosophy.

The inconsequential discourse of the devils bounces back and forth
between opposites, evoking the Derridean difference, the opposite term
suppressed in each (like "passion" in "apathy," etymologically linked
words), and finds no end to this dialectic.

And chiasmus shapes this discourse to reveal what this endlessness
implies. A common feature of epic structure is "ring composition," or
what ancient critics called *hysteron-proteron*. In its most elaborate instance
we find Odysseus asking his mother's shade seven questions, to which
she replies in exactly the reverse order, answering the last question first,
the first last.[40] Milton constructs the two lines 559-60 in exactly that
way, so that the four terms of the first line reappear in reverse order in
the following line, except that the first term is missing: the devils add
adjectives to complete the pentameter, and so they find "no end, in
wandering mazes lost." The term to which the devils cannot get back is

---

[40] *Odyssey* 11.170-203. See Samuel E. Bassett, *The Poetry of Homer* (Berkeley: Univ.
of California Press, 1938), 120-24. I have discussed these ideas at greater length in
"Regeneration and the End of *Paradise Lost*," in *Anglistentag 1982 Zürich*, ed. Udo
Fries and Jörg Hasler (Giessen: Hoffman Verlag, 1984), 221-34.

*Providence.* The Miltonic paradox of freedom and God's absolute foreknowledge remains an intellectual conundrum: it cannot be resolved by the inward experience of freedom, for these devils are in Hell. The frustration of the devils' reasoning is mirrored by the frustration of the conventional epic syntax. To be in Hell is to be denied access to Providence. It is not just "hard and rare" (in Milton's variation of Virgil's *hic opus, hic labor est*) to get back out of Hell; it is, for a devil, impossible. These lines, like the Mt. Niphates speech, show what that might feel like.

As Rajan points out,[41] the devils here have lost touch with the intuitive aspect of discourse, to which Raphael refers at 5.487–88:

> discourse
> Is oftest yours, the latter [intuition] most is ours,
> Differing but in degree, of kind the same.

Innocent discourse ought, then, to be possible, but Raphael's idealized vision of the future, to which these lines belong, with mankind gradually moving up the scale of being, never comes to pass, and it is already threatened by what we have seen of the devils' discourse in Hell. Eve, conversing with Adam, can forget all time—indeed she tells him this in loving dialogue (4.639). But Adam feels the risk, as he tries to explain to Raphael (8.551–53):

> All higher knowledge in her presence falls
> *Degraded*, wisdom in *discourse* with her
> Looses *discountenanced*, and like folly shows.

Raphael is unimpressed by Adam's argument, and tells him to show more self-respect, but Adam's play with *dis-* is deeply serious, and goes to the root of the *twoness* from which the prefix derives. Even in his unfallen state, the *running to and fro* of language between the partners of a *dialogue*, which is the etymology of *discourse*, quickly becomes a loss of something, here the loss of wisdom's face in *discountenanced*.[42] It reminds us of that endless bouncing back and forth that is the devils' discourse in Hell. And Adam's worry brings us back to that subsequent

---

[41] Balachandra Rajan, *John Milton: Paradise Lost Books I and II* (Oxford: Oxford Univ. Press, 1964), 83. See also the discussion in Fowler's note ad loc.

[42] See above the discussion of *defaced*, and n. 8.

use of the word *discourse* in the poem (9.5), near the point of departure for this essay, and helps to explain why the word there should be so anxiously hedged about: *venial discourse unblamed.*

The words of Adam's confession to Raphael anticipate the discourse that man and woman are to have in book 9.205–385, the dispute that will lead to the separation and fall, when all the angel's warnings go for naught. Discourse might be innocent for angels, as in God's instructions to Raphael (5.230–35):

> Converse with Adam . . .
> . . . and such discourse bring on
> As may advise him of his happy state,
> Happiness in his power left free to will. . . .

But among human beings, at least, such innocent discourse is scarcely possible. Indeed such discourse, in Eve's mind at least, becomes a reason for the separation. "Let us *divide* our labors," she says (9.214–24),

> For while so near each other thus all day
> Our task we choose, what wonder if so near
> Looks intervene and smiles, or object new
> *Casual discourse* draw on, which intermits
> Our day's work brought to little. . . .

This is exactly what will happen anyway, as Ricks point out, and the serpent, as object new, does indeed distract Eve from her labors. In one sense his discourse is not casual at all, but in another, deeper, sense it is precisely, in the root sense of the word *casual*, a discourse of the fall.[43] With such ironies at work in the poem's language, it is not surprising that neither Adam nor Eve is able to avoid the separation to which their discourse leads—for the word is already infected by death. Indeed, the Roman god of the dead is already there in Para*DIS*e.

University of Lausanne

---

[43] Ricks, 146. He cites as a parallel the "casual fire" (lightning) of 11.562.

HIROKO SANO

# The Lily and the Rose:
# Milton's Carpe diem Sonnet 20

SONNET 20, WHICH MILTON ADDRESSED to Edward Lawrence around 1655, is an exhortation to enjoy youth.[1] It opens with an Horatian address, as in *Odes* 1.16.1: "O matre pulchra filia pulchrior" ("O maiden, fairer than thy mother fair"), and thereby introduces the reader to the Horatian world.[2] Among many echoes, the most significant is the *carpe diem* ("seize the day") theme. This paper examines how Sonnet 20 is in the Horatian *carpe diem* tradition. The sonnet indicates that Milton was familiar with, and conscious of, various traditions, classical and biblical, medieval and Renaissance, Horatian and Puritan, and above all, his Italian cultural milieu.

The season is winter, when "the Fields are dank and ways are mire" (2). In the damp English winter and in his total blindness, Milton looks forward to spring, when he can take his customary afternoon walk. He invites his younger friend, saying,

> Where shall we sometimes meet and by the fire
> Help waste a sullen day, what may be won
> From the hard Season gaining?          (3-5)

The reader must not be misled by the word "waste" (4) but must interpret the phrase "waste a sullen day" as "seasonable recreation," the only form of gain in mid-winter.[3] Here Milton suggests not idleness, but, paradoxically, the most profitable use of time. The situation is similar to that in Horace's passage:

---

[1] Milton's verse quotations are taken from Hughes.

[2] Latin quotations and translations of Horace's *Odes* are taken from the Loeb Classical Library edition, *Horace: The Odes and Epodes*, ed. and trans. C. E. Bennett (London: William Heinemann, 1914; repr. 1968).

[3] E. A. J. Honigmann, ed., *Milton's Sonnets* (London: Macmillan, 1966), 179-80.

dissolve frigus ligna super foco
large reponens

. . . . .

quid sit futurum cras, fuge quaerere et
quem Fors dierum cumque dabit, lucro
    appone nec dulces amores
        sperne puer neque tu choreas,
donec virenti canities abest
morosa.                                    (1.9.5-18)

Dispel the chill by piling high the wood upon the hearth....
Cease to ask what the morrow will bring forth, and set down as
gain each day that Fortune grants! Nor in thy youth neglect sweet
love nor dances, whilst life is still in its bloom and crabbed age
is far away!

The Roman poet exhorts his friend to enjoy the delights of wine, song,
and love—that is, the delights of youth.
    Milton anticipates that

                    Time will run
On smoother till *Favonius* re-inspire
The frozen earth, and clothe in fresh attire
The Lily and Rose, that neither sow'd nor spun.
                         (5-8)

This passage is an echo of a spring scene described by Horace: "Solvitur
acris hiems grata vice veris et Favoni" (1.4.1) ("Keen winter is breaking
up at the welcome change to spring and the Zephyr"), where Venus
leads her dancing band, and the Graces linked with nymphs tread the
earth with tripping feet. Yet rather than anticipating the delights of
spring, Horace's poem casts a shadow of death. The poet here is conscious of "vitae summa brevis" (1.4.15: "life's brief span") and so he
sings "carpe diem" (1.11.8: "Reap the harvest of to-day").
    Milton invites his friend to "neat repast ... light and choice, / Of
Attic taste, with Wine" (9-10) and music afterwards. He offers an invitation to wine and song, the leisure of cultured men in the three great
civilizations—Horace's Rome, Plato's Athens, and Renaissance Florence.[4] Milton then closes the sonnet thus: "He who of those delights

---

[4] Anna K. Nardo, in *Milton's Sonnets and the Ideal Community* (Lincoln: Univ. of

can judge and spare / To interpose them oft, is not unwise" (13-14). The meaning of "spare" has been debated, and two interpretations have been put forward: "forebear to" and "spare time for."[5] The former interpretation has been long recommended, in accordance with Milton's image as a dour Puritan. As E. A. J. Honigmann suggests, "the recent tendency is to relate sonnets XX and XXI, stressing that the drift of the two is the same."[6] If we understand Milton's inclination toward *carpe diem* poetry, however, we may interpret the problematic phrase "spare / To interpose them oft" as his expression of "affording time to enjoy them [those delights] often" rather than "refraining from enjoying them often."

The Puritans in Milton's day argued about what recreation a Christian could permit himself. The closing of the theaters (1642) and the ban on Christmas festivities (1644) were the strictest measures they took against amusements.[7] Richard Baxter, a Presbyterian divine, says, "We may use the Creatures for delight, when that Delight itself is a means to fit us for the work of God, and is sincerely sought for that intent.... If you deny not your sensitive appetites, you will never be acquainted with *heavenly delights*."[8] His idea that "past-time is to be denied"[9] sounds very strict, but it is based on his sense of redeeming time: "*Opportunity* or *Season* is the flower of Time! *All Time* is precious; but the *season* is *most* precious: The *present Time* is the *season* to works of *present necessi-*

---

Nebraska Press, 1979), 92, interprets the feast offering pleasures enjoyed by the three great civilizations as "a shadowy type of the true heavenly feast" and thereby suggests that "Milton would want to 'spare' time to interpose such graceful intervals among the worldly bus[i]ness a wayfaring-warfaring Christian must conduct on his temporal pilgrimage to Grace."

[5] *Variorum* 2:474-76. Stanley E. Fish, in "Interpreting the *Variorum*," *Critical Inquiry* 2 (1976): 466-69, suggests that a pressure for judgment generated by the lines is transferred from the words on the page to the reader (the reader is "he who"), who has the responsibility of deciding when and how often to indulge in "those delights."

[6] Honigmann, 180-81.

[7] Honigmann, 178. I am indebted to Honigmann's book for pointing out the relevance of Richard Baxter.

[8] Richard Baxter, *A Treatise of Self-Denyall* (London: Robert White for Nevil Simmons, 1660), 102, 105.

[9] Baxter, *Treatise*, chapter 23, "Vain sports and past-times to be denied," imposes ten conditions on recreations, one of which is "If we have an holy Christian end in them, to fit our bodies and minds for the service of God: and do not do it principally to please the flesh."

ty: And for others, they have all their *particular seasons*, which must not be let slip."[10] Puritanism emphasized the dignity of labor and elevated the Sabbath.[11] However, Christopher Hill says, "Milton's approach would have left everything to the individual conscience—whether one went to church or not, whether one worked on the Sabbath or not."[12] Milton's idea of recreation can be seen in Sonnet 21 (c. 1655), in which he persuades Cyriack Skinner to leave his pondering over mathematics and foreign affairs:

> To measure life learn thou betimes, and know
>     Toward solid good what leads the nearest way;
>     For other things mild Heav'n a time ordains,
> And disapproves that care, though wise in show,
>     That with superfluous burden loads the day,
>     And when God sends a cheerful hour, refrains.
>
> (9-14)

Milton thinks it important to work for "present necessity" and also thinks it good to enjoy the given leisure. His use of the word "measure" in the Aristotelian sense suggests the balance of work and recreation. Sonnet 21 is a modest exhortation in the spirit of *carpe diem*; so is Sonnet 20, which ends not with a moral lesson, but not with an exhortation to excessive feasting either, as Horace often proposes.

So-called *carpe diem* poetry can be traced back to the following phrase in Horace's *Odes*:

> sapias, vina liques, et spatio brevi
> spem longam reseces. dum loquimur, fugerit invida
> aetas: carpe diem, quam minimum credula postero.
>
> (1.11.6-8)

---

[10] Baxter, *A Christian Directory: or, A Summ of Practical Theologie and Cases of Conscience* (London: Robert White for Nevil Simmons, 1673). 283. See also 275 for his definition of redeeming time: "To Redeem Time is to see that we cast none of it away in vain; but use every minute of it as a most precious thing, and spend it wholly in the way of duty."

[11] Christopher Hill, *Society and Puritanism in Pre-Revolutionary England* (New York: Schocken Books, 1964; 2nd ed., 1967). See especially chapter 4, "The Industrious Sort of People," and chapter 5, "The Uses of Sabbatarianism."

[12] Hill, 212.

Show wisdom! Busy thyself with household tasks; and since life is brief, cut short far-reaching hopes! Even while we speak, envious Time has sped. Reap the harvest of to-day, putting as little trust as may be in the morrow!

We find that Horace tries to be essentially wise while enjoying today, and that such a code of living is the spirit of *carpe diem*. As J. B. Leishman maintains,

> In their poetry on the topics *carpe diem* and *carpe florem* the ancient poets and their imitators are, one might almost say, re-commending a co-operation with Time, submission to the conditions it imposes; urging those they address to seize Time, to make the best use of Time, to be (in every sense) *in time*, to be and do what is timely, to remove, so far as they can, all possibility of later regrets for lost time, for lost opportunities.[13]

To Milton, both Horatian epicureanism and the Puritan idea of recreation endeavor to redeem time. The world of *carpe diem* is not incompatible with Milton's Puritan sense of time. Rather, it had a magnetic attraction he was powerless to resist.

Sonnet 20 is not merely a social invitation to temperate feasting, but rather a suggestion of a lifestyle and a whole view of life. Milton, like Horace, offers an invitation to wine and song. What about love, then? Milton does not explicitly mention love, but "Lute" and "artful voice" (11) do suggest to his friend that he be ready for love, and "Warble" (12) reminds him of the amorous evening when nightingales warble, as in Sonnet 1. Thus, Sonnet 20 includes some elements of love. Milton pictures the bright season of love in southern Europe, writing this sonnet in the dead of the gloomy English winter.

Critics have commented on line 8, referring to Matthew 6.28-31:

> Consider the lilies of the field, how they grow; they toil not, neither do they spin: And yet I say unto you, That even Solomon in all his glory was not arrayed like one of these. Wherefore, if God so clothe the grass of the field, which to day is, and to morrow is cast into the oven, shall he not much more clothe

---

[13] J. B. Leishman, *Themes and Variations in Shakespeare's Sonnets* (London: Hutchinson, 1961), 100.

you, O ye of little faith? Therefore take no thought, saying, What shall we eat? or What shall we drink? or, Wherewithal shall we be clothed?[14]

Anna K. Nardo shows a tripartite movement: the mechanical measurement of time, the recurrent seasonal rhythm, and the day of the Kingdom of God to come. Commenting on "the lilies," she says, "As the flowers wait through the winter to be reclothed in the spring and cultured men weather a 'hard Season' of political unrest to reestablish their ideals of civilized life, Christians await the resurrection when they will likewise be reinspired and reclothed 'in fresh attire' to join the final heavenly community."[15] But why does Milton add the rose to Christ's parable of the lily? I suggest that he wants to see the classical beyond the biblical, contrary to Christ's warning that "after all these things [thoughts about eating, drinking, and clothing] do the Gentiles seek" (Matthew 6.32).

In the classical tradition, the rose is an attribute of Venus, the goddess of love. In the Middle Ages, the rose won the supreme position as a symbol of love; *The Romance of the Rose* exemplifies the allegory of love in the light of the European tradition of love poetry. The lily, on the other hand, is known in Christian symbolism as a symbol of the Virgin Mary for the whiteness of its flowers and the sweetness of its scent,[16] yet we recall that the lily has a sensuous connotation in the Song of Solomon.[17] Solomon's garden with lilies and roses in bloom is a garden of love. Paul F. Watson points out that

When the Duecento poet Guido Guinizelli sings "I wish to praise my lady and liken her to the rose and the lily," he condenses thereby the general image of a *locus amoenus*. Guido's synecdoche brings to mind a well-worn biblical image, "I am the

---

[14] Biblical quotations are taken from the Authorized Version.

[15] Nardo, 90.

[16] George Ferguson, *Signs and Symbols in Christian Art* (New York: Oxford Univ. Press, 1954), 33-34. See also 37-38: the Virgin Mary is called a "rose without thorns" in reference to the legend that the rose without thorns grew in Paradise before original sin).

[17] The Song of Solomon 6.2-3: "My beloved is gone down into his garden, to the beds of spices, to feed in the gardens, and to gather lilies. I am my beloved's, and my beloved is mine: he feedeth among the lilies." The Song of Solomon is a collection of secular love songs, which has been interpreted mystically.

rose of Sharon and the lily of the valleys" (Song of Solomon 2.1).[18]

Watson further points out that "As we know from Ovidian mythology, the Christian tradition, and the *dolce stil novo*, roses and lilies pertain to ladies especially well beloved."[19] It is no wonder that "the Lily and Rose" together in Sonnet 20 evoke the sensuous as metaphors of love.

The context of "the Lily and Rose" is pagan as well as sensuous. *Favonius* (6) is Zephyr, the west wind which ushers in the spring. Zephyrus is familiar to Milton. In *Paradise Lost*, Adam and Eve can appreciate "cool *Zephyr*" after their labor (4.329). One morning Adam whispers to Eve, touching her hand softly, "as when *Zephyrus* on *Flora* breathes" (5.16). In Elegy 3, "Zephyro Chloris amata levi" (44: "Chloris, the goddess beloved by delicate Zephyr") decks the Elysian fields with various flowers. We read also: "Serpit odoriferas per opes levis aura Favoni, / Aura sub innumeris humida nata rosis" (47–48: "Through the perfumed opulence stole the light breath of Favonius—the dewy breath that is born beneath myriad roses").

The story of Zephyrus is vivified in Botticelli's famous companion paintings: the *Primavera* (1477-78), and the *Birth of Venus* (c. 1485). The former, representing Venus Genetrix, and the latter, representing Venus Urania, are thought to visualize the Neoplatonic theory of love.[20] In the *Primavera*, Zephyrus has pursued Chloris, a Greek earth-nymph, blowing wind on her. Chloris desperately flees him; when he catches her, she is transformed into Flora, the goddess of flowers. Roses

---

[18] Paul F. Watson, *The Garden of Love in Tuscan Art of the Early Renaissance* (Philadelphia: The Art Alliance Press, 1979), 37.

[19] Watson, 45. See also Tadao Kaizu, *Ai no Niwa: Kirisutokyo Bijutsu Tankyu* (Liebesgarten: A Quest of Christian Art) (Tokyo: Nihon Kirisutokyodan Press, 1981). The motif of Mary with a unicorn in the *hortus conclusus* (Solomon 4.12: enclosed garden) was very popular in Northern Renaissance works of art, where the topoi of *Minnesang* (love song) were brought into mysticism. The etchings of *Liebesgarten* (the garden of love) in 1440/50 by so-called *Meister der Liebesgarten* bear some resemblance to a 1480 tapestry on the "unicorn hunt in *hortus conclusus*" in Schweizerisches Landesmuseum in Zurich. The words "sicut lilium inter spinas sic amica mea inter filias" (Solomon 2.2: "as the lily among thorns, so is my love among the daughters") are inscribed over the lilies in the tapestry. Thus Solomon's garden can be interpreted as a prototype of *Liebesgarten*.

[20] Edgar Wind, *Pagan Mysteries in the Renaissance* (New York: Norton, 1958; repr. 1968), 138-40.

dropped from Chloris's mouth form the pattern of Flora's robe. In the *Birth of Venus*, Zephyrus, embracing and entwined with Chloris, blows the newborn Venus on a huge shell toward the shore. Roses flutter about Zephyrus and Chloris. Hora, the goddess of the Hours, steps in to clothe Venus in a red mantle. Milton's passage suggests the imagery of Botticelli. Critics have noted a resemblance between the *Primavera* and the spring scene of *Paradise Lost*:[21]

> The Birds thir choir apply; airs, vernal airs,
> Breathing the smell of field and grove, attune
> The trembling leaves, while Universal *Pan*
> Knit with the *Graces* and the *Hours* in dance
> Led on th'Eternal Spring.                          (4.264–68)

During Milton's Italian journey, the pagan subject treated in Botticelli's paintings might have impressed him, whereas religious paintings might have appeared a form of idolatry to him.[22] In his own account of his grand tour (*Defensio secunda*), Milton mentions the people he met during his stay in Florence but not the places he visited. Nevertheless, his description of his contact with a group of people of rank and learning and his attendance at their private academies[23] allows a guess that he was given a chance to see Botticelli's paintings in the Medici Villa at Castello,[24] while he stayed in Florence for about four months

---

[21] See Roland M. Frye, *Milton's Imagery and the Visual Arts* (Princeton: Princeton Univ. Press, 1978), 230–31. The theme of Botticelli's *Primavera* is found in the following pasage in *Comus*:

> Along the crisped shades and bow'rs
> Revels the spruce and jocund Spring,
> The Graces and the rosy-bosom'd Hours,
> Thither all their bounties bring,
> That there eternal Summer dwells,
> And West winds with musky wing
> About the cedarn alleys fling
> *Nard* and *Cassia's* balmy smells.                          (984–91)

Even before he went to Italy, Milton was familiar with the image of the three Graces dancing hand in hand, which Horace describes in the spring scene in *Odes*.

[22] Lois Potter, *A Preface to Milton* (London: Longman, 1971), 15.

[23] CPW 4.1.615–17.

[24] Caterina Caneva, Alessandro Cecchi and Antonio Natali, *The Uffizi: Guide to the Collections and Catalogue of All Paintings* (Florence: Becocci/Scala, 1986), 66. Both

on his way to and from Rome. It remains to be proved that he actually saw the paintings; if he did, they may be the source of inspiration for the rose of Sonnet 20. That is, he may have thought that Botticelli's Zephyrus, with the Hours, is about to "clothe in fresh attire" the rose representing Venus.

The rose also influences the spirit of Sonnet 20. The rose is associated with a variant of the *carpe diem* theme, the *carpe florem* theme. That even the beautiful rose withers implies that beauty is transitory, and so the lover is urged to pluck it while it is fresh. Comus cites the withering rose as an image of transitory beauty:

> List Lady, be not coy, and be not cozen'd
> With that same vaunted name Virginity;
>
> .  .  .  .  .  .  .  .  .  .  .  .  .
>
> If you let slip time, like a neglected rose
> It withers on the stalk with languish't head.
>                                   (*Comus*, 737–44)[25]

Milton was enamored of "the smooth Elegiack Poets"[26] in his youth. He enthusiastically read and enjoyed the romantic and sensuous sentiments of the Roman elegists such as Ovid and Horace, and cultivated a classical background. He has celebrated the coming of spring and the power of love in Sonnet 1, Elegies 5 and 7, where he is eager to serve the God of Love. His mind is broad enough to accept the delights of wine, song, and love. Milton is never insensible to love. Rather, he is

---

the *Primavera* and the *Birth of Venus* were painted for Giovanni and Lorenzo di Pierfrancesco de' Medici at Castello. They were housed at the Uffizi in 1815.

[25] See the rose song in the Bower of Bliss in Spenser's *The Faerie Queene* 2.12.75:

> Gather therefore the Rose, whilest yet is prime,
> For soone comes age, that will her pride deflowre:
> Gather the Rose of loue, whilest yet is time,
> Whilest louing thou mayst loued be with equall crime.

See also "To the Virgins, to make much of Time" in Herrick's *Hesperides*:

> Gather ye Rose-buds while ye may,
>     Old Time is still a flying:
> And this same flower that smiles to day,
>     To morrow will be dying.

[26] *An Apology against a Pamphlet* in CPW 1:889.

at heart still capable of love even after he suffered an unhappy married life, lost his sight and his first wife and son, and underwent trying political experiences in his so-called prose period, during which he wrote Sonnet 20. He has never lost the sentiment of love, and wants to encourage his young friend to enjoy love, since youth is short.

We have examined the notion that Sonnet 20 presents a view of life rather than an actual invitation to dinner. The lily alludes to Christ's admonition to take no thought for tomorrow (Matthew 6.34: "Take therefore no thought for the morrow: ... Sufficient unto the day is the evil thereof"). The rose alludes to Horace's epicurean unconcern about tomorrow (*Odes* 1.9 and 11: "Cease to ask what the morrow will bring forth, ... Reap the harvest of to-day"). Milton absorbs the essence of, and makes healthy modifications of, both Horatian epicureanism and Puritan ideas of work and recreation. In Milton's time-consciousness, the evangelical labor-leisure discipline is incorporated into the *carpe diem* frame. Milton has a positive attitude toward life in which he can appreciate the delights of youth. Sonnet 20 is Milton's *carpe diem* poem.

Aoyama Gakuin University, Tokyo

CHARLES ROSS

# False Fame in Paradise Regained: The Siege of Albraca

A REFERENCE TO MATTEO MARIA BOIARDO'S *Orlando Innamorato* occurs in *Paradise Regained* when Satan's vision of the Parthians and Scythians at war is compared with a battle invented by the fifteenth-century Italian poet:

> Such forces met not, nor so wide a camp,
> When *Agrican* with all his Northern powers
> Besieg'd *Albracca*, as Romances tell,
> The City of *Gallaphrone*, from thence to win
> The fairest of her sex, *Angelica*,
> His daughter, sought by many Prowest Knights,
> Both *Paynim*, and the Peers of *Charlemagne*.
> Such and so numerous was thir Chivalry.    (3.337–43)

The exact nature and purpose of this allusion to Boiardo have yet to be determined. One reason for this uncertainty is that the state and nature of Boiardo's text render problematic any attempt to identify what Milton may have had in mind when he thought of Boiardo's poem.

Two books of Boiardo's *Orlando Innamorato* were in print by 1483. When Boiardo died in 1494 he left behind a fragmentary third book (eight cantos and part of a ninth), and the poem ends with a stanza bewailing the invasion of the French king Charles VIII in that year. Today, Boiardo claims our attention in several ways, once we concede that the unity of the poem derives not from a *taxis* of cause and effect but from a thematic organization to which modern tastes may not be accustomed. Boiardo's special brilliance as a writer lay in developing to the full the limiting conventions of romance. He carefully coordinated his duels and battles. Employing the medieval technique of *entrelacement*, he gave variety to his story by shifting among protagonists. And he created that web of interrelationships from which irony inevitably arises, and which makes any stable interpretation difficult if not undesirable. The plot structure he developed, typical of romances in which a constant number of heroes face a stream of varying antagonists, inevitably raises the issue of a hero's relationship to Fortune; and Boiardo thematizes this aspect of his story when Orlando enters the underworld domain of the fata Morgana, an allegorical figure of fortune.

To identify these technical achievements, we have to isolate Boiardo's original text, written for the Este court of Ferrara, from the context of its production and printing. For the text we read today is unhistorical for the early modern period, when both Boiardo's story and his language were profoundly altered. The narrative of the poem, incomplete despite its 35,440 lines, allowed for a series of sixteenth-century continuations. The most famous is Ariosto's Orlando Furioso, which has no beginning of its own. A bulky continuation by Niccolò degli Agostini, which eventually reached three books, began to be printed with Boiardo's text as early as 1505, but most editions do little to indicate the shift in authorship. A more insidious erasing of Boiardo's original vision occurred when Francesco Berni reworked Boiardo's language, producing a rifacimento that replaced with Tuscan forms Boiardo's Emilian dialect, the koinè of the Ferrara region and Po valley. Besides forcing Boiardo's text into conformity with the usages established by Dante, Petrarch, and Boccaccio, Berni expanded prologues, interspersed stanzas dedicated to his own acquaintances, and eliminated some of Boiardo's vigorous figures of speech. Where Boiardo's Orlando is a chaste figure (if only due to incompetence), Berni hints at homosexuality.[1] Destined to achieve its greatest fame in the eighteenth century, Berni's version was printed only twice in the cinquecento, yet it has not inconsiderable merits of its own—and Milton read it. Moreover, as Neil Harris has shown, the several editions of Boiardo's "original" that were available to Milton picked up influences from Berni's version as well as alterations by the original publishers and such later editors as Lodovico Domenichi.[2]

In addition to the problems involved in establishing a text that Milton knew, the very size of the Innamorato should give us pause in

---

[1] Elissa Weaver, "Erotic Language and Imagery in Francesco Berni's 'Rifacimento,'" MLN 99 (1984): 80-100.

[2] Neil Harris, "John Milton's Reading of the Orlando Innamorato," La Bibliofilia 88 (1986): 25-43.

attempting to apply it in a positivistic way to a "reading" of *Paradise Regained*. Boiardo was known even during the Renaissance for his invention; and the sixty-nine cantos of his masterpiece contain hundreds of characters and many rapidly changing stories. Moreover, although Milton studied Arthurian romance, no one has claimed that the English poet was so well read in Carolingian epic that he was able to distinguish those characters that Boiardo inherited (most of the Christians, and among the pagans, Feraguto, Grandonio, Marsilio and other Spanish Saracens) from those he invented (e.g., Gradasso, king of Sericana, whose invasion begins the *Innamorato*). It would be unwise to base an argument on whether Milton knew that, in point of fact, Boiardo invented Agricane and the siege of Albraca (mentioned in no earlier poem), as well as his heroine Angelica.

This long preliminary helps explain why what follows ought to be confined to the larger movements of Boiardo's legacy. The *Innamorato* tells the story of Orlando's pursuit of Angelica from Paris to distant Albraca and back. Threatened by unwanted suitors, Angelica first flees from France to avoid one unwanted lover (Feraguto), and then seeks refuge in Albraca (an eastern fortress) to fend off another, King Agricane, who raises an army to pursue her. The siege of Albraca intermittently occupies the *Innamorato* from the point when Orlando learns Angelica's location from a sphinx (1.5), to when the citadel burns (2.18). The siege itself outlasts King Agricane, whom Orlando kills during a nighttime duel about a third of the way through the poem. Angelica tends to fade from the action after her castle is destroyed, as the themes of courtesy and marriage take over and attention shifts to Rugiero and Bradamante, the mythical progenitors of Boiardo's patron, Ercole d'Este.

From the countless details of Boiardo's fantasy, these two aspects, the failure of King Agricane and the family romance of Rugiero, point to a plausible explanation of why Milton alluded to Boiardo at a key moment in *Paradise Regained*. Milton's allusion is a comment on Satan, and the key to its meaning is not a minor detail but the irreducible fact that in referring to the seige of Albraca, Milton fails to mention Orlando. In what follows I will argue that Agricane and Orlando represent competing systems of values that inform Boiardo's romantic epic, just as Satan's opposition to Christ structures Milton's brief epic. The suppression of the name Orlando is an ironic illustration of false fame that highlights Satan's confusion over who is Christ's real opponent.

## Fraternal Strife

Satan's confusion is determined, in part, by the genre of Boiardo's poem. Our clue to this connection is that Satan wants to be paternally related to Christ. This desire arises from his failure to comprehend how the "Sons of God both Angels are and Men" (4.197). Confused about what it means for Jesus to be called the Son of God "which bears no single sense" (4.516), and more and more desperate to win control of his opponent as his temptations fail, Satan suggests that he too is a son of God: "The Son of God I also am, or was, / And if I was, I am; relation stands" (4.517-19). According to Satan's reasoning, his battle with Christ is fraternal strife, since "All men are Sons of God" (4.520).

The script Satan writes for himself, in which he is Christ's sibling, perhaps casts him as an unjustly treated older brother. Genesis is filled with older brothers tricked out of their primogeniture by clever siblings (e.g., Cain slays Abel, Jacob tricks Esau, and Joseph makes good even though his older brothers abandon him). Moreover, one always has the impression (even if just because *Paradise Lost* starts *in medias res*) that Satan exists before Christ is begotten. But Satan's fancy is not limited to male roles. In defending his practice of lying (a charge traditionally leveled at demons and women), Satan uses the rhetoric of the submissive wife: "But thou art plac't above me, thou art Lord; / From thee I can and must submiss endure / Check or reproof, and glad to scape so quit" (1.475-77).

Satan's supposition of kinship extends, finally, almost to full identity. Satan is the "Adversary" at the beginning of the poem when it is said of Christ that "Heav'n pronounc'd him his beloved Son" (1.32). At the end of the poem he attempts to identify Christ and himself by calling Christ his "Adversary" (4.527). For at least one commentator Satan's strategy succeeds: Kerrigan argues that Christ and Satan are identified at the point on the temple pinnacle where one pronoun ("him") confuses the two: "So Satan fell; and straight a fiery Globe / Of Angels on full sail of wing flew nigh, / Who on their plumy Vans receiv'd him soft" (4.581-83).[3]

Such a merging of identities is common in romances, including

---

[3] William Kerrigan, *The Sacred Complex* (Cambridge: Harvard Univ. Press, 1983), 90: "Syntax, the medium of discursive thought, is made intuitional when Christ and Satan inhabit for a moment the same *him*. The poem stops, arrested in mystery."

Boiardo's. To take examples that Boiardo would have known in some form, the French prose *Tristan* (thirteenth century) posits a second Isolde of the White Hands in addition to the original heroine. Moreover, a vague Christian mythology often lurks in romance, as when in the cyclic versions the mysterious appearances of Lancelot uncannily imitate Christ's sudden comings and goings in Mark. In Boiardo, the Christian co-identity of Father and Son gives a distinct resonance to reduplications of Rugiero, who is both his father and himself.

The hero of Boiardo's poem is actually the third Rugiero. Rugiero I is a direct descendant of Hector of Troy by way of Boiardo's romance versions of the Roman emperors. Duke Rampaldo is the descendant several generations later of this distant, spiritual father. Rampaldo's son is Rugiero II, whose son, Rugiero III, is destined to marry Bradamante, Ranaldo's sister, and found the line of the Este family, for whom Boiardo wrote.

Rugiero III incorporates all virtues and is described in terms similar to the Jesus of *Paradise Regained*. Compare Christ's "Perfections absolute, Graces divine, / And amplitude of mind to greatest deeds" (2.137) to the qualities of Rugiero, "qual fu d'ogni virtute il più perfetto / di qualunche altro che al mondo si vanta" ("Blessed with all virtues and outshining / Every man that the world has known," 1.29.56).[4] Rugiero II is also highly praised:

> Lui de Rampaldo nacque, e in quel lignaggio
> Che avesse cotal nome fu secondo;
> Ma fu tra gli altri di virtute un raggio,
> De ogni prodezza più compiuto a tondo.       (3.5.33)

---

[4] This and other translations of Boiardo are from Matteo Maria Boiardo, *Orlando Innamorato*, trans. Charles Stanley Ross (Berkeley: Univ. of California Press, 1989), which reprints the Italian text edited by Aldo Scaglione. This article follows the orthography of the translation (e.g., Albraca). Until Rugiero appears in book 2, the courteous and ardently romantic Brandimarte represents Boiardo's ideal figure. Rugiero, who falls in love at the first opportunity (when Bradamante unhelmets, 3.5.40-42), moves beyond Brandimarte, however, for he is cast in the mold of a classical hero: Like Achilles, who was discovered by Ulysses, Rugiero is found by clever Brunello after a magician claims that victory requires him—in Boiardo, the king of Garamante replaces the Greek Calchas. Rugiero will die young, it is said, slain like Achilles by treachery (I am paraphrasing Aldo Scaglione's note in his edition, *"Orlando Innamorato" / "Amorum Libri" di Matteo Maria Boiardo*, 2 vols. [Turin: Unione Tipgrafico-Editrice Torinese, 1963], 2:9-10).

> Rugiero was Rampaldo's son,
> The second so named of that line,
> And he, among them, was a beacon
> Of grace and prowess—sheer perfection.

Even Satan's assumption of a feminine voice corresponds to the romance tendency toward duplication; for Boiardo suggests that Rugiero has a twin sister (whom Ariosto will identify as Marfisa):

> Nacque con esso ancora una citella,
> Ch'io non l'ho vista, ma ha simiglianza
> Al suo germano, e fior d'ogni altra bella,
> Perché esso di beltate il sole avanza.
> Morì nel parto alor Galacïella,
> E' duo fanciulli vennero in possanza
> D'un barbasore, il quale è nigromante,
> Che è del tuo regno, ed ha nome Atalante.
>
> (2.1.73)

> A little girl was born with him.
> I have not seen her, but if she
> Is like her brother, whose looks pass
> The sun's, she must be beautiful.
> Their mother died delivering,
> And these two children reached the care
> Of Atalant, a vavasor
> And necromancer in your realm.

So strong is the tendency of romances toward self-replication that Jameson has claimed that the ideology of romance is revealed in the moment of class solidarity when the hero unhelmets his opponent and sees something identical to himself.[5]

---

[5] Fredric Jameson, *The Political Unconscious: Narrative as a Socially Symbolic Act* (Ithaca: Cornell Univ. Press, 1981), 118-19, sees in romance "an emergent class solidarity. Romance in its original strong form may then be understood as an imaginary 'solution' to this real contradiction, a symbolic answer to the perplexing question of how my enemy can be thought of as being *evil* (that is, as other than myself and marked by some absolute difference), when what is responsible for his being so characterized is quite simply the *identity* of his own conduct with mine, the which—points of honor, challenges, tests of strength—he reflects as in a mirror image. . . . This moment, in which the antagonist ceases to be a villain, distinguishes the romance

Nonetheless, Satan's assertion of identity with Christ is misguided. The poem itself never doubts the difference between Christ and Satan, and Satan's delusion seems typical of the erring, serpentine wiles of Satan's thought, which keeps harping on the same tedious point.[6] The "symmetrical effect" produced by doubling, as Angus Fletcher has pointed out, "makes it easy to narrate the testing of mythic parodies" in the romantic epic.[7] Christ makes of Satan an antichrist, just as Boiardo's heroes, moving through the labyrinth of fairyland, find that enchanted gardens operate as parodies of Eden. The feminization of Satan may be read as another such parody.

Moreover, for all Satan's confusion in the fourth book about what it means for Christ to be called the Son of God, "which bears no single sense," for most of the poem, Satan's language has assumed that God is Christ's father, not his own: He speaks of "his Father's glory" (1.93), "Thy Father" (1.487), and "Thy Father's ire" (3.219). Although a full identification of Christ and Satan never takes place in *Paradise Regained*, Satan's confusion over whether he is in some sense a son of God reveals, paradoxically, the fraternal strife that animates his opposition to Christ. Psychoanalysis traces fraternal strife to obsession with the father. Satan's problem is that he won't admit the father's authority.

In failing to realize the implications of interpreting his opposition to Christ in terms of fraternal strife, including his inescapable inequality, Satan falls victim to the discourse of romantic epic. We may approach this theoretical problem by considering that, as a late development of romance, the Italian romantic epic adds a political dimension to the economic basis of romance identified by Jameson. The particular symbolism of romantic epic can be seen if we consider that Jameson's unacknowledged inspiration for the romance hero's identification with

---

narrative from those *chansons de geste* and the Western at the same time that it raises a new and productive dilemma for the future development and adaptation of this form."

[6] Annabel Patterson, "*Paradise Regained*: A Last Chance at True Romance," *MS* 17 (1983): 187–208, has cleverly noticed that Satan's mind imitates certain precepts of Seicento romance theorists: Besides "mixing somewhat true to vent more lies" (1.433), which recalls Tasso's argument that poets "intermingle fiction among true things," Satan lives in the kind of narrative suspense that Pigna said results from the wandering poetry of romance.

[7] Angus Fletcher, *The Prophetic Moment* (Chicago: Univ. of Chicago Press, 1971), 36.

his unhelmeted enemy is a comment on Machiavelli's *Prince* by Merleau-Ponty: "And yet when the victim admits defeat, the cruel man perceives another life beating through those words; he finds himself before
*another himself.* We are far from the relationships of sheer force that
hold between objects. To use Machiavelli's words, we have gone from
'beasts' to 'man.' "[8] The transition from mere force to more subtle
forms of coercion characterized the early modern period.[9] The problem,
which Machiavelli concedes that the Este of Ferrara solved, was how to
avoid the dissolution of the consensus of power.[10]

Without going into detail about the particular policies that perpetuated the relative popularity of the Este despotism, it can be said that the
Este's solution provided the political world that informs the masterpieces of romantic epic by Boiardo, Ariosto, and Tasso, all written for the
one small but culturally innovative northern Italian court.[11] Among
the legitimate and bastard sons of Nicolò III were three brothers—
Leonello, Borso, and Ercole—who ruled consecutively for sixty-four years,
despite the fact that no fixed code assured succession to power, and
Leonello's son offered a serious challenge to Ercole's claim to the title.

The cousins of Carolingian epic serve as surrogates for the brothers
in the Este family. I would go so far as to suggest that, as the archetypal
theme of comedy is the battle of generations; and the conflict of good
and evil marks the *chansons de geste*; and Jameson's class solidarity
marks romance; so the derivative genre, Boiardo's romantic epic, talks
about a world of fraternal struggle for identification with the father.[12]

---

[8] Maurice Merleau-Ponty, *Signs*, trans. Richard C. McCleary (Evanston: Northwest-
ern Univ. Press, 1964), 212, citing chapter 18 of *The Prince*.

[9] Compare the notion of tension and relaxation, repression and legality, whose
secret is held by authoritarian regimes, in Stephen Greenblatt, *Shakespearean Negotiations* (Berkeley: Univ. of California Press, 1988), 135-38.

[10] Machiavelli signals the peculiar appropriateness of romance, with its repetitions
and duplications, to the Este's maintenance of power (by the force of custom and
traditional rule) when he conflates Ercole (who reigned from 1471-1505) with his son
Alfonso (to 1534): "As an example, we have in Italy the Duke of Ferrara, who
withstood the assaults of the Venetians in 1484 and those of Pope Julius in 1510"
(Niccolò Machiavelli, *The Prince*, trans. Peter Bondanella and Mark Musa [1979; repr.,
Oxford: Oxford Univ. Press, 1984], 8).

[11] The standard work remains Werner Gundersheimer, *Ferrara: The Style of a
Renaissance Despotism* (Princeton: Princeton Univ. Press, 1972).

[12] R. Howard Bloch, *Etymologies and Genealogies: A Literary Anthropology of the
French Middles Ages* (Chicago: Univ. of Chicago Press, 1983), sees the *Lancelot*'s sets

Such a dynamic helps account for the interplay of cousins (Orlando, Ranaldo, Astolfo, Malagise, etc.), prophecies of future genealogies, founders of noble houses, and compliments to Chiaramonte and Mongrana. Everyone of importance in Boiardo's poem is ultimately related, through Bevis of Hampton and Rugiero I, to Rugiero, the ultimate peer.

Fraternal strife—the struggle between close kin for legitimation by the father—is thus characteristic of both the form and the society from which the oppositional mode of romantic epic grew. Moreover, the conflicts the genre accomodates are homologous to the balancing act the poet performs as, in order to praise the duke of Ferrara, he creates a mythical ancestor for the Este family. This true son of Troy and Rome and the medieval dynasties will naturally display *virtù*: Rugiero, whose twin nature and perfection are fitting for one who is meant to symbolize a synthesis of romance and epic qualities, has a genealogical history that is almost a case study of the perils of fraternal strife. Although Rugiero has no male sibling (a fantasy devoutly to be wished), his father, Rugiero II—who, we have seen, was "più compiuto a tondo" ("sheer perfection," 3.5.33)—was betrayed by Beltramo, his brother:

> Morto fu poscia con estremo oltraggio,
> Né maggior tradimento vidde il mondo,
> Perché Beltramo, il perfido inumano,
> Traditte il patre e il suo franco germano.     (*OI* 3.5.33)

> That knight's betrayal and his murder
> Were the world's most unnatural:
> Inhuman, infamous Beltramo
> Sold out his father and his brother.

Beltramo murdered his brother and *may* have raped his brother's wife, and might therefore be the real father of his brother's son:[13]

---

of similar names as problematizing lineage, which depends on the proper name: "This incestuous onomastic mixing is also accompanied by a more general formal scrambling practically synonymous with the prose romances' overall narrative design . . . that of interlace" (211). This issue of the proper name is one Satan cannot win, for he has no legitimate patronymic, and in *Paradise Lost*, his sexual activity subsumes the transgressions of incest and bastardy that threaten the stable economy of lineage into which he tries to insinuate himself in *Paradise Regained*. What separates the Italian poems and Milton's from the Arthurian prose cycle is the ability of Rugiero and Christ to accommodate oppositions, not least because they die young.

[13] Ariosto does not support this reading. His Beltramo besieges Reggio because he

La voglia di Beltramo traditore
Contra del patre se fece rubella;
E questo fu per sclerato amore
Che egli avea posto alla Galacïella.

                                         (*OI* 3.5.31)

Beltramo's lust made him rebel
Against his father. His betrayal
Arose from his illicit love
For Galaciella.

The name Beltramo may suggest "fine plot," i.e., intrigue, which fits
Satan's usurping function. Moreover, the relationships that Rampaldo's
unrepentant son Beltramo has with the three Rugieros are several—
distant male descendant, wicked uncle, possibly adulterous father, and
murderous brother. I don't wish to argue that Milton intended for
Satan to subsume all these roles. Yet these obscure moments of intrafa-
milial conflict stress the importance for romantic epic of the theme of
fraternal strife, a theme whose evil allure Milton could have registered
even without reference to these isolated particulars.[14]

Favored by his father, confident in his talent, and as invulnerable as
Orlando, Milton was comfortably distanced from the strains that rack
Boiardo's world. Yet studies such as that by Philippe Ariès and the
iconographical work of Jonathan Goldberg indicate that the concept of
family that developed in the fifteenth and sixteenth centuries reached its
full expression in Milton's era.[15] *Paradise Regained* may be considered
a literary battlefield where the old concept of the family line (Boiardo's
houses of Chiaramonte and Mongrana—and Este) fights it out with the
rising importance of the private, individual family unit that required
brothers to live apart.[16] Satan's interest in fraternal family matters

---

has not yet gained his way with Galaciella: "così sperando acquistar lei; aperse Risa agli
nimici" ("hoping to win her, he opened [the gates of] Reggio to the enemy," 36.74).

[14] Ariosto sufficiently recuperates Boiardo's story of Rugiero's lineage (*OF* 36.72 ff.).

[15] Jonathan Goldberg, *James I and the Politics of Literature* (Baltimore: Johns
Hopkins Univ. Press, 1983), 84–112.

[16] By "fraternal" I include the contest among close kin, such as first cousins. I
base this broad category on the living arrangements posited by Philippe Ariès, *Centuries
of Childhood: A Social History of Family Life*, trans. Robert Baldick (1960; trans. New
York: Knopf, 1962), 353: "The basic idea of the historians of law and society is that
the ties of blood composed not one but two groups, distinct though concentric: the

(which he misreads) would be another example of his literary anachronism, making him a throwback to a time when "one has the impression that only the line was capable of exciting the forces of feeling and imagination. That is why so many romances of chivalry treat of it."[17] The point, then, is not that *Paradise Regained* is a family romance, but that within a set of conventions anticipated by Boiardo, the attempt of Satan to identify himself with Christ is in line with what Patterson ("Last Chance") has called the "obsolete, generic expectations" that delude and defeat him.

## Parthians and Scythians

Satan's confused values are mirrored in the illusion he conjures of

---

family or *mesnie* which can be compared with our modern conjugal family, and the line which extended its solidarity to all the descendants of a single ancestor." Similarly Angus Fletcher categorizes as fraternal crime Bolingbroke's murder of his cousin Richard, "by the hand of Exton, who for his crime must now 'with Cain go wander through the shades of night' " (*The Prophetic Moment*, 256-57). Orlando's deep feeling for Ranaldo leads to several laments over the shame they incur when they duel instead of cooperating. I would like to further suggest that if "brothers" are always at odds, genuine twins are an image of concord. The only two actual twin brothers in Boiardo's poem, Aquilante and Grifone, are remarkably congenial to each other. The only triplets in the *Innamorato*, the three sons of Elidonia and Alexander the Great (2.1.6-14), after whom Tripoli is named, are remarkable not for strength or wisdom but for their natural ability to rule:

> Non per prodezza né per vigoria
> Non per gran senno acquistâr tutto il stato,
> Ma la natura sua, ch'è tanto bona,
> Tirava ad obedirli ogni persona                    (*OI* 2.1.11)

James Nohrnberg, *The Analogy of "The Faerie Queene"* (Princeton: Princeton Univ. Press, 1976), 368, has noticed that they recall the three sons of Geryon, "a type of fraternal concord," like Priamond, Diamond, and Triamond in *The Faerie Queene*.

By contrast, twin brothers and sisters—Rugiero and Marfisa, Ranaldo and Bradamante—never meet in Boiardo's work. And, finally, *false* twinship is unforgivable, as when Satan attempts to identify with Christ. Inherent in the Agricane story, as I shall show, this theme is foregrounded in the critically overlooked story of Origille, where knights who impersonate others must die (*OI* 1.29).

[17] Ariès, 355.

Parthians and Scythians; and his incomprehension is emphasized by
Milton's allusion to Boiardo's siege of Albraca, which focuses on Agricane's conflict with Angelica, rather than his more deadly conflict with
Orlando. But we need to understand how the allusion functions before
turning to the self-deception of Satan's doomed duel with Christ.

The historical account of the Parthian armies that Milton read in
Plutarch's *Life of Crassus* tells how their commander Surena, whenever
he traveled *privately*, "had one thousand camels to carry his baggage,
two hundred chariots for his concubines, one thousand completely
armed men for lifeguards, and a great many more light-armed; and he
had at least ten thousand horsemen altogether, of his servants and
retinue."[18] When such a man went to war, as in the vision Satan
conjures before Christ, he would naturally *augment* his forces. The main
function of what I will call Milton's simile is to stress, first, the variety
of Parthian and Scythian armies—the horsemen, foot soldiers, elephants,
archers, and pioneers—and, second, the resulting size. Thus the "forces"
around Albraca were both "such," that is, varied, and "so numerous"
(*PR* 3.344).

Boiardo, for whom hyperbole was second nature and whose favorite
word was "smisurato," was an obvious choice for Milton to turn to when
he created a figure of scale. The *Innamorato's* wildly ranging clashes of
interest, its plots, subplots, and vast range of characters make us feel
intuitively that in whatever form he read Boiardo, Milton associated him
with size and variety. Moreover, the geography of Boiardo's fairyland,
which the Italian poet located in Central Asia, coincides with that of
Satan's Parthians.[19]

---

[18] Milton's source has never been properly identified. See Plutarch, *The Lives of the
Noble Grecians and Romans*, trans. by John Dryden and rev. by Arthur Hugh Clough
(1864; repr., New York: Modern Library, n.d.), 664. Hughes argues in a note that "the
description of the Parthian equipment seems to be drawn from Montaigne's *Essays* II,
ix, or from Montaigne's source in Ammianus Marcellinus' account of the Parthian
cavalry" (512). But Montaigne, who does cite Ariosto in his essay, "Of the Arms of the
Parthians," talks only about the Parthians' supple body armor, made in part from
feathers. Plutarch thus seems a better source, although in light of my argument that the
allusion suppresses heroic chastity, it may be relevant that in another essay, Montaigne
mentions that Julian the Apostate, whose great virtues included chastity—so that, like
Alexander and Scipio, he would not even look at captive women—was slain at the age
of thirty-one by the Parthians. See *The Complete Essays of Montaigne*, trans. Donald M.
Frame (Stanford: Stanford Univ. Press, 1958), 507 (essay 2:19).

[19] See Michael Murrin, *The Allegorical Epic: Essays in Its Rise and Decline* (Chica-

Yet Milton's geographical vocabulary registers how difficult it is to gauge the extent of Boiardo's contribution to *Paradise Regained*. The main problem is that Ariosto's recapitulation gives most, if not all, of the information contained in Milton's reference to the siege of Albraca.[20] Although Albraca, mentioned only three times in minor contexts, plays no role in *Orlando Furioso*, and Agricane and his "Northern powers" are long gone by the time King Agramante crosses the sea to avenge "la morte di Troiano / sopra re Carlo imperator romano" ("the death of Troyano on King Charles, the Roman emperor," *OF* 1.1);[21] nonetheless, Milton's particular phrasing differs enough from what actually happens in Boiardo's poem to provide conclusive evidence that Milton read the siege of Albraca partially, if not almost entirely, through Ariosto's eyes. It is Ariosto, not Boiardo, who refers to Agricane's forces as Scythians: He does so when describing Angelica as "la gran beltà, ch'in India il re Agricane / fece venir da le caucasee porte / con mezza Scizia a guadagnar la morte" (*OF* 8.62) ("the great beauty for whom King Agricane brings, through the passes of the Caucasus mountains, half of Scythia to die." Where the *Innamorato* catalogues Tartar-led armies from Russia, Mongolia, Organa (a region near the Caspian Sea), Gothland, Norway, Sweden, and Denmark, which fit Milton's description of "Northern powers"—although without quite the sinister, demonic polarity that direction held in Milton's imagination—Ariosto uses the classical term ("Scizia") generally associated with the east Crimea, from the Danube to the Don. Superficially, Milton had every reason to compare Satan's Parthians to Agricane's "Scythians." The narrator of *Paradise Regained*, who favors Christian-era literary references, takes advantage of Ariosto's habit of classicizing Boiardo's images, and chooses Boiardo's siege of Albraca for the poem's simile because Ariosto had made the connection palpable.[22] The blurring of

go: Univ. of Chicago Press, 1980), 75, for the location of Boiardo's marvels in Turkestan and the equation of "Albraca (al-Bracca) with Bukhara." Murrin augments the geographical work of Giovanni Ponte, *La personalità e l'opera del Boiardo* (Genoa: Tilgher, 1972).

[20] Cervantes also has a reference to the siege of Albraca that may have prompted Milton. He too remarks on the size of Agricane's army: " 'You are wrong about that,' said Don Quixote, 'for we shall not be two hours at these cross-roads before we see more armed men than came to the siege of Albraca to carry off the fair Angelica' " (*Don Quixote* 1.10; trans. J. M. Cohen [Harmondsworth: Penguin Books, 1972], 82).

[21] Translations from Ariosto are my own.

[22] The characters, however, are locked into pre-Romance forms of dialogue and

Boiardo and Ariosto, as when the narrator attributes to what "Romances tell" a story that is fully told *only* in Boiardo's poem, coincides with other distortions. Deliberately or not, Milton's simile wrongly inflates the nature and number of those "Prowest Knights" seeking Angelica. The fact is that in the *Innamorato*, although at least thirty-one people fall in love with Angelica during her day in Paris—and we suspect that Boiardo can switch anyone's passion on or off as he wishes—by the time Angelica retreats to Albraca, she is being sought, erotically at least, not by "many" but by a comparative handful.[23] Even those actively engaging her attention must be qualified. Agricane, who besieges her city, is so insulted by her refusal of him that he calls her a whore (*OI* 1.11.5). The king of Circassia, melancholy Sacripante, "che lungamente li era state amante" ("who had loved her for a long, long time," *OI* 1.9.40), comes to her defense because she sends for him. It is barely possible to include the king of the Turks, Torindo, among the "Paynim," but the Spanish Saracen Feraguto, although at one stage impetuously bold in Angelica's pursuit, never comes near Albraca. The paucity of pagan lovers indicates that, as with the plural romances, Milton's simile distorts its originary source. Although the distortion is consistent with its main purpose of figuring plenitude by recalling the swarming troops of Agricane's army, one aspect of the distortion has a further significance: Among all the "Peers of *Charlemagne*," only Orlando is in pursuit of Angelica; in this instance, the plural is false. The others from the highest rank of Christendom (the traditional twelve paladins—particularly Astolfo in this case) who arrive at her city do so not for love of her, but because they are looking for Orlando, who has disappeared from Paris.

The pattern of distortions contained in Milton's simile is relevant because the lines about the siege of Albraca are not a mere borrowing, a register of unmediated influence, but a passage that exploits the "critical potential ... inherent in all allusions."[24] John Hollander has

---

mythology. Satan, for example, refers to the forelock of Occasion, the classical name, rather than of Fortune, the more medieval goddess (*PR* 3.173).

[23] This estimate is based on the number of names drawn in the lottery to determine the order of precedence for those seeking to battle Argalia for the right to his sister Angelica (*OI* 1.1.58).

[24] Alan Nadel, "Translating the Past: Literary Allusions as Covert Criticism," *The Georgia Review* 36 (1982): 639-52.

called the Miltonic simile "a form which likens A to B *in that* X is palpably true of both, but with no mention of W, X, and Z, which are also true of them both. As a heuristic fiction, the simile will eventually call on the reader to consider the unmentioned."[25]

Basing their analyses on the fact that Satan's vision of Parthians and Scythians is an illusory image of false power, critics have identified the missing variable, the metaphorical function of the allusion to Boiardo, as deceit. Barbara Lewalski points in the right direction: "Many of Charlemagne's knights were enticed to this siege through Angelica's deceit and thereby defaulted in their proper service to their king."[26] This interpretation is elusive enough to suit Hollander's notion of "metalepsis," redefined as the trope that enacts the elliptical recovery of "transumed material," the unstated middle term between a text and an alluded-to text. Our critical premise about the unlikelihood that Milton referred to anything in Boiardo other than the large oppositions that structure the *Innamorato* helps us overlook the fact that although Angelica has moments of deception, her retreat to Albraca is not one of them. (True, she initially appears at Charlemagne's court under false pretenses, but she does not deceive Agricane, who never visits Paris. Rather, she tells him she would rather die than marry him, thus provoking the Tartar king to mass his forces beneath the high walls of Albraca. Similarly deluded by love are Orlando and Sacripante, Agricane's rivals.) Yet Angelica does manipulate knights to her own advantage, as when, to save Ranaldo's life, she sends Orlando to Falerina's garden, an allegory of deceptiveness (as indicated by the name, from *fallare*, to deceive).

In a variant analysis of deceit as the key to Milton's reading of Boiardo, Annabel Patterson defines the deception not just as a truancy (from Charlemagne, from Christ's true mission) but as the pursuit of an illusory goal. She links the simile to another allusion in *Paradise Regained*, the famous comparison of dancing and singing women (who attend on the banquet Satan prepares), to "Fairy Damsels met in Forest wide / By Knights of *Logres*, or of *Lyones*, / *Lancelot* or *Pelleas*, or *Pellenore*" (2.359–61). The use of Boiardo is taken to mean more than that the pursuit of women in general is illusory, although eroticism

---

[25] John Hollander, *The Figure of Echo* (Berkeley: Univ. of California Press, 1981), 114–15.

[26] Lewalski, 267.

instigates Boiardo's poem. For Patterson, Angelica is the "symbol of a mistaken ideal." In the context of an image of false power—the mustering armies of Satan's temptations of kingdoms—the matter of France, represented by the siege of Albraca, "appears as a metaphor of power abused and confused."[27]

We may push this analysis further. Boiardo's heroic poem offered Milton examples of such power, specifically in figures of fame, which, like eros, Christ rejects. Christ argues that fame can be false for three reasons. First, it can result from the abuse of power. Such fame is "false glory," he says, and "They err who count it glorious to subdue / By Conquest far and wide" (3.69-72). Second, fame can be sought for its own sake instead of God's. Although Christ is not explicit on this point, the problem, as Stanley Fish has argued, is that the seeking of *anything* except God is a temptation, and the point of every temptation in *Paradise Regained* is the same. Each offer must be carefully evaluated in itself; nothing is indispensable, but neither can anything be rejected *a priori* as unnecessary.[28] For this reason, Christ must balance his condemnation of conquerors—who "overrun / Large Countries, and in field great battles win, / Great Cities by assault" while they "rob and spoil, burn, slaughter and enslave" (3.72-75)—against the example of one whose military deeds were defensive, Scipio Africanus, who "his wasted Country freed from *Punic* rage" (3.102). Third, fame can be false because those upon whose "tongues" fame is registered don't know what they are talking about. Although the examples of "patient *Job*" and "poor Socrates" (3.95-96) indicate that earthly fame is not always unjustified, Christ's evenhanded judgment does not hide a disposition to condemn the rabble, just as he condemns most conquerors. He is at pains to point out that Job's fame depended on divine intervention to spread the word. The present is miserable, for "Who names not now with honor patient *Job?*" (3.95); but there was a time when "Famous he was in Heaven, on Earth less known" (3.68). Moreover, Christ says that fame is fickle because the people are fickle; for what are the people "but a herd confus'd, / A miscellaneous rabble, who extol / Things vulgar, and well weigh'd, scarce worth the praise?" (3.50-51).

---

[27] Patterson, "Last Chance," 203.

[28] Stanley Fish, "Things and Actions Indifferent: The Temptation of Plot in *Paradise Regained*," MS 17 (1983): 163-85.

If Agricane resembles the figure of a conqueror whose fame results from an abuse of power, his "Northern powers" easily represent those hordes of humanity who cannot recognize true fame. Orlando slays each of the seven kings who are Agricane's generals, and turns the Tartar hordes into quivering leaves whose cowardice infuriates their leader. Only Agricane (not his men) eventually recognizes the Count as the great Christian hero, not least because Orlando fights incognito. Agricane's recognition comes during a pause in his famous nighttime duel with Orlando:

> Disse Agricane, e riguardollo in viso:
> —Se tu sei cristïano, Orlando sei.
> Chi me facesse re del paradiso,
> Con tal ventura non lo cangiarei.
>
> (OI 1.18.37)
>
> Agrican watched his face and said,
> "If you're a Christian, you're Orlando!
> I would prefer to fight you than
> To be the king of Paradise!"

The allusion to the armies at Albraca thus recalls two ways that false fame deceives: by promoting a bad person and by overlooking a worthy one.

But the suppression of Orlando's name involves another form of deceit as well, by stressing one conflict, that between Agricane and Angelica, at the expense of another, Agricane's more deadly duel with Orlando. For Agricane labors under a deception similar to Satan's self-delusion that he is what Shoaf would call Christ's dual and as such can engage Christ in an equal duel.[29] For the sake of the story alone Agricane *cannot* defeat the hero of Boiardo's romantic epic, although to maintain a modicum of suspense the storyteller must puff the prowess of the loser-to-be and somehow disable the one who must win (as Lancelot is wounded from behind by an arrow before entering a tournament). But the values which Orlando represents also justify his victory.

Orlando is far from perfect—arms had a place in Milton's thought, but not a priority. Yet by suppressing Orlando's name, Milton's simile

---

[29] Shoaf gives a linguistic basis for the opposition I find in the romantic epic genre.

seems to keep it untainted, "above Heroic" (PR 1.15), and representative of values that Milton cherished but knew were unpopular—chastity,
individuality, and learning—values he associated with the romantic
epic,[30] even if he regretted the sullying of the pastoral and chivalric
modes by politics and his own lost innocence.[31] For Orlando, even if
to Ariosto's amusement, practices chastity, which Milton valued. As an
invulnerable warrior in the *Innamorato*, Orlando is a type of Abdiel,
able to stand alone against any multitude. And compared to Agricane,
who claims to have broken his teacher's head (*OI* 1.18.42), Orlando is
something of a scholar, able to recite the Old and New Testaments
(2.12.13) or to argue the value of learning when he and the Tartar king
pause for the night:

> Rispose Orlando: —Io tiro teco a un segno,
> Che l'arme son de l'omo il primo onore;
> Ma non già che il saper faccia men degno,
> Anci lo adorna come un prato il fiore;
> Ed è simile a un bove, a un sasso, a un legno,
> Chi non pensa allo eterno Creatore;
>
> Né ben se può pensar senza dottrina
> La summa maiestate alta e divina.

(OI 1.18.44)

> Orlando answered, "I agree

---

[30] My evidence is the well-known passage in "Apology for Smectymnuus" (Hughes,
694): "I betook me among those lofty fables and romances, which recount in solemn
cantos the deeds of knighthood founded by our victorious kings, and from hence had
in renown over all Christendom. There I read it in the oath of every knight, that he
should defend to the expense of his best blood, or of his life if it so befell him, the
honor and chastity of virgin or matron, from whence even then I learned what a noble
virtue chastity sure must be, to the defense of which so many worthies, by such a dear
adventure of themselves, had sworn.... So that even those books which to many
others have been the fuel of wantonness and loose living, I cannot think how, unless
by divine indulgence, proved to me so many incitements, as you have heard, to the love
and steadfast observation of that virtue which abhors the society of bordelloes." Notice
the reference to cantos, which would seem to rule out Malory (to whom Hughes's note
points) in favor of Italian romantic epic and Spenser's work.

[31] Patterson is convincing in her demonstration that Milton associated pastoral
romance with Henrietta Maria and as a consequence rejected "romance as a mode of
behavior," just as he rejected Charles I ("Last Chance," 193–94, 196).

> A man's first honors are in arms,
> But learning does not lessen men—
> It adds, like flowers in the field.
> Not to acknowledge our Creator
> Makes you an ox, a stone, a log.
> Unschooled, you cannot well conceive
> The heights of holy majesty."

From this perspective, the missing Orlando represents the higher heroic values missing from Satan's illusion of war, the true, spiritual sources of power whose absence vitiates Satan's offer of kingdoms.

On the other hand, the theme of false fame might imply a negative perception of Orlando and the values Milton associated with him. The satire of Berni, which Milton knew, offered a debased Orlando that Boiardo's own irony often supports. For example, the great warrior is, in matters sexual, what Turpin calls a "baboon"—unresponsive in Angelica's bath, timid in the saddle with the seductive Origille, and envious of Ranaldo's way with women.[32] Orlando's truancy from Paris during Gradasso's invasion, one of the keys to the main plot of the *Innamorato*, is mentioned several times: The Count chooses to defend Angelica rather than Charlemagne when Agramante threatens, and during the battle of Montalbano he childishly stands aside until his entry into the fray can gain him maximum credit. By channeling his invincible might into the pursuit of a woman instead of the defense of Christianity, Orlando becomes indistinguishable from Boiardo's other military strongmen, who characteristically use exorbitant means for achieving small ends. This topic is a constant theme in the *Innamorato*, which opens with a remark about the abuse of power by King Gradasso, who levies 150,000 soldiers merely to win a sword and horse:

> E sì come egli avviene a' gran signori,
> Che pur quel volgion che non ponno avere,
> E quanto son difficultà maggiori
> La desïata cosa ad ottenere,
> Pongono il regno spesso in grandi errori,
> Né posson quel che voglion possedere;

---

[32] *OI* 1.25.39; 1.29.47; e.g., 2.20.53.

> Così bramava quel pagan gagliardo
> Sol Durindana e 'l bon destrier Baiardo.
> (*OI* 1.1.5)
> And as it happens to great lords
> Who only want what they can't have,
> The greater obstacles there are
> To reaching what they would obtain
> The more they jeopardize their realms,
> And what they want, they cannot gain.
> Thus that bold pagan only craved
> The horse Bayard and Durindan.

Quattrocento humanists were often preoccupied with the liabilities to which monarchs were subject. One of the passages from Berni that Milton included in his *Commonplace Book* concerns "the true nature and duties of kingship."[33]

Yet all heroes have had their bad reputations: Aeneas, in one tradition, betrayed Troy; Hercules was as well known for his lust as his prowess;[34] Julius Caesar was both tyrant and victim; and Ulysses was the dignified hero as well as the "polytropic villain," both of which Milton exploited.[35] A Christian hero who uses force, as does Orlando, creates a similar ambivalence. As Fletcher explains, "to fight for the good as one of the saints is to use a *virtù* which the good itself transcends. Power, even reproductive power, and grace are at odds." Orlando could have presented such a paradox to Milton (or Spenser), for as Huizinga points out,

> those who upheld the chivalric ideal were aware of its falsity, and it is for this reason that—almost from the very beginning—there was a tendency for the ideal to deny itself from time to time in irony and satire, parody and caricature. *Don Quixote* was merely the last, supreme example of that irony; the line runs through the whole of the Middle Ages.[36]

---

[33] Harris, "John Milton's Reading," 30. The other three Boiardan citations refer to the evils of court, of cursing, and of lying.

[34] Fletcher, *The Prophetic Moment*, 155.

[35] D. C. Allen, *Mysteriously Meant: The Rediscovery of Pagan Symbolism and Allegorical Interpretation in the Renaissance* (Baltimore: The Johns Hopkins Univ. Press, 1970), 297.

[36] Johan Huizinga, "Historical Ideals of Life," in *Men and Ideas*, ed. and trans. J.

Elsewhere I have shown that the marvels of the fata Morgana's enchanted underworld, for example, offer an ironic reading of Orlando as a
representative of *virtù*.[37] The myth of Geryon, which Boiardo drew on,
represented the war of flesh and spirit as well as fraternal concord.[38]
Since strife can produce concord, prophecy "can be enlisted to support
even the original fraternal crime, by which, having murdered Remus,
Romulus is in a position to develop a genuine government."[39] Falerina's Garden is, among other things, an allegory of political justice.[40]
The result of such examples is that Boiardo's poem contains a doubled-
edged critique of power in the theme of fraternal strife, the source of
Satan's confusion.

Whether the values Orlando represents are negative or positive is
less important, however, than his structural opposition to Agricane. The
Tartar king is not the other side of a neat partition of good and evil, but
rather a useful antagonist, a romance Other, even if, as Jameson notes,
one that is recognized as an image of oneself. If the negative Orlando
has affinities with Agricane, the Tartar king is not without redeeming
qualities. He is surprisingly polite in a world of chivalry; he too is an
individual, disgusted at being saddled with cowardly hordes; he converts
to Christianity; and as the following response to Orlando shows, he
represents one of the oppositional poles that are not so much definitions of Boiardo's world as systems of competing values that characterize
the romantic epic:

> Disse Agricane:—Egli è gran scortesia
> A voler contrastar con avantaggio.
> Io te ho scoperto la natura mia,
> E te cognosco che sei dotto e saggio.
> Se più parlassi, io non responderia;
> Piacendoti dormir, dòrmite ad aggio,
> E se meco parlare hai pur diletto,

---

S. Holmes and Hans van Marle (New York: Meridian Books, 1959), 89, cited in
Fletcher, *The Prophetic Moment*, 178.

[37] Charles Ross, "Angelica and the Fata Morgana: Boiardo's Allegory of Love,"
*MLN* 96 (1981): 12-22.

[38] Nohrnberg, *The Analogy of "The Faerie Queene,"* 368-69.

[39] Fletcher, *The Prophetic Moment*, 163.

[40] Murrin, *The Allegorical Epic*, 53-85.

De arme, o de amore a ragionar t'aspetto.

(*OI* 1.18.45)

"It's impolite," said Agrican,
"To argue. You have the advantage.
I told you what my nature is,
And I know you're well-read and wise.
I won't respond if you go on.
If you prefer to sleep, then sleep,
But if you want to talk to me,
Then talk of either war or love."

The day he dies, Agricane pretends to flee to draw Orlando away from the field of battle. Orlando accuses him of failing to stand firm, just as the son of Crassus did when the Parthians fled during Crassus's great loss in 53 BC. Agricane, who leads Scythians—his "Northern powers" acts like a Parthian. Moreover, Plutarch makes it clear that Parthians imitated Scythians, who themselves practiced tactical retreats. Satan's illusion displays a similar schizophrenia, for there too, Parthians and Scythians are scarcely distinguishable. The Parthians are supposed to be streaming forth to war, but the syntax makes it difficult to tell to which army belong the camels, axmen, pioneers, and "clouds of foot" (3.327). Why is there a "sharp sleet of arrowy showers" (3.324) if the Parthians have not yet engaged their enemy? Just as *no troops* are yet in the field for Angelica when Agricane first sets his siege, one doubts whether Satan's Parthians will find any more fleeing images of themselves at the end of their march than they may, or may not, have met already.

The blurring of differences between opposed forces recreates Satan's tactics in confronting Christ. Merely to attain to a level where confrontation is significant, he overreaches himself, positing identity with Christ, equality, twinship. His grand illusion of fraternal strife, based on equality that produces glory (easily allegorized as what Frye calls "the female figure over whom physical wars are fought"),[41] blinds him to

---

[41] Northrop Frye, "The Typology of *Paradise Regained*," *MP* 53 (1956): 227–38. For comments on this article I would like to thank the members of a draft group at Purdue in 1988: Anne Astell, Tim Brennan, Geraldine Friedman, Stan Goldman, Nancy Kelly, Alan Nadel, and Irwin Weiser; also Neil Harris who, after offering me several helpful suggestions, has gone on to produce his own reading, stressing Milton's debt to Berni—his point is that Berni more consistently belittles Orlando than Boiardo does. See "Notes on Milton and the 'Orlando Innamorato': The Albraca Simile in

the necessity of his defeat in the name of justice. Satan never learns, and cannot overcome the fact, that Christ's only true opponent is Christ himself. Agricane is likewise undone by the very similarity to Orlando that makes rivals of them. The moment he discovers that Orlando, whose fame he has known, is in love with Angelica and refuses to yield her, his death is imminent.

To conclude, Orlando's omission from the simile of the siege of Albraca mocks Satan's illusion that he engages Christ as an equal. The seeming oversight of Orlando suggests the vanity of fame that derives from the kind of single combat Satan seeks with Christ. The irony that Christ defeats Satan by refusing combat gives point to the pattern of distortions Milton's simile imposes on its source, a pattern that culminates in the suppression of Agricane's Parthian flight from Orlando, which fails to lure the Christian hero to his death. The omission of Orlando's name, finally, disengages *Paradise Regained* from the oppositional mode of the romantic epic which the poem with its fraternal combats and wars and fame and "Fairy Damsels met in Forests wide" (2.359) otherwise imaginatively recalls.

Purdue University

---

'Paradise Regained,'" *Rivista di letterature moderne e comparate* 42 (1989): 325-47, which the author kindly sent me while this article was already in proof.

ROY ERIKSEN

# God Enthroned: Expansion and Continuity in Ariosto, Tasso, and Milton

PARADISE LOST IS, IN JOHN STEADMAN'S PHRASE, "a poetic heterocosm."[1] If we remain within the context of his chosen metaphor, our efforts to interpret Milton's *magnum opus*[2] inevitably appear microcosmic when compared to the wealth of images and rhetorical forms woven into the textual macrocosm of the poem. We know that the poet achieved such cornucopian profuseness partly because he wrote within a tradition of great epic poems, both classical and Renaissance; in this sense, Milton's themes and techniques are truly traditional. The rich Italian tradition in heroic poetry offered Milton many useful models of epic construction for the various levels of *Paradise Lost*. Steadman's masterful examination of the poem against a sizable body of Renaissance critical theory has demonstrated once and for all Milton's response to and interpretation of the works of leading cinquecento theorists, among them influential poets like Torquato Tasso.[3]

Leaving aside on this occasion the complex issue of the structure of the entire poem, I wish to carry out a topomorphical analysis[4] of one

---

[1] John Steadman, *Epic and Tragic Structure in Paradise Lost* (Chicago: Univ. of Chicago Press, 1976), vii.

[2] The editions and translations used for this paper are: John Milton, *The Poems of Milton*, ed. John Carey and Alastair Fowler (London: Longman Group Ltd., 1968); Lodovico Ariosto, *Orlando furioso*, in *Opere*, ed. Adriano Seroni (Milan: U. Mursia, 1970); John Harington, *Orlando Furioso in English Heroical Verse* (London, 1591), *The English Experience* 259 (Amsterdam and New York: Da Capo Press, 1972); Barbara Reynolds, trans., *Orlando Furioso (The Frenzy of Orlando): A Romantic Epic by Ludovico Ariosto* (Harmondsworth: Penguin Books Ltd., 1975); Torquato Tasso, *La Gerusalemme liberata*, ed. Lanfranco Caretti (Turin: Giulio Einaudi, 1971); and Edward Fairfax, *Jerusalem Delivered* (London, 1600), ed. Roberto Weiss (New York: Centaur Press, 1962).

[3] *Epic and Tragic Structure*, 1-19. Tasso is discussed throughout.

[4] A topomorphical approach to a text involves studying the distribution of topoi

of its important microstructures: the topos of God enthroned in book 3.55-79. I propose to read this textual segment against its possible antecedents in the epics of Ariosto and Tasso, more particularly against *Orlando Furioso* 8.70 and *La Gerusalemme liberata* 9.55-58. These are all passages depicting actions which have far-reaching structural implications in the sense that each contains, or prepares for, an important *peripeteia* in the plot of the respective epics. In addition to this shared structural role, the passages also exhibit strong indications of having been executed according to a similar kind of balanced rhetorical design, which again suggests that all three poets deployed chiastic patterning in order to increase the impact of their plot reversals. In the course of this analysis I will moreover turn to other patterned textual segments in the works of these poets, segments which exhibit textual phenomena similar to those discussed, to illustrate and broaden the base of my argument. It needs pointing out that the kinds of enclosing rhetorical structures explored in this essay belong to the compositional repertoire of the Renaissance and are not characteristic of these writers only, nor of the epic. These configurations appear in a number of Renaissance literary forms and are deployed by most writers of the period, albeit to different degrees.[5]

With the exception of the ironical line "Things unattempted yet in prose or rhyme" (*Paradise Lost* 1.16), *Orlando Furioso* has not frequently figured among the poem's principal models. The entirely different scope and tone of *Orlando Furioso* and *Paradise Lost* naturally explain this situation, but the state of affairs still open a range of possible intertextual dependencies of technique and minor themes. The dominant theme of Ariosto's witty poem is the romantic quest for honor and chivalrous love, the *fiero* and the *dolce assalto*. The serious epic strand, the defence of Paris against the infidels and the implicit religious con-

---

and themes, or textual segments devoted to specific topoi, with particular reference to their structure and the interrelationships they form. As is the case with *Paradise Lost*, poets often combine an overall plan with individually patterned segments, particularly elaborate segments often coinciding with specifically significant episodes or themes. For a sustained use of this type of rhetorical analysis see my *The Forme of Faustus Fortunes: A Study of The Tragedie of Doctor Faustus (1616)* (Atlantic Highlands, NJ, and Oslo: Humanities Press and Solum Forlag, 1987).

[5] The varying degrees to which individual dramatists rely on such patterning when they shape single speeches is the topic of *The Forme of Faustus Fortunes*, chap. 6.

cern, is textually of minimal importance in comparison, even though later theorists strove to interpret the poem according to the four-fold method of scriptural exegesis.[6] Where the religious-political strand appears in the poem, it is never allowed to dominate and occupy the center of interest for long. One brief, but significant, example of such intrusion we witness in canto 8: Ariosto here interrupts his description of the fair Angelica, who is fettered Andromeda-like on a naked rock, deftly inserting some *ottave* which focus directly on the epic's politico-religious overplot. The situation is critical: Paris is ablaze and about to fall into the hands of Agramante and the attacking Saracens. At this crucial point Charlemagne implores God to intervene and save "il santo Imperio e 'l gran nome di Francia" ("the sacred Empire and the great name of France," 8.69.8).[7] God turns his eyes to Paris and promptly sends a heavy rainfall which rapidly quenches the threatening fire:

> Il sommo Creator gli occhi rivolse
> al giusto lamentar del vecchio Carlo;
> e con subita pioggia il fuoco tolse:
> né forse uman saper potea smorzarlo.
> Savio chiunque a Dio sempre si volse;
> ch'altri non poté mai meglio aiutarlo.
> Ben dal devoto re fu conosciuto,
> che si salvò per lo divino aiuto.          (70.1–8)

> For God to Charles's just lament paid heed
> And from the conflagration's raging threat
> The Christians by a sudden downpour freed.
> (The flames might otherwise be burning yet.)
> Wise is the man who turns to God in need.
> Where else will he find help when he's beset?
> This miracle for Charles, who is devout,
> Was aid divinely sent, he has no doubt.[8]

Ariosto's *ottava* describes the close harmonious relationship between the devout old king and the Deity, who allays his just wrath and extends grace to his loyal subject. Upon closer examination we note that the

---

[6] See Barbara Reynolds, 1:78–79.

[7] Unless otherwise stated, the translation is my own.

[8] Reynolds, 1:280.

stanza falls into two parts: the four initial lines contain the entire action—Charlemagne's lament, God's survey of the situation, and his intervention. The four remaining lines comment on the wisdom of one who in his hour of need, addresses God in the way Charlemagne does. Ariosto pulls these elements together in a balanced rhetorical structure which hinges on lines 4 and 5. Unfortunately, this rhetorical design is reflected neither in Reynolds's version, nor in Harington's translation of 1591,[9] so I supply my own translation of the key phrases involved. The words and related concepts Ariosto repeats symmetrically are: "Il sommo Creator" in line 1, which counterbalances "lo divino aiuto" in line 8; "vecchio Carlo" in line 2 corresponds to "devoto re" in line 7, and two versions of human wisdom in the central lines. Practical knowledge, "uman saper" ("human wisdom"), in line 4 yields to divine wisdom in the ensuing fifth line of the *ottava*: "savio chiunque a Dio sempre si volse" ("wise is whoever has always turned to God"). The same impulse towards a symmetrical distribution of thematically related words appears in the inversion seen when "uman saper" balances "savio chiunque." And we cannot but observe that the concepts of divine creation and assistance encircle the particular notions of human wisdom, as if in a protective manoeuver.[10]

The rhetoric of Ariosto's ottava may be said to embody a reversal, which is highly appropriate, of course, because it signals a reversal, or a *peripeteia*, of the action of the epic's overplot. The fortune of war changes dramatically when God intervenes, so what we actually witness at this point is one of the many *peripeteias* found in single episodes of

---

[9] Harington renders Ariosto more freely than Reynolds at this point, as often is the case in a version which is 728 stanzas shorter than the original. Harington writes:

> For when that now the citie was on fire,
> And when all hope of humane helpe was past,
> Then mightie God forgetting wrath and ire,
> Vpon their tears, repentance true, and fast,
> At Charles his humble prayer and desire,
> With helpe from heau'n releeu'd them at the last:
> Sending such raine, to ayd the noble Prince.
> As seld was seene before, and neuer since.    (8.62)

[10] Note that Ariosto connects the middle of the stanza with the end by way of the rhetorical figure *epanados* ("Dio," 5 and "divino," 8)—i.e., when the same word or sound is repeated in the beginning and the middle, or the beginning and the end, of a text element. Abraham Fraunce defines *epanados* purely in terms of sound, see n. 36.

the poem. The use of dramatic reversals in individual cantos or in other textual segments of varying length is a well-known device, recognized by Harington and employed by both Tasso and Milton.[11] If we turn briefly to Harington's rendering, which is by no way an attempt at a stanza-by-stanza translation, we note that his version of 8.70 lacks Ariosto's balanced design altogether. Instead Harington concentrates on underlining the dramatic contrasts between the different strands of action described in the contingent stanzas 61 and 63 (according to his numbering).[12] We will later see that Milton follows Ariosto's practice in favoring a balanced design in his version of the topos.

The absence in Harington's version of the sort of rhetorical patterning found in Ariosto does not, however, turn *Orlando Furioso* 8.70 into a special case. For its careful recurrences by analogy are of the type which adorns, for example, the central *ottava* of Tasso's *Gerusalemme liberata* 11.10, repetitions which are typical of the style of literary *maniera*. Tasso, in that stanza, underlines the sacramental centrality of Mount Olivet within Christian doctrine and his poem:

> Così cantando, il popolo devoto
> con larghi giri si dispiega e stende,
> e drizza a l'Oliveto il lento moto,
> monte che da l'olive il nome prende,
> monte per sacra fama al mondo noto,
> ch'oriental contra le mura ascende,
> e sol da quelle il parte e ne 'l discosta
> la cupa Giosafà ch'in mezzo è posta.          (11.10)

> Singing and saying thus the camp devout
> spread forth her zealous squadron broad and wide,
> Towards mount Olivet went all this rout,
> So call'd of olive trees the hill which hide;

---

[11] Basing himself on the authority of Aristotle and contemporary theorists, Harington claims that "an heroicall Poem (as well as a Tragedie) [should] be full of Peripet<e>ia." For multiple *peripeteias* in Tasso, see *The Forme of Faustus Fortunes*, 112–14. For *peripeteias* in Milton, see *Epic and Tragic Structure*, 41–59.

[12] Ariosto aligns the furious battle at Paris with the storm that rages within Orlando's mind. Harington foregrounds this alignment by beginning his stanza 61 ("Now in this time to Paris siege was layd") with words which link up with the first line of stanza 63 ("Now lay Orlando on his restlesse bed").

A Mountain known by fame the world throughout,
Which riseth on the city's eastern side,
From it divided by the valley green
Of Josaphat that fills the space between.[13]

As I have discussed the placing of this *ottava* within the nineteen-stanza
processional *peripeteia* of the poem elsewhere (11.1-19),[14] it here
suffices to indicate the discrete convolutions of its rhetoric. As a firm
point in the poem's structure, the anaphoric repetition of "monte" in
lines 4 and 5 marks the two central lines of the entire poem by line-
count. Around this structural tribute to Christ's sacrifice on Mount
Olivet, Tasso groups synonymous verbs in symmetrical fashion, in the
manner seen in Ariosto: "si dispiega" and "drizza a" are balanced by
"contra . . . ascende" and "discosta." The syntactical inversions strength-
en the impression of the poet's firm control over his design of *contrap-
posti*. Tasso, moreover, foregrounds the centrality of this stanza by
suggesting that it, like the deep gulf of Giosafà, "in mezzo è posta" ("is
placed in the middle"). As was the case with Ariosto's structural compliment to a vigilant and benevolent deity, here too, it seems reasonable to
see the rhetorical shape of Tasso's *ottava* as a conscious design aimed at
reflecting the order of the creation and God's providential plan, as well
as a device which signals the reversal of the fortune of the Christians in
their campaign against the infidels. We note, also, that Mount Olivet
and the valley of Josaphat symbolize the two opposite aspects of God,
mercy and justice. Mount Olivet reminds us of the sacrifice of Christ
for the benefit of mankind, while Josaphat—so Dante points out—figures
as the future site of the Last Judgement.[15]

*Orlando furioso* 8.70 and *Gerusalemme liberata* 11.10 demonstrate
how subtly Italian poets distribute their signs, illustrating, too, how they
do not readily employ rhymes as structural tokens on such occasions.
The particular technique found in connection with individual *ottave*
would seem to originate in the rhetorical strategies deployed by Italian

---

[13] Tr. Fairfax, 275.

[14] " 'What resting place is this?' Time and Place in *Doctor Faustus* (1616),"
*Renaissance Drama*, n.s., 16 (1985): 51-54.

[15] Cf. *Inferno* 10.11 where Dante mentions "Iosafàt" as the place from which the
souls return after the day of universal judgement; cf. *La Divina Commedia*, ed. Alberto
Chiari (Sesto San Giovanni: Bietti, 1974), 56.

sonneteers from Petrarch onwards, and from there, spread into the more prestigious and elevated genre of heroic poetry.[16] It would also appear that both Ariosto and Tasso sometimes turned to various sorts of chiastic dispositions when it came to giving added emphasis to reversals of fortune in their poems. That this type of structuring may extend to several *ottave* and go well with the kind of triumphal motif found in the topos of God enthroned in *Orlando Furioso* 8.70, we discover both in canto 45 of Ariosto's poem and in canto 9 of *La Gerusalemme liberata*. Let us consider the earliest example first.

Ariosto's poem contains numerous *peripeteias* or "mutazioni di fortuna," one example being the unexpected turn of fortune which befalls Ruggiero in canto 45, where the Christian champion is first captured by Ungiardo and later tortured by Teodora. Before Ariosto launches the reader into a series of swift and incredible reversals, he halts his narrative for a moment while commenting on the principle at work in such changes of fortune. He does so in four *ottave* in which he draws on the medieval metaphor of the Wheel of Fortune and a series of exempla taken from de casibus-literature. What is remarkable from my point of view is the manner in which he knits the *ottave* tightly together by way of verbal reiterations, italicized in the following:

> Quanto più su l'instabil *ruota* vedi
> di *Fortuna* ire in alto il miser *uomo*,
> tanto più tosto hai da vedergli i piedi
> ove ora ha il capo, e far cadendo il tomo.
> Di questo *esempio* è Policrate, e il re di
> Lidia, e Dionigi, e altri ch'io non nomo,
> che ruinati son da la suprema
> gloria in un dì ne la miseria estrema.
>
> Così all'incontro quanto più depresso,
> quanto è più l'uom di questa ruota al fondo,

---

[16] The balanced rhyme scheme of the octave in a sonnet invites such patterning, even though rhetorical structures which comprise the whole of a sonnet occasionally were found as early as in the sonnets of *Il Canzoniere*; see Sonetto 352, which displays a chiasmus ("dolcemente" [1], "'l sole" [2], "'l sol" [13], and "dolce" [14]) and central accent through a pun in verse seven ("sole"). I quote from the edition by Mario Marcazzan (Basiano: Bietti, 1966), 494. Mannerist sonneteers such as Tansillo and Bruno delight in such designs, as do several Elizabethans, e.g., Daniel and Shakespeare.

tanto a *quel punto* più si trova appresso,
c'ha da salir, se de' girarsi in tondo.
Alcun sul ceppo quasi il *capo* ha messo,
ch'altro giorno ha dato legge al mondo.
Servio e Mario e Ventidio l'hanno mostro
al tempo antico, e *il re Luigi* al nostro:

*il re Luigi*, suocero del figlio
del duca mio; che rotto a Santo Albino,
e giunto al suo nimico ne l'artiglio,
a restar senza *capo* fu vicino.
Scorse di questo ancor maggior periglio,
non molto inanzi, il gran Matia Corvino.
Poi l'un de Franchi passato *quel punto*,
l'altro al regno degli Ungari fu assunto.

Si vede per gli *essempii*, di che piene
sono l'antiche e le moderne istorie,
che 'l ben va dietro al male, e 'l male al bene,
e fin son l'un de l'altro e biasmi e glorie;
e che fidarsi a *l'huom* non si conviene
in suo tresor, suo regno e sue vittorie,
né disperarsi per *Fortuna* avversa,
che sempre la sua *ruota* in giro versa.

(45.1-4; my emphasis)

Looke how much higher fortune doth erect,
The clyming wight, on her vnstable wheele,
So much the nigher may a man expect,
To see his head, where late he saw his heele:
Polycrates hath prou'd it in effect,
And Dionysius that two true did feele:
Who long were luld on high in fortunes lap,
And fell downe sodainly to great mishap.

On tother side, the more man is oppressed,
And vtterly ou'rthrowne by Fortunes lowre,
The sooner comes his state to be redressed,
Whe[n] wheele shal turne & bring the happy houre:
Some from the block haue grown to be so blessed,
Whole realmes haue bin subiected to their powre

As Marius and Ventidius sample is,
In former age, and Lews of France in this.

That Lews of France (the storie well is knowne)
That to Alfonsus sonne, did giue his daughter,
Who was at Saint Albinos ouerthrowne,
And eu'n with much adoe escaped slaughter;
A like misfortune by like daunger growne,
Mathew Coruino scapt a little after:
And hauing past that moment by good chance,
One ruled Hungarie, the tother France.

Tis manifest in stories new and old,
That good and ill, each other do succeed,
And worldly blisse hath but a slender hold,
Wherefore a man of wisedome, will take heed;
And on his fortune neuer be too bold,
Although his state and riches farre exceed:
Nor yet in fortune ill, dispaire or doubt,
For euermore her wheele doth turne about.

Harington, 45.1–4

As will appear in the italicized words of Ariosto's text, seven keywords found in the two first *ottave* recur in inverse order in the following two *ottave*. A chiastic pattern thus emerges which may be said to reproduce the idea behind the sequence: the vicissitudinous rotations of Fortune's Wheel. The pattern is completed by the symmetrical insertion of two small-scale chiasmi within the larger rhetorical structure at 45.1.7–8 ("da la suprema / gloria in un di ne la miseria estrema"; "from the highest glory in one day to the deepest misery") and at 45.4.3 ("l'ben va dietro al male, e 'l male al bene"; "good follows upon bad, and bad upon good").[17] Additional syntactic inversions throughout the *ottave* further cement the chiastic grid built into the sequence.

---

[17] Shakespeare employs a similar technique when he fills out the symmetrical rhetorical structure of Sonnet 129. In that poem, sequences of repeated words ("extreme," "had," "mad," "mad," "had," "extreme") expressing the whirligig of sexual passion, are reinforced by the symmetrical placing of chiasmi in lines two ("Is lust in action, and till action, lust") and thirteen ("All this the world well knows yet none know well"). I quote from John Dover Wilson, ed., *The Sonnets* (Cambridge: Cambridge Univ. Press, 1966), 67.

Ariosto's argument in this brief excursus on Fortune is hopeful and applies directly to the outcome of the crises which await Ruggiero: man should not despair when in grave adversity, because a change for the better is imminent. This is indirectly an appeal to the divine plan behind the seeming confusion and chaos in human affairs. The poet's symmetrically disposed visible signs testify to that same divine *ordo*. In his commentary, Harington commends the "excellent Morall" of canto 45, adding that he does not know "whether any thing in this whole worke hath beene, yea or can be said to better purpose, not onely for humanity but in some sort for diuinitie."[18] But in addition to providing an example of heavenly order, Ariosto's sequence of *ottave* also makes a structural tribute to worldly power. In the central two lines, he locates a repeated reference to the son-in-law of his own patron, Alfonso d'Este ("il re Luigi, suocero del figlio / del mio duca": "King Luigi, the son-in-law of my duke's son"). This, of course, is in complete accordance with the conventions of the Renaissance triumphal style[19] where figures of authority often were awarded the central position in a structural array. In this manner, the Fortune-sequence exhibits most of the formal and symbolic properties of the passages by Tasso and Milton to which I now turn.

§

Within the much debated "unità mista" of Tasso's *La Gerusalemme liberata*, the serious epic elements dominate, and a situation like the one discussed in *Orlando furioso* 8.70 receives full treatment. But when Tasso in canto 9 describes how God sends Michele to ward off an attack by the forces of evil, he nevertheless takes his cue from his predecessor's swift thumbnail sketch:

> Gli occhi fra tanto a la battaglia rea
> dal suo gran seggio il Re del Ciel volgea.

> Then from his great seat the King of Heaven
> to the wild battle turned his eyes.          (55.7–8)

---

[18] Harington, *Orlando Furioso*, 392.
[19] See Alastair Fowler, *Triumphal Forms: Structural Patterns in Elizabethan Poetry* (Cambridge: Cambridge Univ. Press, 1970).

These verses amplify Ariosto's "Il sommo Creator gli occhi rivolse" ("The highest Creator turned his eyes"). Tasso, however, seizes the opportunity to elaborate upon the idea of the power God exerts over his creation from his "trono augusto" ("august throne"). He focuses first on God's role as the giver of just laws and the creator of fair forms, rendering homage to divine proportion in the chiastic form of his argument ("dà legge al tutto e 'l tutto orna e produce": "gives laws to all things and everything adorns and creates" [56.2],[20] which recalls the message of God's ordering of his creation in Wisdom 8:1). Chiasmus and antithesis, we remember, are favorite rhetorical figures with Tasso.[21] He next casts the deity as a monarch who sits in triumph on his throne, treading under foot Fate, Nature, and Fortune, who both distribute and subvert worldly riches and empires (56.7–57.4). The topos of God enthroned concludes with an almost Dantesque vision of the Deity surrounded by light and innumerable immortals who make the celestial palace resound with joyful praise (57.7–58.2). It is only when Tasso has presented the topos of God as a ruler of the universe that we learn how God intends to intervene at this critical moment in the history of mankind (58.3 ff.). He sends Michele to force the infernal multitudes to return to hell (9.58.3–66). And the intervention itself is, of course, one of the most important *peripeteias* of Tasso's poem.

When considering the rhetorical structure of Ariosto's *ottava* in *Orlando Furioso* 8.70, and the comparable example of Tasso's *Gerusalemme liberata* 11.10, it comes as no great surprise that the latter's expanded version of the topos of God enthroned displays rhetorical markers of the kind deployed by his predecessor. The textual segment itself comprises twenty lines of verse (55.7–58.2), arranged as follows: 2 + 16 + 2 lines. In the two lines which introduce the topos, Tasso places the phrase "il *Re* del *Ciel*" ("the King of Heaven" [55.8]), which he later echoes and inverts in the phrase "la *celeste reggia*" ("the royal palace of heaven" [58.2]) situated in the concluding two lines. It would

---

[20] This line of verse deserves a commentary of its own: the three verbs—"dà legge," "orna," and "produce"—reflect the shaping power of the Trinity—to create, adorn, and give laws. And we note that their distribution within the chiasmus itself forms the harmonious proportion 1:2. We shall see below that Fairfax tries to play similar games in his rendering of this *ottava*, but without hitting Tasso's high mark.

[21] Fredi Chiappelli, "Struttura inventiva e struttura espressiva nella *Gerusalemme liberata*," *Studi Tassiani* 15 (1965): 15-18.

seem that Tasso draws attention to his verbal echo in a self-referring passage which is replete with musical imagery: We notice in particular the phrase "Al gran *concento* de' beati *carmi* / lieta *risuona* la celeste reggia" ("at the great harmony of holy songs the royal palace of heaven resounds with joy"), where "lieta" ("joyful") picks up "letizia" ("joy") from two lines above.[22] Together with the adjective "gran" ("great") found in *"gran seggio"* ("great seat" [55.8]) and repeated in *"gran concento"* ("great harmony" [58.1]) these verbal recurrences consolidate the structure. Such reiterations, perhaps to be likened to the musical figure of *circulatio*, the dwelling on one note, often occur when a poet wishes to draw attention to a more prominent verbal sign. Good examples that come to mind are the points of transition between *Gerusalemme liberata* 10.78 and 11.1 and 11.19 and 20.[23] On those occasions the verbal reports help to mark the borders of the segment, indicating a wish to foreground the topos in question.

When Fairfax translates Tasso's topos, he reveals that he is aware of the embedded rhetorical structure, but he chooses—possibly due to difficulties of translation—to mark the symmetry at the center of the segment, rather than at its borders. His text thus becomes an important intermediary step between Tasso and Milton. Fairfax does not link the concluding couplet of stanza 55 to the two first verses of stanza 58 by way of repetitions as Tasso had done; instead, he locates his structural markers in the main body of the segment:

> From whence, with grace and goodness compass'd round,
> He ruleth, *blesseth*, keepeth all he wrought,
> Above the air, the fire, the sea, and ground,
> Our sense, our wit, our reason, and our thought;

---

[22] This musical "report" also contributes to linking the concluding two lines of the topos closer to its main textual body. Similarly, "seggio" in the segment's second line links up with and is a variation of "[s]edea" in the third.

[23] Tasso joins the end of the epic's "first movement" (1-10) to the opening of its processional centerpiece with seemingly insignificant verbal repetitions. Yet insignificant they are not, as they work on the reader's memory and create coherence. Thus, the underlined words in the final line of canto 10: "ma i suoi *pensieri* in lui [i.e., Piero] dormir non ponno" ("but his thoughts in him could not sleep") crop up again in the two first lines of canto 11, immediately before Piero enters the scene again in 11.1.4: "Ma 'l capitan de le cristiane genti, / vòlto avendo a l'assalto ogni *pensiero*, . . ." ("But the leader of the Christian peoples having turned his every thought to the attack, . . .").

Where persons three (with *power* and glory crown'd)
Are all one God, who made all things of nought,
Under whose feet (subjected to his grace)
Sit nature, fortune, motion, time, and *place*:

This is the *place* from whence, like smoke and  dust,
Of this frail world the wealth, the pomp, and *pow'r*,
He tosseth, tumbleth, turneth as he lust,
And guides our life, our death, our end, and hour:
No eye (however virtuous, pure and just)
Can view the brightness of that glorious bow'r;
On every side the *blessed* spirits be
Equal in joys, though diff'ring in degree: ...

(9.56–57; my emphasis)

I have italicized the words which Fairfax distributes in a chiastic pattern; they may not be impressive, but he reinforces the idea of the formal balance between the two stanzas which is in keeping with Tasso's original version. We note the rather heavy-handed and rigid effect created, for instance, by the catalogue of "[o]ur sense, our wit, our reason, and our thought" (56.4) which is counterbalanced by another list of four concepts in the ensuing *ottava*: "our life, our death, our end, and hour" (57.4).[24] Fairfax's rhetorical response to Tasso also is evident in the two series of three verbs (55.2 and 56.3) and the two groups of three nouns (56.2 and 4) which may be interpreted as alluding to the trinity, thus confirming that he perceived and appreciated his predecessor's art.

Turning now to the internal organization of Tasso's segment, we initially note that the two *ottave* (9.56 and 9.57) are continuous. But Tasso at the same time contrasts the presentation of God's eternal reign in *ottava* 56 ("e de l'Eternità nel trono augusto / risplendea con tre lumi in una luce": "and of the Eternity in the august throne shone three lights in one" [5–6]) with the fickle power of earthly kings in *ottava* 57 ("la gloria di qua giuso e l'oro e i regni": "the glory of this world and its gold and kingdoms;" [1–3]). At the textual center of the

---

[24] Because the context is one involving the trinity, it could be observed that Fairfax creates two "trinitarian" verb groups: "He ruleth, blesseth, keepeth" (56.2) and "He tosseth, tumbleth, turneth" (57.3).

segment by line-count are positioned the humble ministers of divine omnipotence, Fate, Nature, and Fortune,[25] themselves checked by God's feet in a posture well known from the iconography of the triumph. In a much more direct manner than witnessed in Ariosto's Fortune-sequence, Tasso here makes Fortune subservient to divine control. (Fairfax on the other hand, refers in the two central lines of his segment, to the abode of God's ministers and "the place" from which he controls them, repeating the word "place" at 56.8 and 57.1 to signpost his pivotal point.) Tasso thus creates a celebration of heavenly triumph, where the images of God enthroned enclose the passage cataloguing the forces subjected to God's power. In a similar way, we recall, Ariosto in canto 8.70.1 and 8.70.8 places the references to God as creator and protector of his children so as to circumscribe the presentation of the two forms of human knowledge at the centre of that ottava (8.70.4-5). Returning once more to the rhetoric of the topos as presented in *La Gerusalemme liberata*, we notice that Tasso—in contrast to Fairfax—uses verbal repetitions sparingly in this section. We nevertheless observe that the verb *risplendere* ("*risplendea* con tre lumi in una luce": "shining with three lights in one" [56.7]) reappears in connection with the idea of infolding, which is echoed in similar circumstances in the ensuing *ottava*: "Quivi ei così nel suo splendor s'involve" ("Where he so envelops himself in his own splendour" [57.5]).[26] What Tasso adds in his version of the topos apart from increased length and wealth of descriptive detail, is a pronounced sense of movement; we are brought from the throne of God in heaven down to earth and the fickle affairs of men before soaring upwards again to where God is seated in glory. Such swift movement and compositional symmetry are again the basic ingredients, when Milton—or so I would argue—elaborates on Tasso's survey of God's works.

---

[25] In accordance with Augustine's argument in the *De trinitate*, Tasso may here have intended Fate, Nature, and Fortune to be an analogue or a type of the trinity, which he mentions in the preceding line.

[26] On the principle of infolding in connection with the trinity, see Edgar Wind, *Pagan Mysteries in the Renaissance* (Harmondsworth: Penguin Books Ltd., 1966), 120 ff. The verb "s'involve" strengthens the suggestion that we are dealing here with the principle of infolding.

§

In book 3 of *Paradise Lost* (56-79) we once again encounter a situation of imminent threat: Satan is approaching the world, and human history rapidly approaches one of its decisive *peripeteias*. Like Tasso before him, Milton in this situation chooses to focus directly upon God seated in glory; but he also introduces Satan into the panoramic vision of his works, stressing divine prescience in relation to the threat posed to mankind. The opening of the twenty-four line segment,

> Now had the almighty Father from above,
> From the pure empyrean where he sits
> High throned above all highth, bent down his eye,
>
> (3.56-58)

reads like an inventive expansion of Tasso's phrase "Gli occhi ... / dal suo gran seggio il Re del Ciel volgea" ("from his great seat the Heavenly King turned his eyes"), where "gli occhi ... volgea" matches "bent down his eye" in *Paradise Lost*, because God directs his attention to the threatening situation building up down below. We also remember Fairfax's rendering of Tasso at this point:

> The Lord of heaven meanwhile upon this fight
> From his high throne bent down his gracious sight.
>
> (55.7-8)

However, the verbal echoes are of less consequence than the fact that we here find a system of structural markers similar to those found in the textual segments in Ariosto and Tasso.[27] In this manner, the phrase which introduces the segment "the Almighty Father from above, / High throned above all *highth*, bent down his eye," appears to be summarized and alluded to in its conclusion: "Him God beholding from his prospect *high*" (77). Thus the images of God surveying the world from his throne define the borders and circumscribe the main body of the segment.

---

[27] We know, however, that Milton echoes Tasso in connection with other topoi. Theodore M. Anderson, "Claudian, Tasso, and the Topography of Milton's Paradise," *MLN* 91.6 (December, 1976): 1569-71, has successfully shown that Tasso's description of Armida's mountain (*La Gerusalemme liberata* 15.55-57) provides the source for Satan's first view of Eden in *Paradise Lost* 4.131-45.

Turning to the inside of the segment itself, we note that the description of "all the Sanctities of Heaven," which ensues, recalls Tasso's image of the innumerable immortals surrounding God in heaven (9.57.7-8), but apart from this similarity Milton treats the topos freely and in accordance with his particular thematic concerns. He reinforces the triumphal motif considerably by creating what Alastair Fowler would term an array with "strong central accent,"[28] a device of the kind already encountered in Ariosto's Fortune-sequence. In this instance, too, the pivot falls on the segment's textually central lines, in the passage telling of Adam and Eve:

> On Earth he first beheld
> Our two Parents, yet the onely two
> Of mankind, in the happie Garden plac't,
> Reaping immortal fruits of *joy* and *love*,
> Uninterrupted *joy*, unrivald *love*
> in blissful solitude.                              (64-69)

This does not imply that the center of the triumph "merely" celebrates Adam and Eve, but rather that the principle of divine love at work in the universe—"l'amor che move il sole e l'altre stelle" ("the love which moves the sun and the other stars;" *Paradiso* 33.145)—is the most important theme. Indeed, the unusual rhyme effect created by the homoeoteleutonic repetition of "love" helps to single out the thematic and structural centrality of the concept, and so does the repetition of "joy." Reduplication of rhetorical markers was, we recall, a distinguishing feature also in the central passages of *Orlando Furioso* 8.70 and 45.1-4, as well as of *La Gerusalemme liberata* 9.10.

In fact, Milton may in this passage be adding a theological finesse, because the repetition of "love" possibly alludes to the diapason, the harmonious principle of two into one, that Augustine saw in God's two works of creation and redemption.[29] Similarly, the nexus of three co-equal terms—*immortal, uninterrupted, unrivald*—may be seen to allude to the Trinity, because these epithets reflect three aspects of divine bliss.

---

[28] Fowler uses this characteristic of the centralized temporal scheme of *Paradise Lost* (*Triumphal Forms*, 132). Fowler also discusses central emphasis in *Paradise Lost* 11.388-407 (118).

[29] Augustine discusses this on a number of occasions, e.g., *De trinitate* 4.2, and *Enarrationes in psalmos*, "In psalmum LVIII" and "In psalmum CXXIX."

Such formal *jeux d'ésprit* were introduced into English at least as early as Gascoigne, and are well known in Jonson, Vaughan, and Herbert;[30] and we have already noted that Fairfax plays similar games. As regards the reduplication of thematic and rhetorical markers at the center of the textual segment, it is not inappropriate to claim that its function within the segment is analogous to the role of the double center within the poem as a whole.[31] But such finessing of the center, often found in combination with a recessed symmetrical structure, does not preclude the use of graded arrangements.[32]

§

That Milton's topos of God enthroned can be shown to possess a clearly marked beginning, middle, and end is no coincidence, as we see from his further distribution of subject matter and rhetorical markers within the segment, and also from comparable examples of the same technique found elsewhere in the poem. Thus, the saviour of mankind and his prime adversary are placed on either side of Adam and Eve and connected, among other things, by a distant rhyme. On God's "*right, /* The radiant image of his glory sat, / His onely Son*" (62-64), while Satan, his antagonist, is seen "[c]oasting the wall of Heav'n on this side Night / In the dun Air sublime" (71-72). The opposites of radiant "glory" and "dun Air sublime" become linked through the shared rhyme sound in the reference to God's "right" side and the phrase "this side Night." A similar link exists between the segment's third line (3.58) and the third line from the end (3.77), where—in addition to the repetition of the adjective "high"—we note another "distant" rhyme. The third line, on how God "High Thron'd above all highth, bent

---

[30] In "Gascoignes good morrow," 28-29 the rhyme-word "face" occurs twice at the center of the stanza (4) which holds the topos of divine revelation. An elaborate system of symmetrically disposed rhetorical markers centers on the fourth stanza, which also divides the poem into a sequence of 3:1:6 stanzas. See Roy Eriksen, "Two Into One: The Unity of Gascoigne's Companion Poems," *Studies in Philology* 81 (1984): 275-98. Examples in the poetry of Jonson and Vaughan are referred to on 284n and 293n.

[31] Alastair Fowler argues that *Paradise Lost* retains "some mannerist complexities of structure" (*Triumphal Forms*, 116-17); one instance is the double center which holds the Raphael episode.

[32] See Maren-Sofie Røstvig, "Canto Structure in Tasso and Spenser," *Spenser Studies* 1 (1980): 177-200.

down his *eye*" rhymes with the third from the end: "Him God beholding from his prospect *high*." This rhyme repeated *longo intervallo*,[33] is
solidified by the strong thematic link existing between the lines, both
relating to God and to the act of seeing. Rhyme used for a slightly
different effect, but also then in combination with chiasmus, has been
discussed by Christopher Ricks, who has drawn attention to the following passage further on in book 3:

> Beyond compare the Son of God was seen
> Most glorious, in him in all his Father shon
> Substantially express'd, and in his *face*
> Divine compassion visibly appeer'd,
> Love without end, and without measure *Grace* ...
>                                         (3.138-42; my emphasis)[34]

Examples of this kind are legion in *Paradise Lost*; another case in point
is the rhyme "own"/ "known" in book 8.103-5, which also coincides
with a chiasmus.[35]

Milton thus fairly frequently employs masked rhymes and rhetorical
recurrences to give a topos like that of God enthroned a symmetrical
and "perfect" shape. And when we add that the first line of the textual
segment under discussion concludes with the word "above," which
rhymes with "love" in the two central lines, we perceive that the blank
verse paragraph possesses the following embedded rhyme structure:

     above     eye     right     love     love     night     high

The rhetorical figure which is used to connect the beginning to the
middle, as in this case, or the middle to the end, is termed *epanados*,

---

[33] This is the term the Byzantine rhetorician Hermogenes uses to describe *epana-
lespsis* employed over a long distance. See Hermogenes, *Ars oratoria absolutissima, et
libri omnes*, ed. G. Laurentius (Cologne, 1614), 1.11.337.

[34] Ricks, 140.

[35] This passage may not be as elegant as the one quoted by Ricks, but its motif of
building goes well with the rhetorical constructivism it exhibits in the rhyme and the
chiasmus:

> That man may know he dwells not in his *own*;
> An edifice too large for him to fill,
> Lodged in a small partition, and the rest
> Ordained for uses to his Lord best *known*.      (8.103-6)

when occurring at period level.[36] An even more comprehensive large-scale variant of this figure, which comprises the first half of book 3, is found when God is hailed as "Light" in line one and in the opening lines of the hymn commenced at the midpoint of the book (3.372 ff.).[37] A shorter segment in which the same technique is deployed in combination with a rhyme scheme embedded in the flow of blank verse, is a 113-line paragraph in book 8, which Fowler analyses in terms of central accent.[38] What these textual segments of varying length demonstrate is that the compositional formulae inherent in Milton's topos of God enthroned in book 3 are essential to his art of composing on various levels of *Paradise Lost*. It may be appropriate, too, to consider such rhetorically bi-partite structures in the context of the metaphor of the divine *logos* as a two-edged sword, in the manner suggested by Sanford Budick, who identifies a principle of division as the principal component of Milton's divine universe.[39] Like a double-edged sword, the divine word cuts through and shapes the narrative of human history.

§

If, by way of a conclusion, we consider Milton's topos of God en-

---

[36] Abraham Fraunce defines *epanados* as "regression or turning to the same sound, when one and the same sound is repeated in the beginning and the middle, or middle and end": *The Arcadian Rhetorike* (London, 1588), book 1, chap. 23 (sig. D 4r-5r).

[37] The whole book could be said to be included in this rhetorical figure, because the very last words on Satan's descent on the world, "Nor stayed, till on Niphates' top he *lights*" (741), punningly hark back to the opening apostrophe and the centrally placed hymn on God as light.

[38] Fowler, 820n. Fowler notes that "the word *sun* is placed in the center of the 113-line paragraph," but he does not comment upon the prominent rhetorical structure which supports his observation. The beginning, middle, and end of the paragraph are linked by the symmetrical distribution of the word "heaven" (66, 120, and 178), and the middle of the segment is linked with the end by the repetition of the words "earth" and "high[est]": At the paragraph center, God has "placed heaven from *earth* so far, that *earthly* sight, / If it presume, might err in things too *high*, ..." (120-21); which is echoed in the finale's "not of *earth* only but of *highest* heaven" (178). Reinforcing this system of verbal linkage is the following imperfect rhyme scheme:

| heaven | moved/seem | | seem/move | heaven |
|--------|------------|---|-----------|--------|
| (66) | (116) | (117) | (129) (130) | (178) |

[39] See Budick. I regret that I did not have access to Budick's study or to Michael Lieb, *Poetics of the Holy: A Reading of "Paradise Lost"* (New York: Harper and Row, 1987) when I first wrote this essay.

throned against those of Ariosto and Tasso, we observe that some ingredients have remained more or less constant: the emphasis on God as
creator, his place in initial and final position within the segment, and
the balanced rhetorical structure found in all three versions. Moreover,
the chiastic patterns the poets inscribe into textual segments which
depict vivid changes of action and scene, are put there, or so I would
argue, to reinforce the impact of these passages as instances of *peripeteia*.
In *Paradise Lost*, however, we witness a double *peripeteia*: within the
segment itself a reversal to the worse is announced when Satan enters
the world, whereas Christ's decision to intervene and counter that attack
follows immediately upon our topos. Thus, Milton skillfully delays the
decisive intervention in order to create dramatic suspense. In this sense,
my examination of these microstructures bears directly on what Steadman refers to as the "epic and tragic structures" of *Paradise Lost*; that is,
on the poem's macrostructure in terms of plot. Also, I would claim that
Milton continues the English practice of using rhymes as structural
markers, a technique established by Gascoigne, and perfected by Spenser,[40] and one which Milton had availed himself of in *Il Penseroso* and
*L'Allegro*.[41] This technique is well-adapted to blank verse, and the way
in which it is deployed by Milton here recalls its similar use in long
speeches in the blank verse dramas of Marlowe and Shakespeare.[42] It
should be pointed out, however, that this technique is used in a number of other passages in *Paradise Lost* than those holding instances of
*peripeteia*. Also, such structures do not always bear directly on the
meaning of such passages, but operate on a verbal-structural level to
unify the particular paragraph. In such cases, they function simply as a
compositional tool, or reflect an ingrained habit of writing. The rhetorical pattern of the particular passage analyzed here, however, by far
exceeds these purely compositional functions, bearing directly on the
theme presented.

---

[40] For Gascoigne see note 30; for Spenser consult Maren-Sofie Røstvig's cited essay,
"Canto Structure in Tasso and Spenser," and Marianne Brown, "Spenserian Technique: *The Shepheardes Calender*," REAL 2 (1984): 55–118.

[41] The first rhyme of *Il Penseroso* ("Melancholy," "unholy") is repeated at the exact
midpoint of the companion poems combined ("holy," "Melancholy": *Il Penseroso*,
11–12). Once again the rhetorical figure is a large-scale *epanados*.

[42] See, e.g., *1 Tamburlaine*, 2.7.12–29, *2 Tamburlaine*, 5.2.176–200, and *2 Henry
VI*, 1.1.212–57.

Milton's most important addition to the topos as it was left by Tasso, is no doubt the strongly emphasized triumphal center, where instead of emphasizing God's "ministri umili" ("humble ministers"), prominence is given to the principle of divine love, which is further illustrated in the ensuing dialogue between Father and Son, where the Son freely declares his willingness to die for mankind. Apart from the intensified dramatic element in Milton's treatment of the topos, the expansion to twenty-four lines may be significant. Against the background of Gunnar Quarnström's important observations on speech length in *Paradise Lost*[43] it may here be relevant to note that the line total of twenty-four is meaningful in relation to orthodox interpretations of "all the Sanctities of heaven" (59) and the idea of God's reign over the created universe.[44] But these possible "numerological" aspects of Milton's patterned topos of God enthroned are less important than what we may term the topomorphical ones, that Milton was working within the context of a method of signification practiced by his Italian predecessors.

Since this essay has concentrated on potentially tedious details, I wish to draw attention to the words of E. A. Armstrong, and urge the importance of such investigations: "Why should ... the study of the relationship of the bricks and buttresses, foundations and finials ... diminish our delight in the building itself or our appreciation of the skill with which it was designed and constructed?"[45] By applying a simple method of pattern recognition to Milton's art of construction, we can discover new aspects of his indebtedness to a tradition of structural aesthetics, here traced in the works of Ariosto and Tasso, but whose roots lie deep in classical and Christian antiquity. Milton's art manages to make that world of the past truly new.

University of Tromsø

---

[43] Gunnar Quarnström, *Poetry and Numbers*, Scripta minora regiae societatis humaniorum litterarum lundensis, 2 (Lund: Lund Univ. Press, 1966), 93. Quarnström discusses the number 23 in relation to Christ.

[44] Pietro Bongo, *Mysticae numerorum significatione liber* (Bergamo, 1591), "De numero XXIV," 443-49.

[45] E. A. Armstrong, *Shakespeare's Imagination* (Lincoln: Univ. of Nebraska Press, 1983), 8.

WYMAN H. HERENDEEN

# Milton and Machiavelli:
# The Historical Revolution and Protestant Poetics

I intend not with controversies and quotations to delay or interrupt the smooth course of History; much less to argue and debate long who were the first Inhabitants, with what probabilities,
and authorities each opinion hath bin upheld, but shall endevor
that which hitherto hath bin needed most, with plain, and
lightsom brevity, to relate well and orderly things worth the noting, so as may best instruct and benfit them that read. Which,
imploring divine assistance, that it may redound to his glory, and
the good of the *British* Nation, *I now begin*.[1]

THIS RATHER IDIOSYNCRATIC OPENING TO THE *History of Britain*—written sometime around 1650—shows Milton folding
various poetic tropes into his historical prose, and is likely to
give his audience (of whatever century) confusingly contradictory signals.
It sounds as though Milton the poet forgot that he was writing history
that morning, or that Milton the historian wished he could get back to
his biblical narrative. His profession of originality, perhaps an echo of
the opening of Machiavelli's *Discourses on Livy*,[2] his questioning of
authorities, qualified by his refusal to be distracted by petty details, his

---

[1] John Milton, *The History of Britain*, ed. French Fogle, in CPW 5:4. References
to Milton's prose are to CPW; references to the poetry are to Hughes. Because our
concern is with historiography rather than history *per se*, the exact generic classification
of Milton's prose works does not pose a problem; they regularly reveal the author's
historical methods and concerns.

[2] Compare the preface of Machiavelli's *The Discourses*, ed. Bernard Crick, trans.
Leslie J. Walker, rev. Brian Richardson (Harmondsworth: Penguin Books, 1970),
97–99, and 1–4 of the *History of Britain*. Some of the echoes (present also in the
Italian) may, of course, simply be the result of shared rhetorical conventions, which
Secretary Milton would have recognized in the work of Secretary Machiavelli.

promise of plainness, "lightsom brevity," and orderliness, and his invocation of divine assistance to help realize a divine purpose, show us Milton the historian shaking hands with Milton the poet. The lines also show us a Milton keenly aware of his own historiography—that is, of the discourse, or the movement between representational and rhetorical modes. And, for Milton, awareness and moral choice go hand in hand; this interplay between icastic and fantastic within an historical framework represents Milton's chosen form of self-expression, and his choice is deliberately made with full understanding of recent innovations in historical writing and of the uncomfortable relationship between representational and rhetorical modes by the middle of the seventeenth century. Virtually all of Milton's work, concerned as it is with history of one sort or another, contends with the facts, the art, and the divinity of experience. Milton knew, as any Renaissance writer would, that each of these dimensions has its different claim on reality and on the reader's knowledge.[3] Their different status is the subject of much debate in the Renaissance and is the central concern of Sidney's *Defence of Poesie*, as well as a fundamental question raised by Milton's prose and verse, where the reader must eventually reconcile divinity, art, and history. From Milton's gestures towards history, the imagination, and divinity, emerges a distinct Miltonic historiography the Protestant elements of which are severely modified in ways that are explained by his response to the new Italian historiography of Machiavelli and Guicciardini.[4]

---

[3] In presenting this central issue in Renaissance poetics, I have adapted some of the language of recent scholars who have discussed the subject (particularly as it bears on Catholic and Protestant poetics) including Rosalie Colie's *The Resources of Kind: Genre-Theory in the Renaissance*, ed. Barbara Kiefer Lewalski (Berkeley: Univ. of California Press, 1973), 8-9; Stanley Fish, *Self-Consuming Artifacts: The Experience of Seventeenth-Century Literature* (Berkeley: Univ. of California Press, 1972), 153-80; Barbara Kiefer Lewalski, *Protestant Poetics and the Seventeenth-Century Religious Lyric* (Princeton: Princeton Univ. Press, 1979), 3-13; and Thomas Amorose's very germane study of apocalyptic history and *Paradise Lost*, "Milton the Apocalyptic Historian: Competing Genres in *Paradise Lost*, Books XI-XII," MS 17 (1983): 141-62. See also Lauro Martines, *Society and History in English Renaissance Verse* (Oxford: Basil Blackwell, 1985), 97-127.

[4] That Sidney's *Defence of Poesie* articulates a Protestant poetic is often overlooked, and it provides an instructive gloss to Milton's use of mixed genres. The specific rhetorical strategy that he uses to elevate the poet to divine status is to undermine the historian's and philosopher's claims to truth and knowledge, to ally poet and priest, and subsume the historian's role in that of poet-prophet. In Sidney's hands, the debate

We see Milton self-consciously positioning himself in the controversies about historical writing when he announces in the *History of Britain* that he is not interested in the troublesome antiquarian controversies about historical accuracy that greatly concerned older contemporaries such as Daniel, Drayton, and Selden. In rather playfully—and yet seriously—adopting the role of divine poet and historian ("Which, imploring divine assistance ... I *now begin*"), Milton turns away from the more "realistic" and empirical trends in historical writing that began in Italy but persisted in England after Sidney's *Defence* and after the death of the Fairy Queen. He is doing something decidedly unlike what most recent scholars see as the tendency in seventeenth-century historical writing, and renouncing the path followed by English and Continental writers who were emulating Italian historiographic reformers including Bruni, Guicciardini, Biondo, as well as Machiavelli.[5]

The peculiarity of Milton's position is striking when set against Herschel Baker's description of the state of the art of history at this time. He and others stress that "free" or uninhibited movement between history and poetry was not what it had been for Spenser, and less so since William Camden (in 1586) and, later, Francis Bacon brought the practise and theory of new historical methods from Italy to Britain: "As the gap between literature and history deepened, there was less and less exchange between their methods and materials."[6] While correct

---

questions the modes of knowing, representing, and utilizing "truth," and reveals close knowledge of recent historical methods. Katherine Firth, *The Apocalyptic Tradition in Reformation England, 1530–1645* (Oxford: Oxford Univ. Press, 1979), 232-37, locates Milton in the tradition of apocalyptic history after the Reformation, and Amorose refines the argument significantly. As I try to suggest, much needs to be done to bring together the study of Protestant poetics and Protestant historiography.

[5] Studies in European historiography universally locate the beginnings of the modern phase in Italy, and, with greater or lesser emphasis, identify Machiavelli and Guicciardini as landmarks in its development. See, for example, major studies by Eric Cochrane, *Historians and Historiography in the Italian Renaissance* (Chicago: Univ. of Chicago Press, 1981); F. Smith Fussner, *The Historical Revolution: English Historical Writing and Thought, 1580–1640* (New York: Columbia Univ. Press, 1962), esp. pp. 5-10, and *Tudor History and the Historians* (New York: Basic Books, 1970); Christopher Hill, *Intellectual Origins of the English Revolution* (Oxford: The Clarendon Press, 1965); and F. J. Levy, *Tudor Historical Thought* (San Marino: The Huntington Library, 1967).

[6] *The Race of Time* (Toronto: Univ. of Toronto Press, 1967), 90. Baker's study, at this point concerned with Milton and his generation, is determined to show the separation of disciplines; his comparative disregard for the rhetorical overlap between

about the gap between the disciplines, Baker's statement is truer of the period up to 1625 than it is for Milton in 1650. Milton obviously does combine the methods and materials of the poet and the historian: he does so fully aware of the gap that he is bridging and of his political and moral reasons for doing so. Furthermore, his historiography shows him reacting against major secular and religious modes of the seventeenth century and reverting to earlier sources that transcend confining methodologies and political dogma. Thus, when he assumes the Puritan historian's roles of prophet, priest, and polemicist, he consciously turns away from the current trend in empirical history. But, as we will see, Milton wanders from this path too in ways that show how strongly his Protestant sense of history was influenced by Machiavelli and Guicciardini, both of whom he was reading at this time.[7]

Particularly during the last major creative phase of his career, while he was working simultaneously on portions of the Commonplace Book, the History of Britain, and his major epics, Milton was doing something significantly different from what his major predecessors among the "poets-historical" had been doing—something better understood by direct reference to his Italian precursors.[8] In Paradise Lost and The

---

the two suggests also how much our approach to such questions has changed in twenty years, and since C. H. Firth's useful study, Milton as an Historian (London: British Academy, 1908). For the new historiography and English poetry, see W. H. Herendeen, "Wanton Discourse and the Engines of Time: William Camden: Historian Among Poets-Historical," in Renaissance ReReadings: Intertext and Context, ed. Maryanne Cline Horowitz, Anne J. Cruz, and Wendy A. Furman (Urbana: Univ. of Illinois Press, 1988), 142–56.

[7] For the dating of Milton's reading of these authors, see Ruth Mohl's excellent study, John Milton and his "Commonplace Book" (New York: Frederick Ungar, 1969), 36–38 and 161–64. Milton seems to have been reading Machiavelli around the time of the Italian journey, and again, quite intensely, around 1650.

The link between the historical revolution and religious reform is an important one but still inadequately studied; Baker virtually ignores the influence of Protestant thought on historical writing of the period. There are incongruities in the development of empirical methods in the early Reformation and the apocalyptic history discussed by Amorose (although see p. 143) and Firth; some of these are answerable through rhetorical analysis and the view of baroque and Counter-Reformation historiography offered here.

[8] For discussion of Milton's precursors, Spenser, Drayton, and Daniel, and their relation to the historians, see Herendeen, "Wanton Discourse"; for the difficulties in accommodating demands for historical accuracy and the need for coherent organization, and for the development of thematic focus to histories, see Cochrane, 380–82.

*History of Britain*, Milton makes history an essential part of his poetic. In giving his history a thematic focus that coordinates fact and fiction and gives them the same status without losing sight of the distinction between them, Milton, in his own way, resolves a problem that had troubled English writers since the time of Spenser and breaks away from the influence of Camden's brand of new historical writing. In so doing he not only moves closer to Spenser and other Tudor poets working in the spirit of reform, but, paradoxically, he turns back to the original Italian reformers and away from historically nearer intermediate Protestant figures.

We can begin to demonstrate this by identifying more particularly the characteristics of the historical revolution that is associated first of all with Machiavelli and Guicciardini, and then, in its later forms, with Camden and Bacon in England. Thanks to modern scholars such as Smith Fussner, F. J. Levy, and Eric Cochrane, these characteristics are generally well known and do not need much in the way of synopsis here. Having its roots in Italy, it is marked by self-conscious revolt against classical and medieval rhetorical histories where truth and accuracy are subordinated to the rhetoric of patriotism and a moral order based on largely fictionalized *exempla*. Machiavelli's and Guicciardini's importance for this new realism and reformed rhetoric is well-known and documented. It is their lead that is followed by the early Protestant reformers, such as the influential chronicler of the Reformation, historian, and translator of Guicciardini, Joannes Sleidanus. Making a direct link between reformed historiography and reformed religion, he distinguishes between his own modern style and that of the classical and medieval (what he calls the "papal") historians, whose writing, "especially after the Greek fashion," was "very much Oratoricall" rather than true.[9] Succeeding generations of Protestant historical writers put these methods to different uses, but for our immediate purposes it is sufficient that for Sleidanus and his generation, there can be no doubt that historical forms implicate religious ideology, and this is a major concern of Milton's as well.

---

[9] Johannes Sleidanus [John Philippson], *The Key of Historie. Or, A most methodicall Abridgement of the foure Chiefe Monarchies, Babylon, Persia, Greece, and Rome* (London, 1627), The Epistle, 5. Sleidanus (1506–1556), whose work was regularly assigned by Mead (see Harris Francis Fletcher, *The Intellectual Development of John Milton*, 2 vols. [Urbana: Univ. of Illinois Press, 1961], 2:614), provides a striking example of the relationship between new historical methods and the emergence of a Protestant rhetoric.

Methodologically, the historical revolution is identified with the growing concern to obtain authentic primary materials and historical data, and to use them more scientifically and "objectively." Milton himself provides one of the best descriptions of such modern historical methods in the *Areopagitica*, when he offers John Selden's *De jure naturali* as an example of how historical truth, scientific accuracy, and sound scholarship ultimately support virtue: his "volume of naturall & national laws proves, not only by great authorities brought together, but by exquisite reasons and theorems almost mathematically demonstrative, that all opinions, yea errors, known, read, and collated, are of main service & assistance toward the speedy attainment of what is truest" (2.513).

There is no need to rewrite the history of the Reformation here; most modern scholars are in agreement on the salient points and concur that these new historical methods are part of the revolution in the related areas of biblical, bibliographical, and textual studies; in rhetorical modes through the reaction against Ciceronian style; in the collection and use of documents and data; and in the rejection, by writers of every sort across Europe, of the poetic fluff of legendary and invented histories. Scholars have traced the historical course of the evolution in historiographic method, and it is only recently that the subtler political implications of this original "new historicism" are beginning to be explored.[10]

Nor can there be any doubt that Milton was aware of this revolution and its Italian roots. This was not the sort of silent reform discovered after the fact by modern scholars, but was one cultivated by men like Sleidanus, and consciously assimilated into the ways of thinking and working by men like Selden and Milton. They knew, as well as modern scholars do, where the process of reform began, and what were its rhetorical and methodological characteristics: as Bacon says of his own experiments in historical writing "we are much beholden to Machiavelli

---

[10] See discussions of these topics in Cochrane, Fussner, and Levy. A careful analysis of aspects of religious reform and the growth of the print culture is John N. Wall, Jr., "The Reformation in England and the Typographical Revolution," in Gerald P. Tyson and Sylvia S. Wagonheim, eds., *Print and Culture in the Renaissance: Essays on the Advent of Printing in Europe* (Newark: Univ. of Delaware Press, 1986), 208-21; the subject figures prominently in Elizabeth L. Eisenstein's *The Printing Press as an Agent of Change* (Cambridge: Cambridge Univ. Press, 1979)—see especially 1:300-313.

and other writers of that class ... who openly and unfeignedly declare or describe what men do, not what they ought to do."[11] Milton, as well versed in Machiavelli as he was in Bacon and Camden, shared this indebtedness to Italian influence, and recognized the modern distinction between history and rhetoric, and that a new history requires a new language—as he makes clear when he writes of the composition of *The History of Britain*: "The decorations of style I do not greatly heed: for I require an historian, and not a rhetorician."[12]

The range of political and religious perspectives in Protestant historical writing from Bale through Clarendon is considerable, and we must recognize that although Milton was aware of the historiographic reform stemming from Machiavelli, his relationship to it is very different from what Camden's was in 1586. When he employs the methods of the new history, they naturally lack the innovativeness that they had sixty-five years before: his debunking of some of the legendary history of Britain, for example, is hardly original. We have seen that he applauds the new scholarly methods and pretends to (if only that) a plainer rhetoric. But his historical writing is anything but objective, scientific, and disinterested. Here we have only to refer to the Digression that Milton added to the *History of Britain* and later suppressed: it is an impassioned excoriation of the British penchant for servitude, and an explicit application of history to contemporary politics. In this we can see Milton deviating from one major manifestation of the reformed historiography which pretends to empirical objectivity—the whole bleak sequence of books 11 and 12 of *Paradise Lost* can be seen as an exponent of that unidealizing historical poetic converted through the elements of revelation and prophecy to Protestant historiography. Thus, it takes only a cursory reading to see that his historical writing differs markedly from the new methods and objectives described by Fussner and Levy and illustrated by Camden and other English innovators; in spite of his scholarship, Milton shows none of their reluctance to draw moral conclusions, and is in no way content to reserve judgment, to let the facts speak for themselves. But neutrality, which distinguishes

---

[11] From his *De augmentis*, 9, cited by Fussner, *The Historical Revolution*, 264.

[12] *Prose Works*, 3:515; as the *Commonplace Book* shows, Milton was a close reader of Machiavelli, and *Areopagitica*, in its rejection of idealized Platonic political theories, reflects an implicit affinity with the *real politik* of the sixteenth-century Italian historical reformers.

Camden's work, is not Milton's moral tone: his Puritan polemics reveal their affinity with earlier, Italian sources, particularly in Machiavelli.[13]

To appreciate the significance of some of these differences, and to understand exactly what Milton found in the Italian writers that was lacking in the work of some of his English compatriots, we need to recognize that Milton positively rejects some of the secular and religious trends in new historiography. To this end, a comparison of his references to Machiavelli and Guicciardini with those to Camden and the English breed of new secular historian is revealing. For example, part of the evolution of historiographic writing was the growth of archival and other data used to analyze historical accounts and problems with increasing empirical precision, and the revival (in more modern guise) of various "metahistorical" forms such as chorography; beginning in Italy, these developments are part of the growing antiquarian movement that flourished in England. As we saw in the introductory passage from the *History of Britain*, Milton has no time for the quibbles about place names and the like. While he takes what he needs from Holinshed and Camden, he clearly has no time for the irrelevant minutiae that the modern historian clutters his narrative with: "neither do I care to wrincle the smoothness of History with rugged names of places unknown, better harp'd at in *Camden*, and other chorographers."[14] His

---

[13] For Camden's impartiality, see Fussner, *The Historical Revolution*, 243–52, for example, although the link between "impartiality" and the politics of Protestant history needs fuller examination. Camden's role in the complex developments in historical enquiry up to 1625 are discussed in W. H. Herendeen, "William Camden: Historian, Herald, and Antiquary," *Studies in Philology* 85 (1988): 192–210. It is an irony usually overlooked that Machiavelli and Guicciardini, whose historical writing is so politically engaged, outspoken, and bent upon reform, are the precursors of objective empirical history in Protestant countries. Thus, it is significant that Milton's politically revolutionary historical writings bear such close resemblance to these Italian writers. A fuller, detailed study of similarities between Guicciardini's *Italian History* and the *History of Britain* would be revealing; both these writers and Machiavelli focus much of their view of human history on themes of treachery. Something of the range of Protestant responses to history is suggested by Christopher Hill's *The Experience of Defeat: Milton and Some Contemporaries* (New York: Viking Press, 1984), which characterizes individuals and ideologies struggling for expression and power between 1649 and the Restoration. In *Intellectual Origins* (174–77) Hill suggests Machiavelli's influence on the revolutionary writers and their ideas, but does not expand on the idea.

[14] *History of Britain*, 5:239–40; see also, for example, the *Commonplace Book*, 1:365. I emphasize Camden not only for his historical importance, but also because of Milton's documented interest in him.

frequent references to Camden are to facts—data, details, dates—but they barely conceal his disdain for the idolatry of detail. Milton is a very astute reader of historical genres; his rejection of antiquarianism is also part of his rejection of one kind of Protestant, even Jacobean historiography and its analogue in the episcopacy.

For Milton, literary form and genre have moral and social implications, just as they do today for students revising the canon of literary studies. His reaction against the current kinds of historical writing reflects his critique of his own generation. Social reform and amelioration should shape literary genre; literary fashions, such as the vogue of antiquarianism, he sees as no less than an aspect of cultural decay. In his historical analysis of the Reformation he names antiquarians as one of the three major impediments to true reform: in characteristic Miltonic fashion he means "antiquarian" writ both large and small:

> From this Period [the beginning of Elizabeth's reign] I count to begin our Times, which because they concerne us more neerely ... and will require a more exact search ... I shall distinguish such as I esteeme to be the hinderers of *Reformation* into 3. sorts, *Antiquarians* ... 2. *Libertines*, 3. *Politicians*.[15]

His abruptness with historical controversies at the beginning of the *History of Britain* is part of this impatience with those who "over-affect Antiquity." Milton is the precursor of modern iconoclasts who see political and moral implications in all gestures towards genre—as we see in his condemnation of Camden as "a fast friend of Episcopacie ... who cannot but love Bishops, as well as old coins, and his much lamented Monasteries for antiquities sake."[16] It is ironic that in such almost universally admired Protestant, English historians Milton sees the seeds of servility, resistance to change, and more specifically, the essence of prelaty.

While Milton *uses* his contemporary modern Protestant historians for data of various sorts, we see, in contrast, that he *identifies* with those

[15] *Of Reformation*, 1:541. This text is a good illustration of Milton's fusion of new history and ideology.

[16] *Of Reformation*, 1:541-42. Milton's distrust of Camden stands out against an almost universal respect for him and his work, and marks an important shift in English interpretations of historical writing: he was perceived by his contemporaries as a virulent anti-Catholic.

Italian historians who share the *"Philosophic* freedom" that resists tyranny, and that his historical writing resembles theirs in significant ways.[17] Thus, to continue our comparison, his citations of Machiavelli in the *Commonplace Book* are functionally different from those of his other, more modern, native sources in that they are used to state political theories or to buttress Milton's own essential polemical points. They are organized around crucial Miltonic headings dealing with monarchy, tyranny, religion and its relation to the state, and sedition.[18] Milton obviously viewed Machiavelli not as the source of the satanic rebel of stage and screed, but as a political historian dealing with the fundamental questions of freedom, social covenants, and reform. With similar purposefulness, he cites Guicciardini to illustrate the historical limitations on monarchic authority: "The Kings of Aragon do not have royal authority that is absolute in all things."[19] In Machiavelli he finds support for the idea of government by consent which curbs the power of the state:

> The Kingdoms that have good rule do not give their kings absolute power [over them] except over their armies, because in that case alone a sudden decision is necessary.[20]

Significantly, as early as the late 1630s, Milton looked mainly to Catholic and a few early Protestant writers—notably Machiavelli and Sleidanus —to support the legitimacy of violence against a tyrant. He asks

> Whether it be permissible to kill him [a tyrant]. Against a bad ruler there is no other remedy than the sword. "To cure the ills of the people, words suffice, and against those of the prince, the sword is necessary." Macchiavel. discors. c 58. Book 1.

---

[17] The passage from *Areopagitica* (2:537) should remind us how strongly Milton identified Italy with forceful resistance to the papacy.

[18] Passages are located at 1:477, 452, 471, 475, 505. Milton's *Commonplace Book* resembles the usual literary miscellany of the seventeenth-century less than it does the polemically designed commonplace book compiled under Henry VIII's direction by men such as Cranmer for use in the debates over papal authority, and I would suggest that Milton's work was designed with these models in mind.

[19] *Commonplace Book,* 1:442. Here and elsewhere Milton indicates the precise location of his citations.

[20] *Commonplace Book,* 1:443; see also 449. The consistency, fullness, and accuracy of these citations is revealing.

Nor do the Princes of Germany, for shameful acts that he has done, fear to bring pressure to bear upon the Emperor ... and no one should think it is a crime to attack a king with accusations for just reasons. See Sleidan. Book 18. 299.[21]

Milton recognized that in the hands of these pre-Reformation historians, the "new" methods were used not for "simple veritie" (Spenser's phrase for Camden's history) but to address the fundamental issues of self-determination and social reform. He obviously did not perceive them in terms of hostile cultural or artistic stereotypes: he invokes their judgment and understanding about the proper use of history—even if it is to be used to legitimize civil violence. Thus, Milton again cites Machiavelli, as both source and political theorist, in defense of violent rebellion as a means of regaining freedom:

> "I say that those who condemn the riots between the nobles and the common people thereby, in my estimation, blame those things that were the principal means of keeping Rome free." For good Laws were derived from those disturbances.[22]

Here, the break between quoted material ("I say that ... in my estimation ...") and Milton's own observation ("For good Laws were derived ...") is not very clear, because what is Machiavelli's "estimation" is also Milton's; their affinity is startlingly manifest. In each of the above passages from Machiavelli, Milton's strategy is to state a political premise that is reiterated or reinforced in principle (and not just illustrated) by the citation. In contrast, passages from English Protestant writers simply provide historical information. The political theses articulated in the quoted passages, identifying the civic benefits deriving from sedition, are ones that, even in the most theoretical contexts, would be unthinkable for Camden or Bacon, both of whom, from motives of political caution or conservatism, would never step out from among the ruins of history to draw such politically sensitive conclusions.[23]

---

[21] *Commonplace Book*, 1:456. In bringing together Machiavelli and Sleidanus, Milton makes clear his association of Machiavelli with the forces of reform.

[22] *Commonplace Book*, 1:505.

[23] The absence of political theory in these writers offers a striking contrast with Milton. While Bacon might seem to approach Milton in some of his essays, his history

Many other examples might be offered to illustrate how Milton found quite different kinds of inspiration and information in his Italian and English models. It is always clear, however, that the Italian histori-ographers spoke more immediately to him about matters of fundamental importance. I would suggest that the reason for this is thematic more than it is political; that is, it is not primarily the result of a strong political affinity between Milton and *seicento* Italian brands of republi-canism. Machiavelli's populism is at best suspect, and he ultimately sides with autocratic power. Guicciardini is decidedly conservative and politically incompatible with Milton. Both are temperamentally attractive to Milton for their anti-papal sentiments, but Milton does not make any such specific political or religious identification; even in the privacy of the *Commonplace Book*, he does not invoke Machiavelli as the propo-nent of republicanism, although the *Discourses* certainly provides ample opportunity for such an argument. It would seem that something other is at work here.[24]

Why Milton was drawn more strongly to these early modern histori-ographers of a century and a quarter before him than he was to the innovative work of his contemporaries has to do in part with their similar view of history and the individual, and with the human dynam-ics of reform. It is significant, from a literary-historical perspective, that, in their thematic and psychological focus, Milton's historical writings

---

of Henry VII is remarkably old-fashioned and tame, and falls short, methodologically, of his more theoretical statements in the *De augmentis*.

[24] Milton frequently (and freely) renders the Latin "res publica" as "common-wealth"—when he wants to make Italian republicanism serve his commonwealth politics he readily does so, and that he does not do so with either Machiavelli or Guicciardini is important, and a bit surprising. He probably recognized their respective monarchic and oligarchic politics. For full discussion of the ambiguous politics of these figures, see Mark Phillips, *Francesco Guicciardini: The Historian's Craft* (Toronto: Univ. of Toronto Press, 1977); Peter E. Bondanella, *Machiavelli and the Art of Renaissance History* (Detroit: Wayne State Univ. Press, 1973); Felix Gilbert, *Machiavelli and Guicciardini: Politics and History in Sixteenth-Century Florence* (Princeton: Princeton Univ. Press, 1965). Oddly, Charles R. Geisst, *The Political Thought of John Milton* (London: The MacMillan Press, 1984), and Stevie Davies, *Images of Kingship in "Paradise Lost": Milton's Politics and Christian Liberty* (Columbia: Univ. of Missouri Press, 1983), say virtually nothing about Milton and Machiavelli. Achsah Guibbory, *The Map of Time: Seventeenth-Century English Literature and Ideas of Pattern in History* (Urbana: Univ. of Illinois Press, 1986), 1-10, though not concerned with specific links with Milton, identifies Machiavelli's view of history in ways that complement what I have to say about Milton.

resemble Machiavelli's and Guicciardini's far more than they do Camden's. In the *Discourses*, the *Florentine History*, in Guicciardini's *Italian History*, as well as in Milton's *History of Britain*, we see historical examination of the individual's potential for change, the ability to resist the immoral tone of society, and to affect the course of history.[25] In their defense of rebellion, of leadership, and in their attacks on the seemingly omnipresent force of the papacy, Milton found a political and psychological view of history that, like his own, strove to capture the rhythms of a person's inner life, and, in so doing, he transcended individual political differences.[26]

This interest in early historiographic innovators puts Milton's Protestant historiography in an unusual light. In each case his interest is generalized and becomes identified with the original spirit of the Reformation and the belief in change—that humanity can be other than it is, that it can step out of the determinist course of history onto a path of reform; hardly typical of Protestant histories, this is exactly the force of change that Machiavelli says his *Discourses* is meant to serve.[27] Both he and Guicciardini were reformers whose view of human potential was important for Milton around 1650. In more ways than one, theirs are histories of a culture breaking out of the moral habit of its times, and for this reason their lesson continued to be important.[28] Even though the course of social and religious reform had not gone smoothly since Savonarola, self-determination and moral reform through the individual

---

[25] Each of these three authors uses his history to develop vivid portraits of politically or morally exemplary characters—Machiavelli of Cosimo de' Medici, Guicciardini of Lorenzo the Magnificent, and Milton of Alfred (in the *History of Britain*); Milton's history, in fact, devolves into a series of character sketches. For Machiavelli (see 98–99), history serves to show readers how they can break from the moral habit of their age, and affect change; his prefatory pages offer a view of history very close to Milton's and quite distinct from that of Elizabethan and Jacobean historians.

[26] Cochrane, xii, uses the phrase "inner rhythm of life" and "the organic character of reality" to describe the preeminent concerns of the baroque historian, and it is precisely this focus that we see in Milton, and that reconciles him to the Italian writers.

[27] Machiavelli, *Discourses*, 98–99; see Guibbory, 169–80, for discussion of Milton in similar terms.

[28] We must remember that Machiavelli and Guicciardini saw the end of the Florentine Republic, the fall of Rome, the struggle of autocratic and oligarchic governments, and the growth of a papacy from a local to a national and international force—all of which testified to the power of the individual to shape history. It is this tradition that seems to inform Milton's identification with Italians in *Areopagitica*, for instance.

is possible. In *Of Reformation* Milton saw as clearly as Erasmus, More, or Sleidanus did that the original Reformation (and England's in particular) was the real fruit of that view of history and the individual, that first seeding of rebellion.

Milton's use of and interest in Machiavelli and Guicciardini, then, are part of his attempt to break out of the framework of current Protestant history, and also out of current Protestant historiography that he associates with England's inability to see how its reform has run aground since Calvin, Luther, and Zwingli:

> The light which we have gain'd, was given us, not to be ever staring on, but by it to discover onward things more remote from our knowledge. It is not the unfrocking of a Priest, the unmitring of a Bishop, and the removing him from off the *Presbyterian* shoulders that will make us a happy Nation, no, if other things as great in the Church, and in the rule of life both economicall and politicall, be not lookt into and reform'd, we have lookt so long upon the blaze that *Zuinglius* and *Calvin* hath beacon'd up to us, that we are stark blind.[29]

The passage, illustrating Milton's sense that England must shake off the bondage of the Reformation, clarifies his interest in Italian historiography. For him, "reform" is a verb, not a proper noun. His view of historical events emphasizes the evils arising from the lack of change as much as it does the possiblity of change. In this context, Milton sees his place in history as resembling Machiavelli's more than it does Camden's. Thus, where supposedly secular Tudor and early Stuart historians fear change and write with a disengagement which implicitly sustains the success of Anglican reform, Milton, like his earlier models, greets change, even foments it.

This predilection for pre-Tridentine writers (in this context, a better descriptive label than pre-Reform) points to another major aspect of explicitly Protestant historiography which Milton found particularly uncongenial and chose to suppress, or at least deemphasize in his own work. It can be illustrated by a brief consideration of Johannes Sleidanus's work, *The Key of Historie*, which Milton used and, for political and religious reasons, liked. Anti-papal, modern in his scholarly tech-

---

[29] *Areopagitica*, 2:550; see also 541, 543, 552–53, for other illustrations of this idea.

niques, as politically engaged as Milton was, his view of human history is often regarded as typical of Protestant historiography.[30] Both a humanist and a reformer, Sleidanus offers a perceptive analysis of patterns and causes in the developments of societies, identifies the beginning of reform with the revival of learning in Italy, and sees the advent of printing and the recovery of scripture as part of the emancipation from the papacy.[31] His analysis of the complex forces at work in social change has both the complexity (and modernity) of Machiavelli and the humanist values which appeal to Milton. So far so good.

But his overriding view of history is prophetic, and identifies the corruption and decline of Rome as the beginning of the end, as the fall of the last monarchy prophecied in Daniel 8. The overwhelming sense of historical and cultural predestination precludes any powerfully evoked individual as an effective force or exemplum in history; his insistence on divine revelation and election denies the possibility of change and civil reform. Having seen the light of Reformation, humanity now faces "the last age of this fading world" when "Satan shall be Prince." With the decay of the fourth monarchy, there is no prospect of change, and for the elect, no need for it. He explains that "to ... chear up, and sustaine those, that shall then live ... [God] places the resurrection of the dead ... that we may finde joy and comfort."[32]

This lesson in passivity is very different from the patience-that-serves in Milton's work. Sleidanus's social view in 1550 is as cheerless as Milton's is a century later, but for him, now that Reform has come, all that remains is the resurrection:

these our times, being the most miserable, we ought considerately to ponderate and dilengently look into this Prophet, who preaches to us now acting the last scene upon the world's stage: that we may fortify ourselves ... with true and assured consolation, as with a certaine rampire and bulwarke. (374-75)

---

[30] For Sleidanus as Protestant historian, see Cochrane, 315, 321, 358; Fletcher, 614; and Firth, 69-76.

[31] Sleidanus, 352. The historical recovery of scripture is part of the process of overthrowing the papacy: "And because the holy Scriptures foreshadow the Papall kingdome, we must search out the beginning, together with the progresse and increase therof" (Epistle).

[32] Sleidanus, 374 (the reference is to Daniel 12); also pp. 360, 353, 372.

This reformed view of history, characteristic of one strain of Protestant historiography and having its literary analogue in the poetic of silence (to use Fish's phrase) that we meet with in Herbert's verse, is absent from Milton's prose and verse.[33] When we compare Milton's response to Machiavelli and Sleidanus (and other northern writers), we see the extent to which he curtails this aspect of prophetic Protestant historiography and its denial of the importance of the individual.[34] While he incorporates much else in the way of reform politics and mood, his historical writing always focuses on the individual will and the capacity for freedom, change, and moral independence—qualities that John Steadman sees specifically as the element of Machiavellian *virtù* in Milton's work.[35]

Of course, in identifying Milton's response to what might be called establishment and deterministic approaches to history, we do not want

---

[33] See Fish, 21–30 and Lewalski's discussion, 3–13.

[34] Firth's survey of the apocalyptic tradition makes clear that this is not just an isolated difference from Sleidanus's view of history. Sleidanus's is not, of course, the only response to apocalyptic history, and indeed his own views are more complex than represented here, where my main concern is his overriding theory of history. *The Apocalypse in English Renaissance Thought and Literature*, ed. C. A. Patrides and Joseph Wittreich (Ithaca: Cornell Univ. Press, 1984), surveys the background, literary treatments, and political uses of apocalyptic views of history in Renaissance England. In this volume, Jaroslav Pelikan's essay "Some Uses of Apocalypse in the Magisterial Reformers" (74–92), and Bernard Capp's, "The Political Dimension of Apocalyptic Thought" (93–125), both illustrate how Puritan views of history were also used to justify political activism and reform. The use of history that they identify differs from Sleidanus's, although the view of history is effectively the same: it is characterized in Hill (*Intellectual Origins*, 179–82) as cyclical, mechanistic, basically subsuming the individual within a divine pattern. Apocalytic themes go beyond historical concerns: for a full examination of the importance of subject for Milton, see William Kerrigan, *The Prophetic Milton* (Charlottesville: Univ. of Virginia Press, 1974), and Joseph Anthony Wittreich, Jr., *Visionary Poetics: Milton's Tradition and His Legacy* (San Marino: The Huntington Library, 1979); other critics less concerned with themes of history have stressed Milton's individualism, and Wittreich, *Visionary Poetics* (186–93), links this with the need to break from deterministic historical cycles. Christopher Kendrick, *Milton: A Study in Ideology and Form* (New York: Methuen, 1986), 43–77, though less concerned with history than I am here, studies the ideology of Milton's individualism.

[35] John M. Steadman, *Milton's Epic Characters: Image and Idol* (Chapel Hill: Univ. of North Carolina Press, 1959), 200. This is a concept of *virtù* which can be converted to either moral or immoral action. Steadman would agree that Milton's view of Machiavelli is not the negative stereotype that is commonly associated with him, and that might emerge from the view of Satan in *Paradise Lost*, 4.998–99.

to over-simplify the range of Protestant historiography. But through this glimpse of Sleidanus's history we see the unique combination of pre- and post-Tridentine elements in Milton's own eclectic thinking. His treatment of human history is unflattering, realistic, and sensitive to all the Machiavellian psychological inconsistencies, although confident of the potential for reform also characteristic of the Machiavellian historian's complex view of humanity. Milton is also indefatigably, even dogmatically, engaged politically, and in this, truer to the spirit of Counter-Reformation politics and history than to what we might call the disengaged historiography of some of his Protestant predecessors. In his belief in the ability and even the need to break away from historical cycles, he differs from those apocalyptic historians and polemicists who invoke the patterns of divine history to legitimize reform.

Milton's Puritan perspective, then, captures the original spirit of reform and the polemics of counter-reform, both of which emphasize the potency of the individual to break from history. What we have, in the treatment of Enoch and Noah in book 11 of *Paradise Lost*, and in the eloquent praise of Alfred in the *History of Britain*, is a vision of the rebel able to resist the tyranny of an immoral age. In these figures we have the Machiavellian hero placed in the moral miasma characterized by Sleidanus and the Protestant historians. The result is a baroque history in which powerful Protestant typological figures stand out against the chiaroscuro of their age, rather like the Old Testament figures of Rembrandt's paintings. Thus, at the end of the Digression in the *History of Britain*, Milton sets out to "speak a truth not oft spok'n" and bleakly characterizes Britain "as ... a land fruitful enough of men stout and courageous in warr, so it is naturallie not over fertil of men able to govern justlie & prudently in peace." Supporting his opinion with the ungilded facts of history, he speaks with the scepticism of the modern historian, whether it be the Lutheran Sleidanus justifying faith and resignation, or the worldly humanist defending monarchy and the need for absolutist leadership (as Machiavelli does). But Milton specifically steps out of the world of reform, of prophecy, and historical recurrence. Addressing his own generation in the Digression, he offers not a religious or political solution to historical decline, as these early reformers did, but one nevertheless that he associates with Italy. It is first of all personal, then civic; we can learn it by going out of ourselves to learn about ourselves—a process denied by Puritan historiography. In the foreground of his bleak landscape is the individual illumined by a ray of sun and fed with wine and oil; he gives us a baroque portrait of the individual (neither courtier nor Puritan) finding sustenance by reaching outside of his own country's stores:

> For the sunn, which wee want ripens witts as well as fruits: and as wine and oyle are imported to us from abroad, so must ripe understanding and many civil vertues, bee imported unto our minds from forren writings & examples of best ages: wee shall else miscarry still and com short in the attempts of any great enterprise.[36]

Perhaps part of Milton's "climatic theory . . . of national characteristics," as French Fogle's stringently depoliticized reading suggests, it is also a tactful reminder to his compatriots that they can still learn from Italy. Milton's expressly natural imagery tells his readers not only that the sun, wine, and oil are freely given mankind by God, not by pope or bishop, and that they may be freely taken by all, but also that we must take our understanding and civil virtues from beyond England's histori-cal and geographical borders.

University of Windsor

---

[36] From the conclusion of the MS Digression, 5:451.

DAVID REID

# Tasso and Milton on How One Sees Oneself

I N JERUSALEM DELIVERED, TASSO CATCHES the fall and recovery
of a Christian hero in three images. Two of the three images
represent the hero in eclipse. Rinaldo has been seduced from his
heroic enterprise, the delivery of Jerusalem, and carried away to its
opposite, the enjoyment of an earthly paradise, by Armida, a beautiful
pagan enchantress. While he dallies, the Crusade languishes, and so
two Crusaders are sent to call him back to himself and Christian
warfare. The narrative follows them on their journey to the point where
they break in on the garden and spy on the lovers. And we too are
given a view of what is going on:

> Downe by the loures side there pendant was
> A Christall mirrour, bright, pure, smooth and neat,
> He rose and to his mistresse held the glas,
> (A noble Page, grac'd with that seruice great)
> She, with glad lookes; he with enflam'd (alas)
> Beautie and loue beheld, both in one seat;
>    Yet them in sundrie obiets each espies,
>    She, in the glasse; he, saw them in her eies.
>
>                                  (16.20)[1]

Armida is called away, and the two Crusaders seize the opportunity
to present themselves in full armor and hold up a diamond shield
before him. This is the second image. Here again Rinaldo beholds
himself, this time, however, not in the mirrors of love, which are

---

[1] Citations of *Jerusalem Delivered*, unless otherwise noted, are to Edward Fairfax's
translation, *Godfrey of Bulloigne*, ed. Kathleen M. Lea and T. M. Gang (Oxford:
Clarendon Press, 1981).

Armida's eyes, but in the hard pure surface of the shield of Christian
warfare:[2]

> Vpon the targe his lookes amas'd he bent,
> And therein all his wanton habite spide,
> His ciuet, baulme, and perfumes redolent,
> How from his lockes they smoakt, and mantle wide,
> His sword that many a Pagan stout had shent,
> Bewrapt with flowres, hung idlie by his side,
> > So nicely decked, that it seemd the knight
> > Wore it for fashion sake, but not for fight.
>
> (16.30)

The effect of this severe reflection on himself is to make Rinaldo angry
with himself (16.34). It stirs up the warrior within against a self now
seen, in Fairfax's phrase, as "a carpet champion for a wanton dame"
(16.32). And that, as far as Rinaldo is concerned, is the end of love,
though not of Armida. He returns to the Crusade in a hurry.

But before he can take up his warfare, a religious operation is
required. He has repented of love in the sense that he has undergone a
complete change of heart. Yet the change has to be sanctified before his
restoration is complete. And so it has to go through the Church. Under
the ministrations of Peter the Hermit, Rinaldo confesses his sins and is
directed to pray for forgiveness. This he does with his armor beside him
on Olivet, repenting "The sinnes and errours ... / Of mine vnbridled
youth" (18.14), and while he does so it dawns:

> The heau'nly dew was on his garments spred,
> To which compar'd, his clothes pale ashes seame,
> And sprinkled so, that all that paleness fled,
> And thence of purest white bright raies outstreame;
> So cheered are the flowres late withered,
> With the sweete comfort of the morning beame;
> > And so returned to youth, a serpent old
> > Adornes her selfe in new and natiue gold.
>
> (18.16)

---

[2] A. Bartlett Giamatti, *The Earthly Paradise and the Renaissance Epic* (Princeton:
Princeton Univ. Press, 1966), 206, calls attention to the contrast between the eyes and
shield as mirrors.

In this third image we have the hero restored, irradiated, like Achilles, with a more than earthly light before he goes to war.[3] Rinaldo's glory is heroic, but the supernatural suggestions are Christian. The "heau'nly dew" diffuses on him like grace, making his garments dazzling. And it is the purity of the beams he gives off that Tasso speaks of rather than their brilliance.[4] Tasso represents his god-filled hero as a Christian restored by grace, not as a Homeric berserker warrior discharging violent power.

It is striking how completely these three images epitomize the action of the poem, where Rinaldo is concerned. They sum up the whole complicated business of volition involved in turning from love to duty, or sin to repentance and renewal, as Tasso imagines it. They are incisive but, I think it is fair to add, they are also curiously external. That fairly leaps to the eye if we bring to mind Milton's study of the will in *Paradise Lost*. We can certainly call up images of a visual sort that catch what is going on—the scene of parting when Adam gazes after Eve, her return to him with a false look, their discovering their nakedness as they look at each other with distaste, and so on. But such pictures in Milton's poem are supplementary to a detailed representation of the processes of fall, guilt, and repentance, especially in soliloquy, in what the characters say to themselves. There is very little of that in Tasso.

The externality of Tasso's treatment of volition has probably something to do with the literary mode he was working in. The standard Renaissance humanist defence of literature was that it supplied examples that not only showed ideas of virtue and vice but showed them in action and above all actually inspired the reader to imitate or shun them. This theory of applied literature as a sort of moral rhetoric lies behind Italian criticism of the sixteenth century. It comes out explicitly in Sidney's *Defence of Poetry*.[5] It can even be discerned in Milton's dictum that

[3] *Iliad* 18.207–14.

[4] Judith A. Kates, *Tasso and Milton: The Problem of the Christian Epic* (London and Toronto: Associated Univ. Press, 1983), 121–22, calls attention to images of baptism and rebirth.

[5] See, e.g., Sir Philip Sidney, *A Defence of Poetry*, ed., Katherine Duncan-Jones and Jan van Dorsten, in *Miscellaneous Prose of Sir Philip Sidney* (Oxford: Clarendon, 1973), 85, 98. For humanist thought about the literary exemplum, see Eckhard Kessler, *Das Problem des Frühen Humanismus: Seine Philosophische Bedeutung bei Coluccio Salutati* (Munich: Fink Verlag, 1968), 152–200. Bernard A. Weinberg, *A History of Literary*

poetry is "more simple sensuous and passionate" than those other arts of discourse, logic, and rhetoric; the idea of "pietas," for example, has its complications, and logic or rhetoric might unfold them at length, but poetry makes it simple by fashioning Aeneas as an image of that virtue and the imagination grasps the idea all at once; such an image is sensuous at the same time because it is present to the mind's senses and passionate because it excites the will through engaging the passions.[6] An image of this sort need not be a single speaking picture. Aeneas is not. But still in Tasso's hands the action is cast in visual emblems as strikingly as in a more old-fashioned allegorical epic like the *Faerie Queene*.

Ideal imitation works particularly well with a moral psychology of self-regard.[7] Its visual images, whether glorious or shameful, are self-images and involve the self-image of the reader. In the course of defending the poet Archias, Cicero expatiates on what the humanist study of literature has done for himself. He testifies how the glorious examples that literature holds up have inspired him and how, "me consule" ("when I was consul," the irresistible topic), they guided and sustained his heroic labors to preserve the state against Catiline.[8] He also lets drop that Archias is writing an epic on his consulship so that we may suppose Cicero thinks that he will in turn be fashioned into an

---

*Criticism in the Italian Renaissance* (Chicago: Univ. of Chicago Press, 1961), 1:72, 350, makes it clear that Renaissance critics were unable to take in the newly discovered *Poetics* of Aristotle because of their rhetorical theory of poetry derived from Horace and Cicero. Tasso himself thinks that the excellence of poetry lies in its answering to the profit and delight formula; see *Discourses on the Heroic Poem*, trans. Mariella Cavalchini and Irene Samuel (Oxford: Oxford Univ. Press, 1973), 10: "Poetry . . . is an imitation of human actions fashioned to teach us how to live." His "Allegorie" prefixed to *Godfrey of Bulloigne* analyzes his poem as a concatenation of moral examples, and in book 1, st. 3, he speaks of his poem's rendering moral truths palatable by fiction in the same way as a sweetened cup does bitter medicine (cf. *Discourses*, 11).

[6] *Of Education*, ed. Donald C. Dorian, in CPW 2:403.

[7] "Ideal imitation" is used by Joel E. Spingarn, *Literary Criticism of the Renaissance* (New York: Harcourt Brace, 1963), 19, to cover a theory he thinks Aristotle and the Renaissance critics held in common. I use the term for the fashioning of images of moral ideas as distinct from Aristotle's "imitation of an action." That is more or less how John M. Steadman speaks of ideal imitation in *The Lamb and the Elephant: Ideal Imitation and the Context of Renaissance Allegory* (San Marino, Calif.: Huntington Lib., 1974).

[8] Cicero, *Pro Archia* 5.14, ed. James S. Reid (Cambridge: Cambridge Univ. Press, 1928), 26.

inspirational example of public virtue. Alas, the great work has not survived, if indeed it was ever completed, and though Cicero himself took the important theme in hand, only a fragment or two, such as the immortal "o fortunatam natam me consule Romam" ("O Rome reborn, happy in my happening to be consul") have come down to us.[9] Cicero is not a Renaissance humanist, and the references to the *Pro Archia* among the Italian theorists are, as far as I can see, fugitive. But his defense of the study of literature shows with paradigmatic simplicity how heroic poetry could be moralized. The lustre of the image of the hero moves the reader to moral imitation. He fashions his character like an inner statue in the image of the shining one, and in this way heroes and hero worship can be harnessed to moral and civic designs.

Heroes are notoriously jealous of their self-image. In Homer, Achilles' sense of himself cannot tolerate a superior. Even where the idea of the hero has been moralized, the hero carries an unwieldy ego apparatus—Cicero's heroically fashioned self-importance is an amusing example. Virgilian and post-Virgilian epic tries to disown the narcissism of heroes like Achilles by representing it as anarchic and self-destructive in figures like Turnus in the *Aeneid* or Argantes in *Jerusalem Delivered*. And yet epics escape from schemes of self-regard only by a sort of self-contradiction while they remain heroic poems, certainly as long as they are cast in military fictions. It is true that Virgil's Aeneas and Tasso's Godfrey tend to efface themselves in favor of serving destiny or God. But they are not very inspirational figures. Godfrey, indeed, in book 7 of *Jerusalem Delivered*, refuses a duel with the pagan champion, Argantes, for to endanger himself would endanger the Christian enterprise. This is sensible, but if heroic, only in too attenuated a sense to be compelling. The active hero of *Jerusalem Delivered*, the one who does the hero-work and wins heroic lustre, not just for himself, but for Godfrey's expedition, is Rinaldo, and he has more than enough of the hero's self-regard.

Rinaldo originally leaves the Crusade because he has killed Gernando in a fit of heroic pique. Gernando felt his glory was impaired by Rinaldo's and so cried it down. Rinaldo resented this as an injury to himself and could not stop himself until "in Gernando's breast / He

---

[9] See G. B. Townsend, "The Poems," in *Cicero*, ed. T. A. Dorsey (London: Routledge, 1964), 118-19.

sheathed once or twice" "His thundring sword" (5.31, 29). After that he leaves the Christian camp and lets himself go with Armida. From this he is recalled to himself when the two Crusaders hold up the diamond shield and he sees himself as amorist. Tasso both in his narrative and in the allegory he furnished to his poem makes out that Rinaldo's ruling passion is anger or fiery spiritedness. So in the first scene he is furious with Gernando; in the second he is furious at himself and his shameful appearance in the shield (16.34). But in both scenes, self-regard is behind the anger. In each, Rinaldo finds the image of himself impaired. And it is because he takes himself with such passionate seriousness that he is such a hero.

It is hard for love to coexist with such heroism. So it is not surprising that with Rinaldo the hero is undone in the lover. As lover, the image he regards and even loves to see reflected in himself is Armida's, not his own. That is the drift of the mirror and eyes conceit we began with. There Armida gazes at herself in a mirror, while Rinaldo gazes at himself in the pupils of her eyes. Tasso (not Fairfax) has it that they view in different objects a single object (Mirano in varii oggetti un solo ogetto).[10] The single object of their gaze is puzzling. In the following stanzas, however, Rinaldo pleads with Armida to gaze at herself in him:

> For painted in my hart and purtrai'd right
> Thy woorth, thy beauties, and perfections bee,
>    Of which the forme, the shape, and fashion best,
>    Not in this glas is seene, but in my brest.
>
>                                                    (16.21)

I take it then that the single object is Armida, whether directly imaged in the crystal mirror or indirectly in Rinaldo, who declares he is the true glass of her perfection. A. Bartlett Giamatti has argued that what is wrong with the love shown here is its narcissism.[11] Certainly Armida's enchantment with her own image seems narcissistic and suggests that she loves herself, not Rinaldo. Rinaldo, however, is not concerned for once with his image or the figure he cuts. If Freud's discussion of narcissism is relevant, he has transferred "the original narcissism of the child" to "a love object."[12] He is not narcissistically absorbed in his

---

[10] *Gerusalemme Liberata*, ed. Luigi Bonfigli (Bari: Laterza, 1930).

[11] Giamatti, 199 ff. Tasso compares Armida to Narcissus (4.66).

[12] Freud, "On Narcissism: An Introduction," *Collected Papers*, trans. Joan Rivere

reflection in Armida's eyes but in his own reflection as a reflection of her. At this point the conceit trembles on the edge of the imagery so habitual with Donne that looks for love given and returned in the mutual reflections of lovers in the glasses of their eyes. But in Tasso's conceit the looks glance away from mutuality. This is just as well, for if the love had involved an exchange of selves, Rinaldo could not have left Armida with clean hands. As it is, Tasso represents Rinaldo's love as a self-depleting pursuit of a vain object so that Rinaldo can return to heroic self-regard and Christian warfare with a good conscience where Armida is concerned. His conscience is indeed so excellent that when Armida appears before him in the enchanted grove, he lifts his sword to her without hesitation. It is true that this Armida is a phantom, but it is not clear that Rinaldo knows it. At any rate, after he has come through this test, he is a complete man and can offer the real Armida marriage in the end without the least fear for himself.

The sort of morality that Rinaldo exemplifies both as sinner and as hero is not one that is concerned with other selves, except as rivals or conquests. In public life his heroic self-regard is serviceable in so far as it makes him a good soldier and fits into the designs of the commander, Godfrey. Then his high spirit is to be distinguished from the pride and envy of the pagan champions and of his detractor, Gernando. It is not just to be admired for its heroic brilliance, but approved and imitated because of its social and political function. But the community it serves is an abstract idea, like Plato's *Republic*, whose Guardians Rinaldo is modelled on.[13] It is not imagined as a community of other people, and notably the idea of order that Rinaldo's self-regard serves has no place for love. Again, on the level of private morality, Rinaldo exempli-

---

(London: Hogarth Press, 1925), 4:45. "Mourning and Melancholia" in the same collection, 152-70, also has a bearing on heroic self-regard.

[13] For the scheme of the poem as an allegory of order in the state and the human soul on the model of Plato's *Republic*, see "Allegorie," *Godfrey of Bulloigne*, 88-93. On the idea of order, see Thomas Greene, *The Descent from Heaven* (New Haven: Yale Univ. Press, 1963), 189 ff. Tasso both in his narrative and in his "Allegorie" makes out that Rinaldo represents the irascible powers of the soul, the "thumos" of Plato's *Republic*, 439e-441c. He adds that Rinaldo also represents the concupiscible powers of the soul. It is possible that even in Tasso a feeling, much developed in seventeenth-century heroic drama, that the same vigor impels the lover as the soldier makes itself felt here. Or it may be that he could think of no other way of formulating how Rinaldo's free will might dispose him either to war or love.

fies a self-centered ethic of temperance. He is a heroic exemplar of that irascible or spirited faculty that corresponds in Plato's scheme of the psychological faculties to the Guardians in his scheme of the body politic, and under the government of reason may control the appetites or be let loose to them. Here again the ideal is self-regarding. Virtue is imagined in terms of self-control and the attaining of a perfect character rather than in terms of transactions with other people. So it often seems that we are to imagine Rinaldo's rejection of Armida more as a rejection of his own sensuality or lower nature than as a dealing with someone else. In his *Enchiridion*, Erasmus reduces Eve to an allegory of Adam's lower nature. Tasso has not really got beyond such platonizing ideas of Christian warfare.[14]

The self-regard of this ideal may be elevated, but hardly transformed, by religion. When Rinaldo is touched by the divine light as he prays on Olivet, it is a sign that his making war on the enemies of the Christian state and his making war on his own lower self have God behind them. Partly this is for the benefit of the reader. But it is also for the benefit of Rinaldo, who on his way to Olivet has shown a mind to rise above the stars. In this spirit he prays for himself to be freed from earthly pollution and it is in answer to this that there comes over him and his clothing a radiance, which he looks at with wonder and which supplies him with an image of himself glorified.[15]

In *Paradise Lost*, Milton's treatment of the motions of the will, such as error, guilt, and repentance, and of the way people live with other people, goes beyond Tasso's rather limited set of ideas. And yet there is certainly a side to *Paradise Lost* that seems to make much of heroic self-regard in rather the same way as Tasso's poem does. After all, Milton's succinct description of poetry in *Of Education* falls in with the humanist theory that poetry educates through moral images. And so in *Paradise Lost* Milton makes his moral and religious ideals shine with heroic glory. God has engrossed all true glory to himself, but no doubt because he is God this is to be seen as something different from more than heroic self-regard. True glory in others can only be conferred on them by God and only won by the hero's investing his self-esteem

---

[14] *Enchiridion* (London, 1533), cap. 1.

[15] "The louely whiteness of his changed weed / The prince perceived well, and long admirde" (18.17).

entirely in God. This has been supposed to transform the idea of heroism and glory by a sort of "Copernican revolution."[16] Certainly it makes the hero's glory quite unworldly, transferred from an earthly to a heavenly kingdom, and it ensures that the heavenly sovereign is the absolute fount of honor, while admiration and self-affirmation such as Satan wins from his peers count for nothing in themselves. But I am not sure that this makes so much difference in practice. There is a heavenly honor system in which glorious acts are recorded on banners. Good angels confront bad ones with as jealous a sense of their worth, however heavenly, as earthly heroes do other earthly heroes. Consider the splendid exchanges between the loyal angels and Satan in Paradise. Or think of Abdiel defying the rebel angels in a flame of zeal. To respond to that is to feel for his thrilling with an intense consciousness of uprightness. It is true that his sense of worth comes to him through the regard of the great Taskmaster: "for this was all [his] care / To stand approved in  sight of God, though worlds / Judged [him] perverse" (6.35–37).[17] But this simply makes self-regard sublime; it does not change it into something else. Moreover, the ethical scheme of the poem also is partly one of self-regard. Raphael, for instance, tells Adam that the best way to prevent his admiration for Eve making him forget himself is to cultivate his self-esteem, and a good deal of moralizing of the poem by the narrator and by Michael takes the view that the fall is a failure in temperance, in the wary self-regard that should see to it that a lower version of oneself does not take over.[18]

But temperance and the ethics of self-regard supply only a partial and impoverished account of what Milton shows, whatever he or the angels tell us to think. For his poem traces in often beautifully intricate detail how one self is implicated in another. That comes out, for example, in the reflexiveness of looks. A look is at once a glance and the appearance of the face as it takes in what it looks at. Milton dwells on

---

[16] Kates, 123–24, argues that Tasso, and John M. Steadman, *Milton and the Renaissance Hero* (Oxford: Clarendon, 1967), v–vii, that Milton brought about a "Copernican revolution" in the heroic ideal. My point is that, however reformed ethically or religiously, the original self-regard is still intensely present in any figure who remains heroic in an unattenuated sense. See Steadman, 177–78, for an argument that Milton's idea of heroism transcends self-regard in giving all glory to God.

[17] All citation of *Paradise Lost* are from Fowler.

[18] E.g., 9.1127–31; 11.476, 515–19, 634–36.

this reflexiveness wherever he draws relations between persons.[19] This too starts with God, in the way the Father looks at the Son and sees his glory "In full resplendence" (5.719-20) reflected in him. The Son looks at the Father and in his look "Divine compassion visibly appeared" (3.141) reflected from the Father, and this compassion his face also gives expression to in speech.

Between Father and Son the reflexiveness of one in another can run in only one way, from Father to Son and back again. But among creatures such as angels and men the interchange is truly mutual. This emerges clearly where something has gone wrong with the looks among the fallen angels. They have lost God's countenance. Satan, whose countenance in heaven shone "as the morning star" (5.708), in Hell no longer returns God's glory to him directly. Yet some reflection of the Creator remains:

> his form had yet not lost
> All her original brightness, nor appeared
> Less than archangel ruined, and the excess
> Of glory obscured.                    (1.591-94)

His legions come to his call,

> but with looks
> Down cast and damp, yet such wherein appeared
> Obscure some glimpse of joy, to have found their chief
> Not in despair, to have found themselves not lost
> In loss itself; which on his countenance cast
> Like doubtful hue.                    (1.522-27)

Here the looks of the fallen angels brighten as they take in the look of their leader, whose look in turn brightens as he looks on them. And behind this exchange of looks, there lies a suggestion that they find themselves in each other. This reciprocated look of fear and hope is taken up in the magnificent half-light of the images Milton finds for Satan's appearance:

---

[19] The discovery of one self in another and its reflection in another's eyes goes back to Plato's *Alcibiades*, 1, in *The Dialogues of Plato*, trans. B. Jowett (Oxford: Clarendon, 1871), 4:556-57, cited by Albert Fields, "Milton and Self-Knowledge," *PMLA* 83 (1968): 392-99. See also Don Parry Norford, "The Separation of the World Parents in *Paradise Lost*," *MS* 12 (1978): 12-18, and Jun Harada, "The Mechanism of Reconciliation in *Paradise Lost*," *PQ* 50 (1971): 543-52.

as when the sun new risen
Looks through the horizontal misty air
Shorn of his beams, or from behind the moon
In dim eclipse disastrous twilight sheds
On half the nations. (1.594–98)

It is easy to suppose that there is something innately false in the way Satan needs others to supply his sense of himself. In his speaking, where one-anothering rules as much as in the conversation of looks, he believes his own rhetoric because he sees it impress others. But in a universe where everything seems to be an energy in interchange with other energies and where angels as well as humans are what they are in conversation with each other, it can hardly be wrong in itself that Satan finds himself in the answering looks and responses of others. When Adam talks to Eve in book 4, he "Turned him all ear to hear new utterance flow" (1.410). "Moving speech," he speaks for the response of Eve.[20] That of course is an Edenic ideal of "apt and cheerful conversation." Satan's talk is usually oratory. But even there it is the misuse of the reflexiveness of speech upon the speaker, not the reflexiveness itself, that is wrong.

The way in which human creatures need other humans to be themselves is made clear in what both Adam and Eve tell of their origins. Adam tells Raphael how after he was made and transported to the Garden, he found himself incomplete by himself. God told him to enjoy the society of animals "and seemed / So ordering" (8.376–77). But Adam persists in uttering his intuition of full humanity and speaks of his need for fellowship "Fit to participate / All rational delight, wherein the brute / Cannot be human consort" (8.390–92). Undismayed by God's teasing, he points out that while God may be perfect in oneness, "man by number is to manifest / His single imperfection, and beget / Like of his like, his image multiplied" (8.422–24). God not only accepts this, saying that it was what he had meant all along, but actually finds in Adam's rational freedom of creative judgement his own image. With that he gives Adam Eve, "thy likeness . . . thy other self" (8.450).

---

[20] Fowler, note to 1.410, argues that "him" is Satan on the grounds that Adam's speech is too long to be spoken to elicit a reply from Eve. This disregards the length of speeches in epic conversation and misses the reciprocity motif Milton makes so much of.

Eve in turn on waking from creation wonders what she is and seeks
herself first in her reflection in the lake. She is, however, prompted by
either God or "the genial angel" to think of herself as the image of
another with whom she will "bear / Multitudes like [her]self" (4.473–
74), and Adam adds his entreaties that she is his "other half" (4.488).

The enchantment of Eve's account lies partly in her "unexperienced
thought" (4.457), her uncertainty about above and below and about
herself and the images that approach and fly from her. Adam is more
in command of the situation. The charm of his account lies in his poise
and freedom with God. Yet there are suggestions, even with him, of
Eve's sort of self-bemusement. When he falls asleep before being carried
to Paradise, he not only sees himself, a frequent enough experience in
dreams, but sees the dream itself, in which he sees himself, stand at his
head. And again when he falls asleep at Eve's making, it is to see Eve
being taken out of himself. On both occasions not only is there play
with the image of himself, but with dreaming and waking consciousness, inside and out of himself, for each time he wakes up to find what
he has dreamed going on in the world.

Both accounts of waking from self-bemusement to a world with
others convey an idea that one becomes human in exchange of like with
like. This is carried on in the intercourse of looks that runs through
books 9 and 10, even where the mutuality of Adam and Eve has been
corrupted and they reflect each other askew. When Eve comes back with
the fruit, "in her face excuse / Came prologue, and apology to prompt"
(9.853–54), and the theatrical metaphors convey the false appearance
that she presents to Adam, a falsity which his look at once sees through
("How art thou … / Defaced" [9.900–911]) and accepts. Then comes
the scene in which they discover an appetite for their fallen selves and
the exchange of looks becomes lascivious. After their lovemaking "each
other viewing, / Soon found their eyes how opened" (9.1052–53); they
come to themselves and a consciousness of their nakedness in their
guilty exchange of looks.[21]

---

[21] In *Christian Doctrine*, 1.11, in CPW 6:388–89, Milton talks of the loss of the
divine image visible in the human face. In *Comus*, 68–74, the idea that concupiscence
disfigures appears. Both ideas are worked out in *Paradise Lost* in terms of a psychology
of the mutuality of looks. Ricks, 89 and 140, points out the importance of the face in
the imagery of the poem.

Finally in book 10 it comes to the point where in his self-hatred Adam, who in happier times had called Eve "Best image of myself and dearer half" (5.95), calls her "serpent," as if she had taken on the shape of his sin, a metaphor that recalls the horrible complicity of looks between Satan and Sin.[22]

In *Jerusalem Delivered*, Rinaldo is shown as losing himself when he sees himself as a reflection of Armida. He can only recover himself by returning to the stern self-regard of the Christian hero. But in Milton's universe one finds oneself in mutuality. That at least is part of what he shows. There is, however, that other part in which self-regard is approved, and that cuts across the ideal of mutuality in a perplexing way, particularly in the domestic relations of Adam and Eve. On the one hand, God seems to endorse Adam's ideal of human society as a mutual relation of equals in which friendship as equality combines with love as an interchange of selves.[23] But at the same time Eve is not an equal in the ordinary sense of the word. Eve is Adam's image, but it is not said that he is hers. Notions of domestic hierarchy seem to cancel the way in which the selves of Adam and Eve are given to each other and in insisting on what is owed to a man, not his wife, to leave room for an ethic of heroic self-regard. The two ideals work against each other. But because each is strongly present, Milton's treatment of temptation and fall is more interesting than Tasso's. Adam faces a choice more complicated than one between reason and appetite. Eve is part of himself, not as a personification of his sensuality or even of his desire for companionship, but as another person, who gives him back the image of himself. He is called to discriminate between objects outside himself in the field of this world, not to make war on himself. Moreover, Eve's temptation is as interesting as Adam's, and the fall

---

[22] See 2.764, "Thyself in me thy perfect image viewing." Milton was perhaps recalling the iconographical motif of the serpent with the woman's face reflecting Eve's, such as can be seen in Raphael's painting of the fall, but displaced it for psychological and mimetic probability.

[23] Adam asks for an equal ("Among unequals what society / Can sort"), and God seems to endorse this Renaissance and classical idea of "amicitia aequalitas" (see Erasmus, *Adages*, 1.1 to 1.5, trans. Margaret Mann Philips, *Collected Works of Erasmus* [Toronto: Univ. of Toronto Press, 1982], 31:31). But both the narrator and Raphael insist on Eve's inferiority.

involves them together; it is not something going on separately in each of them.[24]

At the same time Milton gives self-regard an inward turn. Besides representing guilt in corrupted mutuality, he shows it as a lethal pursuit of the self toward death. Of this, there is a hint in *Jerusalem Delivered*, not in *Rinaldo*, where Tasso is not greatly concerned with the motions of guilt and repentance, but in Tancred. Tancred has the misfortune to plunge a sword into the bosom of his love, Clorinda. He is prostrated by guilt. The official view, expressed by Peter the Hermit, is that his love is sinful; the grief he feels is an expression of that love and so at once sin and punishment of sin (12.87). To this Tancred listens and rouses himself as far as is compatible with gallantry and sensibility. But the Hermit seems rather to have deflected him than brought him to repent the real source of his grief. Like other loves in the poem, Tancred's has typically expressed itself as hate, and what he laments is not loss of his love but murder, however accidental. His grief is a guilt that pursues him toward death, "A wofull monster of vnhappie loue" (12.76): "Swift from my selfe I ronne, my selfe I feare, / Yet still my hell within my selfe I beare" (12.77).[25] That in its succinct, if undeveloped, way points toward the great soliloquies of guilt and self-hate in *Paradise Lost*.

In his first two soliloquies in book 4, Satan is moved by an impulse of love toward the God-like sun and the image of God in man. But this reflects painfully on himself and in turning to hate drives him inwards into the self experienced as an abyss:

> Which way I fly is hell; myself am hell;
> And in the lowest deep a lower deep

---

[24] This is not an answer to the argument of David Aers and Bob Hodge, "Rational Burning: Milton on Sex and Marriage," *MS* 13 (1979): 3–33, that Milton suppresses and distorts the relationship of Adam and Eve in important ways. But it is to claim that Milton did grasp "that the life and development of individuals depends unequivocally on social reciprocity, that the individual can only become a human individual through social relationships" (Aers and Hodge, 12). Milton's realization of this insight may have been imperfect but to have realized it with the intensity he does in places is a remarkable thing in a neoclassical epic.

[25] Tasso has "Temero me medesmo, e, da me stesso / Sempre fuggendo, avro me sempre apresso" ("I fear myself and always flying from myself I am always close to myself") which, like Fairfax's splendid embroidery, looks forward to "Which way shall I fly / Infinite wrath, and infinite despair? / Which way I fly is hell; myself am hell" (4.73–75).

Still threatening to devour me opens wide.
                        (4.75-77)

This guilty process takes the form not only of a continuing fall into the
self as hell but of the discovery of death as a deformed image of oneself.
So when Satan approaches Death at Hell's gates, Death approaches
Satan; Death swells and Satan grows like a comet, and each confronts
the other with matching looks and gestures. The point seems to be that
Death, "the meagre shadow" (10.264), is an unrecognizably deformed
reflection of Satan. He is at least a reproduction of Satan upon Sin, we
learn. This is allegory, but it has its counterpart in Adam's soliloquy in
book 10, where Milton represents a wretched confrontation with oneself
as a human action.

Unlike Satan, who is defiant, even in despair, Adam is all prostra-
tion and self-accusation and so in him the pursuit of the self in self-
hatred toward death is undisguised. In him, the self-involved process of
negation takes the form of blame. Consciousness of the self he has lost
forces on him the consciousness of a self utterly execrable. He begins by
mourning the loss of "this new glorious world, and me so late / The
glory of that glory" (10.712-22) and his fall into a condition in which
he cannot meet "the face / of God" (10.723-24). The reflection of what
he has lost brings on a sense of the self as "Accurst of blessed"
(10.723). Part of the glory in Paradise was to have been his becoming
the father of a race of fellow human beings. But now that happy multi-
plication of himself turns on him, "for what can I increase / Or multiply but curses on my head?" (10.731-32). The process of reversal upon
the self, for which Milton has a vocabulary of "reflux," "recoil," "re-
dounding," reduces Adam to seeing himself at the center of a universe
not returning up through him to its creator in praise but rather returning upon himself as a center of cursing:[26]

                             all from me
        Shall with a fierce reflux on me redound,
        On me as on their natural centre light
        Heavy, though in their place.        (10.738-41)

His thoughts circle in helpless involution continually returning to this

---

[26] On the center of the universe see Fowler, note to 10.740-41.

intense self-execration. Like Satan, he experiences a continuing fall from hell to hell within himself:

> O conscience into what abyss of fears
> And horrors hast thou driven me; out of which
> I find no way, from deep to deeper plunged.
>
> (10.842-44)

And like Satan too, he finds himself horribly involved with death. As he pursues himself downward, he naturally asks for death as extinction, only to discover a guilty fear that

> Comes thundering back with dreadful revolution
> On my defenceless head; both death and I
> Am found eternal, and incorporate both.
>
> (10.814-16)

Death has become part of himself and also, as he goes on, part of those multiplications of himself, his children.

From this despair, Adam is turned by Eve, who interposes between him and himself. Though he begins by directing the hate he has felt for himself upon her, she brings him to relent "Towards her, his life so late" (10.941), and with that to relent towards himself. But it is not necessary in a comparison with Tasso's treatment of self-regard to follow that process of recovery in detail.

One's first impression of how Milton's representation of the motions of the will stands toward Tasso's is that *Paradise Lost* displays a much more inward understanding of how people work. And that seems to me a sound enough generalization. It is striking, though, that Milton's representation of choice has much more to do with a world in which other selves have part than does Tasso's. The imagery of the reflection of one self in another that Milton elaborates on does give a subjective slant to dealings between selves. But at the same time that it brings out an inward involvement between people, it stresses that they do not live in solipsistic moral worlds but become themselves in communication with other selves. If *Jerusalem Delivered* has not quite escaped the self-enclosed, platonizing moral psychology of the kind to be found in Erasmus's *Enchiridion*, it is not, I hope, a wild exaggeration to suggest that in some ways *Paradise Lost* looks forward to the analysis of volition in *Middlemarch*, where the choices reveal inward impulses of the individual precisely as they bear on others.

With the representation of guilt we do enter on self-enclosure. That is implied by guilt itself. Even here, though, what comes out from the comparison is not necessarily Milton's greater inwardness; the strained sexuality of Tasso's epic, after all, carries with it a powerful subjective charge. It is rather that Milton enormously develops the psychology of self-pursuit, so succinctly touched on in Tancred. In doing this he was partly bringing to bear the scheme of the divine image, which runs through his poem. The self-regard of guilt with both Satan and Adam is a consciousness of having lost God's regard, and willingly or helplessly they see their self-images become deformed and death-bound. But the self-regard of the epic hero also enters into the loss of the divine image. I have perhaps taken too dismissive a line with the human possibilities of heroic narcissism. At least where Milton elaborates on its inversion as self-execration, the self-regard of the hero does provide a rich moral psychology. And whether treating the reflexiveness of the self in others or its collapse upon itself in guilt, Milton seems to have gone beyond ideal imitation with its attempt to work on the reader morally through heroic self regard and turned the epic toward more commanding ways of representing what people are like. If we are to speak of "Copernican revolutions," this, not his transformation of Christian heroism, is what I should point to.

University of Stirling

ROBERT L. ENTZMINGER

# The Politics of Love
# in Tasso's Aminta *and* Milton's Comus

ILTON'S COMUS HAS PROVED AS OFTEN to be a vexation to
critics as a delight, and much of its problematic character
derives from the matter of genre. Milton himself called the
piece simply *A Maske*, but it is by common consent a masque of a
curious kind. Like virtually all his poems, *Comus* is a composite, deriving a large measure of its stylistic richness from such authors as Spenser, Shakespeare, and Jonson, and incorporating elements characteristic
of a number of genres other than the masque as well. Many of these
resonances have been noted and fully explored, but one that has received only cursory attention is the debt to pastoral drama, an Italian
import that achieved its greatest popularity at precisely the same time
*Comus* was being written, and that addressed itself to the same aristocratic audience to whom Milton owed his commission. In particular,
*Comus* reveals a special debt to Tasso's *Aminta*, the source and paradigm for later Italian and English plays, but the relationship is not a
simple one. Like the masque itself, pastoral drama was designed to
satisfy a social and political agenda from which Milton in the 1630s was
becoming increasingly alienated, and just as in *Comus* he expands the
scope and possibilities of the masque beyond the bounds of its original
purposes, so he also undertakes the rewriting of pastoral drama, transforming its politics in the process.

## I

More than the typical seventeenth-century masque, *Comus* introduces
dramatic elements into its pastoral setting, and it is this conjunction of
masque and drama which has proved troublesome. To Samuel Johnson
*Comus* was just dramatic enough for him to wish it more so, and he

criticized it, among other reasons, for its breaches of dramatic decorum.[1] Don Cameron Allen, on the contrary, has found it too dramatic
already, complaining that its greater length and intensity disqualify it
from the category to which Milton, whether casually or combatively,
assigned it.[2] These and other divergences from an assumed generic
norm have prompted a number of recent attempts to define its character
more precisely by attaching adjectives such as "transcendental," "Puritan," "reformation," or "anti-Laudian."[3] But the fault, perhaps, is less
in the work than in a neoclassical conception of genre more rigid and
narrow than the Renaissance would recognize. In practice if not always
in theory, Renaissance writers tended to think of genre in inclusionist
terms. Sometimes the result was a genuine hybrid, Guarini's pastoral
tragicomedy being a prime example. More frequently, though, elements
of one kind were routinely, if silently, incorporated into particular
examples of other kinds. Sidney scorned the former route as mongrel-
izing, but as Rosalie Colie has shown, he allowed the latter in the
Apologie and produced with the Arcadia a model of the genera mista.[4]
Milton's own works, from the heroic sonnets to the encyclopedic epic,
consistently verify Colie's argument, and Comus proves no exception.
Where Johnson in calling it "a drama in the epick style" meant like
Allen to criticize its mixture of kinds, a contemporary of Milton's found
in its generic complexity a cause for praise. Lacking Johnson's hindsight
as well as his neoclassical tastes, Sir Henry Wotton wrote in a letter to
the author, "I should much commend the Tragical part, if the Lyrical

[1] Samuel Johnson, The Lives of the English Poets, in The Works of Samuel Johnson,
LL.D. (1825; repr. New York, 1970), 7:123.

[2] Don Cameron Allen, The Harmonious Vision: Studies in Milton's Poetry (Baltimore: Johns Hopkins, 1954; enlarged ed. 1970), 31.

[3] See Cedric C. Brown, John Milton's Aristocratic Entertainments (Cambridge:
Cambridge Univ. Press, 1985); Angus Fletcher, The Transcendental Masque: An Essay
on Milton's Comus (Ithaca: Cornell Univ. Press, 1971); Maryann Cale McGuire,
Milton's Puritan Masque (Athens: Univ. of Georgia Press, 1983); Leah S. Marcus, The
Politics of Mirth: Jonson, Herrick, Milton, Marvell, and the Defense of Old Holiday
Pastimes (Chicago: Univ. of Chicago Press, 1986), 169–212; and David Norbrook,
Poetry and Politics in the English Renaissance (London: Oxford Univ. Press, 1984),
235–85.

[4] Sir Philip Sidney, An Apology for Poetry, ed. Forrest G. Robinson (Indianapolis,
1970), 77; Rosalie L. Colie, The Resources of Kind: Genre Theory in the Renaissance
(Berkeley: Univ. of California Press, 1973), 20–28.

did not ravish me with a certain Dorique delicacy in your Songs and Odes."[5] And if Wotton was untroubled by Milton's development of dramatic possibility in the masque, its exploitation in a specifically pastoral setting must have seemed particularly unremarkable, for pastoral drama in the 1630s was an especially fashionable form.

Pastoral drama owes its inception to Italy, and much of its impact in England is traceable to two preeminent Italian models, Tasso's *Aminta* and Guarini's *Il Pastor Fido*. First performed in Ferrara in 1573, the *Aminta* was translated into English in 1587 by Abraham Fraunce, who relied not on the original but on Thomas Watson's Latin translation of 1585. *Il Pastor Fido*, published in 1590, was translated in 1602, and this work like Fraunce's went through a number of editions. Subsequently the form was imitated by Samuel Daniel, in the *Queen's Arcadia* (1605) and *Hymen's Triumph* (1614), and adapted by Fletcher in *The Faithful Shepherdess* of 1609.[6] Guarini's influence, at least, was sufficiently felt in 1606 for so alert a monitor of literary fashion as Lady Would-be to remark to Volpone while brandishing a copy of *Il Pastor Fido*:

> All our English writers,
> I mean such as are happy in the Italian,
> Will deign to steal out of this author mainly;
> Almost as much as from Montaignié;
> He has so modern and facile a vein,
> Fitting the time, and catching the court-ear.[7]

Yet in this if in little else, Lady Would-be is ahead of her time, for the interest in the form under James was at best modest. In fact, despite Jonson's praise to Drummond, that Fletcher's tragicomedy was "well done" (*Conv.* 600), its debut was a disaster. In his dedicatory poem

[5] Henry Wotton, in *The Life and Letters of Sir Henry Wotton*, ed. Logan Pearsall Smith, 2 vols. (1907; repr. Oxford, 1966), 2:381.

[6] See Walter W. Greg, *Pastoral Poetry and Pastoral Drama* (London, 1906); and David Orr, *Italian Renaissance Drama in England Before 1625: The Influence of Erudita Tragedy, Comedy, and Pastoral on Elizabethan and Jacobean Drama* (Chapel Hill: Univ. of North Carolina Press, 1970).

[7] Ben Jonson, *Volpone* (1.4.87–92); in *Ben Jonson*, ed. Ian Donaldson (Oxford: Oxford Univ. Press, 1985). Subsequent references to this edition will be cited by work and line or page number.

Jonson acknowledges that the audience "had, before / They saw it half, damned thy whole play, and more" (Ungathered Verse no. 8, lines 7-8). Under Charles, however, the popularity of the genre accelerated, and Henry Reynolds's re-translation of the *Aminta* in 1628 was the first indication of a new level of interest that reached its peak in the early 1630s. In a posthumous revival of 1634, Fletcher's play finally achieved the success Jonson predicted for it, following the similarly enthusiastic reception in the previous year of Walter Montagu's *The Shepherd's Paradise* and Thomas Randolph's *Amyntas*. Though it was never performed and cannot be positively dated, *The Sad Shepherd*, Jonson's incomplete attempt at the genre, almost certainly is a product of this enthusiasm as well, as is Joseph Rutter's *The Shepherd's Holiday* (1635) and Abraham Cowley's *Love's Riddle* (1638), among others. A kind of drama that was by and large too languorous and refined to catch the ear of the boisterous Jacobean court had found an appreciative audience and a sponsor in the sophisticated, "Continental" court of Charles and Henrietta Maria.

In literary terms the distance between masque and pastoral drama is easily negotiated. Both typically employ mythology, rely on Neoplatonic philosophy for their themes and resolutions, and offer an idealized version of the courtly audience to whom they were primarily addressed. More important, however, is the social function which produced these common characteristics. Like the masque, pastoral drama is inherently political, its aesthetic refinement functioning to promote a vision of society which places its patrons at the center. Louis Montrose's description of Elizabethan pastoral serves equally well to characterize Caroline pastoral drama: "The Neoplatonic affinities of Renaissance court pastoral inevitably involve a transposition of social categories into metaphysical ones, a sublimation of politics into aesthetics. These pastoral processes are intertwined with the growth of autocratic government, the concentration of power in the person of a prince."[8] Though Shakespeare's lovers often challenge the social order as embodied in their elders, the older generation in Tasso and his followers tend to be benign hermits or shepherd-kings who recognize the appropriateness of the sexual pairings that become the means of accommodating everyone within the

---

[8] Louis Adrian Montrose, "Of Gentlemen and Shepherds: The Politics of Elizabethan Pastoral Form," *ELH* 50 (1983): 46-47.

existing social structure. Presenting the love intrigues of Golden Age shepherds, the genre offers a sentimentalizing image of an innocent past whose only real concern is the satisfaction, under socially acceptable and philosophically justifiable circumstances, of sexual passion.

These comedic pairings moreover reinforce a set of symbols through which the Stuart monarchs presented themselves. If Elizabeth the Virgin Queen meant in claiming to be pledged only to her country to emphasize the completeness of her dedication, James drew upon the analogy of the family to justify his authority. As the husband to his country he functioned, employing the traditional metaphor of marriage, as the head to the body; and as father he was not simply the loving *paterfamilias* but patriarch.[9] Charles and Henrietta Maria were even more concerned to offer their own marriage as the symbol and model for a harmoniously ordered society, and the pastoral drama they sponsored adheres to this political agenda. Thus as they offer the opportunity for the expression of refined sentiment and pledges of eternal devotion, these plays also present as the ideal human community a hierarchical social order which works to satisfy the deepest longings of its members. But where James employed the iconography of the family in an aggressive propagandistic campaign, Charles appears himself to have been seduced by the ideal, for it at once provided a model of an attractively harmonious society and offered him a means of escaping into a simplified past, substituting the rarefied aesthetic pleasures of the shepherds for an engagement with the growing political turmoil around him. Increasingly besieged by dissenting voices, Charles ultimately gave over the attempt to persuade his subjects, resting content to find presented on the stage a vision of unity and concord that the nation at large was in the process of disowning.

It is not surprising then that Milton, preparing in 1634 his compliment to a member of Charles's Privy Council on the occasion of his assuming an important political office, should turn for his example to those works and their Italian antecedents which were currently finding so favorable an audience at court, and the early reception of *Comus* confirms its appeal to current aristocratic tastes. Henry Lawes published *Comus* in 1637 the more efficiently to meet the requests for copies, and

---

[9] See Jonathan Goldberg, *James I and the Politics of Literature: Jonson, Shakespeare, Donne, and Their Contemporaries* (Baltimore: Johns Hopkins Univ. Press, 1983), 85–112, 141–47.

the circumstances of its coming to the attention of Wotton likewise suggest a contemporaneous perception of its links to courtly pastoral drama. Wotton, who advised Milton on his Italian itinerary and provided him with letters of introduction which surely facilitated his entry into the company of many of those Italians whose good opinion he so valued, praised the excellence of *Comus* in a letter which Milton reprinted when he published the work in his 1645 *Poems*. Though Milton had himself sent Wotton a copy, the latter had already encountered it, without knowing the identity of its author, in the 1637 edition provided him by "our common friend Mr. R," together with a posthumous collection of Thomas Randolph's work which included *Amyntas*.[10] If the pairing is more than arbitrary, it must suggest that for Wotton's correspondent *Comus* bore an affinity to Randolph's play close enough for them to be commended in the same gesture, and that their common Italian heritage might appeal especially to the former ambassador to Venice.

## II

Despite these indications that it was perceived from the beginning in relation to pastoral drama, the connection has not been pursued. Although Mario Praz urged that "Tasso's *Aminta* is the real model" for *Comus*, the suggestion has suffered rather casual dismissal, both by F. T. Prince and by the editors of the *Variorum*.[11] The editors are certainly correct to stress the dissimilarity in "theme and tendency" between *Comus* and the *Aminta*, but as recent researches have shown, *imitatio* is a dialectical rather than an evolutionary process, an active rewriting of one's models and not simply a development of them.[12] In fact, for

---

[10] Wotton, 2:381.

[11] Mario Praz, "Milton and Poussin," in *Seventeenth-Century Studies Presented to Sir Herbert Grierson* (1938; repr. New York, 1967), 202; F. T. Prince, *The Italian Element in Milton's Verse* (Oxford: Oxford Univ. Press, 1954), 66; *Variorum* 2:767. See also Milton's nineteenth-century editor Henry J. Todd, who noted parallels between the prologue of *Comus* and those of both Tasso and Guarini (*The Poetical Works of John Milton*, 7 vols. [2nd ed., 1809; repr. New York, 1970], 2:237); and Watson Kirkconnell, who also lists analogues in Tasso and Guarini but takes issue with Praz's assertion, in *Awake the Courteous Echo* (Toronto: Univ. of Toronto Press, 1973), 34.

[12] See, for instance, Thomas M. Greene, *The Light in Troy: Imitation and Discovery in Renaissance Poetry* (New Haven: Yale Univ. Press, 1982); and Richard S. Peterson,

Milton Italy itself was first of all a body of historical as well as literary texts, and even before his Italian journey he had acquired a fixed yet complex attitude on the basis of which he was to approach Italian culture. On the one hand openly admiring the grace and elegance achieved by Italy's authors, Milton on the other regarded Italian religion and morality with profound distrust. Though he claims in the *Second Defense* not to have subscribed to the common prejudice that identified Italy as "a refuge or asylum for criminals," he registers no surprise in the discovery that what he knew to be "the lodging-place of *humanitas* and of all the arts of civilization" was at the same time a locale "where so much licence exists" that he had to remain constantly vigilant to resist "the slightest sin or reproach."[13] Fortunately Milton had devised some strategies for dealing with such interpretive ambivalence. One is simply to distinguish the work from the moral character of its author. Though he can praise without reservation those who, like "the two famous renowners of *Beatrice* and *Laura*," enlist their eloquence in the service of virtue, with writers whom he finds "speaking unworthy things of themselves; or unchaste of those names which before they had extoll'd," he is more circumspect: "their art I still applauded, but the men I deplor'd" (*Apology* 1.890). Another strategy, the one for which he argues in *Areopagitica*, involves a willed and thoroughgoing conversion of the work itself to the reader's own purposes. Medieval romances, for instance, "which to many others have bin the fuell of wantonnesse and loose living," become in Milton's misreading an incitement to chastity (*Apology* 1.891). And just as this latter maneuver allowed him to appropriate and recast elements of romance throughout his career, so it also provides the dynamics whereby he assimilated some of the other genres and works which fell short of his standards of moral seriousness.[14]

Of the two primary examples of pastoral drama in the Italian, Guarini's play is the more overtly moralistic and exerted a stronger influence on the English stage as a whole, yet Milton turned rather to Tasso. His preference is based partly on his sense of Tasso as a source

---

*Imitation and Praise in the Poems of Ben Jonson* (New Haven: Yale Univ. Press, 1981), esp. 1–43.

[13] Milton, *Second Defense* (1654), trans. Helen North, CPW 4.1.609, 620; subsequent references to the prose will be cited from this edition.

[14] For Milton's use of romance, see Annabel M. Patterson, "*Paradise Regained*: A Last Chance at True Romance," MS 17 (1983): 187–208.

of worthy models in other genres: he cites with approval Tasso's theory of epic (*Of Ed* 2.404) and includes *La Gerusalemme liberata* among the great models of the kind (*RCG*, 1.813); and his heroic sonnets are indebted to Tasso's example. He gave further evidence of his admiration by paying his respects in Naples to Manso, whose patronage of Tasso and Marino Milton later praised in a Latin poem. In practical terms, Tasso's play offered a more serviceable prototype as well. With its simpler plot, the *Aminta* provided a structural model more easily abbreviated to conform to the strictures of time to which the occasion limited him. Yet for all his admiration of Tasso and the utility of his model, Milton was obliged to resort in his adaptation to the same principle of literary conversion that he was to practice with the related genre of romance. Written originally for the court of Ferrara, the *Aminta* no less than other plays of its kind lent itself to a political program from which Milton in the mid-1630s was becoming increasingly disaffected. He was after all at leisure to accept the commission to write *Comus* because he had deferred taking orders that would have required his pledging an oath of allegiance he found repugnant, and though there may have been other factors involved in his decision, in memory the issue was clearly one of conscience. He had been, he wrote in 1642, "Church-outed by the Prelats" (*RCG* 1.823). Thus it may be that the *Aminta*, like those other English and Italian plays of the genre, served for Milton both as a model to emulate and as a challenge, a stimulus to appropriate and recreate his literary ancestors after an image more congenial to him.

Although courtly pastoral had become in the sixteenth and seventeenth centuries a means of advancing the centralizing policies of its aristocratic patrons, pastoral is always a potentially volatile genre. For if the presentation of an idealized past can reinforce hierarchy, it can also have the opposite effect, the nostalgia turned to an indictment of the present, and for a courtly audience the range of available interpretations must therefore be carefully circumscribed. Montrose argues that with Elizabeth and James, the occasional anticourtly sentiment of pastoral functions simply as "an aspect of courtly or aristocratic culture ... an authorized mode of discontent."[15] But the destabilizing element in pastoral is pervasive and must in most instances be strictly managed in order to control its disruptive potential. In a telling passage of the

---

[15] Montrose, 427.

*Aminta,* Tirsi disabuses Aminta of his admiration for Mopso, recounting how Mopso had warned him away from the city with its "deceitfull
crafty Cittizens" and "evil minded Courtiers."[16] The entire exchange,
including both Mopso's indictment and Tirsi's response, was presumably not a part of the initial production since it first appears in the 1590
Italian edition, at a safe enough distance from the original occasion for
its denunciation of courtly corruption to be innocuous.[17] And when it
does appear, its subversive potential is carefully neutralized. Aware of
the latent capacity of pastoral to be read as a critique of courtly intrigue
and corruption, Tasso counters Mopso's indictment with Tirsi's en-
dorsement, and the only function of the entire passage is at once to
acknowledge the possibility of subversion and then to defuse it. Tirsi's
experience at court, he assures Aminta, has been very different. Welcomed by the Lord "with a benigne, and milde, though grave aspect,"
Tirsi discovers a vision "unvayl'd unclouded" of Phoebus and the
Muses, and as he finds himself transported, his art is transformed.
Though he returns to his pastoral home, he retains "Part of that Spirit;
nor yet sounds my pipe / So lowly as before, but shriller farr, / And
through the woods sings with a trumpets voyce."[18]

*Comus* too addresses the relationship of court to country, but where
Tasso neutralizes the pastoral potential for subversion, Milton insists
upon it. Following Comus in his pastoral disguise, the Lady remarks,
"Shepherd, I take thy word, / And trust thy honest offer'd courtesy, /
Which oft is sooner found in lowly sheds / With smoky rafters, than in
tap'stry Halls / And Courts of Princes, where it first was nam'd, / And
yet is most pretended."[19] Her prejudices here are misapplied, of
course, but they reflect, as John Cox has shown, a growing schism

---

[16] *Torquato Tasso's Aminta Englisht,* att. Henry Reynolds (London, 1628); the
original reads, "gli astuti e scaltri cittadini / E i cortigian malvagi" (1.2.242-43), in
*Opere Minori in Versi di Torquato Tasso,* ed. Angelo Salerti, vol. 3 of 10 (Bologna,
1895). Subsequent quotations will be from the Reynolds translation, with the original
quoted in the notes by act, scene, and line number according to the Salerti edition.

[17] C. P. Brand, *Torquato Tasso: A Study of the Poet and of His Contribution to
English Literature* (Cambridge: Cambridge Univ. Press, 1965), 38-39.

[18] "Che, con fronte benigna insieme e grave," "Senza vel, senza nube," "Parte di
quello spirto: ne gia suona / La mia sampogna umil, come soleva, / Ma di voce piu
altera e piu sonora, / Emula de le trombe, empie le selve" (1.2.291, 296, 309-12).

[19] Milton, *Comus* (322-26), in Hughes; subsequent references will be cited parenthetically, the dialogue by line number, the stage directions by page number.

between the court and the country, with virtue being attributed almost exclusively to the latter.[20] The Lady, in fact, assumes the stance here of the naive viewer of courtly entertainment, but she quickly learns better. Accepting the simplicity of Comus's disguise at face value, she finds its humble innocence to be a façade concealing decadent sophistication, the shepherd himself both prince and revels-master. Holding her captive at his Palace "set out with all manner of deliciousness; soft Music, Tables spread with all dainties" (p. 105), he plots to make her his queen and offers to display her in a masque: "Beauty is nature's brag, and must be shown / In courts, at feasts, and high solemnities / Where most may wonder at the workmanship" (745-47).

More important, though, than Milton's reversal of the implications of the court-country confrontation is the contrasting way in which the Lady's virtue is treated. In its concentration on sexual love, even domesticated and idealized as it tends to be, pastoral drama exalts the passions rather than bringing them strictly to the heel of reason, and, almost universally, chastity is regarded as an aberration. The genre works systematically to undermine the stance of those who seek, especially on moral grounds, to remain apart from their peers, excluding themselves from this generous order and consequently defying nature and threatening to frustrate the happy ending. In fact, it is Sylvia's attachment to the cult of Diana that provides the primary obstacle to an early resolution of Tasso's play, for even after Aminta saves her from the Satyr's attack she continues to reject his devotions. It is only when she finally recognizes the merit of Aminta, miraculously delivered from a suicide attempt provoked by the belief that she has been killed by a wolf, that she relents and permits the inevitable resolution to occur.

Milton, on the contrary, gives us a heroine with no worthy suitor, and in place of Amore as the presiding deity he substitutes the Attendant Spirit, an Orphic figure whose concern is not to advance the cause of true love but to protect and reward virtue. Orpheus, of course, is not a figure necessarily alien to the thematics of love, for his relationship to Eurydice is the subject of early pastoral drama on which the first operas

---

[20] John D. Cox, "Poetry and History in Milton's Country Masque," *ELH* 44 (1977): 622–40. For a reading which sees in those lines, and in other places in the masque, the expression of a more radical political agenda, see Michael Wilding, *Dragon's Teeth: Literature in the English Revolution* (Oxford: Oxford Univ. Press, 1987), 28–88.

are based. Even in treatments of his ascetic life after losing Eurydice, he is interpreted as the prophet of a heavenly love, a singer of the removed mysteries that order and move the universe in harmony.[21] Milton in "Elegy VI" sets the way of Orphic asceticism against Bacchic excess as equally appropriate routes to poetic inspiration, but in *Comus* complementarity has become antagonism. Despite his occupying in terms of the plot a role analogous to that of the lustful Satyr in the *Aminta*, Comus in fact resembles more closely Tasso's Amore himself. A supernatural being, he advances the cause of passion through trickery and illusion, and the Orphic Attendant Spirit, instead of being subordinate as Tirsi and Elpino are in the *Aminta*, is Comus's chief adversary and ultimate vanquisher. Indeed Tasso does more than simply subordinate; he discredits. The most thoroughgoing Orpheus-figure in the *Aminta* after all is Mopso, "who knowes the hid language of birds, / And understands the force of herbs and founts,"[22] but as his account of the court is denied, the whole Orphic mode is called into question. Thus while courtly pastoral drama neutralizes and absorbs figures whose moral stance exists as an implicit indictment of the values of their society, Milton not only tolerates but actively promotes obedience to a more strict standard of behavior.

The political sensitivity of the Lady's virtue is apparent in the textual variants of *Comus*. Chastity or virginity is exalted in three passages as *Comus* is typically printed: one spoken by the Elder Brother ("'Tis chastity, my brother,..." 420-75), and two by the Lady ("O welcome pure-ey'd Faith...," 205-20; and "... the sage / And serious doctrine of Virginity...," 780-89). The Brother's speech and the first of the Lady's exist in the original state of the Trinity MS, probably the earliest extant version, as well as in the printed versions. The Bridgewater MS, however, taken to represent the production text, retains only the Brother's speech.[23] Although other explanations have been offered for

---

[21] See Edgar Wind, *Pagan Mysteries in the Renaissance* (1958; rev. ed. New York: Harper and Row, 1968), 17-18; and *Orpheus: The Metamorphoses of a Myth*, ed. John Warden (Toronto: Univ. of Toronto Press, 1982), esp. Timothy J. McGee, "Orfeo and Euridice, the First Two Operas," 63-81, and Patricia Vicari, "The Triumph of Art, the Triumph of Death: Orpheus in Spenser and Milton," 207-30.

[22] "Mopso, ch' intende il parlar de gli augelli / E le virtu de l' erbe e de le fonti" (1.2.214-15).

[23] See E. S. Sprott, *John Milton: A Maske: The Earlier Versions* (Toronto: Univ. of Toronto Press, 1973).

the de-emphasis of chastity in the production, it is likely that its presentation as an absolute virtue was softened because for an aristocratic audience it was thought inappropriate: the Lady's speeches appeal to a source of meaning outside society, and they entertain the prospect of permanent exclusion from a community whose goal and model is an ideal marriage. The Brother's speech was allowed to remain, on the other hand, because its terms conform to those of the courtly cult of love rather than to the ascetic ideal the Lady affirms. His faith in chastity's power, as Maryann Cale McGuire has shown, echoes an emphasis in courtly drama under the Queen's sponsorship on the Britomart-like qualities of the chaste heroine.[24] But in these plays chastity is provisional, always contemplating marriage as its aim; and in any case, subsequent events belie the Brother's faith. Although her purity is unassailable, the physical danger is real, and neither she nor heaven can repel it as easily as he expects.

Even without the Lady's speeches, however, it is clear that *Comus* works in a direction counter to that of the masque and the court drama, for as the Brother's easy idealism illustrates, court productions assert a direct affinity between the real and the ideal, between what is and what ought to be. *Comus*, however, affirms throughout a virtue that is inward, not capable of being fully realized either in Comus's Wood or in terms of the socializing pressures the conventional plot offers. In her resistance to Comus's arguments, the Lady comes to rely less on the support of what she can see, more on what she believes, despite present evidence to the contrary. And by the time she comes to refute Comus's argument, she appeals to a Nature the Wood does not acknowledge in order to support a morality whose only apparent sustenance is her own conviction. The most serious challenge to the conventions of the drama, however, has occurred before she presents her case, at the beginning of the temptation scene. The Neoplatonic foundation of pastoral drama, like that of the masque, rests on the belief that ideal form and particular embodiment are sacramentally related, immutably connected. The means by which the Lady deprives Comus of his victory, however, works at the same time to contradict this assumption. "Fool, do not boast," she tells him, "Thou canst not touch the freedom of my mind / With all thy charms, although this corporal rind / Thou hast im-

---

[24] McGuire, 130-66.

manacl'd, while Heav'n sees good" (662–65). Withdrawing her mind from her body, she demonstrates that not the outer form but the inner commitment determines one's suitability to represent an ideal. As Milton will later question the eternal character of marriage, church government, and kingship, so here he suggests that the Lady's beauty is no more an index to her virtue than her noble birth is a guarantor of her uprightness. Rather, in a world where evil exercises such potency, nobility is a matter not of lineage but of individual acts of will, capable always either of renewal or of suspension. And the Lady, rather than having to surrender her devotion to chastity in order to become a full member of her society, instead earns her assimilation through her refusal to compromise.

Thus, as he supplants Amore with a Spirit who sanctions sexual abstinence and offers a heroine who embodies it "while Heav'n sees good" (665), Milton accomplishes a reorientation of the genre. It is no longer what Renato Poggioli calls a "pastoral of love," sentimental, nostalgic, and above all politically conservative.[25] Instead *Comus* is an example of what might be termed "prophetic pastoral," a type which derives from Christian readings of Vergil's Fourth Eclogue and becomes associated in the late Middle Ages and during the Reformation with radical social and political programs.[26] We get a sample of prophetic utterance in the Elder Brother's grim assurance that "evil . . . shall be in eternal restless change / Self-fed and self-consum'd" (593–97), but it is in the epilogue, spoken by the Attendant Spirit, that we are presented with the positive counterpart to the Elder Brother's apocalyptic vision. There we see at last an image of pastoral harmony expressed in terms of sexual concord, but it is presented as a reward for suffering and dedication, and it is located firmly in an unspecified future. Moreover, even its pleasures are incomplete. Adonis after all is still convalescing from his wound, and the birth of Youth and Joy is only anticipated. Sexual satisfaction then becomes, as in *Lycidas*, a symbol for the rewards of

---

[25] Poggioli, *The Oaten Flute: Essays on Pastoral Poetry and the Pastoral Ideal* (Cambridge, Mass.: Harvard Univ. Press, 1975), 42–63.

[26] Peter Lindenbaum, in *Changing Landscapes: Anti-Pastoral Sentiment in the English Renaissance* (Athens: Univ. of Georgia Press, 1986), includes Milton among the writers of what he calls anti-pastoral literature, but I believe "prophetic pastoral" more accurately describes the peculiarly Miltonic appropriation and recasting of pastoral materials.

virtue and not itself the goal toward which society's energies are directed.

It is further significant that the apocalyptic section of the epilogue
was not included in the 1634 production, nor is it in the original
manuscript. It first appeared in the privately printed 1637 text along
with the second, and more passionate, of the Lady's affirmations of "the
Sun-clad power of Chastity" and "the sage / And serious doctrine of
Virginity" (782, 786–87). It is as if Milton, recognizing even more
clearly by this time the inadequacy of Royalist policies, wished to assert
with increased force the need to stand apart from a corrupt social order
even as he underscores the prospect of future reward for such steadfastness. And the placement of *Comus* in the 1645 *Poems* brings this
tendency to its culmination. Following *Arcades* and *Lycidas* to conclude
the English portion of the volume, *Comus* completes the pastoral
segment of the collection, and while *Arcades* is a more or less conventional masque, both *Comus* and *Lycidas* show Milton's development of
the pastoral capacity for political critique. As a conclusion at once to the
work and to the section, the epilogue carries a political message resonant with Milton's millenarian optimism of the early 1640s: while like
the courtly pastoral drama it presents an idealized vision, it locates its
paradise not in a remote and irrecoverable past but in a millennial
future whose imminence its readers are urged to anticipate.

Rhodes College

MICHAEL R. G. SPILLER

# "Per Chiamare e Per Destare": Apostrophe in Milton's Sonnets

MILTON'S ITALIAN JOURNEY BEGAN LONG BEFORE he sailed for the Continent in the late spring of 1638. It seems likely that his father arranged for him to study the language, along with French and Hebrew, in the early 1620s—under whose instructions we do not know. By 1629 or 1630 he was reading Italian poetry, and purchased for himself, for the quite considerable sum of tenpence, a copy of Giovanni della Casa's *Rime et Prose* (Venice, 1563).[1] Of all the sonneteers of the Cinquecento, della Casa is probably the one whom, with hindsight, we should single out as the most congenial to Milton in tone and temperament; at the time of the purchase, however, Milton was probably in quest, not so much of the very great *gravità* for which Tasso praised della Casa,[2] as of the idiom of the "lingua di cui si vanta Amore" to impress his friend Emilia. (It is possible that it was from della Casa's sonnet "Amore, per lo tuo calle a morte vassi" that Milton obtained the "varco"/"parco" rhyme which enabled him elegantly to conceal Emilia's name in his very first Italian sonnet—the word "varco" is not, after all, a very common one.) However, Milton chose not to imitate in his Emilian sonnets the tone of proud and lonely suffering that della Casa adopts: his love is full of springtime enthusiasm, and an engaging sense of superiority in having sufficiently mastered the language of the Arno to praise his lady in accomplished verse. His most obviously della Casan moment comes after that, in the "Petrarchan stanza" of the Trinity MS., when his meditation upon "Time, the subtle thief of youth" catches more nearly

---

[1] Maurice Kelly, "Milton's Dante-Della Casa-Varchi Volume," *Bulletin of the New York Public Library* 66 (1962): 499–504.

[2] *Lirici del Cinquecento*, ed. Daniele Ponchiroli (Turin: Unione Tipographico, 1958), 311.

than any other of his Italian verses the severe self-reckoning, the regret over the inexorable advance of time, and the submission to the will of God, that occur in many of the older della Casa's sonnets.

Whatever his models may have been (and we are ignorant of how much, and when, he had read in Dante, Petrarch, the sonnets of Tasso, and the other writer whose works he may have owned early in his career, Benedetto Varchi),[3] one stylistic mannerism appears throughout his sonnet writing: the use of the apostrophe.[4] Fifteen of Milton's twenty-three sonnets apostrophize the addressee in the first line, and in thirteen of these, the addressee's name or appellation is the first word. (The two in which it is not are "Per certo i bei vostr'occhi, Donna mia" and "Avenge, O Lord, thy slaughter'd Saints.") This is a very high proportion: Petrarch uses the apostrophe less than fifty times in the *Rime*, Shakespeare twelve times in his *Sonnets*, Sidney—commonly thought a very direct and conversational sonneteer—some forty times in the 108 poems of *Astrophel and Stella*, and Spenser twenty times in the *Amoretti*. Della Casa shows no particular fondness for it. The English sonneteer who most often resorts to Miltonic apostrophe is, not surprisingly, the poet whose conception of the function of the sonnet was closest to Milton's, William Wordsworth, from whose sonnets come the most notorious of English apostrophes, "Jones! as from Calais southward you and I...."

An apostrophe calls into existence another presence alongside those of speaker and reader, another and temporary hearer, whence of course come the sense embedded in the etymology that the speaker's attention has been diverted from a reader to a hitherto uninvolved bystander, in what Milton's nephew, Edward Phillips, called "a converting of one's speech from one party to another."[5] A certain interruptive violence is often thereby introduced: as Puttenham says in his *Arte of English Poesie* (1589),

---

[3] Milton's purchase of the della Casa volume is recorded on its title page: December 1629. Kelly has shown that Milton owned the Varchi volume, but it is not known when he purchased it.

[4] Used here in the sense of a direct address to some person, place, or thing, without the often attached qualification that the address involved turning away from a previous addressee. But see n. 6 and the accompanying text.

[5] Edward Phillips, *A New World of English Words* (1658), s.v. "apostrophe," sig. c2v.

Many times when we have runne a long race in our tale spoken to the hearers, we do sodainly flye out and either speake or exclaime at some other person or thing. . . .

And yet when apostrophe is employed as the single or dominant trope, as it is for example in *Lycidas*, which has nine apostrophes in its twelve verse paragraphs, the figure is not so much violent as profoundly social: it acts to summon bystanders or presences to an event, where the reader makes only one of a group. Roman Jakobson has offered the term, "split addressee"[6] to cover the problematics of offering the reader a poem formally addressed to someone else (the reader is only noticed in the very last verse paragraph of *Lycidas*). This may be extended to larger groupings of poems, such as Petrarch's *Rime*, in which Petrarch begins by apostrophizing the general reader, "Voi ch'ascoltate in rime sparse il suono . . . ," but then addresses the particular sonnets directly to named friends, such as Sennuccio del Bene. The reader's privileged status is attenuated, and he or she returns back into the mimesis of a specific social utterance, into the group of persons whom the poem or collection of poems addresses.

In addressing further this very social trope, of which Milton was so fond, it may be useful to distinguish between weak and strong apostrophe, and again between apostrophe and invocation. The distinction between weak and strong apostrophe depends on the figure of *prosopopoeia*, so commonly associated with it in the rhetorical manuals of the time. When the speaker addresses a figure not properly human, using a *prosopopoeia* to anthropomorphise it, we have a weak apostrophe, in which the "feigning of a person"[7] is patent; the more vigorous the *prosopopoeia*, the greater the extent to which the addressee is imagined as existing externally apart from speaker and reader, and the stronger the reader's sense of having lost the speaker's attention to another person.

"In Apostrophes are contained invocations,"[8] and we may make note that, whether the apostrophe is weak or strong, whether the addressee is fully human or only feigned to be so, an invocation is an

---

[6] Roman Jakobson, "Linguistics and Poetics," in *Style in Language*, ed. Thomas Sebeok (n.p.: The Technology Press of M.I.T., 1960), 371.

[7] John Smith, *The Mystery of Rhetoric Unveiled* (1567), 157.

[8] Abraham Fraunce, *Arcadian Rhetoric* (1588), sig. F8v.

apostrophe which then invites the addressee to act in some manner
essential to the subject of the poem: for example "Avenge, O Lord, thy
slaughter'd Saints." The addressee is thus a participant in the action. In
Milton's sonnet, "Diodati, e te 'l dirò con maraviglia," on the other
hand, Diodati is merely named as a hearer of or witness to the succeeding statement, and is marginal to the to the poem's content, which
tends therefore to revert back to the reader as addressee. Invocation can
thus be reckoned a strong form of apostrophe, which may itself be
strong or weak, depending on the nature of the addressee, human or
not. Milton and Wordsworth favor strong apostrophe with a preference
for invocation, and the effect is that the reader is marginalized as a
bystander in a social group where the speaker's attention is concentrated
upon someone else for the moment of the poem.

There is no clear Italian source for Milton's devotion to strong
apostrophe, in the sense that we can find a single author who was to
Milton as Milton was to Wordsworth: whom, that is, Milton is known
to have read and in whom the practice was so dominant as certainly
have furnished him with a model. But if we consider the rise of apostrophizing in the sonnet, it has much to do with what is regarded as the
distinctively Italianate use to which Milton put the form.

J. C. Scaliger remarks in his *Poetices libri septem* that *efficacia*, the
power of convincing, is enhanced by various rhetorical strategies:
exclamations, interrogations, and apostrophes all have great efficacy.[9]
The earliest Italian sonnets, the first sonnets of all, by the Sicilian
school of the mid-thirteenth century, are reluctant to employ these
devices. Typically, the octaves of these sonnets relate a state of affairs or
offer one half of a simile: the sestet then may apostrophize the Lady, or
Love, attributing some sort of responsibility or applying the simile to the
poet's condition. In one lively sonnet, however, attributed to the Abbot
of Tivoli, we find the devices of exclamation and apostrophe brought
forward to the first line:

> Oi! Deo d'amore, a te faccio preghera,
> ca m'inteniate s'io chero razone,
> cad io sono tutto fatto a tuo manera,

---

[9] J. C. Scaliger, *Poetices libri septem* (Lyons, 1561), book 3, chap. 27, p. 118.

> aggio cavelli e barba a tua fazone,
> ed ogni parte mio, viso e cera.[10]

Oh! God of Love, I make my prayer to you, that you may hear me if I ask for justice, for I am wholly fashioned in your style: I have a beard and hair like yours, and every bit of me, face and complexion.

It is particularly interesting to note that with this more direct opening goes a lowering of tone—the lofty "maniera aulica" of Sicilian love discourse gives way to a jocular assumption of good fellowship. The sonneteers who follow, such as Rustico di Filippo and Cecco Angiolieri, move the sonnet away from quasi-philosophical musing to "vers de société," roughening it and colloquializing it as they do so. The sonnet begins to function as a small letter, in which, of course, it is essential to identify the addressee:

> Con vostro onore faccio un' invito,
> Ser Giacomo valente, a cui m'inchino. . . .

To your honor I proffer a request, noble Ser Giacomo, to whom I bow. . . .

> Dante Alighier, s'i'so' bon begolardo. . . .
>> (Cecco Angiolieri)
> Dante Alighieri, if I'm a real comic. . . .

The *stilnovisti* may sweeten their style, but they retain the sense of the sonnet as a social communication:

> Dante, un sospiro messagier del core
> subitamente m'assali in dormendo. . . .
>> (Guido Cavalcanti)

Dante, a sigh bringing news from the heart assailed me as I slept. . . .

> Novelle ti so dire, odi, Nerone. . . .
>> (Guido Cavalcanti)
> I've got news for you: listen, Nerone. . . .

---

[10] *The Poetry of Giacomo da Lentino*, ed. Stephen Poplizio (Ann Arbor: University Microfilms, 1980), 233. The second quotation from the Abbot of Tivoli is on p. 249.

And if the letter is a public one, it is necessary to establish one's
audience by calling for attention:

> A voi che ve ne andaste per paura,
> sicuramente potete tornare. . . .
>
> (Rustico di Filippo)

You who fled away for fear, you may now safely return. . . .

> Voi che avete mutate la maniera
> de li piacenti ditti dell'amore. . . .
>
> (Buonagiunta Orbicciani)

You who have changed the style of the pleasant songs of love. . . .

> Voi che per li occhi passaste il core. . . .
>
> (Guido Cavalcanti)

You who through the eyes have reached my heart. . . .

(The *voi che* . . . opening became so usual that three hundred years later
Lorenzo da Ponte used it as a generic signal in that most wonderful of
all Petrarchan spoofs, Cherubino's aria "Voi che sapete" in *The Marriage of Figaro*.)

The writer who, more than any other, confirmed the "letter sonnet"
as a part of the currency of public affairs was Guittone d'Arezzo (1225?-
1294). In both his secular and religious phases, Guittone, like Milton
and Wordsworth, shows a strong desire to challenge the attention of his
addressee, and it was he who developed the technique of the arresting
first line. Now an apostrophe is, grammatically, a vocative, and is thus
parenthetical in the syntax of one's opening line: it can be used to
interrupt, with an effect of immediacy:

> Credo savete ben, Messer Onesto,
> che proceder del fatto il nome dia. . . .
>
> (234)[11]

I think you well know, Messer Onesto, that the name should
emerge from the reality. . . .

---

[11] The sonnet numbers are those in Francesco Egidi's edition, *Le Rime di Guittone
d'Arezzo* (Bari: Laterza, 1940).

> Dett'ho de dir: dirò, gioia gioiosa,
> e credo piaccia voi darmi odienza....
>
> (37)

I have something to say: I shall say it, my joyful joy, and I think
you will be pleased to give me a hearing....

> O tu, om de Bologna, sguarda e sente....
>
> (213)

O thou, man of Bologna, look and realize....

> A te, Montuccio, ed agli altri, il cui nomo
> non gia volentier molt' agio 'n obbrio....
>
> (237)

To you, Montuccio, and the others, whose names I have unwill-
ingly much neglected....

Milton uses the interruptive apostrophe only twice in his sonnets, once
conventionally in "Per certo i bei vostr'occhi, Donna mia," and once
quite tremendously, in "Avenge, O Lord, thy slaughter'd saints"; he
evidently preferred, as did Guittone, to place the apostrophe first,
sounding the name as a call to attention, like an opening chord. It is
possible that the rather contrived interruptive apostrophe of "Per certo
i bei vostr' occhi, Donna mia / Esser non puo che non fian lo mio
sole," drawing attention as it does to the divorce of subject from verb
and thus to the distortion of the word order, may have been suggested
to him by della Casa's liking for a similar effect:

> Il tuo candido fil tosto le amare
> per me, Soranzo mio, Parche troncaro....

The Fates, bitter to me, my Soranzo, have cut your white thread....

> Fuor di man di tiranno a giusto regno,
> Soranzo mio, fuggito in pace or sei....

Fled from the grasp of tyrants to the realm of the just, Soranzo,
you are now at peace....

Delaying the apostrophe and then inserting it to prise apart words
normally conjoined is of course a trick borrowed from Latin, where
word order is not so strongly determinative, and has the effect of

Latinizing della Casa's style, enhancing its *gravità* by echoing the run of elegiacs:

> Multas per gentes et multa per aequora vectus
> advenio has miseras, frater, ad inferias. . . .
>
> By ways remote and distant waters come,
> brother, to thy sad grave-side I am sped. . . .
> (Catullus, trans. Aubrey Beardsley)[12]

However, if he noticed this device and appreciated its weight, Milton chose not to extend its use in his sonnets, but to reserve it for the grandeur of that most wonderfully delayed of all English apostrophes, to the Muse of the opening lines of *Paradise Lost*.

In his sonnets he preferred the simpler approach to his addressee, naming him or her at once. But after the name is sounded, there are two options: the poet may begin at once with his statement, as Milton does in his second sonnet to Cyriack Skinner, thus marginalizing the addressee and returning the reader to a privileged place:

> Cyriack, this three years' day these eyes, though clear
> To outward view of blemish or of spot,
> Bereft of light thir seeing have forgot. . . .

Or, as Milton does in his first sonnet to Cyriac and in every other sonnet which uses an opening apostrophe except his Italian sonnet to Diodati, the poet may extend the apostrophe by attaching a dependant clause to the name, thus making the addressee the focus of at least the octave, and effectively invoking him or her:

> Cyriack, whose Grandsire on the Royal Bench
> Of British *Themis*, with no mean applause
> Pronounc't and in his volumes taught our laws. . . .

This has the effect almost opposite from immediacy: the name is expanded in a kind of *pronominatio*, giving the apostrophized person an honorific, which suggests a ceremonial introduction upon a definite social occasion. The mimesis suggests that the addressee is *not* the main object of attention, since the information given in the dependent clause

---

[12] *The Limits of Art*, ed. Huntingdon Cairns (London: Routledge and Kegan Paul), 234–35.

is designed to introduce him to others, who require it either to identify him or to praise him as he deserves.

Further, a kind of grammatical ominousness[13] is created, because the dependent clause suspends the main statement of the sonnet: the reader, who is summoned by the dependent clause to stand by while the praise of the addressee is recited, then must expect some further social direction or placing of the apostrophized person. This ominousness Guittone could use tellingly, producing a kind of civic challenge to those whom he felt inclined to rebuke upon the public stage, or exhort to virtue:

> O grandi secular, voi che pugnate
> con bombanza si grande in cortesia,
> e chi v'onora e ama, intendo, amate,
> e chi vo serve non per voi s'obbria,
> e per niente altrui servite e date,
> e in despregio è voi far villania—
> ahi, come Dio mertar solo obbriate?        (160)

O you great ones of the State, you who strive in courtesies with such great display, and whoever honors you and loves you, you love, and whoever serves you, you do not forget, and you help and give to others gratis, and it's unthinkable to behave ignobly—ah! how is it that you forget only to make yourselves acceptable to God?

Here it is not until the seventh line of the sonnet that the main statement begins, punctuated, as it were, by an exclamation. The anaphoric run ("e chi ... e chi ... e ... e") has taken the salutation of the letter and turned it into something much more forensic, a rhetorical or even theatrical challenge in the piazza.

So Milton, in his sonnet to Fairfax, suspends the main statement until the second quatrain ("Thy firm unshak'n virtue ever brings / Victory home"), but one has only to substitute "whose" for "thy" to see that the whole octave is in sense, if not in grammar, a dependent clause, awaiting the great challenge of the future that comes in the sestet, after a series of "ringing" anaphoras and rhymes. His sonnet to Cromwell

---

[13] The first critic to comment on the effect of the initial apostrophe is Ludovico Castelvetro, in his remarks on Petrarch's opening sonnet in *Le Rime del Petrarca ... sposte di L. Castelvetro* (Basle, 1582), 2.

runs the apostrophe anaphorically through the whole octave into the ninth line ("and ... and ... and ... and Worcester's laureate wreath"). As in Guittone's sonnet, the arrangement of name + dependant clause(s) + main statement is a way of controlling time: past achievement is subordinate to future challenge.

Wordsworth's declaration that in Milton's sonnet writing "the Thing became a trumpet" is extremely acute: the extended apostrophe functions like a tucket, heralding the arrival on the civic stage of some champion. When the apostrophe is restricted to the name itself, and the speaker begins immediately after with his own material, there is still a strong element of challenge, enforced by the abruptness of the break between the vocative of the name and the ensuing context. As Scaliger said, when the apostrophe is used like this there is discontinuity and greater difficulty.[14] Guittone developed what one might call the civic challenge to a very high degree, particularly when, after his religious conversion, he began to experiment with extended sonnets, favoring especially the *sonnetto rinterzato*, in which a number of short lines, usually of seven syllables, are inserted in the quatrains and tercets. Milton was clearly interested in and adept at the insertion of short lines, as the poems "On Time," "Upon the Circumcision," "At a Solemn Music," and of course *Lycidas* demonstrate; but he does not appear to have known of the *sonnetto rinterzato*, which indeed fell out of favor after Guittone's time. Dante and Petrarch make almost no use of it, and writers who wished to extend the sonnet form usually employed the tailed sonnet. Milton would have known the tailed sonnet as a form appropriate to satire (and, if he knew his Tasso, to writing about cats!), and his only use of the form is the rough satire of "On the New Forcers of Conscience under the Long Parliament." He therefore, in pursuit of the *gravità* appropriate to civil utterance, avoided the tailed sonnet, and cultivated the apostrophe, extended or simple, in its strong form, as Guittone had developed it and put it into currency before the sweeter and more introverted Petrarchan model monopolized the imagination of the Cinquecento.

If the sonnet is a genre, then the apostrophe functions as a sub-

---

[14] Scaliger, book 2, chap. 27, p. 118. Castelvetro claims that readers have been disturbed by the omission of a main verb in "Voi ch'ascoltate ..." and defends Petrarch by explaining how apostrophes actually work.

generic signal: a name in the opening line, or a *pronominatio*, such as
"Daughter to that good Earl...," places the sonnet firmly in the mode
of what George Pettie called "Civile Conversations," whether the
purpose is to praise, reprove, or exhort. Within that mode, one can
begin to distinguish subtleties in the signal, to which Milton, with his
sharp sense of decorum, seems to have been responsive. While it is
difficult to catch the overtones of names as they were used in the early
Italian sonnets, it seems that diminutives, such as Cecco Angiolieri's
Becchina, or Christian names or nicknames, indicate a more familiar
sonnet in a low style: the name is not usually attached to a dependent
clause, and the writer launches straight into his business. When the
surname is prefaced by *Ser* or *Messer*, or is followed by a dependent
clause, one is prepared for loftier discussion of civic or moral matters,
as in della Casa's stately compliment to his friend Girolamo Correggio:

> Correggio, che per prò mai ne per danno
> discordar da te stesso non consenti,
> contra il costume de le inique genti,
> che le fortune adverse amar non sanno....

Correggio, who hast never, for gain or in loss, consented to be
untrue to thyself, against the wont of unjust men, who know not
how to embrace ill fortune....

So Milton apostrophizes the civic leaders of his age, but signals the
more familiar, artistic area of discourse to Henry Lawes by beginning,
not with the surname, nor even with the Christian name, but with the
diminutive "Harry"—a little touch of Harry in the line, and for the same
reason as Shakespeare's.

One may wonder whether the opening of his first sonnet to Cyriac
Skinner gave him pause (it is transcribed by an amanuensis in the
Trinity MS, interestingly, with the first quatrain missing). The decorum
of the subject matter would suggest an apostrophe using the Christian
name, as in the published version; and yet the opening dependent
clause, with its lofty reference to the highest of civil offices, might have
called for a surname. Here Milton would have encountered what, after
Wordsworth, one might call the Jones problem: some British names
have connotations of commonness or uncouthness (one thinks of
"Colkitto" or "Gillespie") such that they might emit the wrong sub-
generic signal—Wordsworth's sonnet to his no doubt admirable friend

Jones is the most famous instance. "Lawrence, of virtuous father virtuous son" is entirely decorous, but "Skinner, whose Grandsire on the Royal Bench ..." would, by the rules of the apostrophic code we have been considering, have started the sonnet calamitously. It is interesting that none of Milton's sonnets addressed to women begins with a woman's name—we know little about the nuances of everyday women's names (as contrasted with classical or pseudo-classical ones) in Renaissance verse.

Milton is the only British sonneteer to use apostrophic openings so frequently, and with an acute sense of their decorum; while it is almost impossible that he could have learnt his tact from the sonneteers of the Duecento, such as Guittone d'Arezzo, among whom the sonnet was first made an instrument of civic humanism, he may very well have observed the continuation of their practice among the Cinquecento writers whom he admired, particularly in Tasso. His own insistence upon the apostrophe shows that their addiction to Petrarchanism was much less important for him as a writer than the less frequent, but still common employment of the sonnet as a civic instrument to show oneself, in Brunetto Latini's phrase, as "dittatore perfetto e nobil parladore."[15]

University of Aberdeen

---

[15] Bianca Ceva, *Brunetto Latini* (Milan: Ricciardi, 1965), 71.

ANNA K. NARDO

# Milton and the Academic Sonnet

ACCORDING TO THE MINUTES OF THE FLORENTINE Accademia degli Svogliati, on March 24, 1639 "a sonnet [was] recited by Signor Cavalcanti . . . and various Latin poems by Signor Milton"; then on March 31, at a meeting Milton also attended, Alessandro Adimari "recited a moral sonnet."[1] It would have been surprising if Milton had not heard sonnets at these meetings. Throughout the seventeenth century sonnet recitations were regular features at academic gatherings, and the Crusca and Apatisti, two other prominent academies whose membership included most of Milton's Florentine friends, "always ended with the recitation of a new sonnet."[2] Although most academic sonnets were uninspired "literary exercises," they helped create and sustain the academy's identity as a community, and expanded Milton's experience of the range of the sonnet form.

In the 1630s every Italian town of considerable size had one and often many more academies devoted primarily to literary study. They identified themselves by their noble protector, patron saint, symbolic names for the academy and each member, *impresa*, and motto; for example, the *impresa* of the Incogniti of Venice depicted the Nile descending from the mountains, fertilizing Egypt, and flowing into the Mediterranean, with the motto: *Ex ignoto notus*. Scholars, prominent

---

[1] Atti dell' Accademia degli Svogliati, Biblioteca Nazionale, Florence, MSS. Magliabecchiana, cl. IX, cod. 60, fols. 52–52v. French, 1:409. Andrea Cavalcanti was a learned teacher and charter member of the Svogliati, which met in his house in the 1640s. He also attended symposia held by the Accademia degli Apatisti. See Michele Maylender, *Storia delle Accademie d'Italia*, 5 vols. (Bologna: L. Cappelli, 1926–30), 5:288–89; Edoardo Benvenuti, *Agostino Coltellini e L'Accademia degli Apatisti a Firenze nel Secolo XVII* (Pistoia: Officina Tipografica Cooperativa, 1910), 251.

[2] Eric W. Cochrane, *Tradition and Enlightenment in the Tuscan Academies: 1690–1800* (Chicago, Ill: Univ. of Chicago Press, 1961), 19. See also Benvenuti, *Coltellini*, 275.

citizens, noblemen, ecclesiastics, and other literati devoted their meetings primarily to analyzing Trecento masterpieces, discussing theories of decorum, criticizing original compositions, and debating what properly constituted the Italian language. Academic charters in Tuscany required that only Tuscan be used for academic business and discussion.[3]

In all their activities the sonnet figured prominently. The Florentine academicians took Petrarch and his Cinquecento followers, Bembo and Della Casa, as models of the purest Tuscan. Since, it was preeminently in the sonnet form that these masters had perfected the language, academicians read frequent disquisitions on Petrarch's sonnets, emphasizing correct usage. They also presented their own sonnets for criticism: sonnets were recited, analyzed by the standards of the masters, sent back for revision, and, if certified by vote of the academy, copied into the records.[4] By virtue of its rigor and brevity, the sonnet was an appropriate form for studying and polishing style, and academicians included sonnet decorum in their frequent debates on genre theory.[5]

Not all their sonnets were exercises in imitation. On every important occasion, and many not-so-important ones, they exchanged sonnets with one another and with nonmembers, frequently gathering them into volumes of sonnets and poetic miscellanies under the academy's name. Even in the miscellanies, sonnets predominate: one representative volume of 185 poems contains 133 sonnets.[6] From the mid-sixteenth through the early eighteenth centuries, academies published hundreds of such volumes; many more remain in manuscript. Although they are not available in the United States, Michele Maylender's five-volume history of the Italian academies includes sufficient descriptions and examples to provide a survey of the range of academic sonnets.

Members addressed encomiastic sonnets to princes, patrons, dignitaries, and other academies deemed worthy of official praise, and those honored typically replied in kind. Sonnets commemorated local or academic events: victories in battle, the carnival season, the academy's patron saint's day, the opening of an academy sponsored theater, the

---

[3] For Incogniti, see Maylender, *Storia*, 3:205. For background of academies, see Cochrane, *Tradition*, 1-34.

[4] Cochrane, *Tradition*, 1, 12, 19-22.

[5] Bernard Weinberg, "The Accademia degli Alterati and Literary Taste from 1570 to 1600," *Italica* 31 (1954): 209.

[6] Maylender, *Storia*, 1:374.

weddings, births, deaths, or consecrations to the religious life in members' families. Members conducted intra- and inter-academic quarrels in sonnets, and praised or debated the appropriateness of academic names or *imprese*.[7] Among themselves they recited a wide range of *giocosi sonetti*. Some academies sponsored *simposia*, light banquets where members enjoyed learned conversation and jocular poetry, including sonnets, as well as wine and food. In this tailed sonnet of homophonic feminine rhymes, a member of the seventeenth-century Accademia delle Cene celebrates his gluttonous and noisy feasting with puns and a mocking allusion to Dante:

> Chi vuol ricreazion, chi cerca spasso,
>> E quel che importa più, senza interesso,
>> Faccia come fo io, che spesso spesso
>> Con la conversazion me ne vo in chiasso.
> Qui vi si sente un rumore, un fracasso,
>> Che con l'arco dell'osso ognun s'è messo.
>> Anzi il Padrone stesso fa l'istesso
>> Col Sopran, col Tenor, coll'Alto e Basso.
> E tanto, più col capo s'è sì fisso,
>> Che, se non vi paresse paradosso,
>> V'è più che Satanasso nell'abisso.
> Qui 'l male è penetrato fin all'osso,
>> Anzichè, per non v'esser più prolisso,
>> Anch'io mi ci son messo a più non posso.
>>> E poi mi veggo addosso
> All'Accademia un dì flusso e reflusso,
> Talchè s'abbia a poter poi dir: che i' russo.[8]

---

[7] Cochrane's description of academic sonnets confirms that this survey taken from Maylender is representative: "sonnets on love, birth, and death, sonnets on the soul of Christina of Sweden rising to God, sonnets on the coronation of Clement XI or the election of the doge of Genova, sonnets comparing the Spanish general Montemar to St. Jerome, sonnets celebrating the terror of the Infidels before the Venetian fleet, sonnets on the retirement of an *arciconsolo* or the beginning of academic vacation, all in impeccable Trecento speech and all adorned with elaborate footnotes explaining the oblique references to ... the hidden compliments to friends or relatives" (*Tradition*, 21).

[8] Some academies originated in such social gatherings. See T. C. Price Zimmermann and Saul Levin, "Fabio Vigile's *Poem of the Pheasant*: Humanist Conviviality in Renaissance Rome," in *Rome in the Renaissance: The City and the Myth*, ed. P. A.

He who wants fun, who is looking for a pastime and, what is more important, one without care, let him do as I do, who very often get myself into an uproar with conversation. Here one hears a din, a racket, to which everyone has put himself with the bow of the bone. In fact, the boss himself does the same with soprano, tenor, alto, and bass. And, if it would not seem paradoxical to you, he has his head set to it even more than that big Satan in the depths of hell [fixed in ice, gnawing sinners: *Inferno*, canto 34]. Here the sickening evil has entered clear to the bone; nay, even I, not to be more wordy, have so put myself to it that I can do no more. And then one day at the Academy I feel myself seized by such a flux and reflux that one might come to say: how I snort. [*russare* = snore; *ruzzare* = romp; *che russia* = what a mess!]

Even at regular meetings, some gifted literati improvised witty sonnet responses to the *lezioni*, serious lectures, and to the *dubbi*, mostly frivolous mind teasers, proposed for debate. Some academies, like the Florentine Apatisti, played such games as *Sibilla*, in which a blindfolded child utters a nonsense syllable, then two academicians argue learnedly that the sibyl has spoken well; in this same sportive vein members recited macaronic sonnets parodying pedantic Latinists.[9]

In the academies, as among Petrarchan lovers, sonnets seemed to breed more sonnets. The brevity and strong closure of the form leave no place to go but to start over again, either to reimagine one's subject or to reply. Maylender includes several examples of such academic sonnet exchanges, some in which the reply uses the rhyming syllables or words of the initiating sonnet.[10] Most of these sonnets are amateur

---

Ramsey, Medieval & Renaissance Texts & Studies, vol. 18 (Binghamton, NY, 1982), 265–78; and Maylender, *Storia*, 2:124; 5:370–71. On banquets among the Apatisti and Alterati, see Benvenuti, *Coltellini*, 251, 273; Weinberg, "Alterati and Literary Taste," 207. For the tailed sonnet, see Maylender, *Storia*, 1:532–33. I would like to thank Robert McMahon and Joseph V. Ricapito for help with this and other sonnet translations.

   [9] On improvisation, see Cochrane, *Tradition*, 19; Benvenuti, *Coltellini*, 275–76; Maylender, *Storia*, 5:370. On sonnets and academic games, see Weinberg, "Alterati and Literary Taste," 207; Cochrane, *Tradition*, 4, 7, 27; Benvenuti, *Coltellini*, 155–62, 273–76.

   [10] On sonnet proliferation, see Judith Scherer Herz, "Epigrams and Sonnets:

productions, but in the following witty exchange, Tasso, a member of
no less than nine academies, and Don Angelo Grillo vie with each
other in Neoplatonic definitions of the sleep of the Addormentati of
Genoa.[11]

Tasso

Qual sonno è il vostro, o chiari, e pronti ingegni,
Da cui rimedio avea l'altrui letargo?
E chi richiuder può tant'occhi d'Argo,
Pur volti al Cielo, e ne' superni regni?
    Vi desti il suon degli amorosi sdegni,
Mentre di bei colori in versi io spargo,
Seguendo chi cantò di Troia, e d'Argo,
E mostrò al poetar le mete, e i segni,
    Se pur è sonno, e se terreno affetto
V'adombra; ma se l'alma in voi non dorme,
E se qui l'una è chiusa, e l'altra trista,
    E su nel cielo aperta; a qual diletto
D'immagine io vi chiamo oscura, e mista,
Dal contemplar lucenti e pure forme?

What slumber is yours, o bright and prompt wits, who cured the
lethargy of others? And who can shut the many eyes of Argus,
always turned to the sky and the celestial realms? If it really is
slumber and if earthly affections darken you, may the sound of
amorous rages awaken you, while I scatter some lovely tones in
verses, following the one who sang of Troy and Argos and
showed to the writing of poetry its goals and aims; but if the soul
does not sleep in you, and if here, one soul is closed and the
other is wretched, and above, the soul is opened unto heaven; to
what enjoyment of a dark and confused image do I call you from
contemplating luminous and pure forms?

Don Angello Grillo

E qual sonno è sì grave, e sì l'ingegni
Lega, o sì l'alme accieca empio letargo,

---

Milton in the Manner of Jonson," *MS* 20 (1984): 31. For exchanges, see Maylender, *Storia*, 1:173–74, 499–500.

[11] Maylender, *Storia*, 1:62.

Che non sian sciolti, e ch'occhi assai più d'Argo
Non apran volti agli alti empirei Regni,
　　Tasso, al tuo canto? ch'ire, o guerre, o sdegni,
O paci, o amori esprima, io sempre spargo
Voci di meraviglia: e Troia ed Argo
Quand'hebber sì gran tomba, e sì bei segni?
　　E 'n te rivolgo ogni più caro affetto,
Che (benchè addormentata) in me non dorme,
E spero rischiarar l'interna vista
　　Alla tua viva voce, il cui diletto
Fa vile questa gioia, a pena mista,
E 'n terra contemplar celesti forme.

And what slumber is so heavy and so binds the wits, or what impious lethargy so blinds the souls, that they may not be freed, and that, Tasso, at your song, they may not open their eyes, many more than Argus's, turned toward the lofty empyreal realms? That your song may express rage, or war, or scorn, or peace, or love, I always marvel: and when did Troy and Argos have such a grand memorial and such beauteous emblems? And I address to you every dearest affection, which (although dormant) does not sleep within me, and I hope to illumine my inner sight upon hearing your living voice—such pleasure makes worthless this earthly happiness tainted by suffering—and here on earth I hope to contemplate heavenly forms.

Whereas Tasso calls the Addormentati, who are asleep only to earthly things, from their contemplation of heavenly forms to the shades of those forms in his poems, Grillo praises the poet for awakening the slumberers to the contemplation of celestial forms. This polite exchange highlights features often present in academic sonnets: elegant play with the name or *impresa* of the academy, mutual adulation, and the enhancement of mutuality by the form (in this case the choice of the same controlling image and rhyme words).

Indeed, academic activities seem virtually synonymous with sonneteering; even into the eighteenth century, when science, agriculture, political economy, and other worldly studies largely supplanted "literary exercises," academicians continued to compose sonnets commemorating the opening of botanical gardens, sonnets invoking God to unveil His hidden wonders to scientists, even a sonnet "upon seeing the finger of the great Galileo" during a celebration for his reinterment.[12] The triviality of some (such as those Maylender mentions on St. Jerome's self-flagellation with a rock after being tempted by the memory of Roman dancing girls, or a bone found in an Englishman's heart sculpted to his perfect likeness, or the dead wife of an innkeeper who opened her eyes) and the hyperbolic, self-congratulatory rhetoric of others have led historians to judge these sonnets as but another indication of the decline of intellectual life in post-Renaissance Italy. According to this view, absolutist regimes, especially in Florence and Naples, and the Counter-Reformation mounted by Rome stifled all dissent, thereby forcing men of considerable talent and erudition to turn away from the world. Many academies, like the Oziosi of Naples founded by Milton's host Giovanni Battista Manso, followed charters "vietando che non si debba leggere alcuna Materia di Teologia e della Sacra Scrittura, delle quali per riverenza dobbiamo astenerci: è medesimamente niuna delle cose appartenenti al publico governo, i quali si deve lasciare alla cura de Principi che ne reggono" ("forbidding that any material concerning theology or holy scripture be read, from which we ought to abstain out of reverence: and likewise nothing pertaining to public government, which ought to be left to the care of princes who govern these matters"). Abandoning political and religious debate, some academicians took up Neoplatonism and piety, but more debated fine points of grammar, played parlor games, argued interminably over names and *imprese*, or composed fulsome sonnets.[13]

Milton and his contemporaries seem to confirm this view. Jean-Jaques Bouchard, a French visitor to Naples, excoriated the Oziosi as mere "amateurs de madrigaux et de versiculets" ("dabblers in madrigals and little verses") who applauded every praise of the viceroy and the house of Austria. Giordano Bruno, himself a Neoplatonic sonneteer,

---

[12] Cochrane, *Tradition*, 70–71, 104n, 114n.

[13] On the triviality of sonnets, see Eric W. Cochrane, *Florence in the Forgotten Centuries: 1527–1800* (Chicago: Univ. of Chicago Press, 1973), 193, and Maylender, *Storia*, 2:54–55. For the effects of political and religious repression on the academies, see Florence Trail, *A History of Italian Literature* (Boston: Richard G. Badger, 1914), 158–59; Francesco de Sanctis, *History of Italian Literature*, trans. Joan Redfern (New York: Barnes & Noble, 1968), 2:541, 635, 709, 856; Cochrane, *Tradition*, 29–33; Masson, 1:762–65; Arthos, 97–98. For the Oziosi charter, see Maylender, *Storia*, 4:184. On debates over names and *imprese*, see Maylender, *Storia*, 5:289, 373.

mocked academic sobriquets by calling himself "an academician of no academy, named the Disgusted One." And Milton reported in *Areopagitica* that his Italian friends "bemoan[ed] the servil condition into which learning amongst them was brought ... that nothing had bin there writt'n now these many years but flattery and fustian." Their complaints notwithstanding, some of his friends played at *dubbi*, *Sibilla*, and macaronic sonneteering.[14]

Seeing the academies as a symptom of intellectual decline is, however, a partial perspective. They also created a structure for dialogue among men (and in rare cases women) of letters—an institution based in cities, not courts, governed by constitutions and elections, with participation determined by talent, not birth. As Eric Cochrane has shown, when the political and social climate began to change in the eighteenth century, the academies already had in place a structure for discussing reforms, a school for citizenship in their debates over laws and elections, and a network of correspondence with an international republic of letters.[15] We may be tempted to dismiss academic practices as narcissistic, even decadent. But their written constitutions and elaborate election procedures, their much discussed and widely displayed symbols, and their mutual encomia and self-congratulations, most often voiced in sonnets—these are the very rituals that create and sustain communal identity. Such forms helped focus the energy that creates and confirms the institutional structure necessary for an autonomous community to persist, especially in times of political and social demoralization.[16]

Above all else, Milton saw the academy as a community of learned

---

[14] Lucien Marcheix, *Un Parisien á Rome et á Naples en 1632 D'après un Manuscrit inédit de J. -J. Bouchard* (Paris: Ernest Leroux, n.d.), 91-94. De Sanctis, *History*, 2:718. John Milton, *Areopagitica* in CPW 2:537-38. (All subsequent references to Milton's prose will be cited in the text.) On the trivial pursuits of some of Milton's Italian friends, see James A.Freeman, "Milton's Roman Connection: Giovanni Salzilli," MS 19 (1984): 89-91; Edward Rosen, "A Friend of John Milton: Valerio Chimentelli... ," *Bulletin of the New York Public Library* 57 (1953): 162-63; and Benvenuti, *Coltellini*, 160, 273, 276. The Apatisti records, however, mention no games of *Sibilla* until 1649, long after Milton's Italian visit: Alessandro Lazzeri, *Intellettuali e consenso nella Toscana del Seicento: L'Accademia degli Apatisti* (Milan: Istituto di Storia del Diritto Italiano e Filosofia del Diritto, 1983), 103.

[15] Cochrane, *Tradition*, xiii-xiv, 52-54, 247.

[16] On academic formalities, see Cochrane, *Tradition*, 4-6. Arthos emphasizes the importance of civility and brotherhood to academicians, 20-22, 41, 107.

friends. He remembers the Florentine academicians in "Epitaphium Damonis" as the singing shepherds of a pastoral idyll, and in *A Second Defense* as members of an "institution which deserves great praise not only for promoting humane studies but also for encouraging friendly intercourse" (4.1.615–16). Indeed, this community is what Milton remembered most about Italy, not the paintings, sculpture, palaces, ruins, and manners that impressed other Englishmen on the grand tour.[17] Its linguistic and literary activities did not, he believed, turn men from the world; rather, studies like Benedetto Buonmattei's Tuscan grammar served the larger community of the state. In a letter, Milton reminds this prominent academician that citizens need a strong and elegant language to sustain the mental alacrity necessary for the freedom and survival of the nation (1.329–30). Also in *The Reason of Church Government*, while explaining the poet's call to write what is "doctrinal and exemplary to a Nation," he urges Englishmen to "civilize, adorn and make discreet our minds by the learned and affable meeting of frequent Academies, and the procurement of wise and artfull recitations sweetned with eloquent and gracefull inticements to the love and practice of justice, temperance, and fortitude, instructing and bettering the Nation at all opportunities" (1.815, 819). For the rest of his life, Milton sought this community of the learned in service to the community of the state.

So far we have explored how Italian academicians articulated their ideals, practices, and communal identity in sonnets. Now let us turn to

---

[17] On Milton's appreciation of the academic community, see Parker, 1:171, 180, 182; Wilson, 81; Freeman, "Salzilli," 87. Richard Lassels's influential guidebook, *The Voyage of Italy* (Paris: John Starkey, 1670), praises the academies where wits "spend the week in making of Orations and Verses" rather than "in drinking of Ale and smoking of Tobacco" (1:67), but after describing the sights of each town in detail, he merely lists the name of the local academy, sometimes mistakenly. Richard Symonds and John Evelyn attended meetings of the Umoristi in Rome in 1651 and 1645. Although Symonds seemed more interested in art and heraldry than academic exercises, Evelyn tried unsuccessfully to found a literary academy in London. See Arthos, 90 n. 24; Mary Beal, *A Study of Richard Symonds: His Italian Notebooks and Their Relevance to Seventeenth-Century Painting Techniques* (New York: Garland, 1984); *The Diary of John Evelyn*, ed. E. S. de Beer (Oxford: Clarendon, 1955), 2:364; *Diary and Correspondence of John Evelyn*, ed. William Bray (London: Henry G. Bohn, 1863), 3:310–11. According to John Walter Stoye, Milton was the "almost solitary instance of an English traveller who assiduously attended Italian literary societies" (*English Travellers Abroad: 1604–67* [London: Jonathan Cape, 1952], 222–23).

Milton's experience of academic sonnets and consider what he gained. Before his trip, he had written seven sonnets and a canzone that show his debt to the tradition of Bembo and Della Casa, the touchstones for perfect Tuscan in the academies.[18] Either shortly before, during, or soon after his trip, he carefully read the social sonnets that Benedetto Varchi, academic historian and grammarian, addressed to friends and fellow literati.[19] At meetings of the Svogliati, Milton heard sonnets and, since he describes academic recitations in The Reason of Church Government as tests of "wit and reading," he probably heard the rigorous critiques of sonnets so often part of academic discussions (1.809).

By reading some of his Latin poems, Milton had passed these tests and his subsequent welcome into the academic community moved him deeply. Eight years after his return, amid loneliness and wearying company, he writes to Carlo Dati, remembering "so many companions and at the same time such good friends" now so far away (2.763). Even after fifteen years, in A Second Defense, he praises these men by name. Almost all the Italians whose attentions Milton valued so highly were members of academies in Florence, Rome, or Naples, and several were sonneteers.[20] Agostino Coltellini, founder of the Apatisti, wrote a typical encomiastic sonnet to Dati exhorting him to abjure earthly grandeur and follow the path of virtue to eternity.[21] Dati and Buonmattei read sonnets at Svogliati meetings, and Milton may have heard Buonmattei.[22] Giovanni Salzilli, with whom Milton exchanged exaggerated verse compliments in Latin, published eleven sonnets—some Petrarchan exercises and some encomia to poets and other academicians—in

---

[18] Prince, 89–102.

[19] Maurice Kelley, "Milton's Dante-Della Casa-Varchi Volume," Bulletin of the New York Public Library 66 (1962): 503. The two-volume De Sonetti di M. Benedetto Varchi (Florence, 1555, 1557) at Harvard includes hundreds of sonnet-exchanges, and Wilmon Brewer takes Varchi as the prime example of the social sonneteer: "Often . . . a sonnet was written to some one as a graceful compliment or an elegant letter. . . . Custom required the person receiving such an honor to reply with another sonnet, which had the same pattern of rhyme and even the same rhyming syllables. And so common were these occasions that the poet Varchi composed two hundred and twenty acknowledgments of this kind" (Sonnets and Sestinas [Boston: Cornhill, 1937], 120).

[20] See Masson, 1:768–824; Parker, 1:170–77; 2:824. Arthos also discusses the likelihood that Milton attended academies in Rome, Naples, and Venice.

[21] Benvenuti, Coltellini, 135; Arthos, 18.

[22] Atti dell' Accademia degli Svogliati, fols. 46v, 54. There are four certain and two possible records of Milton's attendance at meetings of the Svogliati: French, 5:385–87.

a poetic miscellany of the Roman Accademia degli Fantastici.[23] Because Milton found these friends so congenial, he probably read or heard some of their sonnets.

Antonio Malatesti, one member of the Apatisti and also a friend of Dati, presented Milton with a volume of sonnets—fifty lewd equivocations addressed to a peasant girl. The Apatisti were known for their jokes, and Matatesti's gift of *sonetti giocosi* to an English visitor so upright and outspoken in religion and morality was probably intended as an academic prank. These sonnets speak not in the elocutions of Bembo and Della Casa, but in slang from the Tuscan countryside. Since Milton was touted for writing and speaking Tuscan "so correctly and in so polished a manner" even by a prominent member of the Accademia della Crusca, the foremost purifiers of Tuscan (letter from Dati, 2.766), Malatesti might have intended his gift to test and tease the foreigner's linguistic skill.[24]

Another academician, Alessandro Adimari, whose moral sonnet Milton heard at a Svogliati meeting, was a prolific sonneteer. He regularly recited sonnets at the academy and gathered them into six volumes, each including fifty sonnets and each named after a muse: *La Polinnia*, sonnets based on sentences of Tacitus "which united together form a brief political and moral discourse," 1628; *La Tersicore*, jests paradoxically praising various forms of female ugliness (the hunchback, the squint-eyed, the mute, etc.), 1637; *La Clio*, tributes to members of the venerable Adimari family, 1639; *La Melpomene*, funereal sonnets on eminent men and women, 1640; *La Calliope*, moral sonnets based on sentences from sacred scripture, 1641; and *L'Urania*, spiritual sonnets on saints and holy days ordered by the liturgical calendar, 1642. All these volumes are elaborately structured. Each sonnet fills a page, and the facing page presents an argument, a sentence, an elegy, or a prose account of the sonnet's subject, with learned marginal notations. Each volume begins with an emblematic frontispiece and title that announces Adimari's academic affiliation, and each ends with a summary of sentences

---

[23] Freeman, "Salzilli," 97–98.

[24] Donald Sears, "*La Tina*: The Country Sonnets of Antonio Malatesti as Dedicated to Mr. John Milton, English Gentleman," MS 13 (1979): 275–317. Masson also speculates that the sonnet gift might have been a joke, 1:786. Anthony Low has shown Milton's willingness to exchange erudite jests with another academician, Manso: "*Mansus*: In Its Context," MS 19 (1984): 105–26.

or arguments, a table, or a poem that brings the volume into unity.[25]

So, in Italy Milton had ample opportunity to experience a wide range of academic sonneteering—sonnet exercises in perfect Tuscan, encomiastic sonnets, jocular sonnets, and occasional sonnets on every facet of social life, later published as sequences. Some of his own sonnets show traces of academic practice. In Sonnet 10 he describes Lady Margaret Ley as a living emblem of her father's virtue, shining in a tainted world. To emphasize her symbolic function and highlight the contrast to her darker surroundings, he culminates the sonnet with a submerged pun on her name: *margherita* is pearl in Italian. Thus, he honors her in the image of a pure and radiant pearl, with all its biblical resonances of feminine virtue (Proverbs 31:10 ) and of the superiority of heavenly to earthly worth (Matthew 13:45-46). This etymological pun recalls the play with symbolic names so common in academic sonnets. Milton's Sonnet 21 invites Cyriack Skinner to drench deep thoughts in mirth, while offering itself as a sample of the sparkling wit that will grace their "cheerful hour." The sonnet is full of puns (some vinous, some geometric), recondite allusions, and academic jokes between teacher and former pupil which recall with amusement that, despite their brilliant discoveries in scientific measurement, Euclid and Archimedes sometimes failed at humane measurement. This witty invitation to share a "gawdy-day" recalls the *sonetti giocosi* recited at academic symposia.[26]

Still, Milton's experience with the academic sonnet had a more pervasive influence. Rosalie Colie and Barbara Lewalski have shown how literary kinds in the Renaissance offered author and reader not just external form, but "a set of interpretations, of 'frames' or 'fixes' on the world."[27] The Italian academy considerably expanded Milton's understanding of what the sonnet might interpret. After the early love sonnets in the reformed Petrarchan mode of Bembo and Della Casa and the meditative "How soon hath time . . . ," Milton dropped the form for ten

---

[25] These volumes are available at Harvard and the Biblioteca Nazionale in Florence. On Adimari, see *Enciclopedia Italiana di Scienze, Lettere ed Arti* (Rome, 1949), 1:508.

[26] Anna K. Nardo, *Milton's Sonnets and the Ideal Community* (Lincoln: Univ. of Nebraska Press, 1979), 52, 187-90, 94-99. I follow the numbering in *Milton's Sonnets*, ed. E. A. J. Honigmann (New York: St. Martin's Press, 1966).

[27] Colie, 8. For Milton's use of generic frames of reference in *Paradise Lost*, see Barbara K. Lewalski, *"Paradise Lost" and the Rhetoric of Literary Forms* (Princeton: Princeton Univ. Press, 1985).

years, including his years in Europe. When he returned to England to practice his vocation as a man of letters in an embattled state, he also returned to the sonnet form, steadily producing social and political sonnets as events prompted: a sonnet defending his home from Royalist plunder (8), sonnets commending or eulogizing friends (9, 10, 13, 14), sonnets satirizing the ignorant or vicious (11, 12, "Upon the New Forcers . . ."), sonnets praising and advising statesmen and generals (15, 16, 17), a sonnet deploring a massacre of Protestants (18), and sonnet invitations (20, 21). Then he ended his period of writing sonnets as he began it, with meditations on his career and love (19, 22, 23). This marked shift expands the sonnet from a minor lyric form for personal expression toward, as I have argued elsewhere, a sonnet sequence dedicated not to an idealized lady, but to an ideal community—a highly original sequence defining relationships between self, family, friends, the state, and God.[28]

Of course, written sources influenced many of the occasional sonnets: the invitations are Horatian, the *sonetto caudato* (or tailed sonnet) on the forcers of conscience employs Berni's satirical form, the sonnet on the Piedmont massacre echoes Petrarch's anti-papal sonnets, and the calls to Fairfax, Cromwell, and Vane recall Tasso's heroic sonnets. But his reading of Roman and modern Italian poets did not impel him to write such sonnets before his trip. In Italy Milton actually lived in a community that marked its values and identity with the sonnet, and this experience, coupled with his extensive reading, enabled him to see far more of the world through the sonnet's narrow "frame." When he returned, he used the sonnet as his Italian friends did, as a gesture toward community.

Perhaps, as Judith Herz has persuasively argued, Milton learned much about writing a collection of short poems centered on the ideals of a community from Ben Jonson's epigrams.[29] And according to Alastair Fowler, the epigrammatic mode came to dominate lyric forms during the seventeenth century.[30] But unlike Jonson, Milton did not choose to articulate his ideals in epigrams. Before and during his Italian

---

[28] Nardo, *Milton's Sonnets*, 4–26.

[29] Herz, "Epigrams and Sonnets," 29–41.

[30] Alastair Fowler, *Kinds of Literature: An Introduction to the Theory of Genres and Modes* (Cambridge, Mass.: Harvard Univ. Press, 1982), 108, 195–202, 222–23.

trip, he used the epigram for occasional poetry, never the sonnet. Afterwards, however, he wrote only two epigrams, and sixteen sonnets. His experience with academic sonnets may also have influenced this shift.

Renaissance critics frequently paired the sonnet and epigram, some limiting the former to the *mel* of love song and the latter to the *sal* of social wit. In practice Renaissance poets wrote reams of amatory epigrams modeled on the Greek anthology and social sonnets with the pointedness of epigrams. As Colie has demonstrated, both epigram and sonnet spanned a wide range of subjects and tones. But poetic forms sometimes became associated with specific languages. One French critic considered "the sonnet simply the perfect Italian epigram, as the dizain was the perfect French epigram."[31] Likewise, Milton practiced the epigram almost exclusively as a Latin or Greek form—perhaps because epigrams were common school exercises in composition.[32] In Italy, he presented himself primarily as a Latin poet, reading Latin poems at academic meetings and composing and receiving Latin encomia, including epigrams. In his prose letter in Latin to Buonmattei, he gracefully defers his use of Tuscan until Buonmattei publishes his grammar (1.331–32). So, despite the epigram's potential range and Milton's use of it at home and abroad, when he sought a poetic form to express the values of the community he was working to create in the 1640s and 1650s, he chose not the Latin epigram, but the sonnet, a preeminently Tuscan form.

Not long after his Italian trip, Milton published his hope to do "what the greatest and choycest wits of *Athens, Rome,* or modern *Italy,* and those Hebrews of old did for their country," to be "an interpreter & relater of the best and sagest things among mine own Citizens throughout this Iland in the mother dialect" (RCG 1.811–12). As we have seen, the sonnet contributed to this project in Italy. In sonnets, masters like Dante and Petrarch had matured the language and rivaled the ancients, and as part of their efforts to perfect Tuscan, academicians

---

[31] Rosalie L. Colie, *Shakespeare's Living Art* (Princeton: Princeton Univ. Press, 1974), 68–96. Colie translates on p. 88 from Thomas Sébillet, *Art poétique françoyse* (Paris, 1548).

[32] Milton's one English epigram is an epitaph for Shakespeare. On the relationship between epitaph and epigram, see Fowler, *Kinds of Literature,* 197. Fowler also notes "the wide use of epigram composition in schools" (222).

polished their style in imitative sonnets. As the communal identity of the academy was manifest in the sonnet, so was its dedication to proper use of the vulgar.

In Italy Milton saw the sonnet serve a living community in its own language. When he returned, he understood the province of the genre quite differently. He pressed the sonnet into the service of his ideal community in its native tongue, all the while maturing his poetic style in sonnets before attempting the promised masterwork, "doctrinal . . . to a Nation."

Louisiana State University

STELLA P. REVARD

# Milton and Chiabrera

GABRIELLO CHIABRERA, CELEBRATED BY HIS contemporaries as the new Pindar, died in Rome at the age of 86 in 1638, the very year Milton first came to Italy.[1] Accomplished not only in pindarics, but also in a wide range of lyric, dramatic, and narrative genres, Chiabrera was one of the most important poets in Italy since Tasso. Writing for an aristocratic and intellectual society that valued the Muses, Chiabrera was almost exactly the kind of poet the young Milton of the 1630s was aiming to be, Milton himself having composed in many of the modes in which Chiabrera excelled. Milton would have almost certainly have known Chiabrera's poetry before coming to Italy, for he was well versed in contemporary Italian poetry; he would certainly have discussed Chiabrera with his Italian friends, for Chiabrera had had close ties to the court and the academies of Florence.[2] Moreover, in a letter written on November 1, 1647, eight years after Milton's return to England, Carlo Dati comments on one of Chiabrera's *canzonette* in such a way as to suggest previous conversations about Chiabrera and Italian poetry. This letter gives us insight not only into the kind of literary discussions Milton might have enjoyed in Italy, but also into the special interest Milton might have had in a recent poet skilled in vernacular ode and other lyric genres. If we look closely at some of Chiabrera's poetry, we may be able to determine the reason for such an interest. First, however, we must begin with Dati and Florence.

Probably neither Dati nor any of the young Florentines in Milton's

---

[1] See *Enciplopedia Italiana* for Chiabrera's life; also see Alberto Viviani, *Gabriello Chiabrera* (Rome: A. E. Formiggini, 1938).

[2] For Milton's knowledge of Italian literature see Prince. Milton owned a copy of Giovanni Della Casa's *Rime e Prose* (Venice, 1563), which is in the New York Public Library.

group knew Chiabrera personally.[3] The years of Chiabrera's closest association with Florence were 1585 to 1619; although he remained in correspondence with members of the court and with friends until his death, he probably did not visit after 1619.[4] Chiabrera had achieved tremendous success in Florence for his pastoral masque, "Il Rapimento di Cefalo," written for the wedding of Maria de' Medici to Henri IV of France in 1600 and set to music by Guilio Caccini. He had written his most ambitious biblical narrative, "Il Battista," a poem in three cantos, for Duke Ferdinando I, and he continued to write verse for Ferdinando's successors, Cosimo II and Ferdinando II, as well as for other members of the court. He sent a copy of his epic poem, Firenze, to Giovanni Medici in 1615 and dedicated it to Ferdinando II on its publication some years later. His verse to friends in Florence, including ladies and gentlemen of the court, ranges from heroic odes to canzonette, scherzi, sermoni, and canzoni morali. Chiabrera had been, moreover, closely connected with several of the academies in Florence, particularly the Accademia degli Alternati, whose leading member, Giovanni Baptista Strozzi, had died in 1634, at which time the academy closed. Although Milton could not have known Strozzi, he did know Coltellini, Strozzi's protégé and one of Milton's close associates.[5] Another member of Milton's group, the Neo-Latin poet Jacopo Gaddi, who was about forty when Milton came to Florence, certainly knew Chiabrera, for Chiabrera had addressed one of his sermoni to him. The years of close association would have kept Chiabrera's name fresh among the aristocrats and literati in Florence, and news of his death in 1638 would not have gone unnoted.

The admiration that Carlo Dati expresses for Chiabrera in his 1647 letter to Milton and that he echoes elsewhere in his letters and papers is for a poet that he regarded as one of the leading lyric voices among vernacular poets, the best of the moderns. Throughout his life, Dati was a passionate supporter of vernacular poets. Although himself a thor-

---

[3] For information on Dati and on the other men Milton associated with in Florence, see Masson (1946 reprint), 773–81. Also see Parker, 1:170–72.

[4] For Chiabrera's relations with Florence, see Laura da Riva, Gabriello Chiabrera e Firenze (n.p., n.d.).

[5] See Arthos, 18.

oughly trained classicist, who, like Milton, knew both Greek and Latin and composed Latin poetry (he was to advance to Doni's chair in classics in Florence in the late 1640s), Dati urged the use of the vernacular for poetry and, like Dante, argued the superiority of the Tuscan dialect, comparing its beauty, flexibility, and refinement to Ciceronian Latin and Attic Greek.[6] For Dati, Chiabrera was an important poet who continued the tradition begun by Dante and continued by Ariosto and Bernardo and Torquato Tasso of writing verse principally in Italian rather than Latin. In his preface to the collection of orations from the Accademia della Crusca, Dati twice cites Chiabrera's poetry with approval, not only for the beauty of the verse, but also for preserving the traditions and the metrical forms of ancient poetry while writing in his own native language. With Testi, Dati says, Chiabrera illustrates the excellence and glory of the Tuscan tongue. Quoting from Chiabrera's translation of a cantica to the Virgin, Dati praises Chiabrera's melodic lines and commends the use of the term "colombella" for its play on the words "colomba" and "bella."[7] Dati concludes his remarks on Chiabrera by affirming that the Tuscan Parnassus considered his poetry the standard in Italian for Pindaric and Anacreontic adaptations.

Dati's comments on Chiabrera in his letter to Milton in 1647 take up this very question of classical adaptation, for in a letter replete with references to classical and other poets Dati focusses on Chiabrera's skillful imitation of Horace and Tibullus in his *conzonetta*, "Non si temono i tormenti d'Amor." Quoting from the conclusion of the *conzonetta*, Dati remarks that Chiabrera has presented a composite of

---

[6] [Carlo Dati], *Discorso Dell'Obbligo di ben parlare la propria lingua*, di C. E. (Florence, 1657).

[7] *Prose Fiorentine Raccolte dallo Smarrito Academico della Crusca* (Florence, 1661), 1:3-4. The text that Dati quotes from Chiabrera is as follows:

> Come sei bella, o del mio core amica,
> O come amica del mio cor sei bella:
> Gli occhi di colombella
> Acciocchè del' interno altro io non dica.

Dati notes that Strozzi objects to the use of "colombella" as ugly in so elegant and noble a verse. Evidently Dati continued to admire Chiabrera until the end of his life, for he cites with approval some songs of Chiabrera in a letter to Ottavio Falconeri in 1675 (*Lettere di Carlo Roberto Dati* [Florence, 1825], 81).

Horace and Tibullus, for like Horace he calls Venus cruel and, like
Tibullus, he attributes her cruelty to her nativity from the sea.[8]

> Ah, che vien cenere
> Penando un' Amator, benchè fedele,
> Cosi vuol Venere
> Nata nell' Ocean, Nume crudele.

> Ah, how a lover's suffering
> Comes to ashes,
> Although he is faithful;
> So wills Venus,
> Born of the sea, a savage deity.

Although he obviously admires Chiabrera's *canzonetta* as a lyric, which,
as he says, surpasses even Tibullus, Dati does not elaborate on Chiabrera's poetic performance. Yet, he tells Milton that one of his aims was
to "illustrate" Chiabrera. Instead, he goes on to cite in his letter further
support for the motion that Venus's cruelty is the result of her nativity
from the sea, and he argues at length the case for emending a word in
Tibullus, quoting innumerable passages from other classical writers to
lend support for the emendation. We are left, therefore, with this
question: why should Chiabrera specially be cited in discussion that
finally breaks down to a sequence of philological and mythological
footnotes? That these kind of remarks would have been interesting to a
man of Milton's classical training we need not doubt. Yet Dati's introduction of Chiabrera as the Italian master of the Pindaric and Anacreontic manner had seemed to promise some discussion of contemporary Italian poetry that might be pertinent to Milton's own interests and
practice. It is tempting to speculate that Dati had begun by remarking
on Chiabrera's Horatian imitation because he knew that Milton, while
highly skilled in Latin verse, was attempting, like Chiabrera, to adapt
classical material for vernacular performance. Although Dati was primarily interested in Milton's Latin verse (Milton had promised to send him
the Latin volume of the 1645 poems), he might well have known that
Milton had rendered Horace's fifth ode into English, a lyric, like Chiabrera's, which describes a lover's shipwreck at the hand of that same

---

[8] "Dati to Milton," "Miscellaneous Correspondence in Foreign Tongues," 34, in
CE 12:296-313.

savage shipwrecker born of the sea, Venus. But, even if Dati did not have this particular reason for citing Chiabrera's work, we may take for granted that he felt that the Italian poet and his poetic techniques would be of interest to his English poetical friend.

But what of Milton? What might his principal interest in Chiabrera have been? We need not assume that he shared Dati's preoccupation with Chiabrera's *canzonette* and lyric works, for Chiabrera had a wide-ranging poetic output that Milton could have known. Some critics believe that Chiabrera's dramatic or narrative works might have been of greater interest to Milton as the composer of *Comus* and *Arcades* and as the future author of the biblical narrative in blank verse. Indeed, Chiabrera's pastoral plays in the style of *Aminta* or *Pastor Fido*, for example, his *Favola boschereccia*, *Gelopea*, or his mythological masque to music, *Il Rapimento di Cefalo*, might easily be added to the analogues or sources of Milton's masques.[9] Further, Chiabrera had ventured beyond pastoral to epic, composing *Ruggiero* as a continuation of Ariosto's and *L'Erminia* of Tasso's epic, and even aspiring to produce a national epic in *Firenze*; these experiments in epic could hardly have been without note to the English poet who was then planning his own *Arthuriad*. Casting about for predecessors to Milton's blank verse, F. T. Prince has suggested a generic resemblance between it and the *versi sciolti* that Chiabrera uses both for secular and sacred narrative; he cites a passage from Chiabrera's "Il Diluvio" as an example of the particular adaptability of this verse to biblical themes.[10] Milton's apostrophe to Vida in his incomplete ode, "The Passion," testifies to his interest during the 1630s

---

[9] For analogues see Watson Kirkconnell, *Awake the Courteous Echo: The Themes and Prosody of "Comus," "Lycidas," and "Paradise Regained" in World Literature* (Toronto: Univ. of Toronto Press, 1973). Also see *Variorum* 2:766-68. Among Chiabrera's dramatic works is also a regular Greek tragedy, *Ippodamia*, complete with choral and lyric sections, the prosody of which surely would have interested Milton. The tragedy, which recounts the love of Ippodamia for Achilles and her suicide at his death, was not printed until the eighteenth century (*Alcune Poesie di Gabriele Chiabrera* [Genoa, 1794]).

[10] In the preface to *Firenze*, a poem in *ottava rima*, Chiabrera argues the case for using *versi sciolti* (blank verse) for the heroic poem, rather than *terza rima* or *ottava rima*. He cites Trissino, Alamanni, Annibal Caro, and Tasso as poets who have successfully used *versi sciolti* for longer poems. The implication of these arguments and precedents for *Paradise Lost*, is, of course, interesting. (*Firenze*, Poema di Gabriello Chiabrera [Florence, 1728]). See Prince, 175-77.

in biblical epic; Milton might have found Chiabrera a worthy successor to Vida.

Yet, whatever Chiabrera's achievements in the dramatic and narrative modes, we must not forget that Chiabrera's contemporaries (and, most likely, Milton as well) found his greatest strength in his lyric perfor- mances. He adapted, for example, the Virgilian style successfully for the series of seven eclogues that he wrote, some time after 1602, for the death of his close friend, Jacopo Corsi, the Florentine nobleman and musician, who was a patron of early opera and who probably was concerned in the production of "Il Rapimento di Cefalo."[11] Milton would have been interested in this set of eclogues both because they were written for a artist-friend by a poet and because they adhere closely to classical form, as do *Lycidas* and *Epitaphium Damonis*. Chiabrera manages, particularly in the fourth eclogue, where Damon comes to adorn his friend Tirsi's grave with flowers, to infuse the well-worn form of pastoral lament with new life and to use ancient formulas freshly. Like Milton's shepherds, Damon comes to pluck the symbolic laurel, to say a repeated farewell, and to reflect on the evil of the present day as he evokes memories of yesterday's shady valleys, sweet breezes, and murmuring streams: "Per ombra di sì fresco valoncello, / Ove sì dolci corrono l'aurette, / Ove sì chiaro mormora il ruscello" (22-24)[12] ("through the shade of so fresh a little valley, where the little breezes so sweetly course, and where so clearly murmurs the brook"). Even like Thyrsis in *Epitaphium Damon*, in what is perhaps an interesting antici- pation of Milton's refrain, he bids his little lambs and goats to go and seek fresh pastures with green grass, while he laments: "Itene pecorelle, ite caprette, / Mandra forse non è, che in altro prato / Aggia da pas- colar sì molli erbette" (25-27) ("Go little lambs and goats: perhaps there is not a herd which in another meadow takes pleasure in pastur- ing on such sweet grass"). Interesting through Chiabrera's eclogues may have been for Milton, Chiabrera was only one of many models for *Lycidas* and *Epitaphium Damonis*, there being an abundance of Italian,

---

[11] See the article on Corsi in the *New Grove Dictionary of Music and Musicians*, ed. Stanley Sadie (London: Macmillan, 1980). Besides writing this sequence and the epitaph on Corsi's death, Chiabrera wrote verse to Corsi during his lifetime; see the *canzoni morali* in *Rime del Sig. Gabriello Chiabrera* (Venice, 1605), 2:139-40, 151-52.

[12] All quotations, unless otherwise noted, are from *Rime di Gabriello Chiabrera*, 3 vols. (Milan, 1807). *Le Egloghe* in *Rime*, 2:269-81.

French, English and Neo-Latin poets who in the Renaissance attempted Virgilian pastoral. His position as a Pindaric imitator was more exclusive and potentially of more moment for Milton.

From his first early ode, "On the Death of a Fair Infant," through the Latin ode composed in 1646 to John Rouse, Milton had displayed interest in the ode as a genre of lyric; he singled out Pindar, moreover, with Callimachus, as writers of the most noble kind of ode. Milton had determined by the time he had returned from Italy that the proper end of his poetry ought to be to adorn his native language; he pronounced, further, that the most acceptable models for him were "the greatest and choycest wits of *Athens, Rome,* or modern *Italy.*"[13] Among modern Italians Chiabrera had a special place, for he too, like Milton after him, was bent on the study of the poets of Athens and Rome as models to adorn contemporary Italian poetry. In turning particularly to Anacreon and Pindar, Chiabrera was following the path taken by Ronsard, and he became in turn the most notable practitioner of Pindaric and Anacreontic style on the continent after his great French master. If he aspired to Pindaric imitation, Milton could find, aside from Jonson and perhaps Drayton, no models in English poetry for Pindaric imitation. He had to turn to continental models—Neo-Latin and vernacular poets—and among the vernacular poets who practiced the Pindaric style in the late sixteenth and early seventeenth centuries, Chiabrera was the outstanding poet. Although Alessandro Adimari, the first poet to translate Pindar into Italian, was living in Florence at the time of Milton's visit, we have no record that the two met.[14] Further, it is Chiabrera and not Adimari, whom Dati names the exemplar of the Pindaric style. Given the concurrence of Milton's poetic interests during this period and Chiabrera's well-known accomplishments in the genre in which Milton was interested, we can hardly avoid speculating that Milton knew and had explored Chiabrera's Pindarics.

Chiabrera's Pindaric odes fall into two groups: heroic songs of praise (*lodi*), addressed to both the important political leaders and to friends, and religious odes (*canzoni sacre*), addressed to the Virgin and to the saints. Both kinds of odes have relevance for Milton. Chiabrera's heroic *canzoni* celebrate the leading aristocrats of Italy and record some of the

---

[13] "The Reason of Church-Government," in CE 3.1.238, 236.
[14] Arthos, 19–25, 124; Masson, 1:787.

most important political events that concern them. In time of war with the threat of the Turk to the east and foreign armies to the north, the political Pindaric was a particularly apt form; Pindar's odes to the tyrants of Sicily and the noblemen of Greece often concern the problems of war and peace that beset the Mediterranean world in the fifth century BC. The fifteenth-century Italian poet Filelfo, who first brought manuscripts of Pindar's odes to Italy, created the modern political Pindaric in the odes that he wrote to the ducal leaders and kings of his time. Lampridio and Alamanni follow Filelfo's example, the first writing Latin Pindarics, the last vernacular. Alamanni bequeaths the vernacular Pindaric to Ronsard, who in turn hands it down to Chiabrera. Chiabrera's first collection of heroic *lodi* was published in Genoa in 1586 and celebrates members of the same aristocratic families that had been celebrated in Pindarics since the time of Filelfo. Two years later, in 1588, the *canzoni sacre* appear; in these Chiabrera adapts his Pindaric methods to praise the Virgin, Saints Peter, Andrew, Paul and Stephen, and several female martyrs of the early church—Lucy, Cecilia, and Agatha, two of which with their associations with Sicily evoke an interesting combination of Christian and classical imagery.

Both Chiabrera's heroic and religious odes are written in a variety of stanzaic forms, some monostrophic, some triadic. (Pindar's own odes, though mostly triadic, include monostrophic examples.) An accomplished prosodist, Chiabrera employs a great number of different strophic patterns both in triadic and monostrophic ode. Sometimes he writes in the long thin stanza pattern that was so common for Pindaric ode in the sixteenth century; other times he writes stanzas five or six lines long in pentameters or hexameters.[15] In a sequence of ten odes written to celebrate Urban VII's ascendancy to the papacy in 1590, Chiabrera begins with a monostrophic ode and continues with triadic odes, each ode, however, employing a different triadic pattern. This kind of poetic virtuosity clearly had its effect on the English poets of the late sixteenth and early seventeenth centuries and so also perhaps on Milton, who experimented with different strophic patterns in the odes he wrote between 1628 and 1646.

But whether he wrote in monostrophic or in triadic patterns, Chiab-

---

[15] Carol Maddison, *Apollo and the Nine* (Baltimore: Johns Hopkins Press, 1960), 12 (Renaissance versification), 178–83 (Chiabrera).

rera clearly was imitating Pindaric style, incorporating the techniques of the Theban bard into those secular and religious odes he thought most properly suited to the Pindaric mode. Several of the odes made direct claims of imitation. At the end of his ode on Saint Cecilia, he asserts that he will raise the saint to Castalian heights by praising her in the Theban mode. He tells Enrico Dandalo, the duke of Venice, that, as friend to the swan of Dirce, he is adopting the Theban lyre to celebrate him. He announces to Pope Urban that he is employing the Pindaric mode to celebrate his virtues because in the ancient world Pindar had so often composed odes to reward the virtue of royal subjects: Hieron, Theron, and the king of Cyrene.

Certain Pindaric signatures mark the Pindaric style as clearly as the use of triads, for example, the use of the invocation or the extended figure that so often marks the opening of the ode. Chiabrera consciously emulates these, sometimes simply as the invocation to the Muse that opens his *canzone sacra* to the Virgin or the address to Ferrara or to Florence, in imitation of Pindar's apostrophe to Syracuse or to Acragas. Other times we have a more complicated figure. As Pindar opened Olympia 6 by describing the golden columns of a splendid dwelling or Olympia 7 with the figure of the offered bowl of wine, so Chiabrera creates for the duke of Genoa an ode that begins by describing a shining gold-studded scepter. In his ode on the capture of 320 Turkish slaves at Rhodes, he pays close attention to Pindar's own ode to a victor from Rhodes, mindful of Pindar's description in Olympia 7 of the island rising from the sea to be claimed by the sun god Helios and of Pindar's association of Rhodes with rose. Hence he begins by alluding to the garland of flowers that he weaves, before he apostrophizes Rhodes: "Rodi diletta al Sol, Rodi famosa" (1-4), combining both the allusion to sun and flowers (1.157).

Chiabrera follows Pindar also in using both the short mythic reference and the longer more extended digressive myth. Like some of his predecessors he does not restrict himself to classical myth, but alludes to biblical and classical stories in the same ode. In his fifth ode for Urban VII, he invokes the true Apollo and then uses the story of Moses' exodus from Egypt to celebrate the pope's leadership in the struggle against the Turks. In the seventh ode in this sequence, he alludes to Jove's conquest of Typhon, making, as Pindar does in Pythia 1, the righteous leader's resistance against pagan forces analogous to the true god's victory over monsters from the underworld. In his heroic *canzoni,* however, Chiabrera follows Pindar closely in evoking traditional classical heroes, such as Achilles and Hercules, to celebrate the modern heroes of his own time. For example, Hercules appears and reappears in the political odes.[16] The duke of Guise's exploits are compared to Hercules' triumph over the hydra. Giovan-Giacopo Truultio is not only a Milanese Ulysses, but also a glorious and venturesome Alcides. Giovanni Medici is both Jove defeating the aspiring Titans and Giants and Hercules, who showed promise of his future feats by strangling the serpents in his cradle. Yet the fullest use of the Hercules story is probably in the ode for Emmanuel Filiberto di Savoia, where he starts with Hercules' cleansing of the Augean stables and runs through the entire sequence of labors. These are not mere political compliments. Chiabrera takes the Pindaric example seriously, and as Pindar drew comparisons between the lives of the ancient heroes and those of the modern kings, tyrants, and nobles that he wrote for, so Chiabrera attempts the same. In Olympia 2, for example, Pindar reassures Theron that there is good fortune after ill, by recounting the history of his Theban forebears—Cadmus and his daughters, Oedipus and his unfortunate sons—who survive the misfortunes that beset them and finally come to fortune in the surviving son of Polynices, Thersander, who is the founding ancestor of Theron's Sicilian home. Chiabrera's retracing of the Theban story in his ode for Enrico Dandolo makes a similar point—that true valor can finally assure good fortune. Like Pindar, he is drawing a parallel between an ancient city besieged by foes and a modern one likewise in danger. For Ercole Pio, the leader of the Venetians against the Turks, who died at the battle of Lepanto, Chiabrera creates a different kind of ode. Probably modelling his *canzone lugubro* on Pindar's Isthmia 8, Chiabrera recounts, as Pindar had, the fall of Achilles at Troy, pointing out that Achilles died because he sought revenge for his friend and because by resisting the powers of Asia he made possible a safe homecoming for his other comrades. After Patroclus dies on Hector's sword, Achilles ignores his mother's pleas, seeks the making of the shield,

---

[16] Reference to Hercules (Heracles) are to be found throughout Pindar's verse; see, for example, Olympia 10 on Heracles' founding of the Olympic games; Nemea 1 on Heracles' birth and strangling of the serpents, Nemea 3 on the slaying of monsters and the taking of Troy; Nemea 4 on the battles with the giants at Phlegra; Isthmia 1 on the subduing of Geryon, and Isthmia 4 on the defeat of Antaeus.

returns to battle, filling the Xanthus with enemy bodies, and finally kills Hector, even though he himself is killed soon after. The details of Achilles' warfaring are told with the heroic Pio in mind, for after he recounts the grief of Peleus at his son's death, Chiabrera returns to raise the funeral song for Pio, commenting that, like Achilles, this happy-unhappy hero died taking his enemies with him in his death and guaranteeing safety for his friends.

To a degree, the style of address and mythic references that Chiab-rera uses in his Pindaric odes he extends in miniature to the heroic sonnets that he writes to different princes. References to Hercules or to Achilles reappear in small in the sonnets to Carlo Emanuele di Savoia. In one, Chiabrera invokes the watchful protection that Thetis provided for her son and the Greek fleet crossing the sea as he sends his good wishes to the duke travelling over the sea to Spain. In another, encour-aging the duke in his efforts to win Geneva, Chiabrera remarks that it was not without labor that Hercules put down the hydra or conquered Antaeus. In these political sonnets, Chiabrera takes sides and urges action. Noteworthy particularly are the number of sonnets that concern the question of war in Italy, Italy's relations with Spain, and the prob-lem of not only resisting the Turk, but pressing onward against the Ottoman Empire and regaining Jerusalem. Many political sonnets, address the same persons and take up issues similar to those Chiabrera explores in his odes. There is, for example, an ode to Emmanuel Filiberto di Savoia on his victory over the French and his signing of the peace treaty, as there is for Carlo Emmanuele, his son, on pursuing his father's policies and taking Saluzzo. Chiabrera's heroic odes complement his heroic sonnets.

Milton wrote no political odes, but the political sonnet was an important form for him in the 1640s and 1650s. Different though Chiabrera's politics were from his, the techniques of Chiabrera's heroic odes and political sonnets had something to teach Milton, who had been an admirer of the sonnets of Tasso and Della Casa. Although the figure of Hercules as virtue putting down the hydra of rebellion has its source in Horace (and before him in Pindar), it appears again in Pet-rarch and Dante and once again in Chiabrera, who pays homage to its classical and Italian precedents. The reappearance of this figure in Milton's sonnet to Fairfax makes Fairfax a Herculean leader in the line not only of the classical originals but also the Italian dukes and princes who follow: "Thy firm unshak'n virtue ever brings / Victory home,

though new rebellions raise / Thir Hydra heads" (5-7).[17] It also suggests Milton's indebtedness to the line of Italian sonneteers that stretch-
es to Chiabrera, whose technique of using a classical-drawn figure might
easily have recommended itself to Milton. As a political sonneteer
Milton frequently uses allusion to classical or mythic stories to drive his
point home. In Sonnet 12, for example, he alludes to the story of the
transformation into frogs of those who "Rail'd at Latona's twin-born
progeny / Which after held the Sun and Moon in fee" (6-7) in order
to silence the "barbarous noise" of those who preferred license to
honest liberty. In Sonnet 10 he opens up a comparison of Sir James
Ley to Isocrates in order to liken the "dishonest victory / At *Chaeronea*,
fatal to liberty" to the dissolution of the Parliament in 1629, which
ended parliamentary government in England for over a decade. Or, in
a different mood, he appeals in Sonnet 8, "When the Assault was
Intended to the City," for a wartime society to respect the Muses by
alluding to two classical stories—Alexander's sparing of the house of
Pindar and the Spartan generals' mercy towards the city of Athens
because of respect for the poets Pindar and Euripides respectively. Here
Milton's and Chiabrera's views would have been at one, for as a poet
Chiabrera urged Carlo Emmanuele and other leaders to restore peace as
the proper climate for poetry. Milton's sonnets to Fairfax and Cromwell
voice a similar plea for peace. Yet neither Milton nor Chiabrera shrink
from demanding action when the issue is religious freedom—albeit their
definition of religion and freedom might be different. Chiabrera urges
the Christian princes to move their armies against the Turk and free
Jerusalem; he begins the poem with a passionate exhortation—trample,
he cries, those vestiges of the Turk that pollute Jerusalem; he ends
plaintively with the lyre mournfully lamenting the desecration of the
holy altars and the Way of the Cross. In a similar mood, yet for a
different cause, Milton calls upon God to avenge the massacre of the
Waldensians in Piedmont. Milton's techniques of exhortation, if not his
religious allegiance, resemble those of Chiabrera's sonnet.

If the Pindaric ode in the Renaissance naturally inclined to celebrating modern political leaders in place of Pindar's athletes and kings, it
also just as naturally moved to celebrating the Christian God and the

---

[17] Quotations from Milton's poetry are from Hughes. See Hughes's note on the
classical and Italian sources of the hydra metaphor in the Fairfax sonnet (159).

saints in place of Zeus, Apollo, and the gods of the Olympian pantheon. The heroic event celebrated in the ode to the saint was the contest for immortal rather than mortal garlands and the mythic digression often recounted the saint's martyrdom. Such is the case in the first of the three monostrophic odes that Chiabrera wrote for Santa Lucia and in the triadic odes for Santa Celia and Santa Agata. The odes could have been models for Milton. In these, the virgin martyr is likened both to the heroic athlete of Pindar's ode and the hero of his digressive myth—and because she is a Christian she is victorious above both her prototypes. Since Sicily, the land of Ceres, Proserpine, and Theocritean pastoral, gave birth to two of the saints—Lucia and Agata—celebrated in Chiabrera's odes, the odes are rich in associations with pastoral and ancient myth. The flowers that Proserpine let fall bloom again in Lucia's lilies, which Chiabrera describes as earthly flowers only less pure than the saint herself, a bloom who is to be translated to heaven (1.290–91). Agata too resembles a Sicilian nature deity; the flowers of April spring from her martyred blood like the flowers of the metamorphosed heroes of myth. As Proserpine's release from Hades prompts the return of spring, Agata's ascent to heaven makes April smile at Primavera's coming. As he evokes the pastoral beauty of Sicily and recalls Sicilian myth, Chiabrera also echoes some of the mythic references in Pindar's odes—the invocation of Demeter and Persephone from Pythia 12 and Olympia 6, the reference to Alpheus and Arethusa in Nemea 1, and the description of Aetna in Pythia 1. In the ode to Santa Lucia, Chiabrera describes the flames of Aetna and alludes to Alpheus's pursuit of Arethusa, as Milton was later to do in his own pastoral *Lycidas*.

But even as he uses classical myth to adorn his odes to Christian saints, he carefully disclaims the truth of such myth. While he may liken his female martyrs to classical goddesses and invoke the Muses to celebrate them, he asserts, as humanist poets before and after him, that he will raise his saints above Pindus, Permessus, and Parnassus (1.291). Lucia is the elect and spouse of God, who does not owe her grace to a fabled lyre, but stands at the summit of Sion with palms won from Jordan. Celia's name will be famous as an "ammirabile Diva" (1.297); Agata, the true soul, is to be preferred to the goddesses Pallas or Juno, whom men so often celebrate, for she sits enthroned in heaven as the true spouse of God (1.302). Yet Chiabrera constantly alludes to and measures his saints by the standard of classical heroic myth. Referring to expeditions such as the Argonauts, he asserts that Agata's deeds of

heroic martyrdom far surpassed the deeds of ancient heroes; she coura-
geously resisted tyranny and impious pride and by suffering won tro-
phies that are immortal. In the ode to Santa Cecilia, Chiabrera uses an
Old Testament story—the account of Tamar's rape and Absalom's
revenge of his sister's shame—to praise Cecilia's preservation of her
virginity and her refusal to honor false gods. Whether affirmed or
denied, the classical world is a constant presence in Chiabrera's odes.

With their mixture of classical and Christian, Chiabrera's odes have
something to tell us about how to approach Milton's odes of the 1620s
and 1630s with their proclaimed Christian subjects and their very
conscious mythologizing. "On the Death of a Fair Infant," Milton
attempts in an English monostrophic ode to use some of the techniques
of the vernacular Pindaric; he opens with an apostrophe to the dead
child as a flower and uses several brief mythic allusions and a short
digressive myth on Winter's ravishing the pure Virgin Soul. Like
Chiabrera's odes to Lucia, Celia, and Agata, Milton's "Fair Infant"
combines the classical myth of the short-lived flower with the Christian
account of the saint. In Milton's ode the dead child is lifted to heaven
to dwell with God in eternity like the pure virgin martyrs of Chiabrera's
odes. But the "fairest flower no sooner blown but blasted" (1) also
shares a heritage with those flowers of Proserpine that faded; she is
directly compared by Milton to Apollo's transformed hyacinth and
without demur to several other mythological characters—the Athenian
damsel abducted by Aquilo, "some goddess fled / Amongst us here"
(47–48), and to Astraea, the last of the immortals to leave earth. Yet
even as he makes these comparisons, Milton wants us to remember that
this is a Christian soul who has gone to heaven. Like Chiabrera, Milton
uses his mythological references to reinforce his conviction that though
the child may resemble, as Lucia or Celia or Agata do, the golden
goddess, she is truly one of the saints.

Sicilian flowers return for Milton's pastoral ode or monody, Lycidas,
and for his pastoral elegy, Epitaphium Damonis, where, as in "Fair
Infant," he makes liberal use of pagan mythology to construct a Christian account of the saint's progress to heaven. For, though both Lycidas
and Epitaphium Damonis begin as pastoral laments, they conclude with
scenes, much like those in Chiabrera's odes to Lucia, Cecilia, and
Agata, where the once stricken mortal triumphs as a saint in heaven. In
Lycidas, the youth, whose fate has been has been compared to Orpheus
and whom the poet urged to be, like Arion, wafted by dolphins, mounts

at the conclusion of the poem like the saint to the "blest Kingdoms meek of joy and love" to hear the "unexpressive nuptial song" and to be entertained by all the saints (176-78). Just as Lucia's lilies are eternized as the emblems of the risen saint, so the flowers that once were gathered to strew the laureate hearse (133-51) become part of the undying landscape of "other groves" and "other streams" in heaven (174).

The kind of interweaving of pagan and Christian that occurs in Milton's pastoral monody also occurs in his pastoral elegy, *Epitaphium Damonis*. As the sisters of the sacred well have been invoked in *Lycidas* or Euterpe in Chiabrera's odes, the nymphs of Himera are summoned for Damon, who is identified with the classical Daphnis and Hylas. Pastoral mourners lament Damon as they do Lycidas, and if we do not find side-by-side Apollo and Saint Peter, we find real persons, such as Manso, inhabiting the landscape with Tuscan shepherds with pastoral names. In place of the so-called digressive myth that characterizes the Pindaric ode, we find a digressive passage where Milton alludes to his Italian journey and proposes those stories from England's mythic past that he will recount in lieu of a Greek or Roman myth. Further, as he concludes his elegy, he lifts Damon to a semi-classical, semi-Christian heaven that seems an extension of the scene he describes on Manso's cup. There Damon dwells in pure aether, aether pure enough for him to inhabit. Protestant though he may be and opposed to the martyrology of the Catholic Church, Milton resembles the Catholic Chiabrera when he describes the saint's rewards in heaven. Just as Chiabrera's virgin martyrs ascend to a heaven pure enough to hold them and celebrate the nuptial joys that they were denied on earth, Milton's Lycidas and his Damon find in heaven a reward for their pure virtue. Unmarried on earth, Damon will be crowned with glory in heaven, and, holding the palms of victory, take part in an immortal hymenael under a thyrsus both of Bacchus and of Sion. In writing odes to saints inspired by the odes Pindar wrote to athletes, Chiabrera in a sense showed Milton the way to crown his Lycidas and his Damon with the garlands of an Olympian Sion.

For both Milton and Chiabrera the Pindaric ode was the most magnificent genre of lyric poetry, to be used to celebrate the heroic, to lament the tragically lost, and to crown the saint with glory. As he moved through his youthful period of lyric experimentation that culminated with the publication of the 1645 poems, Milton was essentially, as Chiabrera had been, a humanist poet intent on finding the best among classical and modern as models for vernacular verse. Consistent as his interest had been during this period in modern Italian poetry, it would have been odd if he had not discovered, as a model for his own verse, that poet whom contemporary Italian opinion thought had most successfully met the challenge of the loftiest and most serious of ode forms.[18]

Southern Illinois University

---

[18] I wish to thank the Folger Shakespeare Library for a short-term fellowship, during which time I was able to revise this article.

ESTELLE HAAN

# "Written encomiums":
# Milton's Latin Poetry in Its Italian Context

I N THE COMPOSITION OF LATIN VERSE, Milton takes his place among the many Renaissance *literati* in England and on the continent who, largely as a consequence of the emphasis on Latin in the educational system,[1] produced a vast body of Latin poetry on a wide variety of topics. The practice, however, was much more than a purely academic one, since Latin was a universal language which enabled the aspiring poet to win acclaim both at home and abroad.[2] An Englishman who wrote in Latin was heir not only to a well-established Anglo-Latin tradition, but also to the great exemplars of Renaissance Italy —those bilingual poets who saw Latin as a living medium capable of expressing contemporary ideas in vivid and often very original terms.[3]

Milton's output of Latin poetry is impressive: seven Latin elegies on such themes as death, love, spring and the nature of the poet; a miniature epic and five epigrams on the Gunpowder Plot; poems of a philosophic nature; a poem to his father; encomia addressed to, and in praise of, Italian friends; epigrams in praise of an Italian soprano; a pastoral poem on the death of his friend Charles Diodati; and an ode accompa-

---

[1] See W. H. Woodward, *Studies in Education During the Age of the Renaissance 1400–1600* (Cambridge: Cambridge Univ. Press, 1906); F. Watson, *The English Grammar Schools to 1660: Their Curriculum and Practice* (Cambridge: Cambridge Univ. Press, 1908).

[2] Cf. Milton's acknowledgement of the fact that his use of the English language will automatically mean that his reading public will be confined to his native land: *Epitaphium Damonis* 171–78 and *The Reason of Church Government* in CE 3:236. All quotations are from this edition.

[3] See F. A. Wright and T. A. Sinclair, *A History of Later Latin Literature from the Middle of the Fourth to the End of the Seventeenth Century* (London: Routledge, 1931); Paul van Tieghem, *La Littérature Latine de la Renaissance: Étude d'Histoire Litteraire Européenne* (Paris: Droz, 1944); John Sparrow, "Latin Verse of the High Renaissance," in *Italian Renaissance Studies*, ed. E. F. Jacob (London, 1960), 354–409.

nying a replacement of a lost copy of the 1645 edition of his poems. A rough dividing line can be drawn between those poems written while he was still at Cambridge and those composed during or after his trip to Italy. Some are marked by their autobiographical content, others by their sharp invective and anti-papal tone, and others by their rich mythological flavoring and polished elegance. Moreover, they bear an individual stamp whereby, in the true Renaissance spirit, ancient themes and *topoi* are recast and remolded in an often strikingly novel setting. In short, the Milton of the Latin poems reveals himself, not as a mainly vernacular poet who happened to "try his hand," as it were, at the composition of Latin verse, but as a Renaissance Latin poet, the heir of a great European tradition, ranking with his contemporaries on the continent.

More specifically, some of his Latin poems assume particular significance when viewed in their Italian context. Firstly, they may be considered in relation to Latin works by Petrarch, Politian, Mantuan, Vida, and Castiglione; secondly, some of them constitute skillful replies to Latin verse tributes received from Italian friends. For Milton was very much a man of his time, attracted to the "modern" as well as to the classical world. This is amply attested by his visit to Italy, his praise of that country, its practices and *literati*[4]–praise which constitutes his own *laudes Italiae*–and, more explicitly, by his statement to the Italian Benedetto Bonmattei that his literary interests are not confined to the classics, but include Dante, Petrarch *aliosque ... complusculos*.[5] While it is only rarely that he mentions contemporary or recent Latin authors by name,[6] a close reading of his Latin poems often suggests parallels with Latin poetry of the Italian Renaissance.

Even such a youthful piece as "Apologus de Rustico et Hero" merits consideration in an Italian context. Milton's poem is modelled on a

---

[4] See, for example, *Defensio secunda* (CE 8:122).

[5] *Epistolae familiares* 8 (CE 12:34).

[6] See, for example, his allusion to Petrarch (*Apology Against a Pamphlet* [CE 3:309]). More implicit is his reference to the *Christiad* of Vida (a native of Cremona):

> These latest scenes confine my roving vers,
> To this Horizon is my Phoebus bound,
> His Godlike acts; and his temptations fierce,
> And former sufferings other where are found;
> Loud o're the rest Cremona's Trump doth sound.
> (*The Passion*, 21–26)

Latin fable by Mantuan, describing the transplanting of an appletree and its subsequent decay,[7] and is an example of an exercise in imitative verse-composition practised at St. Paul's School. It conforms not to the double translation system, as Fletcher has assumed,[8] but to an educational practice known as the "turning of verses,"[9] whereby alternative nouns, adjectives, or verbs are substituted and a similar idea is expressed in different terms. Indeed, Milton improves upon the original by, for example, including extra sibilants to convey the enticing juices of the apples, creating a stark contrast between fertility and decay, establishing a more personal tone, and emphasizing the master's sense of regret at the loss of the apples. As I have illustrated elsewhere,[10] this poem anticipates Eve's plucking and eating of the apple in *Paradise Lost* 9.

Links with the Italian poet Vida are apparent in Milton's *Ad patrem* and *Elegia quinta*. *Ad patrem* recalls Vida's *De arte poetica* 1 in its fusion of the themes of education and the defense of poetry, and draws upon Renaissance educational theory. Vida's didactic poem outlines the qualities of a father as an ideal Renaissance educator: he must take great care in his son's education, provide him with excellent tutors, teach him to avoid lucrative pursuits and to devote his time to poetry, and enable him to withdraw from the noise of the city. Milton's poem presents his father in this role and seems to imply that he has fulfilled in a practical sense the recommendations laid down by Vida. The young Milton thanks his father for enabling him to learn a wide variety of subjects, for discouraging him from wealthier occupations, such as the legal profession, and for permitting him to retire into the peaceful countryside. Moreover, Milton's defense of poetry in the same poem recalls that of Vida, which in itself is modelled on lines from Politian's *Nutricia*.[11]

*Elegia quinta* contains a passage which can be compared with lines from Vida's *De arte poetica* 2. Milton, in paralleling the arrival of spring

---

[7] See Harris F. Fletcher, "Milton's *Apologus* and Its Mantuan Model," *JEGP* 55 (1956): 230-33. Mantuan's poem is to be found in his *Opera* (Paris, 1513 edition), folio 194v.

[8] Fletcher, "Milton's *Apologus*," 230-33.

[9] I have argued this viewpoint in my doctoral dissertation, "John Milton's Latin Poetry: Some Neo-Latin and Vernacular Contexts" (The Queen's University of Belfast, 1987), 23-35.

[10] Ibid., 28-35.

[11] For a full discussion, see ibid., 2-22.

in the natural world and the onset of inspiration in the poet's breast, inverts lines 395-454 of Vida, in which the arrival and subsequent departure of inspiration are likened to nature's cycle as manifested in the season of spring: just as spring does not always adorn sunny fields, Vida says, so inspiration does not always attend the poet. Unlike Vida, however, who concentrates upon the negative side, stating what will happen if the season is unsuitable and inspiration absent, Milton presents an essentially positive view, thereby inverting the whole. Thus, the very features which Vida had bewailed as lacking are depicted by Milton as actually present. Vida had conveyed the sluggishness which oppresses the poet, with the result that the strength to compose *carmina* weakens; Milton announces the great urge to compose. His *redeunt in carmina vires* (5) inverts Vida's *languent ad carmina vires* (414). Vida had bewailed the absence of the Muses; Milton feels their presence. Where Vida had conveyed the fear that Apollo would never return to the poet, Milton celebrates his arrival.[12]

Milton's pastoral lament *Epitaphium Damonis* merits comparison with a Latin poem by Castiglione, the author of *The Courtier*.[13] Castiglione's poem, entitled *Alcon*, is, like Milton's, a lament for a dead friend of the poet: Falcone in the case of Castiglione; Charles Diodati in the case of Milton. In both instances, grief causes the mourner to remain in solitude during the night and to blame the gods. Both describe in some detail the past joys which characterized the friendship which has now been severed by death; the speaker recalls the presence of his companion in the cold of winter, the heat of summer, by day and by night. Excessive grief causes him to neglect his normal pastoral tasks. Thus, both poems describe the rapid deterioration of the entire countryside and the neglect of flocks. Both mention barren fields, blighted corn, and neglected sheep in the same order. Milton contrasts the sorrowful lot of man with that of other creatures, and inverts lines from Castiglione's poem. There, the grieving speaker was compared to a nightingale who has lost her young ones or a turtle-dove bereft of its mate, whom a shepherd has killed. Milton, on the other hand, states

---

[12] See ibid., 37-45.

[13] See T. P. Harrison, "The Latin Pastorals of Milton and Castiglione," *PMLA* 50 (1935): 480-93. I have elaborated upon and developed Harrison's argument in my dissertation, 198-217.

that even a bird, unlike man, can easily find a substitute for a lost companion. One particularly striking parallel between the two poems is the fact that the speaker was absent at the precise moment of his friend's death and was unable to stand at his bedside and close his eyes. Falcone died in Mantua while Castiglione was in Rome; Diodati died in England while Milton was in Italy. In both instances the speaker feels a deep sense of guilt and regret on this account. In both poems he recalls idle dreams which he had cherished—fanciful thoughts which were very far removed from reality. Ignorant of his friend's death, he vainly speculates about what he may be doing at that very moment, or looks forward to their reunion. Castiglione's speaker indulges in vain daydreams as he imagines that Alcon will leave his old pastoral world and come to him in Rome; he envisages their meeting and embracing, the conversation which they will enjoy, and their delight in speaking of pastoral life. Milton's speaker likewise indulges in vain day-dreams in a passage which, like Castiglione's, contains a strong element of wish-ful-fillment. He imagines that his friend is performing his usual pastoral tasks, and looks forward to the pleasant conversation which they will share. Unlike the pagan world of the *Alcon*, however, in which the speaker's only form of consolation is the erection of a monument in his friend's honor, Milton's poem achieves a positive *consolatio* whereby death is seen, not as final in itself, but as a gateway to a happier and fuller existence, since the deceased friend does not dwell in a pagan underworld, but conquers death itself by rising to heaven.

Hitherto, the phrase "Italian context" has been interpreted largely to mean those possible links between Milton's Latin poetry and Renaissance Latin poems composed by learned Italians. The phrase, however, may be applied in a much more specific sense to the personal contacts which Milton made while in Italy and the various ways in which these are reflected in his Latin poems of that period.

During his sojourn in Italy, Milton made the acquaintance of many Italian *literati*. This is attested by references in his prose works, his Latin correspondence and, most notably, by Latin poems in praise of Italian addressees—poems which are marked by the consistently encomiastic nature of their subjectmatter and their particularly Italianate flavoring. In *Ad Salsillum* and *Mansus* he cleverly replies to "written encomiums" which, as he states in *The Reason of Church Government*, he had received from Italians in recognition of his Latin poems, some of which he had recited before Italian academies:

But much latelier in the privat Academies of Italy, whither I was favor'd to resort, ... some trifles which I had in memory, compos'd at under twenty or thereabout (for the manner is that every one must give some proof of his wit and reading there) met with acceptance above what was lookt for, and other things which I had shifted in scarsity of books and conveniences to patch up amongst them, were receiv'd with written Encomiums, which the Italian is not forward to bestow on men of this side the Alps.[14]

Like contemporary Italians, he addresses encomia to such celebrated figures as the poet Manso and the soprano Leonora Baroni, both of whom had received numerous tributes in their honor. The present study will examine Milton's Latin encomiastic verse in its Italian context by discussing the ways in which Milton replies to "written encomiums" from Salzilli and Manso respectively—whereby he inverts, as it were, features of the original Latin distichs and applies them in a totally different context—and by illustrating on a more general level some hitherto unnoticed parallels with seventeenth-century Italian poems composed by, or in praise of, his Italian addressees.

It was probably during Milton's first visit to Rome that he met the poet Giovanni Salzilli and received from him a four-line encomium:

Ad Ioannem Miltonem Anglum triplici
poeseos laurea coronandum Graeca nimirum,
Latina, atque Hetrusca, Epigramma
Ioannis Salsilli Romani.

Cede Meles, cedat depressa Mincius urna;
Sebetus Tassum desinat usque loqui;
At Thamesis victor cunctis ferat altior undas,
Nam per te, Milto, par tribus unus erit.

An Epigram by Giovanni Salzilli, of Rome, to John Milton, an Englishman, who deserves to be crowned with a threefold laurel-wreath of poetry: Greek certainly, Latin and Tuscan.

Yield Meles; let Mincius yield with lowered urn; let Sebetus cease to speak constantly of Tasso. But let the victorious Thames carry

[14] CE 3:235–36.

his waves higher than all the rest, for through you, Milton, he
alone will be equal to all three.[15]

Milton himself replies to this in his Latin poem *Ad Salsillum poetam
Romanum aegrotantem*. In the prose heading, Salzilli states that Milton
deserves to be crowned with a threefold laurel-wreath of poetry—one of
Greek, one of Latin and one of Tuscan. The chief feature of the tribute
is the use of an appropriate river to represent a famous poet: Meles
(Homer), Mincius (Virgil), and Sebetus (Tasso). These three rivers are
to yield to the Thames, representative of the London-born Milton,
which as a victor carries its waves higher than all the rest since, through
Milton, it alone is equal to the other three taken together.

That *Ad Salsillum* is a reply to the Latin tribute is suggested by the
occurrence of some of these features.[16] Milton actually mentions the
extent to which his poetry has been admired by Salzilli and alludes to
his judgment. He invokes the Muse:

> Adesdum et haec s'is verba pauca Salsillo
> Refer, camoena nostra cui tantum est cordi,
> Quamque ille magnis praetulit immerito divis.
>
> (6–8)

Be present, and carry, if you will, these few words to Salzilli, to
whose heart my poetry is so dear and which he preferred, quite
undeservedly, to the mighty gods.

The perfect tense *praetulit* (8) seems to point to one occasion in particular—the writing of the encomium—while the *magni ... divi* are Homer,
Virgil and Tasso, said to be surpassed by Milton in the encomium
itself. In qualifying his statement by saying that this preference was
undeserved (*immerito*), he expresses in a miniature or condensed form
that element of modesty evident on a much grander scale in the Latin
prose preface prefixed to the "written Encomiums" as a whole, which
states that the following terms of praise go far beyond what he actually
deserves. In *Ad Salsillum*, Milton uses the Latinized form *Milto* to refer
to himself. It may be significant that he should choose this rather than,

---

[15] All translations of both Latin and Italian are mine.

[16] As briefly noted by Parker, 173, and by Anthony Low, "*Mansus*: In Its Context," *MS* 19 (1984): 105.

say, *Miltonius* or *Miltonus* (forms which occur in other tributes in his honor), since this is the form which had been used by Salzilli both in the prose heading (*Ad Ioannem Miltonem*) and in the distich proper.[17] Moreover, Milton introduces himself as *alumnus ille Londini Milto* (9), the emphatic *ille* perhaps suggesting "that same *Milto* mentioned by you in your encomium."

Implicit in Salzilli's tribute is the contrast between the *Ioannes* who is an Englishman (*Ad Ioannem Miltonem Anglum*) and the *Ioannes* who is an Italian and native of Rome (*Epigramma/Ioannis Salsilli Romani*). This heading may be echoed in the title of Milton's poem (*Ad Salsillum poetam Romanum*). Milton develops the contrast in lines 9–16 as he describes the different climates of England and Italy.

Perhaps the closest parallel between Salzilli's encomium and Milton's poem is the motif of a river associated with, and even representative of, the poet of its region. Milton describes the effect which Salzilli's *cantus* will have upon his native river, the Tiber:

> Tumidusque et ipse Tibris hinc delinitus
> Spei favebit annuae colonorum:
> Nec in sepulchris ibit obsessum reges
> Nimium sinistro laxus irruens loro:
> Sed fraena melius temperabit undarum,
> Adusque curvi salsa regna Portumni.          (36–41)

And the swollen Tiber himself, charmed by the strains, will favor the yearly hope of the farmers and will not seek to besiege kings in their tombs by rushing along with the left rein too slack, but he will keep the reins of his waves under better control all the way to the salty kingdom of curved Portumnus.

This develops the river motif which was the characteristic feature of Salzilli's compliment. Now Milton inverts the whole, for whereas Salzilli had described the Thames, representative of Milton, carrying its waves higher than all the other rivers (*At Thamesis victor cunctis ferat altior undas*), Milton depicts Salzilli's river, the Tiber, as curbing its waves (*Sed fraena melius temperabit undarum* [40]) and hints at a parallel between the envisaged healing of Salzilli, who had required *levamen* (30), and the

---

[17] As noted by Bush, *Variorum* 1:264.

calming of the Tiber which had been *tumidus* (36)—an adjective which could also imply ill-health. Neither will have any connections with death: Salzilli, it is hoped, will recover his strength; the Tiber will not invade the tombs of kings. Milton echoes Horace, *Odes* 1.2.13-20, describing the swelling of the Tiber:

> vidimus flavum Tiberim retortis
> litore Etrusco violenter undis
> ire deiectum monumenta regis
>     templaque Vestae;
>
> Iliae dum se nimium querenti
> iactat ultorem, vagus et sinistra
> labitur ripa Iove non probante
>     uxorius amnis

We have seen the yellow Tiber, his waves hurled violently back from his Tuscan bank, advance to lay low the king's monument and Vesta's shrine, while he boasts that he is the avenger of Ilia's importunate complaints, and over his left bank glides far and wide, without the approval of Jupiter—a river too devoted to his wife.

Whereas Horace's Tiber invades the *monumenta regis* (15), the Tiber of Milton's poem will do no such thing (*Nec in sepulchris ibit obsessum reges* [38]). Horace had described the Tiber flooding on the left bank (*vagus et sinistra/labitur ripa* [18-19]); Milton states that this will not occur (*Nec in sepulchris ibit obsessum reges/Nimium sinistro laxus irruens loro* [38-39]). Finally, he seems to play on Salzilli's name (*Salsillus* is the Latinized form) in the last line (*Adusque curvi salsa regna Portumni* [41]).

It is also possible to view Milton's poem in relation to an Italian sonnet by Salzilli himself, which was included, together with several other of his poems, in a collection of Italian verse by members of the Academy of the *Fantastici* in Rome, published in 1637 and undoubtedly available to Milton during his stay:

> Ricco Mercante ucciso in duello,
>   per volersi vendicar d'una parola ingiuriosa
>
> D'Humano fasto a le grandezze intento,
>   Lunga stagion per l'Oceano infido
>   Mendico errai, fin ch'al bramato lido

Ricco m'addusse poi tranquillo vento.
Hor mentre qui nel cumulato Argento
D'un' eterno gioir la speme affido,
Ecco, ò folle pensier, nel patrio nido,
Di propria voglia al mio morir consento.
D'acerbo detto un momentaneo scorno
Vendicar volli, e la nemica sorte
Spense del viver mio l'ultimo giorno.
Flutti, e scogli nel Mar con petto forte
Sostengo, e poscia di lontan ritorno,
Da un falso accento a mendicar la Morte.[18]

A Rich Merchant killed in a duel through wishing to
avenge an insult

Intent on the grandeur of human pomp, I wandered as a beggar
for a long time across the treacherous ocean until a gentle wind
brought me as a rich man to the shore for which I had yearned.
Now while I was trusting in the hope of eternal joy in the money
I had made, behold, o foolish thought, in my native nest, I of
my own free will agreed to my death. I wanted to avenge the
temporary shame of a harsh word, but hostile Fate extinguished
the last day of my life. With a strong breast I endured waves and
rocks in the sea, and then I returned from far away to beg for
Death in a false tone of voice.

The *argumentum* of the poem is rather odd: the speaker, a merchant,
recalls the many sea voyages which he had to endure as a beggar until
a gentle wind brought him to his native land as a rich man. Some
insult which he received led him to participate in a duel which brought
about his own death. While links with Milton's poem have been briefly
noted by James Freeman,[19] there are some further points of contact.

The merchant, "intent on the grandeur of human pomp," was
assisted by a "gentle wind" ("tranquillo vento" [4]) which brought him
ashore. He describes the land as his "native nest" ("nel patrio nido"
[7]). Milton's situation is exactly the reverse:

---

[18] *Poesie de' Signori Accademici Fantastici di Roma* (Rome, 1637), 155.
[19] "Milton's Roman Connection: Giovanni Salzilli," *MS* 19 (1984): 100.

Diebus hisce qui suum linquens nidum
Polique tractum, (pessimus ubi ventorum,
Insanientis impotensque pulmonis
Pernix anhela sub Iove exercet flabra)     (10–13)

[Milton], who recently left his own nest and region of the heavens (where the worst of winds, powerless to control its madly
heaving lungs, swiftly puffs its panting blasts beneath the sky).

He too has travelled, but has *left* his native land—his "nest" (*qui suum
linquens nidum* [10])—in order to see the cities and learned youth of
Italy. Moreover, he describes a wind which, far from being "gentle" and
of assistance to the traveller, is in fact a *pessimus . . . ventorum* (11) which
almost prevented his journey. In Salzilli, the "nido" is closely associated
with death (7–8). Milton inverts this. The fact that he is leaving his
"nest" is balanced by the dismissal of death as he invokes Salus (23)
and Phoebus (24), opponents of death and restorers of life. Thus,
instead of a merchant begging for death, Milton is virtually begging for
a life as he prays for the speedy recovery of Salzilli.

Indeed, the situation of Milton's poem is quite the reverse of Salzilli's. Unlike the merchant who has received an insult and is seeking
vengeance, Milton has received words of praise—the encomium itself
(described in lines 7–8)—and wishes to return a compliment. Instead of
bringing death upon himself by avenging "un momentaneo scorno,"
Milton praises Salzilli and wishes him every good fortune (*Tibi optat
idem hic fausta multa Salsille* [17]).

Milton, in replying to Salzilli's Latin distich, inverts features of the
tribute itself and may also echo an Italian sonnet by Salzilli. *Ad Salsillum* thus moves beyond its ostensible purpose as a get-well wish for
an Italian friend to constitute a highly skillful reply to a commendatory
poem.

*Mansus* is another Latin poem which, like *Ad Salsillum*, replies to a
"written encomium" which he had received. This has been discussed by
Anthony Low,[20] whose points I shall develop, while suggesting some
further links. The poem, moreover, can also be viewed in relation to
seventeenth-century Italian literature—in this instance, certain Italian
tributes which Manso had received from his contemporaries.

---

[20] "*Mansus*: In Its Context," MS 19 (1984): 105–26.

Milton's visit to Giovan Battista Manso, Marquis of Villa,[21] was undoubtedly one of the most memorable incidents of his Italian trip. In the *Defensio secunda* he describes the hospitality which he received from Manso, who led him on a guided tour of Naples and visited him at his own lodgings.[22] The theme recurs in the Latin prose preface to *Mansus* where Milton states that he has composed the Latin poem as a token of sincere gratitude to his host. *Mansus*, however, is a poem of gratitude in a much more specific sense also, since it replies to Manso's tribute composed in Milton's honor:

> Ioannes Baptista Mansus, Marchio
> Villensis Neapolitanus ad Ioannem
> Miltonium Anglum.

> Ut mens, forma, decor, facies, mos, si pietas sic,
> Non Anglus, verum hercle Angelus ipse fores.

> Giovan Battista Manso, Marquis of Villa, a Neapolitan,
> to John Milton, an Englishman.

If your religion were as your mind, beauty, honor, appearance and moral character, you would not be an "Angle," but, by Hercules, a very "Angel."

Read superficially, Manso's distich seems to amount to no more than a tribute to the physical and moral qualities which Milton possesses, praising his *mens, forma, decor, facies* and *mos*. But with the phrase *si pietas sic*, a different note is struck. Manso is emphasizing what he sees to be one possible shortcoming: Milton's religious convictions: if his *pietas* were as outstanding as his physical appearance, he would be an "Angel" as opposed to an "Angle." The pun is not, of course, original with Manso. Rather it recalls the words of Gregory the Great, as narrated in Bede's *Ecclesiastical History* 2.1.[23] On seeing strange youths who had been brought to Rome for sale, Gregory made inquiries about their nationality and punned that because of their fair appearance

---

[21] On Manso, see Angelo Borzelli, *Giovan Battista Manso* (Naples: Federico & Ardia, 1916).

[22] CE 8:124.

[23] See B. Colgrave and R. A. B. Mynors, eds., *Bede's Ecclesiastical History* (Oxford: Clarendon Press, 1969), 132–34.

they were not "Angles," but "Angels." Manso's use of the pun has a wide range of humorous connotations and implications.[24] He is assuming the stance of the Catholic Gregory, pitying the handsome and "pagan" newcomer, Milton, and thereby hinting at the religious tension between Manso, a devout Roman Catholic, and Milton, an ardent Protestant—a tension which was acknowledged and outlined by Milton in the *Defensio secunda*, in which he states that as he was leaving Naples, he received an apology from Manso, who regretted the fact that he had not been able to show him as much attention as he would have liked. This was because Milton himself had not thought it proper to be more guarded on the subject of religion. Milton proceeds to admit that when asked about his religious convictions, he did not dissemble in spite of the consequences.[25]

Milton does not fail to recognize the implications of the distich and adapts and inverts some of the features in Bede's account. (He was later to cite Bede when narrating the incident in the *History of Britain* 4.)[26] It is possible to go even further than Low suggests by arguing that Milton is echoing specific details in Bede, turning the whole upon its head, alluding to such themes as physical beauty, the contrast between the civilized Italian and the barbarous foreigner, the notion of an angel, and including an element of wordplay himself. Thus, he cleverly recognizes the sting implicit in Manso's distich and sets out to counter those very implications by inverting particular details of the story, applying them in a totally different context and, in short, making Manso the butt of the joke!

One important theme underlying Bede's version and implicit in Manso's tribute is that of a foreigner coming to a new land. Both allude to the handsome appearance of the newcomer. In Bede, Gregory noticed boys who were fair-skinned (*candidi corporis*), had charming faces (*venusti vultus*) and beautiful hair (*capillorum forma egregia*)—features which led Gregory to remark that they resembled angels. Manso's distich likewise emphasizes beauty. Assuming the stance of Gregory, he praises the newcomer's *forma* and *facies*, but goes a stage further as he admires his intellectual and moral qualities: his *mens*, *decor* and *mos*.

---

[24] As noted by Low, "*Mansus*," 107.
[25] CE 8:124.
[26] CE 10:142.

The theme recurs in an inverted form in *Mansus* as Milton applies it to Manso himself and, subtly replying to the distich, he too praises both physical beauty and intellectual prowess:

> Hinc longaeva tibi lento sub flore senectus
> Vernat, et Aesonios lucratur vivida fusos,
> Nondum deciduos servans tibi frontis honores,
> Ingeniumque vigens, et adultum mentis acumen.
>
> (74-77)

Hence your old age is spring-like with late blossom and vigorously acquires the spindles of Aeson, preserving the glory of your brow not yet fallen, your intellect active and the sharpness of your mind mature.

Manso, he says, possesses an old age which is spring-like: his handsome features are still intact, and his intellect and wit are very alert indeed. There is a stark contrast between the essential youthfulness of the boys in Bede and Manso's old age (*longaeva senectus* [74]), which seems to be struggling to preserve its youthful looks—as implied by the reference to Aeson, who was rejuvenated by the magical powers of Medea. This contrast and the parallel with Aeson are all the more striking if, as scholars have suggested,[27] line 76 is an allusion to Manso's wig, which indeed attracted a contemporary's notice.[28] Milton with ironic skill thereby inverts Bede's *capillorum forma egregia*. The theme of physical appearance is later associated with Milton himself:

> Forsitan et nostros ducat de marmore vultus,
> Nectens aut Paphia myrti aut Parnasside lauri
> Fronde comas, at ego secura pace quiescam.      (91-93)

And perhaps he may carve my face in marble, binding my hair with Paphian myrtle or Parnassian laurel, but I will rest safely in peace.

Just as Bede had described the "charming faces" (*venusti vultus*) and

---

[27] David Masson, *The Poetical Works of John Milton* (London, 1874), 3:535; Low, 119.

[28] Masson, *The Poetical Works*, cites evidence from the *Pinacotheca* of a certain Janus Nicius Erythraeus that Manso wore a wig.

"beautiful hair" of the boys, so Milton alludes to his own face (*nostros ... vultus* [91]) which, he hopes, will be carved in marble, and to his own hair (*comas* [93]), which will be crowned with laurels.

Both the tribute and Milton's poem imply a contrast between the civilized Italian and the barbarous Englishman. Gregory's pun was the consequence of questions about the region from which the boys had come. He is told that they are pagans who have come *de Britannia insula*. Milton describes himself as a young man (*iuvenis* [26])–like the *pueri* in Bede–and thereby contrasts sharply with Manso, the old man (*senex* [49 & 70]) and father-figure (*pater* [25]). Milton moreover is a "young foreigner" (*iuvenis peregrinus* [26]) and describes Britain (lines 24–29) from the viewpoint of the Italian–cold and northern. However, he proceeds to defend his native land. As opposed to the implications of Manso's distich, Britain does not produce an uncultured race (*genus incultum* [35]) since it is possessed of eloquent poets.

Another feature of Manso's distich which recurs in *Mansus* is the element of wordplay. This occurs no fewer than three times in Bede's account: *Angli/Angeli*; *Deiri/de ira*; *Aelle/Alleluia*.[29] Milton, in describing the withdrawal of Apollo to Chiron's cave, perhaps plays on Manso's name in the line *Nobile mansueti cessit Chironis in antrum* (60), thereby linking the two hosts Chiron and Manso. Indeed, the phrase *Nobile ... antrum* could describe Manso's dwelling–his villa where the Academy of the Oziosi held its meetings.[30] Significant in view of the name *Oziosi* is the setting of Chiron's cave amidst pastoral *otium*.

The final point of Manso's tribute in relation to *Mansus* is the reference to an angel. Gregory had likened the boys to angels because of their physical appearance. Manso states that Milton could be an angel if it were not for his Protestantism. It is possible that Milton reacts to this notion and turns the whole upon its head in the closing lines of the poem:

> Tum quoque, si qua fides, si praemia certa bonorum,
> Ipse ego caelicolum semotus in aethera divum,
> Quo labor et mens pura vehunt, atque ignea virtus

---

[29] See Bede, 132–34.

[30] On Manso and the Oziosi, see Borzelli, *Giovan Battista Manso*, 88–100. On the Oziosi in general, see Camillo Minieri-Riccio, *Cenno storico intorno all' Accademia degli Oziosi in Napoli* (Naples, 1862).

Secreti haec aliqua mundi de parte videbo
(Quantum fata sinunt) et tota mente serenum
Ridens purpureo suffundar lumine vultus
Et simul aethereo plaudam mihi laetus Olympo.

(94–100)

Then also, if faith exists anywhere, if there are fixed rewards for
the virtuous, I myself, removed to the ethereal regions of the
heavenly gods—those regions to which toil, a pure mind and fiery
virtue conduct—, will behold all this from some part of the
hidden world (as far as the fates permit) and as I serenely smile
with my whole heart, my face will be suffused with a scarlet light
and at the same time I will joyfully applaud myself on heavenly
Olympus.

Here, he depicts himself transcending the boundaries of his earthly
existence, looking down from heaven and smiling in defiance upon
Manso and his world. Although there is no mention of an angel, the
description of the smiling and blushing Milton (*Ridens purpureo suffundar lumine vultus* [99]) can be compared with Raphael's "smile that
glowd Celestial rosie red" in *Paradise Lost* 8.618–19. Furthermore, the
notion of applause (*plaudam mihi* [100]) may recall the angelic hosts of
*Elegy* 3 who applaud the Bishop of Winchester with their jewelled wings
(*Agmina gemmatis plaudunt caelestia pennis* [59]). The implication of lines
94–100 is that even Milton, the supposed "pagan" (*Ipse ego* [95]), *can*
be an "angel"; but since Manso is not willing to acknowledge this fact
on earth, Milton will have to applaud himself in heaven. Milton has
inverted Manso's tribute by subverting the pagan world of *Mansus* and
ascending to a Christian heaven, just as Chaucer's Troilus transcended
his pagan existence and, assuming a Christian stance, laughed at the
world which he had left behind.

*Mansus* not only replies cleverly to Manso's distich, but can also be
compared with the many Italian tributes which Manso had received
from his contemporaries and which, some three years before *Mansus*
was written, he had appended to the collection of his own verse (*Poesie
Nomiche* [Venice, 1635]). While points of similarity are inevitable in
view of the encomiastic nature of these pieces addressed to a great
patron of the arts, there are some hitherto unnoticed links with Milton's
poem which may be sufficient to suggest that he was familiar with these
tributes and is even echoing them in one or two instances. This is all

the more likely if, as Black and De Filippis have argued,[31] the two cups (bina ... pocula) presented by Manso to Milton, and described in Epitaphium Damonis (181-97) were in actual fact two books of Manso's Italian compositions: the Erocallia and the Poesie Nomiche itself. In any case, in view of the friendship between the two men, it is evident that Milton would have been eager to read Manso's compositions. It is certainly true that he was very much aware of the great esteem in which Manso was held by his fellow Italians—as can be appreciated from an examination of the prose preface and the poem proper. In the preface, he states that Manso has achieved distinction "among the Italians" for his intellectual ability, his devotion to literature and his bravery in war. Other contemporary tributes had likewise stressed Manso's skill in the fields of literature and warfare. Antonio Biaguazzone praises Manso's "hand which is employed in arms and in writing about love," and marvels at the way in which he has won renown in battle and in poetry alike with the "sword" and "golden plectrum" respectively[32]—a theme which recurs in several other of the tributes.[33] In the opening lines of Mansus, Milton states that his poem is not the only one (haec quoque [1]) which the Pierides are singing. Manso is extremely well known to the chorus of Apollo (Manse choro notissime Phoebi [2]) and, like Gallus and Maecenas, has been honored by the god. Milton is echoing Virgil's sixth Eclogue in which the Phoebi chorus rose up to honor the poet Gallus. So it has honored Manso through the composition of many tributes. Now, if Milton's muse proves adequate, Manso will sit among victorious wreaths of laurel and ivy. The three features: Pierides, the chorus of Phoebus, and laurels occur in an Italian tribute by Don Vincenzo Toraldo:

> Restar le figlie di Pierio (à prova
>     Con le Muse cantando) e dome, e vinte,
>     Voi lor vincete, e le palme, onde cinte
>     Fur quelle, à voi tesson ghirlanda nova.
> Sì che ne l'età nostra in voi rinova
>     Le glorie Febo del suo Choro estinte;

---

[31] John Black, Life of Torquato Tasso (Edinburgh, 1810), 2:467; Michele De Filippis, "Milton and Manso: Cups or Books?" PMLA 51 (1936): 745-56.

[32] Poesie Nomiche, 266.

[33] See, for example, 280, 301, 302, 304, 310.

Per voi crescon gli allori: e in voi distinte
Par, che le gratie sue largo il Ciel piove.

(1-8)[34]

The Pierians (singing in competition with the Muses) remained
subdued and vanquished. You conquer them [i.e., the Muses]
and they are weaving the palms with which they had been
adorned as a new garland for you: in such a way that in our age
Phoebus renews in you the extinct glories of his Chorus. For you
the laurels grow and it seems that Heaven generously rains down
her own graces especially upon you.

Here, as in Ovid's *Metamorphoses* 5.663, the daughters of Pieros ("figlie
di Pierio" [1]) are conquered by the Muses. They in turn are surpassed
by Manso, who receives a new garland and for whom "the laurels
grow" ("crescon gli allori" [7]). It is in him that Apollo has renewed the
"extinct glories" of his "chorus."

Not surprisingly, both *Mansus* and the Italian tributes equate Manso
with Maecenas, the great ancient prototype of the generous patron.
Since Gallus and Maecenas, Milton states, Apollo has deemed no one
so worthy of honor as Manso. Estonne Stordito calls Manso "a new
and glorious Maecenas."[35]

Milton proceeds to present Manso in relation to Tasso and Marino.
Later he introduces himself as a "young foreigner" who has come to
Italy:

Tu quoque si nostrae tantum valet aura Camoenae,
Victrices hederas inter, laurosque sedebis.
Te pridem magno felix concordia Tasso
Iunxit, et aeternis inscripsit nomina chartis.
Mox tibi dulciloquum non inscia Musa Marinum
Tradidit, ille tuum dici se gaudet alumnum,
Dum canit Assyrios divum prolixus amores;
Mollis et Ausonias stupefecit carmine nymphas.

. . . . . . . . . . . . . . . .

---

[34] *Poesie Nomiche*, 262.
[35] *Poesie Nomiche*, 286.

Ergo ego te Clius et magni nomine Phoebi
Manse pater, iubeo longum salvere per aevum
Missus Hyperboreo iuvenis peregrinus ab axe.
Nec tu longinquam bonus aspernabere musam,
Quae nuper gelida vix enutrita sub Arcto
Imprudens Italas ausa est volitare per urbes.

                                    (5–12, 24–29)

You too, if my Muse's inspiration is so great, will sit amidst
victorious wreaths of ivy and laurel. A happy friendship once
united you and the mighty Tasso, and he inscribed your name in
his eternal pages. Then the Muse with full knowledge entrusted
the sweet-voiced Marino to you. He was very pleased to be called
your nursling as he luxuriantly sang of the Assyrian love-affair of
the gods and with his gentle strains amazed the nymphs of Italy
. . . . . Therefore, father Manso, in the name of Clio and of
mighty Apollo, I, a young foreigner sent from the Hyperborean
skies, wish you a lengthy and healthy life. You in your goodness
will not spurn a muse who has travelled a long distance and,
having with difficulty found nourishment beneath the frozen
Bear, has recently ventured in her rashness to fly through the
cities of Italy.

The general thematic and structural progression of these lines bears a
striking resemblance to an Italian tribute entitled "Il loda nelle lodi del
Tasso e del Marino" ("Praise Included in the Praises of Tasso and
Marino") by a certain Angelita Scaramuzza:

>     Gloria di Pindo, honor del secol nostro,
>         Pregio di Febo, e Marte, al cui gentile
>         Eccelso nome Io riverente humile,
>         MANSO, inchino'l pensier, sacro l'inchiostro.
>     Cedano à voi l'alte corone, e l'ostro,
>         Voi, cui la fama oltre a l'estrema Thile
>         Porta raccolta in sen d'heroico stile
>         Di saver, di valor mirabil mostro.
>     Voi protettor de l'alta, che Buglione
>         Tromba cantò con celebrato grido,          10
>         Voi del plettro dolcissimo d'Adone.
>     Di me peregrin tratto à questo lido

Per sì, di veder voi, nobil cagione,
Gradite il cor divoto, il voler fido.[36]

Pride of Mount Pindus, honor of our age, glory of Phoebus and
Mars, to your noble, sublime name, Manso, I reverently and
humbly incline my thought and consecrate my ink. Let lofty
garlands and purple pass to you, whose fame a collection [of
poems] carries within its heroic style beyond furthermost Thule—
a wonderful manifestation of your wisdom and valor. You were
the patron of the lofty trumpet which sang of Godfrey of Bouillon with its renowned blare; you were the patron of the sweetest
plectrum of Adonis. Accept my devoted heart and loyal wishes—I
who as a foreigner have been drawn to this shore to see you—a
noble reason.

In both instances Manso is presented as a victor (*victrices hederas
inter* [6]; "Cedano à voi l'alte corone" [5]); this is followed by a reference to the renown which he will achieve through the heroic writings of
Tasso (7-8)/(9-10). In Milton, Tasso has written Manso's name in his
eternal pages—a theme which occurs in one of Tasso's tributes to
Manso, which states that Manso's name is inscribed by the gods not
only in a thousand pages, but also in beautiful metal or in stone.[37]
Milton's line is a reference to the fact that Tasso mentioned Manso by
name in his *Gerusalemme Conquistata* 20—a point made in the prose
preface to *Mansus*. Scaramuzza likewise alludes to Tasso, not to the
*Gerusalemme Conquistata*, as in Milton, but to the *Gerusalemme Liberata*,
the hero of which was Godfrey of Bouillon (hence "Buglione" [9]). In
both poems this is followed by an allusion to Marino. Manso is depicted as Marino's patron: in Milton, Marino is Manso's *alumnus* (10); in
Scaramuzza, Manso is Marino's "protettor" (9). More specific is the
reference to Marino's Italian poem *L'Adone* (1623) and to the "sweetness" of Marino's style.[38] In Milton, he is *dulciloquum ... Marinum*
(9) and *mollis* (12) as he composes *L'Adone* (*Dum canit Assyrios divum
prolixus amores* [11]); Scaramuzza mentions the "plettro dolcissimo

---

[36] *Poesie Nomiche*, 300.
[37] *Poesie Nomiche*, 257.
[38] See J. V. Mirollo, *The Poet of the Marvelous: Giambattista Marino* (New York:
Columbia Univ. Press, 1963), 115-64.

d'Adone" (11). Of particular note is the subsequent progression of the passages in each poem whereby the speaker introduces himself as a foreigner—a *peregrinus*—who has come to a new land. Milton is a *iuvenis peregrinus* (26), whose *musa* (27) has ventured to fly *Italas per urbes* (29); the speaker of the Italian poem is introduced as "me peregrin tratto à questo lido" (12).

Having described himself as a young foreigner, Milton proceeds to defend the literary merits of his native land. He employs the image of the poet as swan, stating that he has heard swans singing upon the river Thames.[39] While the poet/swan analogy finds precedent in both Latin and English literature—notably in the Latin poetry of John Leland[40]—it also occurs in the Italian tributes, where the members of Manso's academy are envisaged as swans. Ferrante Rovitto describes them as "swans who are unique and rare in their song,"[41] while Gio. Camillo Cacace expresses his desire to join the academy, praises Manso and envisages himself as a swan who would sing if admitted.[42] The use of the swan image in the Italian tributes may give special emphasis to Milton's *Nos etiam* (30), as he states that he too (like Manso) has heard swans/poets sing.

Indeed, Milton's poem contains some possible allusions to Manso's academy and its members. These occur in the mythological passage (lines 54-69) in which Milton states that Apollo will be said to have dwelt in Manso's abode, even though it was with reluctance that the same god came to King Admetus's farm. When he wished to avoid the noisy cowherds, he retreated to the cave of the gentle Chiron and found solace in his music. As we have seen, the terms used to describe Chiron's cave are equally applicable to Manso's villa—depicted as a "noble dwelling" ("nobil magion") by Tomaso Ciamboli who, like Milton, conveys the pastoral *otium* ("l'Otio") of the setting.[43] Finally, the previously noted element of wordplay on Manso's name (*mansueti ... Chironis*)—a skillful means of linking the two hosts—occurs in a more elaborate form in some of the Italian poems, which play not only on his

---

[39] Lines 30-33.

[40] See, for example, *Synchrisis Cygnorum et Poetarum* (*Principum ac illustrium ... Carmina* [London, 1589], 1-2); *Cygnea Cantio* (London, 1658).

[41] *Poesie Nomiche*, 288.

[42] *Poesie Nomiche*, 274.

[43] *Poesie Nomiche*, 281.

name, but also on his formal title. This is most clearly illustrated by a poem entitled "Lodi espresse nel nome" ("Praises Expressed in His Name") by Gennaro Grossi—an example of the device on an ingenious level:

> La MAN SOvrana, onde'l Monarca Hispano
> Debellò più d'un campo, e più d'un mostro,
> Voli'hai, Signor, da ogni tenzon lontano
> Solitaria à trattar penna, ed inchiostro.   (1-4)

> Di tue glorie il gran MAR, CHE SEmpre nove
> Piaggie, e Reggie circonda, adduce al Mondo
> Te DI VILLA, e Cittade, hor Pane, hor Giove.
> (12-14)[44]

Sir, you wished, far from every stress, that the sovereign hand, with the help of which the Spanish Monarch won more than one battlefield and overcame more than one monster, should use pen and ink in solitude.... The great sea of your glories, which always encircles new shores and palaces, conducts you to the world—you who are now Pan of the villa and now Jupiter of the city.

Similarly, Margherita Sarrocchi plays on Manso's name in the line "Di Virtu MAN SOvrana altero mostro."[45]

One last point of similarity between *Mansus* and the Italian poems is the association of Manso with such gods as Jupiter and Apollo. Milton says that these gods must have looked with favor upon Manso's birth (70-73). While the general notion of divine favor at Manso's birth occurs in a tribute by Fra. Giulio Carrafa,[46] an explicit reference to Jupiter and Apollo is to be found in a poem by Gio. Ambrosio Biffi, who sees Manso as a second Jupiter brandishing his thunderbolts; he is also a second Apollo on account of his military and literary skill.[47]

*Mansus*, then, not only replies in a most skillful way to Manso's tribute, but also takes its place beside encomiastic poems in Italian of

---

[44] *Poesie Nomiche*, 277.
[45] *Poesie Nomiche*, 303.
[46] *Poesie Nomiche*, 261.
[47] *Poesie Nomiche*, 267.

the seventeenth century. In replying to one "written encomium," Milton has composed another on a very extensive and elaborate scale.

Unlike his encomiastic verse discussed hitherto, Milton's three Latin epigrams in praise of the Italian soprano, Leonora Baroni, were not composed as a response to a tribute which he had received. On the contrary, Milton takes the initiative and conveys his admiration by composing poems in her honor—as indeed many poets of Italian and other nationalities were doing at this time. A collection of such tributes, entitled *Applausi Poetici Alle Glorie Della Signora Leonora Baroni*, was published in 1639. Although Milton's poems do not appear in this volume, it is possible that he saw in manuscript some of the encomia which were to be included and which may have been circulating in Rome during either or both of his sojourns in that city.[48] It is difficult to believe, for example, that he did not read such a tribute as that by Lukas Holste,[49] who actually conducted him around the Vatican Library, showed him manuscripts, presented him with copies of Greek texts which he had edited, and introduced him to important musical circles in Rome.[50] Furthermore, his eagerness to meet Italian *literati* and his attendance at notable academies might in themselves strengthen the possibility that he had read some of these poems in Leonora's honor. The composition of Milton's epigrams may thus reflect participation in, or a reaction to, a literary trend current at the time.

The *Applausi*, some 267 pages in length, contains poems in five languages. The majority are in Italian, others in Latin, Greek, Spanish, and French. The volume as a whole is marked by the highly extravagant nature of some of the pieces which praise not only Leonora's voice, but also her beauty, chastity and moral character.[51] Milton's poems, on the

---

[48] It is not certain on which of Milton's two visits to Rome he heard Leonora sing. The reference to Tasso's madness in the second epigram may perhaps favor the second visit since, after leaving Rome, Milton had visited Naples and met Manso, the great patron of Tasso, who had written a *Vita* of the poet (see *Mansus* 20-23). It was after his stay in Naples that Milton made his second visit to Rome. The reference may thus reflect conversations which he had with Manso on this subject. For this view, see Ewald Pommrich, *Miltons Verhältnis zu Torquato Tasso* (Halle: Druck von Ehrhardt Karras, 1902), 9-10.

[49] Holste's Latin tribute is on pp. 201-3 of the *Applausi*.

[50] See *Epistolae familiares* 9 (CE 12:40).

[51] See, for example, Berlingiero Gessi, who praises Leonora under the three titles: "La Bellezza" (31-38); "L'Honesta" (39-46); "La Musica" (47-54). On Leonora in

other hand, are much less extravagant; they do not mention her beauty or chastity, and they emphasize more the effect of her song upon the listener than the quality of her voice *per se*. There are, nevertheless, a number of minor parallels which, while certainly not indicating *imitatio* on the part of Milton, do serve to create an interesting perspective from which to view his poems, illustrate some common reactions to the beauty of her voice, and highlight an important seventeenth-century Italian context.

One aspect of Milton's treatment which merits comparison with the poems of the *Applausi* is the association of Leonora's song with a divine presence. This is the major theme of his first epigram, in which her voice is depicted as proclaiming the very presence of God. Thus, she surpasses the common fortune of man, in whom is present not God, but a guardian angel. When she sings, God himself speaks. The *Applausi* likewise emphasizes the other-worldly, and indeed divine, nature of Leonora's singing.[52]

Closely related to this is the notion that Leonora's song transports the harmony of the spheres to an earthly and human level, thereby enabling mortal hearts to grow accustomed to an immortal sound. This is implicit in Milton's puzzling reference to a *mens tertia*[53] which has left the heavens, entered Leonora's throat and makes its presence felt among mankind. Similarly, in the *Applausi*, Andrea Barbazzi states that Leonora's notes transport the heavenly spheres to the earth; Giovanni Bentivoglio says that when Leonora sings, the harmony of the spheres, which is unfamiliar to mortal men, comes and actually dwells in their midst.[54]

Another shared theme is that of the soothing power of Leonora's song. In the second epigram Milton speaks of Tasso's love for another

---

general, see A. Ademollo, *La Leonora di Milton e di Clemente IX* (Milan: Ricordi, 1885); Eugene Schuyler, "Milton's Leonora," *Nation* 47 (18 October, 1888): 310–12; M. Allessandrini, "Una celebre cantatrice alla corte di Urbano VIII," *Scenario* 11 (April, 1942): 152 ff.; *The New Grove's Dictionary of Music and Musicians* (London: Macmillan, 1980), 2:171–72; *Dizionario Biografico Degli Italiani* (Rome: Istituto della Enciclopedia Italiana, 1964), 6:456–58. (For a full bibliography, see 458.)

[52] See, for example, 61, 121, and 142.

[53] For an interpretation of this phrase in the context of contemporary angel lore, see Diane K. McColley, "Tongues of Men and Angels: *Ad Leonoram Romae Canentem*," *MS* 19 (1984): 127–48.

[54] *Applausi*, 19, 174.

lady named Leonora—a love which in fact drove him insane. If Tasso had heard Leonora Baroni singing, his madness would have been assuaged. Even if he had rolled his eyes more fiercely than Pentheus, Leonora's song would have soothed his aching heart and restored him to his senses. The *Applausi* contains several references to the soothing power of Leonora's *cantus*. Fabio Leonida states that her song has the power to calm the Furies themselves. This is extended to embrace the fury of war. Gasparo de Simeonibus asserts that as a result of her singing both swords and hearts are appeased.[55]

The most striking point of similarity is the depiction of Leonora as a Siren, and more specifically, as Parthenope, reputed to have been washed ashore near Naples, where a tomb was erected in her honor. This equation is particularly apt and perhaps inevitable since, like Parthenope, Leonora herself was a Neapolitan noted for her singing. Milton's third epigram is devoted entirely to this theme:

### Ad eandem

Credula quid liquidam Sirena Neapoli iactas,
  Claraque Parthenopes fana Acheloiados,
Littoreamque tua defunctam Naiada ripa
  Corpora Chalcidico sacra dedisse rogo?
Illa quidem vivitque, et amoena Tibridis unda
  Mutavit rauci murmura Pausilipi.
Illic Romulidum studiis ornata secundis,
  Atque homines cantu detinet atque Deos.

### To the Same

Why, credulous Naples, do you boast of your clear-voiced Siren and of the famous shrine of Achelous's daughter, Parthenope, and that when she, a Naiad of the shore, died on your coasts, you placed her sacred body upon a Chalcidian pyre? In actual fact, she is alive and has changed the murmurs of the hoarse Posillipo for the pleasant waters of the Tiber. There, honored by the favorable enthusiasm of Roman audiences, she captivates both men and gods with her song.

---

[55] *Applausi*, 118, 167.

Lines 1–4 constitute a question addressed to Naples: why does she boast of the Siren and of the famous shrine of Parthenope and of the pyre on which she was placed? Lines 5–8 state that in actual fact this Siren is alive, has exchanged noisy Posillipo for the lovely Tiber and holds her audiences spellbound.

Leonora as a Siren is a recurring theme in the *Applausi*: "ò bella Sirena," "alma e canora / Sirena," "questa Sirena," "vaga Sirena," "la dolce Sirena," "la Sirena immortale," "fastosetta Sirena," *pudica Siren*.[56] The notion that in Leonora the Siren is not dead but alive (*Illa quidem vivitque* [5]) occurs in a different sense in a poem by Giulio Rospigliosi, who, praising an artist's painting of Leonora, states that on account of his skill "questa del cor dolce Sirena / non è finta, ma vive."[57]

One of the Italian tributes by Fulvio Testi resembles Milton's poem in that it depicts the Siren exchanging one dwelling-place for another, and in fact coming to the city of Rome:

> Fastosetta Sirena,
> Che da Partenopei liti odiosi
> Sù la Romana arena
> Se' venuta à turbar gli altrui riposi;
> E con la dolce pena
> Del divin canto, e de' begli occhi ardenti
> Con flagello di gioia il cor tormenti.[58]

O magnificent Siren, you who have come from the tedious shores of Parthenope to Roman sand in order to disturb the repose of others, and with the sweet pain of your divine song and of your beautiful burning eyes torment the heart with a whip of joy.

Thus, just as Milton had described Leonora/Siren abandoning the *rauci murmura Pausilipi* (6) for the *amoena Tibridis unda* (5), so Testi envisages her as a Siren who has left the shore of Parthenope, has arrived at Rome and moves audiences with her singing.

The "Italian context" of Milton's Latin poetry is evident on both a

---

[56] *Applausi*, 19, 117, 118, 121, 129, 155, 157, 201.
[57] *Applausi*, 185. "This Siren of my heart is not fictitious, but living."
[58] *Applausi*, 157.

literary and personal level. He echoes Renaissance Latin poems composed by Italians; he replies to Latin tributes which he had received from Italian friends—"written Encomiums, which the Italian is not forward to bestow on men of this side the Alps"—and he seems to recall in a general, and sometimes more specific, sense Italian poems in praise of, or composed by, his addressees. The visit to Italy, then, represents in concrete terms Milton's close links with that country—links which up until then were apparent on a purely literary level. As he states in the *Defensio secunda*, in Italy he had at last reached "the seat of civilization and the hospitable domicile of every species of erudition."[59]

The Queen's University of Belfast

[59] CE 8:114. I wish to express my thanks to Professor Michael J. McGann of the Queen's University of Belfast for his advice and helpful suggestions in the preparations of this article.

JOHN K. HALE

# The Multilingual Milton
and the Italian Journey

I N ITALY MILTON RECEIVED ACCLAIM for his poems in several languages, yet came back resolved to write in English for the English.
Why should his enjoyment of Italy change a polyglot poet into a
monoglot?

The question can be restated in terms derived from Leonard Forster's study of multilingualism in literature.[1] Forster distinguishes two
kinds of polyglot, whom we may call "occasionals" and "romantics."
Whereas the first select the tongue most apposite to a poem's occasion,
heeding decorum in the choice, the second select in such a way as to
declare spiritual allegiance to a single or mother tongue. Occasionals
predominate among the older polyglots, such writers as Huygens or
Weckherlin, while romantics (as might be expected) cluster during and
after the Romantics. Accordingly, we might place Milton as an early-
modern, transitional figure. We might hypothesize that the experience
of Italy revealed to him his English identity and an allegiance to English; and that, just as Germany propelled Wordsworth to write of his
native Cumbria, Italy turned an occasional polyglot into a romantic one.

Yet the tempting hypothesis is over-schematic. Instead, though
making use of Forster's distinction, let us proceed more inductively,
examining passages which illustrate the polyglot poet's choices—before,
during, and in the wake of the Italian visit. There emerges a winding
and individualistic "journeying" among his languages, in which that
metaphor of journeying explains more than the simple supposition that
Italy triggered a doctrinaire-patriotic monoglottism. In his moments of
choice may be understood, not so much why he chose English, as
how—with what elements of a maturing personality. But indeed, to

---

[1] *The Poet's Tongues: Multilingualism in Literature* (Cambridge: Cambridge Univ.
Press with Univ. of Otago Press, 1970), 54–55.

answer questions about how he chose (questions on which his writings about the Italian experience tell us a good deal) may after all illuminate why.

§

Three poems from before 1638[2] show Milton's involvement with choice of tongue, while they also display his unusual range of choice. They are the poem to his father ("Ad Patrem"), Sonnet 4, and Psalm 114—in Latin, Italian, and Greek respectively.

Milton writes "Ad Patrem" as his only possible, and fitting gift in return for his father's gifts:[3]

> Hoc utcunque tibi gratum pater optime carmen
> Exiguum meditatur opus, nec novimus ipsi
> Aptius a nobis quae possunt munera donis
> Respondere tuis, quamvis nec maxima possint
> Respondere tuis. . . .                           (6-10)

Whether you approve or not, best of fathers, [my Muse] is now engaged on this poem—this little offering—and I do not know what I may give you that can more fittingly repay your gifts to me. In fact, though, even my greatest gifts could never repay yours.

Then, after praising his father's negative gifts (his *not* forcing his son into a commercial or legal career [lines 68-75]), he moves over to the positive ones. At once, lightly leaping over the usual kindnesses of fathers to their sons, he dwells lovingly upon "greater ones"—"maiora [officia]":

> Officium chari taceo commune parentis,
> Me poscunt maiora, tuo pater optime sumptu
> Cum mihi Romuleae patuit facundia linguae,

---

[2] The date of "Ad Patrem" remains disputed. I myself accept arguments for a dating early in the 1630s, for it seems most natural to take "abductum" in line 75 to mean the withdrawal from London to Horton. Yet I would not also insist that the poem precedes the Italian sonnets: it is simply for convenience that my exposition considers these next after it. "Psalm CXIV" is dated to November 1634 by the letter concerning it to Alexander Gill (for which see n.7 below).

[3] Texts and translations, unless otherwise stated, are quoted from Fowler.

Et Latii veneres, et quae Iovis ora decebant
Grandia magniloquis elata vocabula Graiis,
Addere suasisti quos iactat Gallia flores,
Et quam degeneri novus Italus ore loquelam
Fundit, barbaricos testatus voce tumultus,
Quaeque Palaestinus loquitur mysteria vates.

(77-85)

I will not mention the kindnesses which a loving father usually
bestows upon his son: there are more considerable kindnesses[4]
which demand my attention. Best of fathers, when the eloquence
of the Roman tongue had been made accessible to me, at your
expense, the beauties of Latin and the high-sounding words of
the sublime Greeks, words which graced the mighty lips of Jove
himself, then you persuaded me to add to my stock those flowers
which are the boast of France, and that language which the
modern Italian pours from his degenerate mouth (his speech
makes him a living proof of the barbarian invasions) and also
those mysteries which the prophet of Palestine utters.

In other words, once his son had mastered Latin and Greek ("patuit
facundia"), the father urged him to study French, Italian, and Hebrew
("addere suasisti") and paid for the tutoring. Who would have supposed
that the love of languages in Milton needed fatherly persuasion?! Whether or not the words are strategic exaggeration (to win continuance of
subsidy) Milton binds together his language acquirements and his filial
gratitude, to suggest that his love thereby becomes unusual, ergo heart-
felt.

In the two passages together there join the ideas of language endow-
ment, poetic vocation, and the love a son has for such a father. The
poem glows with a sense of occasion, although we do not know what.
It does what it describes, it is what it gives: a unique and fittest present.

What about the choice of medium for this occasion? Why should he
choose Latin, and hexameters, and Virgil as exemplar? Latin is Milton's
first foreign tongue, the tongue of humanist discourse and of commemorative permanence. Hexameters are the highest and gravest Latin meter.

---

[4] Carey translates *maiora* absolutely, as "more considerable things" (Fowler, 154).
I supply *officia* from the preceding line.

They are particularly the medium of Virgil in the *Aeneid* where he celebrates *pietas*, dutiful love.[5] When we reflect that the poem teems with words of relationship, especially for the bonds and gifts between father and son ("quae possunt *munera donis* / *Respondere tuis*"), and when we also reflect that those last four words make a hyperbaton which mimes the idea of reciprocity, we are in position to see that Latin makes part of the decorum and equally of the subject. Through Latin, precisely, the poet glimpses a bond between love for a person and the love of languages, together with wider-reaching intimations of the nature of love.

§

Such connections are sought differently, and more explicitly, in the Italian poems. The climax of the Canzone is the declaration, "Questa è lingua di cui si vanta Amore" ("This, Italian, is the language on which Love prides himself"[15]). Though the idea has ample precedent,[6] it has especial force here—the force of rightness of occasion, as he writes in Italian for an Italian lady whose worth includes her skill with languages (4.10). The truth and worth of his love are shown in his risking mockery to attempt the "strange tongue" (3.7, and Canzone passim). For "Love has willed the attempt": "Amor lo volse" (3.11). That this is not mere conceit but earnest, is affirmed by the echo of Dante ("Amor lo strinse" at *Inferno* 5.129); for along with Dante's words Milton assimilates Dante's steady, idealizing tone.[7]

Sonnet 4 best shows the interlocking of choice of language with ideas about language and about the love-occasion:

> Diodati, e te'l dirò con maraviglia,
> Quel ritroso io ch'amor spreggiar soléa

---

[5] As in the incessant epithet *pius* for Aeneas. It is by his *pietas* that Aeneas can take his father out of Troy and found the new Troy through his own son.

[6] Forster, 47, and notes on the line in Sergio Baldi's edition of Milton's Italian poems: "Poesie italiane di Milton," in *Studi Secenteschi* 7 (1966): 103-30. Carey's translations are at 91-96 of Fowler.

[7] See also Ray Fleming, "Sublime and Pure Thoughts, 'Without Transgression': The Dantean Influence in Milton's 'Donna Leggiadra,'" MQ 20 (1986): 38-44. A further echo from Dante's Francesca may be present in line 4, "Gia caddi," cf. "E caddi come corpo morto cade" (*Inferno* 5.142).

E de suoi lacci spesso mi ridéa
Gia caddi, ov'huom dabben talhor s'impiglia.
Ne treccie d'oro, ne guancia vermiglia
M' abbaglian si, ma sotto nova idea
Pellegrina bellezza che'l cuor bea,
Portamenti alti honesti, e nelle ciglia
Quel sereno fulgor d' amabil nero,
Parole adorne di lingua piu d'una,
E'l cantar che di mezzo l'hemispero
Traviar ben può la faticosa Luna,
E degli occhi suoi auventa si gran fuoco
Che l'incerar gli orecchi mi fia poco.

Diodati, I'll tell you something which absolutely amazes me: I, the coy creature who used to scorn love, I who made a habit of laughing at his snares, have now fallen into his trap (which sometimes does catch a good man). It is not golden tresses or rosy cheeks which have dazzled me like this, but a foreign beauty, modelled on a new idea of loveliness, which fills my heart with joy: a proud, yet modest bearing; and that calm radiance of lovely blackness in her eyes and lashes; her speech which is graced by more than one language, and her singing which might well draw down the labouring moon from mid-air. And such bright fire flashes from her eyes that it would not be much good for me to seal up my ears.

Much here is purely conventional of course, and modelled on Petrarch. Nevertheless, all hinges on the attraction of what is foreign, alien, different—a *pellegrina* bellezza. Milton is extending the range of his admirations, to his own and other people's surprise. But the role of language and of language-choice is crucial.

Behind the manifest influence of Petrarch are sensed those of Dante and Plato. Allusion to Dante, whom Milton preferred as a love poet along with Petrarch ("the two famous renowners of Beatrice and Laura"),[8] is instrumental in creating a steady *ideal* ardour: "sotto nova *idea* / Pellegrina bellezza che'l cuor *bea*" (4.6-7). "Idea" seizes the point of intersection between the Italians together and the Platonic. The rhyming

---

[8] In *Apology for Smectymnuus* (1642), as excerpted in Diekhoff, 78-79.

of idea/bea sounds out strongly at the point where the sonnet turns from negation to affirmation. What is more still, Milton is sharing the new love with his closest friend, Diodati, whose Italian name and understanding of Italian launch the sonnet. The meeting of friendship and eros within the Italian hints at the Platonic belief that other loves contribute to perfect love—presumably because in loving persons for ideas seen embodied in them, and in loving an idea which he finds in Italian, he finds the persons and the language coalescing into a single life-expanding excitement. Since the lady's accomplishments include being multilingual, and he loves her for that, the love of languages is integral to this love. Italian itself resembles a ground where love can meet, a source upon which they draw.

§

In his Greek version of Psalm 114 further loves meet.[9]

Ισραὴλ ὅτε παῖδες, ὅτ' ἀγλαὰ φῦλ' 'Ιακώβου
Αἰγύπτιον λίπε δῆμον, ἀπεχθέα, βαρβαρόφωνον,
Δὴ τότε μοῦνον ἔην ὅσιον γένος υἱες 'Ιούδα·
'Εν δὲ θεὸς λαοῖσι μέγα κρείων βασίλευεν.

When the children of Israel, when the glorious tribes of Jacob left the land of Egypt, hateful, barbarous in speech, then indeed were the sons of Judah the one devout race; and God ruled in great might among the peoples.

The occasion now being the awed love of God, the tongue chosen has a different relation to the subject. One might expect no relation: what has Old Testament theophany to do with Homer's anthropomorphic polytheism? No doubt Milton chose Homer as a model so as to match elevated subject with elevated meter, but I see more of challenge: the challenge to find out whether two opposing loved grandeurs can enhance one another.

At times they can. In the first line, the Greek preserves the parallelism which is so typical of the original, but reshapes it to the elegant

---

[9] The text and translation are from Fowler, 229, except that in some particulars I have made corrections: a full discussion of points at issue is found in my essay, "Milton as a Translator of Poetry," *Renaissance Studies* 1 (1987): 252 n.19.

asymmetry of the hexameter line, which hinges by caesura earlier than mid-line. A mingling of symmetry with asymmetry is gained by the joining of anaphora (on "ὅτε") with amplification (a three-word unit balancing one of two words): "Ἰσραὴλ ὅτε παῖδες, ὅτ᾽ ἀγλααφῦλ᾽ Ἰακώβου." The third line squeezes a most Hebraic thought, the exclusive holiness of Israel, into Homer's Greek. Whereupon the fourth line does the same yet more strikingly. The very Homeric tmesis which divides the prefix "εμ-" from its verb, "βασιλευεν," mimics sense by syntax; for thanks to the inflectedness and hyperbaton of Greek, "God" is literally positioned "among the peoples" ("Among, God, the peoples, ruled"). Milton mates the two loved languages.

Nonetheless, the challenge which I have inferred was not so much conscious as mysterious to him, since he writes that "with no deliberate intention certainly, but from I know not what sudden impulse before daybreak, I adapted . . . this ode of the truly divine poet, almost in bed, to the rule of Greek heroic verse" ("nullo certe animi proposito, sed subito nescio quo impetu ante lucis exortum").[10] Now, this being the time of day at which he begins his *Nativity Ode*, and at which later he habitually composed for *Paradise Lost*, we should note that the psalm, like those works, came to him unbidden: can we conclude that it can in answer to some hidden imperative, an imperative to combine Hebraic and Homeric by idealizing each? At all events, the combining was an act of obeying, of unwilled allegiance.

§

If we now refer the choices so far examined to our opening distinction between occasional and romantic polyglots, we find Milton to be both at once. The choice of tongue suits an occasion *and* declares an allegiance. The choosing becomes part of the subject. If so, however, why did Milton abandon his polyglot excellence to write in English for the English? At least from the present perspective it seems like voluntary self-diminution.

---

[10] The letter is discussed in Fowler, 229, and quoted from CE 12:16–17. It's not certain that this letter to Gil refers to Ps. 114; but the remarks fit it, and no other poem of Milton's which survives does fit.

Common-sense explanations have not been lacking. In the first place, his decision has the normal fitness of occasion, because if his best work is to be a national epic for his own countrymen, and for as many as possible of them, he must address them in their mother tongue. Secondly, it would be natural for him, given the changes wrought in him by extended European travel, to want to renew his sense of roots. Thirdly, we know that during his visit to Italy his mind ran on the political crises back home.[11]

Yet even these truisms do not wholly suffice. The epic of England did not eventuate—not in the projected form of an Arthur-epic, nor in any epic of national history. Milton's subsequent poetry does not interweave the subject and the chosen tongue by the sense of occasion which we have come to expect. He does not renew that romantic allegiance to the mother tongue which we find in the early "Hail native language...." We expect self-sacrifice of Milton, but hardly self-diminution. Part of the conundrum remains.

My own view is this: he did *not* give up his languages, and did not diminish himself; rather, the interinanimating of his languages increased through abrupt zigzags of development, in the course of the Italian visit and in its wake; until his languages came to intersect where they could best intersect, within his English. And this, I believe, is what our inductive method reveals, if we apply it to the crucial, albeit sparse, evidence of Milton's poetic development between 1638 and 1645.

A striking, yet indecisive passage occurs in *Mansus*, written about January 1639 when he was leaving Naples to return north. Here (weaving in a complimentary linking of his host Manso with his poetic aspirations) he adumbrates a poem on the kings of his native land, and singles out Arthur:[12]

O mihi si mea sors talem concedat amicum
Phoebaeos decorasse viros qui tam bene norit,
Si quando indigenas revocabo in carmina reges,
Arturumque etiam sub terris bella moventem;
Aut dicam invictae sociali foedere mensae,
Magnanimos heroas, et (O modo spiritus ad sit)

---

[11] See *Second Defence* (1654), in Diekhoff, 20.
[12] Text in Fowler, 261 ff.

Frangam Saxonicas Britonum sub Marte phalanges
(78-84)

O may it be my good luck to find such a friend, who knows so well how to honor Phoebus' followers, if ever I bring back to life in my songs the kings of my native land and Arthur, who set wars raging even under the earth, or tell of the great-hearted heroes of the round table, which their fellowship made invincible, and—if only the inspiration would come—smash the Saxon phalanxes beneath the impact of the British charge.

Milton does not say what language the poem will be in. One could argue it either way: that he writes of Arthur in Latin here, and only in Latin could Manso and his ilk receive it; or that Italians like Manso would well understand that a national epic went best with the national vernacular. We simply cannot decide the question. What *is* clear, is the manner of the proposal: his eager enthusiasm for the subject of Arthur, the simple patriotism which leads him to envision joining Arthur in the Saxon-smashing. I infer he has just possessed the subject, or it has just possessed him. It has not impinged on him that Arthur may be a myth, nor that an English poet may owe more to the Saxons than to their British predecessors.[13]

The key passage regarding the choice of English for his British epic is a long passage (lines 125-84) towards the end of *Epitaphium Damonis* [14] which, in its eloquence and informativeness alike, best reveals the *manner* of his choosing of English. I quote it in full in an appendix to this article.

The context is quite complex. Milton is writing of his Italian experiences of 1638-1639 from the England of 1640. Moreover, the reminiscences have a mixed value, for even while "Thyrsis" (Milton) was enjoying Italy, his friend "Damon" (Diodati, the addressee of Sonnet 4) was dead in England. Accordingly, it is pain to reminisce; yet not entirely so, for Italy was worthwhile, and good to recall, it has permanently enlarged his being. "O ego quantus eram ..." (129): "how great

---

[13] As argued by Roberta F. Brinkley, *Arthurian Legend in the Seventeenth Century*, Johns Hopkins Monographs in Literary History, 3 (repr. London: Frank Cass & Co., 1967).

[14] Text in Fowler, 273-77

I felt then"—and by extension still do, in recalling. Besides, since the dead friend came from Lucca (128), to visit Italy was in a way to visit him, it was an act of *pietas*.

So, indeed, is the entire reminiscence, and the poem itself. It is a gift: a conversation with the dead, and a praising of the dead. And the fitness of Latin is therefore extraordinary. Latin was the language in which Milton had previously written letters to his friend,[15] as well as the language in which Milton had composed the poems which won him reputation among the "shepherd-poets" of Italy (132-38). This is an internal fitness, of Latin to occasion. The external, wider fitness is simply that Latin is the language of commemoration, be it on statues or on graves: it has the needed dignity and tradition, *gravitas* and permanence. The excellence of the Latin, then, adds worth to what is already the natural gift. More still, however, this most ambitious of Milton's Latin poems is also virtually his last.[16] In view of the further fact that this poem announces his next major poem will be in the mother tongue, not Latin, is Milton in some way laying Latin verse itself—his medium as well as his message—as a votive tribute in Damon's grave? Be that as it may, the sense of occasion in the using of Latin for this farewell is even richer than in our previous examples.

To all this in the manner of Milton's choosing of Latin must be added the manner of the reminiscence itself. He felt excited and proud as he lay beside the Arno and listened to the "singing contests" there (132). He made so bold as to compete himself ("Ipse," 133). He did well, too, for the Florentine poets ("Pastores Thusci," 126 and 134) gave him gifts (134-135)—including poems recording his friendship with Damon (136-38). Still imagining himself back in that past he turns to Diodati in England, who he thinks is enjoying an equivalent pastoral life but alas is already dead (142-54). A tumult of feelings is felt in the manner hereabouts—in the twofold "Ah" (142, 153), or the imprecation upon medicine for failing (153). From grief and love together, he nevertheless continues reminiscing (156).[17] The time is complex, be-

---

[15] Latin letters of Milton to Diodati are nos. 6 and 7 in CE 9. Two of his elegiac elegies (1 and 6) are verse-letters to Diodati.

[16] The ode "Ad Ioannem Rousium" (1647) is his only later substantial Latin poem. It is in completely different vein, meter, genre, and tone, from any previous Latin poem of Milton, though very much an occasional piece.

[17] "Haec" at lines 180 and 181, referring to poetic plans and Manso's "cups"

cause it is excited: he narrates in the present tense as if he were back in that lost happy past, so that two times are conflated. "I myself..." (Ipse etiam): the pronoun makes one of the linking-threads of the passage, and is the pronoun of excited self-discovery and self-assertion.

A third time is now introduced, antecedent to the first recollected time. "Eleven days ago, my pipe was sounding out some grand song: I had just set my lips to a new set of pipes, but they fell apart, broken at the fastenings, and were unable to carry the deep sounds. I hesitate to appear a little puffed up, yet I *shall* tell the tale. Give place, you forests" ("vos cedite silvae"). His state of mind was (and remains) ambitious. The new, grand subject proves too much for his instruments, in spite or because of their newness. He remains proud of attempting. He must confide it, whether in the time recollected or the time of the memorial poem—he must, even at the risk of hubris. Let pastoral therefore stand aside: that is, the next passage will rise above the typical pastoral register (as do some parts of *Lycidas*); and the poem which he now describes will as a whole rise thus higher. The excitement is conveyed by the number of the times incorporated, and if these times coalesce, so much the better for the theme of friendship that mere clock-time can be thus transcended.

The following paragraph,[18] mainly given to summarizing of the British material of the new work, likewise conveys a mingling of concern with the medium and a sense of undergoing rapid (and multiple, hence undifferentiated and unclear) change. "If I have any time left to live, you, my pipe [*fistula* at 169 as at 156], will hang far away on the branch of some old pine tree, utterly forgotten by me; or else, transformed by my [*or*, from your] native muses, you will whistle a British tune. But after all, one man cannot do everything, or even hope to do everything. I shall have ample reward, and shall think it great glory" if, though the outside world does not read my English, all Britain does so.

The passage is central to our topic, yet is not exactly transparent. Is he giving up pastoral, or Latin, or both, or what? *Does he really know yet?* My view is that he does not, and that is the whole point. Let us consider the various ambiguities, one by one.

---

brought back together from Italy, shows that the imagined conversation with Damon proceeds *throughout* the Arthur-passage.

[18] Made a paragraph, a distinct unit of the thought, by the refrain line (161).

Lines 155-60 clearly reject pastoral (the *fistula* broke, therefore *cedite silvae*). But from line 169 onwards, he states some alternative, since *aut* is the conjunction of exclusive alternative (as distinct from *vel*): either he will give up his pipe or else he will exchange muses, British for Roman. This latter option would leave him the possibility of a pastoral in English, since an epic in English is not the sole alternative to a pastoral in Latin. Moreover, giving up his pipe might be a rejection of the *fistula* by synecdoche for *all* poetry. It is not simply that the rejection of pastoral glides somewhere into the rejection of Latin. The passage glides between at least four options. Thus Jerram took *fistula* to mean all poetry whatsoever (and Milton of course did write a prose history of England soon afterwards). But Masson took *fistula* to mean Latin poetry (embracing Latin pastoral, but not excluding Latin epic).[19] We might conclude that *fistula* denotes the one at 156 but some wider class at 169. Yet to localize the shifts of meaning thus upon a glide within one word, albeit a repeated and emphatic one, seems mechanical. My sense of the entire passage is of excited, expansionist self-discovery: the more options, then, the better. Why should a poet know exactly in advance how he would treat material which is susceptible to varying treatment, and which in the event he does treat in more than one language and genre? Instead, the passage (partly because it incorporates three different times and states of thought) explodes with as yet unseparated possibilities.

A further reason for thinking so is that the passage depends on Virgil, in a way which may resolve the problem without being mechanical and reductive. Virgil explains that curiously specific "eleven days ago," because in *Eclogue* 8.39 we read "*Alter ab undecimo tum me iam acceperat annus*" ("My eleventh year being completed, the next had just received me"): compare Milton's "*ab undecima iam lux est altera nocte.*" That eclogue, and the one before it, supply Milton with much of the verbal texture hereabouts. For instance, the idea that a poet's limitations are a special instance of human ones comes from *both* eclogues (7.23 and 8.63). Both eclogues are singing-contests, therefore are poems about poetry. In the second of them Virgil asks himself whether he will ever rise to higher genres (8.7-13): so, too, Milton. Milton places a tag from

---

    [19] C. S. Jerram, David Masson, and others are summarized by Douglas Bush in *Variorum* 1:315-17.

the other eclogue (7.27–28) on the title-page of his published first fruits, the *Poemata* of 1645.

That same eclogue provides the allusion which I find decisive, where Corydon enters the singing contest with a "do-or-die" statement of exclusive alternatives:

Nymphae, noster amor, Libethrides, *aut* mihi carmen
quale meo Codro, concedite (proxima Phoebi
versibus ille facit) *aut, si non possumus omnes,*
hic arguta sacra *pendebit fistula pinu.* (7.21–24)

You nymphs of Libethra, my delight, either grant me a song like the one you granted my Codrus—he makes songs which come closest to those of Phoebus—or else, if we cannot all attain such heights, here on the sacred pine tree my clear-sounding pipe shall hang [henceforth].

I have italicized the words which Milton takes over, not so much to show how many ways there are as to show that they are clearer than his. Corydon prays that the Muses will inspire him: if they will not, he vows to give up composing. In Milton, the alternatives are more numerous, and less clear-cut. But the feeling of standing at a cross-roads is transferred. So too is the atmosphere of do-or-die. Damon *has* died ("Et in Arcadia ego"), and his friend voices the thought of dying before he has written the poetry which it is his vocation and desire to write: "Oh mihi tum si vita supersit" ("Oh, if I have any time left to live").

In short, the passage is a Virgilian palimpsest. Latin, especially Neo-Latin, adores the effect of "palimpsest" (signaled and reworked quotation), and hence a poetic meditation upon poetry emulating Virgil works best in Virgilian Latin. But it is palimpsest in subject as much as in verbal correspondences: the subject is poet-singers at their respective cross-roads. The question for Virgil had been how to rise above pastoral, and it was Milton's also at first; but soon, out of sight in the sub-text, the question is becoming whether to do it in Virgil's tongue or some other. An answer lurks in the sequel, that resounding march-past of British places-names (never heard in Virgil): Usa, Alauni, Abra, Treantae, Thamesis, Tamara, and Orcades. British places, Latin names, in the moment of turning away from Latin: a triumphal, pointed, paradox.

To summarize. Milton does not write informatively so much as excitedly. And some regret is intermingled, for he is forfeiting the

European audience he has just found and gloried in. Self-discovery and self-assertion remain dominant, as seen in the threefold anaphora on "ipse": "I shall write all this," or "To think of *me* doing it!" But another element is tension, the conflict between his languages. When for the first time a language choice means loss as well as gain, the poem weighs them.

§

Both excitement and uncertainty continued. In 1642, writing in *Reason of Church-Government*, Milton expresses an obligation to his native language and his native land together: like Ariosto, he would seek "the adorning of my native tongue; not to make verbal curiosities the end ... but to be an interpreter and relater of the best and sagest things among mine own citizens ... in the mother dialect."[20] Zest and zeal are projected. But in the following sentences we find him undecided about everything else—the genre and the subject and whether it should be sacred or secular.

The uncertainty seems odd, in view of his two previous proclaimings of a British theme which should climax with Arthur. Likewise he plays down British (as distinct from Saxon) history in the Trinity Manuscript list of themes, made 1640–1642. As for Arthur in particular, he is deafeningly absent. The usual explanation given is that an intensive study of his nation's history upon his return from Italy had exposed the British historiography of Geoffrey of Monmouth and his like as untrue; and if untrue, then unfit to be celebrated or to serve for instruction. Roberta F. Brinkley[21] argues that Milton may have found the Arthur-story preempted, and contaminated, by the Stuarts, and certainly he becomes rather suddenly more interested in the Saxons than in the Britons (the reverse being true at the time of *Mansus*). At all events, "England hath had her noble achievements made small by the unskilfull handling of monks and mechanics." Thus we have the ironical situation that he abandoned Latin for Arthur's sake, and then Arthur for the sake of England and English. Where would he look next for his subject? And how secure was his grasp of its medium, too?

---

[20] In *Reason of Church-Government*, 7–8 of Diekhoff.
[21] Brinkley, 126 ff.

Even where truth was not in doubt, he faced a dilemma. Should he honor England's history by seeing it under the eye of God, as history is seen in the Old Testament? or by appropriating the history of Israel to England's destiny? Somewhere in the period of the Trinity Manuscript lists[22] he cuts the knot, going beneath both fallen histories to the Fall itself. The manuscript has more entries on Adam than on any other subject, they are longer entries, and each of them is fuller than the one before it. The tide is setting towards "Adam Unparadized" as his epic subject.

In Satan's address to the Sun, that early portion of *Paradise Lost*, he has found his medium also, has chosen his tongue. How early is that passage? As early as 1642-1643, perhaps? Aubrey's *Life of Milton* dates it to "about 15 or 16 years before ever his poem [*Paradise Lost*] was thought of."[23] The figures are not inherently absurd nor their product unlikely: 1658 minus 15 or 16 equals 1643 or 1642. Edward Phillips says only "several years" before the poem was begun; but since he wrote that in old age and had talked with Aubrey much earlier, Aubrey's specific numbers may be more nearly right. Certainly Phillips connects them with the opening of a draft tragedy on the subject of Adam, such as figure in the Trinity MS, yet a draft later than the four sketches there (none of which begins with Satan and his address). But one hesitates to trust Aubrey on figures, despite the neatness of an inference that Milton searched for a subject and medium together.

Certain is that he now found his voice and tongue. Though his choice still rests with English, it is an English made personal and multiple, and given needed tension, by a domiciling of words and illusions and structures of words from his *other* tongues. I shall explore

---

[22] The lists are dated 1639-1641 by Masson, 2:112-15, and so by others since. Of the non-biblical items only Venutius (AD 51) is British: and his story is in the Roman historian Tacitus.

[23] All material from Aubrey and Phillips is taken from Darbishire, 13 for Aubrey, 72-73 for Phillips. The text and pointing of Satan's address to the sun are also taken from Phillips in Darbishire. Although Phillips may be merely mangling the published text, he may instead recall an earlier state of the text, and I quote him in *case* that should be so. If it were so, we should have the passage built around the figure "Glory . . . Glorious . . . Glorious" (stepping upwards from the Sun's glory to Satan's to the Father's). And in that case, we could ask why Milton should think the concluding "Glorious" inferior to "matchless" (creates a better conflict with Satan's "warring" against such a God, and introduces a more jagged and Anglo-Saxon finish?)

the "hybridized" character of this last of my proof-texts before advancing the hypothesis that its English differs from the style of his English, and his other tongues, of before 1641.

> O Thou that with surpassing Glory Crown'd!
> Look'st from thy sole Dominion, like the God
> Of this New World; at whose sight all the Stars
> Hide their diminish'd Heads; to thee I call,
> But with no friendly Voice; and add thy Name,
> O Sun! to tell thee how I hate thy Beams
> That bring to my remembrance, from what State
> I fell; how Glorious once above thy Sphere;
> Till Pride and worse Ambition threw me down,
> Warring in Heaven, against Heaven's Glorious King.

It has long been thought that the address to the Sun takes off from the *Prometheus Bound* of Aeschylus. Although some scholarship has questioned the idea, it seems probable enough; for Milton knew that play, and to him Prometheus signified a principled, yet ambivalent rebellion.[24] Satan, however, rejects the Sun as well as the ruling deity: the first, with rancor, because of the second. So there emerges in subtext a comprehensiveness and as it were idealism in his hatred, but also there emerges the worth of what he contemns. Milton has made a stunning advance from the idealized loves of earlier poems we have examined. And yet the new idiom is related to them, because the tension between valuations of rebellion—Greek-heroic and Hebrew-diabolic—now proceeds within the English language itself. More than that, since the sun was a divine image in the Greek cosmologies, then in Plato and the Neoplatonic tradition through to Ficino, no less than four of his foreign cultures cohabit in his new-forged English.

---

[24] The play may not in fact be by Aeschylus, according to recent scholarship, but that is immaterial for present purposes. Doubt is cast on most Aeschylean debts proposed concerning Milton by J. C. Maxwell, but could one who read so thoroughly the whole of Euripides be unaware of Aeshylus's Prometheus? Milton's allusions to Prometheus (see Columbia Index, sub nomine) are ambivalent: he is both innovator and thief, the champion of humankind and bringer of ills to us. See, e.g., the opening of the epigram "In Inventorem Bombardae":"Iapetionidem laudavit *caeca* vetustas" (my italics), "*In their blindness* the ancients praised Japetus's son."

"Sole dominion" is made of two words borrowed from Latin, and hints at a pun on *Sol*, the Latin for "Sun." In "Their diminished heads" we find a combining of Latin-derived with Anglo-Saxon words which works powerfully for English poets. By artful placing, too, "diminished" becomes both attributive and predicative, as in Latin: heads which have been, and go on being, diminished. The density and emphasis of "diminished" bring out Satan's obsession with status.

Greek and Latin conjoin in the adjective-phrase "no friendly" voice. As well as being the figure litotes—the negative not of absence but of oppositeness—the phrase is a litotes of idiom. *Inimicus* is the negating of *amicus*, friend, and the Greek ἄφιλος "aphilos" works similarly. (He who is not with me is against me.) For good measure, the litotes glances at the Hebrew of "Satan": the Opposer, the Accuser, the Adversary, he who exposes human offences at God's court, the word being first a noun, then a title, then (as he becomes over-zealous at his work, and is poisoned by it) his individuating name; from the root.[25] It will be Milton's frequent practice in *Paradise Lost* thus to etymologize names for the sake of a witty characterizing, of name and nature together.

With the words "I call" we have at last reached the main verb of this single-sentence utterance. But instead of moving forward smoothly henceforth, the syntax at once writhes more than ever: "I call, / But ... no friendly ... and add ... to tell ... how ... That bring ... from what ... how till...." Of course the syntax by its twists and turns enacts the writhing increase of grudge, but we should remember as instigator of that mimesis the many patterns and hyperbatons by which Bembo and Della Casa gave suspension, hence energy and distinction, to literary Italian.[26] (Nor does it qualify, but rather reinforces, the

---

[25] Name, noun, and verb are of course identical when written in letters alone, i.e., without vocalization. The meaning of the name was common knowledge through expositors, yet Milton would have read passages in Hebrew where all three parts of speech occur.

[26] I follow Prince here, especially chapter 7. Prince says (121) that in Milton and the Italians "a quite direct, simple, or 'logical' order of words is avoided in order to provide one in which the completion of the statement is either postponed or anticipated." A notable example in our passage would be "to thee I call, / But with no friendly voice," because the main line of discourse is at once turned aside into a grudging qualifier. Although Prince's chapter is impressionistic, and Italian is not the only possible origin of the effects being considered, he still most usefully draws attention to the intersectings of languages in Milton's stylistic artifice.

point about Milton's style being hybridized to remember further that his Latin authors practiced the same sort of syntactical arts: presumably the Italians went back to source, too.) After which Milton lets in a ray of New Testament light: "O Sun ... I hate thy beams" calls up St. John's words, "Everyone that doeth evil hateth the light," with their context.[27] To hate the sun, the source of life on earth, is virtual blasphemy in most cultures: Milton had read it in Euripides, for instance.[28] His cultures again corroborate.

§

To engender such magnificent self-exposure in English, no single cause sufficed. A prominent contributor, all the same, is the fertilizing interplay of Milton's languages with his native tongue. The forms of interplay fluctuate. We expect contact between his Latin and English. I myself notice how lively is the conjoining of Greek and Hebrew in his English, probably because the those two languages stand further apart from each other and from English. But in truth, none of the possible conjunctions of his five major languages can be safely ignored.

So whether in Italy or upon return, Milton took firmer grasp of something fundamental to English: not simply that it had absorbed much from Latin and from other tongues, but that—in syntax as well as words—it could absorb more; in short, that absorption suited it. English itself has grown by being eclectic and assimilative, a cheerful borrower; hospitable to what is different, and thereby rendered creative. *Milton's English in the early 1640's grew likewise: in its egotistically sublime way it drew other languages to itself.*

Two natural objections must be stated and given an answer. First, it is possible to agree that Milton's English of Satan's address is superior in its complexity and force to the foreign-language poems here considered, but that there is far less difference between the English of the address and his English of the poems composed before Italy, for example *Lycidas*. I grant that *Lycidas* owes much to the eclogues of Virgil for its ideas and pastoral ambience, and that sometimes Milton even says

---

[27] John 3.20 and cf. 5.19.
[28] *Hippolytus* 355.

the identical thing in his English.[29] He deploys classical names, including the Latinized names of native entities. Less prominent in *Lycidas*, though, is an etymologizing sense of the roots of words borrowed from other languages which is growing in Satan's address ("sole," "no friendly") and which grows further in *Paradise Lost* as a whole. To the contrary, I notice in *Lycidas* some tendency to use native English words or things just where a Virgilian or classicizing flavor might have been added ("Or taint-worm to the weanling herds"). Doubtless, however, the increase of etymologizing which I perceive is a matter of degree rather than of kind; and since too the question of Milton's Latinism is a vexing question, it is something to be examined more fully elsewhere.[30]

As with diction, the choosing of words, so with syntax, their ordering: Italian influence predates his visit to Italy, and is seen in *Lycidas*. My reply is, first, that Milton's sonnets *in Italian* are a very important part of this poetic development; then, that the syntax of the English sonnets written after Italy is more Italianate than the syntax of their English predecessors. But, obviously enough, the influence of Italianate syntax will be different, perhaps greater, where it is not played off against rhyme: to my sense, Comus in *A Masque* does not do through syntax what Satan in his address does. We have still to explain the surge forward to the mature style of the satanic voice, and I propose that the Italian journey and its immediate sequel go *some* way to explaining it.

To the second objection, that the present perspective makes Milton's growth too purely linguistic and too conscious, a similarly modest answer is appropriate. It is not my design to make the process of "domiciling" foreign languages in his English a conscious, or deliberate one. *Paradise Lost* is not *Finnegans Wake* (though the comparison would bear some fruit). The choice of a second tongue to compose in does have conscious purpose, for the choice regularly makes part of the sense of occasion. Yet equally regularly the occasional performance seeks an allegiance which eludes us—and eludes Milton. Whenever, too, he writes

---

[29] As at *Lycidas* 77.

[30] In the larger work, "Milton's Tongues," on which this essay draws. Doubts about the extensiveness of Milton's Latinism are powerfully expressed by Fowler, 430-33.

in a tongue that is not native to him it admits willy-nilly an English-language part of his sensibility, be it the feeling for his father in "Ad Patrem," or the sense of being an outsider to Italian in the Italian poems. For this very reason, however, the sensibility can make the leap forward (out of sight, so to speak) to Satan's "multiple" English. For one thing, there is an element of impersonation in speaking any foreign language, some degree of role-playing and self-experimentation, and so to go playing among languages made Satan easier to impersonate, in a general if opaque way. More important, Satan's English is the reverse case of the of the process (whether of self-suspension or of self-inclusion) involved in composing in the other languages. It is the English with which his other tongues can most readily intersect.

To return to our point of departure, finally: tracing how Milton chose among his languages reveals more and has greater value than conjecturing why; for it reveals why we cannot know why, in that he himself may not have known, beyond a limited extent. Into several passages he writes a discussion with himself about the grounds of choice of tongue, and gives a sense that, as he begins to write, the choice of tongue has already been made. How does any poet begin to find a poems words (as distinct from its subject, though subject and first words may in fact originate together)? Often enough it is from a phrase or rhythm found somewhere within the poet. Milton, then, having the wider resources of competence in his several languages, is a special case of what is very generally intriguing. His language-choices obey personal imperatives which remain interestingly obscure. His uncertainty as to why Psalm 114 demanded to be written in Greek before that winter dawn shares something with the fact "That his Vein never happily flow'd, but from the *Autumnal Equinoctial* to the *Vernal*...."[31] Should we speak, not of Milton choosing a language, but rather of a language choosing him?

Otago University–New Zealand

---

[31] Phillips in Diekhoff, 73.

# Appendix

## Epitaphium Damonis

Quamquam etiam vestri numquam meminisse pigebit
Pastores Thusci, musis operata iuventus,
Hic charis, atque lepos; et Thuscus tu quoque Damon,
Antiqua genus unde petis Lucumonis ab urbe.
O ego quantus eram, gelidi cum stratus ad Arni
Murmura, populeumque nemus, qua mollior herba,　　　　　130
Carpere nunc violas, nunc summas carpere myrtos,
Et potui Lycidae certantem audire Menalcam.
Ipse etiam tentare ausus sum, nec puto multum
Displicui, nam sunt et apud me munera vestra
Fiscellae; calathique et cerea vincla cicutae,
Quin et nostra suas docuerunt nomina fagos
Et Datis, et Francinus, erant et vocibus ambo
Et studiis noti, Lydorum sanguinis ambo.
　　　　Ite domum impasti, domino iam non vacat, agni.
Haec mihi tum laeto dictabat roscida luna,　　　　　140
Dum solus teneros claudebam cratibus hoedos.
Ah quoties dixi, cum te cinis ater habebat,
Nunc canit, aut lepori nunc tendit retia Damon,
Vimina nunc texit, varios sibi quod sit in usus;
Et quae tum facili sperabam mente futura
Arripui voto levis, et praesentia finxi,
Heus bone numquid agis? nisi te quid forte retardat,
Imus? et arguta paulum recubamus in umbra,
Aut ad aquas Colni, aut ubi iugera Cassibelauni?
Tu mihi percurres medicos, tua gramina, succos,　　　　　150
Helleborumque, humilesque crocos, foliumque hyacinthi,
Quasque habet ista palus herbas, artesque medentum,
Ah pereant herbae, pereant artesque medentum
Gramina, postquam ipsi nil profecere magistro.
Ipse etiam, nam nescio quid mihi grande sonabat
Fistula, ab undecima ian lux est altera nocte,
Et tum forte novis admoram labra cicutis,
Dissiluere tamen rupta compage, nec ultra

Ferre graves potuere sonos, dubito quoque ne sim
Turgidulus, tamen et referam, vos credite silvae.                    160
    Ite domum impasti, domino iam non vacat, agni.
Ipse ego Dardanias Rutupina per aequora puppes
Dicam, et Pandrasidos regnum vetus Inogeniae,
Brennumque Arviragumque duces, priscumque Belinum,
Et tandem Armoricos Britonum sub lege colonos;
Tum gravidam Arturo fatali fraude Iogernen
Mendaces vultus, assumptaque Gorlois arma,
Merlini dolus. O mihi tum si vita supersit,
Tu procul annosa pendebis fistula pinu
Multum oblita mihi, aut patriis mutata camoenis                      170
Brittonicum strides, quid enum? omnia non licet uni
Non sperasse uni licet omnia, mi satis ampla
Merces, et mihi grande decus (sim ignotus in aevum
Tum licet, externo penitusque inglorius orbi)
Si me flava comas legat Usa, et potor Alauni,
Vorticibusque frequens Abra, et nemus omne Treantae,
Et Thamesis meus ante omnes, et fusca metallis
Tamara, et extremis me discant Ocades undis.
    Ite domum impasti, domino iam non vacat, agni.
Haec tibi servabam lenta sub cortice lauri,                          180
Haec, et plura simul, tum quae mihi pocula Mansus,
Mansus Chalcidicae non ultima gloria ripae
Bina dedit, mirum artis opus, mirandus et ipse,
Et circum gemino caelaverat argumento. . . .

And yet I shall never be regretful when I remember you, shepherds of
Tuscany, young men formed by the muses: grace and charm dwell with
you. You too, Daman, were a Tuscan, descended from the ancient city
of Lucca. O how grand I felt, lying by the cool, murmuring Arno, in the
shade of a poplar grove, on the soft turf, where I was able to pluck
violets and myrtle-tips, and listen to Menalcas and Lycidas having a
singing match. I was even bold enough to compete myself, and I don't
think that I can have been too unpopular, for I still have your gifts,
rush baskets and wicker baskets and pipes fastened together with wax.
What is more, Dati and Francini, famous poets and scholars both, and
both of Lydian blood, made their native beech trees resound with my
name.

"Go home unfed, lambs, your shepherd has no time for you now."
These were the sounds which the dewy moon would repeat to me
while, happy and solitary, I penned my tender kids in the wattled folds.
Ah, how often I used to say (when in reality the black ashes of death
had claimed you), "Now Damon is singing, or laying nets to catch a
hare, or making baskets of osiers to serve his various needs." All
unsuspecting, I was quick to seize upon the scenes which I hoped for so
longingly in the future, and to imagine them as present: "Hallo there!
What are you up to? If there's nothing else you have to do let's go and
lie down a bit in the chequered shade beside the streams of Colne or
among the acres of Cassivellaunus. Then, as I listen, you can run
through your list of healing potions and herbs—hellebore, humble
crocus, hyacinth leaf—all the plants of the fenland, and all the skills of
medicine." O confound herbs and plants and medical skills: they were
not able to save their master! And I—for my pipe was sounding some
lofty strain, I know not what, eleven nights and a day ago, and I had by
chance set my lips to a new set of pipes, when their fastening broke,
and they fell apart: they could bear the grave notes no longer—I am
afraid that I am being swollen-headed, but still, I will tell of that strain.
Give place, woods.

"Go home unfed, lambs, your shepherd has no time for you now."
I shall tell of Trojan keels ploughing the sea off the Kentish coast,
and of the ancient kingdom of Inogene, daughter of Pandrasus, of the
chieftains Brenus and Arviragus and of old Belinus, and of the settlers
in Brittany, subject at last to British law. Then I shall tell of Igraine,
pregnant with Arthur as a result of fatal deception: I shall tell of the
lying features which misled her, and of the borrowing of Gorlois's
armour, Merlin's trick. O if I have any time left to live, you, my pastoral
pipe, will hang far away on the branch of some old pine tree, utterly
forgotten by me, or else, transformed by my native muses, you will
whistle a British tune. But after all, one man cannot do everything, or
even hope to do everything. I shall have ample reward, and shall think
it great glory, although I be forever unknown and utterly without fame
in the world outside, if only yellow-haired Usa reads my poems, and he
who drinks from the Alan, and Humber, full of whirling eddies, and
every grove of Trent, and above all my native Thames and the Tamar,
stained with metals, and if the Orkneys among their distant waves will
learn my song.

"Go home unfed, lambs, your shepherd has no time for you now."

I was keeping these things for you, wrapped in tough laurel bark, these, and more as well. And I was keeping also the two cups which Manso gave me—Manso, not the least glory of the Neapolitan shore. They are a marvellous work of art, and he a marvellous man. Around them he had placed an engraving with a double subject.

LEO MILLER

# Milton and Holstenius Reconsidered: An Exercise in Scholarly Practice

## The Date Confirmed and the Gift Identified

MILTON'S OWN LETTER OF MARCH 29, 1639, surviving in holograph in the Vatican Library, is a most authentic and complete record of his visit with the eminent Lucas Holstenius, yet at least two unresolved questions have persisted until now: the date of his visit and the unidentified gift he received.

The letter does not date the meeting except as a *terminus ante quem*. Questions arose because of Milton's rather imprecise *Defensio secunda* account of his Italian travels, in which he states that after his first stay at Florence he went through Siena to Rome, "where I was most graciously received by Lucas Holstenius and other men as erudite as they were brilliant."[1] Thereafter he writes of proceeding to Naples, later returning through Rome towards Florence. Both the Earliest/Anonymous Biographer (now presumed to have been Cyriack Skinner) and Edward Phillips (in his 1694 *Life of Milton*) followed *Defensio secunda* in its ambiguity. Consequently David Masson in his monumental *Life* and J. Milton French each postulated a first Milton-Holstenius contact in October or November of 1638.

W. R. Parker (827) disagreed. He saw that there was no direct evidence for a 1638 meeting, and he argued that they could have met only once, when Milton was returning northward in 1639, because Holstenius commissioned Milton to make some inquiries on his behalf in a Florentine library, a mission improbable for someone intending to go on to Naples, Sicily, and Greece.

Parker's suggestion can now be confirmed through the answer now

---

[1] *Pro populo Anglicano defensio secunda* (Typis Neucomianis, 1654), 84; CE 8:122. Translation mine.

available to the second question, the nature of the gift Milton received from Holstenius at their parting, a gift hitherto misunderstood because one word in Milton's letter had been misinterpreted. Milton spoke his thanks by praising the labors of Holstenius in editing manuscripts of ancient writers into printed books, and then acknowledged the gift, *quorum et unius duplici dono abs te auctus dimittor*. Masson (1881 edition, 1:802) translated this as "dismissed, too, richer than I came, with two copies of one of these last presented to me by yourself." This is the text printed in Columbia 12:41. French (1:412), apparently following Masson's *first* edition, also has "two copies of one." In CPW (1:334), W. A. Turner and A. Turner rendered the passage, "I am sent forth enriched by your gift of two copies of one of these." Their footnote adds, "This book has not been identified," while J. M. French's word was "no trace has been found of the presentation volumes described here" (1.391).

It is rather odd, indeed rather extraordinary, for even the proudest author to bestow two copies of one book on a one-time caller at first acquaintance, even to a most appreciative and stimulating visitor. To bypass this anomaly, W. R. Parker chose to blur the clear Latin *unius* ("of one") and implied more than one publication, "two gifts of Greek texts" (176). This he annotated (828) as "The books presented by Holstenius are unknown, but may some day come to light if inscribed. Among the possibilities are his editions of Athanasius (Paris, 1627), Eusebius (Paris, 1628), Porphyry (Rome, 1639) and some axioms of the later Pythagoreans (Rome, 1638)."

Identification of the gift book is actually quite simple. At the time of Milton's visit, the only recent publication by Holstenius, and this after a lapse of eight years, was his DEMOPHILI / DEMOCRATIS / ET SECVNDI / VETERVM PHILOSOPHORVM / SENTENTIÆ MORALES / NVNC PRIMVM EDITAE / A LVCA HOLSTENIO. / (device, a tree) / R O M A E / EXCVDEBAT MASCARDUS, dated 1638 in Roman numerals on the title page, and more precisely by its printed dedication to Carolus and Maphæus Barberini on the *nones* of December, 1638, or December 5.

*Duplici* has repeatedly been mistranslated as "two copies," but what Milton himself meant by *duplex* is manifest immediately on opening the volume. It is printed bilingually, Greek text of the ancient authors in Greek type on even numbered pages, each faced by Holstenius's Latin text in roman letters on odd numbered pages, so that the gift is clearly of one book only (*unius*) which was set in type *duplex*, that is "bipartite" in format.

This one two-fold book came off the press towards the very end of December 1638 and could have been given to Milton only during his second stay at Rome, thereby confirming that there was only one visit, and that was in 1639.[2]

## The Milton-Holstenius Letter, 1639 and 1674 Texts Contrasted

Miltonists are forever grateful to Joseph McG. Bottkol for his recovery of the holograph original of that March 29, 1639, letter from Milton to Lucas Holstenius, for supplying a photograph of the manuscript together with a printed text, and for his further toilsome compilation of an apparatus delineating many differences in its text from the copy printed in the *Epistolarum familiarium liber unus* published in 1674 by Brabazon Aylmer. His study appeared in *PMLA* 68 (1953): 617-27. Bottkol's apparatus tabulated most of their variants: minutiae of punctuation, diacritical marks, and capitalization, as well as changes which he classified as "substantive": editorial and grammatical alterations.[3]

Bottkol was so impressed by these variants that he posed a question and offered an answer (626):

Who made the revisions in the edison of 1674? I see no reason to doubt they are Milton's own. Their delicacy in usage and grammatical precision are those of a most accomplished Latinist.

Earlier (625), Bottkol had offered a more expansive evaluation, and suggested a deliberate purpose:

---

[2] I use the British Library copy of the Holstenius book, 720.b.4. Holstenius in his preface assembled some references from ancient sources about his three Pythagoreans, but could not establish any precise data. Milton may have read the book, but it is doubtful that he ever made any other use of it. In "Milton Dines at the Jesuits," *MQ* 13 (1979): 143, I needlessly speculated on a Holstenius introduction to the Jesuits.

[3] In accordance with too common practice, Bottkol omitted certain "trivial" variants, such as et] &, p] per, and the seventeenth-century squiggle for enclitic -que. In textual studies, especially of holograph manuscripts, no variant should be overlooked. Many an elusive problem is soluble when such "trivialities" are taken into account. Peculiarly, Bottkol omitted to list 1639 demittor] 1674 dimittor.

The text of 1674 is a more polished and orthodox Latin than that of 1639; it has been meticulously revised with an eye to a wider audience.

Bottkol's work shows him a careful scholar. His conclusions have not been challenged. Still, as methods in textual studies undergo refinement, it is sometimes in order to review past examinations and conclusions. Such reexamination need not be and should not be undertaken in any invidious spirit. Confirmation via different methodology is as useful as the derivation of a dissenting conclusion, and in that spirit we review the procedures which Bottkol followed in reaching his thesis, or his conclusion, that Milton intentionally subjected his 1639 letter to extensive revision in 1674 in (1) punctuation, (2) vocabulary, and (3) syntax.

Certain facts are axiomatic. Milton was a reviser. He published second editions, revised and enlarged, of his first *Divorce* essay, his *Tenure of Kings*, his *Eikonoklastes*, his *Pro populo Anglicano defensio* (twice revised), his *Paradise Lost*, and his shorter *Poems*. (He inserted late theological thoughts into his treatise on logic drafted decades before, and he never quite finished revising his *Treatise on Christian Doctrine*.) In each of those published works there was substantial reason for appearing before the public a second time in an expanded and revised form. He also had good reason to expend effort on his English-language *Letter to a Friend*, as seen in the heavily rewritten second draft; but these revisions were done at most a few days apart. It seems rather a different case to visualize Milton in 1674, turning over 139 old state paper drafts with thirty-one private letters from long ago to a printer, in order to redo his copy of a personal letter received by the addressee thirty-five years earlier.

On the other hand it is well known that private letters are not seldom modified before publication by their authors, and are even more subject to bowdlerizing by wives and friends. When the private letters of Claudius Sarravius to Claudius Salmasius (which I am analyzing elsewhere) were printed in 1654, the editor took pains to disguise the identities of many persons mentioned, while the 1697 editor as carefully restored these names for all to see.

Bottkol's investigation was rendered possible because he was able to compare the 1639 holograph side by side with the version printed in 1674. It happens, however, that this availability of two variant texts of a Milton letter is not unique. In the New York Public Library there is preserved the holograph original of Milton's 1647 letter to Carlo Dati, which differs in text from the 1674 printed version. Bottkol gives no indication of having tested his hypotheses to see whether they were supported or negated by any evidence from this second pair, of which he was aware. There is also available for comparison a third such pair, Milton's December 31, 1651, letter to Hermann Mylius, also printed in 1674, although the manuscript in this instance is in the hand of the amanuensis to whom Milton dictated.[4]

When Bottkol did his painstaking labors about 1952, he referred to the 1674 volume as the "Aylmer" edition after the name of the publisher Brabazon Aylmer. In 1952 it was not yet known who the person was who had transcribed and arranged the text of the *Familiar Letters* for the press; it was assumed to have been simply Milton's work, and no consideration was given to any possibilities that the text might have been affected by the secretarial aide in the course of his services. The original manuscripts of the personal letter drafts written or dictated by Milton are all lost. So is the manuscript of the *Familiar Letters* as it was given to the printers; but we now know that it was prepared by Milton's last amanuensis, Daniel Skinner, done together with his less-than-perfect transcript of the state letters which survives as SP 9/194 at the Public Record Office in London. Daniel Skinner also recopied many pages of the still surviving manuscript of the *De doctrina christiana*, and these show him not infrequently setting down on paper something less than an exact representation of what he was trying to copy. Reexamination must keep Daniel Skinner's hand and judgment in mind.[5]

Another consideration. A serious scholar who has made a striking discovery and who is preparing it for publication may weigh favorable evidence most cautiously and may attend fully to unfavorable indications, but still in the heat of enthusiasm may also ably marshal the arts of rhetoric to move a reader to a preferred and plausible conclusion. But

---

[4] I use photographs of the Dati letter from the New York Public Library. The first side of the letter is reproduced in the CE 12 facing page 50. Ink penetrating the paper where it was written on both sides has rendered much of it illegible. The original of the letter to Mylius is reproduced in L. Miller, *John Milton & the Oldenburg Safeguard* (Loewenthal Press, 1985), 122.

[5] See my "Milton's Personal Letters and Daniel Skinner," *N&Q* 288 (1983): 431–32; and "Some Inferences from Milton's Hebrew," *MQ* 18 (1984): 41–46.

plausibility is not proof, and the well-telling of a story does not make it true. Bottkol's study is as well-written as his data is well-expounded: the quotations given above are good examples. Upon the critical reader is imposed the responsibility to pare away any rhetorical fat and concentrate on the lean meat.

Many specific experiences warn against facile verdicts that seen prima facie seem to be well founded. In CE 13:488, in 1937 able scholars Thomas O. Mabbott and J. M. French set a label "doubtfully Miltonic" on a state letter in the Columbia Manuscript, because there is a stroke of cancellation drawn across it there. In their doubt they solicited the expertise of Nelson Glenn McCrea, who translated many Latin documents for that edition, and they recorded his verdict: "Professor McCrea considers the Latin weak" (634). One year later, in volume 18:653, they had recognized that the cancellation stroke was there only because that letter (which was fully and authentically Miltonic) had already been entered once before in that manuscript; still they made no mention that their "doubtfulness" had been enough to mislead and prejudice the translator into a groundless judgment against the quality of its Latinity. Milton's style, or various styles, on the whole, are highly recognizable, but in the short span may not be so distinctive, and we now know that final texts of his state letters were often subjected to some revision by his colleagues.[6]

Because Bottkol's conclusions are carefully formulated and cogently argued, it is desirable to apply close and exhaustive scrutiny to the texts themselves. The first argument offered by Bottkol is based on changes in punctuation, which make up the most numerous kinds of alterations, some fifty on one page. Bottkol editorializes: he sees the 1674 punctuation as "much heavier, more analytic" than 1639; commas, semicolons, and full stops are employed "much in the manner of Restoration prose" and these changes "reflect the great shift that had occurred in the articulation of English prose after mid-century." However, stripped of these evaluatory judgments, the facts are not so clear. Bottkol says: "In

---

[6] It is important to understand that (quite apart from ordinary review by colleagues and protocol experts) Milton's state papers suffered particularly from their substitutions of current Neo-Latin terminology in place of his purist and classical Latin, over his objections. These variants, first elucidated in John Milton & the Oldenburg Safeguard, have been making possible the recovery of hitherto unknown Milton state papers and distinguishing his role from the work of colleagues in jointly prepared documents.

1639 Milton relied heavily on commas; the edition of 1674 has not only *multiplied* these, but altered *many* into the stronger semicolon or full stop." I have ilaticized *multiplied* and *many* here because these words are rhetorical and not factual. In 1674, twenty-four commas were *added* (rather than *multiplied*) but thirteen from 1639 were omitted, for a net rise of eleven, while forty-eight commas are unchanged in 1639 and 1674.

A look at the pair of Dati texts, 1647–1674, shows about four commas from 1647 disappearing, about fifteen added, and ninety-three unchanged.

Bottkol emphasizes the shift from commas to semicolons; actually *nine*, rather than *many*, but he omits notice that two semicolons from 1639 become commas in 1674. (One dubious comma, possible intended as a colon, becomes a full stop). "Five new sentences are created by breaking up the earlier, more ponderous ones": actually, three additional sentences are created, but two other sentences of 1639 are combined in 1674 into one by changing a full stop into a semicolon. In the Dati pair, four commas are replaced by semicolons, but three colons or semicolons are changed to commas; six remain the same.

Bottkol observes that thirty-five of Milton's 1639 diacritical marks have disappeared in 1674. Those that remain are erratic, particularly in the use or omission of â to indicate the ablative case in the first declension. (I count seventeen instances of â in 1639; seven are omitted in 1674, ten retained.) Bottkol offers no suggestion of purpose or design in these variations.

With appropriate caution and rhetorical deftness, Bottkol speaks of "Milton" when describing the stylistic features of the 1639 holograph, but when attributing post-Restoration variants he slips in less specific terms such as, "the editor of 1674" and "the punctuator of 1674." On 626 he ends most reservedly cautious about the foregoing data, while still holding on to the verbal revisions: "It may well be doubted whether the hand that repunctuated, capitalized, eliminated the diacritical marks, and changed the heading was that of a blind old man, but the verbal alterations bear the master's stamp."[7] (However, the diacritical mark-

---

[7] Bottkol briefly touched on the Greek accent marks in the letter, drawing no inferences. The "heading" was not changed, but supplied, in the 1674 edition.

ings, because they are erratic, may convey a message. These marks, common in seventeenth-century Latin, have disappeared from more recent printings. They are not mentioned in recent grammars and their former uses are all but forgotten. Milton did use them in his handwritten texts, and, after his blindness, to the limited degree that he could control his amanuenses. Since in 1674 these diacritical marks were partly disregarded and partly inconsistent, it would appear in this respect the transcription was not closely directed or supervised by Milton.)

In effect, Bottkol has here evaded attributing the changes in punctuation and diacritical marks to Milton himself, implicitly modifying his initial thesis. Whether these changes may be with considerable probability attributed to Daniel Skinner as he prepared copy for the printing, or to the printers, or to both, is moot. Whoever may have made the change, Bottkol may be quite correct as to the motivating reason for the modification of the one long sentence into several shorter: that it reflects "the great shift that had occurred in the articulation of English prose after midcentury" (624). As to the variant commas, if there is some rational to the changes, it might take the most powerful of electronic computers to trace it out.

Bottkol moves on: "More substantive changes are words which are altered, omitted, or added" (625). Again he properly begins with a caveat: "Here we are on very uncertain ground, as there is no way of knowing for certain when the alterations in Aylmer were introduced." Actually he deals with only four such changes, and two of these are negligible. In his first draft Milton apparently wrote Cardinal Barberini's given name, abbreviated *Franc.* for *Franciscus*, so that it turns up in the 1674 copy, but he may just as well have omitted it from the delivered holograph as superfluous. Another omission of four words from 1639 *simul, et quasi congruere* in 1674 may have been a slip in copying. There are at least a dozen such omissions in copying in the state paper transcript which Skinner prepared in the original plan to print the public and the private letters in one volume.

That leaves only two words to be considered, and here the rhetoric flows again:

The verbal changes of the printed version are nearly all stylistic changes. . . . Thus certain exuberances of the holograph are toned down: the violent *arripiuntur* (13) becomes *accipiuntur*; the same caution is apparent in *publice* for *populo* (17); the entertainment is "public," but surely not for the whole of Rome.[8]

Only because Bottkol makes it fit into his thesis can he suggest that *accipiuntur* (Holstenius's books "are recieved") is an improvement over *arripiuntur* ("are snatched up," that is, by eager readers). Only by supplying an interpretation which he can fit into his thesis can Bottkol make the substitution of *publice* for *populo* seem to be a reasonable and reasoned choice.

There is at hand an alternative and much simpler explanation. Daniel Skinner was a scribe whose attention may be seen to have wandered more than once in *De doctrina chistiana*. In his transcript of the state papers his eye passes over the word *nempe* ("assuredly") but he sees it and writes it as *semper* ("always"), which makes as good sense. He reads *exteris* ("foreign" nations) and his hand writes *cæteris* ("other" nations). And when his mind really wanders he reads *littoris* ("shore") and writes *literis* ("letters"); he reads the name of the seaport *Ferrarii* and writes the name of the month *Februarij*. Many more such can be cited. So whether *accipiuntur* and *publice* were Milton's revisions or Skinner's sleepy slips must now remain in suspended judgement.[9]

The last revisions examined by Bottkol are what he classifies as "grammatical alterations." He himself quickly eliminates two: *efficiendæ* (1674) for *efficiundæ* (1639) as merely a matter of alternate spellings, and the correct *Artes Liberales* for the slip of the pen *artes liberas* in 1639. The remaining three are complex issues, and very likely it was his alertness to these three which lead Bottkol to develop his hypothesis that this letter was greatly revised to improve it for the 1674 audience. In handling these three cruxes Bottkol had the impressive support of Anselm Strittmatter, who had edited the *Defensio secunda* (CE 8) and *Pro se defensio* (CE 9).[10]

---

[8] Numbers in parentheses refer to lines in the letter. On 625 *PMLA* misprinted *publico* for *publice*.

[9] These examples from Daniel Skinner's text are taken only from instances where readings in the Columbia Manuscript and the 1676 *Literæ Pseudo-Senatûs Anglicani* are the same and confirm one another. The *Literæ* texts are from "Face" edition, pages 6, 14, and 203, corresponding to CE 13, 16 (line 9), 32 (line 10), 378 (lines 21 17), compared with my photocopies of the Skinner Transcript and the Columbia Manuscript. *Ferrarii* was Porto Ferraio on Elba.

[10] Bottkol identifies his Don Anselm Strittmatter of St. Anselm's Priory, Washing-

First a problem in the idiomatic usage. Milton addressed Holstenius and complimented him for his works edited "by your labor." Milton clearly intended *tuo opere* (in his script *tuo ope*), ablative case of the neuter noun *opus*. In 1674 the text reads *tuâ operâ*, ablative case of the feminine noun *opera*. Both forms mean "by your labor."

Strittmatter observed that the *tua opera* (in the ablative) is a usual form found in the writings of Cicero, Nepos, Plautus, Terrence, and Justinus, and so cited in major Latin lexica, whereas *tuo opere* in this sense is not so cited in the lexica. Strittmatter regarded *tuo opere*, therefore, as a departure from normal Latin idiom, so that for him *tua opera* was a correction made in 1674. So he suggested "it is not unlikely that this curious lapse was due to a certain over-eagerness on the part of the young author, who in his old age was quick to correct it (626).[11]

In the absence of any lexical citations for *tuo opere*, should it be regarded as wrong? A masterpiece in literature has always been given a *magnum opus*, and *opus* was used for literary labor by classical Cicero, Livy, and Quintilian. The great *Thesaurus* of Robertus Stephanus (which was a point of departure for Milton's own Latin thesaurus on which he worked for two and a half decades) lists a huge number of citations for *opus* and *opera* without making a sharp differentiation; likewise the recent *Oxford Latin Dictionary*. However, Lewis and Short's *Latin Dictionary* (1975 impression, also published at Oxford), without citing any authorities, prints a note under *opera*: "opus is used mostly of the mechanical activity of work, as that of animals, slaves and soldiers; opera supposes a free will and desire to serve." Lexicographers do not necessarily agree, and Milton, himself a lexicographer, dictated *militari operâ* in his *Defensio secunda* (1654, p. 159; CE 8: 234).

In the absence of any concordance to Milton's Latin prose, my

---

ton, DC, with the editor of CE 8 and 9, where the editor's name is given as Eugene J. Strittmatter. As editor, Strittmatter did not reproduce the original 1654 and 1655 Newcomb publications of Milton's two works, but prepared an emended text, supplying diacritical marks, correcting misprints, and modifying punctuation. In his appended notes, the bracketed form is Strittmatter's, and Newcomb's follows. A proper edition of Milton's collected works is still needed.

[11] Strittmatter did not identify his lexica. Citations for *tua opera* are given in the *Thesaurus* of Robertus Stephanus and the *Oxford Latin Dictionary*. Lewis and Short cite Plautus and Terence for *mea* and *tua opera*, and Cicero, Livy and Quintilian for *opus*.

examination of his usage is at this moment limited to such instances as I can recall. First we must consider Milton's two other letters to his Italian friends. In the 1674 text of his letter, originally done September 30, 1638, Milton twice refers in laudatory spirit to Bonmatthæus's work as *opus* (once, dative *operi*, once, ablative *opere*) and once he uses *opera* in the idiom *operam navare*, presumably retaining his 1638 forms. Milton uses the idiom *operam dare* in the original 1647 holograph letter to Dati, and retains it in 1674.

In Milton's December 4, 1634, letter to Alexander Gil, he saw little value in expending *studium atque operam* ("study and labor") on composition in Greek (*Epistolarum familiarium*, 1674, page 14; CE 12:16). Should we ask whether this *operam* was written in 1634 or dictated in 1674? In Milton's *Artis Logicæ*, composed about 1645-1647, he emphasizes the value of a unified work, *una opera*, but the work of composing the book is *opus* (1672 edition, Sig. A4v and A5v; CE 11: 3, 6). In *Pro populo Anglicano defensio*, 1651 (Madan no. 3 issue of first edition, page 40; CE in notes, p. 571) Milton taunted Salmasius for his *suomet ipse opere*. In *Defensio secunda* (1654, page 99; CE 8:144) *vel operâ vel otio* is "either my labor or my time." In *Pro se defensio*, *opus* serves for More's writing *datâ operâ* for investigative labor, *operam* twice for "to lose one's labor," and *operarum*, the work of proofreading (1655, pages 25, 26, 96, 174, 26; CE pp. 36, 38, 140, 254, 38). In these instances *opera* is used more frequently than *opus*, but still the choice of opus/ opera, tuo opere/tuâ operâ may have been for Milton as much a matter of his present day fancy as a matter of better idiom. But to this question we shall return.

Strittmatter continued with two other strictures in grammar; adhering to his assumption that the 1674 text represents Milton's late corrections, he writes:

> This may well be the explanation also of the change of the two indicatives *ascenderam* and *accesseram* ... to the subjunctive forms *ascenderem* and *accessissem* which we have in Aylmer's text. Milton was undoubtedly fully conversant with the use of the indicative in *cum*-temporal clauses, but his use of two pluperfect indicatives *ascenderam* and *accesseram* is unusual (cf. Stolz-Schmalz *Lateinische Grammatik* [München, 1928], 749: Der Ind. Plqpf., der zu allen Zeiten selten ist [. . .] behauptet sich in klassischer Zeit nur bei Cicero häufiger...), and it was his conscious-

ness of this fact which prompted the use of the subjunctive in the revision made for Aylmer's printing.[12]

Another recent authority, the standard American *Allen and Greenough's New Latin Grammar* (1903 [repr. 1983], 352, sect. 544), so discusses *cum*:

> With the Indicative, besides the simple expression of definite time (corresponding to simple relative clauses with the Indicative), it has a few special uses, conditional, expletive, *cum inversum*—all easily derived from the temporal use.
>
> In classical writers the narrative *cum*-clause (with the Subjunctive) has pushed back the defining clause (with the Imperfect or Pluperfect Indicative) into comparative infrequency, and is itself freely used where the descriptive or characterizing force is scarcely perceptible.

In Milton's own *Accedence Commenc't Grammar*, issued as late as 1669, he first treated *cum* as a conjunction meaning "seeing that," to be followed by the subjunctive (60) and then as an adverb (62) with two choices of mood:

> Adverbs are joyn'd in a Sentence to several Moods of Verbs. Of Time, *Ubi, postquam, cum, or quum*, to an Indicative or Subjunctive; [several examples follow]

It will be noticed here that Milton has admitted the subjunctive after *postquam*, while some present day grammars (*Allen and Greenough*, 351, sect. 543) appear to restrict *postquam* to the indicative. Whether Milton's flexibility or recent rigidity better describes the grammar of the Latin language, there is evidence to favor the hypothesis of Milton's later preference for the subjunctive in this *cum* construction, while recognizing that his 1639 usage appears to have been correct enough for Cicero and not excluded by Milton's 1669 *Grammar*. Without making an

---

[12] Strittmatter's cited authority is better identified as *Friedrich Stolz & Johann Hermann Schmalz. Lateinische Grammatik. In fünfter auflage völlig neu bearbeitet von Manu Leumann und Johann Bapt. Hofmann*, printed in the *Handbuch der Altertums Wissenschaft, Abt. 2, Teil 2* (Munich, 1928), 749. The Stolz-Schmalz opinion translates as "The indicative pluperfect, rare in all eras, is in the classical era reported frequently only in Cicero."

exhaustive study of Milton's practice, we do see in his very first state paper, August 1649, *cum* followed by three subjunctives, *reduxissent, asseruissent, dededissent* (CE 13:6, 8); in his December 31, 1651, letter to Mylius, *cum . . . incidissem, cum . . . commonefecissem* (12:54); and in *Defensio secunda, cum impedissem* (8:126).[13]

When we turn to the second pair of letter texts (the holograph sent to Dati in 1647 and the version printed in 1674) to test for verbal and grammatical changes, we find five minor variants in text which may be quickly dismissed. The 1674 printing has the word *minori* (distinguishing Milton's Chimentelli from an older brother) and a clause *quem te nuper colere jocaris*; both had been omitted from the letter as sent in 1647. That 1647 text has three words, *in Angliam* and *alicubi*, omitted in 1674 without materially affecting the sense. At this moment any explanations for these four changes are only guesses. The somewhat softer *tolli* in the final 1647 letter replacing the draft *abripi* (as printed in 1674) is a change not unreasonable for Milton to have made in 1647. There is nonetheless one major and conspicuous difference between the two texts:

| 1647 | 1674 |
|---|---|
| Nunc tu omnium primus insperato hoc tuo p̄ literas invitatu, ne dicam priorum illarum jacturâ debitas jam tibi à me respondendi vices reliquorum expostulatione liberasti. | Nunc tu primus & hac amicissime Literarum provocatione, & scribendi officio ter jam repetito debitas tibi, à me jampridem respondendi vices reliquorum expostulatione liberasti. |

If in 1639 Milton, seven years away from the university, may have been occasionally more colloquial than strictly classical, in 1647 he had been for more than five years immersed in teaching Latin grammar and his sensitivity to syntax was acute. We must either choose to regard the 1674 text as the original first draft from 1647, or as a late revision for the sake of style. Here a different impulse may perhaps be seen. Milton's highly motivated drive to compile a purist dictionary of classical Latin seems to have begun late in the 1640s, and his sensitivity on the score of proper vocabulary intensified as his studies went on: terms

---

[13] Lewis and Short admit the subjunctive with *postquam*. Milton used the words *potential* and *subjunctive*; present day grammars use only the term *subjunctive*.

which he used freely in 1650 he questioned sharply in 1652. It is possible that his 1647 use of *insperato* (mainly ante-classical and post-classical) and *invitatu* (rare, though Ciceronian) no longer satisfied his standards when his lexicographical compilations were far advanced.[14]

The two-text personal letter to Mylius is another object lesson in scholarly caution. The omission in 1674 of the name Bulstrode White-locke, a major personality in the Interregnum regimes, might plausibly have been dictated by political discretion, as suggested by the editors in CPW (4:836). Or it may have been lacking in the draft (1674), but was added in the letter sent. Examination of the Skinner state paper tran-script shows a certain political discretion in operation, in 1674; it has deleted epithets and terms which would surely have invited prosecution (these may be seen surviving in the Columbia Manuscript of the state papers). But the names of diplomats who had served Cromwell are not at all omitted. For example, in the instance of Philip Meadowe, the Columbia Manuscript shows that Milton usually dictated the words "our envoy" in some form of *internuntius noster*, leaving it to the option of the protocol experts to add the name of Philip Meadowe to the draft. In the one and only instance where Meadowe's name was included in Milton's draft (as seen in the Columbia Manuscript), it was also re-tained in the 1674 Skinner Transcript. Hence the omission of White-locke's name in 1674 is likely merely to reflect Milton's characteristic mode of operation with his amanuenses in 1651.[15]

I have deliberately withheld up to this point the most important test by which we can judge the 1674 revisions in Milton's letters to his Italian friends: the multitudinous alterations which Milton introduced in 1658 when he published his much re-revised edition of *Pro populo Anglicano defensio*. These include substantial additions in subject matter, changes in word forms (astringam/perstringam), changes in syntax (verb tense and mood) and replacing many terms by synonyms. One change

---

[14] More study is needed about Milton's choices and changes of locution. In his letter to Bonmatthaeus, words which are ante-classical and post-classical, *complusculos* and *pomœria*, are retained in the 1674 text.

[15] Meadowe's name, variously spelled, is included in the *Literæ* ("Face" edition) state paper texts on pages 136, 138 (twice), 173, and 219, reprinted in CE 13:250, 252, 254, 318, and 406; but only in the instance of *Literæ*, 173, was his name included in Milton's dictated draft.

in particular catches the eye. Where Milton in 1651 wrote *suomet ipse opere*, in 1658 (page 32; CE 7:138) he dictated *suamet ipse opera*. Therefore, while not every change in 1674 can be attributed to Milton, it is probable that Daniel Skinner, or someone earlier, reread to Milton at least some of his personal letters, and that Milton did dictate significant revisions to some of his letters long since delivered.

New York City

# Index